Also by James Chace

The Consequences of the Peace:
The New Internationalism and American Foreign Policy

What We Had: A Memoir

America Invulnerable:
The Quest for Absolute Security
from 1812 to Star Wars (with Caleb Carr)

Endless War:
How We Got Involved in Central America—
and What Can Be Done

Solvency: The Price of Survival

A World Elsewhere:
The New American Foreign Policy

The Rules of the Game (novel)

ACHESON

The Secretary of State Who Created the American World

JAMES CHACE

SIMON & SCHUSTER

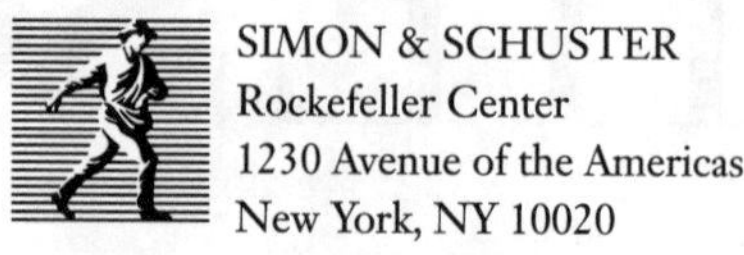

SIMON & SCHUSTER
Rockefeller Center
1230 Avenue of the Americas
New York, NY 10020

Designed by Sam Potts

Manufactured in the United States of America

3 5 7 9 10 8 6 4 2

Library of Congress Cataloging-in-Publication Data
Chace, James.
Acheson : the secretary of state
who created the American world /
James Chace.
p. cm.
Includes bibliographical references and index.
1. Acheson, Dean, 1893–1971.
2. Statesmen—United States—Biography.
3. Cabinet officers—United States—
Biography. 4. United States—Foreign
relations—1945–1989. 5. United States.
Dept. of State—Biography. I. Title.
E748.A15C43 1998
973.91'092—dc21 98-3801 CIP

ISBN 0-684-80843-9

PHOTO CREDITS

Courtesy David C. Acheson 1, 2, 3, 4, 5, 6, 8, 9, 11, 16, 17, 24
Courtesy Mary A. Bundy 7, 10, 12, 13, 14, 32
George Tames, *NYT* Permissions 15
AP/Wide World Photos 18, 21, 26, 29
UPI/Corbis-Bettmann 19, 20, 22, 23, 25, 27
Yoichi R. Okamoto, LBJ Library Collection 28
deKun, Inc., courtesy Mary A. Bundy 30
© Jill Krementz, courtesy of the photographer 31
National Portrait Gallery, Smithsonian Institution 33

This book is dedicated to J. G. Sherman and Peter Collias

CONTENTS

Prologue: The Custom of the Country 9

PART ONE: A BOY'S LIFE

1. Et in Arcadia Ego 15
2. *A World Apart* 21
3. *The Most Dashing of Yale Men* 29
4. *"This Wonderful Mechanism, the Brain"* 37

PART TWO: THE IMPERATIVES OF ACTION

5. *The Heroes* 43
6. *"The Regular Connection of Ideas"* 50
7. *"A Low Life but a Merry One"* 59
8. *"Forces Stronger Than Reason"* 69
9. *Most Unsordid Acts* 82
10. *The New Economic World Order* 93
11. *"The Good Life Is Very Hard"* 104

PART THREE: FROM ALLIANCE TO COLD WAR

12. *"An Armament Race of a Rather Desperate Nature"* 113
13. *No Grand Strategy* 130
14. *"A Graceful Way Out"* 138
15. *Risking War* 146
16. *"Clearer Than Truth"* 156
17. *Reveille in Mississippi* 170
18. *The Habit-Forming Drug of Public Life* 182

PART FOUR: THE SECRETARY OF STATE

19. *In Marshall's Chair* 193
20. *Letting the Dust Settle* 210
21. *"That Moment of Decision"* 225
22. *The German Question, the British Connection, and the French Solution* 241
23. *Putting Our Hand to the Plow* 255
24. *Situations of Strength* 270
25. *"An Entirely New War"* 280
26. *The Substitute for Victory* 304
27. *Entangling Alliances* 323
28. *Endgame* 342
29. *"That Candles May Be Brought"* 349

PART FIVE: THE WARRIOR IN EXILE

30. *Rejoining the Fray* 367
31. *"A Sort of Ancient Mariner"* 381
32. *"The Survival of States"* 395
33. *Contending with LBJ* 410
34. *Into the Quagmire* 418
35. *Seductions and Betrayals* 429

Coda: "A Blade of Steel" 439

Notes 443
Selected Bibliography 489
Acknowledgments 495
Index 497

PROLOGUE

THE CUSTOM OF THE COUNTRY

PRESIDENT HARRY S. TRUMAN knew he was a discredited man. On the day after the congressional elections of 1946, his party suffered its worst defeat since 1928, losing both the House and Senate to Republicans. Under his leadership, Democrats lost badly in New York, California, Pennsylvania, Michigan, and Illinois and did poorly in the border states. The New Deal coalition that FDR had put together appeared shattered. Arriving from Kansas City at Washington's Union Station on a depressingly gray November morning, Truman walked off the train, silent but smiling, and found no one there to greet him.[1]

Politics is an unsentimental business, and the president understood that politicians could not afford to be tainted by too close proximity to failures. It was therefore with some astonishment that he saw there was, after all, someone standing on the platform to meet him. In his elegantly tailored topcoat and homburg was his under secretary of state, Dean Gooderham Acheson. The president was absolutely delighted to see him and asked him back to the White House for a drink.

Dean Acheson, on the other hand, was perplexed and deeply distressed at the absence of any high official from the government save himself. As he later recalled, "It had for years been a Cabinet custom to meet President Roosevelt's private car on his return from happier elections and escort him to the White House. It never occurred to me that after defeat the President would be left to creep unnoticed back to the capital. So I met his train. To my surprise and horror, I was alone on the platform where his car was brought in, except for the stationmaster and a reporter or two."[2]

For Truman, the greatest political value was loyalty. Acheson's uncomplicated display of fealty to his chief was a loyalty as much to the office of the presidency as to the man. But it helped to forge an iron bond between the two men over the next seven years that led to the creation of new institutions so powerful that they came to define—for Americans at home, for allies and adversaries, for good and for ill—an American international order.[3]

Both men were products of small-town life, both were men of action, filled with vitality and endowed with a strong sense of humor, and both were without guile or self-importance. Harry Truman, self-educated, devoted to his wife and daughter, easy with his poker-playing cronies, never really had a close male friend, until, toward the end of his life, he found one in Dean Acheson, who on the surface seemed the most unlikely of choices.[4]

Improbable friends, Truman the bookworm and Acheson the rebel. For Acheson was rarely at peace with the world: he was quick, often impatient, too much at odds with superficial codes of conduct. Tall, slim, dashing, and seemingly remote, the personification of the American notion of a British diplomat, Acheson was, in fact, a gregarious and outspoken man who could easily wound those who he felt were inauthentic. He was said not to suffer fools gladly; in fact, he suffered them scarcely at all.

Like Truman, Acheson believed that most problems could be solved "with a little ingenuity and without inconvenience to the folks at large."[5] Like Truman, Acheson was also something of a stoic, who came to believe what his father, an Episcopal clergyman, taught him: that "much in life could not be affected or mitigated, and, hence, must be borne. Borne without complaint, because complaints were a bore and nuisance to others and undermined the serenity essential to endurance."[6]

When Acheson accompanied the president back to the White House, he seemed to bring a change to the Truman presidency. In a sense he came to the White House to stay. That very afternoon he met with members of Truman's personal staff and urged them not to let the president call a special session of Congress in order to confirm petty political appointments before the new Congress could take over.[7]

The incorruptible figure of Acheson in some sense symbolized the transition from the first phase of the Truman presidency, with all its parochialism and tacking, to the second, more heroic period.

It was Acheson, first as under secretary, then as secretary of state, who was a prime architect of the Marshall Plan to restore economic health to Western Europe, who refashioned a peacetime alliance of nations under the rubric of the North Atlantic Treaty Organization, who crafted the Truman Doctrine to contain any Soviet advance into the Middle East and the Mediterranean. It was Acheson who had already been instrumental in creating the international financial institutions at Bretton Woods that helped ensure global American economic predominance. And it was Acheson who stood by Truman in deciding that the United States must respond to the North Korean invasion of South Korea, who urged the firing of General Douglas MacArthur for insubordination, and who stood up to the vilifications of Senator Joseph McCarthy.

Above all else, it was Acheson who created the intellectual concepts that undergirded Truman's decisions, who had the clearest view of the role America might play in the postwar world, and who possessed the willpower to accomplish these ends. Not long after Acheson joined Truman at the White House on that bleak November day in 1946, the administration finally found its footing in the international arena. With Acheson at or near the helm, its policies started to show a breadth of conception, a buoyancy, and a boldness of action that had not been seen in foreign affairs in peacetime in this century.

Although Acheson was a convinced anti-Communist, he rejected extremes and was far from being a Cold Warrior at the end of World War II. On the contrary, he sought cooperative agreements with the Soviet Union as a great power that had shared in the victory over the Axis with the United States and Great Britain.

But when he determined that it was imperative to contain an expansionist Soviet Union, he was prone at times to employ a rhetoric of anticommunism that, in his own words, made his arguments "clearer than truth" in order to get them accepted by the Congress. These were Faustian bargains, however, and during his last years in office Acheson would be savagely attacked by the conservatives as an appeaser of an ideologically threatening Soviet Union.

In his essence, Acheson was a realist. He never intended, as he testified later, that the United States should embark on a "crusade against any ideology."[8] But he was committed to the defense and to the economic and social construction of Western Europe. An intensely pragmatic man, impatient with abstractions, he saw that American interests required such a policy, one that inevitably entailed the political, and hence military, containment of the Soviet Union. While he did not come to high office with an elaborate plan to establish an American imperium, more than any of his contemporaries, more than Roosevelt, Truman, or General Marshall, he perceived what the interests of the United States and its allies required. In this respect, he did the most to create the world that endured from the outset of the Cold War to the collapse of communism almost half a century later, and beyond.

Nor did Acheson's influence end with the Truman presidency. Out of office, Acheson sat as a member of President John F. Kennedy's executive committee during the Cuban missile crisis. Then, in the twilight of his career, he was asked by President Lyndon B. Johnson to head a group of senior statesmen, the so-called wise men, to see how the United States could extricate itself from the Vietnam quagmire. Although other senior statesmen and military leaders had earlier urged Johnson to avoid a land war in Asia, it was only when Acheson turned against the Vietnam War and told the president that it was time to "take steps to disengage" that Johnson knew it was all over. Later, even President Richard Nixon sought Acheson's counsel, and Acheson reiterated his policy recommendation for Vietnam—to move steadily out; he then broke with Nixon when he extended the war into Cambodia.

The most important figure in American foreign policy since John Quincy Adams, Dean Acheson was the quintessential American realist who most fully understood and mastered the exercise of American power in the American era.

PART ONE

A BOY'S LIFE

CHAPTER ONE

ET IN ARCADIA EGO

DESPITE LATER APPEARANCES, Dean Acheson was not an American patrician. Nor was he born to great wealth. To him, his childhood seemed golden, but its pleasures were the ordinary ones of an American boy allowed to roam free in the safe and seemingly uncomplicated world of a small town in the late nineteenth century. No matter what his studies were during the day, or his scraped knee, or a scuffling argument with his sister at supper, each day at twilight he could anticipate two major events: first of all, the boys and girls would race down to the firehouse, "where every evening," as he recalled years later, "the shining wagon and the well-brushed horses were brought into the street." Firemen slid down poles. Then the horses and wagons were put back into the firehouse. That was all, but this enormous pleasure was followed hard upon by another race to the wharf to watch the arrival of the boat from the state capital at Hartford to pick up passengers en route to New York. To young Dean Acheson, "it seemed that the ladies and gentlemen promenading the deck of that ship were the most fortunate people on earth, and watching them night after night, I imagined myself plowing across the open sea, some nights to Europe, some nights to China, some nights to darkest Africa."[1]

This golden age of childhood, Acheson believed, was able to be fixed quite accurately in the Connecticut valley, in a town in the exact center of the state and "appropriately called Middletown." The Middletown of young Dean Acheson still bore the marks of prosperity because it had once been the head of navigation of the Connecticut River, flowering briefly when clipper ships of the China trade dropped anchor there to service trade to the northern frontier. It was also the site of Wesleyan University. One of the "juicy thrills" of Dean's boyhood was to make for the Wesleyan ball field and hang around the outfield for an hour or so during batting practice. "Sometimes," he said, "if you hung around long enough, a fly ball might come your way and you were allowed to catch it and toss it back to some big boy with a 'W' on his sweater, who could actually say, 'Thanks, kid.' A rather impressive moment."[2] The pattern of one's life seemed to have an "ordered regularity." Life, Acheson believed, "flowed easily and pretty democratically."[3]

At the turn of the century Middletown was a market town with a few small factories—textile, silver, marine hardware. Its great wealth was behind it, but at one time Middletown had promised to be the most important city in Connecticut. Townsfolk prospered by their eager participation in the "triangle trade"—exchanging rum and farm products in the West Indies for slaves, sugar, and molasses, then returning to England for manufactured goods to sell to the colonies. But this trade largely evaporated after the War of 1812, and Middletown turned its energies to manufacturing.[4]

The town remained dominated by sea captains, merchants, and traders, such as the powerful Russell family, which established a merchant house in Canton from 1818 to 1831, importing opium and exporting tea and silk. Perhaps for this reason the ruling families emphasized river and sea over land routes, and Middletown lost out to cities such as Hartford and New Haven that were on the main rail lines. Had Middletown not been bypassed by the railroads, it would have doubtless grown into a large city. Instead it remained a small town of about fifteen thousand when Dean Acheson was born on April 11, 1893, in the brick rectory of Holy Trinity Church, where his father had arrived as pastor a year earlier.

Holy Trinity rose up on Main Street, at the bottom of the hill, which was dominated by the great mansions of the Alsops and the Russells. The rector and his family moved to a more rural part of town and built a large white stucco house, whose door was framed by Ionic pillars and whose bay windows overlooked a flagstone terrace and inviting woods.

In this atmosphere of genteel living, nothing presented any visible hazard to the children. "No one was run over," Acheson recalled. "No one was kidnapped. No one had his teeth straightened. No one worried about the children, except occasionally my mother, when she saw us riding on the back step of the ice wagon and believed, fleetingly, that one of the great blocks of Pamecha Pond ice would fall on us. But none ever did. Unharmed, in hot weather we sucked gallons of ice chips from what was doubtless polluted ice."[5]

As the son of an Episcopal clergyman, Dean Acheson would appear to have adjusted to a world where values were fixed and unquestioned. He was even the proud owner of a pony that did not share its master's passion for imaginative games. "Mean, as well as lazy, and uncooperative," Acheson wrote of the animal, "he knew who was afraid and who would fight back. The timid did well to feed him sugar on a tennis racquet; but he was gentle as a lamb if one had one's fist cocked for a fast punch in the nose."[6] The lesson stayed with Acheson throughout his life.

* * *

The life of a middle-class American was something to which Dean Acheson's father, had he known of it in his early youth, might well have aspired. An Englishman of Scotch-Irish descent, Edward Campion Acheson was born in Woolwich, Kent, in 1857. The Acheson family had apparently lived for centuries in Edinburgh, Scotland, and then migrated to Armagh in Ulster (northern Ireland) in the early seventeenth century, and finally to England. A master sergeant, Edward's father, Alexander Acheson, married Mary Campion, a south Irish woman from Cork, served in the Crimean War, and fought in the battle of Balaclava.[7] There are no family records, but after Edward and his three brothers were born, Mary Campion died, and Alexander married again. Edward was apparently unhappy with his new stepmother and in his teens escaped his unhappy fate and emigrated alone to Canada.

In 1881 this strikingly handsome young man had secured a job in a dry goods company in Toronto as an elevator boy. But soon he found a way to enter University College of the University of Toronto, where he also seems to have inherited his father's bent for military action; while still a student, he enlisted in the Queen's Own Rifles, a militia regiment.[8]

In 1885 his service was in the Northwest Territories to put down a settler-Indian rebellion organized by Louis Riel, a Canadian partially of Indian descent who wanted to establish a separate nation. At the battle of Cut Knife Creek, Acheson was wounded. It appears that the battalion had been ambushed in a clearing and pulled back to seek cover. Edward, seeing that a fellow soldier had been hit and was lying in no-man's-land, ran out to pick him up. After shouldering back the dead man, he then returned to rescue another rifleman who was also wounded. For this he received the Victoria Medal for Bravery.[9]

Perhaps it was his wartime exploits that convinced him to enter divinity school, for he reputedly conducted the first church service at Fort Qu'Appelle west of Winnipeg.[10] In any case, upon returning to the university, he completed his education by studying for the Anglican ministry at a theological seminary, Wycliffe College of the University of Toronto, from which he graduated in 1889, and was made a curate at All Saints' Church in that city.[11] Edward Acheson's sense of order and discipline may well have been reinforced by his military service and his own undoubted self-control and ambition.

Wycliffe College had been founded in 1877 by a local Anglican evangelical movement that had rebelled against the powerful "high-church" Anglicanism that then prevailed at Toronto's Trinity College. Out of this tradition, emphasizing the supremacy of the Scripture accompanied by evangelical fervor, Edward Acheson practiced a Christianity that stressed moral imperatives within a "low-church" ritual.[12]

It was through Wycliffe that he met the Gooderham family, which had long been involved in the Anglican evangelical movement. Soon the handsome young curate was courting Eleanor Gooderham, and in 1892, three years after he was appointed assistant rector of Saint George's Church in New York City, he married her.

Eleanor was the daughter of George Gooderham, one of thirteen children. The Gooderhams had also emigrated from England, but in their case early in 1832, and had become in due course prosperous millers, which had been their calling in England. The processing of grain as a drink soon took the place of the milling of flour, and distilling became the main source of the family's money in the firm of Gooderham and Worts. Only two years before Eleanor's marriage to Edward Acheson, George Gooderham had built a massive red-stone-and-granite house at 135 St. George Street, a mere few blocks from Wycliffe College.[13]

Eleanor herself had been sent to England for schooling. "My mother's enthusiasm for the Empire and the Monarch," Acheson wrote, "was not diluted by any corrupting contact with Canadian nationalism."[14] Eleanor's family was not prepared to have her live as poorly as a clergyman's wife might be expected to. Her father provided her with enough to lead a comfortable existence, and then in 1904, a considerable sum was settled on her, so that the Achesons lived a fairly prosperous life among the gentry of Middletown, where the young couple relocated after less than a year at Saint George's. Their first son, Dean, was born on April 11, 1893.

Despite the Achesons' financial security, they were hardly in the same class as the Alsops and the Russells. They were neither considered, nor considered themselves, part of an American aristocracy. Mrs. Acheson, however, dressed in a stylish manner, rode horseback, and was one of the first in town to own a car. She was also an accomplished sportswoman: her father had taught her to shoot and ride and fish during her childhood summers spent camping in rural Canada. She also got to be a very good shot by practicing at shooting galleries on the Atlantic City boardwalk. The story is told that at dinner Mrs. Acheson, although characteristically dressed in her "long, swishy silks," would spy a squirrel on the terrace, leap from her chair, seize a shotgun from inside the door of the verandah, and bag the importunate intruder who scared birds and broke up their nests. As Dean's wife described it, "on her high heels and her pearls on—always real ones—she'd take a shot and drop the body of the squirrel."[15]

She was an often intimidating woman and became a kind of social arbiter in Middletown.[16] She tended to dominate groups, and, as her granddaughter characterized her, "with her imposing air, she became something of a grande dame." Her friends were "slightly obsequious" and were easily given to flattering her.[17] From a wealthy, relatively cosmopolitan background, she may well have found life in Middletown too confining for her talents, too provincial for someone of her education and upbringing.

Two more children were born to Edward and Eleanor Acheson—Margaret, two years younger than Dean and who was known as Margo, and, a few years later, Edward, who was called Ted. The father's temperament, what Dean called his "wild Ulster streak," was reflected in the children, all of whom seemed determined to avoid conformity.[18] Dean was especially close to his mother, with whom he shared a vivid sense of humor. A boyhood companion remembers the delight in their repartee, and Dean's wife recalled that the first time she visited the Achesons on a college vacation she came up the walk with his sister to see Dean "standing just behind his mother in the open doorway, the two of them laughing over some mutually shared joke."[19] Dean inherited from his mother her forceful character and that somewhat theatrical part of her nature that made her want to stand out from the crowd, to organize things, and to dominate.

Relations with his father were more formal. His father maintained an "Olympian detachment" from the ordinary details of raising children. In the evenings he would retire to his study immediately after dinner, and his most direct influence on the formation of his children tended to come on summer vacations, first on Long Island Sound at Indian Neck not far from New Haven, later at Round Mountain Lake in west-central Maine.

It was a long, rough journey to the north, though it began peacefully enough on the night train, as Acheson later described it, "the rhythm of the clicking wheels beneath, the window curtain raised a cautious inch on the kaleidoscope of dark shapes outside punctuated by a flash of play from lights, the shiver at the lonely, lost-soul wail of the engine ahead."[20] The train dropped off a rail car that took the family to the town of Farmington, and then a short ride to the end of a narrow-gauge logging railroad, where the "buckboards waited for the last excruciating trek to camp." The final few miles were tough ones—"when the forests closed in and the mountains began in earnest, only the luggage rode."[21]

The rector was at ease with his family in the woods. He taught the children canoeing, fly casting, and backpacking, and his stoical attitude was imparted on these camping trips. For he was a man who, though widely read in theology and Christian doctrine, rarely spoke of either. Reflecting his evangelical background, he dealt with ethics and conduct rather than revelation and redemption. "If his goal was the salvation of his soul, it was salvation by works, performed with charity and humor as well as zeal," his son wrote. His code of conduct was "instilled on the trails of our camping trips." Any tendency "to whine or grouse resulted in ignominious dismissal to the end of the line."[22]

Like his father, Acheson was not given to abstract thinking. Like his father, he preferred a code of conduct "based on the perceptions of what was decent and civilized."[23] His father, he said in later years, did not burden him with a guilty conscience; rather, when the boy misbehaved the rector's discipline appeared as "a force of nature." Acheson characterized this aspect of his relationship with his more demanding parent as follows: "The penalty for falling out of a tree was to get hurt. The penalty for falling out with my father was apt to be the same thing.

Result followed cause in a rational, and hence predictable, way but left no spiritual wound. The judgment of nature upon error is harsh and painful, but it is not a lecture or a verdict of moral and social obloquy."[24]

While Dean Acheson came to believe that his father's punishment left no "spiritual wound," he was nonetheless deeply hurt when he sought his father's approval and found it lacking. Time and again he would search for affirmation where he could find it—if not in his family, then within the larger circle of friends whose applause he craved.[25]

In the years immediately ahead, however, at school and at college, Dean almost willfully challenged authority. He seemed to flaunt his rebellious temperament, that "wild Ulster streak" he believed he had inherited from his accomplished father—who in 1915 rose to Episcopal heights as bishop of Connecticut.

CHAPTER TWO

A WORLD APART

"AFTER THE GOLDEN AGE, life lost this pristine, unorganized, amoral freedom," Acheson wrote years later. "The organization of the boarding school, like the wolf, in Icelandic saga, which ran up the sky and devoured the sun, devoured my early freedom."[1] First formally educated at a local private school, Dean continued to enjoy the "amoral freedom" of life in Middletown. It was especially the freedom of "wild things" that he enjoyed, "whose discipline came from pains and penalties externally and impersonally imposed, not penalties devised and inflicted by one's own kind with connotations of personal disapproval."[2] At nine years old, however, he was sent to a nearby boarding school, Hamlet Lodge, in Pomfret, Connecticut; this nonetheless permitted weekend visits from his parents, and he was not yet expelled from the valley that had seemed to him another Eden.

His close boyhood friend, Joe Lawton, remembered driving out with Dean's father to visit the boy. When they reached the top of the steps that led down to the school, they ran into another boy who was walking back and forth. When the minister asked him what he was doing, he explained that he was being punished. Dean's father admonished him to mend his ways and then asked where he might find his son. The boy answered: "He's over there being punished, too." As Lawton recalled it, Dean "did everything that came into his head. He was a good mixer, but very, very independent."[3]

It was an independence that would cost him most dearly in the years ahead, for in 1905, at the age of twelve, he was sent to Groton School northwest of Boston, and the dream of his lost freedom intensified in an atmosphere in which, as a former Grotonian described it, "obedience and conformity were commended by one's teachers as well as by one's peers. Independence, in almost any form, was punished."[4]

Groton was the creation of Endicott Peabody, "the Rector," whose powerful presence was inescapable. He could inspire fear, love, hatred, and loathing, but always respect. As the thirteen-year-old Averell Harriman wrote to his father, "You know he would be an awful bully if he wasn't such a terrible Christian."[5] A man of absolute integrity, from a wealthy and distinguished New England family, Peabody was determined to make Groton New England's new Winchester, and to a remarkable degree he succeeded.

From the outset, Groton School attracted the children of the rich from New York as well as the more patrician offspring of Boston. Peabody saw himself, unlike most headmasters of similar church schools, as the equal of the rich and wellborn, not as their servant. He was eager to enroll the children of American capitalism, in no small part because he believed that certain moral careers, such as public service, were less available to those who had to make money.[6]

Dedicated to service—both to God and to society—Peabody devised as the motto of the school *Cui Servire Est Regnare.* "To Serve Him Is to Rule" is the literal translation, but what Peabody intended was the translation from the Book of Common Prayer: "Whose service is perfect freedom." To Peabody, public service was, above all, the worldly analogue to his rather muscular Christianity. "If some Groton boys do not enter public life and do something for our land," he said, "it will not be because they have not been urged."[7]

Along with his unshakable rectitude, Peabody's imposing height and strength could easily overwhelm those with whom he came in contact. To a boy who was in the wrong, Peabody could be a truly terrifying figure, not because the Rector would harm the boy personally, but because any transgressions on the boy's part would be seen as a violation of right and justice, and Peabody had clearly designed the life of the school to reflect these virtues.

Although Peabody admired the English public school system, he was careful to modify its traditions to American ways. There was no "fagging," whereby older boys held the younger ones as virtual slaves and were allowed to cane miscreants. But Peabody did institute a system of prefects, older boys who were expected to set standards for the younger ones. More important, boys were given "black marks" for misconduct. To receive a black mark, however, did not mean boys were beaten; instead Peabody's system required a boy to work off each black mark with some assigned task, such as shoveling snow or mowing the lawn. The most severe punishment, six black marks, meant a visit to the Rector's study. This subjected the youth to the Rector's Jovian wrath, and that may well have been more daunting than corporal punishment.[8]

There was, however, a method of punishment that was not officially sanctioned but was nonetheless permitted. When younger boys were deemed to have broken the Groton code—by cheating, for example—or were considered too "fresh," physical punishment was inflicted. There were two ways of doing so: the less severe, "boot boxing," consisted of being put into a basement locker assigned to each boy for the boots he wore outdoors. While in the box, the culprit would be painfully doubled up for as long a time as he was forced to remain in his tiny prison.

The second and more terrifying punishment was "pumping." This consisted of having one's face shoved under an open spigot in the lavatory for as long a time as it took to induce a sensation of drowning. If a boy was consistently out of line, two or three pumpings usually sufficed to curb any outward expression of his rebellion.[9]

The hierarchical nature of the system, coupled with the Rector's uncompromising moral stance, produced in Groton a rigid discipline whose effect, as the artist George Biddle (Groton 1904) described it, was "to stifle the creative impulse. Its code could tolerate a feeling of shame for one's brother, and by and large, in many small ways, it was intellectually dishonest."[10]

The curriculum reflected the classical training of the English public school system. Latin was required, Greek optional with a choice between it and extra mathematics, physics, or chemistry. In history, Greece held two and a half years, Rome one year, western Europe and England each one year; the United States was restricted to half a year. French was not taught after the sophomore year (or fourth form), and German was taught the last two years. English was required throughout, but there was no geography, no biology, no music or art, no manual training. There was, of course, sacred studies, taught by the Rector, whose cry "Nails and notebook, boy!" traditionally opened the class.[11]

The true measure of achievement at Groton, however, was athletic prowess. Everyone was expected to play football and baseball no matter how much a boy might dislike them or how indifferently one played. Although scholarship was important to the Rector because the boys had to be prepared properly to enter Harvard or Yale, athletics was believed to build character and excessive bookishness seen as a flaw. When Joseph Alsop, later a globe-trotting columnist, was brought to the school for the first time, his mother started to boast of her son's bookish habits, at which point the Rector told her not to worry, "We'll soon knock all that out of him."[12]

While most Grotonians spent their lives serving Mammon rather than God, a remarkable number entered public service—Groton's first thousand graduates included one president, two secretaries of state, two governors, three senators, and nine ambassadors; few indeed were those who either entered the ministry or pursued the arts.[13]

It was a spartan world that greeted young Acheson as he entered the first form. Bedrooms were six-by-ten cubicles with bare walls, save for the hooks on which suits could be hung. There was no privacy, no door, walls just seven feet high, and only a curtain to be drawn across the entrance to the corridor. Furnishings were minimal: a plain bureau, a table, a chair, a rug, and a narrow bed. At the end of the dormitory was a lavatory with showers and long sinks of black soapstone with tin basins in them.

The regimen began a little before seven in the morning, when the boys were marched to the lavatory, where, under the uncompromising supervision of a prefect, they took a cold shower. After that ordeal, the boys were served breakfast at seven-thirty, followed by morning chapel at eight. Classes began at eight-thirty and continued without interruption until noon, when the main meal of the day was served. In the afternoon were two forty-five-minute sessions, followed in fall and spring by sports. Then, before supper, the boys donned a stiff collar and dress shoes. Evening chapel followed supper, and that was followed by a study period.

At the close of each day every boy lined up to say good night to the Rector and Mrs. Peabody. The Peabodys shook hands with them, and the Rector would often add some personal word. It was a moment when boys would be cast down, should the Rector proffer an unsmiling handshake or a curt "Good night"; on the other hand, should the Rector add a special word of praise and give an especially warm handshake, the boy would be extremely pleased. It was the headmaster's notion of the school as a Victorian family, and even for those boys who never fitted in, it was virtually impossible to rid oneself of the moral shadow of Endicott Peabody.[14]

"We knew that we moved in a world apart—and always of course in a world above," one graduate, who did become an artist, wrote years later.[15] It was this world that Dean Acheson became a part of in the fall of 1905, and it was one that he never accepted. Not only was the regimentation anathema to a boy who had enjoyed an unusual degree of freedom, but also the style of his dress was that of a country boy, as compared with the swells from New York. Schoolboy snobbishness flourished at Groton, and Acheson was hardly in a class with an Auchincloss or a Harriman, yet these were the boys who now attended Groton School. Perhaps the very slights that he may have suffered over his clothes contributed to his later concern with what he wore.

He was doubtless "fresh" and, unlike Franklin Roosevelt a decade earlier, unwilling to bend easily to the rules of the game. Above all, he was unwilling to accept the guidance of Peabody. Not surprisingly his grades suffered, and he was held in low esteem by both the Rector and the masters. Early on, Peabody wrote, "I find [Acheson] a very unexpected sort of person. Irresponsible. Forgets books. Does not remember lessons. Makes excuses. Not quite straightforward. Black marks show conduct not satisfactory. Should have stiff reprimand from home." By spring, Peabody was exasperated and simply noted, "Immature." Four years later, things were no better. "The masters find him disagreeable to teach at times." And a year later, "He is full of immature prejudices."[16]

While there were notations of some improvement from time to time, the overall evaluation was highly unfavorable. At one point the Rector wrote to his parents to ask them to come up and talk with him about their son because he was having such a difficult time with him. His mother took the journey north, and when she was with the Rector, he reputedly said, "Mrs. Acheson, I think it is clear that we will never be able to make a Groton boy out of Dean, and he would do well to go to another school." In her version Mrs. Acheson replied, "Dr. Peabody, I didn't send Dean here to have you make a 'Groton boy' out of him. I sent him here to be educated." "Oh, we can educate him." "Then I suggest you do it. I will leave him here as long as I think you can succeed, though you give me considerable doubt."[17]

The story is indicative not only of the Rector's view of Dean, but of his mother's willingness to defend him at all times, something the boy never doubted. He wrote to her at thirteen, "How dearly I love you and how necessary you are to my happiness."[18]

Acheson graduated at the very bottom of his class of twenty-four, with a sixty-eight average on his final report card. He did, however, make the first crew in his final year. One classmate remembered that "among his schoolmates at Groton Dean was conspicuous for his nimble wit, the independence of his opinions and his courage in declaring them. When the monthly marks were announced by the Rector, his name was seldom, if ever, among the first; because in those days Dean's agile and versatile intelligence was not focused on his classroom assignments to a notable extent, but was spent diffusely, if not capriciously, often to amuse, shock, dazzle, or discomfort."[19]

"At Groton I didn't feel like conforming," Acheson wrote years later. "And to my surprise and astonishment, I discovered not only that an independent judgment might be the right one, but that a man was actually alive and breathing once he had made it."[20] Reflecting on his experience at Groton, Acheson concluded: "The authoritarianism of the English 'public' school, upon which ours was modeled, was not for all temperaments. To adapt oneself to so sudden and considerable a change required what is now called a 'well-adjusted' personality. Mine apparently was not. At first, through surprise, ignorance, and awkwardness, later on and increasingly through willfulness, I bucked the Establishment and the system. One who does this fights against the odds. The result was predictable, painful, and clear."[21]

In his last year he published an essay in the school magazine, the *Grotonian*, called "The Snob in America." In it he spelled out his attachment to democratic values and, one presumes, his implicit criticism of the snobbery that was rampant at Groton and from which he had suffered. He opened his piece by defending the ideal of self-respect and urged the reader not to confuse this with snobbishness. Moreover, "in America especially, the institution of snobbery finds its lot a hard one [for] there is something in the ideal of democracy which is the death knell of snobbery. . . . [T]he essence of democracy is belief in the common people, and the essence of snobbery is contempt of them."[22]

Following his "belief in the common people," and his contempt for the "idle rich," a "class [which] is not American," Acheson, upon graduation, sought out the world of the workingman. Through family connections he obtained a job with the work crew of the Grand Trunk Pacific Railway (now the Canadian National), then being pushed westward across northern Canada. This was to be the great adventure of his youth, and it came none too soon for a boy who felt more than "a measure of self-doubt."[23]

Acheson's eagerness to work on the railroad under conditions of severe hardship reflected what the social historian Nelson Aldrich has called "the ordeal." Working in the wild becomes an occasion for testing oneself in the "rough mercies of the wilderness." There was in the West—whether American or Canadian—a hint of romance and a sense, as Aldrich describes it, "that through a willing exposure of the self to the forces of luck, good and bad, [you] will be led to develop a sense of personal power and consequence, and thereby acquire pride, but not overweening pride."[24] In Acheson's case the summer ordeal was to give him back, as he later recalled, "a priceless possession, joy in life."[25]

On a June day in 1911, Dean set out for the wilderness called James Bay, about 160 miles south of the southern tip of Hudson Bay. From a town called Cochrane, a railroad camp and supply depot, a transcontinental line was being built east and west. This was "Indian country," and after a night spent at the "Four Macs Hotel," he was sent off by construction freight train yet another 160 miles to work at the lowest job available at the residency of the engineer in charge—an axman. Riding in a caboose, Dean was assaulted by smoke, mosquitoes, and blackflies, but, as he later wrote, "Smoke, crying eyes and ravenous insects were as nothing compared to the intoxication of knowing that this was 'life.'"

Summers in the Maine woods proved a boon for the young axman, and within a few days he was sent farther west to the absolute wilderness, where four or five log cabins housed the second group of workmen. There he learned to smoke a pipe and in due course was sent farther into the forest primeval. In a swamp clearing, four or five structures were joined together by a boardwalk. Three or four feet of the walls were made of log; the rest and the ceiling, of canvas: "To have been told that I would become fond of this dreary spot would have been unbelievable. But so it was to be."

Together, Dean and a "French-Indian lad," in addition to working as axmen, took over the jobs of rodman and force accountant—Dean walking over ten miles every day to check off the condition of the thousand or so men working on the railroad.

Life at the residency in the swamp was filled with "songs and talk" that were "noisy, bawdy, often vulgar in the extreme." Dean thrived in this atmosphere of digging latrines, splitting wood, dealing with drunken knife fights—even death "from causes unknown." When he left the camp at the end of the summer to enter Yale College, he was filled with sadness. "These men," he wrote, "had done more for me than they would ever know and, in doing it, had become a part of me. They had given me a new eagerness for experience. The simple, extroverted pattern of their lives had revived a sense of freedom amidst uncoerced order, extinguishing the memory of 'pain as exquisite as any,' in John Adams's words, from suffocating discipline and arbitrary values."[26]

With the money he earned, he bought in Toronto a small gold-filigree brooch studded with pearls for his mother, who wore it until her death. Six months later, on the occasion of her birthday, the eighteen-year-old wrote her a note (which she valued "above all my other treasures") in which he referred to himself in the third person as returning "from his first argosy, bringing his first golden fleece." He goes on to say that "it was not an easy argosy; it was not an easy golden fleece, and it taught him many things. But in one respect he has never changed, that feeling in his heart is the same now as it was in the child's heart over a decade ago. Perhaps there is not the same blindness about it which there was in the child. While to him the mother meant a great, comforting, all-understanding being, now he sees in her all love, patience, goodness, purity."[27]

Through his ordeal in the wilderness, Dean was freed from the unhappiness of Groton, the unremitting discipline, and the Rector's moral strictures. But after graduating from Yale and while a student at Harvard Law School, he came to recognize that he had frittered away too much of his time at the school and tried to make up for it in a letter to Endicott Peabody. This began by apologizing for neglecting his "associations with the school." Yet "I do not want you to think that my attitude has been one of piqued hostility. . . . It was entirely one of shrinking from a place where I knew that I had been a failure and where I felt that the masters and the boys who knew me had an opinion of me far less charitable than the present one of the world at large. . . . All such feeling on my part is quite gone. Of course, I can't deceive myself about my career in school or the memory that everyone has of it. But there was an open mindedness, or rather an eagerness, on the part of every one to find the signs of a redemption which I appreciated a great deal."[28]

A few years later, after the birth of his son, David, he wrote Peabody to ask that the boy be put down for Groton, and years later, in response to an inquiry from Peabody about David's impending admission, Acheson wrote: "I may be wrong about this, but it seemed to me in my own case that being pressed too fast to accept ideas, standards and activities which were foreign to me, led me for many years to take a dissenting point of view—which included dissent from many things which later on I found thoroughly acceptable."[29]

While the mature Acheson admitted the blemishes of a misspent youth, he never became the rebel fully tamed. If anything, he had learned that his refusal to adopt values imposed on him only strengthened his desire for independence. His years at Yale would reveal a temperament that was still far from ready to accept imposed discipline.

CHAPTER THREE

THE MOST DASHING OF YALE MEN

"YOU COME TO YALE—what is said to you? 'Be natural, be spontaneous, revel in a certain freedom, enjoy a leisure you'll never get again, browse around, give your imagination a chance, see everyone, rub wits with everyone, get to know yourself.'"

This was the advice given to Dink Stover in Owen Johnson's classic tale of Yale life at the turn of the century. This was certainly what Dean Acheson intended to do and, to large extent, did. But for most Yalies, the college was a highly competitive institution, and the goal was success. As Owen Johnson remarked of Dink Stover, "What completely surprised him was the lack of careless, indolent camaraderie he had known at school and had expected in larger scope at college. Every one was busy, working with a dogged persistence along some line of ambition."[1]

So demanding was the constant competition among undergraduates that even Henry Stimson, that quintessential Yale man, confessed years later that "the idea of a struggle for prizes, so to speak, has always been one of the fundamental elements of my mind, and I can hardly conceive of what my feelings would be if I ever was put in a position or situation in life where there are no prizes to struggle for."[2] Ambition at Yale, however, did not generally run to scholarship. As a faculty committee described the college a few years before Acheson entered, "Hard study has become unfashionable at Yale."[3]

Organizations abounded, on the other hand, and athletic teams were held in the highest esteem. As freshmen, the members of the Class of 1915 entered the college at the end of the greatest era in Yale football. From 1882 to 1898 Yale produced nine undefeated teams. In 1909 the Yale football team went undefeated, untied, and unscored upon. The Yale competitive spirit was also evident in the proliferation of clubs: between 1900 and 1911 the Yale Dramatic Association was formed, as well as the singing group, the Whiffenpoofs, and the literary society, the Elizabethan Club.

While athletes continued to be held in great esteem, young men who wrote poetry and fiction emerged into what was later called the Yale Literary Renaissance. Between 1911 and 1920 Yale produced poets Archibald MacLeish (1915) and Stephen Vincent Benét (1919); playwrights Donald Ogden Stewart (1916), Philip Barry (1918), and Thornton Wilder (1920); publishers John Farrar (1918), Briton Hadden (1920), and Henry Luce (1920). These young men seemed to embrace the Yale ethos. So prevalent was the organizational impulse that Stephen Vincent Benét and his roommate composed a poem that began

> Do you want to be successful
>   Form a club!
> Are your chances quite distressful?
>   Form a club![4]

In theory all this activity was made possible because of what was termed "Yale Democracy." It did not matter, it was said, who you were or where you came from or how much money you had. Yet, as W. S. Lewis (1918) wrote in his autobiography, *One Man's Education*, "At Yale (as elsewhere, for that matter), it helped to have the right clothes and to know how to wear them. . . . More important than clothes was the air of 'belonging.' The swift appraising eyes of adepts in the art of social intercourse recognized a fellow initiate on sight, the rest might as well not exist, but acquirement of an acceptable appearance was not in itself enough to ensure success. You had to prove your worth, a fact subsumed under the concept of 'Yale Democracy.'

"To the Western boys [like Lewis] who came to Yale . . . without a year or two in a good Eastern prep school, the talk about Yale democracy was ironical. Although it made no difference whether you had money or not (few knew who were rich unless they had famous names) and there was no Harvard Gold Coast into which the *jeunesse dorée* withdrew, by Western standards Yale was anything but 'democratic.'"[5]

Basic to Yale undergraduate life was the institution of the senior society, which was supposed to be reconciled to Yale Democracy by the notion that Yale stood for equality of opportunity but not equality of reward. In Acheson's day there were three senior societies: Wolf's Head, Scroll and Key, and the most prestigious, Skull and Bones. On the second Thursday in May, the junior class, or at least those who thought they had a reasonable chance of being selected, assembled under the "Tap Day Oak" on the campus at five in the afternoon. A few minutes before the hour, members of the secret societies strolled through the Berkeley oval and stood at attention behind the juniors whom they were going to tap. As W. S. Lewis describes the scene: "At the first stroke of five the expressionless Seniors banged the Juniors' shoulders shouting, 'Go to your room!' The crowd burst into nervous applause. This went on for nearly an hour while the excitement grew as the three societies filled up their number of fifteen each and it became evident that some prominent Juniors were going to miss out."[6]

Forty-five men out of 380, or 1 in 8, were selected. They were then expected to spend every Thursday and every Sunday evening meeting with the other members of their society in a "tomb," so-called because of its windowless building. They were not like the social—or "final"—clubs, which flourished at Harvard and were largely given over to dissipation. Yale's senior societies were devoted primarily to self-improvement. They were shrines to good fellowship, minischools of success.

The president of Yale, Arthur Hadley, believed that the "prime necessity" of a course of study was character building, and, in the words of one Yale historian, "after this character was formed it was to be used in public service."[7] The curriculum was devised for the average student, and electives were not encouraged. Yale's president admitted that Oxford and Harvard probably did a better job "in developing independent intellectual activity," but Yale was determined to maintain an educational program that would provide a basic liberal education, which required freshmen and sophomores to take certain core studies in a modern foreign language, history or English literature, mathematics or a modern science, and Greek and Latin (unless a student took both math and a science).[8]

As W. S. Lewis, who later became Acheson's close friend and his colleague on the Yale Corporation, wrote, "What Yale believed was painted on the proscenium over the stage in Lapson Lyceum: *Non Studiis sed Vitae Discimus*. At Yale we learned life, not studies. 'Life' was primarily finding out how to get on with one's fellows and to advance in the never-to-be-relaxed struggle for the first prize, which was not in the minds of most undergraduates the acquirement of bookish knowledge, but an election to a Senior Society."[9] Dean Acheson seems to have shared this belief.

Six feet two, tanned, and healthy after his summer working on the railroad, Dean Acheson came to Yale with the likely belief that he would fit in. Four of his twenty-three classmates at Groton were destined to join him in New Haven (the overwhelming majority of the class went to Harvard). Two of them, Willie Crocker and Joe Walker, were especially good friends and roomed with him his first three years. He was no longer the country lad who had journeyed north to Groton but instead became rather splendid in his dress and possessed of a comfortable allowance. Later he acquired a roadster.

He soon concluded that studying hard at Yale was unnecessary and became a committed bon vivant, so that his grades rarely rose above a C average. He joined a number of clubs, including the Turtles, the Hogans, the Mohicans, and the Grill Room Grizzlies, whose members preferred to drink, sing songs, and tell rather poor jokes, and he became a member of Delta Kappa Epsilon fraternity. Most important of all, he was tapped for Scroll and Key, second only to Skull and Bones in prestige.[10]

Determined to put aside the strictures of Groton, Acheson strove for achievements at Yale that were therefore wholly social, but they were considerable; in essence, Acheson attained the very pinnacle of success by being the wittiest, the cleverest, the most dashing of Yale men. He was known throughout the college for his scintillating wit and was certainly perceived by underclassmen as one of the leading seniors, along with the poet-athlete Archibald MacLeish and the composer Douglas Moore. "Dean moved in a fast circle and seemed to have a great deal more money than he actually had," a former classmate recalled. "He was refreshingly bright, and intent upon enjoying himself. He shunned the abstractions, for example, and kept far from the literary life on the campus, or anything that might have smacked of culture with a capital C."[11]

It is instructive in this respect to compare Acheson's career at Yale with Archibald MacLeish's, for MacLeish became Acheson's closest friend after they encountered each other again at Harvard Law School. At Yale, however, MacLeish seemed to embody everything Acheson detested. A varsity football player, MacLeish was also chairman of the *Lit.*, one of twenty-eight juniors elected to Phi Beta Kappa, and a writer whose poem "Grief" was published in the widely circulated *Yale Review*, the first time the *Review* had ever published verse by an undergraduate.

Acheson, of course, knew MacLeish, whose exploits made the class vote him Most Brilliant and Most Versatile. He was perhaps jealous, but certainly contemptuous, of the image of the striver that MacLeish embodied. When Acheson's future wife, looking over the class book and coming across numerous references to Archibald MacLeish—scholar, athlete, poet—asked, "Just who is this MacLeish fellow?" Acheson replied, "Oh, you wouldn't like him."[12] MacLeish's view of Acheson was no less hostile: "He was the typical son of an Episcopal bishop—gay, graceful, gallant—he was also socially snobby with qualities of arrogance and superciliousness. Dean led a charming social existence at Yale."[13]

The only serious extracurricular activity Acheson permitted himself was to row on the freshman crew, as he had at school. His coach was Averell Harriman, who had been two years ahead of him at Groton and was the son of the railroad baron E. H. Harriman, who had built the Union Pacific.

When Acheson entered Yale, the Harvard oarsmen had defeated the Blues for six straight years. In 1911 even an inexperienced Princeton eight had beaten the varsity. With both alumni and undergraduates favoring amateur coaching by Yale graduates and student assistants, Harriman had volunteered to coach the freshman crew. He also believed that the key to Yale's success might well lie in adapting the Oxford University style of rowing—a long and steady pull. To study Oxford's method, he sailed for England in January 1912 and spent the winter and spring watching the young Oxonians practice each afternoon and taking notes on the way their oars caught the water, how their long strokes swept them forward until their bodies ran almost parallel to the river. He went to Henley on the Thames to observe them as they prepared for their race against Cambridge, and when he returned to Yale in April, he was ready to teach the freshmen new tricks.

At the Harvard-Yale race that June, the Yale varsity lost again, but Harriman's freshmen eight, while also losing, challenged the Harvard boat right up to the finish line. With lanky Dean Acheson rowing number seven, the Yale boat lost by only two and a half seconds. As a result, Harriman was named to coach the varsity.[14]

Although as a sophomore Acheson was not quite big enough to make the varsity crew, Harriman appointed him freshman coach. In the summer of 1913 he asked Acheson to accompany him to England for the crew races at Henley on the Thames and then to Oxford University to pick up some further pointers for the Yale crew. Acheson's first trip to England was filled with rowdy undergraduate parties, exactly the kind of entertainment a twenty-year-old Yale blade reveled in.

Acheson recalled many decades later the dinner following the Grand Challenge Cup at Henley: "All crews entered for the Grand Challenge Cup were present—foreign and domestic. The great Cup was in the center of a long table, beautiful to see, and rendered even more admirable by being filled with champagne." Early in the evening, "someone conceived the happy thought of shaking his bottle, and, as he loosened the wire, pointing it at a fellow guest. . . . The casualties from hostile fire and overrapid consumption of agitated champagne were both heavy and disorganizing—so disorganizing, in fact, that many speeches carefully prepared in English, French, and German perished unspoken."[15]

That fall, Harriman and Acheson returned to New Haven, "as full as Ulysses of esoteric learning about rowing—shell construction, rigging, stroke and training—and with more confidence in our learning than I think I have since felt about anything." Put in charge of coaching at Yale, they arranged a fall race with Princeton University. Yale was soundly beaten, and the following week Harriman and Acheson were dismissed from the coaching staff. In reflecting over the experience of being fired on this occasion, Acheson said that he discovered then that the "sweetest way of being relieved of responsibility without self-reproach is to be unjustly fired."[16]

* * *

While the years at Yale were being "squandered in learning things that were meaningless," as Acheson himself described it years later,[17] there was a troubling episode that Acheson never referred to in any of his reminiscences. During the 1912 campaign for the presidency, Acheson was very much taken by Theodore Roosevelt's Bull Moose campaign against incumbent William Howard Taft and the Democratic challenger, Woodrow Wilson. "I thrilled to every bugle call to action blown by the 'Young Turks,' the 'Progressives,' and most of all by 'T.R.,' the most ebullient of them all," he wrote, "in the revolt against the 'Old Guard,' the 'malefactors of great wealth,' against 'reaction' in the person of Uncle Joe Cannon [the Speaker of the House] and inaction in the benign and ineffective figure of President William Howard Taft. It was springtime and 'T.R.' rode again."[18]

But during a heated discussion with his father about the merits of the candidates, the young sophomore called the minister "a fool." The result was banishment. His father instructed him to pack his bags and not return home for a year. Nonetheless, he was allowed to continue at Yale and to spend his vacations as he chose, which meant rather grand visits to his friends Bayne Denegre in New Orleans and Willie Crocker in San Francisco. Part of the summer of 1913 was spent at Arden House, the Harriman mansion up the Hudson.

Yet the experience was deeply wounding, not only to Dean and to his father, but also, and especially, to his mother. A year to the day after the expulsion, both parents were discussing whether Dean would appear. His mother was especially fearful that he would shun them, but his father maintained that he would be home for dinner. And so he was.[19]

As always when Dean defied his father, the punishment was as swift as it had been in his boyhood. He had disappointed the clergyman both at school and at college and seemed almost determined to stand up to authority. At the same time, while hotly challenging his father whenever he disagreed with him, he very much desired his approval—and, in his view, never got it. Even when he attained high rank in the government in 1933, shortly before his father's death, and acted on moral principles when he stood up to the president himself, he found that his father refused to condone his behavior.[20]

Despite the memory of the banishment, Dean was eager to go home on a given weekend, and his classmates were happy to ride up with him in his Knox roadster for a decent meal. On Thanksgiving Day in his junior year, he arrived for the customary four-day holiday, happy to reconnect with his younger sister, Margo, who was then a freshman at Wellesley College. With her was her roommate, Alice

Stanley, from Detroit, a willowy, strikingly beautiful woman, rather shy but with a strong temperament. She was certainly firm enough in her opinions not to be too intimidated by a dashing Yale upperclassman two years her senior. She was also far more interested in art studies and painting than in a classical Wellesley education, but her father had nonetheless insisted that she finish what she was doing.

The following weekend Dean went to visit her at Wellesley and also asked her to a dance over the Christmas holidays. Unfortunately she had to go home to visit her parents, and after that the courtship lapsed until Dean graduated and stopped off to see her in Detroit en route to Japan on an Asian version of the European Grand Tour.

Alice Stanley's family had originally emigrated from England to Connecticut in the seventeenth century. In 1840 her grandfather, John Mix Stanley, went west, ostensibly as a surveyor but determined to paint portraits and action paintings of Native Americans. He lived among the Indians for ten years and then moved to Washington, D.C., where he tried to persuade the government to buy his pictures of the Plains Indians. In 1868 an exhibition of these works of art was to open in Washington, but it was destroyed by two fires before opening, and Stanley went back to the West to do it all over again.

By this time he had married Alice English, who had come to Washington from New Jersey to help her aunt run a ladies' seminary. Her father engaged the painter to do her portrait; the artist and his subject fell in love, married, and produced a son, Louis. In the 1860s they moved to Detroit, where the painter maintained a studio and where he died in 1872. Among his paintings that now hang in the National Museum of American Art in Washington, D.C., are five that escaped the fire, one of which is the highly naturalistic *Buffalo Hunt on the Southwestern Plains* (1845).

Louis Stanley became a lawyer for the Grand Trunk Railroad, but he was not unmarked by his father's artistic temperament, at least insofar as he chose to marry Jane Caroline Mahon, who played the piano and the violin. They met in Charlevoix, Michigan, a summer resort that fronts on three lakes, where she was playing in a music hall. Louis and Jane were wed in 1890, and six years later Alice Stanley was born. As a girl, Alice spent her summers in Charlevoix or traveling through the Great Lakes on the free passes her father obtained because of his position with the railroad. She painted from an early age, along with her mother, who had become a serious painter.[21]

However much Acheson was attracted to Alice Stanley, he was uncertain of his feelings for her and hers for him when he graduated from college in 1915. Deemed by his classmates to be among the "wittiest" and "sportiest," he was determined to have a last adventure before journeying north to Harvard Law School, where he probably assumed that he would have to work hard. Therefore, with the war in Europe raging on the Western Front, six Yale graduates headed west during the summer of 1915 on their journey to Japan.

* * *

The anonymous log that was kept jointly by the six Wanderers (as they termed themselves) reveals a boyish innocence. They dutifully visited the temples of Kyoto and caught a glimpse of Mount Fujiyama, played bridge interminably on their voyages between San Francisco and Yokohama, and were suitably embarrassed upon entering a Japanese communal bath to find it full of naked men, women, and children. Even their description of a trip to the red-light district of Yokohama concludes with a quintessentially American evaluation of the scene: "We passed down little narrow streets lined on both sides with rows of little Japanese girls all powdered and painted squatting behind bars. They were wonderfully dressed in all sorts of colors and their hair was done up in beautiful and various shapes. Some of them were quite pretty and all of them smiled and waved to us. Dean was by far the greatest favorite. . . . The most extraordinary part of the whole district was the orderliness and total absence of any atmosphere of vice. The pity of it was what struck us most."[22]

In his letters home, Acheson's vivid descriptions of the sights of Japan display a heightened sensitivity to the changes in a country that was undergoing rapid modernization. Sailing up the harbor of Yokohama, he writes: "The glorious green hills and funny twisted trees were symbolic of the way in which nature has put all that is delicate and vari-colored and lovely in these islands. And the forts along the shore which it is said could defy the combined navies of the world are an indication that with all this beauty the new Japan has been sitting at the feet of Germany with very attentive ears."[23]

Acheson seems to have had a shipboard dalliance, but it was of little consequence, for his mind was on Alice Stanley, whom he had seen in Detroit en route to joining his companions in Chicago for the train trip west. In his letters to his mother, he is very direct about his growing feelings for the "Lady Alicia" and very much wants her to approve of her. Arriving in Yokohama, he was keenly disappointed not to find a letter from Alice; finally her letters did reach him, which encouraged him to change his travel plans and return via Detroit. His only apparent care was to make sure that Alice Stanley understood the depth of his feelings for her and, by stopping off in Michigan, to ensure that she would be returning to Wellesley. In a few days he would be entering Harvard Law School.

It is difficult to know exactly what prompted Acheson to study law; he seems to have had no particular calling in this regard. But the law was an honorable profession that doubtless would please his father. Yet it was at the law school that he found for the first time that "excellence counted, a sloppy try wasn't enough."[24] That discovery would change his life.

CHAPTER FOUR

"THIS WONDERFUL MECHANISM, THE BRAIN"

ALTHOUGH ACHESON was now seriously courting Alice Stanley at Wellesley College, only a few miles away, he began his career at Harvard Law School with the same rather carefree and debonair tone he had adopted at Yale.

Nine students roomed together in a rambling wooden house at One Mercer Circle.[1] One was Cole Porter, who had graduated from Yale two years before Dean, where he was also a member of Scroll and Key. A reluctant law student, Porter, in time, transferred to the graduate school of arts and sciences to take courses in music theory. He was also writing and staging musical skits in Boston and New Haven. One after-the-show celebration in the house at Mercer Circle went on until early the next morning; neighbors complained to the dean of the law school, and all were threatened with suspension. As the story goes, Porter told the authorities that the only reason he had entered Harvard was to please his family, so why not expel him and reprimand the others? The solution seemed to please everyone: Acheson was kept on while Porter happily escaped Cambridge for New York, where he staged his first Broadway musical, *See America First*, in 1916.[2]

While America's involvement in the First World War did not come about until the spring of 1917, rumors of war were pervasive. Moreover, Woodrow Wilson realized that the United States had no substantial army. Improvising, the president called out the National Guard by 1916 and mustered it into federal service. Acheson, who had become engaged to Alice Stanley that spring, had no particular plans for the summer after his first year in law school. A devoted believer in "preparedness," he was therefore vulnerable to pressures from his friends to join them for three months in the so-called Yale Battery, Battery D of the Connecticut National Guard's Regiment of Field Artillery.[3]

Armed with his federal warrant, Acheson was shipped off to Tobyhanna, Pennsylvania, for field artillery training. As Acheson described it, it was a classically comic experience of military service. Horses sent to drag the caissons over the Pennsylvania hills turned out to be sick with colds and started to die. Soon, Acheson writes, "we were all pleading with the sufferers to be of good heart, not to give up the battle for life; we put slings under them to keep them on their feet; tenderly gave them the veterinarians' doses; manned round-the-clock watches at the stables."[4]

Promoted to the rank of sergeant and put in charge of the mess, Acheson struggled to keep the cook sober, while hoping that the quality of the food would improve. After spending a few more weeks setting off salvos of gunfire that "blew the hell out of an opposing cardboard artillery position,"[5] Acheson was discharged and returned to Cambridge for his second year at law school.

While Acheson's first year there seemed like an extension of his undergraduate insouciance, at the beginning of his second year he took a class taught by Felix Frankfurter and discovered "the power of thought." Not only did he become aware of "this wonderful mechanism, the brain," but he also became aware of "an unlimited mass of material that was lying about the world waiting to be stuffed into the brain."[6]

Acheson was enamored of Frankfurter's cascade of ideas, his commitment to social justice, his bursts of activity as he scurried about Harvard Square, a peppery little man who was determined to make his views known to the government in power and did not hesitate to take an independent stance on any issue. An intensely loyal man, Frankfurter saw people in hues of black and white—as one friend described it: "The black were of an unrelieved blackness, the white—apart from the gods, [Oliver Wendell] Holmes and [Henry] Stimson—were not exempt from humorous and affectionate discrimination."[7]

As a professor, Frankfurter was dedicated to his students, no matter how busy his life in the great world beyond Cambridge. Legal issues, as he taught them, "were not problems the answers to which are to be found in law books." Like Holmes, who believed "the life of the law has not been logic; it has been experience,"[8] Frankfurter insisted that the "law derives from facts, facts of industry and facts of life. . . ."[9]

Acheson would echo these words: "It was just one step further to the philosophic approach to matters—to learning that you need not make up your mind in advance, that there is no set solution to a problem, and that decisions are the result of analyzing the facts, of tussling and grappling with them."[10]

At the end of his second year Acheson was near the top of his class and was elected to the editorial board of the *Harvard Law Review*. He had also married Alice on May 5, 1917. It was a hasty marriage. Although they had been engaged for well over a year, they were fearful that he would be called up for regular military service. America had entered the war against Germany on April 6, 1917, and even though Alice was to graduate from college in June, they decided not to wait. With less than two weeks' notice, they were married in Detroit. The regulations at Wellesley College at that time did not permit undergraduates to marry, but this was wartime, and Alice received a special dispensation to be able to wed Acheson and still receive her degree. There were few friends as witnesses; while Alice's sister was maid of honor, Acheson chose as "best man" his sister, Margo, who had introduced them at Thanksgiving in Middletown three and a half years earlier.

For the remaining six weeks of Alice's schooling, she and Dean lived in the Waban Hotel in Wellesley. There was still one more year for Dean at the law school, and after finding an apartment in Cambridge, Alice took art classes at the Boston School of Design, near the Isabella Stewart Gardner Museum in Boston. At last, she would follow her bent and make a serious career as a painter even while attending to the novelties of marriage.

Encouraged by Frankfurter and Dean Roscoe Pound, Acheson began a short book, which he completed after the war, proposing a new basis for jurisprudence that would govern labor relations. In defending the interests of the "closed" union shop, Acheson contended that the facts dictated the need for new rules to render justice in industrial relations. He wrote: "If we are passing . . . 'from the day of the individual to the day of the group,' if the press of population, the centralization of power, the intricacies of a highly developed culture are forcing the individual to secure his interests through group rather than solitary action, it is inevitable that the group as an entity should develop interests as real as any with which the law has to deal."[11] Here, Acheson was responding to the spirit of his times, and in Frankfurter he had found an invaluable mentor.

On graduation in June 1918 he would be ranked fifth, which surprised his old classmate Archibald MacLeish, who encountered Acheson on MacLeish's return to the law school from France in January 1919: "The Acheson who had been scornful of zeal, was now full of zeal—zeal for the law."[12]

No longer a student and faced with the imminent prospect of the draft, Acheson felt he had little choice but to enlist in one of the services. Perhaps because of his experience with the artillery, Acheson decided that the navy was a better bet. In any case, he received his commission as an ensign in the naval auxiliary reserve and left for duty with the Naval Overseas Transportation Service, where he was assigned to the operation of navy cargo transports at the Brooklyn Navy Yard. But before he could be sent overseas, the armistice was signed and he was discharged by the end of the year. During his navy service, Alice, who was pregnant, had remained in Connecticut with his parents.

As an expectant father uncertain of his future, Acheson thought it seemed the wisest course to mark time by returning to Cambridge in January 1919 to finish the book on labor law that he hoped to get published. But after a few months working on the manuscript, he found that his decision about what to do with his life was suddenly resolved by Felix Frankfurter, who suggested to Louis D. Brandeis, then associate justice on the Supreme Court, that Acheson go to Washington as his law clerk.

There would be no more "blind alleys," as Acheson put it in a letter to Frankfurter, for a young man with a wife and baby, Jane Stanley Acheson, born on February 27, 1919.[13] The Achesons were to go to Washington, where Dean would spend two years with Brandeis.

PART TWO

THE IMPERATIVES OF ACTION

CHAPTER FIVE

THE HEROES

At sixty-three years of age, Mr. Justice Louis Brandeis was an arresting figure. As Dean Acheson described him, his head was "of Lincolnian cast and grandeur, the same boldness and ruggedness of features, the same untamed hair, the eyes of infinite depth under bushy eyebrows." In later years, law clerks would refer to him as Isaiah, the stern moralist, the Old Testament prophet.[1] With Brandeis, "perfection was the norm and you went up from there." He possessed, as Acheson correctly perceived, "an almost stultifying sense of perfection."[2]

Brandeis had come to the Supreme Court from his law practice in Boston as an acknowledged champion of the people against entrenched economic interests. For Brandeis, bigness was always the enemy, and in business bigness was symbolized by the trusts, those giant machines that would engulf small companies, resources, and individual workers while producing enormous profits for the stockholders.

The problem, of course, was to find a middle way between the trusts at one end and the unemployed and bankrupt on the other. The businessmen, not surprisingly, wanted no government regulation of basic industries. Most Americans, on the other hand, seemed to want neither complete government control nor untrammeled laissez-faire. Brandeis understood this. Although an enemy of bigness he realized that trusts could not be completely destroyed and therefore there was a need for government action to ensure competition. This was the basic course Americans have followed for the rest of this century.[3]

Woodrow Wilson initially considered appointing Brandeis attorney general but bowed before the pressure from New Englanders who had suffered from

Brandeis's uncompromising legal battles and who may have also opposed him as a Jew. Brandeis nonetheless remained a close adviser to the president from his law office in Boston. During Wilson's first term, he was instrumental in drafting the Clayton Antitrust Act, which dealt with business practices that threatened competition, and in drawing up proposals to establish the Federal Trade Commission. The creation of the Federal Reserve Board also reflected Brandeis's views.

His eminence was such that on Independence Day 1915 he was asked to deliver the Fourth of July oration at Boston's Faneuil Hall; previous speakers had included John Quincy Adams, Oliver Wendell Holmes, and Edward Everett Hale. Brandeis spoke of the need to become "our brother's keepers," of the need for each individual to have "some degree of financial independence" for his old age.[4]

Later that year he gave a speech before the Chicago Bar Association, in which he spoke of a man who was an eminent jurist sent to Montenegro to establish a code of law, and "for two years [he] literally made his home with the people—studying everywhere their customs, their practices, their needs, their beliefs, their points of view. Then he embodied in law the life which the Montenegrins lived. They respected that law; because it expressed the will of the people."[5]

On January 28, 1916, Woodrow Wilson nominated Brandeis for the United States Supreme Court.

Dean Acheson became Brandeis's law clerk in 1919. The custom of the time was for each Supreme Court justice to have a "stenographer-secretary" and a messenger. But both Holmes and Brandeis dropped the stenographer and used Harvard Law School graduates (chosen, not surprisingly, by Felix Frankfurter) as clerks. They believed, as Acheson explained it, that "these young men, fresh from the intellectual stimulation of the law school, brought them constant refreshment and challenge, perhaps more useful in their work than the usual office aides."[6] As far as the dictation was concerned, the two justices answered their own mail by hand.

Brandeis took hard work for granted, and he expected the same of his clerks. He was not given to praise in any form, and when he laid blame on a subordinate, the culprit would remember exactly what happened. Acheson's first—and last—experience of his chief's displeasure came early on in his clerkship. As was Brandeis's custom, his brief bulged with footnotes. But when Brandeis went over the case, he noted that two footnotes were not relevant to the case. It had been Acheson's duty to read all the cases cited in the footnotes. Unfortunately, Acheson had checked the wrong notes. When the impetuous young clerk apologized, Brandeis dismissed the matter in a sentence—"Please remember that your function is to correct my errors, not to introduce errors of your own."[7]

Work began on Monday mornings following a Saturday conference of the Court, at which time it was decided what cases were assigned to whom. From the assignment slip, Brandeis would indicate the case on which he was to start drafting his opinion, and he would compose in longhand, while Acheson used the typewriter. When he reached a point in his opinion where he wanted his draft checked, he would give it to Acheson and take Acheson's work, sometimes using parts of it, sometimes not. As Acheson described it, "My instructions regarding his work were to look with suspicion on every statement of fact until it was proved from the record of the case, and on every statement of law until I had exhausted the authorities." Finally, when the time came for a fair copy, "the court printer made it from the nearly indecipherable manuscript put together with the aid of scissors and paste." What Acheson called "a touching part of our relationship" was Brandeis's insistence that "nothing should go out unless we were *both* satisfied with the product."[8]

While Brandeis believed that laws had to reflect the changing attitudes of society, he also believed, as did Acheson, that there were certain transcendent moral principles that always prevailed. By confining his analysis of a case to the effects of prior decisions on the controlling facts involved, Brandeis sometimes misled his admirers. As an instance of this, in the twenties, Acheson took Professor Manley Hudson of Harvard Law School (who later became a judge of the World Court) to meet Brandeis. In discussing the political consequences of Prohibition, Hudson asserted that moral principles were little more than generalizations from the accepted mores and notions of a particular time and place. Acheson writes: "The eruption was even more spectacular than I had anticipated. The Justice wrapped the mantle of Isaiah around himself, dropped his voice a full octave, jutted his eyebrows forward in a most menacing way, and began to prophesy. Morality was truth; and truth had been revealed to man in an unbroken, continuous, and consistent flow by the great prophets and poets of all time."[9]

In his dissents Brandeis was always trying to fulfill his educative purpose and was careful to lessen wounds and to narrow, whenever possible, the gap between the majority and the minority. There would, after all, be other cases. As Acheson concluded, "He was free to look to the future and point out to a wider audience than the Court or the bar the nature of the issue, where its roots lay, future trends which would affect its later manifestations, the possible course of legislation, and so on." It was with this larger audience in mind that he discussed with his law clerk on November 22, 1919, a series of dissenting opinions they were preparing in the Espionage Act cases—that is, prosecuting individuals for publication of views said to impede the conduct of World War I.

"The whole purpose is to educate the country," Brandeis declared. "We may be able to fill the people with shame, after the passion cools, by preserving some of it on the record. The only hope is the people; you cannot educate the Court [on this subject]."[10] He was, he admitted, an incurable optimist.

In a lengthy letter to Felix Frankfurter at the beginning of his second year as clerk, Acheson analyzed Brandeis. He pointed out that the great justice was very wary of "great stupid institutions" that grow larger and larger and "crowd into the little space which the individual has." Above all, Acheson did not believe that the justice put "the slightest faith" in universalistic schemes for mass salvation.[11] This was a sentiment that Acheson himself fully shared.

The Brandeises' weekly "at homes" were purposeful and austere. As Acheson described it, Mrs. Brandeis, "erect on a black horsehair sofa, presided at the tea table." Alice Acheson was expected to assist her in pouring the tea and offering the cucumber sandwiches. The current law clerk presented any new guests. Once this was accomplished, the disciples gathered in a semicircle around the justice. Generally these were young people and their spouses—government lawyers, writers, conservationists, frustrated regulators of utilities and monopolies, and, often, just "pilgrims at the shrine." Other visitors, usually older, were definitely not disciples, and "they were inclined to create a rival center around Mrs. Brandeis."[12]

Acheson's wife was never comfortable at the Brandeises'. A woman who was studying painting while caring for a small child, she was nonetheless seen by the justice only as a wife with no life of her own except that of a mother. The frugal life of the Brandeises—who were quite well-off after years of a lucrative law practice—seemed often absurd. "All that you'd get would be a cup of tea and a sort of ginger snap," said James M. Landis, one of Brandeis's clerks in the twenties. The justice was very much an ascetic. Another clerk commented: "The bed he slept in looked like a camp bed, and the furniture showed distinct signs of wear."[13] This was the way the Brandeises had lived in Boston, and this was how they would live in Stoneleigh Court on Connecticut Avenue. At one point, when a friend asked Mrs. Brandeis if she had something to donate to a thrift shop, Mrs. Brandeis took out a pair of shoes to give her, then removed the laces from the shoes, because "I think these laces are still pretty good." In Alice Acheson's eyes the Brandeises carried pretension to the "simple life" to the "extreme."[14]

In later years, when Mrs. Brandeis was often ill and the justice was alone much of the time, he would welcome a visit from Acheson, who was by then a practicing lawyer. "Being lonely," Acheson wrote, "he would send word that, if convenient, he would welcome an evening call on him in the office. There, with no work to stand between us, and all alone, he would say conspiratorially, 'Dean, what is the latest dirt?'"[15]

Acheson was that rare clerk who became a friend, and it was therefore appropriate that he speak at Brandeis's funeral in 1941. "These were years," he recalled, "during which we were with the Justice and saw in action his burning faith that the verities to which men had clung through the ages were verities; that evil never could be good; that falsehood was not truth, not even if all the ingenuity of science reiterated it in waves that encircled the earth."[16]

* * *

But it was Acheson's relationship with Justice Oliver Wendell Holmes, an almost legendary figure who had fought in the Civil War, that was the last truly formative influence in Acheson's life.

The style of Holmes could not have been more different from that of Louis Brandeis. The great justice was born in 1841 and was sixty-one years old when he ascended to the Supreme Court in 1902. By the time Acheson encountered him in 1919 he was an Olympian figure, a man from the past whose bearing was from another era.[17]

Acheson adored Holmes. In 1960 he could write of Holmes that he "was and is my chalice." He went on to say, "One of the slipperiest words I know is 'great.' But I think the 'greatest' man I have ever known, that is, the essence of man living, man thinking, man baring himself to the lonely emptiness —or the reverse— of the universe, was Holmes. Brandeis was eminent, but not his equal. [General] George Marshall was a peer and in some ways—in transfiguration through duty, for instance—their superior. But there the class closes."[18]

As Holmes lived only a block from Justice Brandeis and neither man would use a telephone, Acheson was able to find many opportunities to encounter Holmes. One rarely got away from 1720 I Street without "a chin," and Acheson invariably made notes of his conversations with Holmes. To the end of his days he would quote Holmes on almost any occasion, often making entries in a notebook reflecting Holmes's wisdom:

> Nov. 29 [1919]—Conversation at 1720 I Street. [Holmes speaking]
>
> "Man is the leader of the whole pageant of the universe! Yes, he is the leader just as small boys lead a circus parade when they walk ahead of it. But if they turn down a side street, the parade goes on.
>
> "I remember once taking an essay I had written on Plato to [Ralph Waldo] Emerson—I was then nineteen. The sage read it and then, 'When you strike at a king, you must kill him!' Rather fine for an old fellow to young man."[19]

As Acheson described him, Holmes was "of a grandeur and beauty rarely met among men. Like General Marshall, his presence entered a room with him as a pervading force; and left with him, too, like a strong light put out. Handsome, and aware of it, with thick white hair, intense eyes under heavy brows, and sweeping white moustache, he had style and dash."[20]

If Holmes seemed a model for Acheson's behavior, Holmes was also emblematic of the pragmatism that Acheson believed was the essence of the law. To Holmes, the "felt necessities of the time, the prevalent moral and political theories, institutions of public policy, avowed or unconscious, even the prejudices which judges share with their fellow men" have the most influence "in determining the rules by which men should be governed."[21]

It was judge-made common law to which Holmes was devoted.[22] Absent some specific constitutional provision, Holmes never doubted that the U.S. Congress and the state legislatures had the supreme right to legislate as they pleased.

Acheson, too, strongly embraced the ideal of judicial restraint. What especially disturbed Acheson late in his life, as it would have Brandeis and Holmes, was "self-conscious activism," which he defined as an acknowledged desire for change in the law in accordance with the decider's own conception of right."[23] He would quote Holmes often to this effect: "General principles do not decide concrete cases."[24]

Acheson admitted that he had "no defense to the charge often made that from the first moment I saw Justice Holmes I succumbed to hero worship."[25] Neither Frankfurter nor Brandeis seemed to embody Holmes's rare combination of style and intellect. Most important of all, Acheson encountered with Holmes that shock of recognition that a young person undergoes when one's own intellectual and moral inclinations are ratified by a mentor of exceptional eminence.

Acheson's development was also stimulated by the new liberalism, wedded to a pragmatic use of the powers of the federal government to restrain the strong from dominating and exploiting weaker groups. At the time of the great coal strike of 1919 and of Attorney General A. Mitchell Palmer's anti-Red drive, when Acheson was introduced to some union officials who were visiting a crusading newspaperman, he was moved by the tales of union busting. Company stores had stopped credit. Union benefits provided only a starvation diet. Evictions from company houses by the state police—whom Acheson termed "Cossacks"—were increasing. Government policy was rigged against the unions, and the Supreme Court was distant and hostile. After this meeting, Acheson concluded that the "essential role of labor unions in the scheme of our times was to me no longer a purely intellectual conclusion. I had passed the first test of a liberal; it was a conviction."[26]

If commitment to the labor movement was one tenet of liberalism, another was the issue of civil rights. The hysteria that swept the United States in 1919 rivaled the McCarthyite madness that terrorized many honest citizens in the early 1950s and deeply wounded Acheson as secretary of state. In words reminiscent of Senator Joseph McCarthy a generation later, Attorney General Palmer told the House Judiciary Committee: "There is a condition of revolutionary intent in the country of sufficiently widespread a character . . . to destroy or overthrow the government of the United States by physical force."[27] As a result of Palmer's anti-Red raids, a new wave of persecution for expressing minority views through the mails, and even for expressing personal opinions, swept the country.

Again and again, Holmes and Brandeis dissented from the Court, which upheld the savage sentences inflicted on those who had exercised their freedom of speech. The most famous of these cases, which Acheson witnessed, was the 1919 Abrams case. In this instance, a small group of about twenty anarchists, recent immigrants from Russia who had welcomed the Bolshevik revolution, protested Wilson's dispatch of about ten thousand troops to Bolshevik Russia in 1918. On an August morning of that same year, they had thrown leaflets out of an open window from a third-floor hatmaker's shop on Broadway, condemning Wilson for his expeditionary force and calling on American workers to resist. All of these anarchists were in their twenties; the oldest, Jacob Abrams, a bookbinder, was thirty-one.

Five were arrested, tried, and convicted of violating the new Sedition Act by making false and derogatory statements about the form of the American government and by their leaflets of trying to obstruct the war effort. They were sentenced to terms of twenty years in prison.

When the case was brought before the Supreme Court in October 1919, Holmes was convinced that the anarchists had opposed not the war against Germany, but the intervention in Russia, and, moreover, that no reasonable person could believe that their statements and leaflets could interfere with the war effort.[28]

The majority of justices tried to persuade Holmes to change his mind, or at least remain silent. Three of them came to visit him in his study to try to dissuade him from doing his duty, and even his wife, Fanny, joined them in urging him not to publish his dissent. But Holmes refused, and in November 1919 he read his dissent:

> But when men have realized that time has upset many fighting faiths, they may come to believe . . . that the ultimate good desired is better reached by free trade in ideas—that the best test of truth is the power of the thought to get itself accepted in the competition of the market, and that truth is the only ground upon which their wishes safely can be carried out. That at any rate is the theory of our Constitution. It is an experiment, as all life is an experiment.[29]

Acheson commented in the 1960s, after the tide of McCarthyism had receded, "Such gallant men as these [Holmes and Brandeis] kept alive faith in the Republic's great traditions of rationalism and restraint. Soon the hysteria passed. But those who had been infected by it were not cured. Distressingly soon they and their spiritual descendants were in its grip again."[30]

CHAPTER SIX

"THE REGULAR CONNECTION OF IDEAS"

As June 1920 approached, Brandeis asked his law clerk about his plans. He had none. He was thinking "vaguely" of teaching law, was considering an offer from the University of Michigan Law School, and had asked his friend Archibald MacLeish "to look into Chicago while he is at home." But Acheson was wary of relocating to the Midwest. "What are these places like?" he asked an old friend from the law school. "I mean are they dominated by sparkplug manufacturers and oily Baptists . . . ?"[1] When Brandeis asked him to stay on for an additional year, Acheson saw the offer as providential. It was highly unusual for a clerk to be asked to remain for more than one year, and this would give Acheson more time to look for a job in the East.

He had already approached Yale Law School for a teaching position, but Thomas W. Swan, dean of the law school, was reluctant to employ Acheson before checking on the book Acheson had now completed on labor relations and the law. He seemed to think that the manuscript might be too liberal and wanted to find out, as Acheson put it, "whether my book was to be published in Moscow." Although Acheson was in contact with both the Harvard and Yale University Presses, neither was prepared to publish his monograph on his terms. As Acheson described it in a letter to the editor of the Yale Press, it had been read by both Frankfurter and Roscoe Pound, dean of Harvard Law School, and Pound had actually accepted it for the Harvard Studies in Jurisprudence.

Acheson, however, became impatient with Harvard because of a delay, which, he believed, "would impair the usefulness of the book." It is unclear what Yale

University Press finally decided, but, in any case, the book was never published, and Acheson's impatience with the pace of university book publishing may have sunk it.[2]

The quest for the right job went on throughout most of Acheson's second year with Brandeis. At one point he contacted a lawyer who was counsel for District No. 12 of the United Mine Workers in Springfield, Illinois, to see if there was an opening in his office. Once again, no offer was forthcoming; had Acheson's approach succeeded, he might someday have worked for the formidable head of the union, John L. Lewis, who, as it happened, became a friendly acquaintance years later.

Although living in a small apartment on Vermont Avenue with a baby had been hard, the Achesons were nonetheless eager to stay on in Washington. Alice was continuing to take art classes at the Corcoran Gallery as well as at the Phillips and had found someone to take care of Jane in the afternoons while she painted. After Dean agreed to another year with Brandeis, the young couple moved to a small house at 1818 Corcoran Street, a block from Dupont Circle, where their son, David, was born in 1921. It was on the south side of the street at its west end, one of a row of small identical houses, each with an overhanging bay window on the second floor, giving, as Acheson described it, "a slightly Walt Disney impression of a twelfth-century Normandy village. In this area existed what might be called a ghetto of near respectability and intelligence in the midst of high position, wealth, and fashion."[3]

Social life centered around a group of young liberals, which included the novelist Sinclair Lewis.[4] One evening the Achesons had dining with them a very proper Bostonian who was Holmes's law clerk. Just as dinner ended, a man wearing a fez, false beard, and "his conception of the probable clothes of an Armenian rug peddler, and with some of his own unimpressive rugs over his arm, pushed past a bewildered cook and stamped muttering up the stairs, the cook protesting behind him. Surprise, embarrassment, and the torrent of his speech as he laid out his wares and pressed a sale on our guest and my wife, as the householders, carried all before him. The performance was first class, but soon ended as the disguise was penetrated and the peddler revealed as our entertaining and then obscure friend, Sinclair Lewis. Our guest was definitely not amused."[5]

"Red" Lewis had already written one novel, *Free Air*, but it had sold few copies, and he was now working on another, *Main Street.* With that book, Lewis's fame was assured, and he and his wife were enormously buoyed by their unexpected success, which none of their friends, most definitely including the Achesons, had believed possible. At one point, invited to tea by the new First Lady, Mrs. Warren Harding, Grace Hegger Lewis declared before the usher could announce her to Mrs. Harding, "I'm Mrs. Main Street."[6]

It was another friend, the muckraking editor of *Collier's Weekly*, Norman Hapgood, who put Acheson in contact with the new law firm of Covington and Burling, beginning to work on an international case to be argued before the World Court at The Hague a year later. The job was not easily won, however, for Acheson's liberalism, and especially his interest in labor law, first made the senior partner, Judge J. Harry Covington, "terrified at the thought of my bringing germs into the office."[7] But Acheson assured him he was no longer interested in being a labor lawyer, and in 1921 the job was finally his.

Judge Covington, an extroverted politician from the eastern shore of Maryland, had been put on the federal bench by President Wilson after delivering the Maryland delegation to Wilson at the 1912 Democratic convention.[8]

With the increasing government legislation that resulted from Wilson's programs and Theodore Roosevelt's trust-busting, government and business were more and more being brought into conflict. Covington soon came to see that there would be a good many new clients for a Washington-based law firm that understood the workings of government and that Covington himself might well represent national clients who now had to contend with the burgeoning government institutions that had grown up over the past two decades. He therefore resigned his judgeship and opened a one-man law office on July 1, 1918, in the Evans Building, at 1420 New York Avenue.[9]

Through another attorney, George Rublee, Covington had met Edward B. Burling, who had left his law practice in Chicago during World War I to become chief counsel to the United States Shipping Board. With the end of the war, he expected to return to Chicago, but after encountering Covington and spending the summer of 1918 at the judge's house on the eastern shore, Burling decided to join him. On January 1, 1919, when both men were in their forty-ninth year, the firm of Covington and Burling was officially founded; six months later it moved to the Union Trust Building, where the firm was to remain for the next half century.

Within two years the man who had introduced the two partners joined the firm in the summer of 1921. George Rublee was a figure of mythological proportions, a Jamesian character who never attained the goals that everyone expected he would achieve. For Acheson, "George Rublee began as a tradition—his name carved in lonely eminence on an oaken panel as the first graduating class of my school, appearing again in the gymnasium as the captain of every team, and in the folklore of [Groton] as the winner of prizes, the setter of standards."[10] One of the initial students of the school, he quickly outstripped his classmates and alone became Groton's first graduating class.

Rublee was a restless figure whose presence was captivating. He had supported Theodore Roosevelt as the Progressive Party's candidate in 1912. After TR was defeated, he worked on Wilson's antitrust measures and then, with the outbreak of the First World War, joined the government to work on pooling the Allied shipping tonnage for war use. With the war's end, he soon joined Judge Covington and Ned Burling, and the firm was renamed as Covington, Burling and Rublee in 1921.[11]

As Acheson saw it, Rublee's flaw, his restless and undirected ambition, came from his never encountering "the discipline of a harder environment, where he would not have been so acclaimed but would have been pushed and buffeted by urgent necessities."[12] For Acheson, the need to prove oneself, as he had as a youth working on the Canadian railroad, was among the necessary ingredients for sustained ambition.

In 1921, when Acheson joined Covington and Burling, he was twenty-eight. Shortly after the founding of the firm in 1919, the Christiana Group of Norwegian Shipowners had offered a retainer of $5,000 to deal with a claim against the United States government. At the outset of the war, contracts had been let out for American shipyards to build ships for Norwegian shipping companies. With America's entry into the war, the U.S. government requisitioned all contracts and insisted that all ships be built for the United States as part of the war effort. At the end of the war, the Norwegian group came to Judge Covington to handle their claims for compensation by the United States.[13]

Norway argued that the United States had seized Norwegian contracts for oceangoing vessels, for which the Norwegians had paid large sums. Its claim was therefore approximately $16 million, including interest for five years. "The United States," according to Acheson, "admitted that something was due, but denied it had taken the Norwegians' contracts. On the contrary, it claimed, what was taken was 'work in progress' in the shipyards." The government offered $2.5 million as the fair value of this work in progress. No interest was to be paid.[14] The way to win the case, Acheson believed, was not to argue "metaphysical and legal arguments," but rather to argue the facts, as Brandeis had trained him to think.

Acheson was expected to work on the pleadings and briefs, then go to The Hague with Burling as a general handyman. As the new firm was overworked and disorganized, Acheson soon found himself far more on his own than he had been with Justice Brandeis. He decided that official U.S. government documents freely available at the Library of Congress—congressional hearings and reports, and records of the various agencies involved—would prove his case for him. The result of his research, "The Case of Norway," filed with the Court on February 6, 1922, left no doubt in Acheson's mind that "the government had said at the time and reported later that it had taken over . . . the contracts with the yards, stepped into the shoes of the former contractors, sought to enforce the contract terms."[15]

On the other side (in Acheson's account), the U.S. government asserted that

$13 million out of $16.4 million was "claimed on the purely speculative nature of transactions conducted by a colorful Norwegian, Christoffer Hannevig, who had important interests both in the shipyards and in the ship companies involved in the case." In short, the government lawyers challenged the legitimacy of the contracts, arguing that they had been "tainted" because most were "purely speculative" agreements negotiated by Hannevig.[16]

The Covington team set off in the early summer of 1922 to Oslo, Norway, on the SS *Stavangerfjord*, an old ship that sailed the northern route along the British Isles to Bergen and then along the Norwegian coast to Oslo. Along with Acheson, Burling, and Rublee was Walter L. Fisher, who had once been Taft's secretary of the interior. Upon their arrival, it fell to Acheson to do extensive interviewing with the indirect clients, the shipowners. He was therefore able to dig into their relations with Hannevig. His research soon convinced him that their association with Hannevig did not have a significant effect upon the fair value of the contracts. Acheson became an expert on this part of the case, which allowed Burling to give him more responsibility than he might otherwise have been granted.

The case opened at The Hague on July 22, 1922, and went on for six weeks. The proceedings at the Peace Palace were dignified "but relaxedly disorganized." Each afternoon and evening Acheson worked with one of the senior attorneys on material for the next day.[17] Although the case seemed to be going well for Covington and Burling, the "taint of Hannevig" persisted and was having a corroding effect. Finally Burling decided that this aspect of the case had to be addressed directly, and while Acheson was untried, he had done most of the preparation and was therefore the best informed. Burling decided that he should argue that aspect of the case before the tribunal.

Aloft in the counsel's pulpit, nervous but prepared, Acheson had a central problem: some way must be found to get the U.S. government lawyers to admit that the contracts were valid and that only their value was in dispute. To accomplish this would not be easy, so Acheson decided to take a chance. To everyone's surprise, the young lawyer decided to attack head-on the American argument that the Norwegian claims were made in bad faith.

"Some very severe things were said about these claims," he declared, "things which look to us as though they related more to the validity of the claims and to the good faith of the purchasers, and, perhaps, in some cases they tended to reflect somewhat upon the Kingdom of Norway in presenting these claims." He challenged the "Agent of the United States" to clear up this implication: "We felt that some statement was due us. We felt that some statement was due the Kingdom of Norway. No statement has been made."[18]

"Do you mean to say that you are demanding an apology from your own government?" one of the presiding judges asked.

"I am, sir," said Acheson.

At this point, Ned Burling experienced a sensation of dizziness: if the lawyers for the United States now decided to respond by pursuing their contention that the contracts were invalid, the whole Norwegian case might be lost. A moment later Acheson was horrified to see Burling reach above his head and shove onto the lectern a pad of paper, on which he had scrawled, "Shut up."

But it was too late for that. Acheson could think of no alternative, so he pressed on until the president of the court broke in: "[I]t is well understood that the validity of the assignments is no longer disputed" and that only the amount was in question. Later Acheson was given a severe dressing-down for risking an all-out attack that had been cleared with no one; but in the final disposition of the case, the risk was justified by the outcome.

The United States was unwilling to make its case rest on the central argument that the claims were not legitimate. The contracts were legitimate, the defense agreed, only their value was in question. The "taint of Hannevig" was contained, if not removed, and the court upheld Norway. In mid-October it awarded $11,995,000 to the plaintiffs. The United States appealed but lost, and in the final judgment an award was paid, which, with interest for that time, came to $12,239,852.47.[19]

Not only did Acheson's foray go unpunished, but he was offered regular employment at the firm. Moreover, his taste for advocacy was only whetted by his dramatic debut at The Hague; in 1926 he was made a partner. He later emerged as a leading appellate lawyer before both the court of appeals in Washington, D.C., and the Supreme Court itself. As Felix Frankfurter recalled, "Dean was a hot-house product in the best sense of the word. Everything conspired to enhance his reputation and position in Washington in those early years."[20]

In 1922 the Achesons bought for $13,000 a brick town house, built in 1843, on P Street in the Georgetown section of Washington;[21] two years later their third and last child, Mary Eleanor Acheson, was born. They remained in the house for the rest of Acheson's life (it was not until she was in her nineties, two decades after her husband's death, that Mrs. Acheson decided to sell it). At the time they bought the house, Georgetown was not fashionable; perhaps the cobblestone streets, the eighteenth- and nineteenth-century houses, many of which had originally been designed for servants, simply reminded Acheson of the small-town atmosphere of Middletown. There were large houses on N Street, but below P Street was a poorer section, inhabited mostly by blacks. In the immediate neighborhood where the Achesons moved, there was still a mixture of blacks and whites.

Despite a community life where the children played in the streets or sat on stoops, chatting with the neighbors, the Achesons wanted a rural setting as well;

Dean also believed that the children would benefit from outdoor activities on the weekends. Escape to the countryside for weekends and summer vacations came in 1924 when they bought Harewood, a small farm eighteen miles north of Washington, in Sandy Spring, Maryland, on which stood a white clapboard farmhouse built in 1795 as a tobacco barn. There was no electricity and little water; lighting was provided by kerosene lamps or candlelight. Fixing up the place was a tremendous task, and everyone in the family was expected to join in.

In fact, the 1920s and 1930s were rigorous years for Acheson. He was working hard as a lawyer and on the weekends always made big plans for the family. Up to the mid-1930s, the roads were poor, and there was no heat on the farm until after the Second World War. Although Acheson had obtained horses for everyone to ride, the family had to do the work of rounding up the horses, which had run wild all week long in a roughly twelve-acre field. The children would be expected to help bring them in and saddle and bridle them. After this came a long ride, and when everyone got back to the farmhouse, they had to unsaddle and unbridle the horses, put them back in the field, and late in the day go into the house for a picnic lunch around a fire. It was very much the strenuous life that Acheson was committed to.

During the summer, Acheson had to commute every day to Washington. He always gave a signal tattoo on his car horn, and when he was approaching the farm on the far side of a fairly large wood, the children could hear him and know it took about five minutes to reach the Quaker Meeting House at the top of the lane. They would then dash ahead to see if they could get there before he did for the ride home. This ritual lasted for many years, as their father was always excited to see them. Acheson, who generally planned the weekend activities, was patient and seemingly inexhaustible.[22]

In his mid-thirties, already a partner in the firm and a kind of adored "son" of Covington, Burling and Rublee, Acheson was being described by George Rublee as "the shiniest fish that ever came out of the sea," the same phrase that William James had once applied to his colleague George Santayana.[23] Although he handled a great many tax cases, Acheson's reputation grew over the years as an appellate lawyer. He was always correct with his clients but felt little obligation to comfort or sympathize with them at any great length.

As an appellate lawyer, as one prominent attorney has put it, "you get cases with a hopelessly sour posture. Once one of our kind gets into the mists and convolutions of appellate work, he is doing splendidly, we like to think, if he emerges victorious in ten percent of his cases."[24] Acheson won around 20 percent of his cases before the Supreme Court, and this enhanced his reputation; indeed, even a lost case often brought him praise from his peers, who were sensitive to his skills in argumentation. He became what physicians call a "garbage surgeon," one who is called in after the case seems hopeless.

Acheson knew the law that came before the Court—which was often constitutional—extremely well and could come at questions with an original slant that gave an extra and uncommon dimension to his legal opinions.[25]

His first appearance before the Supreme Court in the early 1920s, however, was hardly a foretaste of what he was to become. After the required three years as a member of the D.C. bar, Acheson became a member of the bar of the Supreme Court; soon after, an out-of-town lawyer, finding that Ned Burling was away, ran down the short list at the firm and came across Acheson's name. His was a simple request: to move, in a case pending before the Court, to substitute a successor executor for one deceased. The impetuous young Acheson, however, forgot that he was not somberly dressed as he should have been for such an appearance, but "rather sportingly" got up in tweeds and a colored shirt. He hurried up to the Capitol, picked up the briefs from the clerk's office, and tried to absorb them while other cases occupied the Court.

Finally he heard Chief Justice William Howard Taft ask whether there were any motions. Acheson went to the lectern and made his own motion. As he remembered it, "It was followed by complete silence, a sort of perplexed, almost astonished silence, at length broken by an irrelevant question from the Chief Justice—what was my name? I gave it in an agony of apprehension. 'Mr. Acheson,' he went on, 'you have been in the courtroom this morning?' I had. 'How strange,' he added. 'We handed down our opinion and disposed of your case not more than two minutes ago.' Retreating amid titters toward the door, I had covered half the distance when the Chief Justice called me back to the lectern.

"'I am afraid that I exaggerated,' he said. 'It could not have been more than a minute and a half ago.' The courtroom relaxed into a good laugh. Justice Brandeis was not smiling."[26]

Acheson later tried to describe his education as a practicing lawyer and admitted that any account of the cases he had handled would be "an unmitigated bore." Yet "by some alchemy this base material can be turned into insight, judgment, and inventiveness." He liked to quote in this regard Alexis de Tocqueville, himself a lawyer, who once remarked that the study and practice of law produced certain habits of orderly thought, "a kind of instinctive regard for the regular connection of ideas."[27]

What Acheson most admired in lawyers was their ability to "remain detached from the emotional involvement of their client in their purposes or troubles."

This, combined with the need to "spend as much time and thought on learning about and understanding the other parties' business and problems as those of their own client," often provided "practical statesmanship."[28]

On the other hand, Acheson admitted, "Lawyers, who are habituated to having their main choices made for them by the necessities of their clients, are often at a loss when, as in government, for instance, they have wide latitude in a choice of policy."[29]

For Acheson, the practice of law was rewarding because it tended to lead to worldly knowledge and sometimes to worldly wisdom. Intellectual training alone did not necessarily bring forth sophisticated thinking and behavior. A practicing lawyer, however, was "continually made aware of the complex, subtle, and varied nature of human life and human institutions. The simple blacks and whites, goods and bads, rights and wrongs of the village blacksmith under his spreading chestnut tree have to undergo considerable complicating elaboration to become useful aids to judgment in dealing with the inherent ambiguities of modern life."

Here, as in his other writings and reflections, Acheson never ceased to echo Oliver Wendell Holmes's precept that the life of the law was experience.[30]

CHAPTER SEVEN

"A LOW LIFE BUT A MERRY ONE"

FOR A YOUNG LAWYER whose first political enthusiasm had been for the progressive wing of the Republican Party and Theodore Roosevelt, and whose later associations with Frankfurter, Brandeis, and Rublee brought him into sympathy with the New Freedom of Woodrow Wilson, the politics of Republicans Warren Harding and Calvin Coolidge were increasingly repugnant. If Wilson's mistakes were "great and tragic," Acheson wrote, "great also was his understanding of the new role which his country must play in the realignment of power which the crumbling of empires and emergence of new forces necessitated."[1]

In addition to their isolationist stance toward European security, and their rejection of the League of Nations, the Republicans' policies were anti-labor and pro-tariff. As a practicing lawyer with Covington and Burling during this period, Acheson not only kept up his interest in labor law, but also became convinced that the orderly flow of international capital movements, lower tariffs, and reciprocal trade agreements were conducive to international peace and prosperity. He had become a Democrat.[2]

Establishing a residence in Maryland through Harewood offered Acheson a splendid opportunity to engage himself in Democratic Party politics. In the early 1920s he was a member of Washington's Penguin Club, a liberal discussion group often given to evenings of mirth and entertainment; soon he became active in the Maryland Democratic Party of Montgomery County, participating in meetings and local campaigns.[3]

But he was ill suited for the life of an active politician, which called for shaking hands and keeping any controversial opinions to himself. Although he viewed electoral politics as "a low life but a merry one," it soon became clear to him that he would never run for office himself.[4] It was not until the presidential campaign of 1928 that politics more fully engaged him. The Democratic candidate for president, Governor Al Smith of New York, was very much the "Happy Warrior," as Franklin Delano Roosevelt dubbed him at the convention. Acheson thought the phrase aptly described "the sense of joyous, affectionate exaltation his vibrant leadership inspired in us." For almost eight years "the country, in a trance, seemed to have been following a hearse. Now at the touch of this prince in a brown derby, with his East Side accent, gay humanity, and common sense, came an awakening."[5]

In 1928 Acheson campaigned vigorously for Smith throughout Montgomery County. It would have been an uphill battle for any Democrat in an era of Republican dominance and national prosperity. In addition, Smith was a Catholic and in favor of repealing Prohibition. He was doomed to be defeated by Herbert Hoover.

Four years later, Acheson's efforts to elect a Democratic president were vigorous and closer to the power brokers of the party. On June 27, 1932, he attended the Democratic convention in Chicago through the good offices of his friend and neighbor Frank Page, an officer of the Postal Telegraph Company, equipped with credentials that permitted him to go anywhere. With what he called "rare good judgment," Acheson became friendly with the sergeant at arms, who admitted him to the immediate circle of the candidate, "where scotch and soda flowed."[6] Although his own hero, Al Smith, remained hopeful, Acheson believed he would not get the nomination, so he viewed the proceedings with a measure of detachment.

Buttons that read "Anybody but Hoover" captured the mood of the convention. Throughout the long, hot night on July 1–2, delegates voted; a two-thirds majority was required for the nomination. The first vote began at 4:28 A.M., and the roll calls alone for 3,210 delegates, who were allowed to cast 1,154 votes, took three hours. On the first ballot, the results were Roosevelt 666, Smith 201, and Garner 90; on the second ballot, FDR picked up only eleven more votes; on the third ballot, Roosevelt barely held his own with 683 votes. It was now eight in the morning, and the exhausted delegates staggered back to their hotel rooms.[7]

In a day of intense politicking by James Farley, Roosevelt's campaign manager, the opposing camps were warned that if Roosevelt faltered, the likely compromise candidate would be neither Al Smith nor Congressman John Nance Garner, but Newton D. Baker, a liberal Wilsonian progressive. This was the decisive argument that won over the Texas delegation, a state that was committed to Garner. The California delegation was also ready to swing, on conditions that Garner receive the vice presidential nomination and that William McAdoo, who had been Wilson's son-in-law and secretary of the Treasury, control California patronage and be given a veto over the choices for secretaries of state and Treasury. Roosevelt agreed.

Everything went as scheduled. On the fourth ballot, with 945 votes, FDR was the nominee of the Democratic Party. The vice presidential nomination went, as promised, to Garner (who told a friend the office was "not worth a pitcher of warm spit"). Breaking with precedent and setting a new one, FDR flew to Chicago to accept the nomination and pledged himself "to a new deal for the American people."[8]

Acheson was fascinated by the maneuvers he had witnessed. On the other hand, having observed "one of these mad and not a little degrading spectacles, nothing would induce me to do it again."[9] That fall he took an active hand in the local campaigning, organizing meetings, making speeches, meeting with the Democratic Advisory Committee, and writing political pamphlets. It was, predictably, the writing that pleased him the most. Laying out policy issues, which he would do again nearly three decades later for the National Democratic Committee, convinced him that he had made a substantive contribution to American political discourse.

Soon after FDR's massive victory over Hoover, preparatory work for the incoming administration began. Roosevelt had promised to reduce federal government expenditures by a quarter. The president's spokesman in the Senate, South Carolina's James Francis Byrnes (fifteen years later to be Acheson's boss in the State Department), took charge of preparing some of the necessary legislation. Acheson, with the blessing of Judge Covington, volunteered to help Byrnes. Soon after the inauguration on March 4, 1933, Acheson was invited to the White House to attend meetings where the legislative program was being put together. "Thus," he wrote as he looked back on his life's work, "does one get drawn closer and closer to the flypaper of taking part in government."[10]

Acheson hoped for the post of solicitor general—"the adventure for which I yearned."[11] Charged with the supervision of the appellate litigation of the government and with arguing the most important government cases presented to the Supreme Court, this was, from a professional point of view, the most challenging and prestigious appointment for a lawyer of Acheson's caliber.

Felix Frankfurter, a longtime political confidant and admirer of FDR's, was providing any number of names of young men, known as the "happy hotdogs," to staff the new agencies that were being created in Washington under the New

Deal. Frankfurter brought up Dean Acheson's name to the president, who in turn passed it on to the attorney general, Homer Cummings of Connecticut.[12]

The attorney general's reaction to an Acheson appointment as solicitor general was immediate and violent. "No, it's not all right," he told Roosevelt. Acheson was crushed at being turned down without an explanation and only later learned the cause after he went home to see his father in his last illness in 1934. Appointed Episcopal bishop of Connecticut in 1928, Acheson's father took a dim view of Homer Cummings's many marriages. He had refused church sanction to his latest, and Cummings had had to look elsewhere for ecclesiastic blessing.[13]

To get over this disappointment, Dean and Alice left for an extended motor trip to Canada in late April 1933, accompanied by Hume Wrong, a young Canadian diplomat stationed in Washington. "April is a good month for blasted hopes," Acheson later wrote, "for May lies ahead."[14] Sure enough, in May 1933, two good friends, Arthur Ballantine, the Republican holdover undersecretary of the Treasury, and James Douglas, assistant secretary, asked Acheson to lunch with them. They urged him to meet the new Treasury secretary, William Woodin, "a man after our own hearts who will need congenial friends."

Woodin, who had been president of the American Car & Foundry Company, was one of the "Friends of Roosevelt" who had contributed $10,000 to the preconvention campaign. A frail man with no banking experience, he was chosen as Franklin Roosevelt's link to big business. When Woodin and Acheson finally did meet that May, the lunch was "gay, uninhibited; and the Secretary, the same." Acheson was hardly back in his office when Woodin called to ask him to become undersecretary of the Treasury to replace Ballantine. He was formally appointed on May 19, 1933, and was easily confirmed by the Senate.[15]

At this time Acheson's views on economic matters were flexible; he was a reformer like Brandeis and was far from being an ideological opponent of the New Deal. His first experience in government, however, would severely test his ability to master the intricacies of the Treasury and, more important, to understand the delicate relationship between politics and governing.

Not long after Acheson assumed his new post, Will Woodin fell ill. In Woodin's absence, Acheson as acting secretary found himself as head of the Treasury, untrained in monetary and fiscal affairs, at a time of revolutionary change in monetary policy.

In the early stages of the administration, Acheson's relations with FDR were cordial. He was largely supportive of New Deal legislation and impressed with Roosevelt's ability to shift his attention from one project to another with seeming ease. At the same time, he was disturbed by FDR's patrician manner toward those in his administration. Once he was acting secretary, he was at the president's bidding, which was constant, even reporting to FDR at his bedside while he breakfasted. The president's grandchildren might well interrupt, galloping about the room or sitting on the bed beside him. "Then began a game not designed to improve communication between the President and caller," Acheson wrote in his memoir, *Morning and Noon.* "The child, leaning innocently against her grandfather, would suddenly clap her hand over his mouth in the middle of a sentence, smothering the rest of it. The President's counterattack, a vigorous tickling of her ribs, brought her hand down in defense and produced joint hilarity. Conversation became intermittent, disjointed, and obscure."[16]

These performances reminded Acheson of Louis XIV's levees at seventeenth-century Versailles. While they were stiff and formal for outsiders, they were also highly informal among the royals. Acheson recalled the story that Saint-Simon tells of how Madame de Bourgoyne won her bet that she could sit on a chamber pot in the presence of the king himself—which was made possible, however, only because because she was Louis XIV's daughter-in-law and he could and did forgive her. But it was precisely this seignorial right that disturbed Acheson. FDR's attitude reminded him of European royalty. The president could relax with his aides and call everyone from his valet to the secretary of state by his first name—"But he condescended."[17]

In Acheson's view of the presidency, which would perfectly suit his attitude toward Harry Truman, "to accord the President the greatest deference and respect should be a gratification to any citizen. It is not gratifying to receive the easy greeting which milord might give a promising stable boy and pull one's forelock in return." Yet Acheson also admitted that "the essence of [Roosevelt] was force," a man who relished "power and command."[18]

For FDR the immediate task was to get business of all sorts, from farm to factory to services, moving again. In his concern to raise farm prices, which, it was generally believed, would give farmers more money to spend in the market, the president, along with the Congress, became convinced some measure of inflation was necessary. This was an idea that horrified Acheson's old friend, budget director Lewis Douglas, who was determined to restore a balanced budget by cutting spending.[19]

Inevitably, the place of gold in the monetary system came under review, as the value of the dollar was tied to gold; moreover, the gold content of the dollar had been established by Congress, and many people held government bonds whose value would be cut in proportion as the dollar was devalued. Gold had been pegged at $20.67 an ounce since 1900. By buying gold at a higher price, this would effectively devalue the dollar. This adjustment, Roosevelt believed, would have a salutary effect by inducing inflation and thereby raising prices. Raising prices would aid the farmer and stimulate business, and this in turn would lead to recovery from the Great Depression. The question was, did the president have the requisite authority to do so on his own? FDR therefore set about looking for a government agency that could do this.[20]

Over the summer and fall, Roosevelt continued to struggle with his central problem: how to achieve higher prices at home so that business would pick up, for by late July the long upward climb of prices had ceased and a new decline had begun. As near panic was breaking out in the farmlands, the president spoke to Acheson of the imminence of "agrarian revolution" and reported that farmers were stopping milk trucks and pouring their contents on the ground.[21]

Against this background, the debate between two groups of monetary advisers grew in intensity. On one side, the staff of the Treasury Department and the Federal Reserve Bank of New York, urged on by budget director Douglas and with Acheson as an ally, continued to press for a stable dollar tied to gold. Only in this way, they believed, could confidence in the currency be restored to the investing public and recovery achieved.[22] In the opposite corner were the competing theories of another cabal under the leadership of Henry Morgenthau Jr.

At this time head of the Farm Credit Administration, Morgenthau was an intimate of the president. The son of Wilson's ambassador to Turkey, young Morgenthau had found an escape from his father's world of business and diplomacy by buying a thousand-acre farm near Hyde Park in Dutchess County in 1913; soon he and his wife, Elinor, became fast friends of Eleanor and Franklin Roosevelt. Later he became a significant figure in New York State agricultural circles, and Governor Roosevelt brought him to Albany to advise him on agricultural policy. An inarticulate man who displayed great warmth in private but in public seemed worried and suspicious, Morgenthau was absolutely loyal to FDR.[23]

His principal theoretician was George F. Warren, a professor of farm management at Cornell University whom he had frequently consulted about farm problems during his time at Albany; FDR, too, was acquainted with Warren. Both men knew Warren's principal thesis that the price of all commodities varied more or less directly with the price of gold. Controlling the gold value of the dollar and forcing it downward would induce inflation and thereby raise prices. Since the Depression was essentially a phenomenon of price, they thought, it could therefore be cured by higher prices.[24]

Warren's theories gained credibility with the president, who was impressed by the fact that the rise in prices from April to mid-July had coincided with the devaluation of the dollar after he had abandoned the gold standard in March. It was a simple step to conclude that a further depreciation of the dollar would cure falling prices and produce rising ones. Roosevelt expected his subordinates to figure out a legal loophole that would allow him to set the price of gold as he chose without seeking congressional authority to do so.

Early in September, Acheson and his wife had decided to get away from the heat and exhaustion of Washington by joining the Canadian minister William Duncan Herridge and his wife, Mildred, on a fishing trip to New Brunswick. As Acheson described the situation, "An illusion of a lull in the monetary debate was created by the fact that we were in the eye of the hurricane. On September 1, we started off for a two weeks' holiday."[25] Seven weeks after his return, things moved to a climax and Acheson was out of a job.

Acheson's main quarrel with the president was not on strictly economic grounds. He simply did not believe that the executive had the legal authority to buy gold at any price it might set. In short, Roosevelt's determination to purchase gold at a price above the one fixed by statute violated the law. Attorney General Cummings agreed with Acheson. This did not in the least satisfy the president: what FDR wanted was to be told how he could do it, not that it was impossible to do.

At the end of September, Herman Oliphant, Henry Morgenthau's general counsel in the Farm Credit Administration, argued that the Reconstruction Finance Corporation (RFC) had the legal power to pay for gold at changing rates under a complicated scheme that circumvented the congressionally mandated price, thereby giving Roosevelt the power he needed. Stanley Reed, general counsel of the RFC, concurred. There was no turning back.[26]

When Acheson saw the memorandum that finally came out of these discussions, he met with Morgenthau, who told him that FDR was absolutely determined to go ahead with the plan. Acheson neither argued nor quarreled with Morgenthau. But he was deeply troubled and sought advice from Justice Brandeis: if Attorney General Cummings ruled that the new plan was legal, should Acheson forget that he was a lawyer and be governed solely by the opinion of the highest law officer of the land? The justice responded, "Dean, if I wanted a legal opinion, I would prefer to get it from you than from Homer Cummings."[27]

Acheson was encouraged to stand his ground. "This faced me squarely with the legal problem which was my principal difficulty," he wrote later. "Then and since, the plan seemed to me futile, though then it looked more harmful than it proved to be. Not that it ever seemed to me as horrendous as its opponents claimed."[28]

What worried Acheson especially were the ethical implications of initiating a policy of devaluation just at the time when he was about to complete the sale of government securities to the public. If the dollar were devalued under FDR's scheme, the value of these securities would fall proportionately, and the government would have violated its obligation to the bondholders.[29]

Despite his personal concerns, on October 11 Acheson dutifully succeeded in completing a heavily oversubscribed refinancing of the Liberty Bonds.

* * *

By mid-October the president had lost all patience with Acheson's objections to Morgenthau's gold-buying plan. Summoned to the office of Attorney General Homer Cummings, Acheson was joined by the inventor of the scheme, Herman Oliphant, along with Stanley Reed from the RFC (later to be a Supreme Court justice) and Harold Stephens, an assistant attorney general. Cummings stated flatly that upon his informal assurance that the Oliphant plan was legal, FDR had decided to go forward with it. Time to stop arguing and get on with it, Cummings declared.

But Acheson had no intention of accepting Cummings's verbal assurance that all was well. He was the official who would have to authorize the payment of government funds without, as he believed, legal authority to do so. He refused to violate the law. In the hot argument that followed, Stephens supported Acheson, while Attorney General Cummings fumed in what Acheson called "impotent fury" and was doubtless more relieved than ever that he had kept Acheson out of his department as solicitor general. The meeting concluded with Cummings reaffirming his views and saying that he would write an opinion to justify them.

Roosevelt was no less furious at Acheson's continued obstructionism, and on October 19 a climactic conference was held in the White House. Until he had the attorney general's concurring opinion in writing, Acheson refused to sign the order for the devaluation of the dollar. Roosevelt replied grimly, "I say it is legal." Others in the room agreed with the president. "Don't you take my word for it that it will be all right?" Roosevelt asked. But Acheson's temper was fast getting out of control, and he defied the president by reminding him that it was he, not Roosevelt, who had to put his signature on the order. "That will do!" Roosevelt commanded.[30]

Later that day Acheson appeared at the meeting of the RFC board, looking "like a thundercloud," according to Morgenthau, who reported him saying, "I am opposed to our buying gold. The President has ordered me to do it. I will carry out his orders." But he left it to Morgenthau to work out the details of the program with the attorney general. Three days later, in his fourth "fireside chat" to the nation, FDR explained that the RFC would buy newly mined gold in the United States at prices that he and his advisers set. He told Morgenthau the next day, "I have had the shackles on my hands for months now, and I feel for the first time as though I had thrown them off."[31]

Two days later Acheson received a telegram from Secretary of the Treasury Woodin, directing him "in my behalf and in my name" to approve the prices of the debentures that the RFC determined. The first day of RFC buying was October 25, and the president set the purchase price at $31.36 an ounce, $.27 above the London price. The object was always to keep the trend gradually moving upward, a little above the world price, in the expectation that commodity prices would follow. Meanwhile prices generally moved slightly downward, and farm prices remained unaffected.[32]

For the moment, Acheson decided to stay on at the Treasury, hoping the president would abandon his strategy. But stories began to appear in the press hinting that there were those in the administration who strongly disapproved of what was going on. The White House soon became convinced that Acheson was the source. And on October 27 FDR said to Morgenthau, "I guess this boil has about come to a head, and you know me, Henry, I am slow to get mad, but when I do, I get good and mad."[33]

Two days later Acheson was called to the White House for a meeting that included high officials from the Federal Reserve Bank of New York, the RFC, and the attorney general. Sitting behind his desk in the Oval Office, FDR said that anyone who could not accept his decisions about the gold-buying plan could get out, but no one could stay on and oppose them. Nothing specific was stated, no names were mentioned. But Acheson knew that for him the end was near.

In the middle of November, Secretary Woodin, looking very frail, arrived in Washington from New York. He told Acheson that the president wanted Woodin to fire him. Woodin himself would be willing to resign as well, but as it was, he would ask Acheson to give him a letter of resignation. He also told him that Henry Morgenthau Jr. was to be Acheson's successor. (After Woodin's own early resignation on grounds of ill health, Morgenthau became secretary.)

As it turned out, the gold-buying plan never yielded very dramatic results, and in January 1934 FDR unilaterally fixed the price of gold at $35 an ounce, where it remained for almost forty years.[34]

Acheson's letter of resignation was short but without rancor. He wrote that he understood the president's need to have "complete freedom of choice as to whom you will place in charge at the Treasury." And he concluded by expressing his appreciation for the opportunity of serving in the administration "during these stirring times" and offered his "most sincere good wishes for the success of your administration in the years ahead."[35]

All high officials in the Treasury, except Acheson, had been instructed to attend Morgenthau's swearing-in on November 17 in the Oval Office. When Woodin heard this, he insisted that Acheson accompany him, which he did. At the end of the ceremony, Acheson strode over to the president to say good-bye and thanked him for the opportunity to work with him. FDR motioned him to come around his desk, then, taking his hand, pulled him down to him. "I have been awfully angry with you," he said in a low voice. "But you are a real sportsman. You will get a good letter from me in answer to yours."[36]

In fact, FDR never did send the letter. A few days later the press printed an Acheson memorandum on the legality of the devaluation of the dollar, and doubtless this convinced FDR that Acheson had again leaked to the press. Eventually the White House learned that Acheson had never been the culprit; it had probably been the budget director, Lew Douglas, who was to blame, but according to the president's secretary, Grace Tully, "it was too late for corrective action to be taken in regard to Acheson." The president, she said, "acted impulsively and later regretted it."[37]

Acheson also reconsidered his behavior in later years, concluding that, at a time of great crisis in the nation, it had been "tinged with stubbornness and lack of imaginative understanding of my own proper role and of the President's perplexities and needs." Writing after he left office as secretary of state under President Truman, he concluded: "The action I was asked to take was without legal authorization. Was it so horrendous as to require, in the current phrase, making a federal case out of it? Today I am not at all sure."[38]

Nor did Acheson receive any support for his behavior from his father, who made clear his view that Acheson had failed in his duty to the president of the United States. On January 28, 1934, Edward Acheson died, and Dean was left with the feeling that he had never quite measured up to what the bishop had expected of him. Despite an assured manner of self-confidence, Acheson would seek time and again from family and friends the approval that his father had so often denied him.[39]

His troubles with FDR, he admitted later, had a very deep and lasting effect on his judgment: "Whether I was all right or not it warned me that there are terrible problems that an assistant to the President can get into by allowing things to get to the point where trouble occurs, and that, therefore, you ought to be very alert and watchful to consider his position and interests twice as much as your own."[40]

CHAPTER EIGHT

"FORCES STRONGER THAN REASON"

"I UNDERSTAND your difficulty in classifying me as a pro– or anti–New Dealer. I couldn't classify myself," Acheson wrote to a friend in the mid-1930s. "It is much more satisfying to me to consider specific proposals from the point of view of whether they are practicable methods of dealing with immediate problems."[1]

Because of his split with FDR, Acheson was considered a very "sound" lawyer, and his practice prospered. In 1936 Acheson represented electric power utilities that sought to enjoin and prevent the construction of public power utilities by the Public Works Administration under the leadership of Secretary of the Interior Harold L. Ickes. This latter project was dear to the heart of Harry Hopkins, then head of the Works Projects Administration and later one of FDR's closest advisers.

At one point during the process, Hopkins was lunching at the Washington Hotel, where he spied Acheson at another table and scribbled him a note on the back of his menu: "The idea of your claiming that a power project, approved three years ago and still unbuilt, has not provided employment is a clear evidence of prejudice on your part. A good Democratic architect, six detectives and a publicity man have been paid out of this project for years. Their jobs may last forever if you can only keep this in the courts long enough. . . . I can make out a good case to prove that there will be more employment if the projects are never built."[2]

Despite Hopkins's gibe, Acheson said of this period, "Not all my efforts were devoted to representing the forces of reaction in opposition to the children of light." Moreover, after 1935 his writings and speeches began to reveal an increasing admiration for efforts of the New Deal to effect social change. His old interest in labor law was stimulated when the International Ladies' Garment Workers Union, led by David Dubinsky, employed him to argue their appeal in the United States Court of Appeals in Kansas City from an injunction against a strike to unionize the Donnelly Garment Company. Nelly Don, as the company was known in the trade, had authoritarian labor practices and was singularly unwilling to pay a minimum wage or allow its factories to be unionized.

In the courtroom, Acheson was confronted by the vitriolic former senator from Missouri, James A. Reed, who was representing his wife's company. His performance was quite a contrast to Acheson's lower-key, eastern-style argumentation. Well into old age, Jim Reed hobbled to the lectern, leaning on his cane, while his argument rose to a leonine roar. "If the devil scraped the caldrons of hell, and out of the scum created a sensate being, he would not be as vile as this man [pointing his cane at Acheson] who comes here to defend stripping women naked in the streets of this city." Despite having to endure Reed's invective, Acheson insisted nonetheless on shaking his opponent's hand after the arguments had been presented.[3]

David Dubinsky recognized Acheson as a successful advocate of the union's right to organize, describing him in 1940 as a man "not only brilliant as a lawyer, well known as a progressive, but one who could understand the heart of our labor movement."[4]

Acheson, always most happy with appellate work, was nonetheless not content simply to practice law, for his brief experience in government had whetted his taste for public service. As Felix Frankfurter described him then, "The heady experience of being in on big political decisions was like getting used to French cuisine. Once Dean had dined on such rare meat it was painful to return to the hardtack of the law."[5]

No issue was more controversial than the behavior of the Supreme Court, which revealed an eagerness to turn back the legislation of the New Deal and a reluctance to correct the abuses of unregulated corporate power. Roosevelt's plan to overcome the resistance of the Court by enlarging it with justices who would be sympathetic to New Deal legislation did not emerge until after the 1936 presidential election. Acheson, however, was already disturbed by the tendency of the Court to abandon the principles of judicial restraint.

On July 4, 1936, in a speech to the Maryland Bar Association on the hundredth anniversary of Roger Brooke Taney's appointment to the Supreme Court, Acheson devoted most of his address to this point. In recalling that Taney had urged judicial restraint upon a Court faced with the litigation that accompanied the legislation under Andrew Jackson's presidency, Acheson reminded his listeners that Taney had insisted that "the judge, in applying constitutional limitations, must restrain himself and leave the maximum of freedom to those agencies of government whose actions he is called upon to weigh."[6]

For Acheson as for Taney, the best approach would be "to permit the evolution of constitutional practice by actual experience, leaving decisions in the first instance to legislatures, rather than to the a priori reasoning of judges."[7]

Acheson's address was noticed by Norman Hapgood, former editor of *Harper's*, who sent it along to Roosevelt, commenting: "Referring back to our talks about the Supreme Court: it is just possible that you may not have seen notices of Acheson's address on Taney. . . . As he is about 40, I suppose, and has the solid court behind him as a lawyer accustomed to put cases before them, I should think he might well be considered when the time comes."

"Keep on keeping me posted," FDR replied.[8]

In his letters the following year, when Roosevelt's attempt to add more justices to the Court brought this controversy to a bitter head, Acheson was generally sympathetic to FDR's dilemma. To his classmate Ranald MacDonald Jr., he wrote on March 11, 1937: "The present difficulty seems to me to require some present representation on the Court of the current overwhelmingly held point of view, but I do not think that the Ark of the Covenant would be rent if two men were added to the Court who understood the present temper of the country."[9]

The following day he wrote in a letter to his old colleague from Treasury days, James Warburg, "I think it undesirable that the President should demand an immediate majority but he is entitled to representation." Referring to debates at the time of the Constitutional Convention, he wrote: "The conception of the Court as the angel with the flaming sword protecting us from the iniquitous intentions of the legislature and the President was as overdrawn then as it is now."[10]

Acheson's maturing political outlook is well reflected in his remarks before the bar and officers of the Supreme Court in memory of Justice Benjamin N. Cardozo, who died on July 9, 1938. He made a point of eulogizing Cardozo's frank acceptance of the right of government to assert itself, as long as it did so in "the pursuit of legitimate ends by methods honestly conceived and rationally chosen." As always, Acheson was quick to praise pragmatism, noting that Cardozo "struck against the pernicious and inveterate habit of dwelling on abstractions."[11]

If Acheson nonetheless continued to refuse to admit that he was ideologically a New Dealer, this stemmed largely from his belief that it was "profitless to be for or against things in broad categories depending either on the persons who advocate them or upon general principles of a great and sweeping nature."[12]

* * *

While Acheson had shown a growing taste for public service in the 1930s, his work as a practicing lawyer at Covington and Burling as well as raising a family took a great deal of energy. As always, his zest for the active life continued to include making improvements on the farm and riding horses. But eventually his enthusiasm for equestrian sports waned, which his son ascribed to a fall he took in the 1930s during a foxhunt. Although he was unhurt, he had landed in a thornbush, "from which he could not extricate himself for the pain inflicted by the thorns upon the slightest movement." It was one of those "turning points," and Acheson never again urged horsemanship upon one and all.[13]

Shooting clay pigeons was also a part of the regimen of the farm. The launcher was powerful enough to throw the spinning clay disk a good seventy-five yards or more. On one memorable occasion in 1934, Dean's mother, recently widowed and living in Middletown, was visiting the farm, and her son, recalling his mother as a crack shot with a squirrel rifle, suggested they shoot some clay pigeons after lunch. His mother chose a single-shot .410 gauge, the bore little thicker than a cigarette.

"But Mother, you can't hit anything with a .410—the shot pattern is too small."

"Never mind, dear, I like a light gun."

After his mother gave the command "Pull," off went the clay bird, and about thirty feet out Dean and David saw a puff of black clay powder as the shot hit home. "That wasn't hard," said Dean's mother.

The son and grandson gave her three more pigeons—"to the right, and then a sharp rising shot at maximum elevation, and finally a 'grounder,' a quail going for close cover." All were hit, four for four.[14]

Christmas Eve had by the 1930s become a tradition at the Achesons' and revealed Dean at his most genial. The Christmas carol party dated from the early days in Georgetown, and it was geared especially for friends and their children. As Acheson's son described it in an affectionate memoir of his father, "The carol party had two departments—the children's party and the adults' serious singing party. In our dining room in the P Street house, the table was laid out with small sandwiches, gingerbread men with raisin buttons and eyes, cake, and ice cream."

Accompanied by his wife on the piano, Dean managed the singing, reminiscent of his father's Christmas services, where the church featured a brass orchestra, kettledrums, and full choir. In the beginning of the evening, the hymns were sedate—"Silent Night," "O Little Town of Bethlehem"—then rising to a higher level with "We Three Kings" and "O Come All Ye Faithful," and finally reaching a crescendo with "Angels We Have Heard on High." In David Acheson's words: "Dad had a full-throated baritone and opened it up on the first repetitive hammer blows. 'Angels we have heard on high, / Sweetly singing o'er the plain.' He [and his friend Judge Sternhagen] stood together, a powerful bass section, belting out the refrain: 'Glo-o-o-o-o-o-o-o-o-o-o-o-o-o-ria, in excelsis deo.' Dad's throat was distended like a bullfrog's, his eyebrows drawn down in intense concentration. Then, beaming, 'Terrific! Better than last year.'"[15]

His preferred movies were adventure films like *The Prisoner of Zenda*, and he had little taste for the theater, except for musical comedies, especially those of his old housemate Cole Porter; his threshold for boredom was low, and he often left the theater in the middle of a play that was too slow or pretentious. Above all, Acheson was known for not suffering fools easily. He relished clever argument and outrageous humor and hated cant, hypocrisy, the pompous, the obvious, the pedantic.[16]

Vacations in the 1930s also included trips abroad and to Murray Bay in Quebec Province. The summer residents of Murray Bay, near the junction of the Saguenay and St. Lawrence Rivers, were generally well-off and included Republican senator Robert A. Taft, who was to become a stern opponent of Acheson's when he was in government service. Fishing, tennis, picnics in a rocky field: these were the standard diversions, and Acheson was pleased to be in Canada, where he preferred to travel on vacation, renewing his deep ties to the country where he had gained his manhood by working on the railroad.

The last prewar family vacation in Europe took place during the summer of 1938, in the shadow of Adolf Hitler's demands that Czechoslovakia's Sudetenland, which was populated largely by German-speaking Czech citizens, should be returned to Germany. The Achesons spent considerable time in France, ending with a stay in Paris at the Elysée Parc Hôtel. Acheson learned that Endicott Peabody, the aging rector of Groton, was in town and invited Mrs. Peabody and him over for lunch. By now Acheson had established good relations with the rector and had even sent his son to Groton, believing that David needed the discipline of a taut ship.

Over drinks the conversation turned to the crisis in the Sudetenland, the poor state of morale in France, and the question of what England would do. When Peabody expressed confidence in the British prime minister, Neville Chamberlain, Acheson countered that Chamberlain had underestimated Hitler's aims and that perhaps a tougher politician like Winston Churchill was needed at 10 Downing Street. The rector, who knew Chamberlain, questioned Churchill's stability—not quite the gentleman he should be, according to the rector's friends in England.

When the Peabodys had departed, Dean said: "There goes a really great man, but do you know, there's a sad anomaly here. Chamberlain doesn't understand what he's up against, but he would be a great success as a student at Groton. Churchill does understand it. He would be kicked out of Groton in a week."[17]

Acheson had become increasingly active in backing the president, in the first instance for his domestic policy and later in trying to garner support for a more interventionist foreign policy. In 1936 Lewis Douglas and James Warburg—who had shared Acheson's apprehensions over FDR's monetary policies—proposed that he join with them in a "Democrats for Landon" movement. But for Acheson, whatever differences he may have had with Roosevelt were as nothing compared to the gap between Acheson's idea of desirable public policy and those of the Republican candidate, Alf Landon, governor of Kansas.

Finally Acheson went public with his views in a letter to the *Baltimore Sun*, dated October 17, 1936, announcing that he would be voting for the president in the upcoming election. He singled out Landon's opposition to Secretary of State Cordell Hull's efforts to revive international trade through the Reciprocal Trade Agreements Program, calling them "among the most constructive acts of any government in the post war period." In addition, he strongly objected to the charges of communism that the Republican national chairman, John Hamilton, had leveled against the New Deal: "It seems to me utterly fantastic to suggest that Communism is in any manner involved in this campaign. It serves only to arouse a spirit of bigotry. . . . I am against any party which inflames this spirit."[18] Later Acheson learned that both Hull and Roosevelt were surprised and pleased by the letter, which the Democrats then reprinted as a political pamphlet.

Still other obligations continued to infringe on Acheson's law practice. On January 5, 1939, Roosevelt nominated Felix Frankfurter to the Supreme Court of the United States. Within days after the nomination, Frankfurter asked Acheson to be his counsel in Washington during the hearings before a subcommittee of the Senate Judiciary Committee and to help in responding to such requests as the committee might make.

Frankfurter's trips from Cambridge to Washington were frequent; he advised the president even when unasked, and he usually made a point of seeing Acheson. He revealed his deep feelings for his former pupil in a letter to him on Thanksgiving Day 1937. "Dear Dean," he wrote. "This is not a love letter but damn near it. . . . When I think of the spiritual sloth and otiose mentality of most people I encounter . . . I rejoice over the freedom of mind and spirit with which you are enjoying and using the Lord's patrimony to you."[19]

There was, in turn, no one in public life with whom Dean Acheson felt such complete rapport as he did with his former mentor. As he put it in a letter years later when he was asked to discuss Frankfurter, "The Justice is probably the closest friend I have. I cannot write about him at arms length."[20]

Appearing at the hearings as counsel, Acheson wrote later to George Rublee of the odd lot of witnesses: "All were fanatical and some were very definitely mental cases. One poor old fellow informed the Committee that this country was founded on five principles—Christianity, Masonry, checks and balances, the Trinity and God. This was the kind of thing we listened to for two days, interspersed with vicious mis-representation of Felix's views and undisguised anti-Semitism."[21]

Initially Frankfurter had no intention of testifying, since he did not want to look like an office seeker, and it was not customary for the nominee to do so. But after two days of wild charges, FDR's press secretary, Steve Early, called to tell him he had better come down to Washington. At the request of the committee, Frankfurter agreed to do so. In the hearings on January 12, 1939, Frankfurter soon got into a professorial back-and-forth with Senator Patrick McCarran, a right-wing Democrat from Nevada, in which he seemed to be splitting hairs and not coming to grips with McCarran's innuendos about Frankfurter's alleged sympathy for communist doctrines. A typical exchange regarding the work of socialist Harold Laski went this way: McCarran—"Do you know whether [Laski] has a doctrine?" Frankfurter—"I assume he has more than one. All people have." McCarran—"I refer now to a publication entitled 'Communism,' and ask . . . Do you subscribe to his doctrine as expressed in that volume?" Frankfurter—"Senator McCarran, how can I answer that question without making a speech about my views on government and the relations of the various branches of government to one another?"

After more of this kind of interchange, Senator Matthew M. Neely of West Virginia, chairman of the subcommittee, called Acheson over. As Acheson wrote later, Neely told him that McCarran was creating the impression that Felix Frankfurter was a dangerous radical, if not a Communist. The chairman believed that the best thing to do was to bring the matter into the open and ask the witness directly whether or not he was or had ever been a Communist. Acheson agreed and returned to Frankfurter, "urging him to be sensible and not reply by asking the Chairman what he meant by 'Communist.'"

A few moments later Neely asked whether Frankfurter had ever been enrolled as a member of the Communist Party. The witness retorted: "I have never been enrolled, and have never been qualified to be enrolled, because that does not represent my view of life, nor my view of government."

At these words, a great roar of approval came from the crowded room. The chairman, banging his gavel, was all but inaudible. Finally, after order was restored, the subcommittee adjourned to vote favorably on his nomination later in the day.[22]

Acheson and Frankfurter were now due for a lunch with the chairman of the full judiciary committee, Senator Henry Ashurst of Arizona. He greeted them warmly and offered them a brandy as a cocktail. An excellent lunch followed as Ashurst and Frankfurter discoursed on scandals of the post–Civil War period. It was well into the afternoon before the lunch was completed and more brandy consumed to give them a further lift.

As Acheson and Frankfurter made their farewells and headed for the railroad station, Frankfurter put forth a startling proposal that they drop by the White House before going home and tell the president how the hearings went. Acheson had not seen FDR in six years and was apprehensive over such an intrusion. But

Frankfurter insisted he come along, and they were let in through the north gate to the White House because Frankfurter was recognized as a frequent guest.

FDR's secretary, Marguerite ("Missy") LeHand, appeared somewhat distraught at this interruption. The president was already behind schedule, she explained. "Remember, fifteen minutes and not a second more."

Roosevelt greeted Acheson "with genial ease, as though we had parted only yesterday on the best of terms." As Frankfurter recounted the McCarran inquisition, the triumph, and the luncheon, the president howled with laughter. It was three-quarters of an hour later before Missy LeHand was able to force them out of the Oval Office and send them off in a White House car.[23] Acheson always suspected that his future career was made that day.[24]

It was several weeks later, upon arriving home one Sunday after a day at Harewood, that Acheson was given a message to call the White House operator. He believed this was probably just a message from a staff member, but when he reached the operator, she put the president on the phone.

"Hello, Judge," Roosevelt intoned.

"I'm afraid there's some mistake, Mr. President," Acheson said. "This is Dean Acheson."

"Not at all," said FDR. "Judge Acheson of the Court of Appeals for the District of Columbia. Your nomination goes to the Senate tomorrow morning."

"But I don't want to be a judge. Would you?"

Roosevelt admitted that he would not, and Acheson replied, "Well, neither would I."

The president then went on to explain his plan for nominating three judges whom he was convinced the Senate would confirm—the other two, Robert Patterson and Francis Biddle, later became, respectively, undersecretary and secretary of war, and attorney general. After much argument, Acheson finally got FDR to hold off until he could see him first thing in the morning. That night he wrote him a letter, explaining how much he appreciated "the honor of the confidence" that seemed to him "so fine an act of sportsmanship that I shall never forget it." Nonetheless, he believed that he "could not be successful or happy" in the job.[25]

The next day Acheson handed the president the note before he had a chance to speak. That was not enough to deter Roosevelt, who pressed him on his reasons for refusing the job. It finally came down to Acheson's reluctance to serve a life sentence to such "sedentary confinement." The president then switched his offer to create a new post of assistant attorney general for the protection of civil rights. Despite the unsedentary nature of this assignment, Acheson again turned him down. As Acheson described it, "With good grace and in a thoroughly friendly manner the President let me go."[26]

* * *

Despite his reluctance to enter government service, Acheson nonetheless agreed in February 1939 to serve on, and later chair, the Attorney General's Committee on Administrative Procedure, whose task it was to establish procedures assuring fair treatment for persons or concerns falling afoul of the many new federal regulatory laws. The charge had been made that the administrative agencies had become virtually the prosecutor, judge, and executioner in their own causes. As a result, the private citizen was often denied a right to a truly fair hearing. The Acheson committee soon decided that it would study in detail every agency of the government that directly affected persons outside the government, "either by adjudication or by rule-making."[27]

By January 1941, when the committee completed its work, the one thousand-page report recommended separating the judicial and prosecutorial functions; it further called for a speedier and more independent adjudication of disputes between private interests and various federal agencies, as well as simplifying administrative procedures.[28]

Acheson was mightily proud of his handiwork. He called the monographs that the staff produced on each of the agencies "definitive," as they set out "how each actually operated, the reality as opposed to the theory." The act that grew out of the report finally became law in June 1946, and Acheson took satisfaction from Justice Holmes's observation that "legal progress is often secreted in the interstices of legal procedure."[29]

When Germany invaded Poland on September 1, 1939, the Achesons were vacationing in Murray Bay, on the St. Lawrence. Their friend Maude Atherton, the wife of American ambassador to Denmark Ray Atherton, was staying with them and immediately left to try to rejoin her husband. The Achesons soon set about closing the house, and then Dean and his son, David, drove south to get him installed at Yale. On the long drive down to New Haven, father and son discussed the crisis in Europe, and Acheson told him that he was certain that the United States would be drawn into the war in Europe. He suggested that David enlist in a Reserve Officers Training Corps while he carried on with his education. David agreed and, on the way to college, chose the navy; three years later, with a college degree and a commission as an ensign, he went off for three years' duty in the Pacific.

From that day on, Acheson became fully and openly committed to the cause of aiding the Allies. He joined the Committee to Defend America, which had been organized by the editor of the *Emporia* (Kansas) *Gazette*, William Allen White, as well as another group, which had organized itself informally at the Century Association, a private men's club in New York City, and became known as the Century Group.

Since 1936 Acheson had been a member of the Yale Corporation, the governing body of that university, and it was perhaps fitting that he should give his most far-reaching views of the new realities of the global crisis in a speech on November 28, 1939, at Yale's Davenport College. Much of what he said there reflected his belief that the United States would have to learn new ways of exercising power, both in the present conflict and in the postwar world.

Acheson pointed out that the British no longer had the resources either to finance the "means of production of wealth in other countries" or, through its naval power, to "guarantee security of life and investment in distant parts of the earth." Though he did not spell out the specifics of the role the United States should play in the future, he implied that America would to a very large extent have to take Britain's place in the world: "I think it is clear that with a nation, as with a boxer, one of the greatest assurances of safety is to add reach to our power."

In urging a military and naval buildup to make the United States secure in both oceans, he argued for "a realistic American policy." We cannot, he said, be indifferent to the consequences of Russo-German and Japanese victories. The result would be "internment on this continent and such portion of the one to the south as we can physically control."

Acheson then proposed a postwar system remarkably similar to what the United States would adopt in the mid-1940s at the Bretton Woods conference that established a new monetary and economic postwar order. America, he said, could help make capital available to "those parts of Europe which need productive equipment" and provide "a stable international monetary system," remove exclusive or preferential trade arrangements, "cease exporting more than we import and spend abroad," and insist that "the supply of raw materials needed in other parts of the world is not restricted." This vision of a free-trading system undergirded by a stable monetary system became a central building block in the postwar order that Acheson helped create, both at Bretton Woods and as a result of the 1947 Marshall Plan.[30]

This was Acheson's first salvo. His second was an address to a convention of the International Ladies' Garment Workers at Carnegie Hall, June 4, 1940, the week after Dunkirk. Picking up on their slogan, "Dictatorship Dooms Labor; Labor Dooms Dictatorship," Acheson asked, "Do you mean those words?" He urged the United States to find a way "to undo much that has been said and much that has been written into the statute books" prohibiting direct aid to the Allies: "We can and should send to Britain and France food from our surplus."

Equally pressing was "their need for planes and the smaller fighting ships—even those which we class as obsolete." But by far, our "greatest effort must be to turn the vast energy and resources of this country to the production of instruments of war, both for ourselves and others." Confronted with "elemental, unmoral, and ruthless power . . . we can be wrong only once. Remember, I beseech you, that the judgment of nature upon error is death."[31]

With the fall of France in June 1940, a German invasion of England seemed imminent, and the British desperately needed more destroyers to keep the sea lanes open. Soon after Winston Churchill had become prime minister on May 10, he sent FDR a message asking for fifty or sixty overage destroyers. In fact, the navy had in mothballs a large number of old "four stackers" from World War I. Roosevelt wanted to accommodate Churchill; but with FDR facing a run for a third term, the administration was loath to test its legal authority to transfer the old ships. It believed that congressional authority was needed, but the president was wary of trying to obtain it.

Acheson and his friends in the Century Group decided to find a legal means to justify turning over the destroyers to the British in return for leasing American bases located in British possessions in the Western Hemisphere. Under the law, the only equipment that could be released for foreign sale had to be first certified as nonessential to the national defense. Roosevelt hesitated.

This time, unlike his behavior at the Treasury, Acheson felt no compunction in helping FDR to circumvent any legal obstructions to executive action. Benjamin V. Cohen, one of the president's assistants and a good friend of Acheson's, met privately with Acheson to see if they could write a legal opinion setting forth the president's authority and, if possible, get some eminent lawyers to join in publishing it. Together they went to New York and wrote an opinion in Cohen's apartment, putting together an ingenious argument to demonstrate that the transfer of the destroyers would be legal under the law if properly interpreted.

Acheson then took the opinion to several well-known members of the New York bar, who agreed with Acheson and Cohen's argument that there was no reason "to put a strained or unnecessary interpretation on our own statutes contrary to our national interests."[32] Charles C. Burlingham, whom Acheson termed "the patriarch of the bar of the City of New York," Thomas Thacher, former U.S. district judge in New York and solicitor general of the United States under Herbert Hoover, and Acheson's partner, George Rublee, were prepared to sign the document. (John Foster Dulles begged off, apparently because his law firm of Sullivan and Cromwell had German clients—and this may well have been the beginning of Acheson's lack of respect for Dulles.)

Impatient for action, Acheson decided that their five signatures were enough to command respectful attention. His next step was to contact Charles Merz, a Yale classmate and the editor of the editorial page of *The New York Times*, who agreed to publish the lengthy opinion as a letter to the editor on August 11, 1940. After presenting their arguments to show that there was a legal basis for the executive to sell the destroyers, the letter writers concluded by declaring that the executive in an emergency might have to bypass Congress: "To seek an unnecessary reaffirmation of these powers from the Congress now would be to run a serious danger of delay and by delay possibly to endanger the vital interests of the people of the country in keeping war from our own shores."[33]

The letter had an immediate impact. Secretary of War Henry Stimson wrote Burlingham that the opinion "will mark a real turning point in the war and the relations of the U.S.A. and Great Britain."[34] But what Acheson wanted were results, not praise. He decided to contact the attorney general, Robert H. Jackson, who was on a camping trip in the mountains of Pennsylvania with his daughter. Although irritated at being interrupted on holiday, after talking to Acheson, he cut short his vacation and wrote an opinion reaching the same conclusion, though by a different route.

In the days following publication of the letter, Acheson knew that the next move was to persuade the president; Acheson believed that FDR's recent friendliness was not enough to make him the preferred advocate. He found his solution through the good offices of the British ambassador to Washington, Lord Lothian. Roosevelt was soon to meet with the Canadian prime minister, William Lyon Mackenzie King, and at Lothian's urgings King presented to the president the renewed British request for the "overage destroyers."

Roosevelt then sought Prime Minister Winston Churchill's agreement to authorize the use of Newfoundland, Bermuda, the Bahamas, Jamaica, St. Lucia, Trinidad, and British Guiana as naval and air bases by the United States. In this way FDR was able to counter the arguments of the isolationists by insisting that such a deal was concluded solely for the national defense of the United States. On September 3, 1940, by executive agreement, Roosevelt transferred to England some fifty old destroyers in exchange for leases on eight British bases stretching from Newfoundland to British Guiana.[35]

Acheson's efforts to show how the executive could circumvent congressional authorization reflected Acheson's growing belief in the legitimacy of executive action in defense of what he saw as the nation's vital interests. At the outset of the Korean War, when he was secretary of state, Acheson would take the same line with President Truman, asserting the authority of the executive to bypass Congress in a time of national emergency when immediate action is required.

On September 12 Acheson wrote to John J. McCloy, then a practicing lawyer but soon to become an assistant secretary of war: "I continually hear people saying that the President should have gone to Congress. This seems only another way of saying that the transaction was impossible, and I have very little patience with people who insist upon glorifying forms on the theory that another course is going to destroy our institutions. The danger to them seems not in resolving legal doubts in accordance with the national interest but in refusing to act when action is imperative."[36]

* * *

As Roosevelt campaigned for a third term in the fall of 1940, Acheson backed him unreservedly. In a letter to the *Baltimore Sun*, reprinted in *The New York Times*, October 2, 1940, Acheson stated, "Today there is only one test—who can best pilot the ship in this crisis of civilization? For a year now the President has met that test. No one can ask more and no one dare ask less."

FDR wrote him the very day the letter appeared, thanking him for his support, and Acheson replied in kind, writing that it was "a joy and a duty—which Justice Holmes says are all one—to say publicly how essential for our country it is to have you at the helm."[37]

Within a few weeks Acheson was asked to join a White House meeting of Roosevelt and his advisers, who were worried about the campaign. Frank Walker, the postmaster general, Judge Samuel Rosenman, the president's speechwriter, and presidential counselor Harry Hopkins were all fearful that the campaign of the Republican nominee, Wendell Willkie, was catching fire and that the public might perceive him as the man best equipped to keep America out of war.

Acheson remained unusually silent, until the president asked him to speak up. Fortified by a second cocktail, Acheson asserted that the Democratic campaign was becoming "too defensive." In essence, what was needed "was to relate the past eight years of the New Deal and the great horizons it had opened for the common man to the dangers threatening freedom everywhere, including in our own land."

The president paid close attention to Acheson's analysis. "Could you put that on paper for Harry by tomorrow morning?" he asked. Acheson agreed and prepared a memorandum that was filled with heightened rhetoric on how FDR's domestic achievements were linked to the need to marshal "the might of America to guard the New World from the tragic horror which has engulfed the Old World."[38]

The year ended with Roosevelt's reelection, and very soon afterward a call came from Secretary of State Cordell Hull, asking Acheson to accept the post of assistant secretary of state for economic affairs. Although he was earning a good living and had a wife and three children at their most expensive age, and the salary at State would be only about $8,000 a year, his hesitations were hardly serious. He very much wanted to take part in the global struggle against fascism. As he wrote years later about the decision that was to change his life: "How futile these exercises in thought and consultation are! Mere rationalization of decisions already made. Forces stronger than reason determined the result, and the right one, as my life turned out."[39]

On February 1, 1941, Acheson went with his wife, Mr. and Mrs. Archibald MacLeish, Attorney General and Mrs. Francis Biddle, and Justice and Mrs. Felix Frankfurter to Justice Brandeis's apartment, where Brandeis administered the oath of office.

CHAPTER NINE

MOST UNSORDID ACTS

By 1941 war between the United States and Japan seemed to the American ambassador to the Chrysanthemum throne more likely than ever. Joseph Grew, a Boston-bred aristocrat who had known Roosevelt at Groton and Harvard, had spent eight years in Tokyo trying in every way he knew to ease relations between America and Japan. On December 14, 1940, however, Grew sent a despairing assessment of Japanese-American relations to the president personally in a letter addressed to "Dear Frank." In it, he expressed the deepest pessimism he had ever known in his years of diplomacy: "Sooner or later, unless we are prepared . . . to withdraw bag and baggage from the entire sphere of 'Greater East Asia including the South Seas' (which God forbid), we are bound eventually to come to a head-on clash with Japan."[1]

By early 1941 Roosevelt, too, was convinced that the Japanese were bent on war, but he was also hopeful that the United States could avoid a direct conflict with Japan. In the meantime, he hoped to build up America's armed forces, while at the same time denying to Japan iron and steel and, above all, the oil that would fuel the Japanese war machine.

Within his cabinet, the most vocal hawks were Secretary of War Henry Stimson, Secretary of the Interior Harold Ickes, and Secretary of the Treasury Henry Morgenthau. Appointed to FDR's cabinet at seventy-five, Henry Stimson had already served two Republican presidents—as secretary of war under William Howard Taft and as secretary of state under Herbert Hoover. He was paradoxically both an American nationalist and an idealistic internationalist.

Colonel Stimson (a title used by his friends from Stimson's army service in World War I, for which he volunteered when he was almost fifty) was pressed into service by FDR because he needed an eminent Republican internationalist if he was to prepare the nation for the likelihood of war. Moreover, in Stimson Roosevelt found a man who had a record of tireless devotion to his nation, though often carried out in a righteous manner that many found somewhat rigid but all conceded was genuine.[2]

Harold Ickes, known as "the old curmudgeon," was prickly but also high-minded. A grumpy companion for the president, he delighted in controversy. Acheson became close to him during the war when, under gas rationing, he regularly hitched a ride in with Ickes from the farm; he used to say that the secretary of the interior liked nothing better than to win an argument—"and by unfair means if possible."

As Acheson told it, Ickes would back down only after some dramatic gesture. One day, driving home, Ickes launched into yet another diatribe against the shortcomings of Acheson's superiors, Secretary of State Cordell Hull and Under Secretary Sumner Welles. Acheson tried to cut him short, but Ickes pressed on. Finally, as they approached a traffic light, Acheson asked the chauffeur to pull over to the curb so that he could get out.

"How will you get home?" Harold Ickes asked. Acheson replied that it was time he learned how to thumb a ride.

"I believe you're just damned fool enough to do it," Ickes went on. "Sit down and I'll shut up." Acheson relaxed, and the debate shifted to safer ground.[3]

After the fall of France in June 1940, Henry Morgenthau pressed hard to wage a campaign of economic warfare against Germany and Italy, and, as he told Felix Frankfurter, there was no one in State with whom he could talk candidly except for Dean Acheson, the very man he had supplanted at the Treasury years ago.[4] In turn, Assistant Secretary of State Acheson wrote: "There was no one at all with whom I could talk—sympathetically. From top to bottom our Department, except for our corner of it, was against Henry Morgenthau's campaign to apply freezing controls to axis countries and their victims."[5]

Acheson, moreover, worked for the cautious Hull and for Sumner Welles, an imperious fellow Grotonian who tended to encourage the president not to do anything that would box in the Japanese. Much as Acheson bridled under the moralizing secretary of state, he was sensitive to Hull's fears that a total oil embargo might encourage the Japanese to strike out at the United States before America was fully prepared to wage war. Moreover, the president's military advisers believed that they would not be nearly ready to fight before the winter of 1942 and conveyed this to Roosevelt.

Both Morgenthau and Ickes continued to badger the president, and to the extent that he was able, Acheson supported their calls for stiffer sanctions. Throughout 1940 Roosevelt and Hull were all for protecting victims of aggression against the theft of their American assets, but also for still permitting Germany and Japan free use of their own assets. As Acheson commented later, "The

State Department and the White House . . . saw anything more as unneutral, as, indeed, it would have been."[6]

In March 1941 Morgenthau, supported by Acheson, confronted Hull over the question of whether or not to extend the freezing of foreign assets to the Axis countries and their victims. Once again the president backed Hull in his refusal to do so. But by June Hitler's virtual conquest of all of Europe had undermined Hull's position, and on June 14, 1941, the president extended freezing controls on all countries on the continent.[7]

As assistant secretary of state for economic affairs, Acheson became the department's representative on the State-Treasury-Justice policy committee (known as the Foreign Funds Control Committee). This committee, which he chaired, could now turn its attention to the control of Japanese assets in the United States.

The only weapon Roosevelt saw at his disposal was the use of embargoes, for despite widespread isolationist sentiment, the American public supported an anti-Japanese embargo. By the summer of 1939 three-fourths of the nation was in favor of setting an embargo on arms shipments; by October 1940, after Japan had signed the Tripartite Pact with Germany and Italy, 83 percent of the American people favored an embargo on the sale of any war goods, including gasoline.

This gave Roosevelt an opportunity to press forward with his policy of trying to apply pressure on the Japanese, in hopes that a less militarist faction would gain power in Tokyo. When the United States finally did embargo the export of scrap iron and steel in September 1940, 88 percent of the public approved of the action.[8]

The struggle to embargo all oil exports to the Japanese was far more complicated. Not only was oil much more important to the Japanese war effort than scrap iron, but also, as FDR never ceased to remind the war hawks in his family and cabinet, a total ban on all oil exports would probably push the Japanese to invade the Dutch East Indies sooner rather than later. Moreover, both Hull and Welles were apostles of moderation. In July 1940 Roosevelt rejected Morgenthau's call for draconian measures to prevent oil from reaching Japan and yielded to Welles's position, which was to limit the embargo to high-octane aviation gasoline.

The turning point, however, came a year later when Japanese leaders on July 2, 1941, decided to move south, occupy southern Indochina, and prepare to strike at Southeast Asia and the Dutch East Indies. Because of Hitler's attack on Soviet Russia in June 1941, the Japanese were no longer fearful of a Russian onslaught from the north. Later that month Tokyo moved forty thousand troops into southern Indochina, and the way was open to them to obtain the oil reserves of the Dutch East Indies.

Roosevelt and Hull could see the threat and what was about to happen, but neither the admirals nor Hull wanted to do anything that would provoke a Japanese attack on the American air and naval bases in the Philippines. Chief of Naval Operations Harold ["Betty"] Stark personally urged the president not to embargo all trade with Japan.

As a compromise, at a cabinet meeting on July 18, 1941, Roosevelt went along with Hull and Stark and ordered a freeze on all Japanese funds in the United States, but he made the freeze selective. Funds could be released to purchase those goods that Washington deemed the Japanese could have. The president, always determined to retain as much flexibility as possible, wanted to use the freeze as a powerful warning to Japan, but also to allow some give in releasing funds so as to avoid a final confrontation with the Japanese warlords.

Once Roosevelt decided on the freeze, he ordered Sumner Welles to develop the actual plan. Welles therefore sketched out a system that would release enough funds for Japan to purchase gasoline below 86 octane, which could not be manufactured into aviation fuel, but in amounts similar to those of the prewar years of 1935–36. To Acheson as chairman of the Foreign Funds Control Committee fell the responsibility of implementing the freeze.[9]

Acheson drafted an even more sweeping action than Welles intended. He set forth a plan to make the freeze total for the first few weeks, while State and Treasury set up a system that would allow Japan to buy oil only in exchange for goods the United States needed, such as raw silk. Welles, however, deleted Acheson's tougher measures and presented the president with what FDR presumably wanted at a cabinet meeting on July 24.[10]

A week later everything was set. The Export Control Office would decide how much oil Japan would be allowed to purchase, and then the Foreign Funds Control Committee would release just enough dollars to permit the Japanese to buy the oil now licensed for export. Until Export Control could make its final calculations, Acheson's committee would take no action on any applications for funds that the Japanese might submit.

Acheson told the committee that he had talked over the whole matter with Welles, who thought that the "happiest solution with respect to Japanese trade" would be for Acheson's Committee "to take no action on Japanese applications." Acheson, under orders to stall, followed Welles's instructions to the letter. On August 1 all valid licenses for export of petroleum products were revoked.[11]

From August 9 through August 12 both the president and Welles (leaving Hull behind) met secretly with Winston Churchill on the American heavy cruiser *Augusta* and the British battleship *Prince of Wales*, in Argentia Harbor, Newfoundland. Until these discussions were concluded, no action would be taken to allow the Japanese any oil.[12]

In Tokyo, Ambassador Grew was deeply discouraged at the course of events, writing in his diary at the beginning of August after the freeze order went into effect: "The vicious circle of reprisals and counter reprisals is on. *Facilis descensus averni est.* Unless radical surprises occur in the world, it is difficult to see how the momentum of the down-grade movement can be arrested, or how far it will go. The obvious conclusion is eventual war."[13]

Although by early August Export Control notified the Foreign Funds Committee that Japan was entitled to 450,000 gallons of "not so good" gasoline and issued export licenses for $300,000 worth of diesel fuel, a figure substantially increased by mid-August, Japan never got the oil.

Acheson was certainly eager to institute a total embargo. As he explained to Sir Ronald Campbell of the British embassy in Washington, his committee had "discovered by accident the technique of imposing a total embargo by way of its freezing order without having to take decisions about quotas for particular commodities."[14] Acheson wrote later, "The inarticulate major premise was that whether or not we had a policy, we had a state of affairs; the conclusion, that until further notice it would continue." Hull wished this information to be held as closely as possible.[15]

From the beginning of August, no more oil was exported from the United States to Japan. Two Japanese tankers were even left at anchor in the harbor at San Pedro, near Los Angeles, waiting for oil that had already been contracted for.[16] The United States had imposed a de facto oil embargo without saying so.

This was the state of affairs that Acheson reported to Welles the day before Roosevelt returned from his meeting with Churchill in Argentia. Either by phone or in person on August 21 or 29, Welles may well have reported the situation to Roosevelt, and no countervailing directive was issued. Japanese trade, Acheson noted on August 20, was "a matter of confidential discussion between the President and Secretary Hull." In any case, on September 5, a day Hull lunched with the president, the secretary of state gave departmental sanction to these stalling maneuvers.[17]

If Roosevelt had intended to let the Japanese know that they could still obtain some oil, he never made that clear to them. And at this point in time Roosevelt most probably believed that it would be a mistake to make any shift in the embargo policy, which could be interpreted in Tokyo as weakness.[18]

By November 22 Acheson reported to Hull that the freezing controls had brought "a great stillness" over trade and financial relations between the United States and Japan.[19] That stillness lasted only two more weeks.

The diplomacy of proposals and counterproposals between Tokyo and Washington in the summer and fall of 1941 proved ineffective. By early September at an

Imperial Conference in Tokyo, the Japanese leaders decided that negotiations could continue, but parallel plans were to be made for a military assault against the United States, Great Britain, and the Netherlands.[20]

Washington, in turn, had no intention of lifting the oil embargo unless Japan agreed to Hull's four principles: respect for the territorial integrity and sovereignty of all nations; noninterference in the internal affairs of other nations; respect for the equality of commercial opportunity; and support for peaceful change in the Pacific. Perhaps a more flexible negotiator than Cordell Hull would have been able to find a modus vivendi; but for the Japanese the choices came down to fighting the United States or withdrawing from China, and no Japanese leader urged the latter.

On Sunday, December 7, 1941, Acheson and his wife were picnicking with Archibald and Ada MacLeish at Harewood. Right after lunch MacLeish, then librarian of Congress, had to get back to Washington. But no sooner had he gotten in the car than he threw open the door and ran up the drive, shouting, "The Japanese have attacked Pearl Harbor. Turn on your car radio."

Acheson drove forthwith to the Department of State, where Secretary Hull was in a towering rage. The Japanese envoys had left him only a few hours before, when Hull had reportedly castigated them as "scoundrels and piss-ants."[21]

No one knew what was happening. No one seemed to have any orders for Acheson and his cohorts. The scene was an unhappy augury of the next four years. The State Department was not to play a great role in waging the war, but, as it turned out, played a crucial role in planning the peace.

As a longtime internationalist, Acheson had been prepared to let the United States do anything short of war to help the Allies. Moreover, Franklin Roosevelt's determination to arm the Western Allies became a central tenet of his policy after the outbreak of the war in Europe. But as a member of the administration in 1941, Acheson was becoming increasingly aware of the constraints under which Roosevelt operated.

It had been difficult enough for the president to supply overage destroyers to Great Britain in 1940. As it was, FDR had had to present that transaction to a wary Congress as a horse trade in which the United States had emerged the winner.

Throughout most of 1940, Washington sold London war material on a "cash-and-carry basis." Churchill had written to FDR in May that England would go on paying dollars as long as it could. Even after the British evacuation from the French mainland at Dunkirk in June 1940, Secretary of State Hull could tell the British ambassador that Britain must "fight to the last dollar."[22]

This was not a policy that Acheson could admire, but his desire to aid Britain more fully had to wait upon FDR's ability to find a way to win over a Congress suspicious of Britain's cries of poverty. Yet once Roosevelt discovered how to finesse congressional distrust, Acheson would find himself at the very center of the effort to finance Britain's war.

In any case, the American policy of cash-and-carry was rapidly coming to an end when the British ambassador, Lord Lothian, startled the American public by declaring at an impromptu press conference on November 23, 1940, that Britain could no longer pay for the war.

Ten days after Lothian's bombshell, Roosevelt boarded the cruiser USS *Tuscaloosa* for a ten-day cruise. Except for his small office staff, he took only Harry Hopkins aboard. It was to be a carefree post-election vacation, some card playing, fishing, and lolling about in the sun. Roosevelt did leave instructions with Treasury secretary Morgenthau to figure out how to satisfy the British, who wanted about $2 billion worth of goods but did not have enough dollars on hand to pay for them. The very morning the president set sail, Morgenthau informed a small group of the president's advisers that the only direction Roosevelt had given him was to tell him to urge the other relevant cabinet secretaries to "use your imaginations."[23]

At regular intervals, navy seaplanes landed alongside the *Tuscaloosa* and delivered the mail from the White House. On December 9 FDR received a long letter of about four thousand words from Winston Churchill. Most of the missive contained a detailed description of the war situation from the North Sea to Gibraltar, but the real point of the letter was to put before the president the dire financial straits Britain was in and to ask him to find a way for America to meet England's needs.

"The moment approaches when we shall no longer be able to pay cash for shipping and other supplies," Churchill warned. "If, as I believe, you are convinced, Mr. President, that the defeat of the Nazi and Fascist tyranny is a matter of high consequence to the people of the United States and the Western Hemisphere, you will regard this letter not as an appeal for aid, but as a statement of the minimum action necessary to the achievement of our common purpose."[24] Roosevelt said nothing after reading the letter, but he mulled over Churchill's plea and over the next few days invented in his own head the idea of lend-lease.

On December 16 FDR returned to Washington, rested, tanned, and in high spirits. The next day he lunched with Morgenthau, who wrote that Roosevelt was "very proud of the fact that he didn't look at a single report that he had taken with him from Washington." He then explained that he didn't want to put Churchill's request "in terms of dollars or loans."[25]

To the press that afternoon, Roosevelt unveiled his idea: "Now, what I am trying to do is eliminate the dollar sign. That is something brand new in the thoughts of everybody in this room, and I think—get rid of the silly, foolish old dollar sign."[26] He then went on to make an analogy to a man whose neighbor's house was on fire; in such a case that man would not say, "'Neighbor, my garden hose cost me $15; you have to pay me $15 for it.' What is the transaction that goes on? I don't want $15—I want my garden hose back after the fire." If the hose was in good condition after the fire, so be it; if not, the neighbor could simply replace it. So it had to be with munitions.

The president could not say what the exact procedure would be, but he was determined to substitute for the dollar sign a "gentleman's obligation to pay in kind." With that homely image of the garden hose, Roosevelt inaugurated the battle for lend-lease on a high and appealing note.[27]

Roosevelt assigned to the Treasury the drafting of the bill, which fell largely to Morgenthau's general counsel, Edward Foley, and his associate, Oscar Cox. On January 5, 1941, Morgenthau asked Foley to get the advice of Dean Acheson, who had already agreed to become assistant secretary of state for economic affairs but was still at this time a private citizen. Acheson thoroughly approved of the lend-lease idea; after looking over Foley's draft, he said that he wished he could come up with a brilliant suggestion, but he had none.[28]

Roosevelt, to draw the teeth of the opposition, had the bill introduced as H.R. 1776, and after a vigorous debate in Congress, and with important support from Wendell Willkie, the Lend-Lease Act was signed into law on March 11, 1941. Shortly afterward the president asked Secretary Hull to press on with a temporary agreement with the British dealing with the broad principles of a final agreement. Even as the shipments got under way, Hull charged Acheson with the task of producing first the temporary and then the final agreement.

To negotiate the agreement, John Maynard Keynes, who had recently joined the British Treasury as an unpaid consultant, arrived in Washington on May 10, 1941, with his wife, the former Diaghilev ballerina Lydia Lopokova. Keynes was at the height of his fame as an economist. His masterwork, *The General Theory of Employment, Interest and Money*, written during the early 1930s, was influential among many New Deal economists, who were convinced, like Keynes, of the need for active government intervention in the market and, during a recession, deficit spending and easier monetary policies in order to stimulate business activity and thus reduce unemployment.

Here is Acheson's portrait of the man who became a valued friend and with whom he was to spend so much time discussing and at times hotly disputing the provisions of the proposed Lend-Lease Agreement: "Keynes was not only one of the most delightful and engaging men I have ever known but also, in the true sense of the word, one of the most brilliant. His many-faceted and highly polished mind sparkled and danced with light. But not all felt his charm; to some he appeared arrogant."[29]

The Keyneses were shortly welcomed socially by the Achesons, the Frankfurters, and the MacLeishes. As the war progressed and Keynes returned again and again to Washington, he became a familiar figure in their social circle; and Lydia's quips and sallies and her constant struggle with English endeared her to their American friends. "I dislike being in the country in August," she once said, "because my legs get so bitten by barristers."[30]

Keynes's initial business encounter with Acheson was singularly unpropitious, however. He came to see the assistant secretary of state after a meeting with FDR, where he had explained to the president the nature of the temporary agreement Britain proposed. He then presented Acheson with a draft that Acheson described at the time as "wholly impossible": it provided "merely that lend-lease aid should be extended; that the British should return what was practicable for them to return; that no obligation should be created; and that they would be glad to talk about other matters."[31]

By the end of July Acheson's own draft, approved by the president, was ready for Keynes. The first six articles were readily accepted, providing for the United States to furnish the British with defense articles and services, and for Britain to contribute to American defense what it was able to. After the war the British would return whatever material was still in existence if Washington demanded it. But then followed Article VII, which set off six months more of often bitter discussion, in no small part because the secretary of state was a stubborn man.

Cordell Hull was possessed of one controlling idea: that greater freedom of trade would bring about universal peace. He saw Britain's desire to continue preferential treatment, called "Imperial Preference," to members of the British empire as standing in the way of his goal.[32] Because he believed Imperial Preference was a form of trade "discrimination," which amounted to a kind of sin against Hull's god, the State Department had inserted into Article VII of the Lend-Lease Agreement what came to be known as the "consideration." In essence, Britain was required to drop Imperial Preference in return for being let off the repayment of lend-lease goods.

Keynes was not against breaking down the barriers to international trade, but he was very much aware of the appalling problems Britain would face in seeking a favorable trade balance after the war. His overall interest in developing a broad program of international cooperation, designed primarily to rid the industrialized powers of the specter of unemployment, did not include any need to eliminate "discrimination" from trade policy.

Thus, when Acheson presented him with the first draft of Article VII, Keynes lambasted it as "the lunatic proposals of Mr. Hull."[33] Acheson, in turn, accused him of making statements that were "extreme and unjustified." All the Americans wanted was a commitment that the British—after the war and the vast amount of aid they would be receiving from the United States—would not take measures to impede free trade between the two countries.

The next day Keynes wrote Acheson from New York, apologizing for the "vehemence" of his response. Referring to the period of the 1930s when the great powers began to raise tariffs to gain competitive advantage, Keynes explained that he certainly did not want "to discriminate in the old bad sense of that word—on the contrary, quite the opposite."[34]

Negotiations continued throughout the rest of the year. Neither Acheson nor Keynes was wholly committed to his government's position—Acheson was under no illusion that freer trade alone was the solution to all the world's problems, and Keynes was flexible on Imperial Preference.

In the closing weeks of 1941, Acheson produced a new draft that aimed at "the reduction of tariffs and other trade barriers" but did not insist on nondiscrimination as an absolute condition for lend-lease, only for "agreed action" to achieve this end. Acheson thought that this would meet British objections. After all, if the United States someday felt compelled to seriously raise tariffs, it could not demand that the British eliminate all forms of discrimination.

Despite the heroic efforts of Acheson and Keynes, the British cabinet hung back on signing on to Article VII. Many members of the cabinet were opposed to having any reference to trade preferences in the agreement. The only solution seemed to be to appeal to Roosevelt and Churchill.[35]

Pearl Harbor transformed the situation. Only two weeks later, on December 22, 1941, Churchill arrived in Washington and stayed until January 14. Both he and FDR were now preoccupied with the great issues of waging war and putting together a declaration of common purpose by the Allied nations, now to be called, as FDR suggested, the "United Nations." Thus, Hull's entreaties that Roosevelt take up Article VII with Churchill went unheeded. In despair, Hull sent Acheson to the White House at the end of January to see what could be done before new appropriations hearings were held.

The president told Acheson that he had tried in vain to persuade Churchill to resolve the matter. Acheson then asked Roosevelt directly if he agreed with the State Department's position, and FDR said most emphatically that he did. Acheson asked for a note from him, endorsing this position. Roosevelt assented.

Acheson then showed the note to the British envoy, who passed it on to London. On February 6 the British cabinet met and confirmed the ambassador's worst fears. According to the British foreign secretary, Anthony Eden, the cabinet was unwilling "to barter Empire preference in exchange for . . . planes, tanks, guns, goods, et cetera."[36]

In response, FDR fired off a telegram on February 7, 1942, from "FDR to a former Naval Person," urging Churchill to sign the draft agreement. But Churchill echoed Eden. He replied that while he had always been opposed or lukewarm to Imperial Preference, the great majority of the cabinet felt that if the British gave in on this matter, "we should have accepted an intervention in the domestic affairs of the British Empire."[37]

Roosevelt, who understood how beleaguered Churchill felt at this moment, faced with his armies' defeat in Singapore and Libya, wrote back on February 11: "I want to make it perfectly clear to you that it is the furthest thing from my mind that we are attempting in any way to ask you to trade the principle of imperial preference as a consideration for Lend-Lease." On the contrary, "All I am urging is an understanding with you that we are going to have a bold, forthright, and comprehensive discussion looking forward to the construction of what you so aptly call 'a free, fertile economic policy for the post-war world.'"[38]

With this gracious response, Churchill accepted the American position. Twelve days later the revised draft of Article VII was finally signed. Churchill later called the Mutual Aid Agreement, the rubric under which lend-lease eventually emerged, "the most unsordid act in the history of any nation."[39]

In the struggle to define the exact nature of the bargain between Britain and the United States, Acheson had played a central role. In so doing, he was clarifying his own thinking about the part the United States would have to take in planning the postwar international economic order.

CHAPTER TEN

THE NEW ECONOMIC WORLD ORDER

ACHESON'S OFFICES consisted of two large, high-ceilinged rooms in the southwest corner of Old State, adjoining Hull's office. Stifling hot in summer and winter, the outer office housed his assistants—most notably Donald Hiss, who had been a law clerk for Justice Holmes, and Adrian Fisher, another former law clerk for both Justices Brandeis and Frankfurter. Acheson's secretary, Barbara Evans, would remain with him until the end of his life.

Acheson found that the greater part of each day was taken up with meetings. The very fuzziness of the jurisdictional boundaries of the division chiefs made such gatherings inevitable. While these meetings gave "the illusion of action," what generally occurred was the attempt to "reconcile the irreconcilable." For Acheson—and this became his virtual credo—"What was most often needed was not compromise but decision."[1]

In the two years following Pearl Harbor, economic warfare—aimed at cutting the enemy's supplies, information, and funds from foreign territory—became Acheson's most serious concern. In the Second World War, the ancient tactic of the naval blockade was extended to include communication, commerce, and finance, which meant not only direct interdiction of the enemy's control points, but also interference with the rights of neutral nations to ship goods; international legal ideas about the rights of neutrals effectively became irrelevant.

A key aim of economic warfare was also to control overland trade between neutrals and Germany within the continent of Europe. Depending on how they evaluated the course of the war and whom the likely victors would be, the neutrals either pressed to continue their trade with Germany or responded to Allied demands that trade be curtailed. As the neutrals played their hand, they also affected the outcome of the war.

In circumstances of total war, the Allies regarded the neutrals as virtual traitors. Nonetheless, Sweden, Switzerland, Portugal, and Spain were neutral powers that had no intention of caving in to American pressure. It was only because of the increasing success of Allied arms by the end of 1943 that Sweden agreed to deny goods and rights of passage to Germany and German troops.

The Swiss were, if anything, more intractable than the Swedes, and the Spanish were no better. Moreover, the British, fearful of German-Spanish attack on their base in Gibraltar, refused to press Madrid as hard as Washington wanted them to. Once again, Dean Acheson took the bit between his teeth and drafted a speech for Secretary Hull, blasting the neutrals for aiding the enemy.

Despite these warnings, the Swiss held out until April 1945, only a month before the Germans surrendered. The Swedes cracked earlier, and the Spanish cracked last. What Acheson learned from his experience was the power of a weaker ally, in this case Great Britain, to prevent the United States from taking action against Spain, even though America, by far the stronger one, was "charged with ultimate responsibility."[2]

After the 1942 congressional elections saw Republican and isolationist gains, the great potentates of the House and Senate were more often than not impediments to action. This was made abundantly clear the following year, when Acheson tried to commit the United States to planning for and participation in an organization that represented the first cautious steps toward establishing the new foundations for the postwar world.

The immediate task was planning for the relief and rehabilitation of Europe. The European governments-in-exile were eager to find a way to buy supplies for postwar use, while at the same time they understood they must not upset military purchases for a long war. The Russians wanted an internationally controlled relief organization, and the British concurred. The solution to the British-Russian initiative was a proposal, backed as well by the United States and the European governments-in-exile, for a United Nations Relief and Rehabilitation Administration—UNRRA—which Hull asked Acheson to take in hand. It was his first big creative job.

From January to June 1943, four so-called wise men met to work out a draft agreement. Besides Acheson, the congenial group included Lord Halifax, who had been foreign secretary under Neville Chamberlain but became ambassador to Washington following the death of Lord Lothian. Edward Halifax reminded Acheson of an English aristocrat of the second quarter of the nineteenth century, a less amusing Lord Melbourne. As Acheson described him, Halifax, "courteous and apparently hesitating, avoided obstinacy by circuitous restatement of the same position so that it kept reappearing as a new one."[3]

The third "wise man" was the Chinese ambassador, Wei Tao-ming, who had succeeded another Chinese scholar, Hu Shih, from whom Acheson learned that "the Chinese mind, like my own, was baffled by the mysticism of most religious teaching and found itself more at home with ethical and philosophic concepts."[4]

Completing the quartet was the Soviet ambassador, Maxim Litvinov. An old Bolshevik, as prewar foreign minister he had negotiated the 1933 agreements with the Roosevelt administration on U.S. recognition of the Soviet Union. Litvinov was a short, voluble Russian of the old school, who would not last in office during the postwar era of hard-line Stalinism.

No matter how charming, Litvinov was a tough negotiator who represented a Soviet position that would become ever more familiar to American diplomats. He insisted that nothing should be done in any given country "except with that country's consent and as it chose." In vain the other Allies argued, as Acheson recalled it, that relief "must be kept free from politics." This idea greatly amused Litvinov, who believed that in the Soviet Union "nothing is free from politics."[5]

Despite his initial obduracy, Litvinov worked with his colleagues to find points of agreement, largely because the Soviets desperately needed relief assistance. By the first of June 1943, the organizing group was prepared to submit its work to the critical appraisal of "the United Nations." The organization was to be a simple one: the members—present and future signers of the United Nations declaration—would form the council, which was to meet twice a year. A central committee would exercise its powers in between times. A director general was to handle operations. All power to give or not to give would be retained by the member states.[6]

After Roosevelt explained the situation to the leaders of Congress—none of whom, however, was a member of either the Foreign Relations or Foreign Affairs Committee—no one expected any trouble. Then Arthur Vandenberg, the senior Republican on the Senate Foreign Relations Committee, struck. A former newspaper editor from Grand Rapids, Michigan, Senator Vandenberg had been a notorious isolationist who was converted to internationalism after Pearl Harbor. A member of the Senate's inner circle, he was large and vainglorious, occasionally carried away by his own hyperbole. Among Republicans he was the undisputed authority on foreign affairs.[7]

"Suspicion consumed him," Acheson observed, "suspicion in his own words, of 'Executive dictatorship,' 'by-passing the Senate,' 'flouting of the Constitution': suspicion, also, that our Allies were already using for their own ends the victory to which we were contributing so much."[8]

Vandenberg, informed of the plan to make American participation in UNRRA through executive agreement rather than through legislation submitted to Congress, took a dim view of such a procedure. The draft, he said, "pledged our total resources to whatever illimitable scheme for relief and rehabilitation all around the world our New Deal crystal-gazers might desire to pursue." Congress was to be "confronted with a *'fait accompli,'*"and there was to be "no interference with this world-wide prospectus as it might be conceived by Roosevelt, Lehman, Hopkins and Co."[9]

Acheson's and Hull's mistake was not to bring Congress, and especially the Senate Foreign Relations Committee, into the great endeavor—and Acheson vowed never to make it again. The alterations made in the draft to placate Vandenberg were minor, but the senator declared that he had wrung vast changes from the State Department. Yet he also said that he could not "believe that the President will sanction the State Department's wholesale surrender."

Roosevelt, however, did just that—and everything went ahead as planned. From then on, Acheson understood the need to apply what he called "the Vandenberg brand" to any proposal that Congress was expected to endorse, even if that simply meant a minor concession from the administration—as long as it was one for which the senator from Michigan could take credit.[10]

The actual launching of UNRRA came in November 1943 at Claridge's Hotel in Atlantic City. The conference was preceded on November 9 with a convocation at the White House of representatives of forty-four nations to sign the UNRRA agreement to plan and administer "measures for the relief of victims of war" by providing "food, fuel, clothing, shelter and other basic necessities, medical and other essential services."[11] Then, with Roosevelt's blessing, the delegates departed for Atlantic City for the first session of what was to be a precursor of the United Nations. Acheson was elected chairman of the council meeting, and New York's former governor Herbert Lehman became director-general of the new organization. The actual purpose of the gathering was to arrive at some realistic consensus of what the new relief agency could do.

In a letter to his mother, Acheson captured the spirit of Atlantic City, which in his view reflected the very essence of an international conference. He recalled his visits to Atlantic City with her when he was a boy and reminded her of her spectacular marksmanship. "I have passed the shooting galleries or their successors which you and I used to frequent and where you used to so amaze the proprietors," he wrote. He went on to point out that he was elected to run the conference because the Russians insisted that one of the big powers had to chair the meetings (meaning themselves), but this proved impossible because "their delegation had not arrived."[12] The conference lasted three weeks and proceeded relatively smoothly, even though Moscow demanded practically "the entire fund."[13]

More and more, Acheson got a whiff of the difficulties he would encounter in negotiating with the Russians: "The unpredictable element is what our Russian friends may do and what they are thinking," he wrote to his mother. "They are extremely reticent, and several times have come out with decisions which have all the possibilities of trouble and which take many hours of midnight discussion to get into safe channels. This has resulted in my falling into a troubled sleep somewhere between two and three o'clock every night and the most colossal strain on my digestion." Nevertheless, Acheson soldiered on, with "a great deal of improvisation." His rulings started to remind him of those of a judge who once said, "'This Court is often in error, but never in doubt.'"[14]

The UNRRA was in existence until mid-1947: China, Italy, Greece, and Austria absorbed about half of its aid; the other half was spent in the East European countries and the Soviet Union. The organization tried desperately to avoid the politics of the Cold War and to help anyone who was destitute, whether that person was living under a Communist regime or not.[15]

Seven months later Acheson was assigned a far more important and more lasting job. As he wrote to his son, who in 1944 was serving in the navy in the Pacific, "I have to go to the Monetary Conference on July 1 [1944] for three weeks as one of the U.S. delegates. Neither I nor the other delegates know what the hell we are doing and we can't get the Treasury to take time off to work it out with us. But somehow I think we can get along."[16]

Heading the State Department's delegation, Acheson boarded the train for Bretton Woods, New Hampshire, where the economic and financial underpinnings of the postwar world—the International Monetary Fund and the World Bank—were about to be put into place. One participant described the setting as "a quiet, green and soothing garden of the gods, circled by mountain ramparts."[17]

The Mount Washington Hotel, nestled in the lee of the White Mountains, provided a peaceful retreat for about seven hundred people who had gathered there for the conference. A luxurious summer inn, the hotel had been closed for over two years, so that with only about a month to prepare for the invasion of the delegates, everything had to be hastily improvised.

Acheson and his group stayed at a comfortable inn at nearby Crawford Notch. Since he was not billeted in the main hotel, a corner of the ballroom, which had also been fitted up as a bar, became his office, partitioned off with canvas. Moreover, since the lodgings of the State Department delegation were four miles away, as he wrote his son, "transportation was always in default, so that when we got through work about two o'clock in the morning we couldn't get home and to bed. This led to excessive alcoholism."[18]

* * *

The two dominant figures at the conference were John Maynard Keynes and Harry Dexter White. While there were delegates from forty-odd countries, this was an Anglo-American show, and many of the issues had already been worked out by Keynes and White at a preliminary meeting at Atlantic City just before the trip to the White Mountains.

Harry White was the man whom Henry Morgenthau, who admittedly knew little about international finance, relied on to deal with monetary questions. "To make life easier for me," Morgenthau said to his advisers the day after Pearl Harbor, he intended to put Harry White "in charge of all foreign affairs for me. . . . I want it in one brain and I want it in Harry White's brain."[19]

Within a week Morgenthau asked White to start thinking about an inter-Allied stabilization fund. This would be designed to give monetary aid to actual and potential allies and to serve as the basis for postwar arrangements to ensure stable currency values and thus promote an open trading system among nations.

An ardent New Dealer, White found his niche in the Treasury, and his career was meteoric. A disciple of Keynes's, White in 1940 became the Treasury Department's director of monetary research and four years later an assistant secretary of the Treasury. After the war, he came under attack during the McCarthyite period for being allegedly a central figure in a Soviet espionage ring operating within the Treasury. Although he was exhaustively investigated, no official charges were ever brought against him; nonetheless, he died in 1948 with a cloud over his name.[20]

Overshadowing the discussions at Bretton Woods were the dire financial straits of Great Britain. Ever more deeply in debt, England was likely to need piles of dollars to rebuild its economy. Keynes was concerned that British national interests would be harmed if the borrowing privileges available in the International Monetary Fund were restricted. The fund was designed, after all, to provide nations who were running a balance of payments deficit to borrow short-term funds until their payments were in balance.

Keynes had originally preferred a clearinghouse in which virtually unlimited overdraft facilities were available to countries that would then put in place policies designed to right their deficits and so strengthen their currency. This would remove the need to take drastic measures to reduce the money supply, which would have led to greater unemployment. It was simply horrifying to Keynes that the world should return to a time when governments automatically raised interest rates, tightened bank credit, and created unemployment every time their balance of payments was in deficit. Keynes's scheme would certainly favor debtor countries like Great Britain rather than creditor countries like the United States.

White's plan was more conventional. The fund would have a fixed amount of money available, based on sums initially voted by the participating governments. The obligations of the creditor nations to finance the debtors were therefore severely limited.

In a compromise arrived at before Bretton Woods, the British largely accepted the American position. The fund was to hold on deposit a mixed assortment of gold and currencies rather than some new international currency. Moreover, credit would be restricted, and conditions would be set for obtaining the loan.

For their part, the Americans agreed to permit a country that was badly short of dollars (as England most certainly would be) to discriminate against the imports of a trading partner running a trade surplus, the idea being that this would allow the country running a deficit to right its trade balance after a reasonable period of time. It would be the Americans, of course, who would supply most of the gold to make the fund work.

Under the agreement, exchange rates were fixed by having the currencies pegged to gold or to the dollar (which was itself pegged to gold). As a result, since foreign banks could cash in their dollars for gold at $35 an ounce, the dollar, as the principal reserve currency for virtually every country, became world money. In addition, the United States effectively controlled the fund through its vote, which was greater than that of any other because of the size of its contribution.[21]

Keynes may not have been too happy with the outcome. The fund was certainly a less flexible instrument than his scheme. But once the British delegation understood that the U.S. Congress would never endorse the notion of placing the United States in the position of extending almost unlimited credit, Bretton Woods became a relatively friendly negotiation.

Although Acheson played a comparatively small role in actually devising the International Monetary Fund, he was prepared to defend it vigorously before congressional committees. His main job at Bretton Woods was to represent the State Department as the chief American delegate in drawing up the charter for the International Bank for Reconstruction and Development, later known as the World Bank.

The idea for the bank arose out of American concerns for rebuilding those economies destroyed or disrupted by the war. The bank, moreover, would lend money not only to reconstruct war-torn countries but also to aid in the development of poorer nations. Because the borrowings from the bank were unrelated to ownership of bank stock, many smaller nations, conscious that the amount of their subscriptions had no direct bearing on their access to long-term loans, often wanted to make a smaller financial commitment to the World Bank than to the International Monetary Fund. However, a general failure to subscribe would either mean no bank or one financed largely by the United States.

Acheson recalled that Henry Morgenthau put "a great effort" into getting the Soviet Union to raise its subscription to the bank and was able to announce this at the final plenary session. It was, however, a short-lived success, as the Soviet

Union did not ratify the Bretton Woods agreements. Although Moscow sent delegates to the conference, Stalin later concluded that Russia's state-controlled trade and financial policies, which precluded divulging economic data, could not accept the emphasis on "private enterprise."

With Soviet withdrawal, the United States effectively controlled both the bank and the fund. Washington possessed one-third of the votes in the bank by subscribing $3.175 billion of the total of $9.100 billion; Washington also held one-third of the votes in the fund.[22]

The pace of the conference was truly exhausting. Keynes thought the pressure "quite unbelievable" and suffered a mild heart attack after attending some night sessions. As it was, he turned out to be a poor chairman of the sessions he was conducting on the bank, where Acheson was present. Everything was moving very fast. The whole burden of being chairman of the drafting commission of the bank was placed on Acheson's shoulders. As Acheson made clear to White and Morgenthau, "I am playing this by ear." White's meetings were not very organized, Keynes was always in a hurry, and it was not until the Treasury people got through with the fund that the expert help Acheson's group needed was available.[23]

Acheson, by nature more orderly in his procedures, was constantly at odds with Harry White. For White, the only matters that had to be settled were those between Keynes and himself, and, in his view the fund was the principal work of the conference.

Despite his difficulties with the Treasury, Acheson strongly defended State's positions in discussions about both the fund and the bank, at one point insisting that the headquarters of the fund as well as the bank must be located in the United States.

On July 22 the conference ended with a formal dinner. Keynes came in a little late, tired, and pale. Spontaneously, everyone in the room stood up in complete silence in tribute to him, as he walked to his seat. After dinner, he asked to address the conference for the last time, at which point he complimented Harry White for his "indomitable will and energy, always governed by good temper and humor." He even paid tribute to the lawyers, whom he generally detested. "Too often," he said, "lawyers are men who turn poetry into prose and prose into jargon. Not so our lawyers here in Bretton Woods. On the contrary, they have turned our jargon into prose and our prose into poetry." He concluded with the simple statement: "I move to accept the Final Act."

Then, as Keynes made his way toward the door, Acheson led the delegates in a rousing version of "For He's a Jolly Good Fellow."[24]

* * *

In late November 1944 Cordell Hull was in poor health and, as his friend Assistant Secretary Breckinridge Long described him, "tired of intrigue . . . tired of being by-passed . . . tired of being relied upon in public and ignored in private." He therefore resigned.[25]

His relations with Acheson had always been rather formal, and it was only after his resignation that a real friendship developed. Acheson went to see him regularly. Hull, in turn, deeply appreciated Acheson's thoughtfulness, and in 1950 when Acheson was under heavy attack in Congress, Hull came to the State Department to wish him good luck on the eve of Acheson's departure for Europe.[26]

Roosevelt replaced Hull with Edward R. Stettinius Jr., an enthusiastic, good-natured former businessman with prematurely white hair and a gift for public relations. He had been vice president of General Motors and chairman of the board of United States Steel. Stettinius's appointment meant a new under secretary, which turned out to be Joseph Grew, and a new job for Acheson as assistant secretary for congressional relations and international conferences. Will Clayton took over Acheson's post as assistant secretary for economic affairs. As a result, both Acheson and Clayton, in addition to Henry Morgenthau and Harry White, were slated to lead the battle in 1945 for congressional approval of the Bretton Woods agreements.

Will Clayton, a six-foot-three-inch Texan, was the quintessential self-made man. Born in 1880 near Tupelo, Mississippi, by fifteen he had left school to take a job as the personal secretary of a cotton merchant from St. Louis. He never returned to school, educating himself through voracious reading. Later he went to New York City to work for the American Cotton Company. At the age of twenty-four, with a capitalization of $9,000, Clayton, his brother Monroe, and his brother-in-law Frank Anderson started a cotton brokerage business in Houston. By the 1920s, Anderson, Clayton had become the largest cotton brokerage firm in the world.[27]

A classic southern Democrat, Clayton opposed high tariffs and in the late 1930s was, like Acheson, an avowed interventionist. He joined the Roosevelt administration at the outset of the war, first as coordinator of inter-American affairs and later in the Reconstruction Finance Corporation. Like Hull, Clayton wanted to arrange an international economic and financial order that was devoted to lowering tariffs among nations.

The leading opponent of the Bretton Woods accords was Republican senator Robert Taft of Ohio, who had fought unsuccessfully against Wendell Willkie for the nomination for the presidency in 1940; he stayed out of the contest in 1944, but he would try again in 1948 and 1952 and both times would again be denied his party's choice as standard-bearer.

Taft was not an easy man. He was humorless in debate, but well informed, hardheaded, and determined to curb America's involvement in a world beyond its control. "Taft always got the details," Clayton once commented, "but he usually missed the big picture of what we were trying to accomplish."[28] (He would later vote against the Marshall Plan and the North Atlantic Treaty Organization.) He believed it was the duty of the opposition to oppose, and he was adamant in opposing the Bretton Woods agreements.[29]

Taft's main quarrel with the International Monetary Fund was that it would not and could not stabilize unstable and worthless currencies: "If we try to stabilize conditions with this fund it will be like pouring money down a rathole." He feared that under the fund the United States would be playing "Santa Claus."

At one point, during the Senate hearings in June 1945 on Bretton Woods, Taft insisted that a country could withdraw from the fund whatever cash it needed. The exchange that followed between Taft and Acheson was characteristic:

Mr. Acheson: "There is no idea whatever that a person walks in and goes through the empty formality of saying, 'I need this presently to make a payment,' and no one can look into it. That would be too childishly absurd."

Senator Taft: "Well, Mr. Acheson, it is childishly absurd. It is the whole basis on which this whole thing has been negotiated with these countries."[30]

Throughout the rest of 1944 and the winter, spring, and summer of 1945, Acheson and Clayton lobbied hard for Bretton Woods. Acheson worked the Senate and House to counter Taft's arguments and round up votes, while Clayton sought to persuade bankers and businessmen alike that the new international economic order would yield vast benefits for both workers and investors.

"There is not one single element of the 'Santa Claus' philosophy in this policy," Clayton declared before the Economic Club of Detroit. "On the contrary . . . we have the goods for sale, and there are [foreign] buyers who must have these goods; the problem is to find the dollars with which to make payment." Bretton Woods would supply the dollars and the stable currencies needed to make good on the Treasury Department's prediction that Detroit could expect an overseas market of "more than a million cars a year."[31] In his testimony before a congressional committee, Acheson echoed Clayton, declaring that "you must look to other markets, and those markets are abroad."[32]

Although Acheson was too much the realist to embrace Hull's almost mystical belief in the power of an open trading system to ensure perpetual peace, he was of a generation that saw the competitive tariffs that countries employed in the 1930s to save themselves from economic ruin as a leading cause of the rise of Hitler and the Second World War.

On July 19, 1945, by sixty-one votes to sixteen, the Senate passed the Bretton Woods agreements bill.

* * *

Just as the struggle between Acheson and Keynes over the final agreement on lend-lease focused on Britain's desire to retain a preferential trading system within the empire and commonwealth, so, too, the negotiations after the war over an American loan to Britain would center on Washington's insistence that Britain cut these imperial ties and make its currency freely convertible into dollars.

While Acheson was more sympathetic to Britain's travails than many of his colleagues, both he and Clayton were determined to force the British to accept an open trading system, and they were prepared to use virtually any means they had to ensure this outcome.[33]

Acheson later came to believe that the Europeans and the Japanese—at least for a few years—had to be allowed to protect their fledgling economies until such time as they were strong enough to embrace the open trading system Washington had so fervently espoused. Nonetheless, trade and investment, undergirded by the International Monetary Fund and the World Bank, did fuel the prosperity of the West. The volume of trade between America and the rest of the world rose nearly sevenfold in the three decades following Bretton Woods.[34]

For Dean Acheson, the United States was the locomotive and the rest of the world the train. He firmly believed that "the economic aspects [were] no less important than the political aspects of peace."[35] And only the United States had the power and the purpose to yoke them together.

CHAPTER ELEVEN

"THE GOOD LIFE IS VERY HARD"

As DUSK WAS FALLING on Thursday, April 12, 1945, Acheson was having his portrait taken by the famous Canadian photographer Yousuf Karsh. It was a rainy, dismal day outside, while inside his office the room was dark except for the bright lights that were focused on the subject. Suddenly, his secretary, Barbara Evans, opened the door and said, "The president is dead."

Acheson walked to the window and raised the blind. The White House flag was at half-mast. The president had died in his retreat at Warm Springs, Georgia, of a cerebral hemorrhage.

Later, Acheson wrote of his meeting with the president shortly before FDR's fourth-term inauguration on January 20, 1945. He had gone to brief him on his forthcoming meeting with Churchill and Josef Stalin at Yalta, where the Soviet Union's demand for multiple votes for the Soviet republics in the General Assembly of the proposed United Nations would be discussed. Although FDR, as usual, brushed away the Soviet position by joking that he would ask for forty-eight votes for each of the states of the Union, he seemed to Acheson only a shadow of his former days—"thin, gaunt, with sunken and darkly circled eyes."[1]

Over the next few days Acheson's dominant sensation was one of loss. People wandered around in a kind of daze. They came and stood in front of the White House, but there was nothing to see, and they probably did not expect to see anything: "The familiar had given way to an ominous unknown."[2]

Writing to his son in the Pacific not long after the funeral, Acheson admitted that he had never quite realized that for millions of people Roosevelt was like "a parent." He was also pleased to have a last, happy memory of the president. Shortly before FDR's death, Roosevelt had decided to make him solicitor general, the government's lawyer, the post he had always craved. It had been all worked out between the attorney general, the secretary of state, and Acheson himself, and the president was to act on it upon his return from Warm Springs. No one spoke of it again, and Acheson never raised the question with his successor.[3]

"The new President has done an excellent job," Acheson reported to his son a few weeks after Harry Truman was sworn in. "I have seen him off and on for the last four years, but never very much. It just so happened that two days before the President's death, I had a long meeting with Mr. Truman and for the first time got a definite impression. It was a very good impression. He is straightforward, decisive, simple, entirely honest. He, of course, has the limitations upon his judgment and wisdom which the limitations of his experience produce, but I think that he will learn fast and will inspire confidence."[4]

His meetings with the new chief executive became frequent that spring as he worked on Truman's speech closing the San Francisco conference on the United Nations. He also dined and lunched with the new president.

Despite these cordial encounters, Acheson was determined to resign; his income had suffered severely while he was serving in the government, and it was time to return to Covington and Burling. He had never thought much of Ed Stettinius as secretary of state, and now Truman had appointed James F. Byrnes, the former senator from South Carolina, the former Supreme Court justice, the man who had served under Roosevelt as a kind of "assistant president." Roosevelt had even considered asking Byrnes to run with him as vice president in 1944 but had been dissuaded when political advisers pointed out the liability of having on the ticket a southern conservative and former Catholic who had become an Episcopalian. When Truman made Byrnes secretary, he surely realized that Byrnes believed he should be the one sitting in the Oval Office.

Nonetheless, it was not any animosity that prompted Acheson to inform the new secretary that he intended to resign. It was to be a new team, and there was no reason that Acheson should be expected to stay on.

In addition, life for the Achesons had become far more difficult that April. His youngest daughter, Mary, had contracted tuberculosis, and the doctors felt strongly that she should recover at a sanatorium at Saranac in upper New York State.

Mary Acheson Bundy had been married in 1943 to William Putnam Bundy, the lanky older son of Harvey Bundy, who had served as Secretary of War Henry Stimson's special assistant. Her husband, then an officer in the Signal Corps of the U.S. Army, had gone off to the European theater, where he was assigned to cracking enemy codes at Bletchley Park in England. While he was away, Mary lived with her parents in the house at P Street, while working as a cryptanalyst at Arlington Hall, a secret army operation in Virginia. Like all of her colleagues, she took her turn at various eight-hour shifts around the clock, and this exhausting schedule may well have contributed to her illness.

In early May she left for Saranac, and for the rest of that spring Acheson wrote her nearly every day. It had been a habit for father and daughter to sit down in the evening at around ten o'clock and gossip about the day's events, often over milk and crackers. The letters reveal Acheson's increasing impatience with Stettinius and with his immediate superior, Under Secretary of State Joseph Grew, along with his genuine desire to quit government service.

In May, with the San Francisco conference to organize the United Nations under way, Acheson reported to Mary that Archibald MacLeish, then assistant secretary for public affairs, was at the conference, giving him "lyric accounts of Snow White's [Stettinius's] performances, which are beyond belief. The department is beyond belief and God knows how long any sane man can or should stand it."[5]

At another point, when MacLeish urged Acheson to come out to San Francisco to help with the submission of the charter of the United Nations, Acheson refused. He was busy in Washington, working with the Congress to get the Reciprocal Trade Agreements bill passed, and, in addition, had deep misgivings about the efficacy of the United Nations.

The trade agreements bill was yet another building block in Acheson's efforts to lower trade barriers, and at the end of May the House passed it with a final majority of eighty-six. To celebrate, Acheson wrote, "We all went down to the Speaker's room, drank some whiskey, and called Mr. Hull [who had seen the bill as vindicating his policies]. No one thought to call the President who had done a great job for us." Acheson downplayed his own taxing efforts lobbying: "This life is amusing but not calculated to engage or extend all those faculties which when used to the full give one the sense of the good life. But the good life is very hard and takes much courage."[6]

His regard for Under Secretary Joseph Grew did not improve with closer contact. On May 28 he reported, "I have been having a great debate with Joe Grew, who seems to me the Prince of Appeasers."[7] This cryptic reference was to a strong difference of opinion between them over the future of Emperor Hirohito of Japan. As a former ambassador to Japan, Grew had argued for the emperor's retention as the main stabilizing factor in that country, while Acheson called for his removal as a weak character who had given in again and again to the military's demand for war and therefore was not reliable. But not long after, Acheson regretted his position; when he was reviewing his letters to his daughter years later, he added a note: "Grew's view fortunately prevailed. I very shortly came to see that I was quite wrong."[8]

Acheson was also wary of any wholesale anti-Sovietism. As he observed to Mary Bundy of Averell Harriman, who was then ambassador to Moscow, "Averell is very ferocious about the Rouskis—an attitude which is OK for those who can handle it but dangerous medicine for those who want to be ineffectively anti-Russian."[9]

While Acheson was determined to take a tough line with the Russians when called for, he was nonetheless intent on finding ways to resolve tensions between the two powers. What he feared was a return to isolationism and that the Republicans might use anti-Sovietism to challenge the administration's commitment to liberal internationalism. "Perhaps," he mused in May 1945, "the country is going isolationist on the anti-Russian route."[10]

Acheson's work was winding down. Final congressional passage of the charter of the United Nations came on July 28. Congress could now go home. Despite Acheson's reservations about the charter, he had dutifully lobbied for it. But he was especially anxious to prevent the U.S. representative to the United Nations from occupying a seat in the cabinet with direct access to the president, a situation that might well threaten the position of the secretary of state. (Under the Eisenhower administration, however, the UN ambassador was finally granted cabinet rank.)

Acheson later wrote that he "always believed the Charter was impracticable." It was presented to the American people, in his view, "as almost holy writ and with the evangelical enthusiasm of a major advertising campaign." Such hope "could only lead to bitter disappointment."[11]

In an address in 1946, at a time when hopes for the United Nations were at a zenith, Acheson voiced the deepest skepticism over the UN's capacity to resolve great issues of the day. "I am often told," he said, "that the way to solve this or that problem is to leave it to the United Nations. But it still seems to me inescapable that if they are . . . united, they are still nations; and no more can be expected of this forum for political adjustment than the sum total of the contributions. . . . In the Arab proverb, the ass that went to Mecca remained an ass, and a policy has little added to it by its place of utterance."[12]

The creation of the United Nations, in Acheson's view, was yet another example of "the nineteenth-century faith in the perfectibility of man and the advent of universal peace and law." Like his mentor Oliver Wendell Holmes, Acheson did not see any other solution to the problems bedeviling a great nation than to work away at the tangible issues before you. "For my part," Holmes had written, "I believe that the struggle for life is the order of the world, at which it is vain to repine."[13]

Americans in particular, "and none more than Woodrow Wilson," Acheson wrote, were subject to an idealistic belief that gave birth to a number of subsidiary faiths, which all added up to "a grand fallacy." This was the notion that one could—and should—apply to foreign affairs the institutions and practices of legislatures in liberal democracies. Such an approach was deemed preferable to diplomacy "because it reached through a facade to The People." What was reasonable and right would therefore be determined by majority vote—"and just as the equality of man led to one man one vote, so the doctrine of the 'sovereign equality of states' led to one state one vote."[14]

For Acheson, the United Nations was at best "an aid to diplomacy." To the degree that the General Assembly contravened the policies of the great powers, the United Nations blunted the effective use of power among nations. This was the very essence of the realist tradition, and Acheson saw himself as very much a part of it.

After Germany surrendered in May 1945, the president and Byrnes, his new secretary of state, attended the Potsdam summit meeting, July 16 to August 2, with Stalin and Churchill (and Labour's Clement Attlee, who replaced the latter in an election as the summit was under way). They returned on August 7, the day after the United States dropped the atomic bomb on Hiroshima.

Acheson was bent on resigning. There had already been rumors after Byrnes took office that wholesale firings were in order. On June 28 MacLeish asked Acheson whether he too should resign before he was fired. Acheson replied that he should not: "One should not hurry mounting the tumbril." As he wrote to Mary Bundy, "It is said that I will be made Secretary—Under Secretary—Administrator of F.E.A. [Foreign Economic Administration]—Solicitor General—President of Bretton Woods Bank, etc. I say that I shall resign as of the end of this session, rest and then go to the Union Trust Building again. Make your own bets."[15]

As the president and Secretary Byrnes were in almost continuous meetings after getting back from Europe, Acheson found it both impossible and absurd to try to see them. His plans were to travel north with his wife to visit Mary at Saranac, then vacation for a bit at a fishing camp in Canada and after that return to the practice of law.

Some matter of no great importance finally took him into Byrnes's office, and before leaving, he handed him a letter to the president, resigning his office. It was a cordial letter, and on August 9 he received an equally agreeable reply from the president, offering his "best wishes for your success and happiness."[16]

The next day he and Alice packed up and journeyed to New York City. The following morning at the crack of dawn, they boarded a slow train up the Hudson River for Saranac. Upon arriving, they were greeted by celebrations anticipating Japan's surrender. Their daughter, radiant and seemingly well on the way to recovery, was waiting for them in her bedroom. Ray Atherton, the U.S. ambassador to Canada, was driving down from Ottawa to dine with them that evening, spend a day or two with all the Achesons, and then take Dean and Alice on to Canada. Suddenly, after everyone had settled down, Mary remembered that Secretary of State Byrnes had been trying all day to get her father on the phone.

PART THREE

FROM ALLIANCE TO COLD WAR

CHAPTER TWELVE

"AN ARMAMENT RACE OF A RATHER DESPERATE NATURE"

IT WAS ALL A MISTAKE. Neither the president nor the secretary of state wanted Acheson to resign. On the contrary, they wanted him to return to government, this time as under secretary of state, the second in command, and of course as acting secretary in Byrnes's absences abroad, which would be frequent.

But why had it happened this way? There was no ready answer. Byrnes told him on the telephone later that evening of August 11 that the acceptance of his resignation had been an error due to confusion and the pressures of the day. Both the secretary and the president had been consumed with their new responsibilities in July and August, first by the summit meeting in Potsdam and then by the momentous events that led to the surrender of Japan.

Acheson was stunned. He insisted that he intended to return to private life, but Byrnes refused to listen. It was simply too serious and complicated a matter to be decided in a phone conversation. He was prepared to send an army plane to fly him to Washington, where they could discuss the whole matter. But the next day, August 12, was the joint birthday of his wife and his daughter. Moreover, Japan was to surrender on August 14, so Acheson was able to postpone his trip until the fifteenth, when Alice motored to Ottawa to stay at the embassy with the Athertons until Acheson could join her for his vacation, however brief.

In a sweltering Washington Acheson had a first inconclusive talk with Byrnes. The secretary admired Acheson's ability to get things done, and he needed an experienced man to run the department during those periods when he would necessarily be away from Washington negotiating with the Russians.

More important, the new president had met frequently with Acheson in his role as assistant secretary for congressional relations. He was clearly pleased that Acheson was fully at ease with the informality of the Truman White House, while Acheson admired Truman's no-nonsense style of doing business, which was so unlike FDR's.

Acheson had taken his wife's advice and used the time before his meeting with Byrnes to assume for one night what it would be like to accept the job and then on the next night to imagine that he had turned it down, but even then he had still not made up his mind what to do. "Both assumptions depressed me," he wrote.

Acheson was wavering. He spent a restless night at P Street. At one moment he convinced himself that the experience would be a frustrating one; on the other hand, how would he know unless he tried it? So try it he would. He decided to sign on as "mate of the good ship 'Jimmie Byrnes.'" He later reflected: "The frustrations were all that I expected them to be, but for reasons impossible to foresee at the time, the decision was one of the most fortunate of my life."[1]

Perhaps his daughter Jane provided the best answer in a poem she sent him in September, parodying a song from the musical comedy *Oklahoma!*—"I'm Just a Guy Who Can't Say 'No.'"

I'm just a guy who can't say, "No!"
  I'm in a terrible jam.
I always say, "Okay, I'll bite."
  Just when I ought to say, "Scram!" . . .

Suppose they say no other will do;
  They gotta have you some maw?
What'ja gonna do when they talk like that?
  Practice law?

For a while I said, and thought it true,
  I'm a weary and broke old man.
When they said you're the fella to make
    the world new,
  I wonder—Perhaps, I am!"[2]

At the very moment that Acheson was preparing to fly from upstate New York to Washington to answer Byrnes's summons, a weary secretary of war, Henry Stimson, was en route to the Adirondacks to get some rest at the Ausable Club in St. Hubert's. A week earlier, two days after the atomic bomb had fallen on Hiroshima, he had had a small heart attack. With intimations of mortality, Stimson had decided to resign. In a few weeks he would turn seventy-eight.

His deepest concern was over the future of atomic weapons. The reports of what had happened when an American B-29 dropped the bomb on Hiroshima at 8:15 A.M., August 6, 1945, had been highly disturbing. Almost everything was totally incinerated within a radius of five hundred meters of the explosion. Buildings as far away as three kilometers had burned. About seventy thousand died from one bomb, as many wounded. Then a second bomb was dropped on Nagasaki on August 9, killing at least sixty thousand.[3]

Stimson was shaken. He had been instrumental in shepherding the Manhattan Project to build an atom bomb, and he had never opposed using the bomb to end the war and save American lives that would be lost in an invasion of the Japanese islands. Before Hiroshima and Nagasaki, he had even believed that possession of the bomb would be a "master card" in the hands of an American president, which he could use as leverage in settling the great issues of the postwar world. But in the aftermath of the bombings, Stimson had second thoughts.

It was not until August 13, after he received news that the Japanese were about to surrender, that he and his wife, Mabel, were finally able to get away to the Ausable Club, an austere hunting, tennis, and golf club that appealed to men of Stimson's background and class. The idea was to give the members the sense that they were camping out, so the amenities were minimal.

Stimson had been deeply perturbed over the implications for the international community of the American monopoly of the atom bomb. At St. Hubert's, surrounded by old friends in what one biographer described as "an atmosphere of idealism and highmindedness," he concluded that if the United States tried to keep scientific knowledge of how to create an atom bomb secret and then endeavored to use this monopoly to pressure an increasingly truculent Soviet Union to follow domestic and foreign policies that the United States dictated, it was bound to fail.[4] That strategy might even lead, as he later put it, to "a secret armament race of a rather desperate character."[5]

When Harry Truman succeeded Roosevelt, he was unaware of the existence of the Manhattan Project. Stimson informed him about it on April 25, 1945, and Truman showed no inclination to question the prevailing view of the secretary of war and other advisers that it should be used. In addition, it would have been politically unthinkable for the new and unelected president to reverse FDR's policy of demanding unconditional surrender from the Japanese.[6]

Yet the meeting lasted only fifteen minutes, a shockingly short time considering the complexity and ramifications of the project. The only reference to the future of the bomb was Truman's agreement to the appointment of an interim committee of advisers on atomic matters.[7]

Truman himself was already steamed up over the behavior of the Russians over Poland. Stalin had promised FDR at Yalta "free and unfettered elections" in that recently liberated country, but so far nothing had been done to prepare for them. The provisional government was made up of the Moscow-approved, Communist Lublin Poles, whereas the Nationalist Poles in London were being denied places in the government. On the other hand, Truman was not ready to abandon efforts to work out amicably any differences with the Soviet Union.

As Stimson predicted, at Truman's meeting with Churchill and Stalin at Potsdam in July 1945, the "secret" of the bomb affected the president's behavior, as the Big Three deliberated the fate of a devastated Europe. It would be a terrible thing, Stimson believed, "to gamble with such big stakes in diplomacy without having your master card in your hand."[8] Already Stimson thought that the combination of American economic prowess and the possession of an atomic bomb would give the Americans "a royal straight flush and we mustn't be a fool about how we play it."

The Potsdam conference began before a bomb had been tested successfully. Stimson's last advice to the president before Truman embarked on the *Augusta* was to tell Stalin that the bomb existed, but to try to turn aside any of Stalin's inquiries about an atomic partnership with the Americans. Churchill also favored telling Stalin the truth about the bomb in order to gain any possible diplomatic advantage, but to wait until it had been tested successfully.

Byrnes, as both a member of the interim committee and the new secretary of state, hoped that the bomb could be used to end the war before the Russians entered it against Japan and established a base in Manchuria.[9]

While Stimson was present at the Potsdam conference as an adviser, he was excluded from the formal sessions of the Big Three—most likely because Byrnes did not want to be in any way overshadowed by a former secretary of state and now aged but eminent secretary of war. It was at Potsdam that Stimson received news of the successful testing of the bomb at Alamogordo, New Mexico, on July 16.

When Stimson told Truman of the test, the president was ecstatic and said how pleased he was that Stimson had come to Potsdam. Later, after Stimson had briefed Churchill in full, the prime minister noted that at the previous day's meeting of the Big Three, Truman had been much fortified by something that had happened and that he "stood up to the Russians in a most emphatic and decisive manner."[10]

On July 24 Truman casually approached Stalin and told him only that the United States had developed a "new weapon of unusual destructive force." He did not say that it was an atomic bomb. Stalin responded in an equally casual manner, expressing the hope that America would make "good use" of the weapon against the Japanese.[11]

In fact, through secret agents Stalin had known of the existence of the Manhattan Project since 1942, although he may not have known the bomb was ready until Truman's remark. When Stalin told Molotov of his exchange with Truman, Molotov replied, "They're raising the price." To which Stalin added with a laugh, "Let them. We'll have a talk with [Soviet nuclear physicist Igor] Kurchatov today about speeding up our work."[12]

In the Adirondacks a month after Potsdam, Stimson called on his assistant secretary of war, John McCloy, to join him in putting together his thoughts on what to do with the bomb. McCloy, who had been a bluff Wall Street lawyer before the war and whom Stimson admired for his ability to get things done, flew up to work on the memorandum for the president. At a crucial meeting in July 1945, Stimson had permitted McCloy to try to persuade Truman that the Japanese be informed "that we had the bomb and that we would drop the bomb" if reasonable terms of surrender were not promptly accepted.[13] At the core of Stimson and McCloy's thinking was their belief that the United States did not possess scientific atomic secrets as such—only the American technological ability to construct a bomb.

In his last advisory to Truman before leaving for his vacation, Stimson envisioned a "covenant" among the United States, Great Britain, and the Soviet Union. Moscow would halt efforts to develop its own atomic weapons, while Washington would make available information on atomic energy's peaceful application and would also "undertake not to employ the atomic bomb or any development of it as an instrument of warfare."[14]

When McCloy came back to Washington and discussed these ideas with Byrnes, the secretary of state asserted that it would be a "long time before [the Soviets] were at the stage where we were now" in developing the bomb. Looking ahead to the London foreign ministers' meeting scheduled for early September, Byrnes told McCloy, as McCloy later recorded in his diary on September 2: "The Russians were only sensitive to power and all the world, including the Russians, were cognizant of the power of this bomb, and with it in his hip pocket he felt he was in a far better position to come back with tangible accomplishments even if he did not threaten anyone expressly with it."[15] After hearing this, McCloy traveled back to St. Hubert's with a heavy heart to complete his work on the presidential memorandum.

Back in Washington on September 3, Stimson went to a cabinet lunch the next day at the White House, which was pleasant enough but was dominated by Truman and Byrnes reminiscing about old times in the Senate. Afterward Stimson had a long and rather distressing talk with Secretary Byrnes.

"I took up the question I had been working on with McCloy up at St. Hubert's, namely how to handle Russia with the big bomb," he wrote. "I found Byrnes was very much against any attempt to co-operate with Stalin. His mind is full of the problems with the coming meeting of the foreign ministers [in London] and he looks to having the presence of the bomb in his pocket, so to speak, as a great weapon to get through the thing. . . ."[16]

Later that day, Stimson had a fifteen-minute meeting with the president and told him that he was unhappy about Byrnes's approach, which meant a return to "power politics." He also realized he needed more time to explain his own position, so he arranged for a longer meeting with Truman on September 12 to discuss his still unfinished memorandum.

The thrust of the memorandum was that a direct approach to Stalin would be the best way to avoid a devastating arms race. Regardless of how long it might take the Soviets to develop their own bomb, it was vital that the United States work to ensure their cooperation in the postwar world. Because of the issues at stake, Stimson insisted that the president and he read through the finished memo together on September 12.

But before this meeting he sent Truman a covering letter, which referred to a discussion he had had with the president at Potsdam about the question of "whether we could be safe in sharing the atomic bomb with Russia while she was still a police state." He then explained that he had changed his mind on this issue, for "any demand by us for an internal change in Russia as a condition of sharing the atomic weapon would be so resented that it would make the objective we have in view less probable."

By seeming to highlight the issue of *sharing* the bomb, Stimson had obscured his main point. Sharing secrets was never the issue for Stimson; there were no scientific secrets to protect. What Stimson was after was obtaining Russian cooperation in controlling the use of atomic energy and weaponry.[17]

The central argument of the letter was that American-Soviet relations "may be irretrievably embittered by the way in which we approach the solution of the bomb with Russia. For if we fail to approach them now and merely continue to negotiate with them, having this weapon rather ostentatiously on our hip, their suspicions and their distrust of our purposes and motives will increase." By singling out Byrnes's cowboy approach, Stimson was determined to stress the difference between Byrnes's stance and his own.

He concluded by urging a one-on-one approach to the Russians. An offer through the medium of the United Nations, or any other "international group of nations," would not "be taken seriously by the Soviets." It must be "peculiarly the proposal of the United States."[18]

As the capstone to his argument, Stimson reminded Truman: "The chief lesson I have learned in a long life is that the only way you can make a man trustworthy is to trust him; and the surest way to make him untrustworthy is to distrust him and show your distrust."[19]

Harry Truman agreed with Stimson that "we must take Russia into our confidence." But, as events would demonstrate, this was not a hard-and-fast position on the president's part.[20]

Truman then encouraged Stimson to present his views to the whole cabinet on September 21, 1945, the day Stimson turned seventy-eight and his last day in office.

To prepare for the meeting, Stimson sent his memo over to Dean Acheson, who, he believed, "is evidently strongly on our side on the treatment of Russia."[21] Acheson's first reaction to the destruction of Hiroshima had been one of horror: "The news of the atomic bomb is the most frightening yet. If we can't work out some sort of organization of great powers, we shall be gone geese for fair."[22] From now on, the Stimson approach would be in the hands of Acheson, in many ways his moral successor.

"The discussion was unworthy of the subject." This was Dean Acheson's verdict on the fateful cabinet meeting at which Stimson presented his views on the atom bomb and the Russians.[23]

To begin with, no one in the cabinet had had an opportunity to consider the implications of the proposal. Moreover, Stimson was bone tired after a morning of festivities: his aides at the War Department had presented him with a silver tray; he had spoken with General Marshall for the last time; he had lunched in the general officers' mess and had been presented with an enormous birthday cake; he then went to the White House for the president to present him with the Distinguished Service Medal for "service exceptional in the history of the nation." And after all this he went into a full-dress cabinet meeting to defend his proposal.[24]

Before his colleagues, Stimson stressed the distinction between disclosure of basic scientific information and the technological secret of how to make the bomb. He proposed sharing the scientific information with the Soviets as a good-faith gesture; the technology would eventually be developed in any case. "We do not have a secret to give away—the secret will give itself away," Stimson declared.[25]

Acheson, present as acting secretary of state in Byrnes's absence in London, strongly supported Stimson. But the discussion soon veered away from the central issue of how to approach the Russians on questions raised by America's development of the bomb—directly or through the United Nations. In essence, was Stimson's one-on-one approach to Moscow the right one? Instead, the debate, such as it was, centered on the spurious issue of whether or not the United States should "give" the bomb to the Russians.

The fiercest opposition to Stimson's approach came from Secretary of the Navy (and future Secretary of Defense) James V. Forrestal. A self-made, driven Wall Street investment banker before coming to Washington at the outset of the war, Forrestal was already a hard-line anti-Communist; his obsession with the communist menace would finally feed his growing paranoia, eventually forcing him to resign as secretary of defense in 1949 and not long after commit suicide by jumping out of a window at the Bethesda Naval Hospital.

Forrestal viewed both the scientific and technological secrets of the bomb as "the property of the American people" and said he doubted that the Russians, "essentially Oriental in their thinking," could be trusted. He also recorded in his diary that Acheson saw "no alternative except to give full information to the Russians," though in the context of gaining "some quid pro quo in the way of a mutual exchange of information." Acheson, Forrestal noted, "could not conceive of a world in which we were hoarders of military secrets from our Allies, particularly this great Ally upon our cooperation with whom rests the future peace of the world."[26]

Secretary of Commerce Henry Wallace fully supported Acheson, but, as Acheson described it in a letter to his daughter Mary, Wallace "soared into abstractions, trailing clouds of aphorisms as he went."[27]

The meeting was clearly inconclusive. Nonetheless, the president, who professed to find the discussion "exhilarating," ordered the participants to submit their opinions to him in writing.[28]

Four days later Acheson sent an unusually passionate memorandum to the president. He was, Acheson admitted, "deeply influenced by Colonel Stimson's paper."[29] In calling for an approach to the Russians soon and directly, Acheson declared that "what we know is not a secret which we can keep to ourselves. . . .

"This scientific knowledge," he wrote, "relates to a discovery more revolutionary in human society than the invention of the wheel." Moreover, "if the invention is developed and used destructively there will be no victor and there may be no civilization remaining."

He then argued that the joint development of the bomb by the United States, Britain, and Canada "must appear to the Soviet Union to be unanswerable evidence of an Anglo-American combination against them."

His logic was impeccable: "A government as powerful and as power conscious as the Soviet Government" would have to act as vigorously as possible to restore "the loss of power" that the discovery of the bomb had produced. It would most certainly do this if the United States tried to maintain "a policy of exclusion." And for America to declare itself a "trustee of the development for the benefit of the world will mean nothing more to the Russian mind than an outright policy of exclusion."

Acheson proposed approaching the Russians directly, after consultation with the British and after explaining the objective to Congress, in an attempt to work out a program of exchange of scientific information and collaboration in the development of atomic power. No disclosure of the industrial processes used to manufacture atomic weapons would be on the agenda, however. Otherwise, "the public and Congress will be unprepared to accept a policy involving substantial disclosure to the Soviet Union."[30]

He was especially sensitive on this last point, for the press had been full of reports of a so-called Henry Wallace Plan to give away the secrets of the bomb to Russia. Senator Tom Connally of Texas, Democratic chairman of the Senate Foreign Relations Committee, reflected the sentiment prevailing in the Senate when he declared that "complete secrecy should be maintained regarding the atomic bomb."[31] It was surely in response to this criticism that Acheson insisted that discussions with the Russians "need not involve at this time any disclosures going substantially beyond those which have already been made to the world."[32]

But Truman was being pulled in a number of directions. With the growing hostility to the Soviet Union in Congress and the press, he averred that he would not turn over "the plants and equipment" needed to make a bomb; on the other hand, he knew that to try to keep the bomb solely in America's hands might mean the end of the newly born United Nations.[33]

In his message to Congress on October 3, Truman followed Acheson's reasoning; indeed, the opening paragraphs of his speech had been drafted by Acheson's assistant, Herbert Marks. He called for "international arrangements looking, if possible, to the renunciation of the use and development of the atomic bomb." Unless the United States pursued this path, "a desperate armament race" would ensue. Truman affirmed that the theoretical scientific underpinnings of the bomb were already generally known, and he called for discussions, first with Great Britain and Canada and then with other nations.[34]

Despite the fact that Truman or his speechwriter, Samuel Rosenman, had cut the words "comparatively short" from a sentence about other nations catching up "in time," thereby implying that the secrets of the atom could be retained for quite a while, Acheson believed that "the road had been kept open" for the Stimson approach.[35]

Then, on October 8, at an impromptu press conference on the porch of Linda Lodge at Reekfoot Lake, near Tiptonville, Tennessee, Truman erupted. It was "the combination of industrial capacity and resources necessary to produce the bomb" that was "our secret"—"just the same as know-how in the construction of the B-29." He was not willing to share that know-how with anybody: "If they catch up with us on that, they will have to do it on their own hook, just as we did."[36]

Truman's definition of the atomic secret did not differ from Stimson and Acheson's distinction between scientific and industrial information. But while Stimson and Acheson had used this distinction to justify sharing scientific knowledge with the Russians, Truman apparently could see it as a way to justify excluding the Soviets—and, for that matter, even the British—from such an exchange. If no other country could construct a bomb without the combination of industry and resources that the United States alone possessed, there would be no point in giving away either basic scientific information *or* technological "know-how."

Harry Truman was too often tempted to shoot from the hip. Despite his rhetoric, he still concurred with Stimson and Acheson that direct talks with the Russians were necessary. Perhaps some agreements could be worked out after all. At that same press conference, he referred to his meetings with Stalin at Potsdam and pointed out that misunderstandings there had been cleared up. By speaking frankly—which he prided himself on doing—you could get agreements with the Russians. Moreover, he believed he had the right man available to do so: his secretary of state, James F. Byrnes.[37]

Byrnes, however, did not favor dealing directly with the Russians. Although Truman's comments had been in response to the Stimson/Acheson proposals, Byrnes did not consult Acheson as he prepared for a meeting in Washington on this issue with the British and Canadian prime ministers. Instead he solicited advice from Vannevar Bush, the scientist who had obtained FDR's approval in 1940 to organize the scientists needed to construct an atom bomb.

Bush, while eager for cooperation with the Russians, urged a technical approach that was not concerned with questions of political feasibility; his final objective was an inspection system that would offer protection against a surprise atomic attack. Both the technical process and the work of setting it up should be entrusted to a body established by the United Nations that would get started on the long road to control by promoting full scientific exchange.

Byrnes embraced Bush's UN approach. It avoided the difficult task of discussing matters with the Russians on a strictly political basis, of trying to find out what they were willing to negotiate, and it allowed the Americans to safeguard their technological expertise until the Russians proved more cooperative in their dealings on a whole host of other issues.[38]

In Acheson's view, however, by bringing the discussion of atomic energy control to "a large group of nations that included many small ones of no demonstrated power or responsibility," Byrnes was following a course that was "the opposite pole" from what he and Colonel Stimson had proposed.[39]

The meeting with British prime minister Attlee and his Canadian counterpart, Mackenzie King, only reinforced Byrnes's position. In late August Attlee had been convinced that on atomic matters Truman and he and Stalin should "take counsel together." By November, with Britain now preparing to make its own atomic bombs, he decided that "we should all lay aside our nationalistic ideas" and take the problem of control of atomic energy to the United Nations. The November summit in Washington rejected the direct approach to the Russians. No one suggested even talks—let alone "joint action"—with the Soviet Union.[40] The Stimson/Acheson proposed approach was dead.

Soon after the agreement with the British and Canadians to take the issue to the United Nations, in mid-December 1945 Byrnes headed for Moscow—with the British foreign minister, Ernest Bevin, in tow—for a meeting with Stalin. Although the conference was held primarily to try to settle still pending differences among the Western Allies and the Russians over Eastern Europe, Japan, China, and Iran, Byrnes wanted to get the Soviets to agree to sponsor a United Nations commission on atomic energy. Far from keeping the bomb out of discussions with the Soviets, Byrnes now put the question of the atom squarely on the table.

The discussion centered on the proposed United Nations Atomic Energy Commission. No one raised any particular questions about the atomic energy policies of the United States or the Soviet Union. The Russians readily acceded to Washington's proposals, insisting only that the commission be accountable to the UN Security Council, where both the Soviet Union and the United States wielded veto power. "Much to everyone's surprise," noted Harvard University president James Conant, in Moscow as Byrnes's scientific adviser, "the Russians didn't argue or talk back."[41]

As the conference ended, Byrnes, who tended to view foreign affairs in the same light as domestic affairs, believed he was returning home with a good horse trade. (He had once observed that negotiating with the Russians was just like dealing with the Senate: "You build a post office in their state and they'll build a post office in your state."[42]) In addition to Russian agreement to discuss proposals for the UN Atomic Energy Commission, he had secured Russian acquiescence in exclusive American control over occupied Japan and at least tepid support for Chiang Kai-shek as the unifier-to-be in China.

In return, Stalin got American recognition of the Soviet-backed regimes of Bulgaria and Romania (he did agree to include two non-Communists in their respective governments). The only serious question on which there was no agreement was over Soviet troop withdrawals from Iran, but Byrnes did not want to push the issue at that time. He predicted there would be real trouble over that question in the future; however, he did not want to "jeopardize" the good work that had been done.[43]

It was a singular moment of accommodation in what was fast becoming a grim period of confrontation.

* * *

Byrnes may have been successful in Moscow, but he was still facing opposition at home. Not only had he angered Harry Truman by not keeping him fully informed of his deal making in Moscow, but in the Senate, Michigan's Arthur Vandenberg was put out that he had not been consulted. Far from seeing the Moscow conference as a step forward in bettering relations with the Soviet Union, the Republican senator viewed the agreement on the UN Atomic Energy Commission as a possible threat to America's control over the secrets of the atom—"one more American give-away," as he wrote his wife. Fortunately, Acheson suggested a solution to Byrnes's problem with Vandenberg, which the senator was able to call his own: that the Moscow agreements on atomic energy be made "subject to Congressional approval."[44]

But exactly what did the Americans want? No specifics had been decided at Moscow, only the principle of a UN commission. The best approach, as Byrnes saw it, was to appoint Acheson to head a committee to formulate American policy. As Acheson tells the story, Byrnes phoned Acheson, who was in bed with the flu, and asked him to chair a group to devise a plan for the international control of atomic energy. Acheson protested, "Mr. Secretary, I don't know anything about this." But Byrnes was about to depart for London on January 7, 1946, for the first meeting of the UN General Assembly. He said, "My plane's going in a few minutes, and I have no time to argue. The President wants it done, and you are appointed." Acheson claimed his fever went up six degrees.

The other members of the committee were scientists James Bryant Conant, the president of Harvard University, and Vannevar Bush, now head of the Carnegie Institution in Washington; former assistant secretary of war John J. McCloy; and General Leslie Groves, the driving executive who had overseen the work of the Manhattan Project.[45]

Acheson was well aware of his own limitations in understanding the scientific aspects of atomic energy. To assist the committee, he appointed a board of consultants to advise on the technical and scientific aspects of the proposal. Its chairman was David Lilienthal, an energetic, optimistic man who had successfully headed one of the most admired achievements of the New Deal, the public utility known as the Tennessee Valley Authority. But by far the most influential consultant was J. Robert Oppenheimer, the nuclear physicist who had been the director of scientific effort to design and build the atomic bomb at the Los Alamos Atomic Laboratory, which was part of the Manhattan Project. He was now at the University of California at Berkeley.

* * *

Oppenheimer was born in 1904 into a comfortably well-off Jewish family on Manhattan's Riverside Drive. After graduating from Harvard College, he went on to Christ's College, Cambridge, and later Gottingen, where he met the Danish physicist Niels Bohr. After a brief stint teaching in the East, he went to the University of California at Berkeley in the late 1920s, where he lived the life of an unworldly scientist. It was Hitler's coming to power that shocked him into political consciousness, and he soon became acquainted with some California Communists.[46]

In 1943, on a train trip from Cheyenne, Wyoming, to Chicago, he confessed to General Groves, then military director of the Manhattan Project, that "he had probably belonged to every Communist front organization on the West Coast."[47] He had married a former Communist, was the brother of a former Communist, and had had a love affair with a Communist, but he himself had never been a member of the Communist Party. General Groves believed this.[48]

As head of the Los Alamos laboratory, Oppenheimer had demonstrated a singular gift for organization in mobilizing a great number of scientists to work on the bomb and then by managing a workforce of some three thousand people. For Acheson, Lilienthal, and McCloy, he became an indispensable teacher.

At the beginning of their work together, Oppenheimer came to stay with the Achesons. Each evening after dinner he would lecture Acheson and McCloy with the aid of a borrowed blackboard on which, in Acheson's telling, "he drew little figures representing electrons, neutrons, and protons, bombarding one another, chasing one another about, dividing and generally carrying on in unpredictable ways. Our bewildered questions seemed to distress him. At last he put down the chalk in gentle despair, saying, 'It's hopeless! I really think you two believe neutrons and electrons *are* little men.'"[49]

Despite Acheson's grave reservations about exploring the international control of atomic energy through a UN commission, rather than first approaching the Russians directly, he nonetheless labored wholeheartedly to come up with a workable plan. Both he and Lilienthal believed that scientists as well as those "schooled in government or statecraft" should be involved in the plan's formation, so that it might be understood by laymen and experts alike. Without scientific advice, Acheson said, it would be "as if one called in a very intelligent and well-intentioned South Sea Islander and said, 'There are too many cows being killed on railroad tracks and I want you to do something about it.' But the South Sea Islander, although smart and meaning well and wanting to be helpful, has never seen a cow or railroad."[50]

On March 17, 1946, the Acheson-Lilienthal report was ready. The committee and the board of consultants had met for four days at Dumbarton Oaks, the

Georgetown mansion that Mr. and Mrs. Robert Woods Bliss had restored to house their Byzantine collection. The setting, as Lilienthal described it in his diaries, was part of the story. "On the wall," he wrote, "some of the most magnificent tapestries men have ever devised; in a glass case, a priceless ebony cat, Byzantine. The ceiling, three stories high, decorated with the beams of some castle, carved and painted. And dominating the whole thing in a strange and lovely way, a painting by El Greco, 'The Visitation.' . . . And moving by, from time to time, outside the windows on the garden terrace were workmen, the people who had most at stake, and too little to say as to whether someday the order is given and an atomic bomb, perhaps a thousand times greater than Nagasaki, starts on its way against other workmen."[51]

The key to the plan was an Atomic Development Authority that would control the whole field of atomic energy—from mining through manufacturing. Rather than relying on international inspection teams, what might be called "atomic cops," the consultants proposed to control the uranium and thorium mines through the international authority. This solution—Oppenheimer's—Acheson termed "brilliant and profound."[52]

As Acheson and Vannevar Bush stated over the radio after the publication of the Acheson-Lilienthal report, "In plain words, the Report sets up a plan under which no nation would make atomic bombs or the materials for them. All dangerous activities would be carried on—not merely inspected—by a live, functioning international Authority with a real purpose in the world."[53]

The report was endorsed by all members of the committee, although General Groves may have signed on because he did not believe the Russians would ever agree to a workable plan. In essence, the committee recommended that the United States abandon its monopoly on the atomic bomb and rest its hopes on cooperative control of the terrible weapon.

On the very day that Acheson presented the secretary of state with the formal report, Byrnes told him that Truman had asked Bernard Baruch to sell the plan to the rest of the world.

Baruch, a self-styled "park bench" philosopher and self-promoting "adviser to presidents," was seventy-five years old. He had made a fortune speculating on Wall Street and used his lavish hospitality and gifts of money to senatorial and congressional campaigns to further a role in politics. Roosevelt had tried to keep him at a distance, but Byrnes and Truman believed that his influence among senators would help them with the necessary legislation. (Too late, even Truman had reservations, for on the very day he offered him the appointment by telephone, he noted, "Asked old man Baruch to act as U.S. representative. . . . He wants to run the world, the moon and maybe Jupiter—but we'll see."[54])

Acheson and Lilienthal were appalled. Lilienthal wrote in his diary on March 19 that when he read of the news of Baruch's appointment, "I was quite sick. We need a man who is young, vigorous, not vain, and whom the Russians would feel isn't out simply to put them in a hole, not really caring about international cooperation. Baruch has none of these qualifications."[55]

Five days later Baruch made it clear he was not about to accept the report as written and present it to the United Nations; as he put it, he was not going to be "a messenger boy." Moreover, he at first said he would not include any scientists among his advisers—Baruch could, he assured Lilienthal, "smell his way through." In fact, Baruch added three full-time scientists to his delegation.[56]

On June 14, 1946, at the opening session of the UN Atomic Energy Commission in the Hunter College Gymnasium in the Bronx, Baruch set forth his own version of the American plan with the portentous opening words "We are here to make a choice between the quick and the dead."[57]

But he made two key changes in the Acheson-Lilienthal report that proved fatal. There should be "immediate and sure punishment" for violations of the plan; and such punishment should not be subject to a veto by any member of the UN Security Council. Such conditions for a treaty, Acheson believed, "were almost certain to wreck any possibility of Russian acceptance of one."[58]

The Baruch Plan (as it was now labeled) was very much a take-it-or-leave-it proposition. America would give up its stockpile of atomic bombs (which in June 1946 numbered just three) only after firm guarantees were established that no other nation could arm itself with atomic weapons.

General Groves was right when he assured those sitting around him during the translation of Baruch's speech that the Russians would never accept the American conditions. Since Groves believed that it would take the Soviet Union ten to twenty years to develop atomic weapons, this meant an American nuclear monopoly well into the future. (Most scientists, however, believed it would take the Soviets from three to five years to explode a bomb, which was far nearer the mark; the first Soviet atom bomb was tested in 1949.[59])

Nor was it clear what Baruch's "immediate and sure punishment" actually meant. In a talk with Truman, Baruch said that punishment meant "war." Acheson certainly understood that any effective punishment of a great power did mean war, but he also believed that no one would go to war over such an issue. The whole idea of such punishment was an illusion, and Acheson was too much of a realist not to detest "paper police sanctions," as he called them.[60] Controlling uranium through the international authority was the best way to prevent cheating.

Truman, however, endorsed the "no veto" provision, and the plan was effectively dead. Although the Soviet response in July was almost wholly negative, in September Stalin hinted that there might be some way out of the impasse. Baruch, however, was not inclined to negotiate and forced a vote by the end of the year.[61] Not surprisingly, the United Nations Atomic Energy Commission approved the American plan, the Soviet Union and Poland abstaining; it was then killed by a Soviet veto in the Security Council.

Truman later confessed to Acheson that choosing Baruch was "the worst mistake I have ever made."[62] Acheson described Baruch's role more succinctly: "It was his ball and he balled it up."[63]

Was there any real hope of serious negotiation over the control of atomic energy?

Stimson was probably right that the "time had passed," as he wrote Baruch in June 1946, "for handling the bomb in the way I suggested to the President last summer."[64] Once Truman agreed to put the issue in the hands of the United Nations rather than approach the Russians personally, the idea of controlling the future of atomic energy may well have been doomed. But Truman never really concentrated on these issues: otherwise, how could he have both approved the Acheson-Lilienthal report and backed Baruch's veto?

There is also no evidence that Truman really understood the report or even read it with care. Truman's policies, as Kennedy's former national security adviser McGeorge Bundy described them, "seldom went beyond the counsel he had to choose from. He was not an initiator but a chooser; the buck stopped here, but he waited for the buck to arrive."[65]

No one, including Dean Acheson, really pressed Truman to go further than he did. Byrnes, not Acheson, was his secretary of state; just as Byrnes vacillated in his dealings with Moscow from seeking accommodation to hard-line rejection, so did Truman. And Acheson, despite all the efforts expended on the Acheson-Lilienthal Plan, had always doubted whether anything other than the direct approach to the Russians would bear fruit.

As long as the United States possessed atomic bombs, Stalin was determined that the Soviet Union would also have them. In August 1945 he had told his leading nuclear physicist, Igor Kurchatov, to "provide us with atomic weapons in the shortest possible time. You know Hiroshima has shaken the whole world. The equilibrium has been destroyed. Provide the bomb—it will remove a great danger from us."[66]

Yet even if we accept that after Hiroshima Stalin was determined that the United States would not retain its monopoly over atomic weapons, this does not mean that his views could not have been changed. Stimson and Acheson were doubtless right in September 1945 to press for an early direct approach to Moscow precisely to avoid perpetuating a threatening monopoly. Had Roosevelt lived, this might well have occurred. McGeorge Bundy makes the case that "Roosevelt would have taken to heart the quest for a workable international agreement" and "made the matter his most pressing business." Truman did not.[67]

Roosevelt, recognizing that the Soviet Union insisted on being accorded great-power status, would doubtless have understood Stalin's determination to possess atomic weapons as long as the United States did. In this respect, he might well have endorsed Stimson's original proposal to obtain Russian cooperation in controlling the use of atomic energy and weapons. FDR might also have explored an agreement to limit the production of atomic bombs to the great powers and to negotiate some specific number of weapons each might possess. This scheme, however, would have represented a great-power oligopoly with a vengeance, a very hard sell given the postwar rhetoric of collective security.

Acheson himself understood as well as anyone the need to treat the "power conscious" Soviet Union as a great power. This meant that Washington could not—and should not—pursue a policy of atomic exclusion. Had President Truman fully adopted this view and explained to a larger public that discussions with the Russians did not imply giving away some secret scientific information, the Stimson-Acheson proposal for a direct approach to the Russians might have been tried.

But in this period the Truman administration had not yet found its footing in foreign affairs. Dealing with the Russians solely on the basis of great-power relations, when the ideological struggle between the two powers was intensifying, was becoming ever more difficult.

Had the Russians responded favorably to a Stimson-Acheson approach, the history of the Cold War might have been substantially different. Soviet behavior would likely have been far less confrontational, especially after Stalin's death in 1953. A bilateral effort, which Stimson had originally urged, would have provided an even more solid basis for postwar cooperation on a broad range of security issues.

In the end, the Acheson-Lilienthal Plan was the best that anyone could come up with. Then, despite Acheson's best efforts to reopen the path to Moscow, Baruch threw up the final barrier.

Perhaps the direct approach would not have worked in any case—nonetheless, a true test of that approach was never made.

Acheson saw what had happened and why it had happened. If the president did not understand the full implications of what was being offered, if he was not told what was being discussed, as was Byrnes's habit, then his decisions would necessarily be uninformed. For Acheson, the clear imperative was to establish an iron bond between the president and his chief foreign policy adviser—especially at a time when Russian behavior at the periphery of the Soviet sphere seemed more and more threatening.

CHAPTER THIRTEEN

NO GRAND STRATEGY

LIFE ON "the good ship Jimmie Byrnes" was sheer chaos. There was no clear line of command. The secretary was by nature secretive; often even Acheson had no idea what was going on. If FDR had been in effect his own secretary of state, Byrnes acted at times as though he, and not Harry Truman, were president.

With Byrnes away for 350 of his 562 days in office, Acheson frequently found himself, as he explained later, "sitting in a position which was supposed to be important—Under Secretary of State—but I had no idea of what went on. I had no connection with anything. I knew absolutely nothing; I knew nothing of what he was talking about with President Truman. And then I would be Acting Secretary of State, with no idea what it was all about. So I started these 9:30 meetings to pull things together."[1]

The meetings were planned to last no longer than half an hour and were attended by the assistant secretaries and bureau chiefs. The purpose of the meeting was to identify important problems and to assign responsibility for new matters as they arose; above all, it was to make the assistant secretaries responsive to the need to take action. In this respect, Acheson echoed his later chief, General George Marshall, who was famous for telling his subordinates, "Don't fight the problem! Decide it." Then take action.[2]

As time passed, Acheson realized that attendance at these meetings was becoming "a status symbol." Although he believed that "irrelevancy mounted with numbers," he had to institute a large meeting once a week chiefly to keep up morale. Too many meetings, as Acheson saw it, were indicative of "weak leadership." As far as he was concerned, when the department was being run by meetings, it wasn't being run at all.[3]

Despite his best efforts, Acheson was frustrated under Byrnes. In Acheson's view, Byrnes thought of the State Department as himself; Charles ("Chip") Bohlen, the Russian expert who often accompanied him to meetings with his Soviet counterparts; and H. Freeman ("Doc") Matthews, chief of the European Division. In addition, Byrnes's assistant secretary for administration and former law partner, Donald Russell, would often frustrate Acheson's planning by going directly to Byrnes, who would overrule his under secretary.

A struggle to control and organize the State Department took place during the fall and winter of 1945–46, when Russell prevented the State Department from centralizing all the intelligence-gathering agencies, including the wartime Office of Strategic Services, under its wing. Acheson had been firmly opposed to any plan for a central intelligence organization that would remove the primacy of foreign intelligence gathering from the State Department and would therefore operate outside the control of the secretary of state.[4]

Frustrated and feeling his own authority within State was not clear, Acheson decided to leave and gave Byrnes a letter of resignation, dated April 17, 1946, to take effect after Byrnes's return from meetings abroad and at such time as might be convenient to him and to the president.

Byrnes, however, did not like the idea of Acheson resigning. The next day he showed Acheson a letter of his own, stating that he himself would resign after negotiating peace treaties with the East European countries. He had been experiencing chest pains that April, and his letter reported a doctor's finding of a heart murmur. For this reason, Acheson did not press him to act too soon on his own resignation. The upshot of the matter was that Byrnes filed his own letter in the White House but did not file Acheson's.[5]

With Byrnes so often involved in high-level negotiations with the Russians, Acheson was forced to deal with issues on which his personal views differed from the president's. The question of Palestine would surely head such a list. Acheson was never sympathetic to the establishment of a Jewish state, fearing that the mass emigration of Jews from postwar Europe into Palestine would lead to protracted war with the Arabs. It was a position he shared with Marshall, when the general later became secretary of state.

Acheson knew well from Brandeis and Frankfurter, both ardent Zionists, of the deep Zionist commitment to create a Jewish state. Yet he believed that an Arab-Israeli conflict would then threaten American interests in the region and could lead to an American military involvement there. Despite the intimacy of the friendship between Acheson and Frankfurter, both men finally agreed to exclude the subject of Zionism from their daily talks.[6]

Nonetheless, Acheson was prepared to carry out the president's wishes, and in

1946 Truman was becoming committed to the creation of a Jewish state in Palestine. In the wake of the Nazi persecutions of Jews, the moral issue was paramount for the president. Moreover, his former business partner from Kansas City, Eddie Jacobson, was an ardent Zionist and pressed the case for a Jewish state to be carved out of the British mandate of Palestine.[7]

In addition, political considerations certainly favored support for Israel. In 1946, when Truman met with America's Middle East diplomats who warned him of the threat to American prestige because of statements indicating sympathy with Zionism, Truman responded: "I am sorry, gentlemen, but I have to answer to hundreds of thousands who are anxious for the success of Zionism; I do not have hundreds of thousands of Arabs among my constituents."[8]

As under secretary of state, Acheson had to contend with the Department's almost overwhelming opposition to American support for a Jewish state, as well as vacillation from the White House. Should the president support a plan to partition Palestine between the Arabs and Jews, which would lead to a Jewish state, or endorse the British plan to hand their mandate over Palestine to the United Nations?

On Yom Kippur, October 4, 1946, Truman declared his belief that "public opinion in the United States" would support "the creation of a viable Jewish state in control of its own immigration and economic policies in an adequate area of Palestine." In effect, he supported the idea of partition. Acheson, whatever his private reservations, helped him prepare the statement.[9]

By February 1947 the Attlee government was determined to withdraw from Palestine by mid-May 1948. In Acheson's view, "a mere surrender" of the mandate by the British "would be a confession that no solution was possible and an invitation to civil war."[10] For Truman, what was most pressing was to make sure that the British let one hundred thousand refugees emigrate to Palestine. This was a Zionist demand that Truman never backed away from.

The Palestine issue was to come to a head in late 1947 and 1948 during the interregnum when Acheson was out of office. Once Israel was created in May 1948, Acheson came to believe that the unstinting efforts of the UN mediator Ralph Bunche to dampen the conflict through cease-fire and negotiations was the only viable American policy. Soon after he became secretary he offered Bunche the job of heading the Middle East desk as an assistant secretary; Bunche, however, declined the invitation, tired of struggling with unsolvable problems. "His most heartfelt wish," Acheson reported, "was for relief from them, not deeper involvement."

Acheson fully sympathized with him, commenting in later years, "How often I was to remember and echo his wish."[11]

* * *

While Acheson was trying to get a grip on the workings of the State Department, Secretary Byrnes was trying to make progress with the Russians on a host of problems left unfinished at Potsdam. Tensions with the Soviet Union had been mounting in the fall of 1945, especially over Iran, jointly occupied by the Soviet Union and the Western Allies during World War II. The Russians were showing no sign of withdrawing their troops from northern Iran, as agreed, although the British and Americans were taking out their troops from the southern part of the country. Moscow was also pressing forward on its demand for a military role in the Dardanelles, the straits that guarded the entrance to the Black Sea.

Sitting in a gloomy State Department office on Thanksgiving Day 1945, Byrnes decided to go to Moscow, where he could deal with Stalin directly. He informed the British foreign secretary, Ernest Bevin, after he had already approached the Russians about the meeting, and Bevin, although reluctant, had to go along.

The arrival in the Soviet capital in early December was inauspicious. The pilot of Byrnes's plane got lost in a snowstorm trying to land in Moscow and ended up at the wrong airport. Nor was Stalin impressed by Byrnes's effort to distance himself from the British; the Soviet dictator believed that it was "only a cloak to hide the reality of the bloc."[12]

Bluff Ernie Bevin, whose anticommunism stemmed from his experiences as a British socialist labor leader, was suspicious of Soviet behavior in the Middle East and Eastern Europe and thought Byrnes naive. As he told Byrnes, "Just as a British admiral, when he saw an island, instinctively wanted to grab it, so the Soviet government if they saw a piece of land wanted to acquire it."[13]

Although it was at this meeting that Byrnes obtained Soviet endorsement of the proposed UN Atomic Energy Commission, little progress was made on drafting postwar treaties for Romania, Bulgaria, and Hungary. By this time, however, Stalin had stopped arguing over control of Japan and support for the Nationalist Chinese.

Stalin was a realist. Spheres of influence were fundamental to his understanding of foreign relations. "The United Kingdom had India and her possessions in the Indian Ocean in her sphere of influence; the United States had China and Japan, but the Soviets had nothing," he told Bevin. "The Russian sphere extended all the way from Lubeck [on the Baltic Sea] to Port Arthur [in Manchuria]," Bevin retorted.[14]

The Russians, however, insisted on striking any discussion of Iran and Turkey from the agenda. The festering unsolved problems remained: Russia still demanded a coastal strip from Turkey on the Black Sea, parts of Turkish Armenia, and rights in the straits. Soon the American government—and Acheson in particular—would have to focus on Soviet designs in the Middle East. It would prove a decisive turning point in Acheson's approach to the Soviet Union.

* * *

"Chip" Bohlen, who accompanied Byrnes to his meetings with the Russians and acted as both an adviser and a translator, was worried. In the course of the Moscow conference, he noticed that Byrnes was not sending back regular reports to the president. He asked Byrnes why. The secretary brought him up sharply by telling him that he knew when he needed to report to Truman and when he did not. "I was put in my place," Bohlen reported, "and I stayed there."[15]

But Bohlen was right to be concerned. On December 27, Truman was at his home in Independence, Missouri, when a message came through to the State Department from Moscow, announcing the end of the conference and its conclusions. Already news summaries were appearing in the press, and Acheson had to inform the president that Byrnes had cabled him the date of his arrival back home and asked him to arrange a time in the evening when he could make a report to the nation over the radio. This presumptuous request further fueled Truman's anger.

The simplest etiquette required the secretary of state to report first to the president and then get his blessing for a report to the nation. Acting on his instincts, therefore, Acheson told the president that he thought it best if Byrnes met with Truman first and gave his radio talk the next day. Truman agreed, and Acheson now had to break the news to Byrnes.

Driving from the airport to the State Department with the secretary on December 29, Acheson told Byrnes gently that the president was upset with him. Moreover, Truman had boarded the presidential yacht, the *Williamsburg*, and was sailing down the Potomac, leaving word for Byrnes to follow him. This, in turn, maddened Byrnes, who was tired enough after his long flight from Europe.[16] Nevertheless, Byrnes had no choice but to join the president.

The president and his secretary of state closeted themselves for well over an hour in Truman's quarters. What happened there is a matter of some dispute. In Truman's version, he told Byrnes that "it was shocking that a communique should be issued in Washington announcing a foreign-policy development of major importance that I had never heard of. I said I would not tolerate a repetition of such conduct."[17] Byrnes, on the other hand, insisted that the conversation was quite pleasant. In any case, when they came down for dinner, they appeared perfectly friendly.[18]

Acheson, who was not present, thought that both impressions were probably genuine. Truman may well have exaggerated his behavior; Byrnes may well have taken Truman's desire to be informed not as a personal criticism at all. Acheson later noted over this episode that, whatever Truman might say in private, he had never heard him publicly say "a harsh, bitter, sarcastic word to anyone, whatever the offense or failure."[19]

On December 31, 1945, Byrnes told his radio audience that "mobilizing the nation for war is a small job compared with the effort to mobilize the world for peace." He then rejoined the group on the *Williamsburg* for a New Year's Eve party, where they celebrated the evening with old navy songs, and Byrnes, with his Irish tenor voice, took the lead.[20]

Nonetheless, despite the bonhomie of the occasion, a few days later, Truman, still angry, penned a letter to "Dear Jim." In it, he wrote that he had no intention of relinquishing the authority of the president. He claimed later that he read the letter aloud to the secretary—but there is no way of knowing if he actually did so.[21]

What Acheson called "the whole unhappy episode" impressed him with "the reciprocal nature of the President–Secretary of State relationship." If, as he believed, "the President cannot be his own Secretary of State, it is equally true that the Secretary cannot be his own President."[22]

In 1945 and 1946 American foreign policy fluctuated like a compass needle seeking the right azimuth. The uncertainties and fears of this period were reflected not only in Truman's behavior, which too often showed itself in fits of pique toward the rude and recalcitrant Russians, but also in Byrnes, who alternately tried to face down the Russians, as he had at the London conference of foreign ministers in September 1945, or sought compromise, as he did in Moscow in December.

Byrnes, who had served for so long in the Senate, was also especially responsive to the vagaries of public opinion, and by 1946 anti-Soviet attitudes were growing, fueled in no small measure by the Republicans, who hoped to win control of the Congress later that year.

Acheson, less sensitive to domestic politics, viewed relations between America and Russia through the lens of power and interests. Early in November 1945, in an address to the Maryland Historical Society, Acheson said that he feared the emotional reaction that was starting to build up in America against Russia. What was needed was a foreign policy "which will stress the interests of the United States."[23]

In this respect, as he once phrased it, "The sound rule would seem to be that if our interests are hurt enough by the acts of another state, internal or external, we should act to stop them."[24] By the same token, he was fully sensitive to the interests of other great powers. The Russian desire for security, Russian suspicion of American motives if Washington made no effort to give Moscow a stake in controlling the atom, seemed to him perfectly legitimate concerns.

He tried to make these points clear in a speech he was delegated to give in mid-November 1945 at a rally sponsored by the National Council of Soviet-American Friendship, a group that strongly favored a policy of accommodation with the Soviet Union, in Madison Square Garden. In the center of the smoky arena was an elevated boxing ring, where the speech makers and other entertainers performed for a packed house. Most notable was the great actor and singer Paul Robeson, who gave a magnificent rendition of "Old Man River," which became in his interpretation "a swelling protest" ending on a high note of defiance. He was followed by the so-called Red dean of Canterbury Cathedral, whose speech became a veritable antiphony, "the Dean shouting the rhetorical questions, the crowd roaring back the responses."

In this atmosphere, Acheson (in his own words) felt "like a bartender announcing that the last drink before closing time would be cambric tea." He had inserted in his text a paragraph that went beyond State Department homilies to acknowledge the Soviet Union's reasonableness in desiring friendly governments along its borders.[25] Here he insisted on balancing his understanding of the Soviet Union's need for security with a warning: "It seems equally clear to us that the interest in security must take into account and respect other basic interests of nations and men, such as the interest of other peoples to choose the general surroundings of their own lives and of all men to be secure in their person. We believe that the adjustment of interests should take place short of the point where persuasion and firmness become coercion, where a knock on the door at night strikes terror into men and women."[26]

While Acheson wanted a firm policy of opposing excessive Soviet demands, he was not yet ready to contemplate using force to oppose Soviet ambitions. In January 1946, in another speech, he declared, "It is absolutely unthinkable that we should fight Russia. It would destroy both of us and would be the end of the road."[27]

There was, in essence, no grand strategy at this time. The actions that were taken in the early postwar period were often confused, even conflicting—affected not only by the behavior of the Soviet Union, but also by pressures from America's principal allies, Britain and France, and by congressional and public opinion.

Acheson was very much aware of the limitations as well as the abundance of American power. He believed that he had to rein in Truman's initial inclination to confront the Soviets as aggressors, even while he himself grew increasingly uneasy at the truculence of Soviet diplomacy and the unwillingness of Stalin to hold free elections in Poland or withdraw his troops from northern Iran.

Reflecting later on this period, he acknowledged that neither he nor the other American policymakers had fully grasped the profound changes wrought by the Second World War. They perceived Britain as a far greater power than it proved to be, and many saw in London a serious rival as well as an ally. They hoped for a resolution of the civil war in China that would allow China to play a role as an American ally in maintaining the balance of power in Asia. They underestimated Russian scientific know-how and overestimated Russian military strength.

"Only slowly," Acheson wrote in his memoir, "did it dawn upon us that the whole world structure and order that we had inherited from the nineteenth century was gone and that the struggle to replace it would be directed from two bitterly opposed and ideologically irreconcilable power centers."[28]

In this situation, the practical objective of getting the Russians to abandon aggressive moves without making undue threats to their legitimate interests would be tested in Iran, with Acheson in a leading role.

CHAPTER FOURTEEN

"A GRACEFUL WAY OUT"

No one understood more clearly than Acheson that the location of armies at the end of the war would go far to decide the lineaments of the postwar world. Spheres of influence were inevitable, as was evident in the power and presence of the Red Army in Eastern Europe, the British army in Greece, the American and British forces in Italy, and the American army in Japan. But in regions where forces of the Big Three were in place not as occupying or as liberating powers, withdrawals had to be carried out before new spheres of influence were established.

Throughout the fall of 1945 and the winter of 1946, Acheson was increasingly disturbed by the reluctance of the Soviets to pull out of Iran. In 1942 the Soviet Union and Great Britain had sent troops into northern and southern Iran, respectively, to prevent any possible German move to that region, to secure an important supply line from Basra to the Soviet Union, and thus to protect Iranian oil.

At the Big Three meeting in Tehran in December 1943, Roosevelt, Churchill, and Stalin had signed the Tehran Declaration, which affirmed Iran's independence, sovereignty, and territorial integrity. In this spirit they had agreed that their troops would be withdrawn six months after the end of the war. It was essentially an agreement not to carve up a nation that was in no position to protect itself, but there was no mechanism for enforcing the accord. Averell Harriman, present as ambassador to the Soviet Union, later recalled that Stalin never seemed to treat the declaration as a very serious matter; at the last minute Harriman discovered that the Big Three had neglected even to sign the document. They finally did so, however, and with this act Roosevelt bound the United States to uphold its provisions.[1]

Then, in September 1945, a month after the Japanese surrender, the British foreign minister, Ernest Bevin, and his Soviet counterpart, Vyacheslav Molotov, set the date for their troop withdrawals as not later than March 1946.

Throughout the war FDR had been determined not to dispatch large numbers of American troops to Iran. With Soviet troops in the north and British forces in the south, he spent little time trying to think through a coherent American policy toward that oil-rich country. But this did not mean that Roosevelt, when he fleetingly focused on a particular region, did not interest himself in the geopolitical situation there. At one point during the Tehran conference, Roosevelt—without consulting Churchill, the Iranians, or even his own State Department—proposed to Stalin that the Allies establish an international trusteeship in Iran to operate the Iranian State Railroad and a warm-water port on the Persian Gulf. Stalin, doubtless taken aback at this unexpected, generous offer, asked the president if he was serious. When Roosevelt said he was, Stalin first excused himself, conferred briefly with Molotov, and then returned to say the idea seemed fine to him.

And why not? FDR had offered him, with no strings attached, a gift that the czars had sought for well over a century—direct access to a warm-water port. It is no wonder that Stalin went along with the three-power declaration on Iran.[2]

Roosevelt, however, was well aware that the United States would soon become dependent on foreign oil, even though production in the Middle East did not yet amount to very much.[3] At one point, on February 18, 1944, Roosevelt had sat down with the British ambassador, Lord Halifax, and shown him a hand-drawn map that he had made of the Middle East. As Daniel Yergin tells it in his sweeping history of the politics of oil, FDR, determined to avoid a U.S. political or military commitment in Iran, told Halifax that America would take the Saudi Arabian oil, Britain could have Persia (Iran), and the two countries would share the oil of Iraq and Kuwait.[4]

These informal assurances to the British were strengthened when the president told Churchill in a letter that he was not "making sheep's eyes at your oil fields in Iraq or Iran."[5] Churchill, in turn, wrote back: "Thank you very much for your assurances about no sheep's eyes at our oil fields in Iran and Iraq. Let me reciprocate by giving you the fullest assurance that we have no thought of trying to horn in upon your interest or property in Saudi Arabia."[6]

At his death, FDR left behind the suggestion that the Soviet Union had a legitimate desire to seek a warm-water port on the Persian Gulf and the right of access to it. Moreover, he certainly gave Stalin the notion of some form of Big Three trusteeship over Iran. Both ideas threatened to undermine the promise that the Big Three had made to withdraw their troops from Iran six months after the war was won.

* * *

Like Roosevelt, Acheson wished to avoid sending a significant number of American troops to Iran or asserting a major American role in the Persian Gulf region. Acheson had been appalled at a memorandum in January 1944 by General Patrick J. Hurley, FDR's envoy to Iran, suggesting that the United States commit itself, in Hurley's words, "to a world-wide plan of building associated free nations." Borrowing a phrase from the acerbic playwright Clare Boothe Luce, Acheson's aide Eugene Rostow called Hurley's ideas "messianic globaloney."

In addition, Acheson and Rostow saw Hurley's scheme to send American advisers to Iran as nothing less than a "classic device of imperialist penetration." Warning against setting in motion "a chain of events which may have dangerous and unforeseen consequences," Acheson and Rostow had been extremely wary of sending Americans to straighten out the chaos that might accompany a postcolonial world.[7]

For Acheson, the idea of reforming Iran through American advisers and therefore supplanting Russia and Britain as the dominant power in Iranian affairs was fraught with danger. As time passed and as Russia and Britain contested for influence, however, he sought to align America with Britain in an effort to make the Soviet Union comply with its promise to withdraw troops from the country, as both Britain and the United States were doing. But Acheson emphatically did not seek an American protectorate in Iran. In the immediate postwar period, the United States, he believed, had neither the will, nor the power, nor the experience to pursue such a policy in the region.

As the issues involving Russia became more pressing, Ambassador Harriman was eager to strengthen the political reporting and analysis section of his mission. The man he finally chose for the job was George F. Kennan, who on July 1, 1944, flew from the Russian airport in Tehran to Baku, then to Stalingrad, and finally on to Moscow.

Along with Charles E. Bohlen and Loy W. Henderson, Kennan was already considered one of the premier American experts on Russia. Born in 1904, Kennan, who came from pioneer farming stock on his father's side, had grown up in Milwaukee. He described the outstanding characteristic of that side of his family as an "obdurate, tight-lipped independence"; he himself would exhibit that same independence of mind and spirit.[8] As he described himself in his memoirs, he was a shy, dreamy boy, living in a world often peopled with "mysteries, seductive hints, vague menaces." Not surprisingly, Kennan turned out to be an especially gifted writer.[9]

Of great influence on his choice of career was his grandfather's cousin, for whom he was named. The elder George Kennan had traveled through Siberia in 1885 and written an account of the czarist prison system. So it was not surprising that after graduating from Princeton University, where he suffered under the pervasive social snobbery of that time, he tried out for the newly formed Foreign Service; he hoped that by studying Russian, he would follow in the path of his distinguished forebear.

As the United States had no official diplomatic relations with the Soviet Union until 1933, Kennan observed Russia and developed his Russian in the way used by the State Department, serving first as vice-consul in Tallinn, Estonia, and later as third secretary in Riga, Latvia. When FDR recognized the Soviet Union and opened diplomatic relations with Moscow in late 1933, Kennan joined the new staff under Ambassador William C. Bullitt. On December 10 Kennan crossed the border into Russia and, except for a short spell in Austria for his health, remained there until 1937.

It was during these years that he formed his deepest impressions of the Soviet system and concluded that ideology was less important to the understanding of Soviet behavior than Russian history. Without discounting communist ideology, he viewed Stalin more in the tradition of Ivan the Terrible than of Karl Marx.[10]

After service in Washington, Prague, Berlin (at the outbreak of the war), and Portugal, he finally returned to Washington, where he remained until he joined Harriman as his deputy in 1944. In Moscow Kennan would make his reputation as a profound analyst of Soviet thinking, although his analysis tended to rely on metaphoric or figurative language rather than on hard political argumentation.

His mission, he came to believe, was to alert his superiors in Washington to the futility of trusting the Russians to cooperate in the construction of the post-war world, as Roosevelt was attempting to do. Kennan was convinced that the Soviet Union was committed "to the concrete task of becoming the dominant power of Eastern and Central Europe," as he wrote upon his return to Russia in 1944 in a long essay to Ambassador Harriman.[11]

Nor was it simply in Europe that the Soviets were threatening. As Kennan also wrote in 1944, "The jealous and intolerant eye of the Kremlin can distinguish, in the end, only vassals and enemies; and the neighbors of Russia, if they do not wish to be one, must reconcile themselves to being the other."[12] The objective of Britain, and increasingly of the United States, was to see that Iran became neither. Kennan was already keenly suspicious of possible Russian expansion. Should the Soviet Union gain control over Iran and access to the Persian Gulf, the Soviets' political and strategic position would be immensely—and dangerously—improved.

Ten days after the surrender of Germany on May 8, 1945, the shah of Iran informed the American ambassador that he was sending a note to the American, British, and Soviet governments, requesting them to pull out their troops. This was in accordance with the Tehran agreement, calling for them to evacuate Iran six months after the war was over.

Stalin did not dispute this but said at first that he would not do so until after the end of the war with Japan. That came in August, but the Russians still showed little inclination to leave. Moscow now requested oil concessions in the north, where its troops were stationed; this request did not seem outlandish to the Iranian government, nor did the Americans oppose it.

The reluctance of Moscow to withdraw, however, became an issue of grave concern, once the Western Allies perceived in late August 1945 that the Russians were encouraging a separatist Azerbaijan in the northern provinces of Iran. The Soviets denied this, even while their troops were preventing Iranian forces from entering the area.

To Kennan, what was happening in Azerbaijan paralleled events in Eastern Europe. As chargé d'affaires in Moscow in the absence of the ambassador, Kennan noted on September 14, 1945, that the Moscow press was reporting Iranian oppression in Azerbaijan and calling for freedom for the Azeris.[13]

In Washington, Loy Henderson, now head of the Near Eastern desk, shared Kennan's views but urged the rapid withdrawal of the few U.S. troops that had been sent to Iran. Once American forces were out, Washington could pressure the British and the Russians to follow suit. Without force at hand, Acheson was skeptical of this procedure: "I agree [that the troops should be withdrawn]," he said, "but don't see where that gets us."[14]

Truman eventually did order the immediate evacuation of all remaining U.S. troops, as did the British, who were nonetheless doubtful that the Russians would take their own troops out of Azerbaijan by March 2, 1946, as they were supposed to. Kennan continued to make the case that Iran was not an isolated incident but part of a Soviet pattern of expansion in both Eastern Europe and Turkish Armenia.[15]

Then, in December 1945, with Byrnes in Moscow trying to resolve American and Soviet tensions, the Russians decided to consolidate their control over Azerbaijan. When *The New York Times* published an eyewitness report that month that the Azerbaijani capital of Tabriz was lost to the Iranians, Truman was flabbergasted, complaining to his staff that the "Russians confront us with an accomplished fact and then there is little that we can do.... There is only one thing they understand."

"Divisions?" his press secretary asked.

Truman nodded and added, "We can't send any divisions over to prevent them from moving into Bulgaria. I don't know what we're going to do."[16]

Nor did Secretary of State Byrnes. In Moscow he warned Stalin that the Iranians were going to submit a complaint to the United Nations Security Council about Soviet interference in Iranian affairs, and if they did so, the United States would have to support Iran's right to be heard.

Meanwhile in Washington, Acting Secretary of State Acheson met on December 17 with the new Iranian ambassador, Hussein Ala, who told him that Iran had more confidence in the United States than in Great Britain. Ala feared that London might cut a deal with Moscow to split Iran into two spheres of influence.[17]

Acheson reported this message to Byrnes in Moscow, later sending a message to Harriman that elaborated on Ala's thinking and repeated Ala's statement that "Azerbaijan would prove to have been the first shot fired in a third world war."[18] Acheson was determined to avoid any military clash in that part of the world.

Byrnes had no intention of pressing Stalin too hard on Iran. The Soviet leader had said the Russians would be leaving in March and that was that. Stalin reiterated that the Soviet Union had no territorial ambitions in Iran and that he would withdraw his troops as soon as he felt secure about the Baku oil fields in Azerbaijan.

Beneath Stalin's statements, the Soviet leader doubtless wanted a sphere of influence in northern Iran, an oil concession, and a government friendly to the Soviet Union. Beyond that, it was highly unlikely that in 1945 Stalin would use force to drive the British, a wartime ally, out of the Middle East.

Byrnes also had no interest in jeopardizing his other concerns over the Iranian issue. Nor did he have much ammunition. Unless his government was prepared to deliver an ultimatum—and what would it say?—Washington would simply have to wait and see what the Russians did. Stalin was doubtless aware of Washington's anxieties.

Truman was certainly becoming aroused. When Byrnes arrived home at the end of December, Truman wrote a letter to him that he did not send: "When you went to Moscow you were faced with another accomplished fact in Iran. Another outrage if I ever saw one." He concluded angrily, "I'm tired of babying the Soviets."[19]

The Iranian crisis unfolded over the winter and spring of 1946. The shah's envoy was determined to bring Iran's case before the UN Security Council. As the March 2 deadline for withdrawal passed with no Soviet action, George Kennan delivered on March 6 a protest to the Soviet government over its unwillingness to pull out its troops. Cables from the American vice-consul in Tabriz, Robert Rossow, reporting "exceptionally heavy Soviet troop movements" in northern Iran, became so ominous that State Department officials had to consider the possibility of using force against the Russians.[20]

Byrnes was now taking a tough line toward the Russians. On March 7, looking at the blown-up map of Azerbaijan that showed bold arrows representing Soviet forces moving in the direction of Turkey, Iraq, Tehran, and the southern Iranian oil fields, he beat one fist into his other hand and said, "Now we'll give it to them with both barrels."[21]

Two days later Acheson chaired a State Department meeting to deal with the Iranian crisis. Hawks from the Division of Near Eastern Affairs wanted to take a strong line that Moscow had violated its treaty obligations. Charles Bohlen, as a Soviet expert, pointed out that the United States was in no position to confront the Soviets in Iran. America had no substantial forces in the region. Nothing would be more self-defeating than a bluff.

As was his habit, Acheson did not divulge his own position until he had heard all sides of the argument. Then he said firmly that the department should let Moscow know that it was aware of Russian movements in Iran, but "leave a graceful way out" if the Russians wanted to avoid a showdown.[22]

What Acheson did not want to do was threaten force, which America did not possess, over an issue that he believed could be resolved by a show of American firmness without jeopardizing relations between Washington and Moscow.

In Moscow Kennan delivered Acheson's message on March 9, demanding an explanation for the movement of additional Soviet forces into Iran. Truman later declared that he sent Stalin an "ultimatum" on Iran. But there is no record of this. Kennan, who would have delivered it, can recall nothing of this nature. The note that Acheson prepared was doubtless what Truman had in mind. As Kennan wrote later, "It was enough for Stalin to learn that a further effort by the Soviet Union to retain forces in Persia would create serious international complications. He had enough problems, at the moment, without that."[23]

Acheson's note brought the crisis to an end by encouraging Stalin to work out a deal with the Iranians. On March 27 Soviet troops had been withdrawn from Karaj, twenty-four miles outside Tehran. Other forces were leaving other parts of Iran as well.

Washington nonetheless kept up the pressure by supporting the Iranians in the United Nations, where the Russians very much wanted to avoid a public debate. The Soviet representative, Andrei Gromyko, even walked out of a Security Council meeting on the Iran crisis in protest. But Byrnes insisted that the Iranian case be kept on the agenda until the Soviet troops were removed.

For three weeks in February and March 1946 the new Iranian prime minister, Ahmed Qavam, negotiated with the Russians. By April the Iranian crisis was over. In their discussions with the experienced and clever Qavam, Moscow finally agreed to recognize Iranian Azerbaijan as an internal Iranian problem, to be settled by direct negotiations between the rebels and Tehran. In return for withdrawing their troops—though this was never made explicit—the Russians were granted a twenty-five-year oil concession in Iran, subject, however, to ratification by the Iranian parliament (which never took place).

By early May the Soviet forces were gone. There was no doubt that American pressure had been instrumental in furthering the settlement.[24]

On April 4 Walter Bedell Smith, Eisenhower's wartime chief of staff who had succeeded Harriman as ambassador to Moscow, had a late night meeting with Stalin. During the session he presented an invitation from Truman to Stalin inviting the Soviet leader to the United States. Despite his tough talk, Truman was still hoping for better relations.

"How far is Russia going to go?" Smith asked.

"We're not going to go much further," Stalin answered.[25] The Iranian question may have been settled, but any Soviet designs on Turkey remained.

Early in January 1946, before the Iranian crisis had fully unfolded, Acheson had said that he was worried about creating the impression that the "US and UK are forming [a] bloc in [the] Middle East opposed to the Soviet Union."[26] Now the threat to Iran seemed to have brought about the very alliance that the Russians feared—and probably expected. Nonetheless, Acheson was unwilling to concede that only a hard line should be followed in dealing with the Russians. He later admitted he was surprised that the Russians had fully withdrawn from Iran.

"I remember sitting around in the State Department when the row over Azerbaijan was going to the United Nations," he recalled in a speech at the National War College in 1948. "We said, 'This is gallant, but it is futile. The Russians will get out of Persia, they will set up this puppet government, they will subsidize it, it will be stronger than anything else around there, and all this effort is for nothing.' After their troops moved out, the Persians sent a few ill-armed troops into Azerbaijan, a half a dozen shots were fired, all the Russian puppets skipped into Russia taking the assets of the national bank with them, the whole business collapsed overnight, and the Russians did nothing about it. I would have bet a thousand to one that such a thing would not happen, and I was just as wrong as I could be."[27] Acheson, who had been instrumental in having the Russians pull out of Iran, would have settled for far less.

Success in getting the Russians out of Iran did not imply that it would be possible to get them out of Poland. Moreover, any Soviet move to menace Turkey and the Dardanelles would be of a different order. It would mean that the Soviet Union might well be bent on expansion whenever and wherever the opportunity presented itself. This would require a wholly different response.

CHAPTER FIFTEEN

RISKING WAR

EVEN AS THE IRAN CRISIS was being resolved peacefully in the spring of 1946, there was a growing sense that an open conflict might erupt between the United States and the Soviet Union. On March 5, 1946, Winston Churchill, now out of office, had delivered a speech at Westminster College in Fulton, Missouri. He was doing a favor for Harry Truman, who introduced him and sat on the platform as Churchill, arrayed in a flaming scarlet academic robe, gave the world a striking new addition to the vocabulary of the Cold War.

The crux of Churchill's speech was his call for an Anglo-American alliance, which, among other things, would hold fast "the secret knowledge or experience of the atomic bomb." Meeting the objection that such a special relationship would be interpreted by the Soviet Union as a hostile act, he declared that nobody knew what are "the limits, if any, to [Soviet Russia's] expansive and proselytizing tendencies."

Then the former prime minister sounded the warning that reverberated throughout the world: "From Stettin in the Baltic to Trieste in the Adriatic, an iron curtain has descended across the Continent." The audience was silent. Only when Churchill explained that the Soviet Union did not desire war did his listeners applaud. "What they desire is the fruits of war," he went on to say, "and the indefinite expansion of their power and doctrine."[1]

Truman, who had read the speech on board the train from Washington, told Churchill it would "do nothing but good" and surely "make a stir."[2]

That very evening the Achesons were giving a dinner at their Georgetown house. Among others, the columnist Walter Lippmann and his wife, Helen, were invited, as was Australian minister Richard Casey, "Chip" Bohlen, who had been advising Byrnes on Soviet foreign policy, and Secretary of Commerce Henry Wallace, who tended to interpret most Soviet actions as stemming from insecurity. With such a group, conversation was bound to be lively, but at that dinner party, the exchanges grew unusually vigorous.

Acheson and his guests argued the wisdom of Churchill's words. Bohlen dismissed the notion that the Russians were fearful of encirclement; in his view they were the ones who were making threatening moves toward the Middle East, Turkey, and Greece, as well as tightening their grip on Eastern Europe. Wallace, on the other hand, warned that this attitude on the part of the West could lead to war. Lippmann said very little, but the next day in his column he warned that the "line of British imperial interest and the line of American vital interest are not to be regarded as identical."[3] Just because the British had kept the Russians out of the eastern Mediterranean in the nineteenth century did not mean the Americans had to do the same in the twentieth.

Though Acheson forcefully defended Churchill's point that Washington needed to be firm with Moscow, he was deeply troubled by Churchill's call for an Anglo-American partnership that would seem to be directed against Moscow. To show that the administration did not necessarily endorse Churchill's views, Byrnes asked Acheson not to travel to New York to attend a reception for Churchill, and Acheson readily assented: the Iranian situation was still unsettled, the Acheson-Lilienthal Plan was being completed, and he was still trying to test the extent of the Kremlin's desire for expansion.[4]

Despite his reservations over Churchill's rhetoric, Acheson very much admired Churchill as a war leader, and when the former prime minister came to Washington shortly after his Fulton address, Acheson and his wife were invited to lunch by the British ambassador. No statesman had a more devoted admirer than Churchill had in Alice Acheson. Moreover, she told him so. The great British statesman glowed under her praise and then discovered that she was a painter, a common bond. Mrs. Acheson had seen reproductions of his paintings and praised them honestly and warmly.

Expansive with food and drink, Churchill asked her for "a criticism." He would not be put off.

"Very well," she said. "Your palette is keyed too high. Your work would have more depth if it were toned down."

"You are quite wrong. My palette is based on advice of the most eminent painters." But Mrs. Acheson rejected this argument, asserting that the question was one of judgment. As her husband tells it, "She went on to point out specific instances where in her view a lowering of tone would have brought improvement. He fought back with spirit. Neither gave ground nor asked for quarter."

As they rose from the table, Churchill, his cigar "going like a steam locomotive on a stiff grade," turned to Acheson. "A woman of conviction, your wife." It was a good encounter. In later years the Achesons became friendly with the Churchills, lunching with them occasionally both in office and out.[5]

Churchill's Fulton speech was roundly criticized in much of the American press, and Truman lied to reporters by telling them that he had not known what the former prime minister was going to say. In Moscow Stalin labeled it a "call to war."[6]

But Churchill had only eloquently articulated what a growing chorus of advisers inside the American government was saying. Secretary of State Byrnes openly shifted to a harder line toward the Russians after his return from Moscow and his meeting with Truman. Without referring to the Iranian crisis by name, he nonetheless made it clear in a speech to the Overseas Press Club, February 28, that "we cannot allow aggression to be accomplished by coercion or pressure or by subterfuge."[7] Two weeks later he declared, "Should the occasion arise, our military strength will be used to support the purpose and the principles of the [UN] charter."[8]

Much of the stiffening in American policy was as much as anything else sparked by an address by Stalin a month before Churchill's Fulton oration. The Soviet leader delivered his speech at Moscow's Bolshoi Theatre, February 9, 1946, at an election rally on the eve of voting for the Supreme Soviet. It was a lengthy justification in typical Soviet jargon for another series of five-year plans, requiring more sacrifices from the Russian people.

If this had been all, it would have gone unnoticed. But Stalin also contended that World War II had broken out because of the inherent contradictions of capitalism. His most outrageous assertion—from the point of view of the hard-liners—was his argument for the incompatibility of communist and capitalist systems and his forecast of an Anglo-American conflict.[9] Supreme Court justice William O. Douglas labeled the speech a "Declaration of World War III."[10]

Although Justice Douglas's reaction may have been the most extreme, *Time* magazine called it "the most warlike pronouncement uttered by any top-rank statesman since V-J Day," although it noted that Stalin might have delivered it "for purely Russian reasons." Walter Lippmann also thought Stalin's words belligerent. Since Russia possessed both the means and the will to pursue "military superiority," he wrote, the West would have to undertake a "new mighty upsurge of national economy to balance it and withstand it." In response, *Business Week* thought Lippmann had "gone berserk and virtually declared war on Russia."[11]

On the other hand, Truman, speaking as a politician trying to cope with the problems of inflation and the conversion of war industries to peacetime production, said he could understand what Stalin was up to. At a Women's Press Club dinner in early February, he remarked that Stalin's speech reminded him of an amusing story about a fellow senator who said, "Well, you know we always have to demagogue a little before elections."[12]

Within the government, officials were divided. Secretary of the Navy James Forrestal was alarmed, as was Paul Nitze, who had worked with Forrestal at the investment banking firm of Dillon, Read, had joined the government in 1940 at Forrestal's behest, and was now in the State Department's Office of International Trade Policy. After reading Stalin's remarks, Nitze went to see Forrestal at the Pentagon and told him that the speech was a "delayed declaration of war on the U.S."

Forrestal sent him off to see Acheson, whom (according to Nitze) Forrestal viewed as "a seminal source of weakness in the government." When Nitze confronted Acheson with his alarmist view of Stalin's speech, Acheson told him he was "just seeing mirages." "Paul," he said, "you see hobgoblins under the bed. They aren't there. Forget it!"[13]

Two weeks later a Soviet atomic spy ring was exposed in Canada. This further fed anti-Soviet sentiment both in and out of government. Then, on February 22, a dispatch arrived from Moscow. George F. Kennan's eight-thousand-word "Long Telegram" describing Soviet behavior helped to shift many in government—though not Acheson—closer to a stance of grave hostility toward Russia.[14]

Ambassador Harriman was absent, and Kennan was in charge. As Kennan later described it, he was sick with a cold, sinus, and tooth trouble, recovering slowly with the help of sulfa drugs; among the messages brought up to him was a telegram that the Russians were now unwilling to join the World Bank and International Monetary Fund. The Treasury Department was bewildered, and the State Department passed on a general request that he try to explain Soviet behavior in this instance.

At long last, Kennan, who felt that his earlier reports had been ignored, had his chance to try to make Washington understand what the Russians were up to. While he knew that the Soviet desk at the State Department was in sympathy with his ideas, beyond that there was silence, all the more infuriating in the aftermath of Stalin's speech. For weeks he had been so despondent at being on the sidelines that he was thinking seriously of resigning. Now he seized the occasion to put forth far more than a simple explanation of Soviet views of world banks and monetary funds. In his later words, "Here was a case where nothing but the whole truth would do. They had asked for it. Now, by God, they would have it."[15]

To Kennan, it was not an "objective analysis of the situation beyond Russia's borders" that explained Moscow's attitude toward the world elsewhere. At [the] bottom of [the] Kremlin's neurotic view of world affairs is [a] traditional and instinctive Russian sense of insecurity," created in part by frequent nomadic invasions and later by contact with the "economically advanced West." It was impossible for Russia to coexist with the West because Soviet leaders could compensate for their fears only by going permanently on the attack, "in a patient but deadly struggle for total destruction of rival power, never in compacts or compromises with it."

Marxism clothed Soviet purposes, but the dogma should not be underrated: it views the "outside world as evil, hostile and menacing." Above all, he wrote in fevered prose, "We have here a political force committed fanatically to the belief that with the US there can be no permanent modus vivendi, that it is desirable and necessary that the internal harmony of our society be disrupted, our traditional way of life destroyed, the international authority of our state be broken if Soviet power is to be secure."

Kennan outlined a doctrine of containment: "Impervious to the logic of reason, [the Soviet Union] is highly sensitive to the logic of force. For this reason it can easily withdraw—and usually does—when strong resistance is encountered at any point. Thus, if the adversary has sufficient force and makes clear his readiness to use it, he rarely has to do so."

There was no way this could be read without concluding that Kennan would not shrink from using military force to counter Soviet expansion.

The "Long Telegram" ended with recommendations that the public be educated to the "realities of [the] Russian situation" and that the United States keep up the "health and vigor" of its own society, so that communism, a "malignant parasite," would not be able to feed on "diseased tissue."[16]

The influence of the "Long Telegram" in Washington is hard to gauge. Harriman passed it on to Forrestal, with a note to the navy secretary that given his "interest in the philosophy of the present Soviet leaders," Kennan's dispatch was "well worth reading."[17] Forrestal was so taken by the uncompromisingly tough-minded analysis of Soviet motivations that he had it copied and sent on to other members of Truman's cabinet and to officers in the armed services.

Kennan's "official loneliness" came to an end: "My reputation was made. My voice now carried."[18]

Acheson, however, was less impressed with Kennan's analysis, and not at all by his policy prescriptions. "His recommendations," Acheson wrote in retrospect, "—to be of good heart, to look to our own social and economic health, to present a good face to the world, all of which the Government was trying to do—were of no help."[19]

Even at the time, Acheson made no comment on Kennan's interpretation of Soviet motivations. He may have preferred an alternative view of the policy choices facing the administration. In December he had commissioned from State

Department and outside experts on Soviet affairs a study of the Soviet Union as affected by American policy. The final installment, written by Charles Bohlen, was being circulated at about the same time as Kennan's telegram.

Bohlen suggested that Soviet expansion could be limited by using U.S. military bases and economic pressure, but he flatly rejected this approach. Citing America's offensive military—primarily atomic—capability that would remain "manifestly and decisively superior" to that of the Soviet Union for "perhaps five and even ten" years, he thought that the goal should be a collective solution to political and territorial problems through the United Nations.

But that approach might arouse the Soviets to suspect that the United States was trying to mobilize a coalition against them. For that reason, he urged that Britain and the United States meet with the Russians before any kind of international conference took place to make sure that their differences were resolved privately and on a preliminary basis. The decisions of the Big Three could then be considered by the international community. Acheson's only criticism was to ask, "Could such talks remain only *preliminary* and not become definitive?"[20]

During this period of debate, Acheson persisted in trying to find common ground with Russia over atomic energy. But he was also becoming more and more convinced that the United States would have to assume a more prominent moral, military, and economic role in confronting any Soviet probe. This meant voicing a good deal of skepticism over the ability of the United Nations to preserve the peace.

That June of 1946, at the suggestion of Bohlen and others, Acheson delivered a deeply thoughtful speech at the Harvard Club of Boston. In it he tried to deal with the need for resolute action in foreign policy in a postwar world where nations "are still nations." The problems that bedeviled American foreign policy were not like headaches, he wrote—when you "take a powder and they are gone." Instead, "They are like the pain of earning a living. They will stay with us until death. We have got to understand that all our lives the danger, the uncertainty, the need for alertness, for effort, for discipline will be upon us. This is new to us. It will be hard for us. But we are in for it and the only real question is whether we shall know it soon enough."[21]

Acheson was steeped in British thinking and history. Many of the books he inherited from his father were biographies and treatises of nineteenth-century British statesmen—Melbourne, Palmerston, Disraeli. He had been prepared to concede Great Britain its traditional sphere of influence in Iran and to let Britain contest Russia in that region as it had a century ago in the so-called great game in Asia. But now he perceived how weak Britain actually was and its consequent need to rely on America to back it up.

That summer he saw another crisis coming to a head, one that also reflected historic trends and traditions—the Turkish Straits. Unlike northern Iran and Eastern Europe, which Soviet troops occupied as a result of World War II, here was a strategic point that was free of Russian control. The Dardanelles was the stopper in the neck of the bottle, and if Great Britain was too weak to hold it, America must be prepared to take its place.[22]

Stalin had long sought control of the Dardanelles and the Bosporus (together known as the Straits), the vital gateway in and out of the Black Sea for the Russian fleet headquartered at Sebastopol. At the Yalta summit in February 1945 he declared that the Montreux Convention, which the great powers had signed in the 1930s, giving Turkey rights to defend the Straits, must be revised; Churchill and Roosevelt had agreed, but then Stalin spoke in more threatening tones, asserting that he found it "impossible to accept a situation in which Turkey had a hand on Russia's throat."[23]

Stalin's demands escalated after the war, and in June 1945 Soviet foreign minister Molotov insisted that the Kars and Ardahan districts of eastern Turkey, ceded by Moscow to Turkey in 1921, would have to be returned to Russia. In addition, he demanded that the Turks consent to Soviet bases in the Straits.

A month later, meeting with Truman and Churchill at Potsdam, Stalin and his foreign minister, Molotov, said that bases were not enough: Turkey and Russia should become joint custodians of the Straits. Neither Truman nor Churchill accepted this; they fully supported Russia's insistence that its ships move freely in and out of the Black Sea, but they opposed fortifications of any kind in the Straits.[24]

Stalin's desire to acquire the lost territories in eastern Turkey may well have been inspired by Lavrenti Beria, who was the head of the secret police and, like Stalin, a Georgian. According to Nikita Khrushchev's memoirs, at one of many "interminable" suppers with Stalin, Beria "started harping on how certain territories, now part of Turkey, used to belong to Georgia." He then convinced Stalin that "now was the time to get those territories back. He argued that Turkey was weakened by World War II and wouldn't be able to resist."[25]

As Soviet demands rose, Washington took a harder line. By the time Byrnes returned from the Moscow conference in December 1945, Truman was complaining to him: "There isn't a doubt in my mind that Russia intends an invasion of Turkey and seizure of the Black Sea Straits to the Mediterranean. Unless Russia is faced with an iron fist and strong language another war is in the making. Only one language do they understand—'How many divisions have you?'"[26]

The Turks had no intention of satisfying Soviet demands. In the fall of 1945 the American ambassador in Ankara had become convinced that Moscow wanted to convert Turkey into a Soviet satellite, and from Moscow, George Kennan warned that no concessions would satisfy the Soviet Union, whose aim was to establish a "friendly" regime in Turkey.[27]

By March 1946 Kennan believed that Stalin was insatiable: "Nothing short of complete disarmament, delivery of our air and naval forces to Russia and resigning of powers of government to American communists" would alleviate Stalin's distrust, and even then he would probably "smell a trap and would continue to harbor the most baleful misgivings."[28]

In that month there were further Russian troop concentrations pointed toward Turkey, with at least two hundred Soviet tanks crossing the Iranian border, about a third of them mobilizing along the Turkish-Iranian frontier. Despite these intimidating deployments, Ankara stood firm against Soviet demands, while approaching London and Washington to back it up.[29]

As the crisis deepened, former Soviet foreign minister Maxim Litvinov, who had been associated with a more friendly policy toward the United States in the 1930s, gave a surprisingly revealing interview on June 18, 1946, to the CBS correspondent in Moscow, Richard C. Hottelet. The old Bolshevik explained that there "has now been return in USSR to outmoded concept of geographical security." When Hottelet asked if Soviet policy would be mitigated if the West were to give in to Soviet territorial demands, Litvinov said that "it would lead to [the] West being faced after [a] period of time with new series of demands."[30]

On August 7, 1946, Russia sent a detailed note to the Turkish government, with a copy to Washington. Moscow now demanded a joint Turkish-Soviet defense of the Straits, which would necessarily require Soviet bases.

In the absence of Secretary Byrnes, who was in Paris, Acheson called a series of meetings of the Departments of State, War, and Navy, along with the chiefs of staff, to study the situation and agree on a course of action. In Acheson's mind the worst policy would be one of bluff: the Russians must be certain that America would support Turkey if it were attacked.

To that end, Secretary of the Navy Forrestal ordered a naval task force, which included a new aircraft carrier, the *Franklin D. Roosevelt*, and two destroyers, to rendezvous off Lisbon with two cruisers and three more American destroyers dispatched from British waters, and thence to join the USS *Missouri*, which had already arrived in the Dardanelles on April 5.

The pretext on which it was sent there was to bring back the body of Mehmet Munir Ertegun, the Turkish ambassador to the United States, who had died in Washington during World War II. There was an old tradition that chiefs of mission who died in service were returned by warship. Although the direct threat to Turkey was primarily on the ground, Acheson believed the majesty of the *Mis-*

souri, with its sixteen-inch guns, its great bulk, and its strong armor, made it a perfect symbol of U.S. resolve.[31]

The interdepartmental meetings, leading up to a crucial meeting with the president on August 15, produced one of the toughest recommendations for policy yet offered to Harry Truman. Flanked by Forrestal and the top military brass, Acheson presented the joint report. In essence, it stated that where the Russians had valid criticisms of the Montreux Convention, Washington should say so, but the United States government should make it absolutely clear that the Straits were a matter of international concern.

"In our opinion," the report read, "if the Soviet Union succeeds in its objective of obtaining control over Turkey, it will be extremely difficult, if not impossible, to prevent the Soviet Union from obtaining control over Greece and over the whole Near and Middle East."

Should this happen, Moscow would be in a much stronger position to threaten India and China. "The only thing which will deter the Russians will be the conviction that the United States is prepared, if necessary, to meet aggression with force of arms."

The report then concluded: "In our opinion therefore the time has come when we must decide that we shall resist with all means at our disposal any Soviet aggression and in particular, because the case of Turkey would be so clear, any Soviet aggression against Turkey."[32]

The president did not hesitate: "We might as well find out whether the Russians were bent on world conquest now as in five or ten years." He was prepared to pursue the policy to the end.[33]

In Acheson's account, General Eisenhower, then army chief of staff, leaned over and asked Acheson in a whisper if it was clear to the president that the course they were recommending could lead to war. Before he could reply, the president asked whether the general had something to say. Acheson repeated Eisenhower's question.

Truman then took from the drawer of his desk a large map of the Middle East and eastern Mediterranean and asked those present to gather around him. After unfolding the map, he gave a short lecture on the historical background and current strategic importance of the region. Echoing Acheson's report, he said it was vital to protect the Straits from any Russian incursion; otherwise, Soviet troops would soon be used to control all of Turkey, and in the natural course of events Greece and the Near East would fall under Soviet domination.[34]

Four days later Acheson, with Truman's assent, rejected the Soviet demand of August 7. The message dismissed any notion that Russia should share responsibility with Turkey for the defense of the Straits.

Confronted by American resolve and the naval task force in the Turkish Straits, the Russians backed down. A month later their tone on the Dardanelles was much softer. (In due course, after Stalin's death in 1953, Moscow abandoned the question of even revising the Montreux Convention.)

A week after Acheson had sent the American reply to Moscow, *New York Times* reporter James Reston noted a shift in Acheson's thinking. While the under secretary had previously held out for a "liberal policy" toward the Soviet Union, "when the facts seemed to merit a change—as he seems to think they now do in the case of the Soviet Union—he switched with the facts."

Acheson said later that "facts are a matter of interpretation." The more data, the more the interpretation would change. Foreign affairs was "an art and not a science."[35]

In these early decisions Truman's special background played a role. Three years later, Acheson and his wife were dining with President Truman in his private car on the way back to Washington from the dedication of the new United Nations building in New York. They ended up sitting at the table for almost the whole trip because Mrs. Acheson began talking about central Asia. That got Truman started. The waiters cleared away the dishes, and the president took the back of a fork and began to lecture on the history of central Asia, the various emperors, the military campaigns, the migrations of populations. Toward the end of his exposition, Mrs. Acheson said, "This is amazing. I wouldn't have been surprised that you would know all about the Civil War, but this part of the world, I've never known anyone who knew anything about it."

The president laughed and then told her why. "Well, my eyesight isn't any good. I was never any good playing games where you have to see what you're doing at a distance. I couldn't hit a ball if it hit me in the nose, so I spent my time reading. I guess I read nearly every book in the library. I got interested in this part of the world and ever since I've read everything about it I could find."[36]

For Truman, as for Acheson, the Turkish crisis was a clear sign that the Russians would not be content with a sphere of influence in Eastern Europe, but instead were engaged in a policy of renewed expansion. Especially in the Mediterranean and Near East, where the Russians had traditionally sought territory and access to the sea and where the British had historically stood fast against them, the Americans must now be prepared to draw the line.

CHAPTER SIXTEEN

"CLEARER THAN TRUTH"

THE CRISIS OVER THE STRAITS was not the only sign of Soviet expansionism. In the Balkans, Stalin tightened his grip on Romania and Bulgaria, and civil conflict between the Communists and monarchists in Greece further fueled the growing anti-Communist consensus. Among Truman's advisers, Acheson remained buoyant. The atmosphere within the administration, on the other hand, was gloomy.

At the same time, relations between the president and his secretary of state were brittle. Although Byrnes had offered to resign in April 1946, he remained in office for the rest of the year to continue negotiations with the Soviets. Perhaps he never quite believed that Truman would actually accept his resignation. Acheson's resignation was also pending.

After the 1946 congressional elections, then, it appeared that the president would soon be losing both his secretary of state—which he welcomed—and Byrnes's principal deputy, Dean Acheson—which he did not. By now, although Acheson was no longer seeking common ground with the Soviet Union, he was also not considered a hard-liner by his colleagues in the department. Even when he had been willing to risk a military confrontation with the Soviet Union over the Dardanelles, he believed that "the way to impress the Russian political mind is to *understate* what we are doing."[1]

Truman had been buffeted all that fall by the conflicts between hard-liners and the followers of Henry Wallace, who believed that Washington was largely to blame for the worsening relations between the United States and the Soviet Union. In late September Truman's special counsel Clark Clifford gave him a paper on America's relations with the Soviet Union he had prepared with his assistant George Elsey. They had worked on it over the summer, after Truman had asked them to solicit the views of senior officials most concerned with American policy toward the Russians.

Much of the analysis followed the uncompromising lines of George Kennan's "Long Telegram" of the previous February; after reading a draft of the Clifford-Elsey report, Kennan wrote to Clifford that he found the general tone "excellent" and that he had "no fault to find with it." In essence, the report portrayed the Soviet Union as a cunning enemy bent on world domination. As the "language of military power" was the only language the Russians understood, America should maintain its military strength (by then sharply cut) and integrate its foreign, economic, and military policies to counter the Soviet threat. Adoption of such an approach would allow the West "to build up a world of our own [that would] recognize the Soviet orbit as a distinct entity with which conflict is not predestined but with which we cannot pursue common goals."

How much Cifford's document influenced Truman's thinking is not clear. He was certainly not ready to risk a public confrontation with the Soviets with an election pending. The day after he read it, he called Clifford at home at seven o'clock in the morning and asked him how many copies of the memorandum existed. "Twenty," Clifford replied. Truman then asked him to deliver all twenty copies to him at once. "I read your report with care last night," Truman told him. "It is very valuable to me—but if it leaked it would blow the roof off the White House. It would blow the roof off the Kremlin." He took the copies from Clifford, and neither Clifford nor anyone else in the administration ever saw them again.[2] Nor is there any record that Acheson even knew of them.

The White House's harder line toward the Soviet Union surfaced most dramatically over the actions of Henry Wallace. The secretary of commerce (and former vice president) had accepted an invitation to deliver a speech on September 12, 1946, at Madison Square Garden at a rally organized to oppose Republican Thomas E. Dewey's bid for reelection as governor of New York. Wallace seized the occasion to deliver a speech that could be read only as sharply critical of administration policy toward the Soviet Union. Moreover, it was given at a time when Secretary Byrnes was in Paris, negotiating once again with the Russians.

Henry Wallace was an anomaly in the Truman administration. He had already served notice on Truman that he saw the administration's policy toward the Soviet Union as too bellicose. And Truman, while he was cordial to the secretary of commerce and eager to retain him in the cabinet to placate the left wing of the

Democratic Party, saw Wallace as a dreamer. But Truman also admired him and, referring to his position in FDR's cabinet before 1940, called him "the best damn Secretary of Agriculture we ever had."

Fearful of an arms race, Wallace was quite prepared to accord the Russians a sphere of influence in Eastern Europe, where he saw a "complete absence of direct conflicts in national interest" between the Soviet Union and the United States.[3] On July 23, 1946, he had sent a five-thousand-word letter to Truman, stressing his view that Soviet behavior was in no small part a response to American policy. Truman was apparently disturbed by the tenor of the letter but also concerned that Wallace might resign from the cabinet, which could hurt the Democrats in the upcoming congressional elections. He therefore wrote a perfunctory reply, hoping that Wallace would calm down.[4]

But Wallace was determined to try to change the direction of American policy by appealing to the larger public, and a speech in Madison Square Garden seemed the ideal place to do it.

The stage was literally set for a confrontation between the president and his secretary of commerce. On September 10, two days before the speech, Wallace went over his remarks page by page with Truman. But the president was not paying close attention and did not note that Wallace's draft contradicted the policy that Byrnes was following in his negotiations with the allies and the Russians in Paris. In one passage Wallace declared, "The tougher we get, the tougher the Russians will get. . . . We have no more business in the political affairs of Eastern Europe than Russia has in the political affairs of Latin America, Western Europe, and the United States."

What was even more striking were the words Wallace had added to his speech after his meeting with the president: "And just two days ago, when President Truman read these words, he said they represented the policy of his Administration."[5]

At Truman's press conference on October 12, the same day that Wallace gave the speech, the president was asked if he had approved "the whole speech." Truman replied that he had. Then he was asked, "Do you regard Wallace's speech a departure from Byrnes's policy?"

"No," said Truman, "I do not."

When Truman read the newspapers the next morning, he realized he had made a "grave blunder." When he tried to explain away his error by asserting that he had approved only "the right of the Secretary of Commerce to deliver the speech," *Time* magazine rightly branded his explanation "a clumsy lie."[6]

Meanwhile, in Paris Byrnes was threatening to resign in protest, until Truman reassured him that Wallace would never again be allowed to speak out on U.S. foreign policy. Then, in one of his characteristic outbursts, Truman sent an angry letter to Wallace, demanding his resignation. He later realized how foolish he had been and asked Clifford to retrieve the letter from Wallace, who was gracious enough to send it back without making its contents public. He resigned without rancor.

Nonetheless, the incident did not help Truman in the congressional elections, and the Wallace affair doubtless helped to swing the country over to the Republicans.[7]

It was probably fortunate for Acheson that he was absent during the Wallace imbroglio, vacationing in the Canadian Rockies with his wife and the American ambassador to Canada, Ray Atherton, and his spouse. They had ridden north through Jasper Park to the Arctic Circle and back, and when Acheson learned what had happened, he was concerned not only by the tenor of Wallace's speech and the naive behavior of the president, but also by the further deterioration of relations between the president and Acheson's chief, Secretary Byrnes.

Acheson was already aware of Truman's plan to have General Marshall replace Byrnes upon Marshall's return from China, where the general was trying in vain to resolve the civil war between the Chinese Communists under Mao Zedong and the Nationalists led by Chiang Kai-shek. Acheson had come across an obscure passage in one of Marshall's cables from China, and when he asked Truman whether he wanted it clarified, Truman told him of Byrnes's April letter of resignation—about which Acheson already knew—but added that he had explained the situation to General Dwight D. Eisenhower, who was about to leave on a tour of inspection in East Asia and the Pacific, and asked Eisenhower to see if Marshall was willing to serve as secretary of state.

Marshall, out of a sense of duty, agreed to do so, but Truman had not told Byrnes as yet. Unless knowledge of this was restricted to the four of them, Truman explained to Acheson, the usefulness of both Byrnes and Marshall would be destroyed.[8]

Once again, Acheson's own plans to retire were derailed. But George Marshall's appointment as secretary of state turned out to be, in Acheson's words, "an act of God."[9] Marshall took his oath of office on January 21, 1947, and later that day walked with Acheson across the street from the White House to Acheson's office, adjoining General Marshall's new one in the old, colonnaded State Department building.

"Will you stay?" he asked Acheson.

"Certainly," Acheson answered, "as long as you need me, though before too long I ought to get back to my profession if I'm to have one."

"Would six months be too long?"

It would not. Acheson agreed to stay on until the end of June.

Marshall's views as to how to organize the State Department were, not surprisingly, influenced by his military career. He expected Acheson as his under secretary to be his chief of staff and to run things. Everything would come to the secretary through the under secretary unless Acheson chose to decide the matter himself; in turn, everything would flow from the secretary to the department through the under secretary. It was a system that was almost too rigid to work exactly as Marshall described it, but it was far better than the confusion under Hull and the secrecy under Byrnes. Acheson was enormously relieved. Marshall's design also accorded the under secretary enormous power.

At the end of their interview, Marshall declared that he would expect from Acheson nothing less than "the most complete frankness, particularly about myself." He had no feelings, he explained, "except those I reserve for Mrs. Marshall."

There was one other thing: Acheson needed a decision from Marshall on whether the State Department should move into new quarters, as the old building was becoming hopelessly crowded. Marshall asked him what were the arguments against moving.

"Tradition," Acheson replied.

"Move!" said the general.[10]

George Marshall's reserve, which bordered on aloofness, was legendary. The son of a stiff martinet of a father and a warm, affectionate mother, as a boy he had been shy, sensitive, rather gawky. His parents had come from Kentucky but had moved to Uniontown, Pennsylvania, by the time George Jr. was born in 1880. He grew up with some of the courtliness of a southern background and a sense of belonging to history; one of his ancestors was the great chief justice of the Supreme Court, John Marshall. As his biographer points out, though born a Pennsylvanian, he became in his maturity, by schooling, residence, and taste, "a species of Virginian."[11]

Young George Marshall was a poor student, disliked studying, and until the age of nine or ten was badly educated in a genteel private school. By the time he entered public school, he was woefully behind the other students. Hating to be laughed at, he retreated behind a wall of shyness and reserve; he recalled later in life that people "made fun of me a great deal." There was, however, one subject he was devoted to, both in and out of school—history. "If it was history," he said, "that was all right; I could star in history."[12]

Neither of his parents endorsed his notion of making the army a career. But the Virginia Military Institute, which his elder brother had attended, admitted him on the basis of an examination given personally by the superintendent.

Entering VMI in 1897, Marshall found that living conditions were grim: "Rats" (new cadets) were expected to sleep with the windows open wide throughout the year. Hazing was merciless. At one point, after he had been there only a few weeks and when he was still tired from a bout of typhoid fever, Marshall was

1

At twenty-five, faced with the draft, Dean Acheson was commissioned in 1918 as an ensign in the naval reserve.

2

3

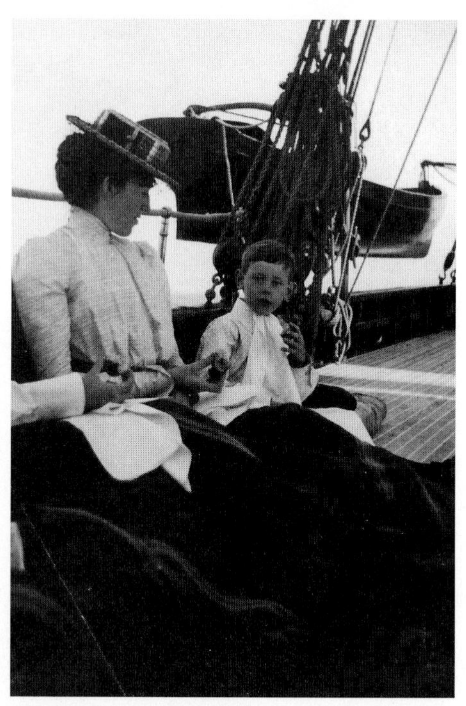

4

Dean's father, Edward Campion Acheson, at the time of the Northwest Rebellion of 1883–85 in Canada (top left). Dean at about seven years old, preparing to fight the Battle of Antietam (bottom left). Dean and his mother, Eleanor Gooderham Acheson, en route to Europe, circa 1902 (above).

5

6

Dean and his mother at Atlantic City, circa 1905 (top left). A senior at Groton, 1910 (top right). The Groton crew, Acheson third from left (bottom).

7

8

9

10

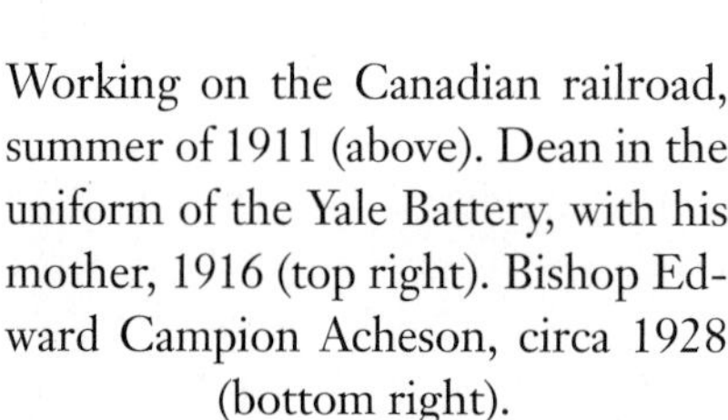

Working on the Canadian railroad, summer of 1911 (above). Dean in the uniform of the Yale Battery, with his mother, 1916 (top right). Bishop Edward Campion Acheson, circa 1928 (bottom right).

11

Dean and Alice Acheson in the 1930s (top). Alice Stanley Acheson at the time of her marriage (bottom).

12

 13

The strenuous life: left to right, Mary, Dean, David, and Jane, circa 1930 (top). The Acheson house in Georgetown (bottom).

 14

Supreme Court justice Felix Frankfurter and Dean Acheson on their habitual morning walk from Acheson's house in Georgetown to the State Department.

 16

The Achesons on the Mediterranean, sailing to a 1951 foreign ministers meeting (top). Vacationing with Ray Atherton, the U.S. ambassador to Canada, in Jasper Park, Canada, summer 1947 (bottom).

 17

18

19

Acheson confers with Senators Arthur Vandenberg and Tom Connally before his confirmation hearing, January 1949 (top). The Achesons with Winston Churchill, 1952 (left). Sworn in as secretary of state, flanked by Harry Truman and Chief Justice Fred Vinson (bottom).

20

21

Meeting in London in 1950 with British foreign secretary Ernest Bevin, center, and French foreign minister Robert Schuman (top). West German chancellor Konrad Adenauer established a warm friendship with Acheson (bottom).

22

23

During the darkest days of the Korean War, Truman greets Acheson and defense secretary George C. Marshall, December 26, 1950 (top). In 1949 in Paris, Schuman, Bevin, and Acheson confronted Soviet foreign minister Andrei Vishinsky over the question of German unification (bottom).

24

25

Acheson called Truman his "constituency of one" (top). Caught by surprise in an elevator in 1951 with Senator Joseph McCarthy, who had attacked Acheson as being soft on Communism (bottom).

26

27

Advising president-elect Kennedy soon after the 1960 election (top). With LBJ during the Vietnam War, 1965 (bottom).

28

Dean and Alice Acheson strolling outside their Maryland farmhouse, Harewood (top). Acheson's study at Harewood, where he died in 1971 (bottom).

30

31

© *Jill Krementz—courtesy of the photographer*

Acheson in his "white garden" in the late 1960s (top). In his beloved woodworking shop at Harewood (bottom).

32

Painting by Gardner Cox, National Portrait Gallery, Washington D.C.

forced to squat over a naked bayonet to test his endurance. He slipped; the bayonet ripped his buttock, and he had to miss drill for several days. Yet Marshall was typically stoic: "It was part of the business," he said later, "and the only thing to do was to accept it as best you could."

The instruction was poor, and Marshall remained a mediocre student. He particularly regretted the absence of courses in history and politics. But he learned "self-control, discipline, so that it was ground in. I learned also the problem of managing men." He was finally named first captain in his senior year, the highest rank in the cadet corps. Cool and austere, he now enjoyed the habit of command.[13]

Commissioned a second lieutenant at the turn of the century, Marshall was sent like several junior officers to the newly acquired Philippines. During the First World War he did outstanding work in drawing up plans for the Meuse-Argonne offensive; he made decisions easily and soon showed himself to be a first-rate administrator. By the end of the war he had come to the attention of General John J. Pershing, who appointed him aide-de-camp and called him "a man who understands the military."

After the war he worked in Washington with Pershing but worried that his career would be stymied if he did not command troops. In 1938, however, Roosevelt needed a new chief of staff, one who could build up the army quickly and therefore had a gift of administration as well as the knowledge of how to train young men as soldiers. On the advice of General Pershing, FDR reached past twenty major generals and fourteen senior brigadier generals and chose Brigadier General George Catlett Marshall.

FDR came to consider him too valuable to use in a single theater of war, so Marshall had to stay in Washington as General Dwight D. Eisenhower took command of the liberation of Europe. Marshall was doubtless crushed but characteristically displayed no sign of temper or bitter disappointment. As he once said to his wife, "I cannot allow myself to get angry. That would be fatal; it is too exhausting. My brain must be kept clear."[14]

Acheson, like many others, felt the power of Marshall's presence as soon as he entered a room. As he described it, General Marshall (and he was always called by that name, never by his first name, by both the president and members of the cabinet) "conveyed intensity, which his voice low, staccato, and incisive, reinforced. It compelled respect. It spread a sense of authority and calm."[15] Harry Truman shared Acheson's admiration. Never, the president wrote, did General Marshall think about himself.

Following General Marshall's instructions, Acheson and his staff were preparing to move out of the old State, War, and Navy building—which both War and Navy had long abandoned for the new Pentagon—to less elegant but more modern quarters farther from the White House. Over the winter, files were being packed for transport to the new building in Foggy Bottom, which had, as James Reston wrote in *The New York Times*, "about as much character as a chewing gum factory in Los Angeles."[16]

It was on a gray Friday afternoon, February 21, 1947, while Acheson was presiding over the packing and hauling, that he received a message from the British ambassador, Lord Inverchapel, asking for an immediate appointment with the secretary of state. The ambassador was to deliver personally to General Marshall a "blue piece of paper," diplomatic language for a formal and important message. (In fact, there were two notes: one on Greece, the other on Turkey.)

But Marshall had already left Washington to deliver a speech at Princeton University's two hundredth anniversary. As a five-star general, he had a plane waiting at all times, and after the speech he was to fly to North Carolina, where Mrs. Marshall was living all winter because of a sinus condition. Marshall would not be returning until Monday morning, and Acheson had no intention of calling him back before then.

Nonetheless, since the matter was urgent, Acheson devised a way to circumvent the ambassador's instructions. Inverchapel could have a carbon copy delivered to the State Department, then formally hand over to General Marshall the original on Monday morning and discuss the contents with him. In the meantime, staff work could begin.[17]

When Acheson read the note, he was truly shocked. British aid to Greece and Turkey was to end in six weeks. Although the note referred to previous conversations in which both governments had agreed that Greece and Turkey should not be allowed to fall under Soviet control, the British could no longer continue underwriting the Greek economy and supplying the government with military assistance and training against a growing Communist insurrection supported by the Soviet Union. Turkey, which for two years now had been resisting Soviet demands for a share in the control of the Straits, also needed aid to procure modern weapons for its armed forces and a program of economic development.

In total, Greece needed between $240 million and $280 million in foreign exchange in 1947 and additional monies for several years. The Turkish needs were to be determined.

Acheson immediately instructed the Near Eastern and European Divisions to get together that evening and work over the weekend to prepare relevant reports on the facts as seen by U.S. representatives on the scene; the American funds and personnel available as well as those needed; and the significance of Greece and Turkey to the West. He then telephoned the president and General Marshall to tell them what had happened and what he had done and to learn what orders they had. They had none.

By Sunday the working groups had finished their studies, and the reports were brought to Acheson's house at P Street for final review. They seemed to Acheson to be in good shape. The chief of the Near Eastern Division, Loy Henderson, then asked him whether they were working on papers in order to make a decision or to execute one. The latter, Acheson replied. Under the circumstances, he asserted, there could be only one decision. At that, "we drank a martini or two toward the confusion of our enemies."[18]

When the British liberated Greece in the fall of 1944, the country was riven by social and political tensions. The spectrum of Greek internal politics ranged from the extreme left to the extreme right, and the country could easily have become a dictatorship. Moreover, the largest and best organized of the resistance forces was led by the leftist National Liberation Front (EAM) and its military arm, the National Popular Liberation Army (ELAS)—both of which contained many Communists. During the fall of 1944 the front acted in a moderate fashion and joined the Government of National Unity. The Greek Communist Party, however, had not decided on a course of action. Should it try to seize power or participate in the political process?

Stalin was reluctant to urge the Greek Communists to try to seize power with no holds barred. His long-term goal may have been to eliminate the British from the eastern Mediterranean and the Near East, but he was wary of urging the Greek Communists to confront the British forces head-on. In 1944 he had given Churchill to understand that Greece would remain within a British sphere of influence, whereas Romania and Bulgaria would necessarily fall within the Soviet orbit, unchallenged in this respect by Great Britain and, as he expected, the United States. Moreover, control of Greece was not essential to the Soviet Union's need for security, as both Bulgaria and Romania were.

Under the circumstances prevailing at the end of the war, Stalin therefore preferred a "gradualist policy" for the Greek Communist Party, one that might serve to establish a strong Communist political presence within a weak Greek government. This would create a "soft" state that would surely frustrate any anti-Soviet moves.[19]

In anticipation of the country's final liberation, the British in the meantime reestablished a predominantly anti-Communist government, and by December 1944 the Greek prime minister ordered the leftist resistance forces disarmed. In response, the leftist ministers resigned from the government and the Communists organized a mass demonstration in the center of Athens. Panicky police fired on the mob, causing many deaths, and fighting broke out in and around the city. After more than a month of desperate street fighting, British reinforcements from Italy drove the leftist ELAS forces out of the capital and won the battle of Athens.[20]

In mid-February 1945 a general peace agreement was signed. It provided for the disarming of ELAS, the restoration of civil authority, a plebiscite on the king's return, and national elections for a parliament. In the aftermath of this agreement, however, the entire leftist coalition of the occupation years became targeted for destruction by the forces of the right. The British, fearing any resurgence of the left, allowed the army and the police to institute a "white terror," which virtually eliminated even moderate leftists from political life. By 1946 the National Liberation Front as a cohesive force had ceased to exist; the Stalinist Greek Communist Party took over what was left of it.[21]

The country's drift toward polarization and violence now reached new heights. The Communists stood alone, their followers harassed and imprisoned. But then they and their leftist allies made a strategic error. They boycotted the parliamentary elections of March 1946, which consequently produced a clear-cut victory for the conservative and royalist coalition. Six months later, a plebiscite, from which many of these same leftist forces abstained, returned King George to his throne.

With the right fully mobilized against the Communists and their allies, the remnants of ELAS took to the hills to launch a new round of guerrilla attacks. After 1946 the Greek Communists were now determined to lead an armed revolution to victory.[22]

Encouraged by the militancy of the Yugoslav Communists, Nikos Zahariadis, the key Communist leader, gave orders for the final offensive. Once the Greek Communists abandoned the cautious strategy Stalin preferred, they necessarily looked to the Yugoslavs for support. The Soviets therefore remained temporarily on the sidelines, refusing to give Zahariadis the full material aid he was asking for.[23]

By early 1947, at the very moment that the British informed Washington that London could no longer sustain the Greek government, Zahariadis declared in a message to Stalin that "the armed struggle has become dominant."[24] By the time of his meeting with Stalin that May, Zahariadis had put the Soviet leader in a dangerous position: there was no longer any point in discussing preventing a civil war. Stalin, unwilling to hand Greek Communist policy over to Tito's Yugoslavs, reportedly offered to provide the assistance he had previously refused.

The aid would not be adequate for the task, however, and it came slowly. In the meantime, the United States was preparing to intervene, which meant that in the larger game that Stalin and Tito were playing for influence and control over the rest of the Balkans, Stalin would be able to mount a powerful argument against Tito's aggressive policies.[25]

On Monday morning, February 24, when General Marshall returned to Washington from North Carolina, Acheson handed him the recommendations for aid to Greece and Turkey, telling him that the papers contained "the most major decision with which we have been faced since the War."[26]

Marshall, who had read the British "blue paper" earlier that morning as well as other relevant memoranda, said that Acheson himself would be principally responsible for carrying through on American policy and plans. He was leaving in a week for another foreign ministers' meeting in Moscow.

Later that morning the journalist Louis Fischer came by the State Department and noticed that Acheson was in a highly agitated mood. As the two men left for lunch at the Metropolitan Club, Acheson closed the window behind the driver and said to Fischer: "The British are pulling out everywhere, and if we don't go in, the Russians will."

At lunch he told the journalist, "There are only two powers left. The British are finished. They are through. And the trouble is that this hits us too soon before we are ready for it. We are having a lot of trouble getting money out of Congress." He threw up his hands. "If the Near East and France go communist, I fear very much for this country and for the world."[27]

But persuading Congress to vote the funds to shore up Greece and Turkey was a formidable task. The new Republican Congress had convened on January 3, 1947. In his opening address to the House of Representatives, Speaker Joseph Martin of Massachusetts had demonstrated how difficult this would be. Although he hailed from one of the poorest districts of the Commonwealth, the Speaker was hostile to the New Deal and determined to push through an across-the-board 20 percent reduction in income taxes and a similar reduction in spending to make this possible.

On February 20 the House voted a $6 billion cut in the president's budget; this included a reduction of 50 percent in the $1 billion requested by the War Department to prevent starvation, disease, and unrest in occupied Germany and Japan. Secretary of War Robert Patterson commented that this would leave the army too weak to carry out its duties and "might compel abandonment of the occupation of Germany and Japan."[28]

Truman scheduled a conference over Greece and Turkey with congressional leaders on Thursday, February 27, a meeting that Acheson viewed with foreboding: "I knew we were met at Armageddon."[29] The day before, the secretaries of war and navy endorsed Acheson's recommendations that the Greek-Turkish crisis needed the fastest possible action. Other countries—specifically South Korea and China—might also need assistance, but these situations required further study. In any case, it would be an error to suggest to a reluctant Congress at this stage that more aid would be needed elsewhere.

Present for the meeting with Truman, Marshall, and Acheson were Senator

Vandenberg, now chairman of the Senate Foreign Relations Committee; Speaker Martin; Democratic House minority leader Sam Rayburn; Senator Tom Connally, ranking Democrat on the Senate Foreign Relations Committee; and Republican senator Styles Bridges, chairman of the Senate Appropriations Committee. (The only congressional potentate who was absent—an accidental omission—was the anti-internationalist senator Robert Taft.)

General Marshall led off the discussion, but his rather summary and even cryptic presentation fell flat. He seemed to imply that the United States should provide aid to Greece for humanitarian reasons, and to Turkey to bolster Great Britain's position in the Middle East. The reactions of the congressional leaders centered on three questions: "Isn't this pulling British chestnuts out of the fire?" "What are we letting ourselves in for?" and "How much is this going to cost?" [30]

Things were going badly. In desperation, Acheson whispered to Secretary Marshall, who was sitting beside him, "Is this a private fight or can anyone get into it?" Marshall asked the president to let Mr. Acheson have the floor.

For Acheson, as he recalled later, "this was my crisis. For a week I had nurtured it. These congressmen had no conception of what challenged them; it was my task to bring it home." In the past eighteen months, he said, Soviet pressure on the Dardanelles, on Iran, and on northern Greece had brought the Balkans to the point where a Soviet breakthrough might open three continents to Soviet penetration. He went on to suggest that if Greece fell, "like apples in a barrel infected by one rotten one, the corruption of Greece would infect Iran and all to the east. It would also carry infection to Africa through Asia Minor and Egypt, and to Europe through Italy and France, already threatened by the strongest domestic Communist parties."[31]

Not since Rome and Carthage had the world been so polarized between two great powers, he continued. Therefore it was not a matter of bailing out Britain and responding to Greece and Turkey on humanitarian grounds, but rather a strengthening of free peoples against Communist aggression. America had no choice, he concluded. It had to protect its own security—it had to protect freedom itself.[32]

A deep silence followed Acheson's passionate call to arms. Then Senator Vandenberg said gravely, "Mr. President, if you will say that to the Congress and the country, I will support you and I believe that most of its members will do the same." Loy Henderson recalled that Vandenberg may have put the message even more bluntly: "Mr. President, the only way you are ever going to get this is to make a speech and scare the hell out of the country."[33]

That was precisely what Truman was prepared to do.

Action followed, along with preparations for Truman to address a joint session of Congress. Although General Marshall would be in Moscow, he told Acheson to go forward "without regard to him and his meeting." The State Department began drafting legislation for a program of economic, military, and technical aid to Greece and Turkey and to set up with the War Department the military training and advisory teams. In the meantime, Acheson urged the British to give a little more time for the Americans to formulate their program. Washington was moving with incredible speed for "so vast a country to assume a novel burden far from our shores."[34]

Acheson was also in charge of drafting Truman's speech, which, of course, would have to be cleared with General Marshall in Moscow. (Much of the language originated with Joseph Jones in the Office of Public Affairs.) Acheson set out the main lines of argument, then sent the third draft to General Marshall en route to Moscow, who cabled his approval. The text was then sent to Clark Clifford at the White House.

George Kennan, too, was shown the message. He was horrified. The highly ideological tone portrayed two opposing ways of life, and the open-ended commitment to aid free peoples, he believed, might lead the Russians to reply by declaring war. He even hurriedly drafted his own version, a more nuanced effort that focused primarily on the problems of Greece and Turkey. Acheson rejected it.[35]

When another State Department official asked Acheson if he believed the United States should bail out every imperiled democracy, Acheson reflected: "If FDR were alive today, I think I know what he'd do. He would make a statement of global policy but confine his request for money right now to Greece and Turkey."[36]

At a cabinet meeting on March 7, Truman approved a request for $250 million for Greece and $150 million for Turkey. By that time he had also doubtless read a memorandum from Will Clayton, urging that a European recovery fund of $5 billion would be needed in the first year alone. Truman was therefore almost surely aware that the funds he said should be appropriated were only the beginning.[37]

On Monday, March 10, Truman convened another meeting of congressional leaders, which this time included Senator Taft. At this far less dramatic meeting, Vandenberg urged the president to lay out the crisis before a joint session of Congress. Two days later the cabinet went in a body to the chamber of the House of Representatives to listen to Harry Truman deliver his message.

It was a warm spring day in Washington as the president mounted the rostrum of the House to speak. The gallery seats had long been taken, and distinguished visitors were now being crowded together on the steps. The diplomatic gallery was also filled to capacity. Three minutes before one P.M., the doorkeeper announced the cabinet of the president of the United States. Then, as Harry Truman entered, all in the chamber rose and applauded. After he mounted to the clerk's desk below the Speaker's rostrum, the president opened his black folder and began to read.

Truman spoke in a flat, high-pitched, but forceful voice. After laying out the physical, financial, and economic conditions of war-torn Greece, the threat to the Greek state posed by the activities of the Communist forces, the appeal of the Athens government to the United States, the financial weakness of Britain, the inability of the United Nations to respond quickly, and the need to sustain an independent and economically viable Turkey, the president proclaimed what would come to be known as the Truman Doctrine: "I believe that it must be the policy of the United States to support free peoples who are resisting attempted subjugation by armed minorities or by outside pressures."[38]

Those present stood, as was customary, when Truman finished his speech and remained standing while the president and his cabinet strode from the chamber. The applause was polite, however, and the president was solemn as he acknowledged it, except for a brief smile to Mrs. Truman in the west gallery.

By using universalistic rhetoric to attain more modest ends, Acheson and Truman laid the groundwork for the belief, which would become ever more widely shared by government officials as well as the larger public, that the United States saw little alternative but to embark on the global containment of communism. Acheson had made the arguments, as he later put it, "clearer than truth." Yet he was well aware that the economic and military means to undertake a broader crusade were neither available nor needed.[39]

Despite the messianic language of Truman's speech, which Acheson himself had evoked in his "rotten apples" imagery, Acheson had a more pragmatic and temperate worldview. When he appeared before the Senate Foreign Relations Committee in the last week of March, he began his testimony by asserting that aid to Greece and Turkey did not establish a pattern for future American assistance elsewhere. This was not, Acheson declared, "an ideological crusade."[40]

Again and again Acheson denied that he advocated giving military and economic aid to countries elsewhere that were under the threat of a Communist takeover. In Hungary, for instance, the administration was not doing the same thing, because the circumstances, particularly for effective action, were wholly different. When Congressman Walter Judd, a China specialist, said that he couldn't understand the Truman Doctrine because the U.S. position toward China was the opposite from its position toward Greece, Acheson pointed out that Washington was giving substantial aid to the Chinese Nationalist government. He also argued that the threat of a Chinese Communist takeover was not imminent.[41]

Finally, to get Acheson off the hook, Senator Tom Connally summed up the administration's position: "This is not a pattern out of a tailor's shop to fit everybody in the world and every nation in the world."[42]

With evident relief, Acheson heartily agreed. Yet these distinctions between vital and secondary interests were never forcefully made to the broad American public.

The congressmen and senators were not the only ones suspicious of an expanded American global role. In his columns Walter Lippmann, while perfectly willing to support American aid to Greece and Turkey, was critical of language that implied indiscriminate intervention in support of far-flung and unstable regimes.

One April evening at a Washington dinner party, Acheson made an impassioned defense of the Truman Doctrine. Carried away by his anger and force of conviction, he accused Lippmann of "sabotaging" American foreign policy. Lippmann hit back. As Ronald Steel, Lippmann's biographer, described it, "Words flew, fingers were jabbed into chests, faces grew red." Finally the match ended in a draw, and the two distinguished adversaries stalked off in opposite directions. Lippmann later described it as a "very unpleasant evening." The next morning he woke up with such a bad nicotine hangover that he gave up smoking. Acheson called to apologize for losing his temper.[43]

America's decision to intervene, and the threat that this posed to the neighboring Communist regimes, paradoxically restored Stalin's dominance in the region and intensified his growing rift with Tito. On February 10, 1948, in his office in the Kremlin, Stalin met with the top-ranking Bulgarian and Yugoslav Communists (though not with Tito, who prudently declined the invitation to travel to Moscow). After haranguing the Yugoslavs and Bulgarians over their differences with the Soviet Union, he suddenly turned to the Greek civil war. "What do you think," he demanded, "that Great Britain and the United States—the United States, the most powerful state in the world—will permit you to break their line of communication in the Mediterranean Sea! Nonsense. And we have no navy. The uprising in Greece must be stopped and as quickly as possible."[44]

By June 1948, fearful that Tito was trying to establish the Balkan federation under his own aegis, Stalin felt strong enough to excommunicate Yugoslavia from the Communist bloc. Moreover, the Greek Communist leader Zahariadis took Stalin's side against the "heretic" Tito; this was enough to cause the Yugoslavs to halt their assistance to the Greek Communist forces, and a year later the Greek Communist uprising tailed to an end. Had Stalin initially chosen to work through the Yugoslavs, had the United States failed to act swiftly and with determination, the outcome of the war might well have been very different.[45]

CHAPTER SEVENTEEN

REVEILLE IN MISSISSIPPI

WHILE GENERAL MARSHALL continued his negotiations in Moscow over peace treaties for Germany and Austria, with no progress, and hearings in the House and Senate were being held on the implications of the Truman Doctrine, the president approached Acheson one Monday in early April 1947 to ask a favor.

Many months before, Truman had agreed to go to Cleveland, Mississippi, to speak at the annual meeting of the Delta Council on May 8. His friends, Mr. and Mrs. William T. Wynne, would be bitterly disappointed if Truman himself did not attend, but the president was wary of making such an appearance at a time when a bitter fight had broken out within the Mississippi Democratic Party over the successor to Senator Theodore Bilbo, who was on his last legs. Truman asked Acheson to speak for him.[1]

Truman and Acheson decided quickly that the subject of the speech should be "the disintegration of Europe." Reports from General Marshall in Moscow and from Under Secretary for Economic Affairs Will Clayton in Europe—and work Acheson himself had begun with the State, War and Navy Coordinating Committee—were making it apparent that the prospects for European economic recovery were worsening. Yet by the end of the fiscal year the United States would have no funds available for Europe except for Greece and Turkey.

Acheson was determined to shock the country—as well as the government bureaucracy and the Congress—into facing the growing crisis. "Did the President agree to this being done?" he recalled later. "To my doing it? I was an eager volunteer and the time was short. If the Delta Council wanted an 'important foreign policy' speech, here was one." The president's reply to both questions was yes.[2]

* * *

On May 7 Acheson and Francis Russell, chief of the State Department Public Affairs Office, boarded a DC-3, assigned by the air force to the secretary of state, to fly to Cleveland, Mississippi, where he would deliver what he labeled a call to "reveille."[3]

Arriving in the late afternoon, Acheson and his aide were met at the airport by the Wynnes. The next morning they were to leave for Cleveland, which was located in one of the most lush and prosperous agricultural regions in the South. Driving through it, Acheson could see dairy cattle "standing knee-deep in rich pastures and new strains of beef cattle adapted to hot weather; fields set aside for new crops to provide an escape from one-crop cotton culture; picturesque but ramshackle shanties giving way to neat, well-fenced farms and painted houses."[4]

The Delta Council itself was an organization of farmers and small businessmen living in the Mississippi Valley. Because cotton was a world crop, they were traditionally internationalists. Once a year, from seven to ten thousand members of the council, their wives, sisters, cousins, and children, congregated for a day of speeches, picnics, and get-togethers.[5]

On the tree-shaded lawn of the Teachers College, the council met, and those interested in the under secretary's speech crowded into the large gymnasium; a sizable overflow listened to him over loudspeakers installed outside. Acheson was happy to conform to the weather and the informality of the audience: he took off his coat, rolled up his shirtsleeves, and did not even read the text he had brought with him; instead he managed to deliver it almost word for word from notes he had made on the plane down.[6]

Acheson was determined to make his words count. Before leaving Washington, he had had lunch with three British newsmen, Leonard Miall of the British Broadcasting Company, Malcolm Muggeridge of the *Daily Telegraph*, and René MacColl of the *Daily Express*. Off the record, he explained to them what he was about to do, why he was doing it, and that he spoke with the president's authority. Although he had told Truman, "I am going to throw up a ball and it's going to have to come down somewhere," he was also well aware that the American press would be largely uninterested in an under secretary's remarks; a far greater impact would be possible if the speech was reinforced by a returning wave of comment from abroad.[7]

At the start of the speech, Acheson described what he called "some of the basic facts of life" in "the conduct of foreign relations." The first was the extreme physical destruction of Europe, on the "borderline of starvation" and "long-established business and trading connections disrupted." The second was that both Germany and Japan, upon whose production Europe and Asia were so dependent before the war, had not even begun the process of reconstruction because no peace settlement had been concluded with them. The third factor was the "unforeseen disasters" of the recent winter's storms and floods and excessive cold. There was little gold or foreign exchange to buy the necessities of life.

Although the United States had already provided loans and humanitarian aid, this was simply not enough. An $8 billion European deficit was likely to result from what America would buy from Europe and Europe from America. For this reason, the United States would have to undertake "further emergency funding."

The connections between Europe's livelihood and America's were clear: unless Europe's acute dollar shortage was overcome, Europe would not be able to finance its imports from the United States.

"There is no charity involved in this," he explained to his audience of farmers and businessmen. "We are today obliged from considerations of self-interest and humanitarianism to finance a huge deficit in the world's budget." Not only do "human beings and nations exist in narrow economic margins, but also human dignity, human freedom, and democratic institutions." It was America's role to widen these margins both for "our national security" and as "our duty and our privilege as human beings."[8]

His eloquence and force of conviction convinced him that his "trumpet did not give an uncertain sound."[9] But he was also right in believing that the speech would get far more coverage in Europe than in America; even there editors were unsure whether Acheson spoke with any authority or solely for himself. James Reston of *The New York Times* decided to find out. He asked Acheson at a press conference after the speech, "Is this a new policy that you are enunciating or is it just a bit of private kite-flying?"

"You know this town better than I do," Acheson replied disingenuously. "Foreign policy is made in the White House—you must ask the President."

This is precisely what Reston did at Truman's next press conference: Did Acheson's speech represent administration policy?

"Yes," said Truman, it did.[10]

Acheson had long been convinced that Britain would need further financial help. The $3.75 billion British loan of December 6, 1945, for which he had keenly lobbied Congress in 1946, had been woefully inadequate; the Americans had "vastly underestimated the extent of British and European economic and financial exhaustion."[11] Yet that loan had been difficult to get through Congress. Republican senator Robert Taft of Ohio saw the loan as a precursor to other loans that America could ill afford. It was only by invoking fears of Russia that the loan was finally approved and legislation authorizing it signed on July 15, 1946.

Acheson, however, had not shared in the general air of satisfaction. The use of anti-Sovietism at that time to sell the loan had disturbed him. The arguments he made in his testimony before the relevant Senate committee therefore stressed the virtues of free enterprise. "We believe passionately that only by continuing a system of free enterprise and having other nations in the same state [can we] continue the same sort of world in which the United States has lived in the past."[12] He was convinced that a multilateral free-trading system, though it would certainly favor the United States, would help create conditions that would lead to general peace and prosperity.

But in the spring of 1946 the Congress was less persuaded by Acheson's views than by the appeal to anticommunism. When the Senate hearings ended in April, the loan's chance of passage was still dim. Finally, Arthur Vandenberg announced on the floor of the Senate that he supported the loan. He warned his fellow senators: "If we do not lead, some other great and powerful nation will capitalize on our failure and we shall pay the price of our default."[13] The allusion to the Soviet Union was clear, and it proved to be the turning point in the Senate debate. The House was even more anti-Soviet in its hearings.

In the end, Acheson had accepted the need to offend the Soviet Union if that was the price to be paid for passage of the loan. He may have also seen more clearly for the first time that a broad appeal to anti-Sovietism was the surest way to secure legislation he deemed vital to American interests.[14]

Moreover, Acheson had opposed the one-year deadline for the free convertibility of sterling into dollars, because he thought Britain's recovery was too doubtful to warrant setting a deadline. Sadly, he proved to be right. Within months of sterling's finally becoming convertible at the end of 1946, the run on the British Treasury to convert pounds into dollars was so great that the effect of the loan was ruined and Britain was virtually bankrupted overnight. It was this emergency, as much as anything else, that prompted the creation of the Marshall Plan.[15]

Even before the Delta speech, and well before the president had offered his version of the Truman Doctrine, Acheson had begun work on studies that led to the Marshall Plan. In early March 1947 Acheson wrote to Secretary of War Robert Patterson and Secretary of the Navy Forrestal to explain that the Greek and Turkish crisis was only part of a much larger problem growing out of the now evident weakness of Great Britain on the world scene.

For this reason, he asked Assistant Secretary of State John Hilldring, as chairman of the State-War-Navy Committee, to consult with the Treasury Department and be ready to propose a much larger program for Europe as soon as they knew the facts.

Their assignment was not only to determine what countries in Europe and elsewhere might need aid, but also to ask: To what extent was each country threatened by internal or external pressures? Would American aid be effective?

and, above all, What were the national security interests of the United States in making any decision to grant or withhold aid?[16]

Acheson was careful not to suggest what other countries the committee should be looking at. As he put it in a later interview, "If you begin mentioning places, they are going to be on your doorstep—'Thank you very much. I'll take it in 20's.'"[17]

On the very day Acheson was writing to Patterson and Forrestal, Will Clayton, ill and on a plane to a favorite ranch in Tucson, Arizona, wrote a short memorandum on the subject of European recovery. "The reins of world leadership," he wrote, "are fast slipping from Britain's competent but now very weak hands. These reins will be picked up either by the United States or by Russia."

Clayton believed that only through American leadership could war be prevented in the next decade. Convinced that other European countries were threatened with economic and political collapse, he urged the president to ask Congress for an emergency fund of $5 billion. The security of the United States, he believed, was intimately bound up with the security of Europe.[18]

In Moscow during the weeks following the March 12 enunciation of the Truman Doctrine, Marshall had become increasingly discouraged by his talks with the Russians. Acheson, reading his reports, came to the view that little could be accomplished in traditional diplomatic negotiations with the Soviets. "I think it is a mistake to believe that you can, at any time, sit down with the Russians and solve questions," he declared in an executive session of the Senate Foreign Relations Committee on April 1, 1947. "I do not think that is the way that our problems are going to be worked out with the Russians. I think they will have to be worked out over a long period of time and by always indicating to the Russians that we are quite aware of what our own interests are and that we are quite firm about them and quite prepared to take necessary action. Then I think solutions will become possible."[19]

At the Moscow conference of foreign ministers, which began on March 10 and lasted until April 24, the impasse in negotiations seemed to bear out Acheson's skepticism. Virtually no progress was made on peace treaties for Austria and Germany. The Russians continued to insist on a strong central government in Berlin and that $10 billion in reparations be in the form of goods out of current German production. The Americans and the British were opposed to a strong central government, which Marshall believed could be converted into a regime similar to the Third Reich and dominated by the Soviet Union; this could eventually lead to the resurrection of German military power.

Moreover, the United States had long insisted that reparations should come only after the Germans had recovered enough economically to subsist without outside aid. Marshall was well aware that Americans would never consent to be taxed at home to help Germany pay reparations to Russia. Now the point had come after the disastrous winter of 1946–47 when Germany, as the potential economic motor for Europe, had to be revived, or there might well be no European recovery at all.[20]

After his April 15 meeting with Stalin, Marshall felt justified in his growing suspicion that the Soviet leader was uninterested in reaching a settlement in Germany and hoped to promote the economic and political disintegration of Western Europe. As was customary in such meetings, it was at ten o'clock at night by the time Marshall's limousine drove through the gates of the Kremlin. Marshall was accompanied by Ambassador Walter Bedell Smith and Charles Bohlen, Stalin by Foreign Minister Vyacheslav Molotov.

The general found that Stalin did not look well; he seemed to have shrunk into his clothes. "You look just the same as when I saw you last time," said Stalin, "but I am just an old man."[21]

After this opening, the talks got down to business; they were frank but without rancor. Bohlen noticed that Stalin doodled by drawing wolf's heads with his red pencil as he talked.[22]

The Soviet ruler seemed sanguine over the lack of progress at the conference and did not find the impasse "so tragic." After all, "differences had occurred before on other questions, and as a rule after people had exhausted themselves in dispute they then recognized the necessity of compromise." He advised Marshall "to have patience and not become depressed."[23]

This was the wrong counsel for General Marshall, whose commitment to action was sorely tried by Stalin's tactics. He left Moscow convinced that "patience" would not lead to compromise and that Stalin's advice was actually an invitation to wait for European conditions to deteriorate so that the Soviet Union would be able to exert greater influence over the continent.

Stopping off in Berlin, Marshall told General Lucius Clay, the American commander in Germany, to proceed apace with the strengthening of the British and American occupation into a single economic unit, which had been formed at the end of 1946 into an entity called Bizonia. The French decided later that they would join their zone to those of other Western allies. The Russians, in turn, decided to set up their economic system in their own occupation zone.

Immediately upon his return to Washington, on April 28, the secretary of state reported to the American people in a nationwide radio address. There was no time to lose in working for the recovery of Europe, he warned: "The patient is sinking while the doctors deliberate."[24]

Marshall then called in George Kennan, who had recently been appointed to head the newly established Policy Planning Staff; he had been enthusiastically endorsed for this position by Acheson. The secretary told him to study the problem of Europe's need for American aid and make recommendations on what should be done. Asked by Kennan if there were any other instructions he wished to give him, Marshall said, "Avoid trivia."[25]

At the same time he decided to meet with Senator Vandenberg, who was disquieted over Acheson's Mississippi speech, and to bring along Acheson as well. They met on May 20 in the quiet seclusion of Blair House, on Pennsylvania Avenue across the street from the old State Department. Vandenberg started off by accusing Acheson of declaring publicly that the United States was prepared to spend vast amounts of money on foreign aid. There was no way he would let this administration get any more money from Congress this session. Furthermore, if there was to be an aid bill, Congress would have to be in on the planning.

Marshall let him sound off for a while and then calmed him by assuring him that he did not intend to ask Congress for any more money at this time. But sooner or later there would have to be a very large program of foreign aid. As the general spoke, Vandenberg cooled off, and the parting was cordial. But in his heart Acheson knew there would have to be a "Vandenberg brand" on the aid bill if it was to get through Congress.[26]

Kennan and his fledgling Policy Planning Staff had little time to prepare the report. Marshall had given them at best two weeks. Everyone worked day and night; discussions were intense; and Kennan recalled one occasion when, to recover his composure, he walked, "weeping," around the entire building.[27]

In Kennan's view, the Russians believed "that Europe is in reality theirs."[28] Like Marshall, he was sure that Moscow was just waiting to see if the Americans would do anything to alleviate the economic conditions on the continent before bringing "the west of Europe into the shadows which have already enveloped the east." To counter this strategy the United States not only had to materially aid in the recovery of Europe, but also to restore German productivity, which was "essential to that rehabilitation."

In his report to Marshall on May 23, Kennan urged a program of American aid that "should be directed not to the combatting of communism as such, but to the restoration of the economic health and vigor of the European society." Moreover, it was not the job of the United States to tell the Europeans what such a program should consist of. "This is the business of the Europeans," he wrote. They should get together and agree on a coordinated program of recovery. If the requests for aid came individually rather than jointly, the United States would be confronted with a series of competing appeals, which would only escalate the sums involved. Washington, of course, would decide how much it could afford to give.

Kennan and his colleagues did not believe the Russians would agree to take part in the European recovery plan. The Communists would doubtless portray the aid program as "a sinister effort to fasten American hegemony onto the people of Western Europe," as he put it later in a speech to the National War College.

Nonetheless, the Russians must be offered an opportunity to take part in the program. If they refused to do so—as was likely, because, as Kennan and Bohlen both believed, they would never accept "American verification of the use of goods and funds"—the onus of refusal would be on their shoulders.[29]

In presenting his report to General Marshall, Kennan advised him, as far as the Russians were concerned, to "play it straight." If they refused to "contribute constructively to the program as well as profiting from it," then "we would simply let them exclude themselves. But we would not ourselves draw a line of division through Europe."[30]

While Kennan's staff recommendations certainly helped to clarify Marshall's thinking, it was the return on May 19 of Will Clayton from a trip to Europe, where he had spent most of April and May negotiating lower tariffs, that probably galvanized General Marshall into taking final action. Over lunch on May 27 at the Metropolitan Club with Paul Nitze and other officials, Clayton spoke with great alarm about the collapse of the European economy.[31]

That afternoon Clayton went back to his office and pressed ahead with a memorandum to Marshall: "It is now obvious that we have grossly underestimated the destruction to the European economy by the war." Without further prompt and substantial aid, "economic, social and political disintegration will overwhelm Europe." A policy must therefore be designed "to save Europe from starvation and chaos (*not* the Russians)." While Clayton urged that a European plan should be worked out by the principal European nations, "*the United States must run this show.*"[32]

At a meeting of Clayton, Acheson, and Marshall the next day, both Clayton's memo and Kennan's paper were at hand. Clayton was also a passionate and persuasive advocate. There was no time to lose. General Marshall agreed wholeheartedly. It would be folly, he said, "to sit back and do nothing."[33]

That noon Acheson lunched with a dozen senators, who were anxious to be briefed on the administration's thinking. Acheson came away from the meeting convinced that further discussion with Congress was vital; otherwise, if the senators were confronted with a fait accompli, they would probably vote against the legislation. Impressed by the seriousness of the opposition, Acheson urged Marshall to begin discussions with the Congress and then give a public talk about the problems Europe was facing.[34]

* * *

The next day, May 29, Marshall summoned Acheson and suggested that the general himself might make a short speech about Europe at Harvard University, where he had been invited to receive an honorary degree on June 5. Acheson didn't think much of the idea on the grounds that commencement addresses rarely got any attention. "You know," he commented later, "it is reported by a fellow from the college paper who gets it all mixed up. To me this was really not the thing to do. But maybe Marshall was smarter than I was: let this come out gradually and take hold rather than have a big build-up."[35]

Marshall went ahead and asked Bohlen to draft a short, simple speech. Armed with the Kennan and Clayton memoranda and the text of Acheson's Mississippi speech, for two days Bohlen shut himself in his office and went to work. Above all, Bohlen wanted to make sure that American policy was directed "not against any country or doctrine," and specifically not against communism, but rather "against hunger, poverty, desperation, and chaos."[36]

Acheson in the meantime decided to garner some attention for the speech by planting a story with James Reston that the administration was considering a four-year, $16 billion program of aid to Europe. On the last Sunday in May, Reston's article appeared on page one of *The New York Times*, but the news was generally ignored.[37]

To make certain that the Europeans did not miss the significance of Marshall's speech, Acheson once again decided to meet with his three favorite British journalists, Leonard Miall, René MacColl, and Malcolm Muggeridge on June 4, the day before Marshall's address. Acheson did not provide them with a copy of the speech. In fact, the general had left for Cambridge with an incomplete text, and Acheson did not have a definitive version until a few hours before the speech was to be delivered.[38]

As Acheson tells it, he informed the journalists that Marshall was to deliver a speech of the greatest importance and he hoped that "they would not fool around with telegraphing the thing." Just get "on the telephone to London and read it, get it over at once. And one other thing, 'One of you have your editor send this to Ernie Bevin and say Dean Acheson wanted him to look at it.'"[39]

The next day Marshall stood on the steps of Memorial Church under a canopy of maple, beech, and hickory trees in the central quadrangle of Harvard Yard, opposite the massive Greek Revival building of Widener Library. T. S. Eliot, who was also receiving an honorary degree, sat nearby. Marshall's words dwelt on the themes that Acheson, Kennan, and Clayton had urged. A policy of aid to Europe was not to be directed against any one country; the initiative must come from Europe, and, above all, any "assistance that this Government may render in the future should provide a cure rather than a mere palliative."[40]

Acheson's work with the British press paid off. Whereas *The New York Times* gave the speech a bland heading (MARSHALL PLEADS FOR EUROPEAN UNITY), London reacted as Acheson had planned. Leonard Miall reported on the speech over the BBC at eight P.M., June 5 (British time), having told his editor that in "an extremely important speech," Marshall "comes out flatly for this great continental plan of help to Europe."[41]

In London, Ernest Bevin was sitting by his radio that evening and heard Miall's broadcast. He later told the National Press Club in Washington, "I assure you, gentlemen, it was like a lifeline to sinking men. It seemed to bring hope where there was none. The generosity of it was beyond my belief."[42]

Seizing on Marshall's words that the "initiative must come from Europe," Bevin acted on his own intuition. When officials at the Foreign Office suggested that Bevin should approach the British envoy to Washington and ask him if Marshall really meant what he said, Bevin said he preferred not to. "I don't want to ask Marshall that question. I want to go on the assumption that it was fully meant, and give an answer myself."[43]

Within days Bevin was in Paris, meeting with French foreign minister Georges Bidault; while both men were wary of Russian participation, they also knew they had no choice but to invite Molotov to join them for a subsequent meeting at the end of June.

Back in Washington Kennan made clear to the British ambassador, Lord Inverchapel, that if the Russians refused to go along with the plan, the Americans were prepared to move ahead with the West Europeans alone.[44]

Molotov's meeting with Bevin and Bidault, which convened in Paris on June 27, began badly. As expected, he objected most strongly to any inquiry into the internal resources of nations that "would violate the sovereignty of the individual countries." Nonetheless, Molotov behaved as though Russia would be a player, and Bidault believed that he was looking for some way in which the Soviet Union could accept Marshall Plan aid.[45]

The wrangling never let up, with France and Britain insisting, as Marshall desired, that a common European plan was called for, not a laundry list of individual needs. In the midst of further haggling over how the Europeans would present their case to Washington, Molotov was suddenly handed a telegram from Moscow, repeating Stalin's final, non-negotiable position. From then on, Molotov hardened his stance and attacked the French and British for trying to create a new organization to force European countries to sacrifice their national independence in order to qualify for American aid. At this point, Bevin whispered to his private secretary, Pierson Dixon, "This really is the birth of the Western Bloc."[46]

On July 2 Molotov quit Paris for Moscow. The Russians refused to take part in the Marshall Plan, and in due time all of the Soviet Union's East European satellites joined it in refusing. To George Kennan, the Western allies had put "Russia over the barrel. Either it must decline or else enter into an arrangement that would mean an ending of the Iron Curtain. When the full horror of [their] alternatives dawned on them they left suddenly in the middle of the night."[47]

Under very different circumstances, Dean Acheson also left the scene of battle. With the Marshall Plan in embryo, Acheson had completed the tour of duty he had agreed to when General Marshall had approached him to stay on. In the six months that Acheson had worked with Marshall, a sweeping new doctrine had been proclaimed that would make containment of the Soviet Union in Europe and the eastern Mediterranean the central focus of American security. The Marshall Plan, in turn, would be the economic analogue to the security concerns that were being met in Greece and Turkey.

Acheson had by now largely abandoned much hope of any productive negotiations with Moscow. Yet he had never embraced a strongly ideological stance toward the Soviet Union; in trying to entice the Russians into a global economic system at Bretton Woods, in discussions over atomic energy, and in the diplomatic maneuvering over Russian troop withdrawal from Iran, Acheson viewed Russia as a traditional great power.

After the Turkish crisis came to a head in August 1946, Acheson concluded that the Russians were now bound on a course of expansion. They had to be stopped, even at the risk of military confrontation. He became more and more skeptical of diplomatic exchanges and was increasingly convinced that the Russians would most likely respond only to decisive action on the part of the West. As secretary of state, he once said, "It takes more than bare hands and a desire for peace to turn back [the Russian] threat."[48]

Like General Marshall, he did not fight the problem. Once policy was decided, action must follow. Time and again he would cite Holmes's advice: "If you want to hit a bird on the wing, you must have all your will in a focus."[49]

On July 1, 1947, however, Acheson was ready to quit high office and return to the law. He felt he was running out of money after years on a government payroll, and he certainly had no expectation that he would ever replace the revered General Marshall. He was perfectly happy to turn over his office to Marshall's choice, Robert A. Lovett, the former assistant secretary of war who had been charged with getting the planes built for the army air force during World War II.

A naval aviator in the First World War, Lovett then became a New York investment banker at Brown Brothers Harriman, managing their currency and lending operations. On his twice-a-year trips he would drive through Belgium, France, and Germany, inspecting their industries and analyzing their finances. A cosmopolitan, rather suave figure, he was most comfortable in Europe and New York.[50]

For a month before he took over as under secretary, Lovett worked side by side with Acheson; he read all the papers, attended all the meetings, and participated in all the decisions. On July 1 he simply moved to the chair behind the desk and took on the task of selling the Marshall Plan and extracting from Congress the necessary appropriations, a task for which this even-tempered man was especially well fitted.

Acheson's leavetaking was marked by a singular display of feeling from the president. In a letter dated May 6, 1947, Truman wrote him: "You have been an arm for me to lean upon. As Marse Robert said when Stonewall lost his left arm at Chancellorsville, 'General Jackson has lost his left arm, I have lost my right'—that's the way I feel when you leave State."[51]

A stunning surprise awaited the departing under secretary. After General Marshall asked him to go over to the White House to discuss one last matter, Acheson was led out into the Rose Garden, where the president pinned on him the Medal of Merit.

That evening he dined with General Marshall and a group of his colleagues Marshall had assembled, and, as he wrote later, "with their generous words still ringing in my ears, I was driven home to a private—or, at least, semiprivate—life."[52]

CHAPTER EIGHTEEN

THE HABIT-FORMING DRUG OF PUBLIC LIFE

THAT SUMMER Acheson found himself in a situation he did not wholly understand. The adrenaline of power had kept him in a state of heightened activity for six and a half years. The tensions of the Second World War and the growing crises of the Cold War had worn away at him. Losing what he called "the sustaining prop of responsibility," he was far more tired than he had imagined. The solution, which his old law firm thoroughly endorsed, was a vacation, first at Harewood, his farm in Maryland, and then on a camping trip with Alice and their friends the Athertons.

Once again he chose to vacation in Canada, where his parental roots were. Their campsite was in the west, beside a lake in the Canadian Rockies at Jasper Park, where they were joined by the park superintendent and his wife.[1]

Back in private life, Acheson discovered how deeply he missed power. He had been able to play such a central role in the formulation and execution of American foreign policy because both Byrnes and Marshall were compelled to spend so much time out of the country. For both men, negotiations with their wartime allies were unusually protracted, not only because of the style of negotiation practiced by their Soviet counterparts, but also because of increasingly divergent views of the postwar settlements.

A month before he was to leave the department, Acheson wrote to his daughter Jane that he felt "very sad and somewhat panic stricken to be going back to the Union Trust Bldg. I like what I am doing and have some sense now of sureness of touch and of a willingness on the part of others to let me drive— Then, of course, one grows into an unconscious acceptance of the side and nonsense of a cabinet position."[2]

Acheson later compared his mood in this period to the "anguish and unhappiness of a drug addict in his 'withdrawal' period." Public life, he believed, "is not only a powerful stimulant but a habit-forming one." Moreover, it was a "seductive" drug, a kind of "happiness" drug, and he cited an old Greek definition of happiness as "the exercise of vital powers along lines of excellence in a life affording them scope."

It was not, he wrote in his memoirs, "an easy or happy" time. Public life, especially on the national stage, did in fact offer scope for the exercise of one's vital powers: "Indeed, so great is the scope, so vast the tasks, so limitless the horizons, that vital powers are exercised far beyond what one had thought of as his strength." Then suddenly it all came to an end. "The stimulation is gone, but the glands go on working for a time." In this period of readjustment, the "outstanding sensation is of the flatness of life."[3]

After his return to Covington and Burling in the fall, Acheson did indeed find that little if anything was likely to come his way that would equal in importance the issues that he had dealt with as under secretary and often acting secretary of state. Nonetheless, he wanted to test his powers as a lawyer, his imagination and judgment—and to make some money. In the months following his return to the law, two cases chiefly occupied him. One required an argument in the Supreme Court of two cases of poor farmers and fishermen of Japanese descent who had been prosecuted under California statutes attempting to exclude them from their means of earning a living. The other, as he described it, was "the defense of one of the industrial giants of our time against an attempt by the federal government to terminate its relations with another giant." In these two instances, his poor clients won and his rich client lost.[4]

His withdrawal period nonetheless did not put him completely out of the public eye. He was expected to testify before congressional committees on the value of the Marshall Plan, and he did so with characteristic force and impatience with congressional nonsense. While Acheson, as a former assistant secretary for congressional affairs, was fully aware of the need to coddle congressmen, he was incapable of holding his barbed tongue at the most egregious instances of congressional inanity. "When you go up to Congress," Dean Rusk, who served under Acheson, once commented, "you should have a little hay behind your ears. Acheson wouldn't do that."[5]

At one point during his testimony Acheson simply stared at a congressman in irritated disbelief and snapped, "If you didn't talk so much and listened more, I think you would understand better what this is all about."[6] In this cutting remark—which Acheson must have later recognized did neither him nor the program he was advocating any good—it is hard not to recall the rebellious schoolboy who refused to defer to any authority he did not respect.

Perhaps the most eloquent and persuasive testimony on the importance of passing the Marshall Plan (or what was officially termed the European Recovery Program) was that of General Marshall before the Senate Foreign Relations Committee. He told the senators that without economic aid, Europe "will take on a new form in the image of the tyranny that we fought to destroy in Germany." There was no doubt in his mind that "the whole world hangs in the balance."[7]

His reference to a new form of tyranny was clearly meant to refer to the Soviet Union; this reflected a growing feeling within the government that the selling of the Marshall Plan required an anti-Communist bias. It is hard to imagine that Congress would have endorsed the program had the Soviet Union finally agreed to join with Britain and France in seeking a formula for overall European recovery.

Bipartisan foreign policy was the order of the day, and Acheson had made sure that Arthur Vandenberg applied his "brand" to the Marshall Plan program in order to win over enough of the Republican opposition to the new internationalism of the Truman administration. "Bipartisan foreign policy," Acheson once suggested, "is the ideal for the executive, because you can't run this country any other way except by fixing the whole organization so it doesn't work the way it is supposed to work. Now the way to do that is to say politics stops at the seaboard—and anyone who denies that postulate is a son-of-a-bitch and crook and not a true patriot. Now if people will swallow that, then you're off to the races."[8]

Very soon Acheson was enlisted in the selling of the Marshall Plan to a broad public. A privately organized Citizens Committee for the Marshall Plan came into being by midsummer 1947, with Henry Stimson as honorary president. Acheson went about the country making speeches before such groups as the National-American Wholesale Grocers' Association at their convention in Atlantic City. Most frequently he spoke at meetings and dinners of citizens committed to an American role in international affairs.

His most grueling engagement came in Minnesota, where he shared a platform with the indefatigable and prolix Hubert Horatio Humphrey, then mayor of Minneapolis and waging a successful campaign for the U.S. Senate. In Duluth, busloads of miners and their families came into the armory to hear the two speakers, each of them for half an hour—Acheson on the Marshall Plan, Humphrey, as Acheson described him, on Humphrey. Then, when they returned to the hotel, a true talk marathon began. For a payment of twenty-five cents and a cup of coffee, first Humphrey, then Acheson, stood precariously on a chair and made fifteen-minute speeches. Then the ballroom emptied, filled again, and there was a rerun.

This went on until the early hours of the morning. As time passed, Humphrey's stamina proved greater than Acheson's. What was left of the group repaired to the only place in town still open for scrambled eggs and dancing to the music of a jukebox. While he liked Humphrey, Acheson finally abandoned him and his friends and snatched a few hours of sleep before Humphrey drove them back to Minneapolis for one more speech before Acheson headed wearily back to Washington.[9]

In addition to his work on the Citizens Committee in the summer of 1947, Acheson also became vice chairman of the Commission on the Organization of the Executive Branch. Chaired by ex-president Herbert Hoover, the Hoover Commission was remarkably nonpartisan in its work, even though much of it took place during the election year of 1948. The most important work the commission did bearing on Acheson's own interests was the National Military Establishment as set up by the act of 1947. This unified the three military services within a strong new defense department, headed by a secretary whose powers would be considerable.

Of surprise to Acheson was the favorable impression Herbert Hoover made on him. The unbending public figure turned out to have "a sense of and enjoyment of the bizarre and ridiculous," as Acheson described him. He wanted his advice unadorned and did not get angry when it was not what he hoped for.[10]

Acheson was a partisan Democrat, loyal to Truman and to the party. On Sunday, April 4, 1948, the president called him at Harewood and asked if he would take the job of running the European Recovery Program. Acheson said, "Do anything you want, but I think it would be a great mistake." Vandenberg was now fully behind the Marshall Plan, and Acheson realized that with the 1948 elections looming ahead, Vandenberg did not want the program to be a credit to any Democrat. Truman, of course, wanted to gain his own political mileage out of the plan. Acheson reminded the president that because of his closeness to him, no one would believe he was nonpartisan.

Moreover, the recent legislation did not provide any money for the program; it was merely an authorization to ask for some. "If you nominate anyone before talking to Van, you will make an enemy of the best friend you have in this." His advice was that Truman consult with Vandenberg about the nomination, tell him that he had thought of Acheson, and ask him for his opinion. Vandenberg was sure to turn Acheson down.

The president then asked, "Who do you think Van wants?"

"No doubt he wants Paul Hoffman," Acheson replied. An ebullient salesman who had risen to become president of the Studebaker automobile corporation, Hoffman was "a good man" in Acheson's view. The president would do well to accept him and, by doing so, "irrevocably commit Vandenberg to support an adequately financed program." On the other hand, if Acheson's prediction was wrong, he would take the job.

Reluctantly Truman agreed to the consultation. Later the president called and said it went precisely along the lines of Acheson's scenario.[11]

Throughout 1947 and 1948 events at home and abroad were moving to create a powerful anti-Communist consensus. The selling of the Marshall Plan required not only public lobbying by Acheson, but also, the administration believed, a heightened rhetoric that would persuade the Congress to appropriate the funds needed to stimulate European recovery, American exports, and the creation of a Western economic bloc. In this effort, Vandenberg's help was vital. A few years later Marshall recalled that he and the senator "couldn't have gotten much closer together unless I sat in Vandenberg's lap or he sat in mine."[12]

One of the most influential articles reflecting the administration's policy of containing Soviet expansion was "The Sources of Soviet Conduct," which appeared in the July 1947 issue of *Foreign Affairs*, the prestigious quarterly of the Council on Foreign Relations. This gracefully written but dangerously ambiguous piece penned by a mysterious Mr. "X" was soon revealed to have been written by George Kennan, then head of the Policy Planning Staff.

Kennan wrote that the United States must adopt a "policy of firm containment designed to confront the Russians with unalterable counterforce at every point where they show signs of encroaching upon the interests of a peaceful and stable world." Applying this kind of pressure, he believed, was someday likely to bring about "the gradual mellowing of Soviet power."[13] The article received immediate attention. *Life* magazine and the *Reader's Digest* published lengthy excerpts from it.

Kennan was vague on whether economic or military means, or both, should be used to implement his policy of "firm and vigilant containment of Russian expansive tendencies." But it is virtually impossible to read the article without assuming, as most did who read it in 1947, that Kennan did not rule out military means, although he later claimed that he had been misinterpreted. In his memoirs he wrote that he meant "not the containment by military means of a military threat, but the political containment of a political threat."[14]

Nor did Kennan distinguish between geographic areas, and therefore he implied that containment was not limited to Europe and Japan, as he later maintained. It was largely for this reason that Walter Lippmann took him to task in a series of twelve columns in the *New York Herald-Tribune* throughout the month of September. While Lippmann supported the program of economic aid under the Marshall Plan, he feared that the language of the Truman Doctrine and the Kennan article would "mean inexorably an unending intervention in all the countries that are supposed to 'contain' the Soviet Union."[15]

Whatever the effects of Lippmann's articles on public opinion, the administration was not about to back off from its policy of persuading the Congress to fund the Marshall Plan by invoking the dangers of communism and the Soviet Union. At the end of September Truman told a small group of congressmen in the Cabinet Room of the White House: "We'll either have to provide a program of interim aid until the Marshall program gets going, or the governments of France and Italy will fall. Austria too, and for all practical purposes Europe will be communist."[16]

That fall, two million workers struck in France, and the main trade union body formally condemned American aid to France. Similar strikes paralyzed Italy. The governments of both countries faced chronic inflation, high unemployment, grain shortages, and serious trade deficits. Both might be forced to curtail imports and further restrict production. Such a course would surely lead to collapse of existing governments and the possible installation of Communist regimes.[17]

A meeting of the Big Four foreign ministers in London in late November 1947 offered little hope of resolving the tensions of what was fast becoming known as the "Cold War" (a phrase for which both Walter Lippmann and Bernard Baruch claimed paternity). Once again the conference bogged down into recriminations over German reparations. Once again the two sides put forth incompatible objectives: the Western allies wanted an independent German state linked to Western Europe and the United States; the Soviets wanted a "unified" Germany, so that Russia would obtain reparations from the Western zones. No German peace treaty seemed in the offing.

The conference broke up in mid-December; it marked the end of the Yalta system of presumed "Big Power" cooperation over a settlement for postwar Europe. Though the Western powers would be willing to make one more try for a united Germany, they were moving inexorably toward uniting the British, American, and French zones into a separate West German state. There would be currency reform and an economic program to counter inflation, done if necessary without the Russians. Bevin and Marshall were determined to go ahead with some kind of Western system, backed, as Bevin believed, "by power, money and resolute action."[18]

* * *

Within three months of the London conference, the Cold War entered a new and even more dangerous phase. In February 1948 came the Czech coup. The coalition of Communists and non-Communists that had governed Czechoslovakia since the end of the war was clearly an anomaly and doubtless could not have lasted much longer. When the non-Communist politicians tried to force President Eduard Beneš to call a new election in February 1948 or to reconstitute the cabinet along more favorable lines, the Communists used the police to search, arrest, and frighten political opponents. Fears of Soviet intervention increased.

In the growing crisis, Beneš gave in. Fearing civil war, he allowed the Communist leader Klement Gottwald to form a new, Communist-dominated government. The politics of social democracy was dead.

In the aftermath there were arrests, purges, and executions, and the government was effectively under Communist control and Soviet domination. On March 10, 1948, Foreign Minister Jan Masaryk, son of the revered founder of Czechoslovakia, fell—or, more likely, was pushed—to his death from his office window.

Seven days later Harry Truman addressed a joint session of Congress to ask for funding of the Marshall Plan program, the restoration of the draft, and universal military training. It was once again a speech with strong rhetoric, denouncing the Soviets for their "ruthless course of action, and the clear design to extend it to the free nations of Europe." Truman then expressed an American interest in a Western military alliance, to follow on the Brussels military pact, which had been signed earlier that day by Britain, France, Belgium, the Netherlands, and Luxembourg.[19]

The president's speech was designed to outflank the Republicans on the right, and on the left to neutralize Henry Wallace, who had announced his third-party candidacy for the presidency at the end of 1947.[20]

The strategy worked. Two days later the House Appropriations Committee endorsed the European Recovery Program in order "to reverse the trend to Communism in Europe." The bill quickly passed in the Senate as well, with even some Republican isolationists shouting their approval.[21]

On June 24, 1948, as Governor Thomas E. Dewey of New York accepted the Republican nomination for president of the United States, the Russians blockaded all rail, highway, and water traffic in and out of Berlin. The Soviet move was a response to the June 19 decision of the Western allies to carve a single economic unit out of their zones of occupation and to proceed with a currency reform that would strengthen western Germany and prepare it for sovereignty. Although Washington recognized that this would be a definite move toward the final partition of Germany, General Marshall and Under Secretary Lovett were prepared to go ahead.

A Western airlift run by the Americans to resupply Berlin with the necessities of life was set up. By July 22 the airlift, involving fifty-two C-54s and eighty C-47s, was bringing in about 2,500 tons of supplies a day; by autumn it had reached a 4,000-ton-per-day minimum. "We stay in Berlin, period," Truman declared.[22]

Throughout this period Truman often had "a terrible feeling" that "we are very close to war." But he remained steadfast in his support of an airlift. He did so without consulting any of his political advisers in the White House.[23]

The airlift went on ceaselessly during the 1948 presidential campaign, and Truman's resolute stance certainly helped him in his astonishing victory over Dewey, Henry Wallace, and Strom Thurmond, who ran for president on a states' rights "Dixiecrat" ticket.

On election night Dean Acheson stayed up at the house of his friend and law partner, Gerhard Gesell, listening to the returns. It seemed impossible that Truman would win, and most of Truman's cabinet were making plans to return to private life. By dawn Acheson was ecstatic. He and Gesell were to catch a train to Wilmington at eight A.M., and in the station Acheson announced, "I'm going to do something I've never done. I'm going to have a highball for breakfast." It was a toast to the president.

Acheson did not expect to return to public life. He was adjusting to work at the law firm, interspersed with his weekends at Harewood. If, as he once said, "To leave positions of great responsibility and authority is to die a little," he would draw sustenance from reading British history and biography and Trollope and Twain.[24]

Buoyed and determined after his victory, Truman was soon busy putting together his thoughts for a new cabinet. There was no question of General Marshall staying on as secretary of state. He was in Walter Reed Hospital having a kidney removed, and by Inauguration Day, January 20, 1949, he would have served two full years at State.

On November 22 Acheson got a call from Rose Conway, the president's secretary, asking him to stop on his way home by Blair House, where the Trumans were living while the residential quarters of the White House were being renovated. As Acheson was putting the final touches on the Hoover Commission report, it was not that unusual for the president to ask him to come by.

Harry Truman was alone in the private study when Acheson arrived. He asked him to sit down, as what he was about to say might be something of a shock. Without hesitation, Truman said he wanted him as secretary of state. For once Acheson was speechless. He then named three or four men who might give the president greater help and support than he could. But Truman said that he had carefully considered his decision. He wanted Acheson.

Finally, when Acheson said that he did not think he was adequate to the task at such a critical time in America's history, the president replied: "Dean, I suppose there are 10,000 people in the United States who are better qualified to be President or Secretary of State than I am or you are. The only difficulty is that we don't know who they are. The fact of the matter is that I have been elected President, and I am President, and I want you to be Secretary of State."

Truman then suggested that Acheson go home and talk it over with his wife. The next afternoon Acheson came back to Blair House and told the president that he would accept the job.[25]

PART FOUR

THE SECRETARY OF STATE

CHAPTER NINETEEN

IN MARSHALL'S CHAIR

IN ACHESON'S CONFIRMATION HEARINGS before the Senate Committee on Foreign Relations in the great Caucus Room of the Senate office building, the Republicans were resentful. The Democrats had recaptured the House and now also controlled the Senate with a twelve-member majority. After Truman's stunning upset, the new Republican minority found itself bereft of any serious alternatives to the president's foreign policies. Moreover, Vandenberg was in ill health, and his power in the Republican Party was declining. As he became less influential, the more isolationist faction, led by Senator Robert Taft of Ohio, grew in importance.

With the Marshall Plan under way and the Berlin airlift triumphant, the best tactic, the Taft Republicans believed, was to accuse the Democratic administration of being soft on communism. The Yalta agreements were seen as having sold out Eastern Europe, and now the Democrats were about to "lose" China to Mao. Surely the reason for these setbacks was the presence of Communists and Communist sympathizers in the government.

Acheson's hearings centered therefore not on the issues of integrating West Germany into the West, or the potential costs of Western rearmament, but rather on the questions of loyalty and subversion—in this case, on Acheson's supposed support of Alger Hiss, who had just been indicted for perjury by a federal grand jury in New York City. Although Whittaker Chambers, a confessed ex-Communist and now an editor at *Time* magazine, had publicly identified Alger Hiss as a Communist and Soviet agent in hearings before the House Un-American Activities Committee (HUAC) in August 1948, he had never accused Hiss of being involved in espionage until Hiss sued Chambers for libel; in a pre-trial examination in November 1948, he then came up with charges that Hiss had given secret government documents to him in 1938.

Hiss had become a member of the State Department in 1936 but worked under Dean Acheson only for about six months before he left the department at the end of 1946 to become head of the Carnegie Endowment for International Peace in New York. At State, Hiss had served in the American delegation at the 1945 Yalta conference and was a member of the team charged with drafting the charter for the United Nations.

Like Acheson, Alger Hiss seemed the prototype of an eastern class that the Republican right especially disliked. Born in Baltimore in 1904, he grew up in shabby gentility, one of five children of an executive in a wholesale dry-goods company who committed suicide when Hiss was two years old. He graduated from the Baltimore public schools, then attended Johns Hopkins University and later Harvard Law School, where he was aided by scholarships. Like Acheson, he became a protégé of Felix Frankfurter's, who recommended him as a clerk to Justice Oliver Wendell Holmes, when Hiss graduated in 1929.

Both Hiss and his wife, Priscilla, were socially conscious New Dealers, and when Roosevelt came to power in 1933, Hiss joined FDR's administration, working first for the Agricultural Adjustment Administration. It was during this decade that Hiss met Whittaker Chambers and, Chambers testified, passed him State Department documents to be transmitted to Moscow.

Unlike Hiss, who sought approval from his elders and a place in the foreign policy establishment, Chambers was a rebel. He left college in 1924 and joined the Communist Party. Soon after, he became a writer and editor for the Party's newspaper, the *Daily Worker,* and then for the *New Masses;* in late 1932 he left the magazine after having been recruited into the Communist underground. In this capacity he worked for the Party until 1938, when he broke from it and took a job on the editorial staff of *Time.*

Chambers stood in marked contrast to the tall, slim, self-possessed Hiss. Richard Nixon, a young congressman on HUAC who would make his reputation by embracing Chambers and doubting Hiss, described him accurately as "short and pudgy," clothes "unpressed, his shirt collar . . . curled up over his jacket"; he spoke "in a rather bored monotone," an "indifferent if not reluctant witness."[1]

Early in Acheson's confirmation hearing on January 13, 1949, Senator Tom Connally of Texas, the Democratic chairman of the committee, put the question. Was it true, he asked, as "has been charged over the radio and in the press and by word of mouth that, while you were Assistant Secretary, Mr. Alger Hiss was your chief of staff or was your special assistant?"

Acheson replied that Hiss was a friend, adding that his friendship was "neither easily given nor withdrawn."[2] He then pointed out that it was not Alger Hiss, but brother Donald, who was also accused of having been involved in espionage, who had in fact been his assistant. Donald Hiss had later joined Acheson's firm as a partner; Acheson felt particularly close to him and gave him unstinting praise for serving both Acheson and the country "with complete fidelity and loyalty." Later, in executive session, Acheson stated that he had never been "close" to Alger Hiss. He "was, and he is—not a close friend, but I am not going to abandon him and throw rocks at him when he is in trouble."[3]

Well before the HUAC hearings, Acheson had apparently known of allegations that Alger Hiss was a Communist sympathizer. They came initially from Adolf A. Berle, who was an assistant secretary of state at the time Acheson joined the government in 1941. According to Berle, also testifying before the House Un-American Activities Committee in 1948, Chambers had told him in 1939 that Alger and Donald Hiss were "sympathetic" to the "general point of view of the Communist Party."[4]

Berle went on to testify that he had asked Acheson about "the two Hiss boys" when Acheson became assistant secretary of state for congressional relations in December 1944 and "Alger Hiss became his executive assistant." (It was not, of course, Alger who was his assistant, but Donald.) In reply to Berle's inquiry, Acheson had (he said) told him that he had known "these two boys from childhood, and could vouch for them absolutely."[5] Berle was surely wrong. It is unlikely Acheson knew them until they came to clerk for Justice Holmes.

Berle also told the House committee that "in the fall of 1944 there was a difference of opinion in the State Department." He felt that "Mr. Acheson's group . . . with Mr. Hiss as his principal assistant" was exhibiting a "pro-Russian point of view." A petty and envious man, Berle doubtless mounted this assault on Acheson because he believed he had lost out to Acheson in the State Department hierarchy.

In his confirmation hearing, Acheson was easily able to refute Berle by pointing out that Alger Hiss had never been his assistant, that Donald Hiss had left his office in the preceding March, and that neither he nor Berle had had much to do with each other in 1944.[6] As for Donald Hiss, after Berle's accusations Acheson did question Donald about "any associations which would embarrass me" and was satisfied with Donald's answer.[7]

In executive session the following day, Acheson was questioned further on his relationship with Alger Hiss. Acheson expanded on how perplexed he was over the whole Hiss-Chambers affair. "If you start with the assumption that [Hiss] is guilty of the things with which he is charged, then he has behaved in a way which leads you to doubt his sanity," he said. "One has the feeling that there is something here that one does not understand."[8]

Acheson, however, had been consulted by Hiss shortly before he left the department to become president of the Carnegie Endowment. Aware that Hiss was under suspicion from FBI chief J. Edgar Hoover, Acheson urged him to get out of government and take the Carnegie job even before these charges might be cleared up. "People will continue to raise these doubts about you so long as you are in a position where you are subject to this sort of attack," Acheson advised, "and if I were you, I would just leave and go to New York."[9]

In addition, Acheson had also helped Hiss prepare for his first statement before the House Un-American Activities Committee in August 1948, before Chambers had accused him of espionage. At this time, Hiss met with his brother and Acheson at the law offices at Covington.[10]

On January 14, 1949, the Senate committee voted unanimously to recommend that Acheson be confirmed, which the Senate did by a vote of eighty-three to six. Vandenberg spoke in support of the nomination, although he said privately that "Mr. Acheson would *not* have been my choice for Secretary of State." Fearing that Acheson was too close to Truman, he worried that the nonpartisan collaboration he had enjoyed with General Marshall and Robert Lovett would diminish, and he predicted that Acheson would be "another Anthony Eden—flashy, brilliant, but soft at the core."[11]

The day after Harry Truman's inauguration on January 20, 1949, Acheson took the oath from Chief Justice Fred Vinson in the president's office. Thinking of General Marshall, who was still in the hospital, he recalled a sentence from the First Book of Kings, often cited by another predecessor, Colonel Stimson, who had been secretary of state under Herbert Hoover: "Let not him that girdeth on his harness boast himself as he that putteth it off." With this admonition in mind, he went to the State Department to sit in Marshall's chair.[12]

Like Marshall, Acheson was orderly in his habits, and the organizational structure and operating procedures that he put in place at State during 1949 were aimed at making lines of command and responsibility clear. The under secretary of state was James Webb, whom Truman had recommended. Webb had been director of the budget and was to be responsible for the administration of the department. But he was not well suited for the job, as he tended to immerse himself in details and had little aptitude for the broader aspects of policy. Although Webb remained for three years in this post, Acheson was probably not sorry to see him leave; he was replaced by David Bruce, an ambassador with great experience whom Acheson knew well.

The department was never happier than under Acheson's reign. After so many years in high positions at State, Acheson knew how the organization worked, and unlike many others who served as secretary, Acheson was willing to share information and ideas with his subordinates. There was a good flow of information from the top down and from the bottom up. He trusted his staff, which included Dean Rusk as a deputy under secretary; George Kennan as counsellor and director of policy planning (succeeded in 1950 by Paul Nitze); Carlisle Humelsine, director of the Executive Secretariat; and Philip C. Jessup, an international lawyer who was named ambassador-at-large. Lucius D. Battle became Acheson's invaluable special assistant.

A tall, thirty-year-old Floridian, Luke Battle had been recommended to Acheson by Carl Humelsine as a bright, energetic young Foreign Service officer who was working on the Canadian desk and was also a bachelor. Acheson had insisted that his special assistant be unmarried, as his assignment would require much traveling and working late hours. As Acheson put it, "At the first twinge of a tender emotion he would be expected to draft his request for other duty." Battle assured Acheson that he was completely free and expected to remain so, but in time Battle did "succumb to the tender emotion." He was heartsick at the idea of ending his work with Acheson. At this point Acheson's personal secretary, Barbara Evans, who rendered her opinions with unstinting candor, told the secretary that he should stop imposing this absurd requirement. He did so, and his relations with young Battle became extremely close. As he wrote in his memoirs, both he and his wife "came to have the same regard and affection for Luke Battle that we had for our own son."[13]

The day began for Acheson when he left his redbrick house in Georgetown at about ten minutes to nine to walk to work. Walking alongside him would usually be Supreme Court justice Felix Frankfurter, who generally stopped by for a chat with the Achesons while they finished breakfast. For the mile and a half from the house on P Street to the State Department in Foggy Bottom, the justice's car would creep along behind them, ready to speed Frankfurter to the Supreme Court building on Capitol Hill after Acheson peeled off at the department.

They made an odd couple, the tall, commanding Acheson and the short, bouncy Frankfurter. Both were renowned conversationalists, and their topics ranged from philosophy to gossip, but, as Frankfurter once reported, "We never talk about the government or foreign policy. We just talk."[14]

Entering into his official world, Acheson would take the elevator to his office, whose size appalled him: "I always have the feeling that I am walking into the cabin-class dining saloon on one of those North German Lloyd liners." At one end was a huge table beneath a large oil portrait of Henry Stimson. The other portrait that Acheson hung was of his most distinguished predecessor, John Quincy Adams.

Acheson's massive mahogany desk had been installed by General Marshall midway along the windowed side of the room. On one side of the desk was an unabridged dictionary, on the other a globe of the world illuminated from within.

Against the wall was a formidable grandfather clock and, above that, two paintings that Mrs. Acheson had borrowed from the Smithsonian Institution, one the signing of the Treaty of Ghent ending the War of 1812, the other a painting by Alice Acheson's grandfather, John Mix Stanley, of the signing of a treaty with the Cherokee Indians. Finally, in the corner of the room was a group of comfortable red leather chairs, a sofa, and a coffee table.[15]

Once Acheson was seated at his desk, either Barbara Evans or Luke Battle would bring him the logbook, a black, leather-bound looseleaf notebook with "Top Secret" stamped in silver across its cover, into which were placed copies of the most important cables sent to and from the State Department in the last twelve hours. Appended to the cables might be a note or two of pertinent information. After studying them for about fifteen minutes, and jotting down in longhand any questions on a lined yellow pad, he would meet for about twenty minutes with a small staff that would usually include Webb, Humelsine, Jessup, who acted as Acheson's troubleshooter and with whom Acheson had a particularly trusting and close relationship, and, of course, Luke Battle.

Occasionally they would be joined by other members of the senior staff—George Kennan, Paul Nitze, or Dean Rusk. The meetings were designed to have a quick look at what had to be done that day. Once or twice a week there would be a larger staff meeting of about twenty-five people at ten o'clock, to which all the assistant secretaries came, or a meeting with a group of departmental experts to discuss something of special importance.[16]

Twice a week—on Mondays and Thursdays—Acheson would have lunch with the president. On Fridays there was a cabinet meeting with Truman, and, in addition, Acheson might see him two or three more times as business required. At his twelve-thirty lunch meetings with the president, Acheson would carry with him a White House book in which Battle and Humelsine would jot down what he needed to be reminded of: choices of ambassadors, whatever required the president's approval. When he returned, he would call in Evans or Battle and inform them what the president had agreed to do, what he wanted to postpone, what further he might need on a certain subject, and what to eliminate from further consideration. He was generally willing to share information with Battle, so that after Acheson returned from the White House, Battle felt free to go into his office and ask, "What happened?"

Battle was instructed to listen in on phone calls and take notes on what was said, except when the calls were to the president or to the family. Over time, Acheson gained such confidence in Battle that he expected his aide to argue with him when he disagreed. As Battle recalled, "I'd say, 'You can't *do* that. That's just wrong of you to do that.'" They might get into a strong argument, but Acheson wanted his subordinates to say what they truly believed and would listen carefully. When Acheson would dictate an intemperate letter, Battle would hold it back until he could persuade the secretary to change or kill it. Acheson used to say, "I dictate the letters—Luke tears them up."

Acheson had the absolute confidence of Harry Truman and felt perfectly free to countermand or overrule directives from the White House staff that Truman himself had not cleared. On one occasion Battle received a call from General Harry Vaughan, a Truman crony who was his military aide and an old pal from the First World War. Vaughan told him that there was a department paper coming up for the secretary of state that recommended a certain course of action. General Vaughan said he thought this was the wrong course and hoped Battle would make this known to Acheson.

Battle decided he ought to bring the matter up with his boss, and when queried by Acheson, Battle replied that he thought the department's recommendation was the right one. Acheson nodded and instructed him that in the future, "When the White House calls, unless it's the President, don't answer it unless you want to." He went on: "Don't ever tell me again what *they* want. As for General Vaughan, I don't ever want to hear anything he thinks about anything." And, "If anybody gives you any trouble, *we* will speak to the President about it."[17]

Press conferences were held every Wednesday. The night before, Acheson would take home a sheaf of reports and memoranda on topics he was likely to be questioned on. After studying these issues before going to bed, he was rarely caught off guard the following morning, and because he was quick on his feet, he was clever at ducking questions he did not want to answer.

"I'll tell you a story," he said one day to avoid responding to a query about something still secret. "My old law partner, Judge Covington, once went to an oyster roast down on the Eastern Shore of Maryland and had a fine time eating those wonderful oysters, until he was handed a red-hot one. Why, that oyster must have been two hundred and seventy degrees Fahrenheit. Old Judge Covington took one look at the oyster and said, 'A man would have to be a damn fool to swallow *that* one.'"[18]

In office, Acheson avoided the Washington social scene. While he kept most of the press at arm's length, he was careful to cultivate certain journalists, such as James Reston of *The New York Times.* On the other hand, he was unwilling to socialize with columnist Joseph Alsop, whose family roots were in Middletown, Connecticut. Alsop resented this distancing by Acheson, but it was Acheson's way of steering a careful course among members of the press while being willing to provide, on rare occasions, carefully calculated leaks to those whom he trusted.[19]

With the most eminent columnist of the day, Walter Lippmann, Acheson's relations were very uneven. Although they had many common friends, Acheson deeply resented Lippmann's criticisms of his policies, and Lippmann rarely hesitated to attack Acheson frontally when he disagreed with him. Precisely because of Lippmann's brilliance and authority, Acheson found his attacks particularly galling.

Most evenings, according to his wife, Acheson enjoyed curling up with a book. He preferred histories and biographies of dashing statesmen, like Disraeli, to social reformers,—"Christers," as he called them—like Gladstone. His taste in fiction ran to the sprawling and picaresque, Tobias Smollett and Charles Dickens. Histories were often stories of war and desperation—Thucydides' *Peloponnesian War* and the American Civil War—though of course he read a good deal of the current literature about American society.[20]

It was in these years that the Achesons constructed a studio at Harewood for Alice and a workshop where Acheson could distract himself with woodworking, which required absolute concentration because of the danger of cutting one's hand with a saw or knife.

Only when absolutely necessary would he attend a diplomatic reception, and even during office hours when he had to meet with visiting dignitaries, he tried to husband his time and energy. In one instance, he knew that a politician who had held high office in a West European country and was trying to make a comeback needed to say he had met with the American secretary of state. Neither Acheson nor the other fellow had anything to say to each other, but because he had been very friendly to America during the war, Acheson let him in. As he told the story later, "He entered ceremoniously, bowed ceremoniously, shook hands ceremoniously, and said, 'Mr. Secretary, what of the future?' 'What of it?' I said, and the man shook hands and left. He had achieved what he wanted, and I had lost, at the most, forty-five seconds."[21]

There was a refreshing informality to Acheson's lunches. In those days the secretary's dining room was right across from his office. Ordinarily he would go into the dining room by himself and sit down with two or three other colleagues wherever he could find an empty chair. If he was at the table that was generally thought of as his, other officials would not sit down with him unless he asked them to, but he would usually wave to someone or other to come over and join him.

It was always a light lunch without cocktails and, for a thirty-year-old like Luke Battle, a pleasant surprise to be able to sit down casually with Philip Jessup or even John Foster Dulles, who often ate there when he accepted an assignment from the department in the name of bipartisan foreign policy.[22]

By the end of the day Acheson would be sitting alone in his office to give himself a little time to think before he returned home for supper. Unless a crisis was all-consuming, he would sometimes call in George Kennan, head of the Policy Planning Staff, and they might have a drink together. His disagreements with Kennan, which intensified later over the issue of Germany and NATO, did not in the early years of Acheson's tenure affect his desire to talk with Kennan informally. Often on Wednesday afternoons toward the end of the working day, Acheson would stroll over to the Policy Planning Staff offices, close the door, and have a fine time batting ideas about, with no one allowed to take notes. These sessions suited both Kennan and Acheson, but after the Korean War broke out, they came to an end.[23]

At the end of the day, after he had had supper with his wife, Acheson might take a call from Felix Frankfurter to discuss a book one of them was reading. Unless a friend dropped by for a late evening chat by the fireplace in the living room, Acheson would generally retire to his study to put in a few more hours before going to bed.[24]

Although myriad problems were facing the new secretary, Acheson was most preoccupied with the commitment the United States had made to a Western alliance, the first one since the alliance with France in 1778. In Asia, on the other hand, events were moving toward a fatal conclusion. By the time Acheson took over, Chiang Kai-shek's Nationalist regime was in the last stages of collapse, and Acheson expected that Washington would eventually have to recognize a new Communist government in Peking under Mao Zedong.

With regard to Japan, both the administration and General Douglas MacArthur, the supreme commander and American proconsul, agreed that the American occupation had to come to an end fairly soon—though what kind of peace treaty should be worked out was not yet clear. In both Indochina and Indonesia, Acheson believed that colonial rule by France and the Netherlands would have to end, though he in fact treated the two countries very differently.

As for the Middle East, a few days before Acheson took office, Acting Secretary of State Robert Lovett had advised the president that Britain's suggestion of an Anglo-American agreement to guarantee the existence of an Israel surrounded by a circle of weak Arab states should be rejected. The only option, Lovett believed, was to press on with efforts to reach a peace settlement between Arabs and Israelis. Acheson heartily concurred, and for the next two years the State Department struggled to accomplish this mission. Not surprisingly, it failed to do so.

Acheson's most pressing task was to conclude a new North Atlantic security treaty with Britain, France, and the three Benelux countries, even as the Berlin blockade was still raging. It was British foreign secretary Ernest Bevin who had originally pushed for a military alliance that would link Western Europe and the United States. Like other leaders of the British Labour Party, he could not forget the Nazi-Soviet pact or ignore postwar Soviet expansionism, and after the early efforts to pursue a policy of accommodation with the Soviet Union waned, he swung the party over to a hard line.

In January 1948 Bevin had told Marshall that he was looking for an "understanding" with the United States and Western Europe that would be backed by "power, money and resolution." His goal was to halt Soviet intimidation of Western Europe and "the piecemeal collapse of one Western bastion after another."

The Brussels treaty of March 1948, binding Britain, France, and the Benelux countries into a defense system, was an essential building block for the hoped-for North Atlantic alliance, and an approach to the United States to link itself with this grouping was implicit in Bevin's thinking.

Toward the end of October 1948, the five members of the Brussels pact did indeed urge the United States and Canada to enter into formal arrangements with them for a security pact, which would eventually become known as the North Atlantic Treaty Organization, or NATO.[25]

At Policy Planning, however, George Kennan opposed the creation of NATO on the grounds that a formal security arrangement would not be the best way to counter Soviet attempts to dominate Europe; he preferred to concentrate on economic recovery and believed that a military pact would deepen the division of Europe into two blocs. Instead he wanted to press for the withdrawal of both American and Soviet occupation troops from Germany and Austria. But the European division of the State Department carried the day. Lovett saw NATO as the military complement to the Marshall Plan.

The leading American policymakers did not view the Soviet threat in strictly military terms. It was, in their view, a question of the power of the Soviet Union to intimidate the West Europeans into becoming a Soviet sphere of influence. Political stability and economic development were therefore to be welded to military containment, which in turn would bind the United States to Europe indefinitely.[26]

Acheson's task was to push ahead with the treaty and gain Senate approval. Moreover, the Berlin blockade, which, along with the Czech coup, had given further impetus to the need for a military pact, was about to come to an unexpected conclusion. Ending the blockade would be rightly seen as a victory for American resolve, but it might also make it more difficult for Acheson to garner support from the Senate for a Western military pact.

In January, with Acheson newly in office, Kingsbury Smith, the European general manager of the International News Service, filed with the Soviet foreign office four questions addressed to Stalin. The answers he received created a sensation. In responding to a query on ending the blockade, Stalin did not mention the ostensible reason for it—the issuance of the new West German currency. Instead, Stalin said that the Soviet Union would lift all restrictions on traffic to Berlin if the three Western allies were willing to discuss with their Soviet counterpart the question of a separate West German state, which he opposed. At a press conference on February 2, 1949, Acheson responded that agreements among the Western allies to end the military occupation in the three Western zones of Germany did not "preclude agreements [with the Soviet Union] on Germany as a whole."

He then instructed Philip Jessup to talk with Jacob Malik, the Soviet representative at the United Nations, to see if Stalin was serious. In March Jessup got an answer. If a definite date could be set for a meeting of the Big Four foreign ministers and if the Western allies were willing to hold up preparation for a West German government until after their meeting, the blockade would be called off.

Jessup told Malik that the West would not hold up its plans for West Germany, but that in any case they could not be completed for some time. If the Russians really wanted to get on with a foreign ministers meeting, they should lift the blockade. The West would not accept any conditions. Moscow finally agreed on April 10 to lift the blockade, and a meeting of the foreign ministers began on May 23 in Paris.

The experience of the blockade only reinforced Acheson's growing view that negotiating with the Russians by traditional diplomatic methods—"that is, by a series of mutual concessions calculated to move parties desiring agreement closer to an acceptable one"—was fruitless. The Russians' "more primitive form" of diplomacy was to try to force an opponent to accept their position. They would abandon this stance only if their adversary demonstrated that it was untenable. It was therefore only by "a calculation of forces" that they could be moved to change their purposes.[27]

Before their conference with the Soviets, the British and French foreign ministers were to meet in Washington at the end of March to discuss the German question. A few days later, on April 4, 1949, the foreign ministers of all the proposed NATO countries (in addition to Britain, France, and the Benelux nations, now including Norway, Denmark, Iceland, Italy, Portugal, the United States, and Canada) were to assemble in Washington for the signing of the North Atlantic Treaty.

Acheson had not met before with his British and French counterparts, Ernest Bevin and Robert Schuman. It would prove to be the beginning of warm friendships with both of them. Never were two people more different in appearance, background, and temperament than Bevin and Schuman. Bevin was short and stout, with a broad nose and thick lips, a man who suffered from attacks of angina but nonetheless continued to eat heartily and drink whiskey and soda. The son of a servant girl from western England and an unknown father, he became a trucker after a few years of schooling. Then he embarked on a career as a labor leader, playing a large part in organizing the giant Transport and General Workers' Union and, with others, in the 1926 general strike. It was Churchill, who as home secretary broke the strike, who nonetheless drafted Bevin into the war cabinet as minister of labour. When the Labour Party took power in 1945, he hoped to become chancellor of the Exchequer, but Clement Attlee chose Hugh Dalton and put Bevin in the Foreign Office. He grew to love his job and to feel at home in Whitehall and with the heritage of his illustrious predecessors.

Bevin began calling Acheson "me lad," an affectionate appellation, and Acheson could catch Bevin's mood from the intonation of that phrase. As Acheson described it, "It could be minatory, as in 'And don't think, me lad, that I'm not on to what ye're up to.' Or warmly reassuring, as when in 1950 Republican legislators were urging my replacement, 'Don't give it a thought, me lad. If those blokes don't want yer, there's plenty as does.'" He had a deep mistrust of the Germans, but, as Acheson wrote, "an even deeper one of the Soviet Union. And he understood power."[28]

Schuman, on the other hand, tall, stooped, bald, with a long nose, was of a more intellectual temperament. A former premier of France who had put the Communists out of government, he had grown up in Lorraine when it was part of Germany after the 1870 Franco-Prussian War and was completely fluent in German. His English was adequate, but he preferred to use an interpreter and had a difficult time understanding Bevin's West Country accent.

Schuman's manner was formal, dignified, and gravely courteous. Acheson always addressed him as "M. le President" (since he had been a premier). But beneath this formality, Acheson recognized "a nature warm and affectionate to those to whom he gave his confidence, feelings which shyness rarely let show through the protective cover." His almost monkish asceticism led him to live in a few rooms over his offices at the Quai d'Orsay, attended by an old woman who had been his nurse. A devout Catholic, he was devoted to the reconciliation of France and Germany so that they could lead Europe within a broader Atlantic community. No aim was more congenial to Acheson.[29]

On the question of Germany, Acheson was highly responsive to the views of his newfound friends.[30]

Senate ratification of the North Atlantic Treaty was not without its travail. The senators were most concerned about ensuring that the NATO treaty, which considered an attack on one as an attack on all, did not automatically commit the United States to go to war. Acheson himself was persuaded that "no power on earth could force any other action upon any signatory" and that for this reason alone the power to declare war still rested in the hands of the Congress.

Nevertheless, as he explained in a press conference and then again in a radio address to the nation in March, "decent people kept their contract obligations." Americans were "decent people, we would keep our promises, and our promises were written out and clear enough. They were to regard an attack on any of our allies as an attack on ourselves and to assist the victim ourselves and with the others, with force if necessary, to restore peace and security." This did not mean that "we would be automatically at war if one of our allies was attacked. We should and would act as a nation in accordance with our promises—not in repudiation of them—and, as a nation, that decision will rest where the Constitution has placed it."[31]

In the course of his repeated attempts to clarify America's commitments under the treaty, under dogged questioning by senators at hearings in late April over ratification, Acheson dropped his diplomatic guard on an important point. Iowa Republican senator Bourke Hickenlooper asked whether we were "going to be expected to send substantial numbers of troops over there as a more or less permanent contribution to the development of these countries' capacity to resist."

"The answer to that question," Acheson said, "is a clear and absolute 'No.'"

Two years later the senator was justifiably bitter when Acheson came before the committee to inform it of the president's decision to send four additional troop divisions to Europe. Although Acheson claimed his earlier response had been given because no unified command was being considered for NATO at the time and American troops were then regarded solely as occupation forces, his answer was, as he admitted later, "deplorably wrong" and "almost equally stupid."[32]

On July 21, 1949, the Senate approved the treaty by a vote of eighty-three to thirteen.

On taking office in January, Acheson had no fixed answer to the question of how reunification of Germany should be pursued. His naturally pragmatic approach made him hesitant to come down firmly on any policy until he had examined all sides of the issue. For this reason he asked George Kennan as head of Policy Planning to prepare a paper on German policy for consideration by the National Security Council (NSC). What finally came out of these discussions was Kennan's proposal, known as Program or Plan A, which sought to avoid splitting Germany into two halves.[33]

Plan A, in fact, had been largely drawn up the year before Acheson returned to office, when Kennan had organized a consulting group of outsiders to work with him on the German problem. Foremost among those was Dean Acheson himself, who did not object to the ultimate aim of Kennan's policy, which was the removal of the de facto division of Germany. In fact, all but two of the consultants supported the main lines of Plan A—withdrawing occupation forces of both the Western allies and the Soviets and the establishment of a German government after elections under international supervision in all four zones. Provision was also made for the complete demilitarization of Germany.

The consultants questioned whether the Soviets would accept such a program on terms agreeable to the Americans. In the meantime, according to the plan, the Western allies should nonetheless proceed with their intention to establish a separate West German state, with a new constitution that was being drawn up by the delegates to a German Parliamentary Council.[34]

In short, a provisional West German state should come into being while at the same time holding open the possibility of four-power agreement over the unification of the whole country. This double-track policy was what Acheson seemed to have in mind when he met with Bevin and Schuman in Washington.[35]

Even before Acheson came into office, however, Plan A had met with much opposition from General Lucius D. Clay, the American commander in Germany, and from his political adviser, the senior State Department official Robert Murphy. Clay was highly skeptical of the troop withdrawal called for by Plan A and believed that it was the presence of the U.S. Army in Germany that was keeping Europe stable. He was also hostile to the idea of American and Russian troops withdrawing to the periphery of Europe, calling it "totally impractical."

Within the State Department, John Hickerson, chief of the European Affairs Division, also wanted to keep the larger part of Germany under Western control. And Kennan's friend and colleague Charles Bohlen predicted that Plan A would meet with strong objections from the French and probably from the Dutch and Belgians as well. As he wrote Kennan, "The one faint element of confidence which [the French] cling to is the fact that American troops, however strong in number, stand between them and the Red Army."[36]

In early March, before Kennan departed for Germany to assess the German situation firsthand, he spoke to Acheson about the opposition to his program from officers in the State Department. He had decided, Kennan said, to defer to their desire to press ahead with establishing a West German government, owing to commitments made within Germany and with the British and French.

Acheson surprised Kennan by his reaction. The secretary said that he regretted Kennan's deferral and told him that he had been "almost persuaded by the cogency of . . . [Kennan's] argument." Acheson strongly implied that he was not that partial to the decision to establish a West German government; he did not understand, he said, "how we ever arrived at the decision to see established a West German government or State." Had this not perhaps been "the brainchild of General Clay"?

Acheson was simply not ready to make a final judgment on his German policy before his planning director's return. At the same time he would not interfere with the program to go ahead with a West German government.[37]

By the time Kennan returned from Europe, however, Acheson, busy preparing for the Washington meeting with Bevin and Schuman, had learned just how fully committed the British and French were to having a separate West German state integrated into Western Europe. By adopting this position, the three foreign ministers moved the discussion along swiftly and smoothly. Acheson, Bevin, and Schuman were now prepared to meet with their Soviet counterpart in Paris.

* * *

For Acheson, however, the matter of the division of Germany had still not been fully resolved. His was a genuinely two-track approach: to proceed with the program to establish a West German government but also to make sure that this did not preclude eventual German reunification. He now decided to ask his closest associate, Philip Jessup, who was not committed to any program, to gather opinions on the matter. Jessup found Kennan's views attractive. "Isn't it true," he asked a member of the Policy Planning Staff, "that everything we can learn from historical experience indicates that the permanent or long-continued suppression of a nation like Germany is impossible?" And if this were so, "shouldn't we keep in mind in framing a long-range policy the eventuality of a restored Germany?"[38]

Two views were therefore put before Acheson in the weeks preceding the Paris meeting. On the one hand, Kennan and Jessup sought to end the division of Germany, as long as the division between Eastern and Western Europe was also liquidated. The other view, pressed by Clay's camp, saw West Germany as more manageable within an integrated Western Europe. Troop withdrawals, he believed, would pose a major threat to the whole security of Europe.

Clay's objections, however, did not kill Plan A in the daily discussions Acheson was holding with his advisers. "Just as the unification of Germany is not an end in itself," Acheson explained to Bevin and Schuman in a note that had been approved by Truman, "so the division of Germany isn't an end in itself."

This suggests that Acheson was ready to investigate whether an all-German settlement was practical. Would it be acceptable to the other Western powers? Could it be achieved under conditions that helped to ensure the security and stability of Europe? Even though he admired Kennan's analysis of the German question, for Acheson the key test for German unification was its practicality.[39]

Now, on the eve of the Paris meeting, a new attack was launched against Plan A. General Omar Bradley, chairman of the Joint Chiefs of Staff, the American ground commander in Europe in World War II, responded that Plan A's proposed troop withdrawals into German port areas would back the British and Americans into indefensible positions, while the Red Army would not be removed far enough east to eliminate its threat to West Germany and all of Western Europe. Bradley's reaction was endorsed by the secretary of defense, Louis Johnson.[40]

The final setback to Plan A came when *The New York Times* on May 12 printed a page one story by James Reston, reporting on Plan A's proposal for troop withdrawals. This "raised hell in Europe," as Bohlen put it, and the French and British reacted violently against the proposal. The British were especially concerned about preventing any Soviet incursion in the West, and the French feared a unified Germany.

Jessup hastily assured Schuman that Reston's story was inaccurate, then repeated these assurances to other suspicious British and French officials. He was struck by the vehemence of the allied reaction and wrote to Kennan from Paris, "Had we come here with 'Program A' (even if unhampered by the really serious effects of the Reston article), I do not think we could have secured tripartite agreement on it." Kennan later concluded that the French and British views had made "a deep impression on Mr. Acheson." They also coincided "with those of our own military establishment [and] they had the support of the Western European Division of the Department of State."[41]

Acheson did not present Plan A to the Europeans in Paris. Two days before he left on May 20, he told the National Security Council that "any unification of Germany as a whole" had to grow out of the formation of a West German state. He saw this as a far less painful approach than trying to unite Germany first.[42]

In meeting twice with his British and French colleagues before the conference began with the Russians at the Palais Rose, Acheson concurred with the outlook of Bevin and Schuman. The American position was set.

The meeting in Paris introduced to Acheson the Soviet foreign minister, Andrei Vishinsky. He was short and slim, given to nervous gestures, and had what Acheson perceived as "mercilessly cold eyes." Although he had been a public prosecutor during Stalin's bloody purge trials of the 1930s, Vishinsky had never been accepted into Stalin's inner circle.

A fin-de-siècle pink marble mansion off the Champs-Elysées, the Palais Rose was built by Count Boni de Castellane for his American bride, Anna Gould, who lent it to the French government in 1949. The Council of Foreign Ministers met in the Grand Salon, where a frescoed ceiling of satyrs in hot pursuit of nymphs gave an "incorrigible musical comedy setting" to what Acheson described as "our wholly unreal meetings."[43]

Neither side budged from its position. The Russians had nothing new to propose for Germany as a whole but sought to prevent any progress in the formation of a West German state. In essence, they called for the status quo and continued four-power control. Bevin countered with a Western proposal for the establishment of a federal government for all of Germany, by extending the new Bonn constitution to the whole country and thereby making it one economic and political unit. But this was really a call for an unconditional capitulation by the Soviets. Predictably, Vishinsky rejected it. The deadlock meant that no more efforts would be made by the victors of World War II to reunify Germany. The division of Germany was formalized.[44]

At one point, it seemed as though some real progress might be made on concluding a peace treaty for Austria, which was still under four-power occupation. But on June 30, the last day of the conference, Vishinsky telephoned Schuman, who was holding a press conference, and demanded that the council reconvene. Apparently, Andrei Gromyko, Vishinsky's deputy, had telephoned him from Moscow and told him in brutal language that the Austrian agreements were unsatisfactory and must be reopened.

As Acheson tells it, he and Bevin had just reached the Quai d'Orsay together. After checking with each other on what each had been told of Viskinsky's change of position, Bevin asked, "Any ideas?"

"I'd tell him to go to hell," Acheson said.

"Me, too."

In the Quai d'Orsay's glass-enclosed elevator, Bevin asked, "Do you know our Labour song, 'The Red Flag'?" Acheson said he did not. "The tune's the same as 'Maryland, My Maryland.' Y'know that, coomin' from there. Let's sing 'em together, a sign of solidarity, as we Labour blokes say."

And so they did, arm in arm, walking through the sedate Second Empire anterooms, with the final bars at the entrance of the meeting room.[45]

Bevin congratulated his Soviet counterpart on a new record. Soviet agreements, he said, were fragile things, but today's was the frailest yet. It had not survived even a day. There would be no Austrian peace treaty until 1954.[46]

George Kennan later acknowledged how unlikely it was that the Russians would have agreed to a withdrawal of forces from Germany on the basis of a continued demilitarization of that country and genuine freedom for German political life.[47] He certainly underestimated the stability that would come to prevail in Europe with Germany divided. And he could not have imagined the peaceful unification of that country four decades later with the collapse of the Soviet Union. By accepting Bevin and Schuman's view that the division of Germany was the best course to follow, Acheson, in French critic Raymond Aron's words, had chosen "the present partition of Europe" as "less dangerous than any other arrangement."[48]

CHAPTER TWENTY

LETTING THE DUST SETTLE

THE VERY DAY Dean Acheson assumed the office of secretary of state on January 1, 1949, Generalissimo Chiang Kai-shek resigned the presidency of the Republic of China. His Nationalist armies, badly led and demoralized, had collapsed before the onslaught of well-disciplined Chinese Communist troops.*

In Nanjing, the last capital of the Chinese Nationalist government, the American ambassador and former missionary John Leighton Stuart had set up "an elaborately decorated tree" to try to provide what he called "something of Christmas cheer in the gathering gloom." Now, with the holiday over and Chiang in his picturesque retreat in the hilly countryside near the Chikiang coast, the last American ambassador insisted he remain at his post and wait for the Communist forces to capture the capital.

Finally, on Sunday morning, April 24, 1949, the Communists easily crossed the great Yangtze River—which American general Albert Wedemeyer had once said could be defended with broomsticks by an army willing to fight—and entered the city. In the face of Nationalist soldiers who deserted their posts and fell

* I will employ current usage in the spelling of Chinese names, but in citations of the period or in secondary sources, the Wade-Giles spelling is more common; thus, Mao Zedong = Mao Tse-tung; Zhou Enlai = Chou En-lai; Taiwan = Formosa; Beijing = Peking or Peiping. On the other hand, I prefer to employ the more commonly used Chiang Kaishek rather than Jiang Jieshi.

apart before the highly motivated Communist troops, the orderly armies of Mao Zedong quietly took over Nanjing.[1]

As total Communist control on the Chinese mainland now appeared inevitable, the Republican opposition bitterly tried to pin the "loss" of China on the Democrats. And as the Republican attacks mounted in fury, Acheson found it increasingly difficult to carry out the policy that he believed was best for the United States—to wait until the Communists had fully consolidated their power (both on the mainland and on the island of Taiwan, where Chiang Kai-shek and remnants of his forces hung on), to recognize Mao's new regime, and to try to prevent it from becoming subservient to the Soviet Union.

The problem that constantly bedeviled him was the willingness of the Republican opposition to hold up appropriations for European recovery in order to force the administration to support Chiang Kai-shek. Acheson's strategy at home therefore was to try to placate pro-Chiang conservatives while the president mobilized suppport for containment in Europe.[2]

How had this all come to pass? To Acheson, the American Congress and public needed and deserved an explanation of U.S. policy for the past four years; in the spring of 1949 he had his staff prepare a one-thousand-page document known as the *China White Paper*. It was designed to provide a dispassionate history of American efforts to hold China together after Japan's surrender, while portraying the increasing Nationalist corruption and incompetence, along with the evidence of Communist determination and discipline.[3]

American attitudes toward China had always been shaped by the missionary and the trader. Along with its traders, America sent missionaries in abundance, and their success was measured less in numbers of converted Chinese than in the importance of their influence in America. By the time Acheson was in college, the Chinese revolution of 1911–12, led by the founder of the Kuomintang Party, Dr. Sun Yat-sen, had overthrown the Manchu dynasty, and Americans tended to feel a sentimental attachment to the Chinese. As Acheson himself described it years later, "I went to Yale, and we had a Yale-in-China in the central part of China. We raised money throughout the years—$10 a year or whatever it was—and we supported this place. And the Chinese came here to every college in the country, and we made pets of them. The boys were taken home for supper, and they'd tell fascinating stories about what it was like in that strange part of the world. . . . We are emotional about this thing."[4]

From the beginning of the century, Washington insisted on an "Open Door" policy, which called for every nation to have economic access to the Chinese market and therefore for the territorial and administrative integrity of China. This allowed the United States to express its traditional distrust of colonialism while at the same time demanding that the United States have a right to establish its own trading relationships with the Middle Kingdom.

Despite American insistence on the principles of the Open Door, Washington nonetheless pursued a foreign policy without giving those principles any support in terms of power. The Chinese civil war, which broke out in 1927 between the Nationalists, led by Chiang Kai-shek, and the Communists, led by Mao Zedong; the occupation of Manchuria by the Japanese in 1931; and the subsequent invasion of China by the Japanese in July 1937 all provoked condemnation by the U.S. government but no military intervention or aid to preserve China's territorial integrity.

The success of the Japanese war machine in China did provoke an ever-stronger American response in terms of economic embargoes on Japan, and American sympathies lay with China. But little or no help was given to the Chinese government, which mended relations with the Communists in 1937 in a halfhearted attempt to form a common front against the Japanese.

The attack on Pearl Harbor changed all this. With the United States now at war with Japan, the Chinese government, which had retreated to Chongqinq in far western China, received an American military mission and extensive aid under lend-lease. Because the Chinese were now allies against the Japanese, American policy was to promote continued cooperation between the Communists and the Nationalists in order to win the war against Japan. But with the American entrance into the war, Chiang Kai-shek concluded that the Americans would eventually win and that they would not desert him, no matter how badly his armies fared against the Japanese. Chiang's cooperation with the Chinese Communists faded.

At the end of World War II, American policy continued to urge cooperation between the Nationalists and the Communists. China had been anointed by Roosevelt to assume the role of one of the "four policemen," along with the Soviet Union, Britain, and America, to help keep the peace in the postwar world. At FDR's behest, Stalin was willing to recognize Chiang's government as the legal government of postwar China; the Soviet ruler had little expectation that Mao would win the civil war between the Nationalists and the Communists once victory over Japan was assured.

Chiang was a devout and practicing Methodist, aided and abetted by his American-educated wife; he himself spoke no English. He read the Bible every day, was puritanical in his own habits, and brooked no licentious behavior among those in his immediate entourage. He neither smoked nor drank, except at ceremonial occasions. He almost always appeared composed and self-confident, though his temper was furious when aroused.

Yet he was also harsh, devious, and cruel, and an incompetent military leader—"a sucker for a feint," as American officers said. He was adept at divide-and-rule politics. He promised his American advisers that he would institute reforms, but he never did so. His troops were to be saved for postwar battles against the Communists. As he said in 1941, "The Japanese are a disease of the skin; the Communists are a disease of the heart. They say they wish to support me, but secretly they want to overthrow me." To the Americans, most of whom had few illusions about his military ability or his attitude toward corruption, he was nonetheless the indispensable man, the inheritor of Sun Yat-sen's revolution, the symbol of the unity of China.[5]

Mao Zedong, on the other hand, controlled much of north China, and without his cooperation the civil war would erupt again at any time. Moreover, his forces were far better trained and motivated than Chiang's; as a military strategist he was far superior, for he recognized that this was a war of movement and that holding cities far from headquarters with dangerously extended supply lines, as the Nationalist forces now did in the north, rendered them highly vulnerable.

Unlike the trim, ascetic Chiang, Mao was stocky, with a round, unlined face; he was more given to expressing his emotions, ready to flash a broad smile, and better at connecting with his audiences through the use of earthy puns and broad gestures. But he was, if anything, even crueller than Chiang to his enemies, willing to eliminate large numbers of those groups that opposed his dictatorship.

Among his closest collaborators was General Zhou Enlai, a brilliant mandarin who was sent to Chiang's capital to see if the two sides could compose their differences in the final struggle against Japan and, afterward, in the rebuilding of China.

Negotiations between the Nationalists and the Communists came to an end in early November 1945. Moreover, the presence of Major General Patrick J. Hurley, who was appointed ambassador to China in the fall of 1944 and remained in that post for a year, only exacerbated the tensions between the two sides. His bizarre behavior, such as the performance of an Indian war dance at an embassy party and his war whoop of "Yahoo!" when he met with Mao Zedong on November 7, 1944, made it difficult for either side to take him seriously. By the end of his stay, Hurley was wholly committed to Chiang Kai-shek.[6]

On November 27, 1945, General Hurley, who was in Washington to consult with Secretary Byrnes, delivered a blistering attack at the National Press Club on the administration for not having a clear policy toward China, and then he resigned. In his letter of resignation, he denounced Foreign Service officers serving in the American embassy in Chongqinq for siding with the Chinese Communists and therefore wanting "to pull the plug on Chiang Kai-Shek."[7]

Acheson, under secretary of state at the time, was puzzled by Hurley's statements. He believed that the administration did have a clear policy: by reconciling warring factions, it was trying to restore a "strong, united and democratic China" without intervening militarily in the Chinese civil war. He later admitted that "few, if any of us, including Hurley, myself, the Secretary, General Marshall, and the President, realized that these admirable aims were mutually exclusive and separately unachievable."[8]

That same afternoon Truman telephoned General Marshall, who was planning to retire from active service, and asked him to go to China as his personal representative.

Just before Christmas, Marshall, having worked out his instructions with the president and the secretary of state, was preparing to leave. At that point he told Truman that "no sensible soldier undertakes a field command without leaving a rear echelon at headquarters." He knew only too well that out of sight was out of mind, and he was determined to leave behind someone who would receive his communications from the field, get answers for his requests, and reply within twenty-four hours. This meant a highly placed representative, who, as Acheson tells it, "could surmount bureaucratic procedure of the sort which let General Gordon be overwhelmed at Khartoum through glacial ponderousness of overpreparation." When asked who this should be, Marshall named Under Secretary of State Dean Acheson. He would be the rear echelon. In this way Marshall would be in direct communication with the president.

In essence, Marshall's mission was to reconcile the warring parties, so that "the reunification of China by peaceful, democratic methods" might be achieved as soon as possible. In addition, Truman instructed Marshall to inform Chiang Kai-shek and the other Chinese leaders that "a China disunited and torn by civil strife could not be considered realistically as a proper place for American assistance."[9]

Marshall remained in China for one year and utterly failed to achieve an end to the civil war. He did obtain a cease-fire and a political conference between the two sides before he returned to Washington in March 1946 to arrange for financial credits for a unified Chinese government; at that time he was hopeful that both an interim coalition government and the integration of the Communist and Nationalist armed forces would be achieved.[10]

But this was the high point of his mission. Almost immediately thereafter, the situation in China deteriorated. As the Soviets pulled out of Manchuria, both the Communists and the Nationalists moved into their place; but as they did so, the communication lines of the Nationalists became dangerously overextended. By the time Marshall returned in May, a full-scale war was about to break out. Nonetheless, he obtained a truce until the end of June, but then the fighting resumed.

Back in Washington Acheson believed that the United States should maintain relations with Chiang's government but also consider withdrawing the residual

U.S. military forces that remained in China and ending all material support to the Nationalists, if the war resumed.[11]

By October Marshall was at a point where he was about to abandon his role as a middleman between the two warring factions. Concluding that the Nationalists were determined to use force to further their aims, he virtually accused Chiang's government of duplicity in its further military activity in the north. Continued efforts at mediation would be fruitless. Neither the Communists nor the Nationalists trusted one another.

By now the Nationalists had reached an apparent peak of their military endeavors, but their gains were illusory. As Acheson later testified, "General Marshall repeatedly pointed out to the [Nationalist] Government that what it was doing was overextending itself militarily and politically, since it neither had sufficient troops to garrison the whole area nor did it have sufficient administrators to administer areas that it was taking over."

Major General David Barr, chief of the U.S. Advisory Group, described the doomed strategy of Chiang's generals in their campaign in northern China: "In modern warfare the most disastrous of all things to do is to retreat into a city behind walls and take a defensive position."[12]

By 1946 the Marshall mission had clearly collapsed, and the general accepted Truman's offer to become secretary of state.

In the two years that Marshall ran the State Department, the bipartisan foreign policy that had been worked out for European recovery fell apart when it came to China. The Republicans, flush with victory in the 1946 congressional elections, centered their criticism of the administration's foreign policy on the China issue.

Senator Vandenberg did point out that it was "a very easy, simple matter to dissociate oneself from a policy," but it "is not quite so easy to assert what an alternative policy might have been." In fact, the senators and congressmen who gave unflinching suppport to Chiang Kai-shek, the so-called China bloc, did have an alternative to the administration's refusal to send in American troops to quell the Communists and appropriate vast amounts of money to prop up the Nationalists.

What China-bloc senators William Knowland of California and Owen Brewster of Maine and congressman Walter Judd of Minnesota wanted was to provide the Nationalists with massive economic and military aid, but without American combat troops. Judd told the House: "Not for one moment has anyone contemplated sending a single combat soldier in."[13]

Since Marshall's unwillingness to use American ground troops reflected almost universal American public opinion, Truman's critics had no other solution except massive military aid. Moreover, in order to get the reluctant administration to pour more money down what seemed to Truman an endless rathole, the Republicans would hold up appropriations on European recovery until the administration agreed to appropriations for China.

To ease Vandenberg's position as a promoter of bipartisan foreign policy and to gain greater support for the European Recovery Program, Marshall believed he had to endorse a policy of limited aid to the Nationalists. The problem with this decision was that such aid merely postponed the inevitable defeat of Chiang's forces on the mainland. In his recommendation to Marshall just before the general left China for home, Ambassador John Leighton Stuart urged that the United States either make a genuine effort to prevent a Communist takeover or do nothing at all.[14]

Stuart's recommendation made sense, but politically it was all but impossible. Nothing was likely to stem the tide of a Communist victory, short of an all-out military effort involving U.S. ground troops. However, to refuse aid to the Nationalists, who seemed to have no intention of making genuine reforms, was abhorrent to many members of Congress. Even Republicans not normally associated with the China bloc joined in an ever more bitter attack on the administration's China policy.

At the end of May 1947 Marshall responded to congressional pressure by lifting the embargo on the shipment of munitions. Over the next six months, as the last American troops withdrew from north China, they left the Nationalist forces some 6,500 tons of ammunition.

Finally, a program of limited assistance became embodied in the China Aid Act of April 1948, which Truman and Marshall reluctantly supported in order to ensure Vandenberg's support for European aid under the Marshall Plan. It provided for $400 million—$275 million in economic aid and $125 million in military aid. Altogether the United States gave the Nationalists approximately $1 billion in military aid and a similar amount in economic aid from V-J Day in August 1945 through 1948.[15]

In yet another effort to gain support for his policy toward China, in mid-1947 Marshall sent to China on a fact-finding mission General Albert Wedemeyer, a tough anti-Communist known as "Barefoot Al" because of his habit of pretending to be humble and uninformed. ("I'm just a farm boy from Nebraska," he would say.[16])

Marshall, in fact, used Wedemeyer to send secret instructions to the American consulate in Mukden, Manchuria, to begin building bridges with the Communists who were in control there. The Wedemeyer report did call for further aid to Chiang, but the entire mission was ordered by Marshall because it might prove useful for him as he approached Congress for European aid early in 1948.[17]

In the meantime, Chiang's military campaign went from bad to worse, as the generalissimo continued to retain incompetent commanders. Not pausing to consolidate their gains in north China, Chiang's armies tried to take over Manchuria as well, which was a task far beyond their logistic capabilities. The Nationalists were finally forced to retreat into walled cities, leaving the Communist forces to cut lines of communications and starve them out. By the end of 1948 the Communists had control of Manchuria and most of China north of the Yangtze.

Consistent with his belief that the Communists would overwhelm the Nationalists even if they retreated to Taiwan, Marshall had decided in October 1948 that the United States would not defend Taiwan, a decision "unanimously recommended" by all the departments concerned.[18]

As Chiang anticipated a Communist victory on the mainland, at the beginning of 1949 he transferred to Taiwan all foreign exchange and monetary reserves. He then requested that the United States ship any remaining military equipment destined for China to his island fortress, where he would now make his headquarters and wait for the United States to restore him to power. By May the Nationalist resistance on the mainland was virtually at an end, and the Communists were firmly in power. Mao officially announced the founding of the People's Republic of China, with Beijing as its capital, on October 1, 1949.

As these events unfolded, on February 7, 1949, Dean Acheson as the new secretary of state met with thirty Republican congressmen to discuss the likely final collapse of the Nationalist government. Asked to predict the course of events, Acheson replied that "when a great tree falls in the forest one cannot see the extent of the damage until the dust settles."

The next day the press reported that his China policy was to "wait until the dust settles." Though Acheson vainly protested that this was not a policy, but rather a confession of his inability to see very far into the future, the China bloc found his imagery invaluable in assaulting the administration's foreign policy.[19]

Ten days before Acheson took over at State, a National Security Council paper had declared that the "immediate aim of U.S. policy should, therefore, be to prevent China from becoming an adjunct of Soviet power."[20] In that same month, Acheson declared to the NSC that for all intents and purposes the Chinese civil war had come to an end. He believed that the Nationalists might survive in south China and Taiwan "for months or years to come," but it would "at best be a local regime with its claims to international reocognition based on insubstantial legalisms." Eventually, he predicted, "most or all of China will come under Communist rule." The last thing the Truman administration should do would be to give any further military aid to the Nationalists, for this would simply solidify the support of the Chinese people for Mao's regime and "perpetuate the delusion that China's interests lie with the USSR."[21]

By the end of February the National Security Council presented a paper to the president that called for the government to "maintain its freedom of action" by pursuing a policy designed "to create serious rifts between Moscow and a Chinese Communist regime."

To this end, Washington should restore "ordinary economic relations between China on the one hand and Japan and the western world on the other." Such an approach would make it possible for the United States "to exploit frictions between the Chinese Communist regime and the USSR should they arise."[22] This strategy might keep Mao from aligning himself too closely to Stalin. Like Marshal Tito in Yugoslavia, Mao would come into power without any significant help from the Soviet Union.

President Truman approved the paper on March 3, 1949.[23]

In early April, when Acheson and his advisers met with Ernest Bevin, they told him that the "Nationalists seem to be washed up, and the Communists able to go wherever they wished." The administration had abandoned "the idea of supporting the regime," but it was difficult "publicly to withdraw support for Chiang." Nonetheless, Acheson, hoping that the United States could eventually recognize Mao's regime, assured Bevin that the "U.S. henceforth will pursue a more realistic policy respecting China."[24]

That spring, with the Communists about to cross the Yangtze on their final push to victory, Acheson successfully resisted a bill introduced by the China bloc to provide an additional $1.5 billion in loans to the Nationalists and to authorize American officers to direct Nationalist armies still in the field. However, in order to win passage of European recovery aid for fiscal year 1950, which would be followed by a push for Senate approval of NATO and its Military Aid Program, Acheson agreed to permit the unexpended portion of the funds provided for in the China Aid Act to be spent beyond the act's expiration date of April 2, 1949; the Senate extended that date to February 15, 1950.

In effect, Congress was making it impossible for Acheson to abandon support of the Chinese Nationalists and move to a realist policy of establishing relations with Beijing on the basis of who represented the effective government of China.

No sooner had the aid bill been modified than Mao Zedong declared on June 30, 1949, that China would align itself with the Soviet Union. To assure the Soviets that he was not about to become an Asian Tito, he asserted, "We must lean to one side. . . . Sitting on the fence will not do; nor is there a third road."[25]

Mao's decision may have been influenced by the extension of the aid bill, but the way had been foreshadowed by Zhou Enlai a few months earlier when he said: "It is a fond dream of the United States to split China from the Soviet Union." However, "The Chinese Communist Party cannot afford to make enemies on both sides; no force can prevent it from having two friends at once."[26]

Although the Chinese Communists might not be able to have close relations with the United States until Washington finally broke with Chiang's Nationalists, they could at least trade with America, and this might lead to eventual diplomatic ties. In fact, ten days after Mao's "lean to one side" statement, Mao dispatched Chen Mingshu, described as a "fellow traveler of the Communists" from the Nationalists, to explain his thinking to the American ambassador in Nanjing. In mid-July 1949 Chen told Ambassador Stuart that Mao's declaration was designed "for his own Party." The Chinese Communists still hoped for formal diplomatic relations between the United States and a Chinese Communist regime.[27]

If Mao and Zhou were moving closer to Stalin, they nonetheless hoped to have good relations with the United States, which could eventually lead to recognition. In this respect, their policies briefly converged with what Truman and Acheson were trying to do. The Americans saw Sino-American trade as a means of weaning away the Chinese Communists from Moscow's embrace; Mao and Zhou saw it as a hedge against too close an alignment with Stalin. At the same time, Stalin, alarmed at the signing of the North Atlantic Treaty on April 4, 1949, perceived China as an increasingly valuable asset in the Cold War.

In August 1949 Acheson released the *White Paper*, seeking to explain and justify American policy toward China since Pearl Harbor. Buttressed by hundreds of pages of documents, it was Acheson's effort as a "frustrated schoolteacher," in Felix Frankfurter's words, to educate the American people as to why the administration should not be held responsible for the fall of Nationalist China.[28]

Though the *White Paper* still holds up as a model of scholarship, as a means of explaining to the public what happened and why, it failed to achieve its purpose of calming American public opinion: its bulk alone simply did not lend itself to serious study except by scholars. More accessible but ultimately more disastrous was Acheson's Letter of Transmittal, drafted by Philip Jessup.

In the Letter, signed by the secretary of state, Acheson was determined to demonstrate that the failures of the Nationalist government "do not stem from an inadequacy of American aid." Pointing out that "history has proved again and again that a regime without faith in itself and an army without morale cannot survive the test of battle," the Letter reiterated that "nothing the United States did or could have done within the reasonable limits of its capabilities could have changed the results."[29]

The Letter was essentially a political document that portrayed the Chinese

Communists as tools of Moscow. It stated that the Chinese Communist leaders "have publicly announced their subservience to a foreign power, Russia."[30] This was a position that Acheson did not hold, according to John Melby, a key adviser on China affairs for General Marshall, who had written the draft of the *White Paper.*[31] He approved this language in order to appease the China bloc and because he thought it would be little noted.

Once again, as he had in 1947 when he used the heightened rhetoric of the "rotten apples" to gain support for aid to Greece and Turkey, in the Letter Acheson dangerously overstated his case. By asserting Beijing's submissiveness to Moscow, he made it much more difficult to pursue a policy of recognition, even should Mao eventually conquer Taiwan and eliminate all domestic opposition.

In fact, Acheson was still searching for a way to separate Beijing from Moscow. He seems to have believed that China's Communist leaders would eventually have to choose between the interests of their own people and those of Moscow. By accusing Mao of kowtowing to Stalin, he hoped to spur on the Chinese to "throw off the foreign yoke."[32]

Not only did the *White Paper* arouse the ire of Walter Lippmann, who attacked the language about China's subservience to the Soviet Union and also believed America had been doing too much in a losing cause, it also enraged the China bloc, which believed America had done too little. General Hurley called the *White Paper* "a smooth alibi for the pro-Communists in the State Department who had engineered the overthrow of our ally, the Nationalist Government of the Republic of China."[33]

Republican senators like Knowland, Styles Bridges of New Hampshire, and Kenneth Wherry of Nebraska, along with Democrat Pat McCarran of Nevada, assailed the *White Paper* as "a 1,054-page whitewash of a wishful, do-nothing policy which has succeeded only in placing Asia in danger of Soviet conquest."[34]

Diplomatic recognition of the Communist Chinese government, which Mao officially proclaimed as the government of China on October 1, 1949, was an absolute necessity in Acheson's view. But it was almost impossible to accomplish, not only because of the strength of the China bloc, but also because Chiang Kai-shek had now established his Republic of China government on Taiwan. Moreover, every abuse by Mao's government, including the detention of the American consul, Angus Ward, in Mukden, Manchuria, from late 1948 to late 1949, added to Acheson's difficulty in proceeding with recognition.

As long as Chiang was in power on Taiwan, the China bloc could present an alternative to recognizing Mao's government in Beijing. Should the United States therefore protect Taiwan from invasion from the mainland? Or should it wait for Taiwan to fall, in which case recognition might come more easily?

In the State Department Walton Butterworth, the assistant secretary of state for Far Eastern affairs, and George Kennan offered different approaches, designed to prevent the island from coming under Mao's control. Butterworth suggested a United Nations plebiscite that would allow Taiwan's population to vote for either mainland control or some form of UN trusteeship, pending independence.

George Kennan proposed a drastic scheme for ridding the island of the Nationalist soldiers but retaining it as strategically valuable to the United States. He urged the use of American forces to throw Chiang's troops out of Taiwan and the adjoining islands and, under American auspices and protection, create an independent country. This was the way "Theodore Roosevelt might have done it," he suggested, with "resolution, speed, ruthlessness and self-assurance."[35]

Acheson rejected these proposals and recommended that the United States abandon any effort to prevent the island from falling to the Communists.[36] In August 1949, in a meeting with members of the National Security Council, the Joint Chiefs of Staff also agreed that military measures would be unwise.[37]

Still, pressures mounted on Acheson to support Taiwan from any attack from the mainland Communists. As Acheson wrote to his old friend Archibald MacLeish in early 1950, "Formosa is a subject which seems to draw out the boys like a red haired girl on the beach. It appears that what you want most is what you ain't got."[38]

When Truman signed a Mutual Defense Act that included an appropriation of $75 million for the "general area of China," Chiang's supporters grew hopeful. But they soon discovered that Truman, on Acheson's advice, did not intend to use the money to aid the Nationalist regime on Taiwan.

In a December 23 meeting between the State Department and the Joint Chiefs of Staff, Acheson argued that "Mao is not a true satellite in that he came to power by his own efforts and was not installed in office by the Soviet army." In his end-of-the-year memorandum to the president he further declared that America should not subsidize attacks by the Nationalists on Mao's government, which "would soon be widely recognized."[39]

By the end of 1949 Acheson had once again persuaded the Joint Chiefs to repeat their opposition to overt military means to protect Taiwan. The JCS now defined an American defensive position based on the Philippines, north to the Ryukyu Islands and to Japan itself.[40]

On January 4, 1950, Acheson advised the president to make known publicly the administration's plan to adopt a hands-off policy toward Taiwan. Truman agreed and the next day announced that the United States would not intercede to prevent a takeover of Taiwan by the Communists.[41] Although the need to combat the spread of communism in Asia was becoming an ever larger goal of American policy, it was by no means a considered policy of containment, as in Greece and Turkey. Acheson did not see the Truman Doctrine as applicable to China.

Along the periphery of Asia, stretching from Korea to Indochina and beyond, the United States would nonetheless look for ways to discourage the Communists from making further inroads.[42] Acheson had said to Philip Jessup in a top-secret memorandum just before the *White Paper* was released that he wanted to make "absolutely certain that we are neglecting no opportunity that would be within our capabilities to achieve the purpose of halting the spread of totalitarian communism in Asia."[43]

On January 10, 1950, Acheson testified in executive session before the Senate Foreign Relations Committee. As far as recognition of Mao's government was concerned, he saw no reason to move too swiftly at this time. He wanted to see how the Chinese Communists would behave toward Americans in China, and their attitude toward the foreign debts of the Nationalist government, but he warned the senators not to get "this thing mixed up with approval or disapproval." Above all, "We should not [use] military forces of the United States to take, secure, or defend Formosa."[44]

Two days later Acheson delivered an important address on Far Eastern policy to the National Press Club in Washington. Tossing aside the speech the department had prepared, which he felt lacked life and had "no continuity of thought," he had made extensive notes for a new speech at his house in Georgetown.

Acheson's press club speech had little to do with military matters, and indeed he had urged his listeners not "to become obsessed with military considerations." In the main, Acheson was repeating for a larger public what he had been saying privately to members of Congress. He reminded his audience that nobody said "the Nationalist Government fell because it was confronted by overwhelming military force which it could not resist"; on the contrary, Chiang's "support in the country has melted away." He warned Americans against "the folly of ill-conceived adventures on our part," which could "deflect from the Russians to ourselves the righteous anger, and the wrath, and the hatred of the Chinese which must develop. It would be folly to deflect it to ourselves."[45]

Acheson did, however, describe the military security of the Pacific area, pointing out that the American "defensive perimeter" ran from the Aleutian Islands to Japan, then on to Okinawa and the Philippine Islands. In South Korea, on the other hand, "initial reliance must be on the people attacked to resist it and then upon the commitments of the entire civilized world under the Charter of the United Nations. . . ." Acheson emphasized, however, that the United States bore "a direct responsibility" for Korea, as it did for Japan.

In thus defining a defense perimeter, Acheson was simply repeating the position of the Joint Chiefs of Staff at the end of 1949, one that MacArthur himself had described in a speech on March 1, 1949.[46] While critics later charged that omitting South Korea from the perimeter gave the Soviet Union and its North

Korean allies the incentive to attack the south, no serious critic argued this at the time. Acheson's assertion of U.S. responsibility for South Korea and his evocation of UN commitments implied that the United States would indeed act if South Korea was attacked, though it was certainly not a clear and open declaration to defend South Korea.

Four years later Acheson said that "that was the warning which the aggressor disregarded." But he also admitted somewhat disingenuously that "in those days I was fresh and eager and inexperienced"; his own "rough notes" had led to a speech that opened him up "for a very serious misunderstanding."[47]

In executive session before the Senate Foreign Relations Committee, January 13, 1950, Acheson was more explicit: "South Korea could take care of any trouble started by North Korea," he said. But if an invasion was started by the USSR or China, "we would take every possible action in the U.N. I do not believe that we would undertake to resist it by force . . . independently. Of course, if under the Charter action were taken, we would take our part in that, but probably it would not be taken because [the Russians] would veto it."[48]

In contrast to his assault on the *White Paper*, Walter Lippmann hailed Acheson's speech as one of "great moment throughout Asia." Acheson had spoken with "great sagacity and deep penetration." It seemed to Lippmann that at long last the administration was ready to break with Chiang and recognize the Communist government in Beijing.[49]

Acheson's press club speech had also been reported to Stalin and Mao in Moscow. When Acheson declared that Russia was going to annex parts of China, a process "nearly complete in Manchuria," this outraged Stalin because it was very close to the truth.

Stalin now had to demonstrate to Mao that he had no intention of seizing Chinese territory; Mao, in turn, could not allow himself to be portrayed as a weak leader who permitted himself to be used as a puppet of Stalin. For Mao, Acheson's hands-off stand on Taiwan was welcome news; for Stalin, it might portend a tacit understanding between Beijing and Washington.

Molotov, now a vice chairman of the Council of Ministers, proposed that Stalin and Mao issue official statements against the "shameless lie" of the U.S. secretary of state regarding Soviet designs on Manchuria and Mongolia. From the language of their statement, there is no doubt that Stalin and Mao coordinated their replies. But the Russian reply to Acheson's speech was far ruder in tone and insult. This allowed the State Department to promote the idea in the press that there were indeed strains between the two leaders. It seemed that Acheson had been on the mark.[50]

On the other hand, Acheson may well have underestimated Stalin's interest in clearing up any divisive issues between the Soviet Union and China in the face of growing Western power, especially in light of the recently concluded NATO pact. Moreover, while identifying nationalism as the principal force in Asian politics, Acheson appeared to discount the possibility that Chinese communism might also be a legitimate expression of Asian nationalism.

On January 14, 1950, Mao's government seized American consular property in Shanghai and Beijing, which led to the withdrawal of all American personnel from the Chinese mainland that spring. A month later Moscow and Beijing signed the Sino-Soviet Treaty of Friendship, a defense pact. Yet despite this rapprochement between Russia and China, Acheson did not give up on the hope of abandoning Chiang, recognizing the People's Republic of China, and then weaning it away from a Soviet alliance.[51]

On March 29, 1950, Acheson once again testified in executive session before the Senate Foreign Relations Committee. "If the devil himself runs China," he said, "if he is an independent devil, that is infinitely better than if he is a stooge of Moscow, or China comes under Russia." Despite the Sino-Soviet agreement signed in February, "the Chinese, inevitably, we believe, will come into conflict with Moscow."[52]

Acheson also told the senators that he was especially wary of Chiang Kai-shek's adventurism, the risk that Chiang, who was running a war against the mainland by "bombing Nanking and other cities," would drag the United States into conflict with China proper.

According to Acheson, Chiang "believed World War III is absolutely inevitable," in which case "the United States will have to go back and conquer China, and he will come riding in on our coat tails." As far as Acheson was concerned, Chiang was actually inviting Mao to invade Taiwan. "The Communists would be criminally crazy," he advised the senators, "if they did not put an end to [Chiang's island bastion] just as soon as possible."[53]

Had this happened, Acheson believed that he could have overcome opposition to recognizing Communist China. He certainly hoped to drive a wedge between the Chinese and the Russians. On the other hand, he was never clear on whether he wanted to persuade Mao to become an Asian Tito or to encourage the Chinese people to overthrow the Communists by depicting them as Moscow's puppets. Nor is it evident that an alternative policy of recognizing mainland China as the legitimate government of China would have been acceptable to Congress.

Nonetheless, Acheson's approach of waiting for the dust to settle, moving slowly in hopes that events in the Far East would ease his task of recognizing Communist China, of driving a wedge between Moscow and Beijing, and of containing communism on the periphery of the Middle Kingdom was each day made far more costly by the China bloc's accusations that he had "lost China."

CHAPTER TWENTY-ONE

"THAT MOMENT OF DECISION"

With Bretton Woods, the Truman Doctrine, the Marshall Plan, and the North Atlantic Treaty, the building blocks of the West's plan to manage the East-West competition were virtually in place by 1950. The most difficult issue still to be resolved was to construct a security system that would provide Western Europe with a shield with which it could defend itself against any Soviet attack and to make sure that the United States Congress as well as the president would be willing to increase the military budget to help make this possible.

At the same time, there was a growing uneasiness in the country. The explosion of a Soviet atomic bomb in late August 1949 revealed that America was likely to become more vulnerable than at the time of Pearl Harbor. Less than six months later, authorities in London announced the arrest of the scientist Klaus Fuchs, who confessed to having spied for the Russians while working on Anglo-American research at Los Alamos, where the U.S. atomic bomb had been built.

In addition, the drumbeat of Republican criticism of the administration's China policy reverberated with the seeming threat of domestic communist subversion and Soviet military prowess. Attacks on Acheson and his State Department aides for their alleged softness toward communism were increasing, especially after Alger Hiss was convicted of perjury in January 1950.

In his own way, Acheson tried to put forth a view of America's role in the world that was deeply grounded in his realist approach to foreign affairs. Acheson was fully aware of the limitations of American power and purpose. On October 20,

1949, he said at the annual Al Smith dinner in New York City: "We cannot direct or control; we cannot make a world, as God did, out of chaos."[1]

Just before Christmas 1949, Acheson spoke at the National War College. Once again he tried to explain that the Cold War was not a struggle between good and evil. America had to deal with the Soviet Union as a great power and not as a monster that had to be destroyed. "Today you hear much talk of absolutes . . . that two systems such as ours and that of the Russians cannot exist in the same world . . . that one is good and one is evil, and good and evil cannot exist in the world." But, "Good and evil have existed in this world since Adam and Eve went out of the Garden of Eden."

Pleading for balance and solvency, Acheson urged his listeners to remember that the "proper search is for limited ends. . . . That is what all of us must learn to do in the United States: to limit objectives, to get ourselves away from the search for the absolute, to find out what is within our powers, to find out how it can be done with the materials at our disposal."[2]

Once again Acheson was writing regularly to his daughter Mary, who had returned to the sanatorium in September with a new bout of tuberculosis, leaving her baby, Michael, in the care of her parents until the fall of 1950. A week before his China speech to the National Press Club, he had written to her that he hoped to be able "to carry some sense of the problem in the Far East, the limitation of our power, the direction of our purpose." He was also proud and pleased with Harry Truman, whose support he required and, as it turned out, would need far more than he had ever anticipated. "The President," he wrote, "has been superb. . . . One could not ask for a commander with more directness, understanding and courage."[3]

Later that month Acheson made a decision that was to make him vulnerable. On January 21, 1950, Alger Hiss, at the end of a long second trial, was found guilty of perjury—for falsely stating that he had not passed secret documents to Whittaker Chambers. (His first trial had resulted in a hung jury the previous July.) Four days later, on the day Hiss was sentenced to five years in prison, Acheson was asked at a press conference if he had any comments on the matter.

Acheson knew he would probably be asked about Hiss. The previous evening his son-in-law, William Bundy, recalled, the secretary of state had been fretting about the press conference the next day and got out a Bible; without saying what he was planning to use it for, he wrote out something from it.[4] Acheson had also told his aide, Lucius Battle, that he would speak about Hiss at the press conference. Unlike others who had known Hiss, he would not "turn and run." Battle, worried about what his boss would say, got in touch with Paul Nitze, who had replaced Kennan as head of Policy Planning, and told him, "We've got to stop him."[5]

At breakfast the next morning, Acheson informed his wife that he was sure to be asked about Hiss and that he was not going to forsake him. Alice supported him. "What else could you say?"

"Don't think this is a light matter," Acheson warned. "This could be quite a storm and it could get me in trouble." When his wife asked if he was sure he was right, he answered, "It is what I have to do."[6]

Upon arriving at the office, he told Battle that he had discussed the Hiss matter with Felix Frankfurter on their morning walk. "Felix does not want me to refrain from commenting," he told his worried young assistant. Battle, who had drafted two or three responses, had finally given up and concluded that Acheson shouldn't say anything. But Acheson assured Battle that all he was going to do was quote Saint Matthew from the Bible.

"Well, that's fine," Battle said. "Wrap yourself up in the Bible."

Acheson could certainly have given no comment, especially when he had no close connection to Hiss or any particular affection for him. But Alger was Donald's brother; Donald had been Acheson's law partner; Acheson's conscience would simply not allow him to act in a cowardly manner. As he wrote to his daughter Mary that night, it had been a "hard and exhausting" day. "Alger's case has been on my mind incessantly. As I have written you, here is stark tragedy—whatever the reasonably probable facts may be." The problem was "to say what one really meant—forgetting the yelping pack at one's heels—saying no more and no less than one truly believed. This was not easy. I felt that advisers were of no use and so consulted none. I understood that I had responsibilities above and beyond my own desires."[7]

It did not take long for one of the reporters to ask for his comment on Hiss. After noting that the case was still before the courts, pending appeal, Acheson plunged ahead: "I should like to make it clear to you that whatever the outcome of any appeal . . . I do not intend to turn my back on Alger Hiss."

He went on to explain that every person who knew or had worked with Hiss had it upon his conscience to decide what position he should take. "This must be done," he said, "by each person in the light of his own standards and principles. I think they were stated for us a very long time ago. They were stated on the Mount of Olives and if you are interested in seeing them you will find them in the 25th Chapter of the Gospel according to St. Matthew beginning with verse 34."[8]

The verse Acheson cited reads: "For I was an hungred, and ye gave me meat; I was thirsty and ye gave me drink; I was a stranger and ye took me in; Naked and ye clothed me; I was sick and ye visited me; I was in prison and ye came unto me."

Had Acheson simply read the selection from Saint Matthew to the reporters gathered there, he might have evoked from them and from the American public a sympathetic response. Instead, what was remembered and reported were the fateful words "I do not intend to turn my back on Alger Hiss."

Although Acheson personally believed that Hiss's testimony about his relations with Whittaker Chambers "did not add up," his statement at the press conference did not reflect views on Hiss's guilt or innocence. Acheson's response was an act of Christian charity, no more and no less.[9]

After sending word ahead asking the president to receive him, Acheson went straight to the White House following the press conference. He told him what had happened and offered his resignation. Truman, however, already had the news ticker report on his desk, and as Acheson wrote to his daughter, the president was, "as usual, wonderful about it and said that one who had gone to the funeral of a friendless old man just out of the penitentiary had no trouble in knowing what I meant and in approving it." (The reference was to the time when Truman as vice president attended the services of Tom Pendergast, the former political boss of Kansas City convicted of bribery and tax evasion, who had given Truman his start in politics.)

"So there we are," Acheson assured Mary, "and as the Persian King had carved on his ring, 'This, too, will pass.'"[10]

He was wrong. The storm of criticism did not pass. And while Acheson's words of compassion may have marked his finest hour, they were also a political disaster both for him and for the president.

On Capitol Hill, Senator Joseph McCarthy of Wisconsin interrupted a Senate session to report the "fantastic statement the Secretary of State has made in the last few minutes." McCarthy wondered aloud if this meant that Acheson would not turn his back on other Communists in government as well. Senator Richard Nixon of California called Acheson's remarks "disgusting."[11]

Few stood up for Acheson in public. Only the *New York Herald-Tribune* called his statement "as courageous as it was Christian." *The New York Times*'s James Reston said later that he should have employed a more earthy idiom like "I won't kick a man when he's down."[12]

Old friends and supporters were heartening. On the night of his press conference, Acheson was applauded at a dinner by John McCloy, the next night by Charles Bohlen. Robert Lovett offered him his house in Hobe Sound, Florida, to rest up in and wrote, "I pray for you—quite literally."[13]

A month later, when Acheson was testifying before a Senate committee, he was asked by Democratic senator Pat McCarran of Nevada to "clarify" his statement on Hiss; Acheson declared to the senators, "One must be true to the things by which one lives. The counsels of discretion and cowardice are appealing. The safe course is to avoid situations which are disagreeable and dangerous. Such a course might get one by the issue of the moment, but it has bitter and evil consequences. In the long days and years which stretch beyond that moment of decision, one must live with one's self. . . . It is not merely a question of peace of mind, although that is vital; it is a matter of integrity of character."

In the atmosphere of the time, however, Acheson also felt compelled to end his testimony by stating "what should be obvious—that I did not and do not condone in any way the offenses charged, whether committed by a friend or by a total stranger, and that I would never knowingly tolerate any disloyal person in the Department of State."[14]

Acheson's words did not quell the growing barrage of criticism. For many Republicans, Hiss and Acheson represented the New Deal on trial. Typical was Republican senator Hugh Butler of Nebraska, who exploded in fury, "I look at that fellow. I watch his smart-aleck manner and his British clothes and that New Dealism in everything he says and does, and I want to shout, 'Get out, Get out. You stand for everything that has been wrong with the United States for years!'"[15]

There was a dark mood in Washington that January as the administration grappled with the crisis in China and weighed the decision of whether or not to build the hydrogen bomb, the "Superbomb." At his press conference on January 27, 1950, Truman was asked first whether or not he would turn his back on Alger Hiss—he answered, "No comment"—and then what his views were on the hydrogen bomb.[16] He refused to say anything about the Superbomb. It was a decision he had not yet faced.

The news that the Soviets had exploded an atomic bomb on August 29, 1949, came to David Lilienthal, chairman of the Atomic Energy Commission (AEC), while he was vacationing on Martha's Vineyard. On September 19, after verifying that the Soviets had indeed exploded an atomic device, the other AEC commissioners agreed that their chairman should bring the news to the president so that he could then announce it to the world. General James McCormack Jr. was dispatched by the commissioners to tell Lilienthal what the Russians had accomplished.

Lilienthal described a Brontë-like encounter: running into McCormack hatless in the middle of the road, squinting into the lights, pretending to thumb a ride, "as if I frequently found him on a windswept moor, in the dead of night, on an island, outside a goat field. . . . No questions; said he had lighted a candle in our house. Had he parachuted; what was this?" Inside the house, General McCormack gave Lilienthal the news by the light of a kerosene lamp.[17]

The next morning, September 20, Lilienthal flew to Washington. There he found Robert Oppenheimer, the head of the AEC's General Advisory Committee (GAC), "frantic, drawn," but positive that the Russians had succeeded. Lilienthal drove through the back entrance of the White House in midafternoon to find the president in the Oval Office, quietly reading the *Congressional Record*—"as quiet and composed a scene as imaginable; bright sunlight in the garden outside, the most unbusy of airs."[18]

Truman was initially skeptical: he could not believe that "those Asiatics" could construct so complicated a device as the atomic bomb. But after a few days of exposure to the evidence he made the announcement on September 23. At that time, the American arsenal of atomic bombs numbered perhaps two hundred. But the American monopoly was broken, and the pressure was on to build the hydrogen or thermonuclear "Superbomb."

At the end of the war, there had been no great push to construct a "Super." When the new Atomic Energy Commission took over the direction of atomic research and production in 1946, the emphasis was to improve and produce atomic bombs. Nevertheless, in April 1946 a conference on the Super was held at Los Alamos with thirty-one participants, including the Hungarian-born nuclear physicist Edward Teller, who had been doing theoretical work on thermonuclear weapons since 1942, and the German refugee scientist Klaus Fuchs, who had come to Los Alamos through the British to work on the A-bomb during the war. Fuchs had already provided the Soviets with information on how the Americans had constructed the atomic bomb, and by 1948 the Russians had decided to abandon their own design and use the American one.[19]

Fuchs also reported to his Soviet masters on the April 1946 Superbomb conference. During 1947 scientists at the Soviet Institute of Chemical Physics explored Teller's "Super" design; the Kremlin then ordered stepped-up thermonuclear weapons research. In 1948, convinced that the Soviet Union needed nuclear weapons to restore the balance of power with the United States, Andrei Sakharov, a twenty-seven-year-old physicist, agreed to work on the Super. Under Sakharov's direction, however, the Soviet scientists did not follow Teller's design. By the end of 1948, well before Russia had even exploded an atom bomb, Sakharov and his colleagues had come up with their own solutions to the Superbomb. The development of the hydrogen bomb now became the top priority for the Soviet government.[20]

Galvanized by the Soviet testing of an atom bomb, two American physicists, Teller at Los Alamos and Ernest Lawrence, the head of the Berkeley Radiation Laboratory, along with former rear admiral Lewis Strauss, a member of the five-man Atomic Energy Commission, pushed for a crash program to develop the hydrogen bomb.[21]

Perhaps the most valuable ally of the adherents of the Super was Strauss. An investment banker before the war, he had been called up from the naval reserve in 1941 and risen to the rank of rear admiral. When he was chosen by Truman to be a member of the Atomic Energy Commission, he was an unabashed conservative; as he told Truman at the time of his appointment, he was "a black Hoover Republican." Strauss soon became a frequent antagonist of the liberal-minded David Lilienthal.[22]

The debate over whether or not to build the Super involved not only the members of the Atomic Energy Commission, but also scientists who had been appointed to the commission's General Advisory Commmitee; this was now headed by Robert Oppenheimer, who in 1947 had accepted the post of director of the Institute for Advanced Study at Princeton. The most influential member of the GAC, however, was Harvard president James Bryant Conant—called "Uncle Jim" by Oppenheimer—who had been second only to Vannevar Bush in the high command of the wartime Manhattan Project.[23]

Meeting in Washington on October 29–30, the GAC first heard a presentation by George Kennan, director of Policy Planning, who left the impression that it might still be possible to negotiate a halt to the arms race with the Soviet Union.

Four of the five AEC commissioners also joined the advisory committee—Lilienthal, Strauss, the attorney Gordon Dean, who would soon replace Lilienthal as chairman of the AEC, and physicist Henry Smyth. To Lilienthal it was "a dramatic setting: Oppenheimer at the end of the table. Conant looking almost translucent, so gray."[24]

After an hour's discussion on the Superbomb program, the Joint Chiefs of Staff arrived. Omar Bradley, chairman of the JCS, was ambivalent. As John Manley, secretary to the GAC, wrote: "Instead of being infatuated with the possibility of a bomb 1,000 times as powerful as our first A-bombs, he thought such a weapon would be useless against most military targets and that its value would be mostly 'psychological.'" Conant expressed his views opposing development of the H-bomb largely on moral grounds; Hartley Rowe, a senior member of the GAC and an engineer who had helped build the Panama Canal, agreed: "We built one Frankenstein," he said.[25]

In the end, all eight members of the GAC (Glenn Seaborg was absent) "agreed that it would be wrong at the present moment to commit ourselves to an all-out effort toward its development." The commmittee did divide on one issue—scientists Enrico Fermi and I. I. Rabi, in the minority, felt that the commitment not to develop the weapon should be "conditioned on the response of the Soviet government to a proposal to renounce such development."[26]

Most important were the expressions of horror in both the majority and minority reports: "The extreme dangers to mankind inherent in the proposal wholly outweigh any military advantage that could come from this development . . . a super bomb might become a weapon of genocide" (majority). In Rabi and Fermi's words, the Super "is necessarily an evil thing considered in any light" (minority).[27]

Five years later, Oppenheimer, reflecting on the meeting, said that the advisers believed that an American decision not to build the H-bomb "would make it less likely that the Russians would attempt [it] and less likely that they would succeed in the undertaking."[28]

When Senator Brien McMahon, chairman of Congress's Joint Committee on Atomic Energy, read the GAC report in the presence of the AEC commissioners, there was an intense discussion. Lilienthal found the whole thing "pretty discouraging. What McMahon is talking about is the inevitability of war with the Russians, and what he says adds up to one thing: blow them off the face of the earth, quick, before they do the same to us—and we haven't much time."[29] The senator decided to go off on a campaign of letters and personal appeals to persuade Truman to embark on a crash program to build the Super.

On Tuesday, November 1, Lilienthal alerted Dean Acheson to what was going on. "He was somber enough when I began," Lilienthal noted, "after a few questions he was graver still." Lilienthal now believed that the issue was not one for the commission. It was a matter of foreign policy, a decision for the president and the secretary of state.[30] The following day, three of the five AEC commissioners, including the chairman, David Lilienthal, voted against the Super development, Lewis Strauss and Gordon Dean dissenting. Truman then received the GAC report and the AEC recommendations.

When Lilienthal presented them to him on November 7, he warned Truman that McMahon and his committee would try "to put on a blitz." Truman reassured him, "I don't blitz easily."[31]

Lilienthal's warning was on the mark. The president received a letter from Strauss a week later, pointing out that the Soviets' success with producing an atomic bomb meant that the hydrogen bomb was certainly within their grasp: "a government of atheists is not likely to be dissuaded from producing such a weapon on 'moral' grounds."[32]

McMahon also sent to Truman a strong letter supporting development of the Super, and the Joint Chiefs of Staff produced a paper on November 23, arguing that "possession of a thermonuclear weapon by the USSR without such possession by the United States would be intolerable."[33] Buffeted by conflicting advice, Truman decided to refer the matter to a "Special Committee" consisting of Acheson, Lilienthal, and Secretary of Defense Louis Johnson.

A former American Legion commander and Truman fund-raiser, Johnson was a most unstable character, given to extreme shifts of mood and temper. After James Forrestal resigned as secretary of defense in March 1949, Truman had appointed Johnson with a mandate to hold the line on military spending. Johnson shouted at generals and admirals and exuded such political ambitions that he had to disavow publicly that he was running for president. He was one of the worst appointments Truman ever made.[34]

Johnson and Acheson clashed on numerous occasions. After a first meeting on December 22, Acheson was convinced that the emotional and intellectual differences between Lilienthal and Johnson were so great that no more meetings of the special committee should be held until he had done what he could to work out an agreed recommendation among the three to present to the president.

Acheson began his deliberations by consulting with George Kennan and the Policy Planning Staff. (Kennan remained director of Policy Planning until the end of 1949, at which time he would assume the duties of counsellor to the department.) At Acheson's suggestion, he had been working on an approach to international control of the atomic race, and the secretary was eager to receive his views.

Both men considered themselves realists. Both men in deep ways admired each other. At the National War College in December 1949, Acheson introduced Kennan by saying, "I have rarely met a man the depth of whose thought, the sweetness of whose nature combined to bring a real understanding to the problems of modern life."[35] In turn, Kennan wrote in his memoirs that his "affection and admiration" for Acheson were so strong that "they would even withstand the public controversy of ensuing years."[36]

But Acheson's relentlessly pragmatic approach often came into conflict with Kennan's policy recommendations, which tended to ignore the domestic political realities. In addition, he was irritated by Kennan's tendency to keep after him once a policy had been decided upon. (This was unlike Kennan's closest colleague, Charles Bohlen, who more easily accepted official policy even if it went against his own views.) In their correspondence, it was Kennan far more than Acheson who seemed to seek the other's good opinion. For Acheson, even while admiring the range and depth of Kennan's thinking, seemed indifferent to Kennan's approval.

As usual, Acheson listened intently to all the arguments at a meeting of the Policy Planning Staff, November 3, 1949. At one point Acheson considered a moratorium of eighteen to twenty-four months on development of the Superbomb, "during which time you do your best to ease the international situation, come to an agreement with the Russians, put your economic house in order, get your people's minds set on what ever is necessary to do, and if no agreement is in sight at the end of that time . . . then go ahead with overall production of the Super bomb and the atomic bomb."[37]

Acheson was not yet prepared to recommend this course of action to the president, but he was nonetheless willing to consider the linkage between some form of international control of nuclear weapons and the development of the hydrogen bomb, which seemed to reflect his efforts to do so at the time of the 1946 Acheson-Lilienthal report.[38]

Acheson's sentiments encouraged Kennan to pursue his investigation into the feasibility of international control. The secretary indicated his further support for Kennan's work by advising Truman that the State Department was making a complete review of the question of international control of atomic energy matters.

Throughout November and December Kennan worked alone on a memorandum, which he presented to Acheson about January 20, 1950; Kennan later called it "one of the most important, if not the most important, of all the documents I ever wrote in government."[39] In essence, he argued that the United States should adopt a policy of "no first use" of nuclear weapons "unless we are forced to it by the use of such weapons against us. Meanwhile, we remain prepared to go very far, to show considerable confidence in others, and to accept a certain risk to ourselves, in order to achieve international agreement on their removal from international arsenals."[40]

In the end, however, Acheson rejected Kennan's advice. He also dropped the idea of a moratorium.[41]

Truman's instructions to Acheson directed the secretary and the other members of the special committee to recommend a decision on the narrow question of whether or not to develop the hydrogen bomb. Neither Acheson's early speculations about seeking a new agreement with Moscow nor Kennan's later paper focusing on "no first use" of nuclear weapons fell within Truman's more restricted assignment.

Paul Nitze, Kennan's deputy who would succeed him as head of Policy Planning, was in favor of testing the Super. He argued that it must be assumed that the Russians were pressing forward to develop thermonuclear weapons and that "the military and political advantages which would accrue to the USSR if it possessed even a temporary monopoly of this weapon are so great as to make time of the essence."[42]

Acheson therefore faced a division within his own department between Kennan and Nitze. But finally he no longer believed that a new effort to reach international agreement on control of nuclear weapons was possible at that time. He was also not convinced by Oppenheimer, who argued against the Super and in favor of efforts—including unilateral ones—at disarmament. As Acheson said to Gordon Arneson, the State Department's expert on nuclear matters, "You know, I listened as carefully as I know how, but I don't understand what 'Oppie' was trying to say. How can you persuade a paranoid adversary to disarm 'by example'?"[43]

Oppenheimer recalled that Acheson "was very depressed" by the whole business and "wished he could go along with [Oppenheimer and Lilienthal's] idea, but didn't think he would be able to." In his view, Acheson simply could not see "how any President could survive a policy of not making the H-bomb."[44]

Acheson's analysis of the Soviet threat and his sense of the president's responsibilities in dealing with it finally overrode all other arguments. Gordon Arneson thought that domestic politics had a significant impact on Acheson's final recommendations: "His sense of realism prompted him to conclude that even if the Soviet Union refrained from undertaking a thermonuclear program as the result of our refraining—a non-existent prospect—the Administration would run into a Congressional buzz saw and the proposal [for a moratorium] would be stillborn."[45]

The moral issue seemed to Acheson unpersuasive. "Reliance on perpetual good will," Acheson later wrote, "seemed to me a terrible policy."[46] What he advocated was what he later called a "strategic morality." He wrote that he took his inspiration in this respect from Abraham Lincoln, whose "moral attitude—excoriated as immorality by abolitionists and secessionists alike—disclosed what we might call a strategic, as against an ideological approach, to great and complicated problems." Lincoln wrote to Horace Greeley in 1862 that his "paramount object in this struggle is to save the Union." If he could do this by freeing the slaves, he would do so. But preserving the Union was his highest priority.

For Acheson, the overriding concern was the national interest as he understood it and the security of the nation. "What may be quite proper and moral for a private citizen . . . often, and rightly, is condemned if done when he assumes legislative or executive powers of government."[47]

When Acheson met with Louis Johnson and David Lilienthal on January 31, 1950, he held the deciding vote. To persuade Lilienthal to go along with his recommendation to develop the Super, Acheson suggested that the president include in his announcement a call for a full-scale defense and foreign policy review. Acheson was sympathetic to objections by Conant and Lilienthal that U.S. defense policy should not rely so heavily on atomic weapons. Johnson, of course, was determined to cut the military budget, but Acheson wanted to reexamine the whole rationale behind our military posture. Acheson recommended that the National Security Council be ordered to undertake that reexamination.[48]

When the special committee met with Truman later that day, the president was not inclined to spend much time discussing alternatives. The Rabi-Fermi notion of approaching the Russians to seek a test ban agreement that could be monitored without inspection was never brought up.

"Can the Russians do it?" Truman asked the committee members.

They all nodded.

When Lilienthal tried to argue at some length that there were problems with the policy of relying on atomic weapons as the country's main defense, Truman cut him short. "What the hell are we waiting for?" he recalled telling them. "Let's get on with it."[49] The meeting took all of seven minutes.

Later that day the president issued a statement saying that he had directed the Atomic Energy Commission to work "on all forms of atomic weapons, including the so-called hydrogen or super bomb."[50] Three days later Klaus Fuchs was arraigned in London on charges of spying for the Soviet Union.

Truman had doubtless made up his mind prior to meeting with the special committee: he knew the views of the Joint Chiefs of Staff, of Senator Brien McMahon, and of prominent scientists such as Karl Compton of MIT, most of whom urged him to proceed with developing the Super. His assistant press secretary, Eben Ayers, wrote in his diary that Truman said that "we had to do it—make the [H-]bomb—though no one wants to use it. But, he said, we have got to have it if only for bargaining purposes with the Russians."[51]

The United States tested its first thermonuclear device on November 1, 1952; the Soviets tested their first device less than a year later. Andrei Sakharov wrote in his memoirs that any American offer of either a moratorium on research or proposals for verifiable arrangements for controlling nuclear weapons would have been destined to fail. Stalin was determined to have the Super.[52]

Nine days after Truman's public announcement that the United States would press ahead with the H-bomb, and barely two weeks after Acheson's refusal to turn his back on Alger Hiss, a relatively obscure senator from Wisconsin made a Lincoln Day speech on February 9, 1950, in Wheeling, West Virginia. Joseph McCarthy was forty-one years old at the time and had been recently voted the worst member of the Senate in a poll conducted among the Washington correspondents. His speech was ill prepared and rambling, and no copy of it is available except one that the senator made later. Though the *Wheeling News-Register* expected that he would champion "adequate old age and other pensions," Joe McCarthy had quite a different talk in mind.

For some time he had been searching for an issue that would give him greater visibility. The previous November, in a speech in Madison, Wisconsin, he had insinuated that the *Madison Capital-Times*, published by an archenemy of his, was "the red mouthpiece for the Communist Party in Wisconsin." But he finally found his theme in early January at a dinner at the Colony restaurant in Washington with Father Edmund A. Walsh of Georgetown University. In no small part because of the Hiss case, the priest suggested that Communist infiltration in government was becoming a salient issue.[53]

Before the members of the Ohio County Women's Republican Club at Wheeling, McCarthy asserted that America had lost ground against the Soviets not because of foreign aggression, but "because of the traitorous actions of those who have been treated so well by this nation," who enjoyed "the finest homes, the finest college education, and the finest jobs in Government we can give." This was "glaringly true in the State Department," where "the bright young men who are born with silver spoons in their mouths are the ones who have been the worst." He waved a piece of paper, saying he had "here in my hand a list of 205 that were known to the Secretary of State and who are nevertheless still working and shaping the policy of the State Department."[54]

Once McCarthy decided to run with this issue, he showed no scruples about using it on any and almost every occasion. He offered wildly different numbers of State Department employees who had been or were members of the Communist Party, although he produced no hard evidence for his assertions.

As he continued on his speaking tour to Salt Lake City and Reno on the weekend after the Wheeling speech, the numbers changed and later they changed again. In Salt Lake City he said, "I have the names of fifty-seven card-carrying members of the Communist Party." He went on to say, "If [Acheson] wants to call me tonight at the Utah Hotel, I will be glad to give him the names of those fifty-seven card-carrying Communists." By February 20 the list had grown to 81, and for the next few months it varied from as low as 10 to as high again as 121. News reports coming in from Wheeling and Salt Lake City finally forced the State Department press officer to announce, "We know of no Communist member of the Department and if we find any they will be summarily discharged."[55]

McCarthy's campaign had begun; he was in the headlines at last; and his main target was Dean Acheson.

McCarthy excoriated Acheson. Referring to the secretary's unwillingness to turn his back on Alger Hiss, McCarthy declared: "When this pompous diplomat in striped pants, with the phony British accent, proclaimed to the American people that Christ on the Mount endorsed Communism, high treason, and betrayal of sacred trust, the blasphemy was so great that it awakened the dormant indignation of the American people." As McCarthy's attacks intensified, Acheson received so many threatening letters that he felt it necessary to have guards posted at his house day and night.[56]

Seeing that McCarthy's tactics were beginning to have an impact on public opinion, worried about his reelection in 1950, and hoping for the presidential nomination two years later, Senator Robert Taft allegedly told McCarthy to "keep talking and if one case doesn't work out, proceed with another."[57]

The Democratic leadership in Congress believed that it could expose McCarthy's baseless accusations by having his charges investigated. A subcommittee of the Senate Foreign Relations Committee was set up, chaired by Millard Tydings of Maryland, and hearings began on March 8. Unfortunately Tydings, a conservative Democrat with a short temper and pompous manner, chose to attack McCarthy personally and to try him rather than to hire a staff to investigate dispassionately his charges. In such a contest, McCarthy stood to win.

Tydings made a shambles out of the hearings, which soon turned into a partisan battle in which Democrats harassed McCarthy even before he could make his opening statement. In the first two days McCarthy failed to substantiate any of his charges, but the Democrats did not succeed in destroying his case. *The New York Times*, hardly a McCarthy supporter, editorialized that he at least "deserved a chance to complete his story."[58]

After a confusing two days, the subcommittee allowed McCarthy to proceed with his charges. Because Truman refused to give the committee access to the confidential loyalty files of the eighty-one employees of the State Department accused of Communist sympathies, the subcommittee was vulnerable to McCarthy's accusation that it was simply trying to whitewash the administration.

McCarthy was particularly eager to assert that China had been lost through Soviet agents in the State Department—such as Philip Jessup, John Service, and Owen Lattimore, who was teaching at Johns Hopkins and was named "the architect of our Far Eastern policy." (Lattimore, in fact, had never been officially connected with the department.)

Eventually Truman gave in to the committee and allowed them to examine the files, but the senators found nothing of substance and soon grew bored with poring through the record. When the Tydings committee finally produced a report in mid-July, the three Democrats accused McCarthy of perpetrating "a fraud and a hoax."[59] However, they did find that China expert Service had been indiscreet by passing classified government documents to the journal *Amerasia* in 1945. In December 1951 Truman's Loyalty Review Board, which he had established in 1947, found Service's actions in the *Amerasia* case grounds for "reasonable doubt as to his loyalty"; Acheson then felt that he could not overrule the interdepartmental Loyalty Review Board and dismissed him.

When a number of Foreign Service officers started collecting signatures urging Acheson to reject the advice of the board, Charles Bohlen, then counsellor of the department, called the officers into his office and assured them that Acheson shared their respect for Service and their desire that Service be retained. But if Acheson rejected the advice of the government-wide Loyalty Review Board, he felt that his only option would be to resign. Accordingly, the Foreign Service officers, who wanted to prevent his resignation at all costs, withdrew their petition and instead raised contributions for Service's legal defense fund, which carried his case to the Supreme Court. In 1957 the Court unanimously ordered that he be reinstated.[60] No other State Department employee was dismissed for security reasons during Acheson's tenure as secretary.[61]

In trying to defuse the issues of loyalty, Truman's 1947 order to establish the Loyalty Review Board may well have contributed to the atmosphere that made McCarthyism possible. The heightened rhetoric over the Soviet Communist threat that both Truman and Acheson used to mobilize public opinion behind their policies surely added to the climate of fear and frustration. Yet it is hard not to conclude that external events—the testing of a Soviet A-bomb, the arrest of Soviet spy Klaus Fuchs, Mao's victory in China, the Berlin blockade—would have made subversion at home a central issue. For the Republicans, it was a whip with which to lash a president who had so destroyed their hopes for power with his "give 'em hell" campaign of 1948.

There were, of course, Republicans who repudiated McCarthyism, notably Senator Margaret Chase Smith of Maine, who organized a "Declaration of Conscience" on June 2, 1950, and was joined in this effort by half a dozen other Senate Republicans and two Democrats. She criticized her own party for allowing the Senate to have been too often "debased to the level of a forum of hate and character assassination sheltered by the shield of congressional immunity."[62]

Senator Smith's words seemed to spur on those politicians who wanted to stand up to McCarthy. At the governors' conference at White Sulphur Springs, Virginia, on June 20, 1950, Acheson discussed the charges being made against the State Department. Standing before the governors for four hours, mostly answering a fusillade of hostile questions, Acheson found two of the governors willing to intervene on his behalf: Thomas E. Dewey of New York and Earl Warren of California, respectively the Republican candidates for the presidency and vice presidency in 1948. With these two men on the field for Acheson, the assailants at the conference lost their zest for the fray.[63]

Throughout the rest of his tenure as secretary of state, Acheson bore the attacks of McCarthy and his followers with stoicism and acerbic humor. Archibald MacLeish recalled staying at the Achesons' house in Georgetown during this time. MacLeish's bedroom was near Acheson's bathroom, and when MacLeish woke up he could hear Acheson shaving while listening to the radio commentator Fulton Lewis launch into another diatribe against him, all the while cheerily whistling away. "It was during this period," MacLeish later said, "that Dean's intellectual arrogance became a great strength." He would come home from a long day at the department outwardly unperturbed by events, then sit down and have a drink as though he had hardly a care in the world.[64]

That spring Acheson did strike back at his McCarthyite critics. In a speech to the American Society of Newspaper Editors on April 22, 1950, he defended the State Department against those who were trying to destroy the institution. To McCarthyite charges that the Foreign Service officers were effete, Acheson spoke of them as "loyal" and "clean-living," citing State's legal adviser, Adrian Fisher, as "a bomber navigator during the war," and attacked those who would "smear everybody's reputation." In closing the address, he evoked Robert Browning's poem in which Caliban, watching a procession of crabs on the sand, compares himself to his god Setebos. Caliban lets twenty crabs go by, then picks up the twenty-first and tears off a claw. Three more go by, and the fourth he crushes with his heel to watch it wriggle. "It is that degree of vicious madness which has been going on here," Acheson said. Then he added these words that revealed his personal anguish:

> Now, I don't ask you for sympathy. I don't ask you for help. You are in a worse situation than I am. I and my associates are only the intended victims of this mad and vicious operation. But you, unhappily, you by reason of your calling, are participants. You are unwilling participants, disgusted participants, but, nevertheless, participants, and your position is far more serious than mine.
>
> As I leave this filthy business, and I hope never to speak of it again, I should like to leave in your minds the words of John Donne . . .
>
> Any man's death diminishes me, because I am
> involved in mankind.
> And therefore, never send to know for whom
> the bell tolls;
> It tolls for thee.[65]

CHAPTER TWENTY-TWO

THE GERMAN QUESTION, THE BRITISH CONNECTION, AND THE FRENCH SOLUTION

THE BUSINESS OF THE STATE could not wait upon the defeat of Senator Joseph McCarthy. The deteriorating situation in the Far East was beyond the control of the State Department, even if Acheson had felt himself free to recognize Mao's China. Moreover, the focus of American internationalism was on Europe: the need to bind Western European nations to the United States was the immediate goal of Acheson's policy.

While the Marshall Plan was fueling the European economic recovery and the North Atlantic Treaty was in place, the question of Germany's role in Europe had to be settled. After World War I, John Maynard Keynes had written of Germany in 1914, "Round Germany as a central support the rest of the European economic system grouped itself, and on the prosperity and enterprise of Germany, the prosperity of the rest of the Continent mainly depended."[1] Acheson fully shared Keynes's view. Now was the time to integrate Germany with the West to ensure full economic recovery in Europe while seeking a political grouping of European nations that could both contain and satisfy German ambitions.

In the fall of 1949 Acheson believed it was too soon to think of Germany once more having arms, but it was time for the three Western allies to end their zones of occupation and allow a West German state to come into being. John McCloy had been appointed U.S. high commissioner, replacing the military government of General Lucius Clay. Elections were held throughout West Germany on August 14, 1949. The new Bundestag, meeting in Bonn on September 15, chose Konrad Adenauer by a one-vote margin as the first chancellor of the Federal Republic of Germany.

Despite West Germany's new status, the allies decided to reserve "supreme authority" for themselves in certain key areas, including foreign affairs, demilitarization, decartelization, and war criminals. Adenauer, however, was determined to lead Germany back into full sovereignty and eventually to economic prosperity—a prospect that frightened the French and troubled the British.

At the very first session of the new Bundestag, the German deputies had asked the occupying powers to reexamine their policy of dismantling German industry for reparations. Acheson supported this request, for he saw German industrial production as imperative for German, and therefore European, recovery; moreover, he believed that dismantling and Marshall Plan aid were inconsistent, and eventually the allies would have to yield on this issue.

Always sensitive to French and British concerns, Acheson wanted to bring Bevin and Schuman over to the American position without generating ill will. At this point, the French were simply opposed to any retreat on dismantling; and the British, while they favored continued dismantling, were approaching the point where they would have to carry out this policy under military protection, so angry were German workers over the program.[2]

In Bonn, Adenauer was adamant on the need to halt the program. He saw it as being the "best propaganda for unbounded nationalism." McCloy joined in the fray, demanding in a public statement an end to "aimless dismantling."[3]

At Bevin's suggestion, Schuman and Acheson were asked to join him at a meeting in Paris on November 9, 1949, to clear up their differences. Acheson agreed, while stressing the need in a letter to Schuman to move only as far as France would allow. But he wrote Schuman that now was "the time for French initiative and leadership of the type required to integrate the German Federal Republic promptly and decisively into Western Europe." Moreover, Acheson came prepared to demonstrate the anomaly of the United States supplying Germany with steel, which Germany itself could make.[4]

The Paris talks, however, began disastrously. As the meeting with Acheson and Schuman opened, the British foreign minister was in a white rage at McCloy for using "pressure tactics" on the allies to cut back on the dismantling of former German war plants. He beat the air with both arms and worked himself into such a passion that Acheson was worried he might have another heart attack, such as had happened when he was in New York at the theater with the Achesons seeing the musical *South Pacific*.

As chairman of the conference, Schuman was at a loss. A polite, careful man who always obeyed diplomatic niceties, he was totally unable to cope with Bevin's hysterical outburst. All of a sudden, Bevin stopped and asked Acheson what he had to say.

The secretary of state paused. The key lay in Bevin's sense of humor. As Acheson described it, it was his memory of Episcopal services in Middletown as a boy that saved the situation: "'*M. le President*,' I said to Schuman, 'all that I can reply to Mr. Bevin is written in an English book, The Book of Common Prayer: "The remembrance of our sins is grievous unto us; the burden of them is intolerable."'

"Waving aside translation, Schuman eagerly interjected, 'It is the same in the Catholic book.'"

Bevin burst into laughter and threw up his hands. As a "bush Baptist," he had never heard of that particular prayer.

The Americans were absolved. But setting the limits on German steel production—Schuman's main concern—was much more difficult. As a result, their sessions on the second day lasted from ten A.M. to four the next morning, with two French ceremonial meals thrown in.

Nonetheless, by the time the Paris meeting was over, there was general agreement to limit dismantling of German industry to those plants that could be devoted to war use, provided there was no increase in the amount of steel Germany was authorized to produce by the Western powers. As the allies had already dismantled about six hundred industrial plants, and were promising to continue dismantling "war plants," Schuman and Bevin were content.

With these agreements in his pocket, Acheson believed he was moving in the right direction—the need to reconcile Germany to its former enemies and to ensure that West Germany would be tied to a West European political and economic grouping. Above all, Acheson, like Adenauer, was determined that Germany not suffer the fate of the weakened and resentful Weimar Republic of the 1920s. Now, at McCloy's urging, Acheson left for the West German republic to pay a visit to the new German chancellor.[5]

On November 11, Armistice Day, Acheson and the American group flew to Frankfurt to stay with the high commissioner and Mrs. McCloy. His first postwar visit to Germany was a sharp reminder that this was "an only recently defeated enemy." War damage was still extensive. After motoring to Heidelberg, the headquarters of the United States commander in chief in Europe, Acheson dined with the McCloys in the university town he had last visited forty years earlier; the following day he took the train down the Rhine to Bonn, the new republic's soporific capital, known mainly for being Beethoven's birthplace.

Konrad Adenauer was seventy-three years old when Acheson encountered him. *Der Alte Fuchs*—the "old Fox," as the Germans called him—had spent most of his working life as *Oberbürgermeister* (or mayor) of Cologne, first taking office in 1917. Autocratic in exercising his authority, he made "Holy Cologne" one of the most beautiful and powerful cities in Weimar Germany, revitalizing its university and institutes.

As a devout and conservative Catholic, Adenauer bitterly opposed Hitler, and in March 1933, two months after the Nazis took power, Hitler dismissed him and later twice imprisoned him over the next ten years. After the Allied victory in 1945, Adenauer became one of the founders of the Christian Democratic Union, a conservative political party, and once political activity was allowed to resume in the British zone, he became active in provincial and zonal affairs.

Adenauer took office as chancellor with certain firmly held convictions. He believed that rapprochement with France was an absolute necessity and that political and economic integration with the West was the only way to ensure Germany's rehabilitation. Ending restrictions on Germany's industrial production would help solve domestic unemployment, and only through a strong economy would the government gain the respect of the people and thus confer on it a legitimacy that the Weimar Republic had lacked.

Finally, he distrusted the German people's propensity to embrace nationalistic romanticism. He was therefore wary of any signs of pan-Germanism and was more committed to anchoring Germany to the West than to pursuing unification with the East.[6]

His friendship had to be earned, and Acheson did so; over time Adenauer became an "uninhibited companion in a good gossip." And after Acheson was no longer in office, the German chancellor did not forget him. He always had the time and the desire to seek out a friend such as Acheson proved himself to be.[7]

After a welcoming lunch at which Adenauer's favorite Rhine wines were served, the chancellor sketched out for Acheson his vision for Germany. His country, he said, "is in some ways just the opposite from your own country. Your rivers run from north to south. In your early days they came from the unknown bearing nothing but water. Our rivers flow from south to north, and in our early days they brought us, here in the Rhineland, civilization and Christianity."

This theory was the basis for Adenauer's judgment that a largely Catholic, romanized Germany was the safest Germany for Europe. According to Adenauer, a German proverb declared that Germans take on the color of the wall, that they tend to conform to their environment. Germans, he told Acheson, would profit from escaping their purely national world by embracing a larger environment "in which their more liberal traditions would find strength through companionship."

His view that a reunified Germany, if that were to come into being someday, would be best served by seeing the Germans join with their European neighbors within a still wider Atlantic setting. For Acheson, these words confirmed and reinforced his own thinking on the security of Europe.[8]

Following the lunch, Acheson had a far rougher encounter at the Bundestag with Kurt Schumacher, the leader of the opposition Social Democrats (SPD). Just as Adenauer epitomized the prejudices of the Rhinelanders, Schumacher incarnated the German temperament of west Prussia. A militant anti-Communist, Schumacher deeply distrusted what he saw as the Slavic barbarism of the East; but whereas Adenauer was a devout Catholic, Schumacher embodied anticlericalism.

He was a Berliner who had enlisted in the army in November 1914 and less than a month later lost his right arm fighting on the Russian front. As he later made his way in the socialist politics of Weimar Germany, he held audiences spellbound by his passionate speaking style, which he emphasized with one-armed gestures. He became known as the "man with one arm and a dozen elbows," and after election to the Reichstag in 1930, he became a scathing enemy of the Nazis, believing that National Socialism appealed to the *innere Schweinehund* (the "intrinsic evil") in man. As soon as Hitler took power in 1933, he was arrested and imprisoned in Dachau.

Here his incorruptibility gained him the admiration of all who encountered him. He helped the sick and starving; he offered friendship to "non-Aryan" prisoners. The Nazis tortured him but never broke him. But when he was released in 1943, one acquaintance described him as "a pitiful walking cadaver, with ulcers, yellowing stumps for teeth, flickering eyesight." He lost a leg in 1948. Nonetheless, he became the most prominent German politician in the Western zones.

Schumacher was a passionate critic of the dismantling program and had expected to ride the issue to victory in the elections of 1949, when he lost so narrowly. He sought for Germany a "third way," something between communism and capitalism. He also spoke in the tones of unbridled German nationalism but hoped to align that sentiment with social democracy. Far from trying to bind Germany to the capitalist West, he opposed a close relationship with France and hoped for a unified Germany that would support his brand of nationalism and progressivism.[9]

It was not surprising that Acheson's meeting with Schumacher went badly. The SPD leader denounced Adenauer as unrepresentative of the German people. Acheson tried to defuse the hostility by responding that a great many Americans had thought the same about President Truman before the 1948 elections. When Schumacher criticized Adenauer for working so smoothly with the British, American, and French occupation authorities, Acheson asked him what alternative was possible. Schumacher responded that the Russians would be induced to reunite eastern and western Germany by a policy of German aloofness toward the West, even though the SPD opposed Russia and not the Western powers.

Acheson was put off by Schumacher's tone as well as his point of view. He warned him that the allies would not tolerate any attempt by anyone to play the Western allies and the Russians off against one another. Breaking off the interview as soon as politeness permitted, Acheson viewed Schumacher as combining "a harsh and violent nature with nationalistic and aggressive ideas."[10]

After going to a reception in Bonn that Adenauer gave for him to meet government officials, Acheson and the chancellor proceeded to the Cologne railroad station. Streetlights were already on, and the motorcade was surrounded by police in white coats and helmets. When Adenauer and Acheson arrived at the station, the square was packed with people being held back by police lines. The two notables proceeded in closed and darkened limousines to the station itself and onto the platform alongside their train.

As Acheson tells it, he protested to Adenauer that that was "a very poor way to do things." The people had been waiting most patiently to see the chancellor and the American secretary of state. "He and I, alone, I proposed, should walk back out into the square, shake hands, and walk back. The security officers had tantrums; Dr. Adenauer agreed." When word got out, the crowd started cheering and police lines bulged. When both men started shaking hands, "everything exploded. The police lines broke; we were picked up and carried to our train, with as many as could push into the station following."

After a half hour more of pandemonium, Adenauer was finally maneuvered back to his car and escorted out of the station by a cheering crowd. Acheson concluded happily that while he had fouled up the protocol of departure, he had introduced "a desirable element of democratic disorder into the political life of the Federal Republic."[11]

Acheson was absolutely convinced that European unity and Germany's integration with the West required French leadership. As he told Schuman on September 15, 1949, "The best chance and hope seems to us to be under French leadership. It doesn't work for us to take the lead. We are too far away."[12]

Moreover, Acheson understood that the British would resist integration with Western Europe, because of their relations with the Commonwealth and the empire. But this did not imply, Acheson told Bevin on October 16, 1949, that there were not steps far greater than any Britain had so far taken to join with the continental Europeans in a common economic grouping.

While the British were eager to enshrine the so-called Anglo-American special relationship, Acheson saw a danger in stressing U.S.-British ties. When he arrived in London for a foreign ministers' meeting in November 1949, he found that the agenda included a paper drawn up by member of the British Foreign Office that was entitled "Special Relationship between the United States and Great Britain." Acheson was "shocked, horrified, and overwhelmed to discover that there was a paper which spelled out this common law marriage in a way which I thought would utterly destroy us if it were ever known, either to our allies or to anybody in the United States." All copies of the paper that could be found were collected and burned.[13]

Acheson was quite prepared to acknowledge privately that "a unique relation existed between Britain and America—our common language and history insured that." But, as he wrote later, "unique did not mean affectionate. We had fought England as an enemy as often as we had fought side by side as an ally." Sentimental impulses, he declared, should be reserved for speeches in London like an address to the Society of Pilgrims.[14]

In January 1950 he made it clear even to his good friend British ambassador Sir Oliver Franks that the United States would not permit Britain's "special relationship" to get in the way of West European efforts at integration. The United States would not try to coerce Britain into joining the movement toward European economic union, but at the same time Britain had no right to try to undermine any efforts the continental Europeans might make along these lines. How else could the United States expect Germany to take its place as a traditional power in Europe![15]

In the winter of 1950 Acheson was worried about the allied position in Western Europe. The Soviet testing of an atomic bomb, the final conquest of China by Mao, and the relative weakness of American military strength at a time of a shrinking defense budget—these seemed ominous trends that put Washington on the defensive.

It therefore became more important than ever to ensure that the Federal Republic would be firmly anchored in the West. And while West Germany's industrial production had reached prewar levels in early 1950, its growing trade deficit, high unemployment at 12.2 percent of the labor force, lack of investment capital, and poor housing appeared so grave that McCloy's economic adviser described the country as "flat on its ass."[16]

At the same time, German steel exports into the European markets were expanding, and the Adenauer government was insisting that the allies lift the production quotas that had been imposed on the steel industry. As the Big Three foreign ministers prepared for a new conference in London in May 1950, Acheson told Schuman that the Americans were growing in favor of liberalizing allied controls over all aspects of German industry.

At this point, McCloy was openly calling for a politically "united Europe" as the only solution to the German question. He urged Acheson to tell the French that this was the basis of "our whole fundamental policy." But Acheson remained skeptical of schemes for a new European confederation. He was also still somewhat wary about accepting West Germany into the Western alliance and convinced that the French had to take the leadership role.[17]

Now, as Acheson got ready for his trip to London, he decided to spend a few days in Paris first. He was weary from an exhausting winter and spring; a rest in the French capital and some friendly talks with Schuman would please the French foreign minister and give Acheson some needed peace. As it turned out, these were far from restful days, and his presence in Paris at that time convinced Ernest Bevin that there was a French-American conspiracy against him.

Ever since Acheson had urged France to take the lead in ensuring the Federal Republic's integration into Western Europe, Schuman had been wrestling with the problem of how to do that. There seemed a vacuum of ideas in the spring of 1950 until Jean Monnet stepped in to fill the gap.

Monnet was a remarkable figure, a man who eschewed public visibility while seeking out those individuals on both sides of the Atlantic who were powerful enough to get things done. Although he had played a central role in organizing the postwar French economy, Monnet hardly resembled a traditional French bureaucrat trained at elite schools. Instead he was a businessman, born in the small town of Cognac, on November 9, 1888. His grandfather had built a thriving business through selling brandy, and Monnet himself had left school at sixteen to be trained to take over the company.

Before the First World War, Monnet spent most of his time traveling abroad, selling his family's cognac, and learning perfect English. At heart he was a born salesman. As his friend André Fontaine, the editor of *Le Monde*, said of him, Monnet's "education, far from being classical, was personal and pragmatic. He knows more English words than he does French." He also came to admire the Anglo-American way of doing things, and it was his pragmatic approach that gave him such success in dealing with the Americans.[18]

Before the Second World War, Monnet had first become deputy secretary-general of the League of Nations in Geneva, then returned to France to work in the family business; later he entered a New York investment bank, where he soon became friendly with such international lawyers as John Foster Dulles and John McCloy.

After the fall of France in 1940, he did not join Charles de Gaulle's Free French in London but returned to Washington to work for the British. After the American landings in Africa in 1942, Monnet started to play a role in French politics; though he was never close to de Gaulle, the general sent him back to Washington toward the end of the war in hopes that his American connections would bring more aid to France. Then, after the liberation, de Gaulle asked Monnet to head the Commissariat-General of the French Modernization and Investment Plan. In this role, Monnet made his reputation inside France.

Monnet detested large bureaucracies, and at his office in the rue Martignac, he worked with fewer than fifty people under him. His approach was to set broad goals and then let the businessmen, farmers, and bureaucrats devise ways of achieving them. By setting targets for French modernization—concentrating on transportation, electrification, and industry at the expense of public housing—Monnet laid the foundations for the modern French state.[19]

For Monnet, personal connections meant everything—the best way to circumvent an obstreperous bureaucracy was to find the right person to push things through. Because he threatened no one, belonged to no political party, and was seen as honorable and wise, he was trusted by almost everyone except the French Communists.

He had one obsession: the unity of Europe. This was clearly not a new idea, but in contrast with the Europe organized under one state that Napoleon had tried to achieve, Monnet's Europe was to come into being through a pooling of economic resources and markets. All else—joint military planning, a political directorate, a European parliament—would follow.

By 1950, when Monnet saw that French steel production was leveling off and German production was rising, he imagined a bleak future: "Germany expanding; Germany dumping on export markets; a call for the protection of French industry; an end to trade liberalization; the re-establishment of prewar cartels; perhaps, eastward outlets for German expansion, a prelude to political agreements; and France back in the old rut of limited protected production."[20]

Drawing on his wartime experiences, he set out to pool the coal and steel resources of Germany and France; other nations that possessed iron ore or coal, like Great Britain, would be invited to join the pool. But the new Coal and Steel Community should not become a cartel that would divide up the markets and assign certain quotas for various companies. Its goal was to eliminate the barriers to competition among states and encourage production to meet the demands of a larger market. It would also make it easier for the victor powers to lift their controls over German steel production by binding Germany and France within this broader economic community.[21]

The man Monnet had to sell this idea to was Foreign Minister Robert Schuman, whose roots in Lorraine made him the perfect vehicle for presenting the plan to the cabinet and the National Assembly. In secret, the two men schemed on how to accomplish this, and they soon concluded that the key to its success was getting the Americans on board. Acheson's fateful arrival in Paris provided them the occasion they needed.

Acheson was met at Orly airport on Sunday, May 7, by the American ambassador to France, David Bruce. The very model of the American establishment diplomat, Bruce had been a contemporary at Princeton of F. Scott Fitzgerald's and Edmund Wilson's, a businessman involved in ventures from denicotinizing cigarettes to racetracks and French vineyards, and had worked with the French Underground during World War II. By the spring of 1950 he had already served as deputy to Averell Harriman, supervising the operation of the Marshall Plan in Europe. Before his diplomatic career was over, he would serve as ambassador to the Court of Saint James's and to the Federal Republic of Germany and, in Acheson's final year in office, as under secretary of state. He was a highly cultivated man of great taste and elegance, with whom Acheson was very comfortable.[22]

On the drive into the French capital, Bruce told Acheson that Robert Schuman was planning to call on him that very day at the ambassador's residence. This was odd for a Sunday. Even more mysterious was Schuman's request that only he, Acheson, and Bruce, along with an interpreter, be present. Bruce and Acheson could not figure out why this request had come about, since Bruce had already asked for an appointment for Acheson to pay his respects to Schuman at the Quai d'Orsay the next day.

They quickly found out.

No sooner were amenities observed than Schuman expounded the essentials of Monnet's idea that the whole French-German production of coal and steel be placed under a joint high authority, with the organization open to other European nations—what would later become known as the "Schuman Plan." It was, as Acheson wrote later, "so breathtaking a step toward the unification of Europe that at first I did not grasp it."

Schuman implored the two Americans not to speak of his plan to any of their colleagues until he had discussed the proposal with the members of the cabinet and, if they agreed, made a public statement in the National Assembly. Schuman said he was consulting Acheson because he believed that the scheme was wholly in accord with American policy, and he needed strong support from Washington to help his government push the plan through.

Acheson was especially impressed by the simple approach that Schuman brought to a big idea, "a far cry from that of American-trained lawyers." It was, as Bruce called it in a cable later that week, "the most imaginative and far-reaching approach that has been made for generations to the settlement of fundamental differences between France and Germany."[23]

Acheson was concerned, however, that the arrangement could become a giant cartel controlling the basic necessities of an advanced industrial society. The allies' occupation policy toward Germany had, in fact, been to break up such cartels. He put the question to Schuman, who was both surprised and annoyed. Yes, he said, a cartel in coal and steel could be created, but his purpose was very different. Underneath it lay a political conception: to move toward the unification of Western Europe by economic means. Provisions could be made to prevent the emergence of a cartel. Nonetheless, Acheson's fears did not disappear in an afternoon, and later, because of his apprehensions on this score, the French added a stronger anticartel statement to their plan.

As Schuman talked, Acheson and Bruce caught his infectious enthusiasm: they imagined a rebirth of Europe, which, as Acheson wrote, "had been in eclipse since the Reformation." Schuman parted from the Americans with a promise that Jean Monnet would meet with them to discuss further details.

Acheson and Bruce felt they needed to know much more about the plan before they could advise the president to support it. The meeting with Monnet made them more confident, and before flying to London on Tuesday, May 9, Acheson sent an "eyes only" cable to the White House, outlining the plan and urging Truman, on its announcement, to express warm and sympathetic interest. Until then, keep everything secret. Truman approved.

Arriving in the British capital, Acheson found Bevin ill and testy. He had recently undergone a painful operation, and the drugs he was taking to quell the pain often made him doze off during discussions.

Acheson told Bevin nothing of Schuman's plan. But at lunch a message was brought from the French ambassador, René Massigli, asking for an appointment with Bevin after lunch and with Acheson an hour later. Acheson suspected that Schuman was unveiling his plan that afternoon at the National Assembly. This was precisely what Massigli had to report, so by the time Bevin met again with Acheson, he was in what Acheson described as "a towering rage."

He at once charged Acheson with conspiring with Schuman to create a European grouping directed against British trade with the continent. Circumstantial evidence seemed overwhelming. Why would Acheson have stopped off in Paris just before the plan was unveiled to the world?

It took some time for Bevin to calm down, and grudgingly he accepted Acheson's explanation that there had been no conspiracy. But Bevin still resented Acheson's advance knowledge of the plan and his unwillingness to inform him of what was afoot. In retrospect, Acheson believed that Schuman should have authorized him to try to persuade Bevin and Attlee to support the plan before Schuman announced it publicly.

Bevin was certainly convinced that Britain could not join a freely competitive system in the basic commodities of coal and steel and still run a controlled domestic economy to advance the social goals of the Labour Party. And if it could not join, how could Britain retain its basic markets on the continent?[24]

Predictably, Britain's rebuff to the coal and steel plan was only the first step in marking a British refusal to join in a West European defense community and a European Common Market over the next decade.

Acheson was right to suspect the danger of Britain's emphasis on the "special relationship" with the United States. Unable to foresee the eventual loss of empire and the hollow advantages of the Commonwealth, Britain repeatedly tried to slow the movement toward European unity. Yet neither Britain's political ties to the United States nor its political and economic ties to the empire and Commonwealth could do anything but mask British weakness.

On May 11 Schuman arrived in London to meet with Acheson and Bevin prior to a gathering of the North Atlantic Council of the Western alliance. Bevin was gruff and unyielding. As occupying powers of Germany, the three countries should have open and frank dealings with one another, not "secret deals." Instead he was confronted with a fait accompli.

As the interpreter was translating Bevin's remark into Schuman's ears, Acheson asked to speak before Schuman replied. He said that he realized that the first requirement of a grand alliance was full consultation among them, but on occasion the need to deal with domestic politics warped the ideal. He then reminded Bevin of a meeting in Washington at which Acheson, Bevin, and the British chancellor of the Exchequer, Sir Stafford Cripps, had discussed the impending devaluation of the pound privately among themselves, while Schuman and the French finance minister had been in Washington. Secrecy had been vital to the British Treasury, even though the devaluation would seriously affect France. Nonetheless, Schuman had never complained, as he'd understood the sad necessity of secrecy.

At this, Bevin had had enough. "Oh, hell," he said, "let's join the others. We're keepin' them waiting."

As they filed out of the room, Schuman squeezed Acheson's arm. "My friend," he said, "you have a large deposit in my bank. You may draw on it whenever you please."[25]

Throughout his ten days in London, Acheson's official duties were interspersed with social engagements. At one point between meetings, Acheson and his wife were to lunch with King George VI, Queen Elizabeth, and the two princesses, Elizabeth and Margaret.

Before lunch Acheson met alone with the king and discussed personalities and policies in Europe, and especially Acheson's impressions of both. Acheson made sure to speak highly of Ernest Bevin, who, he gathered, rather baffled the monarch.

The queen and Mrs. Acheson joined them shortly, but the princesses did not appear, much to the annoyance of their father. He finally ordered two places to be taken away and directed that lunch be served. Not long after, Princess Margaret appeared, described by Acheson as "full of gaiety, explanations, and apologies." Her sister, Elizabeth, who had just returned from Malta, begged to be excused so that she could go home and see her own family. The king was barely mollified, and it was left to Alice Acheson to steer the conversation into happier channels.

That evening Acheson addressed a dinner gathering of the London branch of the Society of Pilgrims. In this company he did not feel constrained to warn Britain not to overstress the advantages of the "special relationship." But beyond the usual homage paid to Anglo-American friendship, Acheson decided to emphasize the need to make common cause with the continental European nations and, in particular, "with our late and bitter enemy, Germany."

With the twelve nations in the North Atlantic Council about to meet, Acheson reminded his listeners that Germany could not remain "a passive spectator of its own fate." The Germans, he warned, must be prepared to assume the full risks and responsibilities of a sovereign nation.[26]

In a private meeting with Schuman and Bevin, Acheson reiterated his view that Germany would soon have to become a full-fledged member of the European community. As he saw it, the Allied High Commission's influence in Germany would not last for more than a couple of years. The allies could therefore not delay much longer transforming the occupying forces into a new concept and organization, "a force for the protection of Western Europe." (Acheson was right about the effective life of the occupation and the Allied High Commission; two years later agreements were signed in Paris and Bonn that signaled their end.)

At the council meeting, the problem of the twelve-member North Atlantic Alliance was obvious. As Acheson described it, the council was experiencing "the frustrations of the Continental Congress in 1776 before the appointment of General Washington. It recognized the need of forces in being and in position, but saw little possibility of getting either without organization, a command, and a strategy."

The council did agree to call for the creation of collective forces rather than separate, national forces for the defense of Europe, each with its own armaments. However, the point was raised that a nation would be in peril if the collective force did not come to its aid. Acheson met the point head-on. As he saw it, such a nation would be imperiled, however its individual defense force was constructed, if the aggressor should be the only likely one, the Soviet bloc. In that case, the effective defense could be provided only through the collective force, which would include all the power of the United States.

Acheson agreed that nations with responsibilities outside the European theater would need forces for these purposes. But in Europe both economic and strategic considerations dictated a collective force rather than a number of national defense forces, which would waste resources in a clear duplication of efforts. Anything other than a common plan, a common effort, and a common strategy would prove self-defeating.

What Acheson emphasized to the council was the limitation of means to achieve the desired end—the defense of Europe against a presumed Soviet threat. The task for the immediate future was to determine what forces would be adequate to this end and then find the means available to provide them.[27]

On May 19 Acheson and his party boarded the boat train for Liverpool, anticipating a relaxed week on the *Britannic* en route to New York. Initially the president wanted Acheson to address a joint session of Congress, as Secretary Cordell Hull had done in 1943 after returning from Moscow. But this seemed unwise to the Speaker of the House, Sam Rayburn. Acheson had become a controversial figure, and the opposition was bent on tearing Acheson down, not building him up.

The solution, in a compromise with the Republican leadership, was to have the Speaker and Vice President Alben Barkley invite Acheson to appear in the auditorium of the Library of Congress to address members of the House and Senate who wished to attend. This meant that there would be little time to relax on the *Britannic.*

Acheson later described the setting of this speech on the future of Europe and the need for a common defense force in a letter of May 31, 1950, to his daughter Mary.

> This was the day of my gala performance. It was a day of sweat. The small, crowded hall was well steamed up with animal heat. Then the television lights went on and it passed 100 degrees. As I spoke I sweated out of me all the sins of a misspent life. My collar went, my shirt became a washrag, even my coat hung in loose, wet folds. But I was determined not to wipe my brow. That might mean to viewers of the airwaves that I was suffering—which I was. But I must always appear gay, cool and confident!
>
> I was none of these. . . .
>
> However, the spies say that it went well. So who am I to complain?[28]

CHAPTER TWENTY-THREE

PUTTING OUR HAND TO THE PLOW

DISTURBED BY THE SIGNING of the Sino-Soviet pact on February 14, 1950, Acheson was determined to press ahead with a Japanese peace treaty that would bind Japan to the West. He was also preparing to help the South Koreans to rebuild their country after the withdrawal of U.S. forces and—reluctantly—to aid the French in their war against the Communists under Ho Chi Minh in Indochina.

In trying to accomplish these goals, the secretary of state often found himself at odds with Secretary of Defense Louis Johnson, who was committed to cutting the military budget; but Acheson remained on such good terms with Harry Truman that he tended to win his battles. Characteristic of the warmth of their relationship was a note that Truman penned to Acheson from the aircraft bearing the president to Key West for a vacation in late November 1949: after thanking Acheson for seeing him off, Truman confessed, "I'm still a farm boy and when the Secretary of State of the greatest Republic comes to the airport to see me off on a vacation, I can't help but swell up a little bit." Acheson responded to the president's note with a brief note of his own in which he expressed his "deepest respect and affection" for Truman.[1]

The often effusive nature of the Truman-Acheson correspondence reflected an intimacy that went undamaged throughout their years in office and after. In letters and conversations with friends and members of his family, Acheson reiterated not only his good opinion of Truman's straightforwardness and lack of guile, but also his surprisingly wide knowledge of history, all the more admirable, in Acheson's view, because it was self-taught and revealed a man thinking for himself.

By giving the president absolute loyalty and being sensitive to his needs, Acheson gave Harry Truman a growing self-confidence in foreign affairs. Unlike Roosevelt, Kennedy, or Nixon, Truman did not want to make foreign policy from the White House; what he wanted was respect, consultation, and the right to make final decisions. Acheson understood this and never failed to provide him with the personal touches that Truman craved. Whenever he was away at foreign ministers' conferences, Acheson sent the president a personal report at the end of each day; when in Washington, they met several times a week. Acheson never let outsiders know of the rare occasions when Truman overruled him or insisted on initiatives that Acheson disliked.[2] Truman was rightly seen as a man of decision; under both Marshall and Acheson, those decisions almost always ratified what his secretaries of state wanted.

In postwar Japan, the United States had absolute control. There were no zones of occupation. Washington made it quite clear to its allies in the Pacific war that while their troops would be welcome in Japan, the allies would have only an advisory function and their soldiers would serve under the direct command of the American supreme commander, General Douglas MacArthur. The emperor and the government would remain in place, subject to the orders of the Supreme Commander of the Allied Powers (SCAP). MacArthur was more than a proconsul, he became an absolute ruler.

Instructions for MacArthur's governance stemmed from the "Initial Surrender Policy" document Truman had approved on September 6, 1945. Its main provisions charged MacArthur with disarming and demilitarizing Japan, creating a democratic society, and directing industry toward a peaceful economy. In accomplishing these tasks, MacArthur turned out to be remarkably successful, except in the creation of a productive economy.

American policy (in line with much New Deal thinking) reflected the belief that breaking up the industrial and financial combines that had so dominated the economic life of Japan would contribute to demilitarization and democratization. In Japan, the system of "private enterprise" had long been controlled by the *zaibatsu*—conglomerates in the hands of a family or families rather than shareholders. As MacArthur himself put it, the system "exploited into virtual slavery the remainder of the Japanese people." The general therefore began to carry out a vigorous program of breaking up the *zaibatsu*.

The danger in doing so, however, was that trust-busting and political purges further disrupted the economic life of the country so that the people became increasingly discontented, and this, in turn, threatened MacArthur's efforts to ensure a stable political life. While the Americans were successful in insisting on the right of labor to organize freely, and in imposing an extensive program of land reform, aimed, in MacArthur's words, to make "every farmer in the country . . . a capitalist," the occupation authorities were less successful in destroying the *zaibatsu.*

What they did succeed in doing was opening up Japan's trading relationship with the outside world and discouraging a return to the nation-centered, mercantilist form of economic organization, which depended on the state promoting economic growth through control of foreign markets. It was this effort to secure markets abroad that had fed Japanese aggression in the interwar period.

As the postwar economies of much of east Asia were in ruins, however, Japan could not seek markets there. In order to support Japanese exports, Washington encouraged Tokyo to look for markets for Japanese goods in the United States. At the same time, Washington sought to rebuild Korea's economy so that Japan and Korea could reestablish a strong trading relationship.[3]

Even in 1946, it was becoming more and more evident to Acheson that the Japanese economy was suffering from MacArthur's policy of breaking up the *zaibatsu.* At war's end, Japan had lost over 88 percent of its merchant fleet, and its industrial production for that year came to just 30.7 percent of its prewar average. Yet Japan depended on foreign trade for its survival. Because the war had destroyed the economies of major trading partners—Korea, Taiwan, and Manchuria—Japan was now dependent on the United States for 92 percent of its imports; but it earned so little from exports that its trade deficit threatened to cripple the economy. Moreover, Japan could not import enough food to feed its people, and the State Department openly acknowledged that Japan's food crisis was "leading to starvation."[4]

To Acheson a radical change of course was needed to strengthen the economy and thereby solidify the domestic reforms MacArthur had initiated. No longer could Japan's problems be left wholly in MacArthur's hands. A new economic team was needed, and Acheson was determined to put one in place. But to do so would require the most careful handling of the supreme commander.

With Acheson's resignation as under secretary of state in mid-1947, the efforts to replace MacArthur's economic team flagged briefly. Nonetheless, in February 1948 Secretary of State Marshall took up Acheson's questioning of the wisdom of dismantling the *zaibatsu.* He decided to dispatch George Kennan, then head of Policy Planning, to visit MacArthur and come back with a full report. Kennan was concerned with the strategic position of Japan and worried that the islands might fall under Soviet influence after an American withdrawal. Only a strong Japanese economy would prevent that. The issue was how to modify the position of General MacArthur.[5]

MacArthur was a commanding presence, possessed of an overweening self-confidence. His headquarters resembled a court: his pronouncements went unchallenged, and everything was done to feed his vanity. His orotund way of speaking, and his imperial manner, often left listeners in awe of him and his genius.[6] Kennan was the highest American official to visit Japan since the beginning of the occupation, and he saw himself as "an envoy charged with opening up relations with a hostile and suspicious government."[7] Secretary Marshall had cautioned him to let MacArthur do all the talking in the first stages of his visit.

MacArthur had little use for the State Department. When informed of Kennan's impending visit, he reportedly said, "I'll have him briefed until it comes out of his ears."

Kennan and two advisers, Brigadier General Cortlandt Van Rensselaer Schuyler and Marshall Green, a Foreign Service officer who had served in Japan before the war, arrived exhausted and thoroughly chilled in a snowstorm. Nonetheless, despite having been without sleep for nearly forty-eight hours, Kennan and General Schuyler were summoned to MacArthur's residence for lunch.

As the meal came to an end, MacArthur turned his back on Kennan and addressed himself exclusively to Schuyler in a monologue that lasted about two hours, with Kennan sitting "motionless in my humble corner." As Kennan recalled in his memoirs, "Caesar's experience in the military occupation of Gaul was cited . . . as the only other historical example of a productive military occupation."

That was it. The envoys from Washington were dismissed, and for the next few days Kennan was indeed briefed and briefed again mercilessly. Although Kennan wrote a note politely thanking MacArthur for his briefings and "the local hospitality," he might not have gained another interview but for the tactful initiative of Marshall Green, who arranged for Kennan to give a talk to a number of MacArthur's aides on the situation in the Soviet Union.

Reports of Kennan's brilliant presentation quickly reached the supreme commander, and on March 5 MacArthur met alone with the diplomat for a long and comprehensive discussion. MacArthur outlined his strategy for defending the islands of the western Pacific, now to be the new American western frontier. Kennan, in turn, put forward his ideas for changing the emphasis of the occupation policy to economic rehabilitation and the restoration of Japan's ability to contribute to the prosperity and stability of the region. Nothing was decided, but the two men parted cordially.

Kennan then traveled about Japan in a special railroad car provided by the supreme commander. He returned to Washington convinced that the occupation had "embraced with an almost wild enthusiasm the trust-busting ideals" that now prevailed in America at the Department of Justice. In addition, Kennan was appalled at the extent to which MacArthur had carried out a wholesale and indiscriminate "purging" of people in government, education, and business who "were suspected of having had militaristic sympathies or of having abetted Japanese aggression in earlier days." At the same time, nothing had been done to provide the Japanese with "any adequate means of looking to their own security." There were no Japanese armed forces, although the Japanese Communists "were increasing their strength rapidly."[8]

In his report to Secretary Marshall on March 25, Kennan urged that the occupation regime be relaxed. The emphasis should be shifting from political reform to economic recovery. The purges should taper off and be terminated as soon as possible. A similar report was made by William H. Draper Jr., the under secretary of the army, whose visit to Japan followed hard upon Kennan's. Both reports made their way to the National Security Council, and on October 9, 1948, President Truman approved a directive, NSC 13/2, altering the thrust of occupation policies from reform to recovery.[9]

Acheson's return to power as secretary of state in 1949 gave impetus to the new course in American occupation policy in Japan. The emphasis on economic recovery included rejecting most of MacArthur's *zaibatsu* dissolution program; the new blueprint for the Japanese economy was to center around fiscal, monetary, price, and wage stability, as well as maximum production for export. Joseph Dodge, a longtime friend of Paul Nitze's and a prominent Detroit banker, was chosen to implement the program. He was to be a senior adviser to General MacArthur, and in a carefully composed and cordial letter Acheson personally informed MacArthur of Dodge's mission and credentials. He also had Max Bishop, his chief of northeast Asian affairs and perhaps the only man in the State Department on good terms with MacArthur, serve as Dodge's escort in Tokyo.[10]

Although MacArthur had welcomed Acheson's appointment as secretary of state, Bishop knew how difficult it would be for MacArthur to relinquish his authority. The plan, as Bishop saw it, was to "give the Japanese a chance to run their own business." Acheson, however, had lined up the president behind the program, and by late July MacArthur declared that his civil affairs teams would be abolished by the end of the year. A few days later he declared that the *zaibatsu* dissolution program had been completed.

The Dodge program—supported by MacArthur, the Pentagon, and Acheson—pressured the Japanese government into accepting balanced budgets and a reduced rate of monetary growth. Dodge's tight monetary policy initially produced a mild recession, but this quickly gave way to a period of sustained economic growth. Japan's industrial production, which had attained only 54.6 percent of its prewar level in 1948, rose to 114.4 percent in 1951.

Meanwhile, the need to secure a peace treaty loomed larger in Acheson's thinking. The Pentagon, however, insisted that the United States retain bases in Japan, and that any peace treaty was "premature" until, in the Pentagon's words,

"Japan's democracy and western orientation first be established beyond all question." Moreover, since neither the Soviet Union nor Communist China would accept any peace treaty that allowed the United States to retain bases, their participation was out of the question at this time.

In the face of these problems, Acheson reorganized his campaign in February 1950. He understood that even if the United States was willing to go ahead with a treaty unilaterally, the Japanese were wary of signing such a document without the signatures of China and the Soviet Union.[11]

At this point, Dean Rusk, the deputy under secretary, offered to take a demotion to become assistant secretary for Far Eastern affairs. Rusk, who had good relations with the Republicans, and who had served in New Delhi under Lord Mountbatten in the China-Burma-India theater during World War II, believed he could help take the political heat off Acheson from Republicans who were lambasting the secretary for "losing China" to the Communists. His offer was gratefully accepted. (Years later, this display of loyalty was central to Acheson's recommendation of Rusk to President-elect Kennedy in December 1960 when JFK was seeking a secretary of state.[12])

Acheson still had to find a way to neutralize potential Republican opposition, which would likely make common cause with the Pentagon's objections. The solution to at least part of this problem came from an unexpected source.

One evening in the late fall of 1949, Lucius Battle received a telephone call from Carl McCardle, the Washington correspondent for the *Philadelphia Bulletin.* About to go out to dinner with his wife, Battle was not eager to spend much time talking with McCardle, who had given good play to Foster Dulles's attacks on the administration during Dulles's 1949 losing campaign for a U.S. Senate seat in New York. But what McCardle had to say kept Battle on the phone for up to an hour.

The thrust of McCardle's message was that Dulles feared his remarks during the Senate campaign would destroy his usefulness to the administration in foreign affairs. Dulles had been in the habit of often attending conferences with foreign ministers as a bipartisan adviser to Byrnes, Marshall, and Acheson; now, after serving four months as an appointed U.S. senator, he had lost a bitterly contested election to former governor Herbert Lehman. Dulles knew that his political career was at an end.

Battle's initial response was far from positive. As Battle put it to McCardle, Dulles had given the president "a pretty nasty roughing up." McCardle replied that Dulles considered it "just the game of politics, and it ought to be forgotten." In short, John Foster Dulles wanted to rejoin the State Department in some capacity.[13]

Battle knew that Acheson detested Dulles. Not only had Dulles played rough during the campaign, but Acheson was generally repelled by Dulles's heavy-handed moralizing and what he saw as a general deviousness—leaking to the press views that conflicted with the official position of State when he was presumably in a bipartisan role of serving the administration.

Dulles certainly expected one day to be secretary of state, as indeed he would have been had Dewey been elected in 1948. His grandfather John Foster had served as secretary of state to President Benjamin Harrison; his uncle was Robert Lansing, who had been Woodrow Wilson's secretary of state during World War I.

Born in 1888, Dulles grew up to become an earnest and disciplined student more than a brilliant one. After graduating from Princeton University, rather than entering the ministry as his father would have preferred, he attended George Washington Law School in Washington, D.C. Through his grandfather Foster, he was taken into the New York office of Sullivan and Cromwell, a firm that would not normally have accepted a graduate of George Washington.

Dulles turned out to be a first-class lawyer; he had the ability to cut through to the heart of the matter and was able to make the issues at hand clear to his clients. Though he could be warm and even jocular with his family, he exhibited a puritanical hardness of nature to outsiders.

During World War II he worked within the Republican Party to garner support for the United Nations. In this capacity he became invaluable to the Democrats as a Republican internationalist, with close ties to Governor Thomas Dewey, who helped Roosevelt and later Truman to establish a bipartisan consensus for their major foreign policies,

Unlike Acheson, who tended to downplay ideology in the context of the Cold War, Dulles, in a book he wrote after his 1949 Senate campaign, declared that "Soviet Communism starts with an atheistic, Godless premise. Everything else flows from that premise."[14] Although he wrote that he supported the Truman administration's policy of containment, believing they had saved Western Europe, Greece, Turkey, and Iran, he also believed that they had failed to save Eastern Europe or China.

The morning after McCardle's call Battle mentioned it to James Webb, the under secretary. Astonished at his suggestion that Dulles receive an appointment at State, Webb retorted: "Have you lost your mind?" Yet a few weeks later Webb suggested to Acheson that Dulles be brought back as a special adviser. "Has he lost his mind?" Acheson muttered. Behind the scenes, Senator Vandenberg had expressed to Webb an urgent need to reestablish "unpartisan unity" following "the fall of China" and had persuaded Webb to support Dulles as the most qualified Republican available.

Finally Acheson, too, came around and allowed Webb to put the case to Truman. Truman was appalled; as one report had it, he exploded: "What, that bastard? Not on your life!" Nonetheless, on April 4, 1950, Truman finally agreed that conditions were such that Dulles could serve as a "consultant," provided

Dulles gave assurance that he would not run again for the Senate. Dulles, though he detested the title he was offered, nonetheless accepted.

Soon after, Rusk urged Acheson to assign Dulles to negotiate the Japanese peace treaty. On May 18, 1950, Truman appointed him to do so, with the final responsibility for the treaty resting with Acheson. With Kennan and Acheson's instructions before him, Dulles prepared his own memorandum. The essence of his approach mirrored Acheson's: first, recalling the lessons of the Versailles Treaty, Dulles believed it would be a mistake to impose a vengeful peace on the Japanese; second, the Cold War made it imperative to align Japanese interests with those of the West.

Acheson was satisfied with Dulles's basic conclusions, and on June 14, 1950, Dulles set off on a reconnaissance trip to Korea and Japan.

Acheson's policy toward Japan was relatively uncomplicated. He needed to rehabilitate Japan so that it could withstand any Soviet pressures in northeast Asia and the western Pacific. In Southeast Asia, Acheson hoped to contain the expansion of Soviet and Chinese Communist influence in Indochina, which comprised the three French colonies of Vietnam, Laos, and Cambodia. His immediate problem was to find in Vietnam a nationalist leader who was also a non-Communist.

In Vietnam, Ho Chi Minh, who had managed to organize resistance against both French colonial rule and the Japanese occupation during World War II and even establish an independent state in northern Vietnam at the end of the war, was surely a tough and uncompromising Communist. But he had also assumed the mantle of Vietnamese nationalism. In November 1946 negotiations broke down between his own movement, known as the Viet Minh, and the French authorities who had returned to North Vietnam in 1945, and the First Indochina War had effectively begun.

From 1945 to 1947, when Acheson was under secretary of state, Washington had rebuffed Ho's entreaties for American aid against the French, while simultaneously pressuring the French to seek a negotiated solution to the growing Indochinese war. Upon his return to office as secretary of state, however, Acheson shifted his policy and with deep reservations came to support France's struggle against Ho's Viet Minh. The Sino-Soviet Treaty in February 1950 had dampened his thinking that Mao might prove an Asian Tito, and he became increasingly doubtful that in Asia a dedicated Communist could also be a convinced nationalist.[15]

Franklin Roosevelt had been especially opposed to the return of Indochina to French rule after the war. He had made a point of opposing colonialism in the

Atlantic Charter and hoped to replace the colonial regimes in Southeast Asia with international trusteeships. On January 24, 1944, he told Secretary of State Cordell Hull that he did not think Indochina should go back to France. "France has had that country—thirty million inhabitants for nearly one hundred years," he said, "and the people are worse off than they were at the beginning."[16]

Characteristically, Roosevelt sought to postpone any final decision about Indochina until after the war. Nonetheless, on April 3, 1945, Roosevelt allowed his new secretary of state, Edward Stettinius, to issue a statement that, as a result of the Yalta talks, America hoped for a trusteeship as a postwar arrangement for "territories taken from the enemy" and for "territories as might voluntarily be placed under trusteeship."[17] Indochina fell into the latter category, so any trusteeship for Indochina would be determined by the French. Seven days later Roosevelt was dead.

With Truman in office, French sovereignty over Indochina was recognized. But in 1945 the United States made it clear to the French foreign minister, Georges Bidault, that Washington was not happy with French colonial practices. Self-government looking toward "eventual independence" was the favored American outcome. In the meantime, at Potsdam, with the Japanese still in the war, Truman agreed to have the British and Chinese occupy Indochina until such time as the territory could be turned over to the French.[18]

For the next two years, with Acheson as under secretary, American policy tried to square a circle. The State Department's Office of Far Eastern Affairs strongly argued that Washington should support Asian nationalism and oppose French colonialism—a continuation of Roosevelt's policy. But the Office of European Affairs cautioned policymakers to pay attention to France's central role in European affairs and the need for a strong France that would not fall under communist influence; this meant taking care not to alienate French policymakers or put too much pressure on the French government.

A rough compromise was worked out in August 1945, whereby the United States did not question French sovereignty over Indochina but reserved the right to reconsider that position if the people of Indochina rejected French rule. Acheson was pretty much put in charge of American policy toward the region by Secretary Byrnes; in turn, Acheson relied on John Carter Vincent, who headed the State Department's branch for Southeast Asia.

With the outbreak of fighting in the north between the Viet Minh and the French troops in late 1946, Acheson called in French ambassador Henri Bonnet that December. He told Bonnet that Washington would be prepared to use its good offices to facilitate a settlement in Indochina. He also urged the ambassador to tell the Foreign Ministry that any attempt by the French to reconquer the country through military force would be wrongheaded, a step that the British had found "unwise" in Burma.[19]

About two weeks later, on January 8, 1947, the State Department informed the American ambassador in Paris that the United States would approve the sale of arms to France, "except in cases which appear to relate to Indochina." On the same day, the French told Washington that they were not interested in Acheson's offer of good offices.

Early in February, Acheson and Secretary of State Marshall instructed their ambassador in Paris, Jefferson Caffery, to remind the Quai d'Orsay that colonial empires "are rapidly becoming a thing of the past." On the other hand, Caffery was informed that "we do not lose sight [of the] fact that Ho Chi Minh has direct Communist connections and it should be obvious that we are not interested in seeing colonial empire administrations supplanted by philosophical and political organizations emanating and controlled by [the] Kremlin. Frankly, we have no solution of [the] problem to suggest," Acheson admitted. The United States, in short, was determined to remain outside the conflict.[20]

Acheson, as planned, left the department at the end of June, and no one else was much interested pressing the French on their handling of the Indochinese war.

Through 1947 and 1948 the French Fourth Republic was chronically unstable (it would have nineteen governments during the twelve years of its existence). In its policy toward Indochina, the United States was convinced that it could neither endorse French colonialism nor support Ho Chi Minh. The United States refused to provide any direct assistance to the French for their war in Southeast Asia but did provide $1.9 billion in unrestricted economic aid to France between July 1945 and July 1948.

These dollars helped stimulate the French economic recovery at home, but they also permitted the French to pursue what many in France called their *sale guerre* in Vietnam.[21] Moreover, the State Department Office of Intelligence Research reported in October 1948 that there was no evidence of Soviet influence in Indochina: "If there is a Moscow-directed conspiracy in Southeast Asia, Indochina is an anomaly so far."[22]

Upon his return to office in January 1949, Acheson found the situation in Indochina very different from what it had been two years earlier. Now the French were seeking a military solution and were about to set up a puppet government in March under the former emperor Bao Dai; they had given up on any further negotiations with Ho Chi Minh. On February 25, in a cable to the American ambassador in Paris, Acheson commented, "Over the past three years" [the] French have shown no impressively sincere intention or desire [to] make [the] concessions which seem necessary [to] solve [the] Indochina question."[23] He was far from prepared to endorse Bao Dai.

* * *

In part, Acheson's reservations may have prodded the French into pushing ahead with the March 1949 Elysée Agreements with Bao Dai, granting autonomy to the Indochinese peoples of Laos, Cambodia, and Vietnam, but with the French retaining "rights of observation" and "intervention." Independence was myth.[24]

At this point, Acheson's advisers in the Office of Western European Affairs pressed him to support the Bao Dai solution, arguing, "While we obviously do not wish to get ourselves involved in a repetition of the painful Chiang Kai-shek situation, we must realize that the only alternative to a Bao Dai regime is one led by [the] Communist Ho Chi-Minh."

The State Department Asian specialists disputed this view. Charles Reed, former consul general in Saigon, argued that Bao Dai had a dubious chance of succeeding and that the United States should not be following France down what might turn out to be "a dead-end alley."[25]

Acheson hesitated to give any premature endorsement or de facto recognition of Bao Dai. But George M. Abbott, the recently appointed U.S. consul general in Saigon, urged Acheson to back the new French policy. "Our support will not insure Bao Dai success," Abbott reasoned, "but the lack of it will probably make certain his failure." From Paris, Caffery endorsed Abbott's views. Nonetheless, Acheson wanted greater study of the situation before he would proceed to full recognition of the Bao Dai government.

At his request, under the supervision of George Kennan, the Policy Planning Staff spent two months producing a comprehensive study on Southeast Asia, which was completed on May 19, 1949. In essence, the report urged Washington to press the French to accommodate themselves to Indochinese nationalism; unless France abandoned its "niggardly" attitude and granted full independence to the Bao Dai regime, the Viet Minh would soon gain control of most of Indochina.[26]

This had long been Acheson's position, but the problem was how to persuade the French to do so. Acheson was well aware of the precarious position that any French government would find itself in, were it to abandon Indochina.

The issue of pressuring the French came to a head in June 1949, when Acheson met in Paris with Ambassador David Bruce. Walton Butterworth, director for the Office of Far Eastern Affairs, had sent Bruce a memorandum on June 6, along with instructions to deliver it to the Foreign Ministry. Butterworth, using the Kennan report to combat (or circumvent) the views of the Office of European Affairs, wanted to tell the French that unless the French government agreed to terms compatible with "Vietnamese national pride," most of the Vietnamese people would support Ho Chi Minh's republic.[27] This was not what the French intended when they were making their arrangements with Bao Dai.

Bruce was shocked by the tone of the message, as well as by the implications for U.S. policy. He therefore decided to show the missive to Acheson, who was in

Paris for a foreign ministers' conference. Bruce told Acheson that while Butterworth's analysis doubtless reflected the situation in Indochina, it did not consider the climate in France. The policy of the United States, Bruce believed, should be to support the French in their promises to Bao Dai; Butterworth's document would "impede rather than encourage" further movement by the French.[28]

In addition, granting full independence to Vietnam would set a precedent for France's negotiations with its other colonies, especially Tunisia and Morocco. French public opinion would oppose the collapse of the empire in such a short time, and therefore the government would fall, endangering the other policies that France was carrying out in regard to German sovereignty and European unity.

Acheson, aware of the cogency of Butterworth's reasoning but also sympathetic to Bruce's rebuttal, came up with a compromise that essentially favored Bruce. He told the ambassador to apprise the French orally of Butterworth's concerns but insist on nothing—just tell the French that he hoped they would adopt "a liberal interpretation of the [Elysée] agreements just already reached and a similarly generous attitude in the negotiations still to be concluded."[29]

Acheson took this course because he believed that additional French concessions at that time were simply not attainable. He had to recognize, as he wrote later, "the limits on the extent to which one may successfully coerce an ally."[30]

On October 1, 1949, Acheson told the Senate Committee on Foreign Relations in executive session that it would be "unwise" to recognize Bao Dai at this point. "We will get nowhere, I think, by supporting the French as a colonial power against Indochina," he declared. "We want to put as much pressure on the French as we can."[31]

The fact is that little pressure was put on the French to do more than formally implement the Elysée Agreements with Bao Dai. Once these were ratified at the end of January 1950, and the proclamation of the independence of Vietnam announced on February 2, Acheson recommended to Truman that he give U.S. recognition of the "three legally constituted governments of Vietnam, Laos, and Cambodia." The main reason to do so was to aid in "the establishment of stable, non-Communist governments in areas adjacent to Communist China." On February 3, 1950, Harry Truman did just that.[32]

When the French ambassador in the wake of U.S. recognition brought up the question of military aid for the French efforts in Indochina on February 16, Acheson refused. Following the meeting with the French envoy, Acheson emphasized to the U.S. embassy in Paris "that our bargaining position disappears the moment we agree to give them aid."[33]

In April, a new National Security Council document (NSC 64) once again spoke of the danger of Communist expansion if Indochina fell and reiterated that the State and Defense Departments should take "all practicable measures designed to protect United States security interests in Indochina." In response to this document and to further French requests for American assistance, on May 8, 1950, Truman finally approved military supplies and economic support totaling $10 million for France and the Associated States of Indochina. Neither Acheson nor the Joint Chiefs of Staff was willing to give any kind of U.S. military guarantee for Indochina, even if the Communist Chinese intervened directly.[34]

As time passed, the United States became increasingly committed to keeping the French from abandoning Indochina, lest America itself become militarily involved in the region. When Acheson spoke in later years of being "blackmailed" by the French, he was referring to their threats to pull out of Vietnam should the United States refuse to provide France with ever increasing amounts of military aid.[35]

When Acheson appeared before an executive session of the Senate Foreign Relations Committee in March 1950, he stated quite candidly, "We do not want to get into a position where the French say, 'You take over; we aren't able to go ahead on this.' We want the French to stay there. . . . The French have got to carry [their burden] in Indochina, and we are willing to help, but not to substitute for them." Acheson cautioned the senators that "the thing that we want to be careful about is that we do not press the French to the point where they say, 'All right, take over the damned country. We don't want it,' and put their soldiers on ships and send them back to France."[36]

In addition, Acheson did not want to destabilize the French government as it was preparing to make concessions to Washington over allied policy toward Germany. In the months and years to come, it was far more the French than the Americans who possessed the greater leverage over policy in Indochina.

In his memoirs, Acheson admitted that critics were accurate in describing the Truman administration's policy toward Indochina as "a muddled hodgepodge." He also admitted that he could not think of a better course, unless it was to do nothing. But for Acheson, while that policy "might have had merit," the United States, "the leader of a great alliance," simply could not easily stand aside.

Once he recommended to the president that military and economic aid be given to France to fight the Indochina War, he decided that "having put our hand to the plow, we would not look back."[37] Throughout his tenure as secretary of state, Acheson did not do so. By mid-1954, within two years after he left office, the United States, under the Eisenhower administration, was poised to supplant the French in their struggle to subdue the Viet Minh—the very course of action Acheson had most wanted to avoid.

* * *

Contrary to later accusations directed at him, Dean Acheson never intended to write off South Korea. The occupation of the peninsula by the Russians and the Americans at the end of World War II had not been expected to be permanent. As in Germany, a temporary demarcation line along the thirty-eighth parallel slowly evolved into an Asian Iron Curtain separating two distinct political and economic systems.

On February 25, 1947, the report of a special interdepartmental committee on Korea, which Acheson personally approved as under secretary, declared that in the event of general hostilities "Korea would be a military liability," and therefore the United States had "little strategic interest in maintaining troops or bases." Nonetheless, the report noted, "control of Korea by Soviet or Soviet-dominated forces . . . would constitute an extremely serious political and military threat to U.S. interests in the Far East." In particular, a Soviet Korea would be "an extremely serious political and military threat" to Japan. Any mutual withdrawal by American and Soviet troops would have to be based on adequate safeguards for Korea's territorial integrity.[38] To this end, the United States should make every effort to hold elections in Korea and then effect a withdrawal of both American and Soviet troops.

At the same time, the special committee recommended "an aggressive, positive, long-term program" for Korea that was estimated to cost $600 million over the next three years. (It is worth recalling that in this same period Truman asked only $400 million for Greece and Turkey combined under the Truman Doctrine.)

In testimony before the Senate Committee on Foreign Relations, March 13, 1947, to defend the Truman Doctrine, Acheson replied to a senator's suggestion that it might be wise to limit U.S. assistance to "certain strategic areas" by first enumerating places where American aid would be ill advised. Then he went on the offensive: "There are other places where we can be effective. One of them is Korea, and I think that is another place where the line is clearly drawn between the Russians and ourselves." Acheson certainly intended to follow up his aid package for Greece and Turkey with one for South Korea.[39]

Despite the worsening relations between the two occupying powers, Washington and Moscow did manage a mutual withdrawal from Korea in 1949, although not by mutual agreement. The United Nations had held elections in South Korea on May 10, 1948—though the Russians refused to allow them in the north—and the United States then began to move out its forty-five thousand troops.

Elections in the south brought to power the authoritarian Syngman Rhee, an aging rebel against the Japanese who had spent much of his life in exile. Rhee went on to install an undemocratic, rabidly anti-Communist government based in Seoul. In the north in Pyongyang, Kim Il Sung, a Moscow-trained Korean, headed his own undemocratic, Communist government.

With Acheson back at his law firm, the State Department in 1948 was now prepared to accede to the Pentagon's desire to get American troops out of Korea as soon as possible. The Joint Chiefs of Staff, led by General Eisenhower, were unequivocal: "The United States has little strategic interest in maintaining the present troops and bases in Korea." (Later, Acheson said that upon his return to office, "I delayed the leaving of the army until July 1949 so that we could have something there."[40])

With Acheson out of office, interest by the administration in providing economic and military aid for South Korea languished. The Pentagon was determined that the United States should not get involved in any conflict on the Korean peninsula, and in 1948 the JCS produced a new study that recommended that the United States should accept as a "probability" the "eventual domination of Korea by the U.S.S.R." after American troop withdrawal. American aid and support should go to "countries of greater strategic importance."[41]

Shortly after he returned to power in 1949, Acheson ordered a policy review on Korea. On March 23 Acheson's new policy, which largely echoed his earlier approach, stated that "the United States must continue to give political support, and economic, technical, military, and other assistance to the Republic of Korea." However, the new policy did confirm the complete withdrawal of U.S. troops by the summer. Concurrent with U.S. troop withdrawal Acheson put forth his request for $150 million for South Korea, but Congress, assured by Acheson that there was "a good fighting chance" that the South Koreans could take care of themselves, felt no pressure to act on the bill.[42]

While Acheson's press club speech of January 12, 1950, had left South Korea outside the American defense perimeter, a far more serious indication to Beijing and Moscow that the United States was not prepared to back up the South Korean regime was the defeat of the Korean aid bill by the House of Representatives (by a vote of 192–191) a week after the press club speech. Stung by this setback, Acheson redoubled his efforts. He urged Truman to make a public statement that the United States was not pulling out of Korea and to tell the Koreans that "we did not intend to write them off." The House soon reversed itself and voted $100 million for fiscal year 1951.

With the passage of the Korean aid bill, with the Japanese peace treaty under way, and with Chiang Kai-shek bottled up on Taiwan, Acheson was confident that the situation in north Asia was fairly well in hand. His aim now was to mount his offensive at home to strengthen American conventional forces in order to defend Europe and, in so doing, avoid depending on the atomic bomb as America's first line of defense.

CHAPTER TWENTY-FOUR

SITUATIONS OF STRENGTH

ALTHOUGH ACHESON was proving successful in mobilizing the Europeans to start mounting an effective fighting force on the continent, the shocks of 1949—the "loss" of China, the testing of a Soviet atom bomb, Moscow's capacity for aggression whatever its apparent intentions—all led Acheson in the winter of 1950 to call for what he termed "total diplomacy" that would allow America to negotiate from a position of strength.

On a number of occasions over the winter and spring of 1950, in press conferences, at universities, and before business groups, Acheson spoke out strongly against the notion, sometimes suggested in the press and in Congress, that a preventive war should be launched against the Soviet Union while America still possessed the lead in atomic weaponry. He argued instead that "the only way to deal with the Soviet Union, we have found from hard experience, is to create situations of strength."[1]

Negotiating from strength meant, in this view, getting the Russians to "agree to terms consistent with our objectives."[2] He was especially wary of allowing the Soviet Union to take advantage of "situations of weakness" that had been created all over the world: "Every time one of those situations exists—and they exist in Asia and they exist in Europe—it is not only an invitation but an irresistible invitation for the Soviet Government to fish in these troubled waters. To ask them not to fish and to say we will have an agreement that you won't fish is like trying to deal with a force of nature. You can't argue with a river—it is going to flow. You can dam it up, you can even put it to useful purposes, you can deflect it, but you can't argue with it. Therefore, we go to work, as I said, to change those situations of weakness so that they won't create opportunities for fishing and opportunities for trouble."[3]

"The times," he asserted in an address at the University of California at Berkeley, "call for a total diplomacy equal to the task of defense against Soviet expansion."[4]

Acheson believed it might be possible to reach "working agreements with the Kremlin because the Soviet leaders were realists and might at some point come to accept 'a live and let live' philosophy." America's moral certainties did not imply that "the two systems, theirs and ours, cannot exist concurrently in this world." But to demonstrate its readiness to deal with the Soviet Union on a peaceful basis, the United States must always be willing to negotiate on concrete issues. It was the policy of the United States, Acheson said, echoing General Marshall, to be "the first to attend at international conference tables and the last to retire."[5] Acheson was convinced that any agreement worth having had to be made by an American secretary of state negotiating from strength.

During this same period when Acheson was traveling about the country, trying to define for a broad public the objectives of American foreign policy, members of the State and Defense Departments back in Washington were working on a new definition of national security. This effort came out of the promise that Acheson and Truman made to David Lilienthal to have the government take a fresh look at American national security needs at the time the president decided to develop the hydrogen bomb. Reliance on atomic weapons for America's defense posture was a dangerous strategy, and the committee to investigate alternatives was now headed by Paul Nitze, who had replaced George Kennan as head of the Policy Planning Staff.

Kennan had become increasingly dispirited in his role as head of Policy Planning. When Marshall was secretary of state, Kennan's influence was at its height, and he conscientiously put together a first-rate staff. But under Secretary Acheson, Kennan saw himself as increasingly marginal to the formation of American policy.[6] While Acheson valued Kennan's analysis, he thought that Kennan did not fully appreciate the realities of domestic politics, which made an ideal solution impossible. While both men saw themselves as realists, and distrustful of moralistic thinking in foreign affairs, Kennan's approach to policy made it very difficult for Acheson to work out a decision with him.

In September 1949, therefore, Kennan decided to resign as director of Policy Planning and to leave government service. The immediate cause of his departure was a directive from Under Secretary James Webb that prevented him from submitting the Policy Planning Staff's papers directly to Acheson. Unhappy with seeing himself as someone who merely stimulated debates which he was then destined to lose, as he had when Acheson turned down his recommendations calling for the unification of Germany, Kennan now realized that Acheson considered him as just another policy adviser, albeit one whose advice he very much valued.

Kennan was certainly not forced out by Acheson. As he wrote Averell Harriman, his decision to leave was "the result of many considerations, most of which are personal. It reflects no bitterness; least of all any differences of opinion with the Secretary, who has always treated me with much greater consideration than I deserve."[7] Many years later he said that "Mr. Acheson did not at all drive me from the Planning Staff. We had . . . high respect and even affection for each other." On the other hand, Kennan also thought it "not unlikely that he was somewhat relieved that I myself decided to go and that he would be able to work with Mr. Nitze on the question of military policy in the coming period."[8]

Acheson offered Kennan the alternative of taking a leave of absence without pay, after which time he would return to the department. Moreover, although Kennan would quit Policy Planning at the end of 1949, he was to stay on as counsellor to the secretary until June of 1950, at which time he would take a one-year leave to join Robert Oppenheimer's Institute for Advanced Study at Princeton.

Acheson appreciated the need for Kennan to take some time off; in December, referring to Kennan's departure publicly, he said that "at first that filled me with despair. He is one of the most distinguished, if not the most distinguished, Foreign Service Officer."[9]

Kennan was much moved by Acheson's tribute, writing to Acheson on that occasion, "As one who was tempted, day before yesterday, to go into the baby's room and say: 'Go on, get up. You're going to work today. I'll get in the crib'—and who has since existed in the reflection that 'This, too, will pass'—I find no words to say how deeply moved I was by what you did and said this morning."[10]

Receiving this note, Acheson must have been convinced of the rightness of his decision to urge Kennan to take some time off before returning to his duties in foreign service.

The appointment of Paul Nitze to head Policy Planning put in place an adviser who was far more clearly attuned to Acheson's way of thinking. Nitze, who had been serving as Will Clayton's special assistant to work on implementing the Marshall Plan, had not been Acheson's original choice for Kennan's deputy; Kennan himself wanted him in that position, in the belief that Nitze's background in business and strategic planning would be useful in tackling problems associated with Britain's financial crisis and trade relations between the United States and Europe. But Acheson, then under secretary, had vetoed Kennan's suggestion. He thought of Nitze as a Wall Street operator, and what Policy Planning needed, he believed, was a deep thinker. Later, however, when Acheson returned as secretary of state, he found Nitze invaluable in discussions on the currency question in

Germany and Austria. Now he endorsed Kennan's desire to take on Nitze as his deputy, and in August 1949 Nitze moved into his new office, only a few yards from Acheson's own.[11]

Although he had grown up in the world of the University of Chicago, where his father was a professor of Romance languages, Nitze spurned the academic life. After entering Harvard in 1923, he began by getting A's but soon started to run with a fast crowd that included Chip Bohlen. Bored with economics, he skipped the final exam to attend a house party in Newport and received a zero. As he said later, "We all drank too much, had girls, and a rich glorious life." In one escapade, he paddled a small craft from the north shore of Massachusetts to New York City with a classmate from the Porcellian Club on a drunken dare after he had just recovered from hepatitis. They made it in eight days, but Nitze ended up in a hospital, half-dead.

In 1929, just before the stock market crash, Nitze joined the investment firm of Dillon, Read, where he grew close to another Dillon, Read partner, James Forrestal, who brought him into government in 1940. By the end of the war Nitze was working on the U.S. Strategic Bombing Survey, and during this period he became a great admirer of the military. He had also become highly distrustful of the Soviets. Returning to Wall Street now seemed unappealing, and he was only too eager to accept Will Clayton's invitation to work in the State Department on European recovery. It was in this connection that first Kennan, and then Acheson, became aware of his talents.[12]

When Kennan left Policy Planning, Nitze used his experience and his intelligence to establish himself as indispensable to Dean Acheson. "In intellectual terms, Dean found Paul very rewarding," Lucius Battle recalled. "He was decisive; he was clear; he was thoughtful; he was an outsider but was also an insider in the sense of knowledge and intellect and associations." He was, as Acheson wrote in his memoirs, "a joy to work with because of his clear, incisive mind."[13]

During the fall of 1949, when Acheson was pondering the decision on whether or not to build the H-bomb, Nitze worked tirelessly to meet Acheson's needs. "If the matter was high on Mr. Acheson's agenda," according to Policy Planning Staff member Robert Tufts, "it tended to be high on Mr. Nitze's agenda. Whatever Acheson was deeply concerned with, Nitze tended to get involved with."

When Nitze took over Policy Planning, the staff responded well to Nitze's methods. Under Kennan it had been "a court," staff member Dorothy Fosdick recalled. "Our role was to help him make up his mind." Kennan wrote most of the papers, and the staff's job was merely to comment on them. With Nitze it was quite different. The director was interested in the staff's views and in their papers. According to Fosdick, "He didn't think he had the answers, he felt he had to seek the wisest brains."

Like Acheson, Nitze was pragmatic; he lacked the intuitive and scholarly character of Kennan but was powerful in his argumentation and command of facts.

As he worked to evaluate American security interests and Soviet capabilities in the winter and spring of 1950, he spurned ambiguity and argued persuasively that the Soviet Union was now in a position as never before to act aggressively against the West.[14]

For Nitze and the other members of the State-Defense Policy Review Group who worked on the paper that eventually was labeled NSC 68, the bedrock assumption they had to deal with was that the president was determined to hold down the defense budget. For fiscal 1950 the defense budget was planned to reach $13.5 billion, and Truman, as well as his secretary of defense, Louis Johnson, believed they could hold it to that figure for the following years as well.

Work on the NSC 68 document began in January and was to be finished by March 31. By February 20, however, Nitze completed his own study of Soviet behavior, in which he argued that "the USSR had already committed itself to the defeat of the United States," although he conceded there was no evidence that "Moscow is preparing the launch in the near future of an all-out military attack on the West." Nonetheless, "the chance of war through miscalculation is increased." Nitze believed that the Soviet Union considered this a favorable time to probe "soft spots" on its periphery.[15]

For Nitze, as for Acheson, Russia's capacity for aggression was more significant than Russia's present intentions, which were impossible to know for sure. Any responsible planner had to place greater weight on the arsenal the antagonist possessed. In short, if the enemy holds a loaded gun, you had better be prepared to respond with even greater force without spending too much time trying to figure out your enemy's intentions.

If the Congress, in the spring of 1950, was not willing to appropriate more funds for conventional defense at a time when the United States had only seven active divisions, then continued reliance on atomic weapons would have to remain the primary military strategy of the United States. This was not what Acheson, Nitze, or indeed Kennan himself wanted.[16]

Although Truman had instructed representatives from both the State and Defense Departments to produce the NSC paper, Secretary of Defense Louis Johnson immediately became suspicious that the State Department was conspiring to make it impossible for him to carry out his promise to hold military spending to $13.5 billion. He therefore issued an order that all contacts between the military and the State Department go through his office, a highly impractical arrangement.

Major General James Burns, Johnson's deputy for political-military affairs, was supposed to be the Pentagon's point of contact with the State Department. But Burns was not in good health and usually worked only half a day. After some delay, Johnson appointed Major General Truman "Ted" Landon of the air force to assume the main burden of the Defense Department work with Nitze's Policy Planning Staff on NSC 68. In fact, the writing of the document was done almost wholly by the Policy Planning Staff, in close consultation with Acheson.[17] Moreover, in the drafting of the document, the group decided to make their appraisal of existing assumptions, strategy, and plans without reference to the budgetary constraints of the Truman administration.

For six hard weeks the group struggled to produce a draft paper. The result was a document that used heightened language to buttress its arguments. Acheson admitted later that NSC 68, which was not made public, was designed, in Acheson's words, to "bludgeon the mass mind of 'top government'" into recognizing the need to greatly increase conventional forces in order to escape the trap of relying on atomic weapons.[18]

The struggle between the United States and the Soviet Union was depicted in Manichaean terms—good versus evil—and even the cautionary notes that were sounded against those who were urging preventive war were obscured by the assertion that "the cold war is in fact a real war in which the survival of the free world is at stake."[19]

In NSC 68's opening paragraph, its authors evoked the balance of power among nations as the desirable state of affairs that had prevailed for several centuries. It had once been impossible "for any one nation to gain such preponderant strength that a coalition of other nations could not in time face it with greater strength." World War II and the possession of atomic weapons, however, had fundamentally altered the historical distribution of powers among great nations. Now there were only two great powers, America and Russia, but the latter, "animated by a new fanatic faith antithetical to our own, seeks to impose its authority over the rest of the world."

Under these circumstances, not only was the Soviet Union acting as a great power that wanted to dominate all else, as Napoleon's France and Hitler's Germany had tried to do, but unlike in the past, only the United States, not a coalition of powers, had the strength to face up to the Russians. Containment, the authors implied, had to be extended along the perimeter of the Soviet empire, not simply at the mouth of the Dardanelles or along the Iron Curtain from the Baltic to the Adriatic. But containment without military power to back it up would be "no more than a policy of bluff."

The 175 divisions that the intelligence community in Washington believed the Soviet Union possessed in readiness were in fact far from the formidable force that number implied. Many were paper units made up of only a skeleton headquarters and staff, but American military intelligence at this time made little effort to distinguish those units capable of fighting from those that existed only on paper.

Nonetheless, the Soviet Union possessed at a minimum about thirty elite divisions, as compared with America's seven, and their presence did create a genuine fear in Western Europe and the United States that they could prove a spearhead for invasion. To stop them without adequate conventional forces would require the United States to hit the Soviet Union with atomic weapons, which in turn could elicit a Soviet atomic response once the Soviets had enough bombs in their arsenal (estimated at this time to reach two hundred by 1954.[20])

Given these fears and force projections, the authors of NSC 68 were determined to increase not only U.S. conventional forces to contain a possible Soviet attack, but also American atomic weapons as a deterrent against any presumed Soviet use of such weaponry. The paper argued that the American economy had the ability to provide "enormous resources for purposes other than civilian consumption while simultaneously providing a higher standard of living."

This Keynesian perspective was eagerly adopted by the planners after discussions with Leon Keyserling, who would soon become chairman of the President's Council of Economic Advisers. Keyserling argued that the government could stimulate the economy and therefore tolerate short-term budget deficits (a $5.5 billion deficit was projected for fiscal 1950) until tax revenues from the increased economic activity started to roll in. According to Nitze, Keyserling was convinced that the country could afford $40 billion for defense if necessary.[21] When former under secretary of state Robert Lovett read the draft of NSC 68, the Wall Street banker told the drafting committee that "there was practically nothing that the country could not do if it wanted to do it."[22]

Expanding means to meet larger ends seemed both feasible and desirable, although the ends as such were never spelled out. Evoking Alexander Hamilton, who wrote in the *Federalist* that "the means employed must be proportioned to the extent of the mischief," Nitze and his colleagues found in Hamilton's doctrine the answer to the question of how a nation that believed itself scrupulous about the means it would use to defend itself would be able to stand up against a power like the Soviet Union, which possessed no such scruples. Beyond doing whatever was necessary to survive as a nation, the United States would employ the means proportional to the extent of the mischief.

This would require a broad range of military responses if America's aim was "frustrating the Kremlin design." But it also meant that the U.S. military buildup should be defensive in nature, that it should not imply a preventive war, and that the United States should not become too reliant on atomic weapons to deter Soviet aggression. A war of annihilation was ruled out.

Nowhere does NSC 68 discuss in any geographical detail where American interests conflicted with Russia's. Although the point of NSC 68 was to call for greater expenditures to defend existing U.S. interests, the authors of the document did not define those interests, only the threat. Interests could therefore expand or contract according to Washington's evaluation of that threat. The possibility that containment could become worldwide—as it did in the 1950s—was inherent in the strategy outlined in NSC 68.[23]

As the work progressed, it became obvious to the drafters that the kind of military buildup that would provide a force strong enough to hold Russia at the Rhine with conventional weapons would cost between $35 billion and $50 billion a year, rather than the $13.5 billion that Louis Johnson had hoped for. Unlike Acheson, Johnson had not kept himself informed of the general progress of the group. Because Acheson did not have adequate conference facilities in the building at that time, a meeting was therefore convened in Nitze's office on March 22, 1950. The group included Acheson and Johnson as well as General Burns, the liaison to the Defense Department; General Landon, who had been the main contributor from Defense; and General Omar Bradley, chairman of the Joint Chiefs of Staff. Admiral Sidney Souers, as the president's consultant for national security, represented the White House.

A two-page summary of the current draft of the paper had been prepared for Johnson, but he had been too busy to read it, and in the end a one-page summary, as well as a copy of the draft paper, was given to him before he went into a session with Acheson and the study group.

The State Department contingent was united in its support of the paper. Skeptics like Kennan and Bohlen, who would probably have been critical of the lack of emphasis on Soviet intentions, were absent. Acheson, while he harbored some doubts as to the value of the document, favored the study. There was already marked hostility between Acheson and Johnson, but no one was prepared for the scene that erupted on that cold and rainy spring afternoon.

After friendly greetings all around, Acheson asked Nitze to summarize the paper and its conclusions. As Nitze started to do so, Johnson leaned back in his chair and gazed at the ceiling, apparently calm and attentive. Suddenly, Acheson recalled, "he lunged forward with a crash of chair legs on the floor and fist on the table, scaring me out of my shoes. No one, he shouted, was going to make arrangements for him to meet with another Cabinet officer and a roomful of people and be told what he was going to report to the president."[24]

Johnson demanded to know who had authorized the meeting and asked if Acheson had read the paper. When Acheson replied that he had, Johnson asserted that the paper had been sent over to him only that morning—actually Acheson had sent him a copy a week earlier—and that neither he nor Bradley "was going to agree to anything" that they had not read. He didn't like being called into conferences without having had time to read the appropriate material, this was the fourth time the Department of State had done this to him, and "he did not want any more of it."

Though Acheson tried to calm him, telling him that they were working under the president's orders and through Johnson's designated channel, General Burns, the secretary of defense would have none of it. General Burns, Johnson barked, "had no authority to arrange such conferences." At that, Johnson gathered General Bradley and other Defense people and stalked out of the room.

As Acheson tells it, "The rest of us were left in shocked disbelief. General Burns, who had stayed behind, put his head in his hands and wept in shame. I was then summoned to my own office, where Louis Johnson began again to storm at me that he had been insulted. This was too much. I told him since he had started to leave, to get on with it and the State Department would complete the report alone and explain why."

The meeting in Nitze's office had lasted only fifteen minutes. Within an hour Truman was told of the incident by Admiral Souers and called Acheson to express his outrage at Johnson's behavior. The review group was to continue its work as before. "From this time on until the President felt it necessary in September to ask for Johnson's resignation," Acheson wrote later, "evidence accumulated to convince me that Louis Johnson was mentally ill. His conduct became too outrageous to be explained by mere cussedness. It did not surprise me when some years later he underwent a brain operation."[25]

Despite this outburst and his differences with Acheson, Johnson endorsed the NSC document that was finally submitted to the president.

After the meeting the report was circulated to other experts. Both Charles Bohlen and George Kennan were highly critical of the scant attention paid to Soviet intentions rather than Soviet capabilities. Both men found the description of Soviet aims oversimplistic and thought it could lead to the conclusion, as Bohlen put it, that "war is inevitable."

Nitze attributed his differences with Kennan and Bohlen to their ignorance of Russia's military capability. At one point in his discussions with Bohlen, Nitze, basing his arguments on CIA estimates, asserted that the Soviets were capable of producing 315 MiG fighters a month, while the United States was producing only half a dozen F-86s. Bohlen said this estimate was preposterous. Nitze decided to test his assertion by getting the CIA to photograph a Soviet air base on Sakhalin Island north of Japan. The CIA had predicted it would probably find about thirty to forty MiGs there. In fact, the spy plane photographed fifty. Nitze felt vindicated. In the end, Bohlen endorsed a higher level of military spending.[26]

Both James Bryant Conant and Robert Oppenheimer also went along with the need to increase spending on conventional forces. Both men also called for a shift away from "complete dependence on the atomic bomb," and Conant believed "we would be better off if we had one million more men under arms rather than more air power."

The strongest support for the document came from Robert Lovett, in private life after his stint as Marshall's under secretary in 1947–48. He not only believed in increasing the defense budget, but also declared that "we are now in a mortal conflict." To Lovett, the struggle was just as severe as Nitze described it: "Just because there is not much shooting as yet does not mean that we are in a cold war. It is not a cold war; it is a hot war."[27]

Acheson agreed later that NSC 68 was "the most ponderous expression of elementary ideas." But he nonetheless defended the document by quoting his hero, Oliver Wendell Holmes, who once "wisely" said that there are times when "we need education in the obvious more than investigation of the obscure." He also thought the extreme language of NSC 68 would serve not only to "bludgeon the mass mind of 'top government,'" but also to persuade Harry Truman that he had to abandon his commitment to a $13 billion defense budget and risk a deficit.

Truman hesitated. When presented with the NSC paper in April, he called in the executive secretary of the National Security Council and told him that before he could sign it, he needed to know just how much the program envisaged in the report would cost.

Acheson maintained that to gain support for a major policy, "qualification must give way to simplicity of statement, nicety and nuance to bluntness, almost brutality, in carrying home a point." In approving NSC 68, Acheson was repeating the process he had used to gain support from senior senators for the Truman Doctrine. He was allowing the authors to make the points "clearer than truth."[28]

As in the case of the Truman Doctrine, the language used may well have given him the support that would have been much harder to achieve had he been more nuanced. The price paid, however, was to convince the senior officials that the United States must prepare to counter the Soviet Union militarily not only along the Iron Curtain, but, if necessary, in far more distant areas.

This was not his intention. Acheson told a Senate hearing in May that the United States had to be wary not to take on more than it could afford. "I think we have to start out with the realization that the main center of our activity at present has to be in Europe," Acheson declared. "We cannot scatter our shots equally all over the world. We just haven't got the shots for that."[29]

Even the rhetoric of NSC 68 was not enough to garner the support Acheson required for the military buildup he believed America needed. Only a crisis would produce that.

CHAPTER TWENTY-FIVE

"AN ENTIRELY NEW WAR"

"SOMEWHERE ACROSS THE BROAD GLOBE the armed forces of some Communist power [are] expecting soon to go into action." In late May or early June 1950, intelligence reports to this effect were reaching the desk of George Kennan at the State Department. Though Kennan would be leaving government at the end of June, he set about determining which Communist state might be preparing for aggression. Satisfied that it was not Soviet forces that would be involved, he later recalled, Kennan and his fellow Russian experts "toured the horizons of the Soviet bloc."

In due course, Korea came up. The Pentagon and MacArthur's headquarters in Tokyo advised Kennan and his colleagues that the possibility of an attack by North Korea against the southern republic was practically out of the question. Despite the withdrawal of most American troops, "the South Korean troops were so well armed and trained that they were clearly superior to those of the Communist north; our greatest task, we were told, was to restrain the South Koreans from resorting to arms to settle their difference with the north."

The likelihood of aggression in Korea was therefore discarded. To Kennan, this offered cold comfort, for "nowhere else . . . could we see any possibility of attack, and we came away from the exercise quite frustrated."

In such a state of mind, Kennan and his wife left for their farm in Pennsylvania on Saturday, June 24.[1]

On that same Saturday, Dean Acheson was winding up a week that had included a Harvard commencement speech, press conferences, and a cabinet meeting, with a welcome day of rest at Harewood. But even in the countryside of Maryland he was prevented from leaving the world of official Washington completely behind by a special white telephone that had been installed at Harewood and hooked up to the White House switchboard. It rang several times that Saturday, breaking the summer stillness and calling Acheson away from the gladiolus gardening that consumed much of his spare time.

None of the news was momentous, however, and Acheson did manage to get in "some hours of gardening and a good dinner" before retiring to read himself to sleep. The only disturbance was the "movements of security officers changing guard during the night." Acheson was not used to such heavy security, but it had become a necessary precaution—his frequent clashes with Senator Joseph McCarthy and his followers had produced hate mail, some of it threatening, and this resulted in "a regimen not conducive to relaxation."[2]

Meanwhile, in Washington, at just past eight in the evening, the public affairs officer of the Division of Far Eastern Affairs, W. Bradley Connors, took a call in his Washington apartment. On the line was Donald Gonzales, Washington bureau chief of UPI, who said he had just received word from the bureau's correspondent in South Korea that the North Korean Communists had launched an attack across the thirty-eighth parallel. Could Connors confirm this?

Connors immediately broke off discussion and tried to call the American embassy in Seoul. But because of the time difference the switchboards in Seoul were closed down. Connors left his apartment and headed straight for State.

By 9:26 Connors was at his post to receive a cable from John J. Muccio, American ambassador to South Korea: ACCORDING KOREAN ARMY REPORTS WHICH PARTLY CONFIRMED . . . NORTH KOREAN FORCES INVADED ROK [Republic of Korea] TERRITORY AT SEVERAL POINTS THIS MORNING. . . . IT WOULD APPEAR FROM NATURE OF ATTACK AND MANNER IN WHICH IT WAS LAUNCHED THAT IT CONSTITUTES ALL OUT OFFENSIVE AGAINST ROK.

Muccio cited artillery, infantry, armor, and amphibious attacks at several points along and below the thirty-eighth parallel; the South Koreans were apparently in full retreat. Connors immediately got on the phone to his chief, Assistant Secretary of State for Far Eastern Affairs Dean Rusk, who was dining at the home of Washington columnist Joseph Alsop.[3]

Rusk made straight for the department, where he found the assistant secretary for United Nations affairs, John Hickerson, and Ambassador-at-Large Philip Jessup. The three immediately called the secretary of state at Harewood. Acheson shared their alarm and ordered that the secretary-general of the United Nations be notified of the attack and asked to schedule an emergency meeting of the UN

Security Council the next day. When Hickerson finally got through to Trygve Lie at the United Nations, the secretary-general reacted with astonishment: "My God, Jack, this is war against the United Nations."[4]

In addition, Acheson asked his aides to inform the chiefs of staff. (Louis Johnson, secretary of defense, and General Omar Bradley, chairman of the Joint Chiefs of Staff, were in Tokyo.) In the meantime, Hickerson, Rusk, and Jessup would work out possible American responses to the North Korean attack with Secretary of the Army Frank Pace. It was now time for Acheson to call the president.

In Independence, Missouri, where Truman was spending the weekend, it was two hours earlier than in Maryland. The president had just finished dinner and was sitting in his library in his home on North Delaware Street when the telephone rang. "Mr. President," Truman heard Acheson say, "I have very serious news. The North Koreans have invaded South Korea."

Truman's first reaction was, "I must get back to the capital." But Acheson urged him to remain in Independence until he could give him a fuller report in the morning. He also told Truman that he had requested an emergency session of the UN Security Council, at which he hoped to secure condemnation of the attack. But for the moment, American actions hinged on the effectiveness of South Korea's resistance. Truman approved both Acheson's actions and advice, and the two men went uneasily to bed.[5]

By late Sunday morning it was clear that the South Koreans were in deep trouble, and Acheson called Truman to tell him so. A North Korean tank column was moving relentlessly toward Seoul, which was less than fifty miles south of the thirty-eighth parallel; it was already time to start thinking about evacuating the South Korean capital. As Truman ordered his presidential plane readied for the trip back to Washington, Acheson got into his convertible and drove top down to the State Department, where waiting reporters noticed that the usually punctilious secretary was in his shirtsleeves, carrying, not wearing, his jacket.

From his aircraft, Truman called for a meeting and dinner with all the requisite people from State and Defense that evening at Blair House, the mansion facing Lafayette Square Park where the Trumans were living while the White House was being renovated. During the day Acheson learned that the military situation had grown worse, but diplomatically the United States scored a victory. The United Nations Security Council had approved an American resolution condemning the North Korean attack as "a breach of peace." Passage of the resolution had been made possible by the absence of the Soviet delegation, which was continuing a boycott of council sessions that had been prompted in February by the UN's refusal to replace the Nationalists, who still held China's seat in the Security Council, with the People's Republic of China.[6]

Meeting with his advisers that afternoon, including George Kennan, who had driven in from Pennsylvania as soon as he learned of the invasion, Acheson found everyone in a hawkish mood. Along with Jessup, Rusk, and the chief of European affairs, H. Freeman Matthews, Kennan urged that the United States react with all the military force needed to expel the North Korean forces from the southern half of the peninsula.[7]

After the meeting, Acheson decided to keep everyone and all messages out of his office for a couple of hours while he pondered the implications of the North Korean attack and what might be the best American response. "'Thought,'" as he wrote later, "would suggest too orderly and purposeful a process. It was rather to let various possibilities, like glass fragments in a kaleidoscope, form a series of patterns of actions and then draw conclusions from them."

He thought it was close to certain that the attack had been instigated by the Soviet Union and that it would not be stopped by anything short of force. Moreover, if the South Koreans could not stop it, only American intervention could. He saw the attack as a testing ground for American resolve—and not only in north Asia, but also in Europe. To back away from the challenge that he believed Moscow had launched would be highly destructive of the power and prestige of the United States. "By prestige," he later wrote, "I mean the shadow cast by power, which is of great deterrent importance." That shadow did not mean the United States had to press on to total victory, "but rather to see that the attack failed."[8]

At the same time Acheson was determined not to get into a shooting war with the Soviet Union. "The whole idea that war is inevitable," he later told Charles Collingwood of CBS in a television interview in early September, "seems to me to be completely wrong and very vicious. I remember looking back over the history of the United States not long ago and reading the terrible things that were said in the 1850s about the irrepressible conflict. It's talk like that, talk of an irrepressible conflict, talk about war being inevitable, which tends to make it so. War isn't inevitable." It was to avoid just such an eventuality that Acheson decided not to brand the Soviets publicly, at least for the time being, as the instigators of the drama that was unfolding half a world away.[9]

By the time he went to the airport to meet the president's plane, Acheson had no specific plan in mind, but he was pretty clear on the course that Truman's advisers were likely to recommend and why it was necessary to follow that course.

At the president's insistence, dinner at Blair House preceded any serious discussion of the fighting in Korea. But Truman had already made up his mind that the North Korean aggression had to be stopped; the parallels with appeasement in the 1930s loomed large. "In my generation," Truman wrote in his memoirs, "this was not the

The War in Korea, 1950–53

Theater of Operations

first occasion when the strong had attacked the weak. I recalled some earlier instances: Manchuria, Ethiopia, Austria. . . . Communism was acting in Korea just as Hitler, Mussolini and the Japanese had acted ten, fifteen, and twenty years earlier." For Truman, if the North Korean attack went unchallenged, "it would mean a third world war, just as similar incidents had brought on the second world war."[10]

Attending the dinner meeting were Louis Johnson and General Bradley, back that afternoon from the Far East, the service secretaries and other chiefs of staff, and from State, Under Secretary James Webb, Assistant Secretaries Hickerson and Rusk, and Ambassador Jessup. (Kennan, whom Acheson had personally invited, was somehow left off the list by the White House.)

Acheson dominated the evening. After the dishes had been cleared from the big mahogany table, and the White House staff left the room, Acheson stated that force was the only answer to what they all believed was a Soviet threat—collective force if the United Nations could be made to act quickly, unilateral force if it could not. But the force used was to be concentrated against the North Korean forces. It was imperative not to threaten Russia itself, which could lead to a third world war.

Specifically, Acheson's recommendations, all of which Truman approved, were that General MacArthur be authorized to provide the South Korean army with all the matériel it required, that the air force cover an evacuation from Seoul, and that the U.S. Seventh Fleet be sent to the Taiwan Strait to ensure that neither Mao Zedong nor Chiang Kai-shek could use the Korean hostilities as a cover for operations against his opponent. Once the administration had decided to defend South Korea, it would be hard to explain why Taiwan should not be defended. By interposing the fleet between the island and the mainland, Acheson effectively ended Mao's preparations to mount an invasion to take over the island. Mao and the Chinese leadership would now focus on Korea.[11]

The following day, June 26, steadily worsening reports were coming in. The war appeared to be a growing rout. After lunch the South Korean ambassador, distraught and weeping, called on Truman to deliver President Syngman Rhee's appeal for help. Truman decided not to address Congress but rather to give out a public statement outlining his actions. At the end of the afternoon, Acheson again withdrew to his office to draw up the statement.

At nine o'clock that Monday evening, the Blair House group met again with the president. Acheson made further suggestions, which included providing direct American air support to South Korean ground forces and dispatching additional troops to the American garrison in the Philippines. He also proposed increased aid to the French in Indochina, on the chance that Korea might be only the first of several Communist attacks in Asia. He then recommended that the United States sponsor a Security Council resolution calling on any and all UN members to aid South Korea. This last suggestion, which Truman approved along with the others, was made after Charles Bohlen and George Kennan gave their opinion that the cumbersome Soviet bureaucracy was not equipped to make a quick decision on whether or not the Soviet representative to the UN, Jacob Malik, would return to the Security Council the next day to veto such a resolution. Bohlen and Kennan proved right.[12]

When General J. Lawton ("Joe") Collins, the army chief of staff, pointed out that the military situation in Korea was so bad that it was "impossible to say how much our air can do," Acheson insisted that "it was important for us to do something even if the effort were not successful."[13] But at this stage, neither Acheson nor the president was yet prepared to sanction American aircraft violating North Korean airspace above the thirty-eighth parallel.

On Tuesday, June 27, Acheson got his UN resolution and with it international sanction for American military action, sanction he and the president greatly prized but had not waited for—American airplanes were already at work in the skies above South Korea.

That morning Truman and Acheson met with a group of congressional leaders to inform them of the events and decisions of the past two days; at the same time Truman sought their views on the statement he was preparing for the press later that day. One congressman asked whether the United States was now committed to defend South Korea. The president answered yes—as a member of the United Nations and in response to the Security Council's resolutions. With their approval for his action, Truman released his statement. It was characteristically forthright: he announced that he had ordered "United States air and sea forces to give the Korean government cover and support." He also declared that the Seventh Fleet was being dispatched to the Taiwan Strait to prevent any attack on Taiwan from the mainland.[14]

To the Soviet Union, Washington had sent a note as early as June 25 (although it was not delivered until June 27), asking Moscow to disavow responsibility for this "unprovoked and irresponsible act" and to use its influence to have the North Koreans withdraw their forces and cease hostilities. On June 29 the Soviets came back with a rather mild response, speaking only of the "impermissibility of interference by foreigners in the internal affairs of Korea."[15]

By deciding to treat the North Korean aggression as a local conflict, even though it was being fought by what Acheson considered a proxy of the Soviet Union, Acheson and Truman established a Cold War precedent for fighting a limited rather than a general war; in short, even if the Soviet Union had approved the attack by the North Koreans and supplied them with arms, Washington would seek to avoid engaging the Soviet Union—or Communist China—in a military conflict.

Throughout the rest of the week, the lessons of the 1930s haunted not only the policymakers in Washington, but also military officers in the Far East as the fighting continued to go badly for the South Koreans. Meanwhile, Averell Harriman, who was administering the Marshall Plan in Paris, wanted badly to return to Washington to be in on the action. At first Truman was reluctant to recall him, fearing that the press would speculate that Harriman was slated to succeed Acheson. But the secretary dismissed this argument: he had known Averell for forty-five years, and he had full confidence in Harriman's integrity. Truman then agreed that Harriman should come back to help Acheson.

While Harriman could not be called a close friend, Acheson admired his energy and tenacity; moreover, like Acheson, Harriman had a reverence for the institution of the presidency. Harriman had been deeply disappointed that Truman picked Acheson rather than him for secretary of state, but he remained an ardent defender of Acheson and was careful never to go behind Acheson's back.[16]

Appointed a "Special Assistant to the President," Harriman became indispensable to Acheson, especially in Acheson's difficult relations with the Defense Department under Louis Johnson. From the time Harriman returned on June 28, he would attend all Acheson's nine-thirty meetings and any other meeting he wished, read all the important cables, and have access to all information.

By Thursday, June 29, General MacArthur's personal representative in South Korea was reporting that despite American air support, North Korean forces could not be pushed back north of the thirty-eighth parallel without the deployment of American ground forces. Truman worried that introducing U.S. ground forces would lead to a similar response on the part of one of the other Communist powers, but Acheson told him "it was State's view that while the Chinese might intervene, the Russians would not."

Meanwhile, back in Tokyo on June 30 after a typically reckless visit to the front by plane, MacArthur cabled that without the intervention of American troops, a military disaster loomed. He asked for authority to send from Japan at once a regimental combat team as the spearhead for a two-division buildup. Army secretary Frank Pace telephoned Truman with this message at five that morning, to find him up and dressing for his early walk.

The president did not hesitate to give immediate approval for deploying the augmented regiment, then called for a meeting of the "Blair House Group" at eight-thirty A.M. at the White House office. At that time he told Acheson and the others that he was looking favorably on Chiang Kai-shek's offer of troops to assist the South Koreans. Acheson, however, was resolutely opposed, believing it might trigger Communist Chinese intervention. Truman therefore decided simply to authorize the two divisions from Japan.

At the end of a momentous week, as Acheson recalled, "We were then fully committed in Korea."[17]

The president's decision to commit American forces to the war met with wide-ranging support both within and outside the administration; even Senator Taft said he would back the action. The public and America's allies alike applauded the unhesitating resolve of Truman and Acheson. But Acheson realized that these sentiments, especially those at home, might well change. Although he was convinced that Truman had the constitutional authority to do what he did, Acheson recommended on July 3 that the president go before a joint session of Congress to report on the Korean situation. He urged that this report to the Congress be followed by a joint resolution approving the action taken in Korea.[18]

Truman, however, was persuaded not to do so by Senator Scott Lucas of Illinois, the Democratic leader, on the ground that "things were now going along well. The President had very properly done what he had to do." Moreover, Congress was not in session; only Republican senators Taft and Wherry had taken the position that Congress should be consulted. It would be enough, Lucas believed, if the president simply reported his actions to the Congress and addressed the American people.[19]

Acheson later said he refrained from pushing for congressional resolution because he shared the view that "the thing to do was to get on and do what had to be done as quickly and effectively as you could, and if you stopped to analyze what you were doing, you immobilized yourself and [tried] to answer a lot of questions which were unanswerable. All you did was to weaken and confuse your will and not get anywhere."[20]

Nonetheless, Acheson was determined to provide historical precedents with which to refute any allegations that the president had exceeded his powers in committing U.S. forces in Korea. To this end he had the State Department prepare a relatively short but key memorandum, which was delivered to Truman and the Congress on July 3.

Listing eighty-five specific instances in which presidents of the United States had ordered American troops into action without congressional authority—ranging from the expulsion of the pirates in Spanish Florida in 1817 to Woodrow Wilson's interventions in Mexico, the Caribbean, and Central America—Acheson's memorandum was a powerful exposition of the expanding power of the American presidency. Citing constitutional authorities such as William Howard Taft and Charles Evans Hughes, as well as a number of other Supreme Court justices, Acheson argued that the "United States has, throughout its history, upon orders of the Commander in Chief of the Armed Forces and without congressional authorization, acted to prevent violent and unlawful acts in other states from depriving the United States and its nationals of the benefits of such peace and security."

Reading like a solid legal brief, the memo came to its central point: The defiance of the United Nations by North Korea represented "a threat to international peace and security, a threat to the peace and security of the United States and to the security of United States forces in the Pacific."[21]

Yet it would probably have been far wiser had Acheson persisted in pressing the case for formal congressional approval. The overwhelming consensus supporting the president that prevailed in the early summer of 1950 would surely have led to rapid endorsement of his actions, without serious doubt or distraction. As it was, that consensus would give way, and the Republicans could and did hold it against the administration that it had not secured congressional sanction for military intervention. It only too easily became "Truman's war."

At the same time, by tying American security to the southern portion of a peninsula that had historically been of little importance to the United States, Acheson knowingly extended the perimeter of American vital interests and signaled to the world that Washington would constantly be on the alert for any threat to that perimeter; the effect was to blur the contours of the perimeter, increasing the chances that America would involve itself in foreign entanglements that only peripherally affected American vital interests.

The Korean War was deliberately designed by the administration as a limited war, but the doctrine of limited containment was moving toward a policy of global containment. When Truman dispatched American troops to fight in Korea, he brought to a crescendo the expansion of American vital interests that had begun in 1941.[22]

It was in the first hours of daylight on a Sunday morning that General Douglas MacArthur, in his bedroom in the American embassy in Tokyo, received the phone call from the duty officer at his downtown headquarters: "General, we have just received a dispatch from Seoul, advising that the North Koreans have struck in great strength south across the 38th Parallel at four o'clock this morning." MacArthur, recalling Manila nearly nine years earlier, experienced "an uncanny feeling of nightmare."[23]

That weekend, MacArthur's moods were uneven. On the one hand, he seemed almost euphoric at the prospect of new action; on the other, he seemed to be trying to convince himself that what had happened was not of such great moment and could be easily dealt with. He told John Foster Dulles, who was then in Tokyo on his Japanese treaty assignment, that it was a mere "border incident." The South Korean army would hold.

On Monday morning Tokyo time—Sunday evening, July 2, in Washington—Truman's order came, giving him full command over all military operations in the Far East. He was told to "support the Republic of Korea" with warships and warplanes.

By now reports were coming in that the invaders could not easily be driven back. "Our estimate," he radioed to Truman, "is that a complete collapse is imminent." In reply, he was cautioned not to send planes or vessels north of the thirty-eighth parallel.

MacArthur had reservations about this order. The notion that the president could confine the war to the terrain he chose seemed to him foolish, and he was prepared to wage the struggle until the enemy was vanquished. None of this was made clear to Washington, however.[24]

This is not to say that MacArthur would disobey a direct order—but unless the orders he received were specific, he interpreted them as he saw fit. As events transpired, however, orders from Washington were often ambiguous or couched as guidance. The Joint Chiefs of Staff, moreover, were men who had been quite junior to him when MacArthur was a very senior commander; in the First World

War MacArthur was a much decorated hero, whereas General Marshall was seen as a consummate staff man. MacArthur's immense prestige had an intimidating effect on military commanders in Washington, and even when the ground war in Korea turned against him they were hesitant to assert their authority.

Writing in *The New York Times*, July 9, 1950, James Reston pointed out that MacArthur, at seventy, was being asked to be "not only a great soldier but a great statesman." Whereas Eisenhower was widely admired for his "international teamwork," MacArthur "is a sovereign power in his own right, with stubborn confidence in his own judgment. Diplomacy and a vast concern for the opinions and sensitivities of others are the political qualities essential to this new assignment, and these are precisely the qualities General MacArthur has been accused of lacking in the past."[25]

As North Korean troops continued to pour down the peninsula, policymakers in both Tokyo and Washington assumed this was a Soviet initiative. But if so, was it designed to divert American attention from the European theater, where Acheson was trying to put together a coalition of forces under the aegis of the North Atlantic Treaty?

Acheson continued to believe that the Russians did not intend to become overtly involved in Korea. Nor did he expect the Chinese to enter the war, for he believed that China remained wary of Moscow's encroachment on its territory, and its interests in Korea diverged from Moscow's. Only if the United States bombed Chinese territory would the Russians and the Chinese act together under the Sino-Soviet Treaty.[26]

In fact, later evidence showed that the Russians had been involved in the final stages of planning the North Korean offensive, but the initiative came from the North Korean leader, Kim Il Sung. As early as 1948 Kim Il Sung had wanted to unify the peninsula by military means, but it was not until January 1950, at the time of Mao's visit to Moscow, that Kim actively sought the full backing of Stalin for his war aims.[27] Stalin, however, was hesitant, explaining that the matter must be organized so that there would not be too great a risk.[28]

Stalin also brought up the Korean situation with Mao and found Mao more cautious than either Kim or Stalin. Nonetheless, Mao was willing to transfer some fourteen thousand Korean Chinese from China to the North Korean army.[29]

If Stalin and Mao were cautious about approving an attack on the south, Kim was reckless. By April he was determined to get the Soviet leader's blessing for a summer offensive. The withdrawal of American troops from the peninsula, the reluctance of the U.S. Congress to vote aid to Syngman Rhee's regime, and perhaps Acheson's reiteration of MacArthur's earlier statement putting South Korea outside the U.S. defense perimeter, even though he promised aid to Korea if attacked and military support through the United Nations—at the very least Kim could use these arguments to bolster his case with Stalin.

It was not an easy sell. When Kim arrived in Moscow on March 31, he recognized that his main problem was to convince Stalin that the United States would not intervene. To this end he explained that the surprise attack would be decisive and that the war would be won in three days. In addition, there would be an uprising in the south against Rhee's government. And, in any case, the United States would have no time to participate.

Stalin reluctantly consented to the plan. But he also urged Kim to consult with Mao because he had "a good understanding of Oriental matters." Then, during his final conversation with Kim, Stalin gave him a tacit but somewhat conditional green light. The Soviet leader warned, "If you should get kicked in the teeth, I shall not lift a finger. You have to ask Mao for all the help."

Two weeks later Kim was in Beijing. At this time, however, he only informed Mao of his determination to reunify the country by military means. He gave neither details on his planning nor the date of the attack.[30]

It may well be that Kim played the two leaders off on one another, exaggerating Stalin's support to Mao, and vice versa. In any case, even before Mao gave his "approval" to Kim, Stalin had ordered weapons sent to North Korea. Further confirmation of Stalin's go-ahead was the dispatch of a team of Soviet advisers, which included three major generals, to oversee the preparation for war.

It is hard to know what changed Stalin's mind from giving conditional to positive endorsement of the invasion, including a clear willingness to participate in the planning. He may have been convinced that the United States would be most reluctant to go to war with the Soviet Union over Korea, and he probably bought Kim's argument that a North Korean attack would touch off support in the south and produce an easy victory. Moreover, with a U.S.-Japanese peace treaty in the offing, it would be to Stalin's advantage to have a unified Korea as a Soviet satellite.

Mao, on the other hand, was preoccupied with his own plans to take Taiwan, and for this reason alone Kim probably kept Mao out of the picture. After the war, the Chinese remained bitter about being ill informed. In the mid-1950s Marshal Peng Dehuai, the commander of the Chinese troops that eventually fought in Korea, was still angry that the Chinese had been excluded from the final decision to launch the invasion and that Kim's "surprise attack" had been designed solely by him and Stalin, without consultation with Beijing but at a terrible price for China.[31]

Over the summer the American troops and their South Korean allies staggered down the peninsula until they held only a precarious bastion at the southeast tip of the peninsula, the so-called Pusan perimeter. Late in August nine North Korean infantry divisions tried to overpower the Pusan defenders along the seventy-by-sixty-mile beachhead, but they were stopped. The first two weeks of September were particularly bloody, but by then MacArthur, with total control of sea and air, assured Washington that he now had a "secure base."[32]

Back in the nation's capital, Acheson was having to deal with peace initiatives from both the British and the Indians. The British tried, through the Russians, to get a cease-fire in Korea in return for the admission of Communist China into the United Nations. Acheson was outraged at the idea of settling the Korean conflict by granting concessions elsewhere. Aggression, Acheson and Truman agreed, could not be rewarded. In any case, the British ambassador in Moscow was rebuffed: the Soviet Union would not use its "special influence" to induce the North Koreans to withdraw behind the thirty-eighth parallel because it was the South Koreans who had "provoked" the hostilities.[33]

Acheson was even more annoyed by the Indian initiative. He had already found Prime Minister Pandit Nehru's moralizing not to his taste when Nehru visited Washington in October 1949. In his private meeting with Nehru, he found that the Indian prime minister would not relax: "He talked to me, as Queen Victoria said of Mr. Gladstone, as though I were a public meeting."[34]

Now Nehru proposed to Acheson and Stalin that the Korean conflict be settled by having the United States support Communist China taking over Nationalist China's seat in the Security Council. Then, whether within or outside the council, the United States, China, and Russia could find a way to end the conflict.

Acheson was appalled at the logic of Nehru's proposal, which would serve to transfer the discussion from North Korean aggression to who should represent China on the Security Council. Meanwhile, American troops would be fighting a rear-guard action in Korea as the Communists tried to drive them into the sea.

As with the British proposal, Acheson believed ending North Korea's aggression should not be made contingent on conceding other questions before the United Nations. In any case, on July 20 Moscow announced that the Soviet UN representative, Jacob Malik, would return to the Security Council, thereby ending the boycott the Russians had staged to force the United States to permit the Chinese Communists to be seated.[35]

The central question for Acheson, the Joint Chiefs of Staff, and the president was whether MacArthur should be authorized to cross the thirty-eighth parallel. The UN resolution of June 27 had asked the members of the United Nations to "furnish such assistance to the Republic of Korea as may be necessary to repel the armed attack and restore peace and security to the area." This could be interpreted to mean that the United Nations command was now authorized to end the main obstacle to peace and security by ending the division between north and south and reunifying the country.[36]

On July 31 planners in the Pentagon recommended that MacArthur, as the UN supreme commander, should be directed to cross the thirty-eighth parallel, defeat the enemy's forces, and occupy the country, *provided* the following assumptions held—that the United States strengthen its position in all other areas of strategic importance; that the Soviet Union not intervene in Korea or elsewhere; and that the United States and the United Nations adopt as a war aim "a united, free, and independent Korea." Acheson later commented that he generally found that military assumptions "as often as not are quite contrary to the facts and yet control the conclusions."[37]

For Acheson, worries over the possibility of Chinese or Soviet intervention—which he displayed time and again during the next few months—nonetheless went alongside a growing belief that Korea might be unified without provoking such intervention. But his confidence that this could be done hinged solely on the conviction that once the North Koreans were defeated, "chances were believed good that neither Russian nor Chinese troops would intervene."[38]

Acheson initially had no thought "of an independent and united Korea as the U.S. or UN war aim."[39] Nonetheless, as the situation on the ground improved in late September, Acheson certainly entertained the hope that such a unification could be accomplished.

On September 11 Truman approved a recommendation of the National Security Council dealing solely with military operations; it authorized ground operations north of the parallel, provided that neither the Russians nor the Chinese entered the conflict or announced their intention of doing so. With Truman's assent to the conditions, the Joint Chiefs now went to work on instructions for General MacArthur for operations north of the thirty-eighth parallel; these were finally dispatched to him, approved by the president and the State Department, on September 27.[40]

In his memoirs, Acheson dismissed the issue of the thirty-eighth parallel in itself. "Troops could not be expected, as I put it, to march up to a surveyor's line and stop. Until the actual military situation developed further," Acheson believed that no one could say for sure "where the necessity for flexibility in tactics ended and embarkation upon a new strategic purpose began. One conclusion was clear: no arbitrary prohibition against crossing the parallel should be imposed. As a boundary it had no political validity."[41]

Doubtless it may have made no military sense to stop precisely at the parallel. But the fears Acheson voiced about provoking Russian or Chinese intervention required a commander who would proceed cautiously once his forces moved north of the parallel. Any hint of foreign intervention should have signaled him to pause and look for political guidance in Washington.

Later, Acheson wrote ruefully: "If we had been able to peer into General

MacArthur's mind, we should have been infinitely more cautious than we were a few weeks later in giving him instructions and in formulating policy in the United Nations."[42]

Already at the end of July, MacArthur had decided without any formal permission from Washington to discuss with Chiang Kai-shek America's decision to deploy the Seventh Fleet to the Taiwan Strait in order to deter an attack on or from Taiwan. Official Washington therefore was startled to read in the press on August 1 that General MacArthur had gone to Taiwan, given what his staff called his "number one" handshake—right hands clasped, his left hand gripping Chiang's elbow—kissed Mme. Chiang's hand, and gone into conference with her husband.

Back in Tokyo, the general concluded that although sending Nationalist troops to fight in Korea was "inadvisable" at this time because it might jeopardize the defense of Taiwan, it had been a great pleasure for him "to meet my old comrade-in-arms" (whom, in fact, MacArthur had never met before).

In Taipei, the generalissimo declared that "victory" over Mao's mainland forces was now "assured." MacArthur reciprocated with praise of Chiang and ordered three squadrons of jet fighters to Taiwan without informing the Pentagon. Truman and Acheson were appalled at his behavior. Explicit orders went out to MacArthur emphasizing the limits of American policy toward Taiwan.

They also dispatched Averell Harriman to the general to reinforce the explanation of U.S. policy. Harriman could assure MacArthur that Washington would do everything it could to meet his request for more troops for Korea; in addition, he could make sure the supreme commander knew that Chiang Kai-shek was not going to be allowed to start a new war with the mainland Communists.[43]

Harriman seemed a good choice to send to MacArthur at this moment. He had known the supreme commander since the early 1920s, and when MacArthur was superintendent of the U.S. Military Academy at West Point, the general was a regular guest at Harriman's palatial country place, Arden House.

Contrary to his custom of not meeting dignitaries at the airport, on August 6 MacArthur was waiting at the ramp when Harriman, accompanied by Lieutenant Generals Lauris Norstad, air force deputy chief of staff, and Matthew Ridgway, army deputy chief of staff, arrived in Tokyo.

"Hello, Averell," said the supreme commander.

"Hello, Doug," said Harriman.

Reporters were stunned by Harriman's informality.

During this visit Harriman and the generals heard the details of MacArthur's plan to encircle the North Korean army by staging an amphibious landing at Inchon near the capital of Seoul. As MacArthur explained the plan, the outcome depended on a successful landing at high tide. The approach to Inchon was so narrow that one disabled ship could damage the whole operation. The tides themselves rose to thirty-two feet at high tide, but at low tide the approach became a broad mud flat, and the marines who would storm the beach could be exposed to deadly fire. Moreover, because of the tides, the marines could not be resupplied, reinforced, or rescued until the next high tide, twelve hours later. If successful—and MacArthur brooked no possibility of failure—the operation would effectively cut off the invaders from their base in North Korea.

MacArthur told his visitors that he needed more troops for his daring plan. He urged Harriman to tell the president that if he provided them, "I will on the rising tide of fifteenth of September, land at Inchon, and between the hammer of this landing and the anvil of the Eighth Army [breaking out of the Pusan perimeter], I will crush and destroy the enemy armies of North Korea."[44]

Harriman spent a good deal of time going over Washington's policy toward Chiang Kai-shek. While the supreme commander promised to abide by Washington's orders, he did not accept Harriman's assessment that the United States would suffer serious consequences in its relations with its allies, and perhaps even be dragged into a world war, if Chiang attacked the mainland.

At the end, Harriman returned to Washington believing that MacArthur did not fully agree with Washington's policy. "For reasons that are rather difficult to explain," he reported, "I did not feel we came to a full agreement on the way things should be handled on Formosa [Taiwan] and with the Generalissimo. He accepted the President's position and will act accordingly, but without full conviction. He has the strange idea that we should back anybody who will fight Communism."[45]

As planning for Inchon moved forward, Acheson hoped that Truman and he could now put MacArthur's visit to Chiang behind them. But before the month was out, MacArthur defied the president once again.

On August 25 the U.S. ambassador to the United Nations, Warren Austin, informed the secretary-general that America would not use Taiwan as a base from which to attack China. That same evening Acheson's press secretary called him at Harewood to read an Associated Press report of a message that MacArthur had sent to the convention of the Veterans of Foreign Wars. In it MacArthur defended the strategic importance of Taiwan (Formosa), saying that the island was an unsinkable aircraft carrier and that it was "appeasement" to assert that "if we defend Formosa we alienate continental Asia."

Acheson was outraged by MacArthur's statement. The next day he met with Harriman and other aides. All agreed that MacArthur had to publicly retract his statement. Harriman then went to the White House to show the proposed dispatch to Truman.

As it happened, a meeting of the secretaries of the Departments of State, Treasury, and Defense had been scheduled with Truman. As Acheson described it, when they filed into the Oval Office, "the President, his lips white and compressed, dispensed with the usual greetings." After ascertaining that no one knew beforehand of the MacArthur message, he ordered Secretary of Defense Louis Johnson to tell MacArthur to withdraw the message.

Johnson waffled. After the meeting in the White House, he called Acheson. He did not want to embarrass the general and posed what Acheson called "an amazing question"—whether "we dare send [MacArthur] a message that the President directs him to withdraw his statement?" Acheson retorted that he saw nothing else to do in view of the president's order.

Truman himself then dictated a message to Johnson, specifically stating that the president was directing MacArthur to withdraw the message because it conflicted "with the policy of the United States and its position in the United Nations."

MacArthur retracted his message.[46]

This incident strengthened Truman's desire to fire Louis Johnson. But it was Johnson's machinations against Acheson that finally convinced the president that the defense secretary had to go. In mid-August, just after Harriman's trip to Tokyo, Johnson told a closed session of the Senate Foreign Relations Committee that the president, Harriman, and Acheson had known about MacArthur's visit to Chiang in advance. After the session, in a conversation with Harriman's chief of staff, Johnson spewed forth more venom against Acheson and said that he was depending on Harriman to help protect him from "that terrible man in the State Department."

Johnson made two fatal moves in the next two weeks. One was to attack Acheson in a telephone conversation with Senator Taft, now Truman's chief critic. The other was to solicit Harriman's help in forcing Acheson from office, promising in return that he would see to it that Harriman was made secretary of state. Harriman reported the entire conversation to Truman.[47]

Already in early August Truman had quietly asked General Marshall if he would replace Johnson. Marshall, whose health had much improved, said yes, and on September 7 Harriman visited the Marshalls in Leesburg, Virginia, to make sure Mrs. Marshall was agreeable. Harriman reported back that, wonder of wonders, she was, and on September 12 the president forced Johnson, weeping, to sign a letter of resignation.

On September 15, three weeks after the ruckus over the message to the Veterans of Foreign Wars, MacArthur sent the Marines ashore at Inchon. It was a landing that was possible only two days a month. Once asked what he wanted of his generals, Napoleon reportedly said, "Luck." MacArthur had enormous luck in his landing at Inchon. It accomplished everything he predicted it would.[48]

It was a massive victory—he defeated between 30,000 and 40,000 men at a cost of 536 dead, 2,550 wounded, and 65 missing. Now the great pincer movement began, and on September 26 the South Korean capital of Seoul was retaken. Meanwhile, the Eighth Army, having broken out of the Pusan beachhead, raced the North Koreans up the peninsula. Intercepted by MacArthur's forces west of Seoul, the North Korean army was virtually destroyed by the two American forces. Perhaps 30,000 stragglers out of an army of some 400,000 escaped without their equipment in full retreat above the thirty-eighth parallel.

MacArthur's forces could approach the parallel without opposition. "There's no stopping MacArthur now," Acheson told Averell Harriman. Not only Republican senators, but *The New York Times* as well, called for MacArthur to make an all-out push to reunify Korea.[49]

On September 27 MacArthur received a directive from the Joint Chiefs of Staff, approved by the State Department and authorized by the president, designed to guide him in his operations north of the thirty-eighth parallel. It was dangerously ambiguous. The general was told to "conduct military operations north of the thirty-eighth parallel" leading to "the destruction of the North Korean armed forces," but under several restraints and conditions, loosely stated.

He was to proceed with his offensive north of the parallel, "provided that by the time of such operations there has been no entry into North Korea by major Soviet or Chinese forces, no announcement of intended entry, nor a threat to counter our operations militarily in North Korea." In addition, he was forbidden to send aircraft or any forces over the Sino-Soviet borders and told that "no non-Korean Ground Forces will be used in the northeast provinces bordering the Soviet Union or in the area along the Manchurian border."

On the other hand, the instructions stated, "You will not discontinue Air and Naval operation north of the 38th parallel merely because the presence of Soviet or Chinese Communist troops is detected in a target area, but if the Soviet Union or Chinese Communists should announce in advance their intention to reoccupy North Korea and give warning, either explicitly or implicitly, that their forces should not be attacked you should refer the matter to Washington."[50]

What these instructions did, of course, was leave it to MacArthur to judge whether the mere presence of Soviet or Chinese troops in North Korea warranted halting his offensive. Acheson's young assistant, Lucius Battle, presenting the orders for Acheson to sign while the secretary was in New York on NATO matters, told Acheson that he was worried that the orders were too broadly drawn. Acheson turned to Battle and snapped, "For God's sake, how old are you?" Battle answered sheepishly that he was thirty-two. "Are you willing to take on the Joint Chiefs?" Acheson asked as he signed the orders and turned back to tending to NATO.[51]

Responding to these instructions on September 28, the supreme commander filed his plan of operations with the JCS. On the west coast he proposed to capture Pyongyang, just north of the thirty-eighth parallel, with the Eighth Army. He would then land the Xth Corps in the east at Wonsan and establish a line across the peninsula from Pyongyang to Wonsan. He would use only South Korean troops north of a line fifty miles above the Pyongyang-Wonsan line and sixty miles southeast of the Yalu River on the Manchurian border. This seemed a reasonable plan in accordance with the instructions from the Joint Chiefs.

MacArthur believed that the Pyongyang-Wonsan line was a strong defensive position against any North Korean renewal of attack. If the South Korean soldiers were strong enough and the Chinese or the Russians did not intervene, he was confident he could achieve the goal of unifying Korea. On September 29 Acheson and Marshall recommended, and the president approved, the plan.

Unknown to Acheson, however, on the same day General Marshall, as secretary of defense, sent MacArthur an "eyes only" telegram with Truman's approval. It said: "We want you to feel unhampered tactically and strategically to proceed north of the thirty-eighth parallel." To which MacArthur replied: "Unless and until the enemy capitulates, I regard all Korea as open for our military operations."[52]

Marshall assented. When MacArthur submitted to him the directive he planned to issue to the Eighth Army on October 2, Marshall further encouraged him: "We desire you to proceed with your operations without any further explanation or announcement and let action determine the matter. Our government desires to avoid having to make an issue of the thirty-eighth parallel until we have accomplished our mission." To MacArthur it was clear that he could proceed at will to use troops other than South Koreans on his offensive north to the Yalu.

Why Marshall sent this "eyes only" message is a mystery. Acheson speculated years later that Marshall was not giving MacArthur leave to abrogate the instructions from the JCS, but rather he was trying to soothe MacArthur's irritation at being required to submit his plan of operation to Washington for approval.[53]

In the meantime, the United Nations General Assembly endorsed an American proposal on October 7 declaring the UN objective to be the establishment of "a unified, independent and democratic government" for all Korea. This resolution was interpreted by MacArthur as a mandate to impose such a government in Korea.

Acheson bears a fair measure of blame, as he admits in his memoirs, for the wording of the UN resolution. Armed with the directive of the Joint Chiefs and Secretary Marshall's "eyes only" telegram, MacArthur saw no reason he should not wrap up the war, declare victory, and present the world with a unified Korea.[54]

* * *

On October 1, 1950, MacArthur called on the commander of the North Korean forces to surrender. The same day Chinese premier Zhou Enlai warned the West that the Chinese people "will not tolerate foreign aggression and will not stand aside should the imperialists wantonly invade the territory of their neighbor." Two days later Zhou Enlai called in the Indian ambassador to Beijing, Kavalam Panikkar, and told him that if American troops crossed the thirty-eighth parallel, China would enter the war. This step would not be taken, however, if only South Korean troops moved north.

Acheson dismissed the Chinese warning as "not an authoritative statement of policy."[55] Moreover, Panikkar was seen by U.S. officials as in Beijing's pocket and therefore not to be trusted. The British were more concerned and urged Acheson to heed Panikkar's reports. But Acheson told the British that "we should not be unduly frightened at what was probably a Chinese Communist bluff."[56]

To his colleagues in the department, Acheson described the Chinese as taking part in a "poker game." While he admitted there was a risk in pushing north, "nevertheless there had been risk from the beginning and at present," and "a greater risk would be incurred by showing hesitation and timidity." He also implied that because the UN's armed forces were advancing, "it was too late now to stop this process."[57]

By mid-October Truman was determined to see Douglas MacArthur. He had never met the general, and doing so would aid the president politically. MacArthur refused to come to the United States, or even to Hawaii, so the two compromised on Wake Island (an island, however, far closer to Tokyo than to Washington).

Acheson was opposed to the visit. He did not like the idea of the president meeting with a "foreign sovereign" such as MacArthur without a specific agenda. Talks such as these were likely to lead to misunderstanding. For this reason, and to stay on the job, Acheson did not go; nor did General Marshall. Dean Rusk, Philip Jessup, and Averell Harriman accompanied the president.

MacArthur, who arrived on Wake Island several hours before Truman on October 15, was on the field at six A.M., ready to greet the president when his plane landed. MacArthur had dressed in his deliberately casual manner, battered cap on his head and shirt open at the neck. The general did not salute the commander in chief, but instead gave him what he called his number-one handshake.[58]

The general and the president went off alone in a 1948 Chevrolet to a Quonset hut, where they talked alone for half an hour or so. No one took notes, but Truman later wrote that MacArthur informed him that victory was already won in Korea, that the Chinese Communists would not intervene, and that Japan was ready to sign a peace treaty. He also apologized for his message to the Veterans of

Foreign Wars and expressed regret that it had caused any embarrassment. Truman replied that he considered the incident closed. MacArthur, in turn, assured him that he was not about to enter politics in any way.

Then the two principals went to another small building, where the other members of the party were gathered. As it happened, Jessup's secretary, Miss Vernice Anderson, without instruction from anyone, took stenographic notes. General MacArthur, according to Truman, "stated his firm belief that all resistance would end, in both North and South Korea, by Thanksgiving." The Eighth Army would be back in Japan for Christmas.

Truman then gave MacArthur an opportunity to repeat what he had said in their private meeting about the Chinese. The supreme commander replied that there was very little chance that the Chinese would come in. At most they might be able to get fifty or sixty thousand men into Korea, but, as they had no air force, "if the Chinese tried to get down to Pyongyang, there would be the greatest slaughter."

A little after nine A.M. the conference was over. "Happy landings," MacArthur said as he bade the president good-bye before lunch. It was a thoroughly "satisfactory conference," Truman reported to the nation in a speech at the San Francisco Opera House.[59]

About the only contribution Acheson made to the Wake Island encounter was a memorandum to Philip Jessup, who went with the president. After going over a draft of the speech Truman was to make in San Francisco, Acheson wrote Jessup that all references to victory in Korea should be removed—"the whole idea of victory should be taken out. We should not be talking about victory. . . . There are no victors or vanquished in this kind of situation, only an adjudication. The only victor is peace."[60]

Even as Truman was flying halfway across the globe for his meeting with MacArthur on Wake Island, Chinese soldiers were crossing the Yalu and marching south.

American intelligence, lacking such assets as large-scale air reconnaissance, never grasped the scale or timing of these Chinese moves. Nor had it a clue about what was passing among the key Communist leaders. In fact, later revelations from Soviet archives in the 1990s showed that until the Inchon landing, China had not decided to enter the war. The more than 250,000 Chinese troops massing on the Chinese-Korean border were not as yet fully prepared; Kim Il Sung still wanted to fight the war with his own forces; and, finally, Stalin had grown even more wary of helping the North Koreans after the United States had entered the war.

Stalin was already alarmed by the fall of Seoul after Inchon. On October 1, after receiving Kim Il Sung's desperate plea for help, Stalin dictated a telegram to Mao and Zhou, in which he placed all the blame for the North Korean army's collapse on its military commanders. He urged Mao, if possible, to "immediately dispatch at least five to six divisions toward the 38th parallel." He also offered to share command and control over the North Korean and the Chinese Volunteer Forces.[61] But Mao was not so eager to get into the fight at this point. In his reply to Stalin two days later, he counseled "patience."[62]

Shocked at Mao's hesitation, Stalin decided to make sure no direct confrontation between the Soviet Union and the United States occurred. He appeared resigned that the North Koreans might well be annihilated. The only decision Stalin made was to press Mao to enter the war.[63]

In this first week in October, Mao confirmed his decision to send Chinese troops to Korea. At the same time Mao decided Zhou Enlai should meet with Stalin to make sure that Stalin would fulfill his promise to provide air cover and matériel.

Zhou left for Russia on October 6, the very day patrols of the U.S. First Cavalry Division pushed north of the thirty-eighth parallel. The Americans had disregarded Zhou's warnings. China's Rubicon had been crossed.

The Zhou-Stalin talks on October 9–10 were central in the efforts to get China and Russia to work together; at the same time they sowed seeds of further distrust between the two great allies. The meeting at Stalin's villa on the Black Sea was hard bargaining. Zhou was one of the members of the Chinese Politburo who had been skeptical of China's entering the war in Korea, and he pressed Stalin hard to fulfill his promises to provide air cover, weapons, and equipment for the Chinese "volunteers," should they enter the war. Stalin, in turn, urged Zhou to enter the war without fear of U.S. retaliation against mainland China.

Yet what Zhou apparently reported to Mao was that Stalin did not object to China's reluctance to send troops to Korea. Certainly this report to Mao reopened the debate on whether to intervene with military force. Finally, in a telegram Mao sent Zhou on October 13, Mao confirmed China's final Politburo decision to enter the war; he would fight even if he had to do so alone and without Soviet air support. Nonetheless, Stalin's eagerness to let the Chinese become entangled in the conflict would make Mao far more distrustful of Soviet promises in the future.[64]

In the end, Soviet air support was forthcoming; there was no betrayal. The involvement of the Soviet air force later grew to substantial proportions, although Stalin was eager to train Chinese pilots as quickly as possible to replace Soviet air crews. In addition, Moscow did provide military supplies and advisers for the Chinese and North Korean war effort.[65]

Warnings that the Chinese were entering North Korea either were discounted by MacArthur or their presence was seen as so slight as to be of no great concern. In the meantime he was pushing north, with no intention of halting at the Pyongyang-Wonsan line above the thirty-eighth parallel. In addition, MacArthur was growing careless. His Eighth Army, now north of Pyongyang, had overextended its supply lines. Aware that winter would be upon him soon and that the Yalu River would freeze and offer a virtual highway for invading Chinese troops, MacArthur lifted his restrictions on non–South Korean troops operating north of the the Pyongyang-Wonsan line. On October 24, four days after he liberated Pyongyang, he ordered the Xth Corps and the Eighth Army to "drive forward with all speed and full utilization of their forces."[66] One element of the Eighth Army reached the Yalu on October 26 without encountering any opposition and then turned back.

Stunned at MacArthur's changes from his own plan of operations of September 28, the Joint Chiefs of Staff sent a rather timorous message to MacArthur on October 24, stating that while he undoubtedly had sound reasons for issuing his order, they would like to know them.

MacArthur sent back a haughty reply. He had lifted the restrictions "as a matter of military necessity," since the South Korean troops were not that strong or that well led. In any case, the JCS September 27 instructions were not a final directive; the Joint Chiefs had not banned the use of non-Korean forces in the extreme north but merely stated that "it should not be done as a matter of policy."[67]

In any event, Marshall's cable of September 29 had allowed him to proceed unhampered. The "entire subject," MacArthur reported, "was covered in my conference at Wake Island." Yet, according to Acheson, Truman said on October 26 that it was his understanding that only South Korean troops would approach the northern border. Of course, no one had been with MacArthur and Truman at all times, and there was no way to dispute the general's interpretation.[68]

On October 26, a regiment of South Koreans, falling back from the Yalu, blundered into a large concentration of Chinese troops and was destroyed. The next day South Korean troops and units of the U.S. Cavalry were attacked with overwhelming force. After four days of fierce fighting, the enemy broke contact, and General Walton Walker, commanding the Eighth Army, regrouped. Walker reported to MacArthur that these Chinese units were "well-organized and well-trained."

Things were getting far more risky. Already there was a gap of fifty to seventy miles between the Eighth Army on the west side of the peninsula and the Xth (U.S. Marine) Corps on the east. MacArthur requested permission to bomb a bridge across the Yalu; at the very last minute, on November 6, Acheson persuaded the president to have the JCS stop him from doing it. Two days later, however, Truman bowed to MacArthur's protests that failure to take out the bridges would endanger his command. As ordered, the Far East Air Command knocked out two 3,000-foot bridges, but by then most of the Chinese troops were already in Korea, hiding in the mountains.

Acheson's policy of a limited war was rapidly falling into ruins. Despite the knowledge that Chinese troops were already in the country, despite MacArthur's deliberate flouting of the Joint Chiefs' instructions, Acheson admitted later that everyone "sat around like paralyzed rabbits while MacArthur carried out this nightmare."

The only way Acheson could later explain why MacArthur was allowed to proceed as he wished was to cite "the power and position of an American theater commander as that developed after President Lincoln concluded that he and General Halleck had made a supreme mess in interfering with the strategy, tactics, and choice of commands of the Federal Armies in the East, and determined to turn all of this over to General Grant."[69]

The "Sorcerer of Inchon," as Acheson called him, simply cowed the Joint Chiefs. Moreover, Acheson believed it was not his place to question military strategy, particularly with General Marshall as secretary of defense. Yet what MacArthur was doing was violating Acheson's *political* goals, and in this respect Acheson could have advised the president that the political as well as the military risks outweighed the advantages of MacArthur's march northward to wrap up the war.

In his private meetings with Generals Bradley and Marshall from November 10 to December 4, however, Acheson apparently did not offer any serious reservations over MacArthur's military strategy. When he did express a layman's concern over MacArthur's scattering of his forces, Marshall and Bradley responded that at seven thousand miles away, they could not direct a theater commander's dispositions; Acheson later wrote that "under this obvious truth lay, I felt, uneasy respect for the MacArthur mystique."[70]

Finally, on November 17 MacArthur informed the JCS that he would start a general offensive to attain a line at the Yalu. A cautionary cable from the Joint Chiefs urging him to stop on the high ground commanding the Yalu was brushed aside as "utterly impossible."

In retrospect, Acheson wrote: "If General Marshall and the Joint Chiefs had proposed withdrawal to the Pyongyang-Wonsan line," and been backed by the president, "disaster would have probably been averted." But this would have meant a fight with MacArthur and "charges by him that they had denied him victory." In turn, they might have felt that this was probably true. "So they hesitated, wavered, and the chance was lost."[71]

On November 24 MacArthur set out to "close the vise" around the enemy. He told reporters that he would "have the boys home by Christmas." Two weeks of probing and extensive aerial reconnaissance, he said, had shown no sign of large Chinese formations. He ordered the Eighth Army in the west and the Xth Corps in the east, now out of touch with one another, to close the gap on the Yalu. No one in the Pentagon objected to his strategy.

Just three days later, on Monday, November 27, MacArthur learned that his plans had gone disastrously wrong. On a three-hundred-mile front, three hundred thousand Chinese, hidden in gorges and ravines, stormed down from what the general had called a "rugged spinal mountain range" too precipitous to shelter troops. With heavy casualties, the American army fled south.

The next day Acheson read MacArthur's desperate cable to Washington: "We face an entirely new war."[72]

CHAPTER TWENTY-SIX

THE SUBSTITUTE FOR VICTORY

IN WASHINGTON, MacArthur's alarm produced a thickening gloom. The danger of a wider war, which Acheson had always feared, was now a reality. And looming over the active involvement of Chinese forces was the somber possibility that the Russians would intervene as well.

On November 28, the very day that MacArthur had reported the Chinese offensive and cabled the Joint Chiefs of Staff that the Chinese wanted nothing less than the "complete destruction" of his army, the president met with the members of the National Security Council. Acheson was determined to make sure that this time MacArthur fully understood his mission: he was *not* to occupy all of North Korea. No matter how he may have interpreted earlier directives, he was to terminate that involvement. The important thing was to find a line and hold it.

General Omar Bradley, chairman of the Joint Chiefs, was grim. He informed the council that there were three hundred aircraft, including two hundred bombers, on China's Manchurian airfields. Yet if MacArthur bombed them, the Chinese and Soviets would doubtless retaliate in kind.

Defense Secretary George Marshall concurred. The war must be kept limited, he said. The United States should neither strike Chinese territory nor use Chiang's Nationalist forces in Korea. Army chief of staff J. Lawton Collins reported that troops to replace MacArthur's losses would not be ready until the new year; no new divisions would be ready until after March 1, 1951.

The meeting ended inconclusively. No one knew what action to recommend to the supreme commander. The council members were united, however, on one point: to pull out of Korea now would be devastating—a humiliation for the United States that would almost surely wreck any hopes of building up allied support for a unified NATO military force.[1]

Two days later, on November 30, the president held a disastrous press conference. Truman was tense as he met with reporters in the Indian Treaty Room at the White House. Nonetheless, the conference began well enough, with the president declaring that the United States was prepared to fight on in Korea, despite the recent military reverses. But then he blundered. After Truman said that he would take "whatever steps are necessary to meet the military situation," Edward Folliard of *The Washington Post* asked if that included the atomic bomb. "That," Truman said without hesitation, "includes every weapon we have."

The room fell very still. Did that mean "active consideration" of use of the bomb?

"There has always been active consideration of its use," said Truman.

Merriman Smith of the United Press tried to give Truman an opportunity to clarify his words. "Did we understand you clearly that the use of the bomb is under active consideration?"

Truman reiterated his position. "Always has been. It is one of our weapons." Unthinking, he added, "The military commander in the field will have charge of the use of the weapons, as he always has."

Within seventeen minutes of the end of the conference, the United Press sent over the wires the following bulletin: "President Truman said today that the United States has under consideration use of the atomic bomb in connection with the war in Korea."

By nightfall, with the House of Commons in an uproar over the report, word came from London that Prime Minister Clement Attlee would be flying to Washington. Truman had failed to declare that he had no intention of using the bomb, so Attlee's visit was not unreasonable. Any American use of the bomb could lead to war with the Soviet Union and the likelihood of direct Soviet air attacks on Britain. Although Acheson drafted a "clarifying" statement for the White House, the damage was not undone. In the statement released by Truman's press secretary, the clarification stated that while the president, by law, could authorize use of the atomic bomb, "no such authorization had been given." Attlee's visit, scheduled for December 4, remained on the docket.[2]

Within forty-eight hours after the initial Chinese attack, MacArthur's armies had suffered one thousand casualties, and the supreme commander was reported by the press to be in a "blue funk," sorry for himself and sending to the press and the Pentagon what Marshall's deputy, Robert Lovett, called "posterity papers."

Meeting at the Pentagon on December 1, Acheson asked the Joint Chiefs if they thought "we would be lucky" to get a cease-fire and agreement to hold the line along the thirty-eighth parallel. The generals agreed. No one, however, was ready to settle for a cease-fire yet, for, as Marshall put it, "the acceptance of a cease-fire would represent a great weakness on our part." He ordered General Collins to go to Korea at once and find out just what was going on.[3]

MacArthur cabled the Pentagon on December 3 that his "small command" was now facing an entire Chinese nation in battle and called for reinforcements. It was becoming a question of whether the Eighth Army and the Xth Corps could hold on or whether a full-scale evacuation—another Dunkirk—would have to take place.

When Acheson met with the president, General Marshall, and General Bradley on December 3, Marshall reported that things were going so badly that "even a Dunkirk-type of operation" might be impossible if the Chinese brought in their airpower. When the president mentioned General MacArthur's view that he needed to launch operations across the Chinese frontier, Acheson said he was opposed to allowing MacArthur alone to make the decision on whether or not to hit the Chinese airfields. Leave that decision to General Collins in Tokyo and to General Marshall at home, and only if absolutely necessary to protect the evacuation of the troops, Acheson advised.[4]

Lieutenant General Matthew Ridgway later recalled his growing impatience on that same dreary Sunday afternoon, as discussions continued in the JCS war room over the deteriorating military situation. No one—not General Marshall or Dean Acheson or the JCS—was willing to issue "a flat order to the Far East Commander to correct the state of affairs that was going rapidly from bad to disastrous. Yet the responsibility and the authority clearly resided right in the room." At last, Ridgway's own conscience overcame his discretion. Immediate action was needed, he said. They owed it to "the men in the field and to the God to whom we must answer for these men's lives to stop talking and act." The answer was complete silence.

As Acheson later wrote, "This was the first time that someone had expressed what everyone thought—that the Emperor had no clothes on."[5] To Ridgway, MacArthur's foolhardy advance to the Yalu, in disregard of the mounting evidence of Chinese intervention, was like Custer's stand at the Little Big Horn, "when the commander's overriding belief that he alone was right closed his mind to all counsel."[6]

In Paris as minister and deputy chief of mission, Charles Bohlen realized that Acheson was without the advice of an expert on the Soviet Union. That weekend he telephoned George Kennan, on leave at the Institute for Advanced Study in

Princeton, at his Pennsylvania farm and urged him to go to Washington and see what he could do to help out.

Acheson enthusiastically accepted Kennan's offer, and Kennan spent most of Sunday being briefed by the under secretary, James Webb. What Webb told him left "substantially no hope that we could retain *any* position on the peninsula," Kennan later wrote Bohlen.

What State Department officials wanted from Kennan was his estimate of the prospects for negotiations with the Russians to obtain a cease-fire. Kennan's conclusions, which he outlined in a paper, were bleak: the Russians would regard an American request for a cease-fire as confirmation that the Americans were faced with the alternative of "capitulation" or a "complete rout." For negotiations to succeed, the United States would have to demonstrate its ability to stabilize the front "somewhere in the peninsula and engage a large number of Communist forces for a long time."

When Kennan was ready to bring the paper to the secretary of state at seven o'clock that evening, he found an exhausted Acheson; Kennan decided he could wait to hand in "so wretchedly unhelpful a paper" until the following morning.[7]

Glad to see an old colleague whose friendship he very much valued, Acheson asked Kennan to come home with him to P Street and spend the night. As they sat down over a cocktail, Acheson was warm and welcoming. Kennan felt deeply for him and wrote later of these feelings: "Here he was, a gentleman, the soul of honor, attempting to serve the interests of the country against the background of a Washington seething with anger, confusion and misunderstanding, bearing the greatest possible burden of responsibility for a dreadful situation he had not created, yet having daily to endure the most vicious and unjust of personal attacks from the very men . . . who, by their insistence on this adventurous and ill-advised march to the Yalu, had created it."

Acheson and Kennan talked late into the night about MacArthur's erratic behavior. Early the next morning, in the hope of strengthening the secretary for the day to come when he must also go to the airport to meet a querulous and troubled British prime minister, Kennan wrote Acheson a note that he would find at his place when he arrived at the small conference room for his regular nine-thirty staff meeting. "Dear Mr. Secretary," he wrote.

> In international, as in private, life what counts most is not what happens to someone but how he bears what happens to him. For this reason almost everything depends from here on out on the manner in which we Americans bear what is unquestionably a major failure and disaster to our national fortune. If we accept it with candor, with dignity, with a resolve to absorb its lessons and to make it good by redoubled and determined effort—starting all over again, if necessary, along the pattern of Pearl

> Harbor—we need neither lose our allies nor our power for bargaining, eventually, with the Russians. But if we try to conceal from our own people or from our allies the full measure of our misfortune, or permit ourselves to seek relief in any reactions of bluster or petulance or hysteria, we can easily find this crisis resolving itself into an irreparable deterioration of our world position—and of our confidence in ourselves.[8]

Acheson was both deeply moved and encouraged by the letter and read it to his advisers. We are all being infected by a spirit of defeatism emanating from Tokyo, he said. A redoubled and determined effort must be made.

At the end of the meeting Acheson called General Marshall. The Korean campaign had been cursed, he said, between exuberant optimism and the deepest depression. Both seemed to him unwarranted. What was now needed was "dogged determination" to find a place and hold and then fight the Chinese to a standstill. Marshall was in substantial agreement with Acheson's position, with two provisos: first, he had to see how successful MacArthur was in getting the Xth Corps out of the east coast; second, the American forces in Korea must not dig themselves in without an exit available.[9]

At the Pentagon, morale had plunged even further as the first reports from General Collins came in from Tokyo. MacArthur believed that without either a cease-fire or a new policy that allowed air attacks against and a naval blockade of China, that provided for reinforcements from the United States and Taiwan, and that left open the possibility of using atomic weapons in North Korea, he would have to evacuate his forces.[10]

Clement Attlee was surely, as Acheson described him, "a Job's comforter." During his five days of talks with Truman and Acheson beginning on December 4, Attlee's thought impressed Acheson "as a long withdrawing, melancholy sigh."

On the third morning of the visit, the possibility that the war in Korea would escalate to a general war with Russia seemed very much at hand. Soon after Acheson arrived at his office, Robert Lovett called to report that radar in Canada had picked up formations of unidentified objects, presumably aircraft, headed on a course that could bring them to Washington in two or three hours. Acheson was to inform the British ambassador that the prime minister should take whatever measures were necessary for his safety.

"Now wait a minute, Bob," Acheson said, "do you believe this?"

"No," replied Lovett, and hung up.

After reaching Sir Oliver Franks by phone, Acheson repeated Lovett's message. The ambassador asked whether the prime minister's meeting with the president scheduled for that morning was canceled. Acheson said no. Before ending their talk, the ambassador wondered about the exact purpose of his message. Acheson suggested "fair warning" and an opportunity for prayer.

By the time Acheson arrived at the White House for the meeting, Lovett had informed him that the unidentified objects had disappeared. He figured they were probably geese.[11]

The meetings went well enough under the circumstances. Truman assured the prime minister that there was no likelihood of any use of atomic weapons in Korea. What Attlee also wanted was for the Americans to end the conflict in Asia and concentrate on plans for European security. Moreover, he believed that the military position of the allies was so precarious in Korea that they would have to pay for a cease-fire in order to extricate their troops. This meant not only withdrawal from Korea, but also agreeing to a seat for Communist China in the United Nations. There was nothing more important, he warned, than retaining the good opinion of Asia. To this, Acheson remarked acidly that the security of the United States was more important. Acheson repeated Kennan's line that negotiating with the Russians now would mean that they would hold all the cards and concede nothing.

Attlee did not achieve what he had most hoped for: a formal commitment that the president would never use atomic weapons without prior consultation with the British prime minister. In a private meeting with Attlee, Truman had agreed to go along with this suggestion; but when Acheson saw this commitment enshrined in a draft of the final communiqué, he insisted that it be revised. Under the law the president could make no commitment of any sort to anyone that would limit his duty and power to authorize use of atomic weapons if he believed it necessary in the defense of the country.

The requisite changes were made. The prime minister had to be satisfied with Truman's promise, written into the official statement, that he desired to keep Attlee at all times informed over any developments that might bring about a change in the Korean situation. The communiqué concluded with the statement that the president declared that "it was his hope that world conditions would never call for the use of the atomic bomb."[12]

By the time Attlee left Washington on December 8, General Collins, who had arrived back from the front, had told the leaders that the long retreat had almost reached the thirty-eighth parallel and that the prospect of extracting the Xth Corps from the east coast appeared good. General Walton Walker of the Eighth Army, General MacArthur, and Collins himself now believed that a line south of Seoul could be held.

Despite General Collins's relatively optimistic report from Korea, the American and UN forces there continued to be thrown back. Then, on December 23, General Walton Walker, commanding the Eighth Army, was killed when his jeep crashed on an icy Korean road. In keeping with a standby selection that had been made long before by MacArthur, General Matthew Ridgway was to succeed Walker as commanding officer.

On Christmas Day Ridgway touched down at the Haneda Airport in Tokyo. The next morning he met with the supreme commander at his office in the Dai Ichi building. That morning MacArthur's talk with his field commander was, as Ridgway later wrote, "detailed, specific, frank, and far-ranging." He told Ridgway to hold a line as far north as possible. As for MacArthur's own goal, the most he had in mind, he said, was "inflicting a broadening defeat making possible the retention and security of South Korea." There was no talk of unifying the country now.

"Form your own opinions," he told Ridgway in closing. "Use your own judgment. I will support you. You have my complete confidence."

Ridgway's final question before leaving for the front was: "If I find the situation to my liking, would you have any objections to my attacking?"

MacArthur did not hesitate. "The Eighth Army is yours, Matt. Do what you think best."[13]

Within a month Ridgway had stabilized the front. The Chinese advance halted. Ridgway did indeed begin laying plans for a new offensive that would soon have the UN forces regain the thirty-eighth parallel. The limited war that Acheson and Truman preferred to fight would remain the military strategy for the rest of the Korean conflict.

With Ridgway's success, Generals Collins and Vandenberg made another fact-finding trip to the front. They saw that GI morale was now high and that Ridgway considered his position impregnable. Collins had arrived in Tokyo believing that evacuation was probably unavoidable; when he reached the front he saw that the danger had been grossly exaggerated by the supreme commander. This discovery marked the end of MacArthur's dominance over the Joint Chiefs of Staff; thereafter he ceased to be a strong force in strategic planning.[14]

As the military situation deteriorated in Korea after the Chinese intervention, attacks against the Truman administration's handling of the war—and against Acheson in particular—reached a crescendo. On December 15, 1950, in congressional party caucuses, Republicans in the House voted unanimously, and in the Senate twenty to five, that Acheson had lost the confidence of the country and should be removed from office.

Six months earlier, shortly after the outbreak of the war when South Korean and American troops were being forced down the peninsula to the Pusan perimeter, leading Republicans had seized upon the crisis to attack Truman and his secretary of state. On August 7 Senator Kenneth Wherry demanded Acheson's dismissal; a week later he declared that "the blood of our boys in Korea is on [Acheson's] shoulders and no one else." At the same time four of the five Republican members of the House Foreign Relations Committee, along with Senator Taft, accused Truman and Acheson of having invited the attack on Korea.[15]

That August Acheson could no longer contain himself from striking out at Wherry. At an executive hearing of the Senate Committee on Appropriations, Senator Wherry began badgering Acheson from directly across a narrow table. Acheson felt his blood rising and his ears getting hot, and before he could control himself he found himself standing up and shouting, "Don't you dare shake your dirty little finger in my face!" Wherry bellowed back that he could and he would, and he did.

What Acheson described as a "rather inexpertly aimed and executed swing" at the senator's jaw was intercepted by Adrian Fisher, the legal adviser to the State Department and a former guard on the Princeton football team. He enveloped Acheson in a bearlike embrace, murmuring, "Take it easy, boss; take it easy."

The next morning Acheson called on the chairman of the committee, Senator Kenneth McKellar of Tennessee, to apologize.

"Not at all, my boy, not at all," he said, beating his cane on the floor. "Do you know what I did after you left? I called Harry Truman and told him we could pay off the national debt by putting you two on the vaudeville circuit."

Curiously enough, Acheson wrote, his relations with Wherry became much better.[16]

But the attacks on him continued unabated. On social occasions he and Mrs. Acheson would encounter newsmen and columnists who were vilifying him, and his critics would sidle away either because they were embarrassed or because they simply did not want to be seen with him.[17]

Even the character of General Marshall had come under attack when Truman appointed him secretary of defense in place of Louis Johnson; Senator William Jenner, Republican of Indiana, accused Marshall of playing "the role of a front man for traitors." As a result, the government had been turned into "a military dictatorship, run by Communist-appeasing, Communist-protecting betrayer of America, Secretary of State Dean Acheson."[18]

Senator McCarthy naturally joined in the chorus. In August he asserted that "the Korea deathtrap" could be laid at "the doors of the Kremlin and those who sabotaged rearming, including Acheson and the president."[19]

During the congressional campaign that fall, McCarthy continued making gibes at Acheson and the "commiecrat Party." With Republican gains in the November elections, and following the Chinese invasion that undid MacArthur's triumph at Inchon, the Republican calls for Acheson's ouster attained new heights and were joined by those from other members of the Washington establishment. "Why, Mr. President," Senator McCarthy intoned, "do you follow the orders of your Secretary of State, who feels that only the sons of American mothers should fight and die?"[20]

Even those who deplored McCarthy's vicious attacks began to question Acheson's usefulness and to call for his resignation. On December 14, 1950, Walter Lippmann, whose column in the *New York Herald-Tribune* was enormously influential, did so. Critical of Acheson for allowing MacArthur to push beyond the thirty-eighth parallel, for apparently seeing the Korean War as part of a broader maneuver by the Russians to prevent the rearmament of Germany and the completion of the NATO military command, Lippmann wrote Daisy Harriman, a Washington hostess who was at one time FDR's ambassador to Norway, that whether Congress lacked confidence in him for good public reasons or bad was "quite irrelevant." It was "impossible to conduct foreign affairs, and especially to conduct wars, without popular confidence in the men who conduct them." Such a situation would be "absolutely unthinkable" in any parliamentary system.[21]

On the other hand, many friends rallied around Acheson, and letters of support poured into his office. On January 21, 1951, Robert Lovett wrote him, "I don't know from what source you draw your courage, but whatever it is, hang on to it—and go on sharing it with the rest of your friends." To reporters, Lovett said of Acheson, "He's a giant."[22]

At his news conference of December 19, 1950, Truman forcefully defended his beleaguered secretary of state. "How our position in the world would be improved by the retirement of Dean Acheson from public life is beyond me. . . . If Communism were to prevail in the world today—as it shall not prevail—Dean Acheson would be one of the first, if not the first, to be shot by the enemies of liberty and Christianity."[23]

The attacks, which were to last throughout the rest of Acheson's tenure as secretary of state, did nonetheless exact an awful toll. In later years his wife would assert that they had truly shortened his life.[24]

"Whom the Gods destroy they first make mad," Acheson later wrote of MacArthur, quoting Euripides.[25]

By mid-March 1951 Ridgway's forces had halted their retreat and regained the thirty-eighth parallel. Washington now hoped to seize the opportunity to obtain a cease-fire without pushing any farther north. This was not what MacArthur wanted, and he set out to sabotage this policy. On March 15 he contacted Hugh Baillie of the United Press and criticized the halting of the Eighth Army's advance at or just above the thirty-eighth parallel, saying that this fell short of "accomplishment of our mission in the unification of Korea." MacArthur, of course, had been told repeatedly that this was not his mission.

As the administration was contacting other governments that had troops in

Korea with a view to arranging a cease-fire, MacArthur exceeded his authority once again. On March 24 (Tokyo time) he issued what amounted to a virtual ultimatum to an enemy that was far from beaten. He taunted China for lacking "the industrial capacity" for "the conduct of modern war." Should the United Nations decide to depart from its tolerant policy of simply containing China, then China itself faced the risk of imminent collapse. He stood ready, he said, to meet with the military commander in chief of the enemy forces, meaning China's, to realize "the political objectives of the United Nations." In short, he delivered a threat that neither the United States nor any other member of the United Nations was prepared to carry out.[26]

When Deputy Secretary of Defense Robert Lovett received a copy of MacArthur's ultimatum, he appeared at Acheson's house in a rage at eleven o'clock that night [March 23 in Washington] and told the secretary of state that MacArthur had to be dismissed at once.

Acheson shared Lovett's sense of outrage, and the next morning they met with the president, who, in Acheson's words, "combined disbelief with controlled fury." Truman, however, was not quite ready to face the political consequences of firing the supreme commander. Instead he sent MacArthur a sharp reminder of his directive of December 6, 1950, ordering him to clear all public statements with Washington.

MacArthur's final act of insubordination was a letter to Joseph W. Martin, the Republican leader of the House of Representatives, written and sent on March 20. Responding to questions posed by Martin, MacArthur said he agreed with Martin that the United Nations command should use Nationalist Chinese forces in Korea. He went on to attack Truman for fighting "Europe's wars" in Asia, asserted that "if we lose this war to Communism in Asia the fall of Europe is inevitable," and concluded with his refrain, "There is no substitute for victory."[27]

On Thursday, April 5, 1951, Martin read the letter on the floor of the House.

Acheson learned of it that same day but waited to react. In order to take his mind off his troubles, Alice had arranged a dinner party and a trip to the theater that evening. Knowing Dean's admiration for the actress Myrna Loy, especially for her performance in the *Thin Man* movies with William Powell, she had asked Myrna and her husband, Howland Sergeant, who was in the State Department, to accompany them to the theater. Acheson's daughter Mary and her husband, William Bundy, completed the group. It proved a joyous evening until the Achesons and the Bundys arrived back at P Street and found Robert Lovett and an aide from the Pentagon sitting in the front study. Tersely Lovett said to Acheson that MacArthur had gone too far and must be relieved. Acheson heartily agreed.[28]

* * *

The next morning Acheson, General Marshall, General Bradley, and Averell Harriman met with the president. Neither of the generals was willing to move forthrightly to relieve MacArthur of his command. Both Marshall and Bradley wanted to consult further with the Joint Chiefs of Staff, who were out of town for the weekend.

Later that day Marshall suggested that MacArthur should be called home for consultation before any decision was made as to the supreme commander's future. Harriman and Acheson expressed strong opposition. To Acheson, that approach seemed "a road to disaster." For MacArthur to return to the capital, with his full panoply of command and his well-known ability for histrionics, would make any decision, especially one to fire him, far more difficult.[29]

As Acheson later described his position and reasoning: "Before MacArthur returned to the United States, he had to be stripped of his power and authority so that he returned as a private citizen with somebody else in command, somebody else already directing affairs, and though we'd have a difficult enough time with that battle, it would still be an argument about the past and not an argument about the future."[30] Truman agreed.

By Monday morning, April 9, Marshall was able to report that the Joint Chiefs of Staff unanimously recommended that MacArthur be relieved of his duties as supreme commander and that Lieutenant General Matthew Ridgway should be designated to replace him. General James Van Fleet would take over from Ridgway as commander of the Eighth Army.

Delivery of the orders of April 10 relieving MacArthur of his command was badly handled. Believing it should be hand-delivered, the White House decided to use Secretary of the Army Frank Pace, then in Tokyo. However, this led to delay, so that advance notice of what was about to happen reached MacArthur before the message was officially delivered. The news was on the radio, and soon after, the message itself was handed to the supreme commander in a brown army envelope, stamped in red letters "Action for MacArthur" on the cover. The general opened it and read it quickly. Drafted by Marshall, the orders were characteristically terse, simply notifying the general that he was being relieved as supreme commander, UN commander, and commander in chief in the Far East. MacArthur turned to his wife. "Jeannie," he said quietly, "we're going home at last."[31]

To Acheson, the issue was simple. It went to the "very root of democratic government"—the control over the military by the president and the civilian side of government. "It seemed to me," he said later, "that we were in the presence of the gravest constitutional crisis that perhaps the United States had ever faced."[32]

Acheson found himself in an awkward and seemingly duplicitous situation on the very day that MacArthur received the news of his dismissal. Unable to release a report of what Truman had done before the general was informed, Acheson kept a strange appointment with Senators Pat McCarran, Democrat of Nevada, and Styles Bridges, Republican of New Hampshire, two of his harshest critics on the Hill. Their purpose in meeting with him, they said, was to ask him to make sure the president did not get into an ill-considered row with MacArthur. They urged Acheson to tell Truman to reconsider his attitude and come to an accommodation with the general.

Acheson replied he would report their views to the White House. Of course when the news broke the next day, the two senators accused Acheson of misleading them by his silence. From their point of view, this was a not unreasonable indictment. Acheson, on the other hand, really had no choice in the matter but to behave as he did.

That evening by telephone Acheson informed other leading senators, and then the ambassadors who had troops in Korea under MacArthur's command, of the general's dismissal. He even got Foster Dulles out of bed to come over to his house and see him. Dulles was not only unhappy with the news, but even more distressed to hear that Truman wanted him to go to Tokyo at once to reassure Prime Minister Shigeru Yoshida that there would be no change in American policy toward Japan.

By four o'clock in the morning Acheson was finished; less than five hours later his next working day, April 11, would begin. It was also his fifty-eighth birthday. He attended a lunch in his honor given by the secretary of the Senate in his dining room in the Capitol. As Acheson put it, "Most of my staunch friends—and other senators—were there."

A couple of days later at the next cabinet meeting, the president asked Acheson to give his impression of the events of the last few days. Acheson responded with a tale that he recounts in his memoirs: what had happened was summed up, he said, "by the story of the family with the beautiful young daughter who lived on the edge of a large army camp. The wife worried continually, and harassed her husband, over the dangers to which this exposed their daughter. One afternoon the husband found his wife red-eyed and weeping on the doorstep. The worst had happened, she informed him; their daughter was pregnant! Wiping his brow, he said, 'Thank God that's over!'"[33]

Upon returning to the United States on April 17, McArthur was greeted by an outpouring of adulation and affection rarely seen in the nation's history, and certainly not for a military officer since the Civil War. Though the general may have been genuinely surprised at his emotional reception, he was fully prepared to take advantage of it. Truman was pilloried, and there were calls for his impeachment across the country. The GOP Policy Committee unanimously approved a statement accusing "the Truman-Acheson-Marshall triumvirate" of planning a "super-Munich in Asia."[34]

On April 19 MacArthur arrived at Washington's National Airport a little after midnight to deliver his speech to the joint session of Congress, scheduled for noon that day. At 12:31 that afternoon, the doorkeeper at the House of Representatives announced: "Mr. Speaker, General of the Army Douglas MacArthur." The audience rose, and many shouted and clapped and thumped desks. MacArthur strode impassively to the rostrum. With his vibrant voice, he never appeared more Olympian—or more melodramatic.[35]

After a sweeping review of Asian history, MacArthur declared that victory had been in his grasp when the hordes of Chinese intervened. Under the circumstances, a new war called for new military strategy, which he said included an economic blockade of China's mainland, a naval blockade of Chinese coastal areas and Manchuria, and no restrictions on using Chiang's Nationalist troops for raids on the mainland. All these steps went precisely against the political/military strategy that the administration was pursuing. He denied that he was "a warmonger." But, once war is forced upon the American people, "there can be no substitute for victory."

The general concluded by evoking his youth, "the oath on the Plain at West Point and the hopes and dreams" that "have long since vanished. But I remember the refrain of one of the most popular barrack ballads of that day which proclaimed most proudly that—'Old soldiers never die, they just fade away.' And like the old soldier of that ballad, I now close my military career and just fade away—an old soldier who tried to do his duty as God gave him the light to see that duty." His voice fell to a hush: "Good-bye."[36]

Most legislators were overcome, sobbing, struggling to touch his sleeves as he walked from the rostrum. One congressman shouted, "We heard God speak here today, God in the flesh, the voice of God!"

At a cabinet meeting after the speech, Dean Acheson had a different reaction. He thought it was "bathetic." Truman said it was "bullshit."[37]

At the hearings in June on the "Relief of General of the Army Douglas MacArthur" before the Senate Committees on Armed Services and Foreign Relations, MacArthur said that he could recall no fundamental disagreements between him and the Joint Chiefs of Staff. But even the fiercest critics of the administration were taken aback when the Joint Chiefs testified that they did not agree with MacArthur's strategy. Instead the JCS informed the senators that they did not believe that the war could be won by an assault on China.

"The strategic alternative, enlargement of the war in Korea to include Red

China, would probably delight the Kremlin more than anything else we could do," General Bradley asserted. It was the Soviet Union that was the real enemy, he added, one that would be only too happy to see American forces tied down in Asia while the Russians themselves "would not be obliged to put a single man into conflict." Bradley went on to declare that "in the opinion of the Joint Chiefs of Staff, this strategy would involve us in the wrong war, at the wrong place, at the wrong time, and with the wrong enemy."[38]

On the crucial matter of MacArthur's sending troops north to the Manchurian frontier, General Collins testified that the Joint Chiefs had instructed General MacArthur to use only South Korean troops on the Manchurian frontier, and the supreme commander had not complied. "He sent American troops directly to the frontier without advising us ahead of time on it, and when we . . . challenged his doing this, he said that he did it because of military necessity."[39]

Acheson was never more masterful than in his defense of the administration's policy. He began testifying on Friday morning, June 1, 1951, and continued all day every day except Sunday until Saturday afternoon, June 9. His was by far the most extensive questioning that any witness had to undergo. He, like Bradley, warned of the danger of getting bogged down in a land war with China—but he also pointed out that in such a war the Soviet Union might be compelled to intervene because of its commitments under its security treaty with Beijing.

He made it clear that the administration's aim was to get a cease-fire "at or near the thirty-eighth parallel" and to agree to remove all foreign troops—both Chinese and those of the United Nations—from Korea. It was still America's purpose to secure "a unified, free, and democratic Korea." This was not "a war aim," but rather something to be achieved diplomatically over the long term.[40]

By the time Acheson finished testifying, MacArthur's strategy had been fatally undermined.

Acheson's reflections, years later in his memoirs, seem to be justified; "Had General MacArthur, who faced no opposition after Inchon and the defeat of the North Koreans, occupied one of the strong positions in mid-Korea, fortified it, and kept his forces collected, he could have shattered a Chinese assault just as Ridgway did."

Moreover, had MacArthur followed this strategy, America's allies would have been far more willing to support the administration's initiatives elsewhere, and public opinion at home would have thoroughly endorsed Truman's policy.[41]

With Ridgway giving the administration confidence that the allies had gained back their strength in Korea, Acheson was able to turn his attention to completing the work of the Japanese peace treaty and the U.S.-Japanese mutual security pact. On September 4, 1951, the San Francisco Opera House became, as it had been for the inauguration of the United Nations in 1945, the setting for a powerful American foreign policy initiative.

At the international conference convened there to sign the peace treaty, a big surprise was the Soviet Union's acceptance of an invitation to attend. This could prove a danger if the Soviet delegate decided to try to present its own proposals for peace or otherwise disrupt the proceedings. To forestall any such tactics, Dean Acheson, presiding as chairman of the U.S. delegation, decided it was going to be "run by bosses," like "a political convention," with the delegates assembled not to debate the merits of the treaty, but to ratify it.

Determined to push on with a Japanese peace treaty, Acheson had spurred John Foster Dulles—his bipartisan negotiator—to complete the task in 1951. The Korean War made it even more imperative to strengthen Japan against both Chinese and Soviet designs through a bilateral U.S.-Japanese defense treaty that would be separate from the peace treaty. Throughout the fall and winter of 1950–51, amid the hopes following the Inchon landing and the despair over the Chinese intervention, Dulles pressed ahead with a determination verging on ruthlessness in dealing with any domestic or foreign opposition.

From the start, Acheson assumed that the Soviet Union was unlikely to fully endorse any American policy toward their common former enemy. But Acheson also had no intention of delaying his peace treaty and expected to go forward without the Soviets if necessary.

Acheson had already overcome the Pentagon's initial opposition to the treaty by September 1950—but up until the last moment and even after the treaty was signed, the Pentagon wanted certain rights in Japan, such as legal jurisdiction over American troops there. The Japanese did not want to be treated any differently from America's allies in Europe, and in the end that was how they were treated. But the Pentagon, according to Dean Rusk, then assistant secretary for Far Eastern affairs, "would have preferred to maintain the occupation indefinitely. . . . They just didn't want to give up their right to take what they wanted, to put what troops they wanted there, to use Japan for whatever purpose they wanted to."

It was the president who finally overruled the military, telling Acheson, "You go right straight ahead, and anyone who wants to argue with you is arguing with me." Acheson and Rusk went ahead to obtain Japanese consent and support for the American bases for the future.[42]

A second big problem was to make sure that those countries that had legitimate claims for reparations against Tokyo because of Japanese actions against them during the war did not tie up the treaty process. To settle these issues would have been impossible in a general gathering, so Acheson devised a series of bilateral meetings to precede the final conference. Promoted to ambassador in early 1951, Dulles had flown off to England, France, Australia, New Zealand, and the

Philippines in order to persuade those countries to allow the Japanese to conclude separate agreements later over reparations.

Another sticking point was the question of who would represent China at the signing of the treaty. The British were opposed to having Taiwan sign for China, whereas the United States would not allow Beijing to sign, as it had not recognized the Communist government. The solution was to have neither the Nationalists from Taiwan nor the Communists from mainland China at the conclave in San Francisco. The British and the Americans decided that it would be up to Tokyo to sign a separate agreement with whatever China it wished after it had regained its sovereignty. Nonetheless, Japan's prime minister, Shigeru Yoshida, produced a letter promising to recognize Chiang Kai-shek's regime as the legitimate government of China; this would ease ratification of the treaty in the U.S. Senate.[43]

The last obstacle to the peace treaty was the desire of other nations in the Pacific for the United States to protect them against any recurrence of Japanese aggression. To this end, Washington signed one security treaty with the Philippines and another with Australia and New Zealand.

These commitments, along with the security treaty with Japan, created a whole new security system in the Pacific, which, according to Acheson, he had not foreseen. Yet neither Australia and New Zealand nor the Philippines would have agreed to a peace treaty with Japan unless they had defense treaties with the United States.[44] With NATO in place in Europe, and the three interlocking security treaties in the western Pacific, the United States was protected from any significant threat to American security that might arise on either ocean front.

To deal with Soviet deputy foreign minister Andrei Gromyko, who led the Soviet delegation, Acheson decided the conference would follow the methods Speaker Sam Rayburn of Texas used to get a bill through the House. Under the procedures of the House Rules Committee controlled by the leadership, a "closed rule" usually permitted no amendments from the floor and set a limited amount of time for debate, after which, "without amendment or further dilatory procedure," the bill was put to a vote. At San Francisco, Acheson as chairman arranged beforehand for a delegate to propose that similar "closed" rules of procedure be adopted. Once this was done, no amendments to the draft treaty would be permitted, and no extended debate; each delegation would be allowed to make a statement not to exceed one hour. Motions to close a debate were to have precedence over all others and could not be debated. These were, as Acheson described them, "severe rules."[45]

Upon arriving in San Francisco, Acheson met with Yoshida of Japan and urged on him the need for complete secrecy regarding the U.S.-Japanese security treaty; otherwise, he feared that the Russians might deflect conference discussions from the peace treaty to the security treaty. He had already arranged with the delegates from New Zealand and Cuba for the former to make a motion to adopt the rules of procedure and the latter to second it.

On September 4, the opening day of the conference, Acheson fell ill with a severe case of ptomaine poisoning. At a meeting with Dulles and some Latin American delegates just before the conclave was to open that evening, he fainted and had to be carried out of the room. His secretary then telephoned the president's physician, Major General Wallace Graham, who gave him some shots and put him to bed.[46]

Acheson nonetheless appeared on the platform that evening to introduce Truman, who welcomed the delegates, after which came a reception for the president, which Acheson hosted in the Pied Piper Room of the Palace Hotel. He seemed to be surviving the party without incident, but just when it seemed his ordeal was coming to an end, Truman invited him and a number of others up to his private suite. There the president began playing requests on a piano amid smiles and laughter; Acheson suffered and said nothing. His aide, Luke Battle, urged his boss to retire to his room for the night, but Acheson refused to do so. Finally Battle had a few words with the president, who immediately abandoned the piano and told the secretary to go to bed, as if he were a small boy who was staying up too late.[47]

The working sessions of the conference opened with Acheson presiding. After the motion had been made and seconded to adopt the rules of procedure, the floor was opened for discussion. Gromyko rose to protest the absence of delegates from mainland China and to move that they be invited; Acheson ruled this motion out of order and then allowed five minutes for a speech on an appeal from the ruling and the same amount of time for one against changing it.

When the Polish delegate, Stefan Wierblowski, opposing the ruling, refused to stop at the end of his allotted five minutes, Acheson kept telling him he was out of order and started banging his gavel. But the Pole would not sit down and insisted on arguing with the chair. As there was no sergeant at arms, and even though he was not feeling well, Acheson decided he was rugged enough to physically throw the Pole off the podium.

Three thousand miles away on Long Island, Robert Lovett was driving through the village of Locust Valley when he was flagged down by a local garageman. "Come here, Mr. Lovett," he said, "and look at the television. Your friend Acheson is going to take a swing at a Pole!" Lovett joined the circle to watch the scene in San Francisco, as Acheson moved threateningly and Wierblowski backed away from the rostrum and scurried back to his seat, accompanied by cheers and clapping. The Locust Valley audience broke into a cheer.[48]

With Acheson's parliamentary procedure sustained, the rules were adopted, confining all deliberations to the existing draft treaty. At this point the fight seemed to go out of the Soviet-bloc delegates. "It took the Russians about three days to discover what had happened to them," Dean Rusk later recalled[49]

The rest of the conference came off well. There were occasional tirades from Gromyko, attacking the treaty and proposing amendments, which, of course, were now prohibited by the rules. On September 8, however, the Communist-bloc delegates did not appear; they seemed to have just faded away. As a consequence, the peace treaty was approved without any dissenting votes.

When the Japanese delegation ended the signing, Acheson, still weak from his illness, thanked his colleagues at the conference and then spoke of the "act of reconciliation" embodied in a document in which "there was nothing mean, there was nothing sordid . . . nothing hidden." He closed the conference, as he put it, "with words which in many languages, in many forms, in many religions have brought comfort and strength: 'May the peace of God which passeth all understanding be amongst us and remain with us always.'"

When he uttered his last words to a hushed audience, Republican senator Alexander Wiley of Wisconsin, a member of the U.S. delegation, jumped to his feet and shouted, "Everybody up!" and led a prolonged and tumultuous ovation.[50]

In Korea, meanwhile, a fairly stable front had been established generally north of the thirty-eighth parallel except in the west, where it dipped south of the Inchon peninsula, and Acheson was eagerly seeking an armistice. In the spring of 1951 he and his diplomatic colleagues, he later wrote, "cast about like a pack of hounds searching for a scent." But nothing came of these soundings.

In mid-May Acheson decided to allow George Kennan to try to make a breakthrough. Kennan was still on his leave of absence at Princeton, so that he could approach the Soviet envoy to the United Nations, Jacob Malik, and talk seriously with him without making any firm commitments. Kennan had been in touch with Nitze and Acheson about a proposal for a cease-fire. In Kennan's view, this would require dealing with the Russians rather than just "their puppets," the Chinese or North Koreans—to "build an arrangement that does not include the [Soviets] would be building on sand."[51]

Kennan decided to send a note in longhand to Malik at his apartment in New York, suggesting that they talk over U.S.-Soviet relations. Malik promptly invited Kennan to his summer house on Long Island. Kennan drove out there, and on June 1 he and Malik met alone and spoke to each other in Russian.

After an embarrassing start when Malik upset a tremendous tray of fruit and wine on himself, the two diplomats circuitously approached the question of an armistice in Korea. Malik said he could give no definite answer to this question, which meant he had to consult with Moscow. But he agreed to meet with Kennan again on June 5, four days later, and this time Malik was able to tell him that the Soviet government wanted a peaceful solution in Korea as soon as possible. As the Soviet Union was not technically a belligerent, however, no representative of Moscow could take part in the talks.

A couple of weeks later, on June 23, Malik delivered a speech on a UN radio program, declaring that Moscow believed discussions should be started between the warring parties "for a cease-fire and an armistice providing for the mutual withdrawal of forces from the 38th parallel."[52]

The negotiations opened early in July at Kaesong and later moved to Panmunjon, but they did not proceed easily or quickly. There were arguments over whether the cease-fire line should be at the thirty-eighth parallel or along the military front. From the American point of view, withdrawing to the parallel would make defending any violation of the cease-fire more difficult. The cease-fire line, Acheson proposed, should be the existing battle line, wherever it was, when the armistice was finally signed. In hard negotiations, the other side agreed to this only on November 27, but a month later there was still no armistice. The fighting went on.

The key sticking point now centered on the repatriation of prisoners of war, which Acheson had never expected would turn out to be "a great issue." Generally, after an armistice, prisoners are exchanged wholesale, and they are happy to return to their families. This had not been the case after World War II, however, when Acheson and others recalled heartrending episodes in 1945 when Russians who fell into American hands after the German surrender committed suicide in preference to being handed over to Soviet authorities. Similarly, many of the North Korean and Chinese prisoners did not want to return to their homeland.

If the United States did not agree to North Korea's demand for forcible repatriation of North Korean prisoners, the war might well continue and lives would be lost. Nonetheless, Truman and Robert Lovett, who had replaced Marshall as defense secretary in September 1951, agreed that there must be no compromise leading to what Truman publicly called "an armistice by turning over human beings for slaughter or slavery." At the same time, he and Acheson were unwilling to escalate the war in hopes of ending it.[53]

Truman and Acheson viewed the Chinese refusal to negotiate a cease-fire in Korea as demonstrating a hostile intent that the administration could now do little to change. By January 1952 Acheson told Churchill at a meeting in Washington that American policy toward China had to be "pragmatic." The United States, he said, "no longer felt, as it had in January 1950, that there was any real possibility of inducing Chinese Titoism in the foreseeable future."[54]

CHAPTER TWENTY-SEVEN

ENTANGLING ALLIANCES

THE BIPARTISAN SUPPORT given to the Japanese peace treaty was not so easily replicated when it came to the issues of German rearmament and the deployment of large numbers of American troops to Europe. The Korean War had, if anything, stiffened Acheson's belief that creating "situations of strength" along the periphery of the Soviet empire was the only way to force a change in Soviet behavior. As NSC 68 had argued, that would require a much higher level of defense spending for the United States and its allies in Europe.

In seeking support for his policy, Acheson knew that the Korean War would probably provide him with enough arguments to persuade the allies of the need for more guns. But to avoid having the allies sacrifice too much butter, the United States would have to help finance the buildup. After the North Korean attack, Truman was now willing to lift his cap on defense spending to fund the NSC program. Within a month after the Korean War broke out, Acheson instructed Charles Spofford, the U.S. delegate to NATO, to tell the Europeans that the United States was prepared to offer $4 billion to $6 billion to NATO countries willing to press ahead with their own rearmament program. In return for their willingness to reorient their budgets to military preparedness, the United States would also be ready to extend Marshall Plan aid beyond 1952.

As for Germany, as late as June 5, 1950, Acheson had repeated before the House Committee on Foreign Affairs that the demilitarization of Germany would continue: "There is no discussion of doing anything else. That is our policy."[1] But on August 9 Spofford came back from Europe to tell Acheson that without a substantial deployment of American troops on the European continent, the Western allies were unlikely to provide a large buildup of conventional forces for the defense of Europe, a policy that Acheson preferred to reliance on atomic weapons for this purpose.

When the State Department therefore proposed to dispatch four to six divisions to reinforce American ground forces in Europe, the Pentagon seized on this initiative to secure their long-held objective of German rearmament; the American military argued that a unified defense of the continent was not really sensible unless Germany, geographically and militarily the linchpin of Europe, was a part of it.

Acheson's conversion to German rearmament and participation in Europe's defense was swift. The question was how to achieve this. Acheson knew that getting allied support for German rearmament would take time, especially with the French. While Acheson told his staff at the end of August 1950 that he was "serious about protecting against the regeneration of 'old German power,'" he now agreed with General Bradley that German rearmament had to be part of any plan to station American forces in Europe.

So far, Acheson and his colleagues in the Pentagon had made no commitments to send ground and air forces to Europe. So far, nothing had been done to give any reality to the concept of an "integrated defense." The Pentagon was now insisting that no more American troops be sent to Europe until the German troops were designated to serve in a unified command, presumably under an American commander.

Acheson, however, believed that the best way to get France to go along with German rearmament was to first establish the unified command and then demonstrate the need for German troops to serve as a part of the NATO force. The Defense Department, still under the direction of Louis Johnson, held firm to their approach, and Acheson finally gave in.

On September 12, 1950, Acheson met with his French and British counterparts, Schuman and Bevin, at the Waldorf-Astoria in New York. It was at this meeting that he proposed in a single package an integrated NATO force under a supreme commander, a major American troop contribution, and the rearming of Germany within this force. This proposal became known as the "bomb in the Waldorf."

Bevin held a deep distrust of the Germans, but an even deeper one of the Soviet Union. The French were adamantly opposed to the creation of a German army. Although Acheson's proposal would directly incorporate German units in the NATO forces, the French were fearful that even NATO would not be able to contain a new Wehrmacht.[2]

Despite his earlier misgivings, day after day in September 1950 Acheson argued his case, first with the French and British and then before the NATO Council, which convened on September 15. At the outset of the conference, fortunately, George Marshall had replaced Louis Johnson as secretary of defense. He joined Acheson in New York on September 22 and 23, and soon the American position became far more flexible. Now, all the Americans wanted was a decision *in principle* on the participation of German units in NATO's defense.[3]

The conference adjourned on September 26 after agreeing to have collective forces under a unified command with an overall supreme commander, who would surely be General Eisenhower. The ministers further recognized that Germany should be able to contribute to the defense of Western Europe, but exactly how this was to be done was left for the future.

When Schuman returned to Paris, he learned that Jean Monnet had come up with a solution to the problem of German rearmament. What Monnet did was to adapt the mechanism of the Coal-and-Steel Community to the creation of a West European army. By merging West European armed forces into a single army that would include Germans and a European minister of defense, Monnet also furthered his ideal of a United States of Europe.

Acheson was extremely skeptical of Monnet's scheme (which became the genesis of the proposed European Defense Community), calling it "a proposal designed for infinite delay on German participation."[4] In any case, he was determined not to let this scheme get in the way of establishing a unified NATO force under an American commander. As for the German question, Acheson and Lovett agreed that they would simply act under the assumption that the French had already accepted German rearmament and a commitment "in principle" for German participation.

The next step forward was the Brussels meeting of the NATO Council on December 18–19, 1950. The West Germans were already making it clear that they would agree to rearming only on the basis of full sovereignty and equality. Acheson fully sympathized with this but was wary of letting the Germans think they held too strong a bargaining position in this respect.[5] At Brussels the other NATO members agreed to the appointment of Eisenhower as supreme allied commander. The Americans were willing to accept a German regimental combat team of between five thousand and six thousand men, even while insisting that the division-size unit was still the most practicable fighting machine.

The atmosphere in the Belgian capital was ominous: American troops in Korea were reeling under the Chinese offensive, the Russians were making threatening noises over the prospect of German rearmament, and speculation was rife that war was imminent. Characteristically, Acheson was fixed on proceeding straightaway with a Western plan of defense. In addition to the Eisenhower appointment, he agreed to two sets of negotiations on German rearmament—one at Bonn among the Western high commissioners on the plan for German participation in NATO, and the other in Paris dealing with the French proposal for a European army. Reluctantly he also went along with a French suggestion to explore four-power talks with the Soviets to see if the wartime allies could resolve their differences over German unification and German rearmament.

Despite the continued French recalcitrance over rearming the Germans at any level, and even Bevin's unwillingness to move too fast on this score, Acheson could count the Brussels conference as a singular success. He had persisted in his aims, and he had gone as far as possible to meet legitimate French concerns. Now he could return to Washington and get the backing from Congress to make the great commitment to send American troops abroad in time of peace.

For a few terrifying minutes, however, he thought he might never see home again. The takeoff on the morning of December 20 was notoriously rough. Freezing fog blotted out the side lights on the runway more than two lights ahead; crews sprayed the plane with glycerin to prevent ice from coating the wings. At last came the signal to take off, and Acheson and his aides, strapped in their seats, went on what he called "a veritable buckboard ride down the runway." Happily, once they were aloft, bright sunlight greeted them, and he finally arrived in Washington at three o'clock the next morning, only to face the news of a full-scale isolationist assault on his foreign policy led by ex-president Herbert Hoover.[6]

The Republican attack on the Truman administration's European policy had been launched a month earlier, in Cincinnati on November 10, when Republican senator Robert Taft had called for a "fundamental re-examination" of the necessity of giving military and economic aid to Western Europe. With Senator Arthur Vandenberg in failing health, Taft felt free to take the lead in spelling out a Republican response to Acheson's foreign policy. But even while Taft specifically repudiated the concept of isolationism, his criticism was fully in the isolationist vein. Moreover, Taft, coming off a smashing reelection victory in Ohio, believed the public shared his views. He was now looking ahead to the presidential campaign in 1952, when he hoped to be the Republican standard-bearer.

A week later, Acheson, in a clever tour de force before the National Council of Negro Women, mercilessly rebutted Taft without naming him directly. "I read in the papers," he said, "that there is a species of *Homo sapiens* which has now become extinct. . . . That is the isolationist. We are told there aren't any more. . . . But there is a new species which has come on the horizon. This new species I call the re-examinist. . . . We need to look at this re-examinist and see what kind of person he really is."

Pointedly leveling his sarcasm at Taft, he went on to ask: "When we re-examine, does it mean that we are like the sound navigator who, after long flight or a long voyage, checks his course by the sun and stars every day? Or does it mean that the navigator says, 'How did I ever get started on this? Do I really want to take this trip after all?'"[7]

Taft had no ready reply at the time, but soon after Acheson returned from Brussels, he would take his revenge.

A second assault on Acheson's foreign policy came on December 12 when former U.S. ambassador to Britain Joseph P. Kennedy, who had been a rabid isolationist prior to Pearl Harbor, described American policy as "suicidal" and "politically and morally bankrupt." He called for the withdrawal of American troops from Korea and Berlin and opposed U.S. participation in the defense of Western Europe.[8]

But the main offensive was launched by Herbert Hoover on December 20. In essence, his approach was to send no more "American men and matériel" to Europe until the Europeans themselves had turned their territories into "an impregnable fortress." Hoover believed that America could not possibly hope to mount a successful land defense in Europe, and the attempt to do so would bankrupt the country. He assured the Europeans that they need not fear the United States would desert them; while no American ground troops would be available, help would be forthcoming from the U.S. Navy and Air Force. "The foundation of our national policies," he asserted, "must be to preserve for the world this Western Hemisphere Gibraltar of Western civilization."[9]

Within twenty-four hours of his return from Europe, Acheson answered Hoover at a press conference. Using only notes he had hastily scribbled after attending several meetings that morning, Acheson told reporters that isolating America as the "Gibraltar of the Western Hemisphere" would give the Soviet Union such a predominant position over Western Europe, with its skilled population and large military and economic resources, that it would put the United States into a position "of sitting quivering in a storm cellar waiting for whatever others may wish to prepare for us." This was a policy that the administration firmly rejected.[10]

Like Hoover's, Taft's next attack, on January 5, 1951, in the Senate, was directed not so much against the deployment of troops in Europe as against the whole internationalist position of the Truman-Acheson foreign policy.

Like Hoover, Taft believed the best military strategy for the United States was to deny Communist influence in areas that could be defended by American air and naval power. As for the cost of Taft's program, the senator simply proposed a budget based on a military establishment of six hundred thousand fewer men than the president was proposing. At the same time, presumably without calculating what it would cost in terms of lives and money, Taft supported MacArthur's call for an all-out war against mainland China—discounting the likelihood that such a conflict would result in war with the Soviet Union as well.[11]

The opening salvos of "the Great Debate" on American internationalism had been fired. These were followed by Senator Wherry's resolution on January 8,

1951, stating that "no ground forces of the United States should be assigned to duty in the European area" under NATO auspices pending Congressional approval.[12] Hearings on the resolution before the joint Senate Foreign Relations and Armed Forces Committees began on February 1, 1951, and would last for a month. The outcome would go far to define the character of American foreign policy for the rest of the century.

General Eisenhower, now NATO supreme commander, returned to Washington from a fact-finding tour of Europe's capitals and gave a report to an informal joint session of the House and Senate on February 1, followed by a private session with the two joint committees. Acheson wrote later that until the election campaign of 1952, his relations with the general were always "cordial," but he was not "drawn to him as were so many who were exposed to his personality." Yet Eisenhower's powers of persuasion were invaluable both on this occasion and later that spring, when the feasibility of the French-sponsored European army was being debated.

Before Congress, Eisenhower declared that American troops in Europe should be increased but that no rigid limit should be imposed. In response Taft wavered in his call for budgetary restraint—he "would not object," he said, "to a few more divisions."

As secretary of defense, General Marshall followed up Eisenhower's report with his own counterattack. Marshall declared that all the president planned to send to Europe were four divisions, making a total of six, or about one hundred thousand men. To reveal this decision to the Russians was unprecedented, and General Marshall indicated he was doing so only because the outcome of a great national debate should not rest on uncertainties.

In response, Senator Taft shifted the grounds of his opposition to constitutional matters. He had no objection to four divisions, he said; the real question was whether these troops should be committed to "an international army" until an agreement was reached with the other members of the Atlantic Alliance and "approved by Congress." Then the administration and Congress could thrash out the question of limiting the number of troops America would provide.[13]

In his riposte, the secretary of state hammered away at Taft's position; he feared a protracted debate could sound the death knell to an integrated NATO command. "Our first purpose," Acheson said, "is to deter the aggressors from attacking Europe. Our primary concern is not how to win a war after it gets started, but how to prevent it, and how to help Europe stay free in the meantime. . . . Our allies are building their forces *now;* the time for our contribution is *now.*"

The somewhat contradictory Taft-Hoover arguments assumed the Soviet atomic bomb made Europe strategically more vulnerable and therefore not worth fighting for; at the same time the two men were urging an American defense of the European continent based on air and sea power. Acheson easily exposed the hollowness of this reasoning. Although the United States now had a substantial lead in air power and in atomic weapons, in time the Soviet Union would possess enough atomic weaponry to diminish the value of that lead. The way to deter Russia after America's atomic advantage was lessened was to build up conventional forces on the continent. With this argument, Acheson went to the very heart of American strategy against a Soviet threat, a strategy embodied in NSC 68 but that the administration had not fully explained to the American people.

Another question that had to be dealt with was whether or not the president had the authority to send troops to Europe without express congressional approval. Acheson argued that the chief executive had a constitutional right to do so but at the same time made it clear that "if the Congress does not provide the funds to raise any army at all," there was no way to carry out plans for NATO or anything else.

The objective Acheson sought was cooperation and a resolution that would demonstrate congressional support without limiting the powers of the president. It was up to the United States to provide "the spark of leadership" for the defense of the West.

The last point Acheson had to answer was why American ground forces had to be sent to Europe when he himself had testified in 1949 that no such forces would be sent there. "I gather from your question," Acheson replied to Senator Alexander Smith of New Jersey, "that you were under the impression that, whereas I had said there was no commitment, that in some sort of weasel way there was a commitment. Now, I tell you there isn't. There isn't any commitment at all on this subject."

He did admit that during the debate over the North Atlantic Treaty two years earlier, he did not think it would become essential to send U.S. troops to Europe. Nor was there any legal obligation under the treaty to do so. But, he believed, under the treaty it was our *obligation* to help and our *privilege* to decide for ourselves just what sort of help would be needed. Now, would the Congress help? Would the Congress support him?

The answer finally was yes. On April 4 Congress approved sending four divisions to Europe, but no more "without further congressional approval." Both sides claimed victory, but the Truman administration's plans for the defense of Western Europe were never again seriously questioned during Acheson's tenure as secretary of state.[14]

The French, who under Monnet's inspiration invented the notion of a European Defense Community as an ingenious way of accepting the inevitability of German rearmament, were now balking. On a visit to Washington in early 1951, the French premier, René Pleven, brought up how the costs of the war in Indochina were making it difficult for the French to do their part in paying for the defense of Europe. Although Washington had been providing money to help cover the French military effort in Southeast Asia since May 1950, Acheson was convinced that "France was engaged in a task beyond her strength, indeed, beyond the strength of any external power unless it was acting in support of a dominant local will and purpose."

Providing U.S. military aid had brought Acheson little or no leverage over France's Indochina policy; on the contrary, what Acheson later called France's blackmail—the French threatening to cut back on their support for European defense unless Washington underwrote an ever greater proportion of their overall military buildup—was successful in letting the French do what they wanted in Southeast Asia. No matter how much Acheson might badger the French to find non-Communist nationalists to whom they could yield power, the French resisted any real abandonment of empire. On the one hand, there was no genuine nationalist alternative to the Communist Viet Minh; on the other hand, turning Vietnam over to Ho Chi Minh would totally demoralize the French. This was a contradiction that Acheson could never surmount.[15]

After returning to France, Pleven and his colleagues made new efforts to spell out what they meant by a European army. In essence, this European Defense Community (EDC) was to be a military arrangement whereby the armies of France, West Germany, Italy, and the Benelux countries (Belgium, the Netherlands, and Luxembourg) would "merge" into a supranational organization. The soldiers in this new European army would wear a common uniform, receive identical pay and training, and serve under an integrated command. There would also be a political commissariat to serve as a European defense ministry with authority to raise, train, and equip these armies, as well as to set, in part, a common budget. The European army would presumably be subordinate to NATO.[16]

Talks on the proposed European army began at the Quai d'Orsay in Paris in mid-February 1951 among delegations from the countries that would presumably become members of the European Defense Community. Six weeks earlier, on January 9, 1951, a different set of negotiations had been convened at the allies' headquarters in the Petersberg in Bonn among the high commissioners and the West German government. These brought forth another route to German rearmament by direct entry of German national units into NATO. The German military experts, represented by former generals Hans Speidel and Adolf Heusinger, ridiculed the Pleven plan's mixed divisions in which, as Speidel put it, "Bavarians would want sauerkraut and beer, French troops white bread and wine, and Italians spaghetti and Chianti."[17]

In June, with the Paris talks over a European army deadlocked and the Petersberg talks completed, Acheson was at first inclined to go along with the Petersberg formula, as it would "produce German units at the earliest possible date." He figured he could bring the French around by expressing support for a European army in the "long range." Yet less than two months later Acheson reversed himself and committed the administration to wholehearted support for Pleven's European army.

Three people—John McCloy, Dwight Eisenhower, and David Bruce—were instrumental in turning him around. McCloy, while eager to offer the Germans genuine "equality" within the Western alliance, saw that the Petersberg formula would produce unalloyed hostility from the French. The European Defense Community, he believed, would be the best means of reconciling French and German views. Then, too, McCloy thought that the United States would eventually withdraw from Europe. Once American troops were gone, national units in NATO would simply revert to national armies unless there was a permanent European political structure.

Eisenhower, too, anticipated an eventual American withdrawal. He told one friend, "If in ten years all American troops stationed in Europe for national defense purposes have not been returned to the United States, then this whole project will have failed."[18] If the Germans were to be armed in a way that would strengthen the Atlantic Alliance, they should do so as part of a European army.

Bruce was especially influential on Acheson. In his own "long telegram" to the secretary of state, he explained that the ineffectiveness of the Paris talks on EDC stemmed from France's uncertainty over Washington's attitude toward a European army.

Then McCloy arrived in Paris on June 17 and asked Eisenhower to urge General Marshall to get behind EDC. Eisenhower's backing convinced Pentagon critics. They could no longer scoff at the "impracticality" of the French proposal.

Acheson's inclination for "orderliness and clarity" had blocked his wholehearted endorsement of EDC. Nonetheless, with some skepticism of tying America "absolutely" to the European army concept, Acheson decided in July to "go all out" for it. At the same time, he insisted on specific arrangements for raising German contingents at the earliest possible date. Germans units were not to be delayed while awaiting the actual formation of a still mythical European Defense Community.[19]

In the meantime, talks among deputy foreign ministers of America, Britain, France, and Russia had been held at the Palais Rose throughout the spring. On June 21 they adjourned without accomplishing their ostensible purpose—preparation of an agenda for a conference of full foreign ministers. The Soviet delegate, Andrei Gromyko, failed to block the Brussels decision to go ahead with the rearmament of Germany. The allies and the Soviets remained at loggerheads, the allied agenda centering on completion of an Austrian peace treaty and preparing a peace treaty for Germany, the Soviets focusing on the demilitarization of Germany coupled with the withdrawal of occupation forces. This allowed Acheson to proceed with his plans for the defense of Europe and for the French and British to be assured that the Russians had no radically new proposals that would impede allied unity.[20]

In a discussion years later on the diplomacy of the Truman administration, Acheson admitted that "our whole purpose in this maneuver was to talk anywhere at any time with anybody, but never stop acting at all and never allow the talk to get us maneuvered in any field which would stop us from acting."[21]

Ernest Bevin was forced by illness to retire in March 1951 as British foreign secretary, and he died the following month. His successor, Herbert Morrison, was not calculated to make Acheson's job any easier. He was a gloomy man with little experience in foreign affairs. Often when he expressed his point of view, Acheson described him as doing so "with insinuations and innuendos in what he said, so that the sum of his expression was disagreeable and slightly insulting."[22]

Meeting in Ottawa from September 15 through September 20, the NATO foreign ministers issued invitations to Greece and Turkey to join the alliance and establish a committee charged with examining each member's economic and fiscal resources and then redirecting the allocation of these resources. Too often the United States had simply urged the other NATO countries to accept economic sacrifices for the greater good. This was a way of helping to persuade the U.S. Congress that the Europeans were making a reasonable contribution to the common defense.[23]

Despite progress on this front, Acheson was dissatisfied with the Ottawa meeting; no matter how deftly he might perform to persuade the allies to work together, he was frustrated that rapid and decisive action was not more forthcoming on an overall West European military buildup. Marshall Shulman, who later became a noted expert on the Soviet Union and was then working for Acheson as a special assistant, vividly recalled a day during the Ottawa meetings when the United States was under assault on the issue of rearming Germany. The room in which this was taking place had stained-glass windows, and the sun shone through in the late afternon, bathing Acheson in a halo of colors as he bent over a yellow legal pad, writing furiously.

When his colleagues had finally worn themselves out, Acheson began speaking from his hastily assembled notes and laid out a masterly brief justifying the American position. His logic was impeccable as he took them step by step through the process, concluding with the phrase "so you see it seems to us there is no escape from the situation." He won the day. The others voted with him, and later the delegates crowded around him to show how much they appreciated his craftsmanship and the trouble he had taken to make his case.[24]

Mercifully, Morrison's tenure as foreign minister was brief, as the Conservatives were returned to power in an election in late October 1951. When the United Nations General Assembly met in Paris in November, Acheson greeted a new British foreign secretary, one far more agreeable than Morrison: Anthony Eden, Churchill's wartime foreign minister.

Tall, carefully tailored, with his aristocratic hauteur and elegant mustache, Eden reminded casual observers of Acheson. Though they became good friends—and remained so after both were out of office—Acheson never developed the genuine camaraderie with Eden that he had enjoyed with Bevin. While Bevin could blow up easily, once the storm had passed he did not hold a grudge and could readily laugh at himself. By contrast, Eden's touchiness was notorious, and he seemed to feel the need to prove time and again that he was at the head of the class.[25]

Although Eden had had great experience in foreign affairs, serving as head of the Foreign Office for many years before Acheson played a significant role in formulating American policy, Acheson found him somewhat out of touch with the postwar realities after six years of Labour rule. Nonetheless, despite Eden's insistence on asserting British power, now greatly diminished, he and Acheson worked in tandem in moving German rearmament forward while searching for ways to reassure the French.

Acheson's most significant encounter in this Paris session was with Konrad Adenauer. This was the first time that the German chancellor had been invited to meet with the French, British, and American foreign ministers. After a lunch given by the American ambassador, Acheson recalled that Adenauer sat down with him in the living room and blurted out what had preoccupied him for the past few years: Was the United States as deeply committed to the defense of Europe as it was asking the Federal Republic to become? Were the Americans and the British playing around with the idea of using plans to rearm Germany in order to back the Russians into a corner? Then, when the allies had accomplished their purpose, would they make a deal with the Russians and sell the Germans out? He made it clear that he had the gravest worries about the British and the French.

Acheson told Adenauer that that was not the way Americans did business. In asking him to come along as partner, Acheson expected this partnership was going to hold, and decisions would be made together. In short, whatever arrangements might be made with the Russians would be arrangements in which there was German participation and willingness. The three of them would not, in Adenauer's phrase, "get together and sell out the Germans."

Adenauer was reassured. As Acheson said later, "It was *our* assurance on which he was going to rely and that was the one that counted with him."[26]

Afterward, John McCloy told Acheson that Adenauer had been much impressed by the relations he observed the next day among Eden, Schuman, and Acheson—the informality, the friendliness, and the mutual understanding that existed among them. It was, McCloy added, a completely new idea for Adenauer that representatives of important powers could conduct themselves with such warmth and understanding and be so frank and friendly and aboveboard.[27]

Little of great substance was accomplished at Paris, and the main problem, determining the final German financial contribution to the defense of Europe, was left to the future. The most important achievement was to create a good atmosphere for subsequent negotiations between the Germans and the allies. In this respect, Paris was a signal success. By the end of the conference, Adenauer and Schuman were speaking German together without waiting for a translation. This did not bother Eden or Acheson, but it greatly upset Schuman's aides from the French Foreign Office, who would pull at his coattails to make him wait until what he had understood perfectly was repeated in French.[28]

From Paris Acheson journeyed to Rome for yet another gathering of the NATO Council, which was followed by a bone-chilling sea voyage across the Atlantic. Yet Acheson felt rested and relatively content. In a speech to Jewish War Veterans in New York shortly after his return, his words were buoyant. Despite the prolonged bloodshed of Korea, the American troops were no longer in retreat and an armistice seemed in the offing; European defense was in the hands of the widely respected Eisenhower; and the question of German rearmament was being resolved, which might well lead to a union of European nations united with America in the containment of the Soviet Union. He therefore left his audience with Lincoln's determined and hopeful words: "With firmness in the right, as God gives us to see the right, let us strive on to finish the work we are in."[29]

The New Year brought news that once again the British were coming, this time in the guise of Winston Churchill and Anthony Eden. Acheson had first met Churchill during World War II when he was summoned to the White House to provide some information that was needed by the prime minister and Harry Hopkins. At that time, he had found them in the Lincoln Bedroom at ten A.M., Hopkins propped up in the high-backed bed and Churchill still in his pajamas and bathrobe, sitting at the foot of the bed, smoking a cigar.

Although Churchill was in his late seventies by the time of his return to office two months before his post-Christmas visit to Washington, Acheson found that "the old lion" was "still formidable and quite magnificent." In his evaluation of Churchill in his memoirs, Acheson believed it would be hard to find his equal in one person—as soldier, as statesman, and as orator.

What Acheson admired especially was the artifice Churchill used to get his way. "Art," Acheson wrote, "great art, transformed courage, right decisions, magnificent oratory into something different and superlative." Everything Churchill embodied wore "the touch of his art—his appearance and gestures, the siren suit, the indomitable V sign for victory, the cigar for imperturbability. He used all these artifices to get his way, from wooing and cajolery through powerful advocacy to bluff bullying; yet he never overruled the Chiefs of Staff." It was a question not merely of "the direction of great affairs, but the creation and development of personality."[30]

The nine days of the Churchill visit were strenuous, not so much because the issues at hand were momentous as because Churchill treated the trip as a kind of family holiday. On Saturday, January 5, after welcoming ceremonies at the airport and an official lunch at Blair House, the British and American contingents met for a cruise down the Potomac on the presidential yacht.

Conversation during dinner was marked by Churchill's mockery of the proposed European Defense Community. He evoked the image of a bewildered French drill sergeant sweating over a platoon made up of Greeks, Italians, Germans, Turks, and Dutch. Rather than the spirited singing to boost morale that Churchill would like to hear, he would doubtless find little enthusiasm in this motley bunch of soldiers singing, "March, NATO, march on!"

Doubtless not for the first time, Eden patiently explained that the proposed EDC contemplated not a heterogeneous mixing of nationalities, but a creation of national units in the form of divisions, or *groupements*, of about twelve thousand men.

The prime minister finally bowed before their arguments, but later he would often evoke the baffled drill sergeant. While he knew that the Americans were determined to press on with EDC, both because Congress had given its approval to the scheme and because it would mollify French worries over Germany, at heart Churchill did not approve of it.[31]

For Churchill, however, the central problem was the issue of the Atlantic command under NATO, which was tackled at the end of his visit. During the Attlee government, the British Parliament had accepted that the Atlantic command, as distinct from the Channel command and the approaches to Britain, should be commanded by an American. Churchill, then in opposition and determined to reassert British primacy in North Atlantic naval affairs, intended to revoke this.

On the last day, after a farewell dinner tendered to him by Acheson and his wife, Churchill met with the president, Acheson, and both British and American high-ranking officers, including the U.S. chief of naval operations, Admiral William Fechteler, and General Bradley, chairman of the Joint Chiefs of Staff.

As the Americans waited in the Cabinet Room for the president and the prime minister, the British delegation came in badly shaken. They had met Churchill in the president's anteroom to show him a draft of an agreement on the Atlantic command. He had read it, torn it up, and tossed the pieces into the air. The jaunty Scottish first sea lord, Admiral Sir Roderick Robert McGrigor, summed up the impending meeting: "Hurricane warnings along the Potomac." At that point the two heads of government entered, and everyone took their seats, the British on one side, the Americans on the other.

Truman opened the meeting in a brusque manner, announcing the unfinished business of the Atlantic command. Had the prime minister any comments? Then followed what Acheson described as "the most eloquent and moving speech" he had ever heard. For centuries England had kept alight the flame of freedom, fighting every tyrant who would have put it out, wresting the command from Spain and then from France, and used it to put teeth into America's defiance of European penetration in the Western Hemisphere. Now, in the plenitude of America's power and with the awful burden of atomic command, surely we could make room for Britain to play her historic role "upon that western sea whose floor is white with the bones of Englishmen."

As the majestic speech progressed, Ambassador Oliver Franks passed on to Acheson a note that read "Be very, very careful." Acheson thought to himself that, indeed, this was no time for a banal reply and pressure for a decision. Sitting to the right of the president, he whispered a request that he be allowed to speak first. Truman nodded.

Acheson knew he had to get the floor, let the tensions pass, and find a way to preclude further discussion. He opened by sympathizing with the prime minister, who was being asked to agree to an idea he had publicly opposed. Churchill nodded vigorously. Acheson went on: How often had all of us found ourselves accepting a course of action that was far from what it should be, in order to get on with the job? Again, Churchill nodded. Then Acheson asked the president and the prime minister to let some of them—Franks, Lovett, the two admirals, Air Marshal Sir William Elliot, and General Bradley—retire and come up with a suggestion.

As the group closed the door, Admiral Fechteler burst out, "How long are we going to fool around with his damned talk?"

"Forget it, Bill," said Lovett. "Dean has got something in mind; but what it is I couldn't guess."

Acheson realized that the problem was asking Churchill to reverse a position he had taken publicly, which he would never do. The trick was to get him to agree to go along with defense measures already in train, while allowing him to go on disagreeing if he chose to. A draft communiqué was quickly typed. "You read it, Dean, and no one else says anything," Franks commanded as they filed back into the Cabinet Room.

Acheson read it with great "expression." After referring to the arrangement about the Atlantic command "recommended by NATO and accepted by the late Government of the United Kingdom," he came to the heart of the matter: "These changes, however, do not go the full way to meet the Prime Minister's objections to the original arrangements. Nevertheless, the Prime Minister, while not withdrawing his objections, expressed his willingness to allow the appointment of a Supreme Commander . . . to proceed with the necessary planning in the Atlantic area. He reserved the right to bring forward modifications . . . at a later stage."

After an interminable moment of silence, Churchill brought down his hand on the paper. "I accept every word of it," he said.

"Shall we have the two press secretaries review it for language, Mr. President?" an aide asked.

"I don't think so," Truman said. "The Prime Minister and I have both been over it, and one of us, at least, uses fair English."[32]

Not long after Churchill's visit, King George VI died. At noon on February 6, 1952, the British ambassador, along with envoys from all the other Commonwealth countries, called on Acheson with the official news of the king's death. As there was a foreign ministers' meeting scheduled in Lisbon to wrap up the questions still pending over German participation in European defense, Truman decided to send Acheson to the king's funeral as his special ambassador. This would allow him to have a four-power encounter with Adenauer, Eden, and Schuman before going on to Lisbon.

Acheson sent a private message to Churchill, referring to the close bond that had existed between the king and Churchill. Waiting for him on his arrival with his wife in London was an invitation to lunch with the Churchills. At the lunch, the prime minister once again spoke of the great respect and affection he had for the king, in much the same tone as the king had spoken of him to Acheson two years earlier.

"How will it be now?" Acheson asked. "The queen is a very young woman. Will you tell her the sort of somber and intricate matters you discussed with her father? And will she listen?"

"Of course I will," he answered. "She is the Monarch; my duty is the same. And," he added, "I think she will listen. She has a good head."[33]

The next three days were filled with the ceremonies of the king's burial as well as negotiations among the allies. The problems over Europe centered on increasing French reluctance in the National Assembly and cabinet to endorse the European Defense Community. Schuman's room for compromise was therefore more circumscribed than usual. Just before Acheson left for London he had received a letter from Schuman insisting that restrictions be imposed on the production of German armaments and that the Germans be forbidden to secede from the European Defense Community and not be allowed to join NATO.

Acheson wrote back to Schuman immediately, explaining that these prohibitions were plainly inconsistent with German sovereignty, so that Adenauer could not possibly accept them. He concluded his letter by urging Schuman to solve the problems in London so that the upcoming Lisbon meeting would approve the establishment of the European Defense Community, its relationship to NATO, and the final arrangements for the German military contribution to European defense. "Either we must guide the events we have set in motion to the goal we have chosen," Acheson wrote, "or they will move themselves, we cannot tell where."[34]

The funeral itself was impressive as was the outpouring of deep affection for the shy wartime monarch by the British people. With other dignitaries, Acheson filed through Westminster Hall by the king's bier, surmounted by orb and scepter resting on a purple-covered catafalque, then "signed the book" at Buckingham Palace, Clarence House (still the new queen's residence), and Marlborough House (Queen Mary's residence).

Then came the pilgrimage to Windsor for the funeral service, which was held not in Westminister Abbey, but in St. George's Chapel at Windsor Castle. It was a cold and foggy morning, with patches of drizzle across the Thames. Acheson first had to stand on the sidewalk outside Westminster Hall, wisely wearing long woolen underwear, rubbers, a thin black raincoat to go under a more respectable topcoat, and, as he described it, "a small container of alcoholic restorative."

The mourners followed on foot at an agonizingly slow pace for three exhausting hours until they arrived at Paddington Station for the train to Windsor. The crowd watched in complete silence. Acheson saw them as "mostly pale," a "tired people."

Into Windsor Castle and through a Tudor courtyard, under an archway marked "E.R. 1583," and into the nave of St. George's Chapel, the coffin was borne. Then, after a brief and virtually inaudible service, Acheson joined his wife and the American ambassador in a short downhill walk to the returning train. There he ran into King Haakon of Norway, who remembered him from the time Covington and Burling represented the Norwegian government some thirty years before. Most likely, Acheson reflected, he remembered him because the judgment that his firm won for Norway was so large. On rejoining his own party, Acheson found an alcoholic restorative far more effective than tea for the ride back to London, where a long, hot bath would soothe his aching muscles.[35]

With Adenauer's appearance in London, matters relating to European defense and the end of the allied occupation of West Germany came to a head. The German chancellor agreed to a board of three allied members and three Germans to review sentences imposed by the allies for war crimes. The German financial contribution to European defense was to be worked out with the British, the Americans, and the European Defense Community.

With these most pressing issues seemingly resolved, Acheson was confident that when he flew to Lisbon the next day, the European Defense Community and the German role in the defense of the continent would be accepted.

The morning before he left for Portugal, Acheson made a farewell visit to the queen. Prince Philip and Anthony Eden were also present. After greeting him, she opened the conversation by regretting the weather, typical of London in February. But Acheson, bearing in mind what Churchill had said a few days earlier about keeping the new monarch informed, decided to make the conversation more interesting. In response to her polite question whether his meetings had gone well, he answered that they had gone only fairly well at times. There were some points on which he and his fellow foreign ministers had not reached full agreement. But he could not blame the Germans for that, for he had generally found himself siding with Adenauer.

Eden was highly annoyed at Acheson. It seemed to him a grave breach of protocol for a foreign statesman to brief the queen, especially when her own foreign secretary was sitting nearby. Later that night, after the flight to Lisbon, Eden went to a dinner with Acheson's party at the American embassy. When he arrived he said, "I don't know why I speak to you. You behaved very badly this afternoon."

"Did Her Majesty say that?" Acheson asked.

"You know very well she didn't," he answered. "That was the trouble. You did it with malice aforethought."

Acheson then cited Churchill as his inspiration and "was finally forgiven under the benign influence of the Ambassador's martinis."[36]

Lisbon entranced Acheson. As he described it, "Mists, rising from the Tagus River and drawing a chilly shroud around the city, were burned away at midmorning by a bright, warm sun." The Achesons stayed with the American ambassador, an old school friend, Lincoln MacVeagh, who had moved to Lisbon from Athens and was now overseeing the negotiations of an Azores Defense Agreement with NATO. That first morning, the Achesons walked undisturbed through the narrow streets, all washed clean every night, and along the Avenida da Liberdade, constructed after the earthquake, fire, and tidal wave of 1755. The next morning, when word got out that the American secretary of state and his wife were again promenading along the same route, Acheson was harassed by hundreds of children wanting his autograph.

During the day, when Acheson was in meetings, Alice quickly became a well-known figure in Lisbon, as she painted seascapes and the hills, and passersby naturally stopped to watch an artist at work. As she had to budget her time carefully between social engagements, she would travel in a small car with a Portuguese chauffeur, who would get out and guard the car while the painter stayed in the automobile with canvas propped from knees to dashboard, paint box on the seat beside her. When it was time to depart to attend a social gathering, the chauffeur would help her clean up, then she would apply new makeup and wave good-bye to the little crowd on the sidewalk amid loud cheers.[37] For Alice, painting was where she could allow her emotions to run freely. Her formal public manner could be cast aside in these private moments at the easel in work that was bold and expressive.

Acheson was much taken with Portugal's premier, Antonio de Oliveira Salazar. A former economics professor, Salazar had been installed by the military as ruler of Portugal in 1928 after a period of economic and financial chaos. He practiced financial stringency and soon brought the nation's budget under control, providing Portugal with a sound currency but at the expense of any dynamic economic expansion.

Under an authoritarian regime headed by Salazar at the army's sufferance, Portugal was a country with little political liberty. It was not, however, a regime of terror—in Acheson's words, "one doesn't feel that this has any of the cruelty that goes on in Latin America"—and therefore was not excluded by the United States and the Western European powers from membership in NATO.

As Acheson described Salazar, what appealed to him especially was the simplicity of Salazar's way of life. His office was in a government building approached by the private entrance and guarded by one old uniformed doorman. His small study was furnished with a desk, no telephone, comfortable leather chairs, and bookshelves with paintings above them. In his conversation with Acheson, Salazar was relaxed, a man seemingly certain of his policies and his ends, which seemed to be stability at all costs and full employment, even at the expense of modernization. He had not a trace of pomposity, a quality that made him especially agreeable to Acheson.

Nonetheless, in Acheson's descriptions of Portugal's dictator, it is hard to discern which of Salazar's policies might have appealed to Acheson or even what his philosophy might be. But the attraction was powerful and must have influenced Acheson in later years to sympathize with the efforts of Salazar and his successors to control growing rebellions in the African colonies of Angola and Mozambique.[38]

Acheson later remarked of the Lisbon conference, "The whole operation was like one of those games where a dozen little shots have to be maneuvered into holes in a cardboard field: the slightest jar in trying to get the last one in shakes all the others out."[39]

Of great importance to Acheson was the endorsement by the NATO Council of the European Defense Community and the resolution approving the establishment of a European army within it. Both were adopted. In addition, plans were approved for an overall European force level of fifty divisions in 1952, rising to seventy-five in 1953 and to ninety-six by 1954. (Nothing remotely approaching these levels was ever attained.[40])

After much wrangling among the British, French, and Germans over their monetary contributions to European defense, this issue, too, was happily resolved. In his cable home to the president, giving him a final report on the conference, Acheson concluded exultantly, "We have something pretty close to a grand slam."[41]

What the NATO leaders wanted above all as a solution to the German question was the permanent engagement of the United States to the Western alliance and the presence of American troops on the European continent.

CHAPTER TWENTY-EIGHT

ENDGAME

IN BONN, High Commissioner John J. McCloy was worried. Over the winter and spring of 1952, Acheson had moved deftly to bring about an agreement in principle on a European Defense Community. American diplomacy had also helped prepare the way for the Western allies to sign a series of accords with the Bonn government. With the issue of German rearmament apparently settled, the Federal Republic would have full political sovereignty, with the important proviso that the Western allies reserved their occupation rights over Berlin, where the Soviet Union also remained an occupying power. These accords—the so-called contractual agreements—were supposed to take the place of a formal peace treaty, for no actual treaty could be signed with Germany except by all of the wartime allies, including the Soviet Union. Moreover, such a peace treaty was predicated on there being a unified Germany.

McCloy was therefore not surprised when, on March 10, 1952, Moscow sent a note that was intended to derail Adenauer's hopes for a political and military alignment with the United States and Western Europe. The progress made at the Lisbon talks that February had clearly alarmed the Kremlin. What Stalin now proposed was a new series of four-power talks to negotiate the reunification and neutralization of Germany. The proposals were seductive. They called for a withdrawal of all foreign troops no later than one year after the signing of a peace treaty and the reunification of Germany based on free elections.

A few days after the Soviet message was received, the high commissioner told his general counsel, Robert Bowie, "It is one I have been expecting for a long time." To McCloy, the issue was simple: "If the Germans were now to delay, the

American reaction might be to wash our hands of the entire project and let the Germans fend for themselves."[1]

In addition—and this was a surprise to Acheson and McCloy—Stalin's note suggested that Germany should be allowed to establish "its own national armed forces," the only restriction being that Germany not enter into any coalition or military alliance against any power that had fought against Nazi Germany in the Second World War. Moreover, Germany would be permitted to have its own armaments industry. The note called for the restoration of all civil and political rights to "[all] former members of the German army, including officers and generals, [and] all former Nazis," except for those already serving court sentences.[2]

But the note was deliberately vague on certain key questions: How would Germany's nonaligned or neutral status be guaranteed? How would an all-German government be elected? Who would monitor the "free elections"? For McCloy, a country as powerful and economically dynamic as a unified Germany could not remain neutral. He believed that a neutral Germany would inevitably fall into a Soviet sphere of influence. Nor did he think that the Soviets would allow genuinely free elections in their zone.[3]

Why would Stalin even entertain such a notion? Did the Soviet dictator truly think that a neutral Germany was preferable to a Germany under the joint control by the Big Four or split between the East and the West?

There is some evidence that in 1952 Stalin believed that a reunited Germany, as he put it elsewhere, might "break out of American bondage" and pose more of a threat to the West than to the Soviet Union. Soviet commentators evoked the memory of the 1922 Rapallo treaty, which had been the first sign of a rapprochement between Weimar Germany and the Bolshevik Soviet Union.[4]

Or was it simply a ploy to persuade the French and the Germans to reject the European Defense Community and the "contractuals" that would permit German rearmament? One Soviet diplomat, Vladimir Semyonov, recalled Stalin asking: Was it *certain* that the Americans would turn the note down? Only when assured that it was did Stalin agree to have it sent.[5]

Acheson understood immediately that the allies would have to be forthcoming. Whether the Soviet note was a bargaining chip or a delaying tactic had to be explored. "It is shrewdly drafted to appeal primarily to the Germans," he wrote to Truman, who was trying to shake off a bronchial infection in Key West, "and it seems clear that we would be ill-advised . . . to turn it down out of hand."[6]

In the State Department, the Policy Planning Staff argued that there was only "one chance in ten" that the Russians were prepared "to pay, if necessary, the price of free elections in order to block West Germany's entrance into EDC." But Acheson could not run the risk of letting the Russians prevent the signing of the EDC and the "contractual" agreements. There is little doubt that Soviet worries in 1952 were focused less on a rearmed Germany than on the danger of a

Germany within a tight Western military alliance.[7] While the Americans did not believe they could fully defend Western Europe without Germany, the Russians had no reason to fear NATO as long as Germany remained outside the alliance.

Those Germans who, as McCloy put it, believed they were being used to further America's policies, "which they consider alien to their interest and contrary to their preference," were likely to mobilize to prevent the "contractuals" from being signed. The Adenauer government was already in a somewhat weakened position during an election year; in April, shortly after the note, the Adenauer coalition lost control of the upper house of the German parliament.[8]

At this juncture, Anthony Eden seized the initiative; he, as well as France's foreign minister, Robert Schuman, wanted to prevent the re-creation of a united Germany, which would reverse "Adenauer's policy of integration with the West and go for a policy of neutrality and maneuvering between East and West." Eden therefore suggested that the Big Three should concentrate on that part of the Soviet note relating to the creation of an all-German government.[9]

Following Eden's approach, the Western allies stressed the need for free elections throughout Germany under the supervision of the United Nations rather than of the four powers, as the Russians suggested in a second note, dated April 9. The Western reply pointed out, in Acheson's words, that "an all-German government was a prerequisite to a peace treaty, free elections were prerequisite to an all-German government, and free conditions prerequisite to free elections."[10]

Acheson was certainly willing to consider "talks of some sort" with the Russians, if for no other reason than "to convince Ger[man]s we mean business and are not afraid to talk," to "expose Sov[iet] insincerity," and "if the Sov[iets] are really prepared to open Eastern Zone, [to] force their hand." Timing would be "about right" for such talks "after signature of EDC treaty and contractuals."[11]

A series of carefully designed exchanges with Moscow—what Eden called the "battle of the notes"—soon became the strategy, designed to delay any action on the Soviet proposals until the "contractuals" were signed by the end of May, terminating the American, British, and French occupation of the Federal Republic and bringing it into the EDC.

On May 25 a third Soviet note, markedly different from the previous two, arrived while the Western leaders were meeting in Bonn. It had a decidedly perfunctory though somewhat bullying tone and showed no signs of making any serious effort to pursue opportunities for negotiation. George Kennan, now serving in Moscow as the U.S. ambassador, cabled back to Washington that the Soviet note seemed remarkable for "its weakness, its mild discursiveness, its lack of enthusiasm."

To Kennan's sensitive and trained eye, the note was not "the authentic, terse, collected, menacing voice of Stalin's Kremlin when functioning in high gear and pursuing an important Soviet initiative. To the contrary, the document seemed to me to show signs of having been prepared by hacks supplied only with grudging, cryptic and guarded [instructions] and told to make the best of it."[12]

As Marshall Shulman later wrote, the third Soviet note did not show any enthusiasm for reunification on terms that would have jeopardized the Soviet position in East Germany, where a forcible program for the "construction of socialism" was under way.[13] Moscow's commitment was to ensure East Germany's survival.

Neither Stalin nor his successors ever revived the ideas of an independent, reunified, rearmed, but neutral state. Ever since the end of the Second World War, Stalin's position had been that only a Germany under Moscow's control could truly ensure the Soviet Union's safety. As historian John Lewis Gaddis noted, the March 1952 note may have represented Stalin's "last fragile hope" that he could achieve the outcome by popular consent. But a Soviet-dominated Germany was his aim and would not have been relinquished. Stalin, as Molotov testified later, "would never have abandoned the conquests of socialism."[14]

There had been one big surprise that spring. Upon returning from Key West, Harry Truman dropped a bombshell at the Jefferson-Jackson Day dinner on March 29. On their way to dinner, Alice Acheson asked her husband if he thought the president might disclose his political future in his after-dinner speech. "Not at all," he said in, as she later told him, "an offensively superior manner." It was far too early to declare his intention to run for the presidency again and, to a large gathering of the party faithful, too disappointing to announce the contrary.

That evening Alice sat next to the president. As the time for speech making approached, Truman opened the binder that held his text and showed her a last page written in his own hand, declaring in his usual terse way that he would not seek the presidency again. "You, Bess, and I," he said, "are the only ones here who know that."

Alice protested and wanted to get Dean to come over and argue him out of it. But the president refused. Acheson was, as he wrote later, "stunned" at the announcement.[15]

In the aftermath, the administration's power to affect events overseas inevitably diminished. The Korean armistice negotiations languished while the Communists waited to see what the next administration would bring. While there was no longer any danger that the U.S. military commanders in Korea would defy the Truman administration in word or deed, there was at one point pressure from the Joint Chiefs of Staff to stage a spectacular air and naval demonstration off the China coast as an inducement for the Communists to settle. Acheson and Lovett were firmly opposed. In the meantime the South Korean government repeatedly complained that its interests were being threatened if Washington accepted anything less than unification of the peninsula under one government. But Acheson made it clear that this was not America's aim.[16]

Not until Eisenhower took office was an armistice arranged on July 27, 1953. The terms on voluntary repatriation of those prisoners, mainly North Koreans, who wanted to remain in the south did not differ significantly from what the Truman administration had offered.

Prisoners on both sides were to be turned over to Indian troops in a newly created Neutral Nation Commission. After six months, during which time the governments involved would have had an opportunity to change the minds of those unwilling to return to their homelands, the prisoners who still wanted political asylum would revert to civilian status and be released. It had taken two years and seventeen days after the peace talks had begun—including the death of Stalin in March and Eisenhower's implied threat to Beijing that he was prepared to use atomic weapons to end the war—to achieve the armistice.[17]

Precisely because time was running out, Acheson was anxious to end his term in office with a Western political and military system in place undergirded by a historic American peacetime commitment to defend Western Europe. It was the culmination of a string of policies that had begun with the Truman Doctrine and the Marshall Plan, not as part of an American grand design, but as a response to specific Soviet threats and to the articulated needs of the allies.

On the afternoon of May 22, the president saw Acheson's party off for Bonn on the *Independence.* The group included Acheson's wife, the Jessups, Assistant Secretary of State George Perkins, Lucius Battle, and Acheson's secretary, Barbara Evans. As Acheson was preparing for his last major European diplomatic rounds and for the signing of the "contractuals" and the EDC treaty, there were still some issues to resolve; he could not yet know the outcome of the "battle of the notes."

Eden and Schuman joined Acheson and the high commissioners at Bad Godesberg, a suburb of Bonn. There Acheson found that Schuman was especially distressed. In London and Lisbon he had seemed in control of French foreign policy; now he seemed not even in control of his own ministry. He was clearly tired, nervous, and depressed and frequently dozed off at meetings. At one point Adenauer said to Acheson, "Can't you give some confidence to our poor friend?"[18]

The French still wanted a guarantee by Britain and the United States against any German withdrawal from EDC. While Eden was ready to negotiate such a treaty with France, Acheson knew this would be almost impossible for him to do in the waning days of the Truman administration. To overcome this obstacle,

Philip Jessup cited an article in the NATO treaty that bound its members to consult together should any member believe its security was threatened in order to find the means to remove the threat. With some reworking, an Anglo-American commitment along these lines satisfied Paris.

The last-minute German problem, largely having to do with the amount of the German defense contribution, was forcefully resolved by Adenauer. Not only had the May 25 Soviet note done nothing to persuade the Germans to resist integration with the West; it had solidified German public opinion behind Adenauer. As Acheson later noted, "We were fortunate in our opponent."[19]

With the most worrisome problems resolved, Schuman started to cheer up, and the signing of the contractual agreements took place on May 26, the day after a gala dinner given by Adenauer in the Palais Schaumburg, the former residence of the archbishop of Cologne, on a bluff overlooking the Rhine. At the ceremony, held in the room where the German Senate met, Acheson welcomed the Federal Republic into "the community of nations." Then, after lunching with the chancellor, he and his party took off for Paris.[20]

The signing of the treaty for the European Defense Community took place the next day in the Salon de l'Horloge at the French Foreign Ministry on the Quai d'Orsay. For Acheson, it was the completion of his efforts to construct a defense alliance that would be the foundation for a European political community, which, forty years later, finally emerged as the European Union. Ultimately the French National Assembly refused to ratify EDC in 1954, largely from continued fears of a German military buildup; ironically, in the aftermath of EDC's demise, the German forces were nonetheless brought into NATO under the same terms and conditions as the other members of the alliance—exactly the reverse of what the French had originally wanted.

At the time the European Defense Community was facing defeat in 1954, Acheson speculated that the European army might well have come into being had the 1952 American presidential campaign not intervened. "I think there was momentum after Lisbon . . . that was so great that if this election had come a year later, instead of the fall of '52, we would have gone through this period and taken steps which would have very greatly conditioned everybody's thinking for the future."[21]

Despite the failure of EDC, Acheson's efforts on its behalf nonetheless contributed to his ultimate objective—providing a strong defense capability for West Europe. His initial skepticism toward EDC had given way to support for the project because he believed at the time that it was the best way to create French approval for German rearmament. Sooner or later the French would have had to face up to the question of German sovereignty and hence a German military contribution to European defense. By embracing EDC, Acheson helped force Paris and Bonn to work together to create a Western security structure.

Moreover, he had been willing to use the economic and military assistance Washington was prepared to provide the Europeans to extract concessions from them for the common good. Acheson may not have come into office with a specific plan for European security, but he had a goal and he was determined to achieve it. In any duel between America and Russia for predominance in Europe, Acheson expected America would be the winner. What Stalin feared—a rearmed and rehabilitated Germany within an American sphere of influence—was now in the offing.[22]

For Acheson, to prevent Russian hegemony in Western Europe, and to bind the Federal Republic of Germany into a democratic political, economic, and military alliance, was to restore the balance of power in Europe—so that American soldiers would never again have to fight a great war on the European landmass. This had been his long-term strategy and would be his lasting legacy.

CHAPTER TWENTY-NINE

"THAT CANDLES MAY BE BROUGHT"

IN THE WANING MONTHS of Acheson's tenure, there were inevitably tributes and farewells. The accolade Acheson most valued was the honorary doctorate he received from Oxford University on June 25, 1952. Other invitations included laying the cornerstone of the American Memorial Library in Berlin and visits to Austria and Brazil. The president insisted that the Austrian and Brazilian visits be regarded as state occasions and therefore made the presidential plane, *Independence*, available. Among those accompanying Acheson were his wife, Luke Battle, Barbara Evans, and Philip Jessup and his wife.

The occasion for the conferring of degrees, what Oxford called an encaenia, turned out to be an idyllic summer day in the ancient university town. At Wadham College, the public orator presented Acheson to the chancellor, Lord Halifax, with a salutation in Latin, and after various dissertations delivered mostly in Latin and Greek, the procession marched to All Souls College for lunch. At one point, as the group descended a narrow staircase, one of Acheson's fellow honorands, author Somerset Maugham, started to plunge to the marble floor but was fortunately intercepted.

That evening, at a dinner known as a "Gaudy," a full-dress affair at Christ Church College, Acheson was called upon to speak. He evoked the ghost of that son of Oxford John Davenport, who had founded the city of New Haven, site of Acheson's own university. As Acheson told the story, some of Davenport's stern training and fearlessness must have passed on to his grandson Colonel Abraham Davenport, who on May 19, 1780, confronted a fearful gathering at Hartford,

Connecticut, on what seemed to be a day of judgment. The sky that day had turned from blue to gray to deepest black. By midafternoon it was midnight. Many of the representatives in the upper house of the Connecticut State Legislature were calling, in fear and trembling, for immediate adjournment. Colonel Davenport asked to be recognized and said: "The Day of Judgment is either approaching, or it is not. If it is not, there is no cause for adjournment. If it is, I choose to be found doing my duty. I wish, therefore, that candles may be brought."[1] It was a fitting sentiment for Acheson himself.

Before and after the Oxford ceremonies, Acheson met in London with Eden and Schuman. Once again, the two foreign ministers of the embattled colonial powers looked to the United States for support. And once again, Acheson sought to avoid too deep an American entanglement while at the same time trying not to break with his most valued allies. Schuman requested more economic aid for France's war in Indochina, but he was unwilling to accept Acheson's more limited offer of U.S. training of Vietnamese forces.

Acheson's belief that American training would improve the fighting capacity of the South Vietnamese may have reflected his continuing view that the United States would not be seen as the colonial power that France was. By this time, Washington was providing Paris with about 40 percent of the military and economic aid for the Indochina War, but the war was going from bad to worse.

Despite these signs of failure, Acheson still put the Indochina conflict in a larger setting. On June 30 the State Department issued a communiqué that depicted the struggle in Southeast Asia as part of the worldwide resistance to "Communist attempts at conquest and subversion." Although Acheson was now willing to contemplate American naval and air action against China should there be signs of any direct Chinese military intervention in Vietnam, he was wholly opposed to using American ground forces in Indochina. In this respect, there must be no more Koreas. Yet he clung to the belief that well-equipped and well-motivated native armies could defend a country, if they were trained by the United States. This was the approach that was now being used in South Korea, and Acheson believed it could work in Vietnam.

At the same time he knew that the French were likely to reject his offer of American training missions in Indochina. Thus France's efforts to win the war were probably doomed. When he briefed President-elect Eisenhower on November 18, he told him that the French lacked the will to fight and the native population was on the fence, waiting to support the side of the victor. As he left office, he could offer no solution to the deteriorating situation in Southeast Asia.[2]

* * *

Anthony Eden's problems that June also centered on the remnants of empire, in this case Egypt. In the aftermath of the Second World War, the Egyptian government was determined to evict the British military presence from the country. In October 1951 it abrogated the 1936 treaty, which had allowed British forces to remain in Egypt to protect the Suez Canal. Cairo wanted full sovereignty and no foreign troops on its soil.

In response, the British placed an embargo on export of oil to Egypt. In November 1951 Acheson urged London to repeal the embargo and said that no settlement achieved by force would last. He wanted to help the British but saw British policy as foolish and obtuse. In late January 1952 fighting broke out between British troops in the canal zone and Egyptian police. Mobs burned Cairo's famous Shepheards Hotel. Eden asked Washington for full support for British military action.

Acheson refused. Egypt was not threatened by Soviet military or political pressure, and he felt that Britain should make concessions to satisfy Egyptian nationalism. This was still his position when he met with Eden in June. Moreover, he brashly suggested that the likely result of the Egyptian dispute was that Britain would lose the Suez Canal, and Egypt, which now claimed the Sudan, would lose that territory as well. He was right on both counts.[3]

In this same period, British policy toward Iran also seemed to Acheson futile and misconceived. On April 28, 1951, Mohammed Mosadeq, a nationalist foe of the British-controlled Anglo-Iranian oil company, became prime minister. Four days later the shah signed a new law passed by the Iranian parliament (Majlis) to nationalize Anglo-Iranian. In response, Britain was threatening by July to use military force against Iran to close the Abadan refinery, which was yielding 80 percent of Iran's income. This would plunge the country into economic chaos and, Acheson feared, might bring about a Communist takeover—in short, a strategic disaster for the United States.

To prevent armed intervention by the British was Acheson's most urgent task. Whereas the British were incensed over what they considered the illegality of Tehran's actions, the Iranians were prepared to risk economic ruin to rid themselves of what they viewed as a remnant of British colonialism. In this climate the Russians might well try to reoccupy northern Iran, and Acheson could imagine Mosadeq asking the Russians to intervene in order to prevent British forces from occupying the refinery and oil fields.[4]

That July, on Acheson's advice, Truman sent Averell Harriman to Iran to see if he could stimulate negotiations between the Iranian government and the British. To Harriman, the British government was taking "a completely nineteenth century colonial attitude towards Iran." He was therefore disposed to support Iran's policy of nationalization. The questions to be decided revolved around accomplishing that—of compensation, of operating the refinery, and of marketing the product.[5]

At the end of August Harriman returned to Washington to report failure on his effort to bring about a successful negotiation between Mosadeq and the Anglo-Iranian special negotiator, Sir Richard Stokes, a socialist millionaire who knew nothing about the Middle East. On September 25, 1951, the Iranian prime minister gave the last remaining British employees at Abadan exactly one week to clear out.[6]

Harriman's mission, however, did succeed in its immediate aim of turning back Britain and Iran from the brink of war. "It failed in its more ambitious purpose to find a solution to the oil dispute," Acheson wrote later, "for the same reason that the Marshall mission to China in 1946 failed, because neither party to the dispute wanted a solution."[7]

As a response to the Iranian action, Britain proposed a condemnatory resolution in the UN Security Council. Mosadeq, in turn, came to New York to argue his case personally before the United Nations. About seventy years old, he was a frail, even decrepit, old man, completely bald, with a long, beaklike face that seemed to come out of his nose. While he was adept at fainting spells, and often took to his bed to negotiate with foreigners, at other moments he would toss aside his cane and scamper over to greet his visitors.

With his customary humor and eccentricities, he soon became a hit on American television. Then, with the British resolution defeated, he made his way to Washington, where he first encountered, and to a large degree amused, Dean Acheson. Arriving at Union Station, he had his arm through his son's arm and was leaning on a stick as he left the train. Spotting Acheson at the gate, however, he dropped the stick, let go of his son, and came skipping down the platform to say hello.[8]

Acheson remembered Mosadeq sitting with the president and him after lunch at Blair House, when he suddenly dropped his air of gaiety and, looking old and pathetic, leaned toward Truman. "Mr. President," he said, "I am speaking for a very poor country—a country all desert—just sand, a few camels, a few sheep—"

"Yes," Acheson interrupted, "and with your oil, rather like Texas."

At this, Mosadeq burst into laughter. He was a gambler, Acheson concluded, and the game had simply not paid off. The president was not prepared to give Iran money to help him fight off the British "imperialists," as Mosadeq had requested.[9]

Mosadeq then entered Walter Reed Hospital, the army's medical center, and was installed to his great delight in the presidential suite. There he remained until mid-November 1951, holding court with Acheson's advisers, who vainly tried to explain oil economics to him. During Mosadeq's stay, the British Conservatives returned to power, but Anthony Eden was no more forthcoming than his

Labour predecessor. A devotee of Persian literature, Eden thought he knew and understood the Persians. In his view, as Acheson said later, "they were rug dealers and that's all they were. You should never give in and they would always come around and make a deal with you if you stayed firm."

Eden also believed that Mosadeq should be ousted. But Acheson was opposed to this, for he believed that Mosadeq was representative of "a very deep revolution, nationalist in character, which was sweeping not only Iran but the whole Middle East."[10]

By mid-November Mosadeq was back in Iran. As he told one American on the eve of his departure, "I return in a much stronger position than if I returned with an agreement which I would have to sell to my fanatics."

The crisis dragged on through 1952. Iran could not sell its oil, it was running out of cash, and conditions throughout the country were deteriorating. In Washington in early 1952, on the occasion of Churchill and Eden's trip to Washington, Acheson blew up and told Eden that it was the British who were behaving like rug merchants.[11]

Acheson's efforts to resolve the Iranian imbroglio got nowhere. By October 1952 Mosadeq broke diplomatic relations with London. When the British suggested to the Americans that they work together to mount a coup to overthrow Mosadeq, Acheson would have none of it.

Nonetheless, Truman and Acheson made one last try. Acheson proposed what was essentially a consortium of oil companies, which would include Anglo-Iranian and American companies, to take over operations. In addition, the United States would advance Iran millions of dollars against future oil deliveries, while the issue of compensation was being settled by international arbitrators. Mosadeq seemed agreeable to an arbitration. But when Acheson tried to press Eden into making concessions, Eden refused, believing it would be better to find an alternative to Mosadeq rather than buy him off.[12]

The haggling went on into January 1953, when Acheson left office. The consortium plan was finally adopted two years later—but only after the shah had fled the country and then been restored to his throne through a coup assisted by the CIA.[13]

Acheson later admitted to "a feeling of dissatisfaction with everything we did in the Middle East." But he was being unduly harsh on himself. He had refused to support the French in their policies of repression in their protectorates of Tunisia and Morocco, whose rulers were demanding political autonomy for their countries. In the fall of 1952 he even had the United States vote with the Soviet Union and the Arab-Asian bloc to place the question of French policies in Tunisia and Morocco on the agenda in the United Nations. The French position—that

France's problems in North Africa were internal matters and could not be discussed by the United Nations—was to him, as to most Americans, "a confession of guilt."[14]

His policy of avoiding any direct application of American military power in the region was sound. Throughout his tenure in office, Acheson believed the West had to accommodate itself to the forces of nationalism that were raging from Morocco to Iran. Yet, as in Indochina, this policy often ran counter to the aims of his principal allies, with whom he had to work most closely if he was to accomplish what he most desired—the strengthening of Western Europe in alliance with America.

Following his June 1952 meeting with Schuman and Eden, Acheson left London for Berlin and Vienna. These visits were almost wholly ceremonial. After giving a short speech on the site of the new American Memorial Library in Berlin, on June 29 Acheson flew to the Austrian capital.

Vienna, which he and Alice had never visited before, enchanted them. Although Austria was still under four-power occupation, passage from zone to zone was less formalized than in Germany. Acheson's party arrived at the Tulln airport in the Russian zone, and during the two-hour train journey to the capital, crowds lined the track. Acheson and Austrian foreign minister Karl Gruber stood on the back platform of the train and were saluted by flowers and cheers.

The Austrian chancellor, Leopold Figl, had arranged a classic Austrian experience for the Achesons. Although Vienna's opera season had ended, Figl persuaded the musicians and a group of singers to return to perform Mozart's *The Marriage of Figaro* in the Redoutensaal, an eighteenth-century theater built for the composer in the Hofburg Palace.

The Achesons spent the next day at the vast complex of the Hofburg, where he met with the president of Austria, General Theodor Koerner, who remarked sadly, "Vienna is an imperial city without an empire. Come, I will show you." As Acheson tells it, "He led us through room after room, stopping to show us a clock, a masterpiece of its time, which had been a wedding present to [Empress] Maria Theresa. When the hour struck, the most complicated maneuver had once taken place, in the course of which, as I remember it, a heavenly host descended to crown Maria Theresa and her bridegroom with celestial garlands. But the clock was not going."

On Acheson's second and final evening in the Austrian capital, the chancellor gave him a state dinner at the Ballhausplatz, where the Congress of Vienna had met in 1815 at the end of the first Napoleonic War. Sitting at the excellently appointed table, with flowers everywhere, a symphony orchestra playing, the crystal chandeliers ablaze with candles, Acheson could imagine, as he wrote later, "the Prince of Benevento, M. de Talleyrand himself, limping from group to group, raising France like a phoenix from the ashes of Napoleon's consuming ambition; Lord Castelreagh, handsome, charming, wise, waiting restlessly for the meeting to end so that he and the wife to whom he remained the lover could hurry off to their dancing lesson . . . Metternich, silent, watchful, a product of the same school as Talleyrand; the Czar Alexander I, talking liberalism and acting the autocrat."

What would they talk about? he wondered. He then remembered asking Justice Holmes a similar question when the old man had commented on the difference in their ages and noted that he had spoken to Lincoln and had talked with a man who had talked with Washington. "But could they talk together," Acheson asked him, "and what would they talk about?"

"They would find a way to talk," Holmes said, "through a series of interpreters; and the talk would be about the one subject they would all have in common—women."[15]

It was a very different world the Achesons traveled to on the morning of July 2—Rio de Janeiro via Dakar.

Unlike most other Latin American countries, Brazil, because of its size and potential economic power, had been visited by other American secretaries of state—Elihu Root, Charles Evans Hughes, Cordell Hull, Edward Stettinius, and General Marshall. Acheson shared the view of his predecessors that Brazil and Mexico were the "key countries" in the development of the hemisphere. His visit to the industrial metropolis of São Paulo impressed him with its air of dynamic capitalism. As a whole, though, Acheson did not pay much attention to Latin America, and his policy toward that continent was one of benign paternalism.

Latin America received little economic assistance from the United States during his years in office. Acheson was especially hostile to extending much military aid to countries in that region on the grounds that arms would simply strengthen the "power of existing regimes, most of which were military dictatorships."

Acheson was remarkably tolerant of Latin American economic nationalism. When Bolivia nationalized its tin mines in 1951, he refused to impose sanctions on that country. In his view, economic sanctions tended to play into the hands of extremists among the Latin Americans, and while he might deplore some manifestations of the new nationalism, he was not about to campaign against it, even though he did expect that foreign owners would be compensated for nationalized industries. He also opposed congressional action to raise tariffs, which he believed would be disastrous for the economies of the countries in question. Above all, it was a cardinal rule of his foreign policy not to use American armed forces in the hemisphere.

No doubt Acheson's policy of minimal U.S. involvement in the region did not aid Latin American countries to modernize or democratize, but his approach cannot be said to have worsened U.S.-Latin American relations, as the more activist policies of subsequent administrations often did. Acheson's relative indifference did not lead to covert operations against elected governments, as occurred in Guatemala in 1954, and there was no instance of overt U.S. military intervention during the Acheson era.[16]

That summer, Acheson, as was traditional for secretaries of state, played little part in the presidential campaign. On July 25 Adlai Stevenson, governor of Illinois, was nominated in Chicago as the Democratic Party's candidate for president. Acheson had known and worked with Stevenson during the war, and his wife had known Stevenson since childhood. The candidate was determined to distance himself from Truman and Acheson as much as he could, and while both men understood his need to do so, they were not happy at the cool treatment accorded them. To Acheson, Stevenson was "a good staff officer but without the stuff of command." Still very much the target of Republican ire, Acheson had no thought of receiving any post in a Stevenson administration; it was likely that Stevenson would have selected a far more idealistic person as secretary of state, perhaps someone like Chester Bowles, rather than a pragmatic realist of Acheson's stripe.

Stevenson did not ask Acheson's advice during the campaign against the Republican candidate, General Eisenhower. Nor did Acheson offer any. Only in his defense of Truman's policies did Acheson indirectly support Stevenson. Nonetheless, while the campaign progressed and the administration found itself hobbled in pushing its policies through a wary or indifferent Congress, Acheson soldiered on. He did make two partisan speeches before trade unions that had been particularly loyal to the president.

In early September he addressed the powerful Machinists Union in Kansas City. There he responded sharply to criticism, leveled especially by John Foster Dulles, of policies that had received bipartisan support. It was a new experience, he told the gathering, to be urged to be dynamic, positive, and bold by those who had hitherto had their hands on the horn and their feet on the brakes. He was fed up with criticism that the Truman administration had been too hesitant in pursuing its chosen policies and was contemptuous of both Dulles's rhetoric of "liberating" the countries of Eastern Europe and his describing the containment policy as "negative, immoral, and futile."

Containment, in fact, was a word Acheson was not particularly fond of, for it seemed to cast him in a passive mode that was far from the reality of his disposition to take decisive action. What "better concrete, specific acts with which to meet concrete specific problems" did the Republicans have in mind? He accused them of believing that words solved problems; instead, he concluded, "The pattern of leadership is a pattern of responsibility."[17]

But he was most bitter in responding to a speech Eisenhower gave in Cincinnati, Taft's hometown, accusing Acheson of inviting the attack on South Korea by putting it outside "America's so-called defensive perimeter." In a press conference on September 26, Acheson scorned Eisenhower's distortion of what the general himself knew to be the official defensive perimeter as developed by the military at that time. "I cannot believe General Eisenhower now means to imply that Korea should have been included by me within the defensive perimeter and that it should have been manned by American troops. Certainly, as Chief of Staff of the Army, his opinion was quite to the contrary and wholly in accordance with the statement I made."[18]

His last speech during the campaign period came in October, to a gathering at the Armoury in Washington, convened by the National Council of Churches to inaugurate a new translation of the Bible. Here Acheson took the occasion to warn his audience against the extremism of those who hated the Soviet Union and, in the heat of the Cold War, had even come to hate their neighbors. His message was simple: One did not have to hate in order to love one's country.[19]

On election night, November 4, 1952, the Achesons were at the house of friends, watching television and listening to the returns. Except for Justice Frankfurter and themselves, most of those present were young people—Acheson's children and their associates from various parts of government—and as the news came in of Stevenson's overwhelming defeat, far greater than the polls had predicted, the young were in despair. They turned to Acheson and asked him, What were they to do?

Acheson spoke as an elder statesman. He believed that despite the bitter tone of the campaign, it was "not necessarily a bad thing" that the Democrats, who had been in power for so long, should lose. "You must accept it," he counseled them, "the way someday you accept growing old."

It might also be no bad thing for the Democrats to have "a fallow period." He urged them to let their emotions "stay barren, let new seeds germinate," at least for a year or so. Except through the exercise and discipline of power, how would the opposition understand the problems that they so easily criticized? Above all, "give them a chance."

What the Democrats needed were new ideas, and if these ideas were wise, they would be picked up by "the new people in the Democratic Party, people whom we don't even know yet because they haven't appeared," and they "will have something to go on."

The next morning Felix Frankfurter sent him a note. “Those words of yours,” he wrote, “could have been spoken only by one who had lived them in the fiery furnace that burns out all that is petty and personal, and sees the contingencies of life in the perspective of the enduring.”[20]

In this spirit, Truman and Acheson were determined to do everything they could to ease the transition. Truman was especially mindful of how little he had been told about FDR’s policies prior to Roosevelt’s death. Obviously the president bore full responsibility for all policies until noon of January 20, 1953, the day of the inauguration. Truman did not expect Eisenhower to share in these responsibilities, but he did want to make sure the new administration was fully informed.

To this end, on November 18 Truman arranged a meeting with President-elect Eisenhower and his aides, Senator Henry Cabot Lodge of Massachusetts, who had engineered his nomination; and Joseph Dodge of Detroit, who had advised Acheson on financial relations with Japan after the peace treaty and who would be named Eisenhower’s director of the Bureau of the Budget. Present from the administration were Acheson, Lovett, and Harriman.

It was not a successful meeting. Acheson went over certain key problems: the question of repatriation of Korean prisoners of war; the state of play in the Anglo-Iranian dispute; and French problems with contributing to European defense as well as France’s war in Indochina, a dual crisis that might well come to a head during the Eisenhower administration.

What was disturbing was Eisenhower’s demeanor—what Truman later called “frozen grimness.” In a preliminary, private meeting between the president and the president-elect, Truman had tried to put the general at ease by offering him a large and magnificent globe that Eisenhower had used in World War II and that he had given Truman at Potsdam. The general accepted the generous offer but remained unsmiling.

In the larger meeting, the general appeared tense. Gone were what Acheson described as the “good nature and easy manner tending toward loquacity.” Eisenhower seemed “embarrassed and reluctant” to be with them—“wary, withdrawn, and taciturn to the point of surliness.” The notion that an efficient and even-tempered changing of the guard could take place now appeared lost.[21]

Acheson’s meeting on December 3 with John Foster Dulles, who had been named Eisenhower’s secretary of state, was no more productive. Dulles said that he expected to devote himself almost entirely to policy matters and not spend as much time as Acheson had on personnel and administrative matters. Acheson was highly skeptical of this approach—it was precisely the secretary's ability to choose and handle those who worked under him that would be crucial to the successful conduct of foreign policy.

The question of personnel was Acheson's greatest concern. He was well aware that those closely associated with him, and especially with his Asia policy, were likely to be treated badly by the new administration. As he wrote later, toward his subordinates the secretary of state "must be their protector and inspirer, their critic, the appreciator of excellence, harsh toward shoddiness or conclusions contrived to comply with the currently accepted notions. He cannot be aloof. He must share and guide their thoughts, partake of their complexities . . . so that the product of their common work is advice which the government of this nation can wisely and practically put into execution in the world as it is." These words aptly described Acheson's own relationship with his colleagues and can also be read as a reproof of Dulles's style of management.[22]

Of special concern was the case of John Carter Vincent, with whom Acheson had worked closely on China matters. Charges against him of disloyalty had been investigated and dismissed by the State Department's Loyalty and Security Board. But in mid-December the President's Loyalty Review Board had reached, by a vote of three to two, a conclusion of "reasonable doubt" regarding Vincent's loyalty. Acheson believed that the charges against Vincent were in reality "based upon the policies that he had recommended and the valuations of situations he had made and that largely I had accepted."

In a memorandum he sent to Truman, Acheson strongly defended Vincent's right to report the facts as he had seen them. While the president's board had noted "Mr. Vincent's studied praise of Chinese Communists and equally studied criticism of Chiang Kai-shek," Acheson replied that it was not Vincent's job "merely to report success of existing policy but also to report on the aspects in which it was failing and the reasons therefor."

Acheson had a good opinion of the State Department's Loyalty Board but a very low one of the President's Loyalty Review Board, which Truman had set up in 1947, and of its chairman, Senator Hiram Bingham of Connecticut, whom he knew well from Connecticut ties. After the presidential board's decision, Vincent was suspended from active duty in mid-December, until the secretary returned from Europe to deal with the problem. Adrian Fisher, Acheson's legal adviser, believed that he could disregard the board and restore Vincent to active duty. In Acheson's view, however, a better course would be to appoint a distinguished panel of impeccable authority and reputation to review the record and the two conflicting recommendations. As chairman, Acheson suggested Judge Learned Hand, the recently retired senior judge for the U.S. Court of Appeals for the Second Circuit in New York. Truman assented.

Before appointing the review board, Acheson again met with Dulles, this time on the afternoon of Christmas Eve. After further briefing him on European matters, he turned to the Vincent case. Dulles listened respectfully to Acheson's suggestion to appoint Judge Hand's advisory group, and he told Acheson that he would be glad to talk to any members of the advisory group who wished to contact him; the appointment of the group was, of course, wholly Acheson's responsibility.

It was a deliberately evasive reply. Once in office, Dulles informed Judge Hand that he did not need the special review group to act on the Vincent matter, and on March 4, 1953, he rendered his own decision. He wrote that he did not find Vincent a "security" risk, but he also wrote that he did not believe that Vincent could usefully continue to serve as a Foreign Service officer. Vincent therefore offered his resignation and applied for retirement, which Dulles granted.

After he left office, Acheson commented bitterly that while Vincent had been vindicated, Dulles had no reason to conclude that Vincent's professional judgment had fallen below some undefined standard. By finding Vincent's judgment and services defective or substandard, Dulles contributed significantly to a lowering of morale of the State Department.[23]

In a further defense of those accused of disloyalty, Acheson during his last weeks in office refused to turn over to the Senate Internal Security Subcommittee a list of Americans employed by the United Nations. Similarly, when a subcommittee of the House Judiciary Committee asked for this list, Acheson replied that to make public the names of those assigned to controversial tasks would put pressure on them to avoid these tasks "or to perform them with an eye to popular emotions and to their own defense."

As far as Acheson was concerned, as he said to the members of the subcommittee, he would not "snatch the knotted cord from the hand of God and deal out murderous blows to my associates."[24]

Escaping from Washington, Acheson attended his last NATO Council meeting in Paris in mid-December. It was becoming increasingly evident that the ratification of the European Defense Community was in deep trouble not only because of French fears of German rearmament, but also because the British remained unwilling to throw in their lot with Europe. Had the British been willing to join the European Defense Community, the French National Assembly would have doubtless ratified the treaty. Acheson well understood the reason for the British position—their desperate need to retain a "special relationship" with the United States, their reluctance to abandon the remnants of empire—but he was also aware of the illusions the British held of their ability to act as a great power.

Meeting with Jean Monnet on December 14, Acheson found the usually ebullient Frenchman despondent over Britain's attitude. If there was to be any real progress toward European unity, Monnet insisted, the British must "support and not impede true unity on the continent and then associate themselves, without giving up their ultimate sovereignty, with the new united Europe."[25]

Acheson pointed out to Monnet how far the United States had come to fulfill European desires—the Marshall Plan, the North Atlantic Treaty, the stationing of American troops abroad in peacetime. However badly the British might behave, it was up to the Germans and the French to create their own future.

In his farewell speech to the NATO Council, Acheson exhorted the Europeans not to falter in their quest for unity. Through continental strength and purpose he believed the British would eventually be brought across the Channel, and Canada and the United States would be drawn into ever-closer association with Europe. These were prophetic words, for it was the success of the European Common Market in the 1960s that finally persuaded Britain to join Europe. But genuine British enthusiasm for Europe would be lacking for the rest of the century. On the other hand, despite Acheson's worries over American isolationism, the United States would remain committed to Europe and even in the aftermath of the Cold War retain military forces on the continent.[26]

With the inauguration of Eisenhower only three weeks away, Acheson made his last farewells. On January 9, at a cabinet meeting, Acheson, on behalf of his colleagues, presented the president with his cabinet chair, which they had bought from the government.[27] At his last press conference, Acheson spoke of the bond of mutual loyalty between Truman and his "chief servants and associates." That evening the president and a group of friends, including Chief Justice Fred Vinson and Clark Clifford, came to dine at the Achesons' house. It was a relaxed evening, with a good deal of banter at the expense of the chief justice, who was alleged to have employed excessive language in addressing the president during a poker game.

On the last day of business, Friday, January 16, several thousand State Department employees gathered in the open space behind the building on 21st Street. Acheson commented later that few experiences had so moved him. As he wrote in his memoirs, his colleagues in the department "had been through three years of bitter persecution and vilification, largely at the hands of fools and self-seeking blackguards."

In thanking them for presenting him with his own cabinet chair, Acheson once again sounded the theme of loyalty. He tried to encourage and comfort them, as he was about to leave and whatever protection he had been able to offer them would be withdrawn. "One thing you are entitled to ask—that you should not be vilified; that your loyalty should not be brought in doubt; that slanders and libels should not be made against you."

Evoking his great predecessor, John Quincy Adams, whose portrait hung in his office, Acheson recalled that Adams "never for one moment believed that the holding of office was a source of power—it was an obligation of service."

All that afternoon his office door stood open, and a steady line of well-wishers passed through to shake his hand.

As Truman knew, Acheson's loyalty to him had been firm and total. Never did Acheson go behind the president's back to further his own agenda, never did he betray to colleagues their differences. Acheson never forgot, as he wrote later, "who was President, and the President most punctiliously remembered who was Secretary of State." Acheson admired "the basic integrity" of Truman's character, and Truman repaid the compliment. Similarly, Acheson wrote that Truman was "free of the greatest vice in a leader, his ego never came between him and his job."

Truman might have said the same of Acheson. While Acheson could be accused at times of arrogance and impatience, his reverence for the office of secretary of state matched Harry Truman's of the presidency. When Truman received Acheson's official resignation from office, he responded that he considered Acheson "among the very greatest of the Secretaries of State the country has had."[28]

On Inauguration Day, January 20, 1953, low clouds hung over the city on a chill morning. But the sun broke through shortly before the new president was to take the oath of office.

Truman accompanied Eisenhower to the dais, as was customary, but the ride from the White House to the Capitol was a singularly cool one. When at eleven-thirty A.M. the Eisenhowers arrived at the North Portico to begin the drive to the Capitol, they refused even to come in for a cup of coffee. Only when the Trumans appeared did the Eisenhowers step out of the automobile to greet them. Truman was deeply hurt by the general's rudeness.

Less than half an hour after the inauguration, Truman and his family were on their way to Acheson's house for a farewell luncheon before taking the train to Missouri. Gathered at P Street were members of the former president's staff and cabinet, as well as their spouses. The street was jammed with friends and admirers. Each arrival at the door was vociferously cheered, and even after all the guests had assembled, from outside the brick town house chants of "We want Harry!" went on and on until the former president stepped out onto the little front terrace to thank them.

After a lunch, described by Margaret Truman as "an absolutely wonderful affair full of jokes and laughter and a few tears," the Trumans retired for a short rest before going to Union Station for their late afternoon train to Kansas City.

The Achesons went to the station to see them off. Much to the astonishment of both Truman and Acheson, the terminal was packed with a vast crowd. Dignitaries from the cabinet and the Senate, generals and ambassadors, all piled aboard the train to shake Truman's hand.

At six-thirty, with the crowd singing "Auld Lang Syne," the train began pulling slowly out of the station, with Truman, his wife, and his daughter waving from the rear platform. How different was Truman's leavetaking from that day in 1946 when Acheson, alone, appeared on the same platform to welcome a discredited president who had led his party to defeat in congressional elections.

As Truman disappeared into the darkness of the winter night, Acheson turned to a reporter and said above the noise, "There's the best friend in the world."[29]

PART V

THE WARRIOR IN EXILE

CHAPTER THIRTY

REJOINING THE FRAY

IT WAS "the longest, gayest and happiest time," Acheson wrote to his friends Archibald and Ada MacLeish. His wife echoed his words: "You really can never know what you did for two ragged and tattered souls."[1]

The Achesons had joined the MacLeishes at their house on the Caribbean island of Antigua for two months of vacation after Acheson left office. For a man who generally preferred his Maryland retreat of Harewood to vacationing in foreign climes, Antigua was a revelation.

The MacLeishes had discovered the island during the Christmas holidays of 1950 and lived at the Mill Reef Club. The "Club" included up to three hundred acres, and charter members were expected to build homes on parcels of land along the water. Located in the Lesser Antilles, Antigua had been a British colony since the time Horatio Nelson sailed into its protected harbor. It was a small island, about 108 square miles, and had survived mainly by producing sugar. By the late 1940s that business was fading.

With warm days and cool nights, MacLeish thought Antigua was "the best climate in the world." For the next twenty-five years the MacLeishes spent part of the winter on the island, a blessed relief from the harsh Massachusetts climate, where MacLeish lived and taught poetry at Harvard.

Not surprisingly, the Mill Reef Club membership came to be made up almost entirely of rich and successful businessmen. To dilute this mix, the MacLeishes wanted the company of the Achesons, who were so taken with its beauty that they would visit the island regularly over the next two decades. Both the Achesons and the MacLeishes found other close friends, especially Betty and John Cowles, the latter an outspoken but warm man who was president of the *Minneapolis Star and Tribune.*[2]

Acheson, thoroughly exhausted after the last, trying years of the Korean War and the attacks he had undergone from McCarthy and his followers, embraced what MacLeish called the "liquid velvet" water of the Caribbean. Above all, he found time to read. He was especially fascinated by the correspondence between John Adams and Thomas Jefferson; writing to former president Truman, Acheson urged him to read these letters, in which "one gets a wholly new affection for Adams."

He was equally delighted by the letters exchanged by Oliver Wendell Holmes and Harold Laski, the British socialist who at one time was acquainted with every intellectual who counted on both sides of the Atlantic. Writing to his son, David, Acheson spoke of Laski as "a gay rascal . . . erudite, facile and really fond of Holmes. He gives the old man a sense of living which in those last years he got nowhere else."

To Jeffrey Kitchen, who had succeeded Luke Battle as his executive assistant at the close of his period as secretary, Acheson extolled the pleasures of being in a "state of nature." "I am brown, saturated with sun, salt water and rum," he wrote, "and full of reading such as I have not done for twenty years. Day follows day without any real working (since I sleep whenever I feel like it regardless of light or dark). If there ever was a lad relaxed or on his way to it, and fast, it is yours truly. As I just read in Holmes to Laski—'At 90 it is time to begin to learn golf and possibly resume horseback riding—but the world is all before you.'"[3]

The return to Washington was less than agreeable. Acheson had cracked two bones in his toe, and Alice's new pictures were temporarily misplaced by the airline. Above all, as he wrote MacLeish in late March, "The political atmosphere in Washington is unbelievable. . . . On one side is McCarthy who has no limit, only infinity; on the other side Taft, his protector, whose limit is not yet in sight."[4]

Before returning to Covington and Burling, Acheson took another month off in order to spend April at Harewood, where he contemplated his future and continued to indulge his passion for cabinet making. He had taken it up after he returned to office in 1949, and it took total concentration to avoid the risk of losing a finger or hand from the electric saw. It was a way, as he wrote later, of keeping "sane when I was Secretary of State."[5]

But he was also frankly concerned that he would return to the law with little enthusiasm and, moreover, that he would find it hard to attract new clients. Felix Frankfurter feared that "he might go stale." The Supreme Court justice believed that the "difference in the two schemes of life is about that between French cooking and hardtack."[6]

Acheson was right to be apprehensive. After his return to the firm in May, he wrote his old partner George Rublee that the period of adjustment was proving to be "a hard one." He admitted that he had been exhausted. "For months I just did not have the energy or desire for much of anything but rest and reading." Worse yet, he found himself in a state of "bewildered emptiness at being so wholly uninformed, impotent, and on the outside." He hoped that work would get him over his uncharacteristic melancholy.[7]

In addition, he had picked up a bacterial infection, and this was a further hindrance to an energetic return to work at the firm. More important, Acheson found himself with not enough to do once he did come back. Considered one of the finest legal minds in Washington, he was now seen as tainted by McCarthy's accusations; quite simply, he was perceived as "controversial," which corporations, especially if their inclinations were Republican, hated. In a city that reflected the mood of a new administration that showed little disposition to curb McCarthy's excesses, Acheson found himself uncommonly isolated. Years later, his wife recalled those days when "people turned their backs" on the Achesons and "wouldn't speak to us." Very few of these people they counted as friends, but nonetheless it was an unexpectedly cruel rebuff.[8]

For the rest of his life Acheson remained at Covington, but he handled very few important cases. Within two years after his return to the firm, he filed two briefs before the Supreme Court that were successful. The only highlight came in the 1960s, when he represented the government of Cambodia in a case against Thailand involving ownership of an ancient temple, before the World Court at The Hague.[9]

For an active mind like Acheson's, there was simply not enough interesting work. As he wrote in 1955 to Sir Oliver Franks, "These past two years have been quiet and uneventful ones with us. In a way that was good because we were tired. But it has also been a let-down. My professional life has not revived with enough vigor to keep the dust out of my mind."[10]

With time on his hands, he soon began to write essays and reminiscences, starting with a book on his lifelong commitment to the Democratic Party.

His devotion to Yale University never flagged. Elected in 1936 as a trustee of the Yale Corporation, the governing body, he served in it for more than twenty years. In the wake of Acheson's first visit to Antigua, MacLeish was asked by Harvard to sound out Acheson to see if he would accept a university professorship, which MacLeish believed he might prefer to returning to the practice of law. "It's perfect, Dean," the poet said. "There are no fixed rules about residence or teaching. We could go to Antigua in the winter just as we do now. The pay is good and the company is wonderful." Acheson admitted that the offer was enticing, but he just couldn't do it. What was the obstacle? MacLeish asked. Acheson responded: "The train to Boston goes through New Haven."[11]

Despite his government posts, Acheson made great efforts to get to the corporation's meetings and follow what was going on during the presidency of Charles Seymour, from 1937 to 1950. Seymour's conservatism helped perpetuate the composition of a traditional Yale undergraduate body that Acheson believed was not as intellectually gifted or oriented as it should be. When Seymour retired in 1950, Acheson and his close friend and colleague on the corporation, Wilmarth Lewis, were eager to rejuvenate the university.[12]

The two men had their candidate—Whitney Griswold, a forty-three-year-old professor of history, who was committed to educational excellence. In the years to come, Griswold, a flinty New Englander—opinionated, witty, and independent—did indeed raise the intellectual level of the undergraduate body. During that time Acheson came to love the man, and on the afternoon Griswold died in 1963, he sat at his bedside and, when talk tired him, held his hand.[13]

Acheson's passion to improve the quality of students at Yale and require more rigorous training of them contrasted vividly with his own behavior as an undergraduate. Just as Acheson later regretted his constant state of rebelliousness while a schoolboy, his commitment to excellence at Yale was in part a reproach to his own extravagant undergraduate days.

In a memorandum he prepared for the corporation in 1957 but sent only to Griswold, he urged Yale to commit itself to educate students of "exceptional talent." He pressed for a highly meritocratic undergraduate body, one that would allow late bloomers "to bloom somewhere else." And he believed "the dogma of the inviolability of tenure" for members of the faculty should be modified "by a plucking board to get rid of dead wood."[14]

Acheson's was a frankly elitist program. It was designed to strip the college of shoddy intellectual standards, brought about in part by admitting such a large proportion of alumni children, and, in a very real sense, to change radically the anti-intellectual Yale of his own youth.

As a noted lawyer, Acheson took a particular interest in the condition of the Yale Law School. In 1939, under the Seymour presidency, he suggested Harry Shulman, who was Jewish, as his first choice to become dean of the school. In his letter to Seymour recommending Shulman, he asserted that the "discussion really comes down to the question of race. You know how I feel about this." He said he felt "stronger than ever that I should like to see some of us act upon a belief in the old decencies which everyone professes, even though there may be some who won't like it."[15]

Although the Yale Law School had had Jewish professors since 1922, there was no question that Shulman, a former clerk to Justice Brandeis and the first choice of the law school faculty, was turned down because he was a Jew.[16]

When the deanship came open again in 1954, Griswold was enthusiastically on

Acheson's side in supporting Shulman as dean. Acheson sent a six-page letter to Griswold on December 18, 1953. Citing his respect for Shulman's mind and character, Acheson noted that "the longer I live the more I find myself stressing character as the indispensable element."[17] His letter proved decisive.

Shulman died suddenly in March 1955, but the mold had been broken. Four of the law school deans who followed him were Jewish, starting with Eugene Rostow, who had served in the State Department under Acheson and whom Acheson warmly supported.[18]

During these years out of government, Acheson's relations with Truman grew, if anything, even warmer. Upon his return to Independence, the former president thanked Acheson fervently for the farewell tendered him by his secretary of state. "It was the happiest luncheon I ever had or ever will have," he wrote. "May we never lose contact."[19]

It was not long before both men were bemoaning the state of the nation under the stewardship of Eisenhower and his secretary of state, John Foster Dulles. Acheson complained to Truman in late May 1953 that "Ike's abdication has given us Congressional government, directionless and feeble, which de Tocqueville feared would result from the Constitution." With Stalin's death in March and an uncertain succession period at hand, Acheson reminded the ex-president that "we used to say that in a tight pinch we could generally rely on some fool play of the Russians to pull us through. Now that is being exactly reversed. They now have, as invaluable allies [in Washington], division, weakness and folly."

He agreed with Truman that "you and I are very likely to be in for another period of attack and vilification." He suspected that "Taft will turn McCarthy loose on us . . . to give Taft the kind of Republican majority which would insist on a policy which Taft would control, and which would make Ike the captive of the right wing."[20]

A Truman visit to Washington in June 1953 was an occasion for much joy and self-congratulation. Averell Harriman and Acheson met with Truman at the Mayflower Hotel and worked on a speech Truman was planning to deliver to the Reserve Officers Association in Philadelphia. They were careful to make sure the former president did not criticize Eisenhower too forcefully, but at the same time they pointed out that "policy consisted of more than mere assertion."[21]

The daily tribulations of life at the farm and in Georgetown, the slow start to his law practice, these Acheson bore with as good humor as he could, but he ached to get back into the public arena. By August he was thoroughly fed up with the purges Dulles was carrying out in the State Department, sacrificing the careers and especially the reputations of those especially connected with Acheson's policies. As he wrote to Luke Battle, now serving abroad, "Dulles' people seem to me like Cossacks quartered in a grand old city hall, burning the panelling to cook with."[22]

It was time for him to rejoin the fray. On October 1, 1953, at a Woodrow Wilson Foundation dinner, he tore into Senator Joseph McCarthy for his "insults" to America's allies and for his "totalitarian" methods. Adlai Stevenson praised him, and the party chairman, Thomas Finletter, encouraged him to speak out as strongly as he wished. For the rest of the decade that was exactly what Acheson did.

What particularly disturbed Acheson was Eisenhower's "New Look," a defense doctrine calling for heavy cuts in conventional military forces and greater reliance on nuclear weapons. As Foster Dulles described it, the United States would "depend primarily upon a great capacity to retaliate instantly, by means and at places of our own choosing." It was a policy that soon became known as "massive retaliation."

Just as Acheson had urged a buildup of conventional forces after 1949 rather than depending on atomic bombs for America's defense, so now he feared that this "defense on the cheap" could turn a border incident into a nuclear war. A policy of what was called the "bigger bang for the buck" seemed to him a dangerous return to an isolationist foreign policy.[23]

In a scathing article in *The New York Times Magazine* in March 1954, Acheson asserted that America's moral position in the world depended on "our very nature" as "defenders, not offenders." It was folly to base strategy on the threat or use of nuclear weapons. Although Acheson believed that the nation required a strong atomic striking force so that "the mutual suicide of general war will be rejected by all," he was convinced that the United States needed strong conventional forces for dealing "with lesser aggressions." For Acheson, the idea that the United States could not afford to fight a conventional war was wholly wrong. The American economy, in his view, was perfectly capable "of supporting what is necessary for its own survival."[24]

As Acheson chafed in exile, he was especially riled at the moralizing rhetoric of his successor, John Foster Dulles, who depicted the Cold War as a struggle that pitted Christianity against godless communism. In the election campaign Dulles had railed against the "treadmill" policies of Acheson, calling for a "policy of boldness" that would not merely contain but "roll back" communism and "liberate" the areas under Communist control.[25]

Acheson was a pragmatic realist whose moral code, like his father's, was embedded in behavior and action. Like the theologian Reinhold Niebuhr, one of the preeminent realists of the period, he believed that power could not be divorced from morality. This meant, for example, that during the Cold War American power had to oppose Soviet power. By disavowing the responsibilities of power, the United States would invoke far worse guilt than whatever guilt came from wielding power.

As Acheson wrote Truman in early 1954, "Power is at the root of most relationships—by no means the only factor, but one of vast importance. A balance of power has proved the best international sheriff we have ever had."[26]

In his book *Power and Diplomacy*, published in 1958, Acheson inveighed against unlimited force and unlimited objectives, which was embodied in the Eisenhower/Dulles rhetoric of rolling back communism in Eastern Europe and elsewhere. On the other hand, the limited use of force for limited purposes, which should have been employed by Britain and France and the United States in the 1930s, could have "preserved a balance, stability, and restraint in international affairs which we might now envy."

Acheson urged moderation in international affairs, which led him to object to threatening adversaries with massive retaliation. The ability and willingness to fight limited wars for limited ends, as he believed the United States had demonstrated in the Korean War, was the prerequisite for a realistic American foreign policy. "A threat," Acheson said, "is not believed and therefore cannot deter, unless there is general conviction that the threatener has both the capacity and the intention to carry out the threat."

Acheson warned against dealing as a nation with the peoples of other nations "through preachments." Not, he cautioned, "because moral principles can, or should be, excluded from the relations of states to one another," but "to characterize conduct between nations as moral or immoral will involve us in confusions of vocabulary and of thought." He made the classic realist distinction between relations between individuals and those between states: "The substance of all discussion, which concerns the conduct of individuals within a society toward one another, is more likely to be misleading if applied to the relations of one society to another."

In his conclusion, he attacked Dulles without naming him: "On one thing only I feel a measure of assurance—on the rightness of contempt for sanctimonious self-righteousness which . . . beclouds the dangers and opportunities of our time with an unctuous film. For this is the ultimate sin."[27]

Fearing Republican attacks on Acheson's loyalty and competence, Adlai Stevenson tried to distance himself from Acheson during his 1952 and 1956 presidential campaigns. Two events, however, brought Acheson back into favor with the leaders of the Democratic Party. The first was Dulles's handling of the October 1956

British-French-Israeli invasion of Egypt following Gamal Abdel Nasser's seizure of the Suez Canal, which was controlled and operated by the British. Acheson attacked Dulles mercilessly for precipitating the crisis by abruptly canceling the financing of the Aswan High Dam project on the Nile River with British, American, and World Bank monies. At this insult to Egypt's national pride, Nasser occupied the canal, an act that, according to Acheson, Nasser might not have taken for a few years more.

Acheson believed that Dulles made matters worse by vacillating once the canal was under Egyptian control. There should have been a forceful Western response; but rather than blaming British prime minister Anthony Eden for failing immediately to reclaim the canal, Acheson blamed Dulles, who kept proclaiming that a peaceful solution was at hand. Then, when the tardy British-French expedition was launched to retake the canal, the United States lined up with the Soviet Union to condemn America's allies. As a result, Acheson charged, Nasser "was given a victory of unprecedented proportions."[28]

The second event involved Dulles's refusal to aid the Hungarian rebels during that same period. In October, young revolutionaries in Hungary had marched and fought against an orthodox Communist regime. When a reformist Communist government then came into power and sought independence from the Soviet bloc, the Russians sent tanks into Budapest on November 4 to restore a regime subservient to Moscow. In part because Dulles had repeatedly called for the "liberation" of Eastern Europe, the Hungarians were encouraged to believe that American help would be forthcoming. None materialized. Hungary was once again in the grip of the Soviet Union. Acheson believed that his own record contrasted favorably with Dulles's false promises and indecision.

In order to help the Democrats in the 1956 presidential campaign, in June 1955 Acheson had published a book, *A Democrat Looks at His Party.* Once again he attacked the doctrine of massive retaliation, asserting that "atomic war has no positive place as an element of policy." He also praised the New Deal as "a clinic in the use of innovation to conserve and strengthen fundamental institutions." The answer to America's problems was clear: The people should elect a Democrat as president in 1956.[29]

But Adlai Stevenson, again the Democrats' candidate that year, did not want Acheson at his side, and Acheson was as deeply skeptical of Stevenson's ability to lead the nation in 1956 as he was four years earlier. As he told Harvard professor Robert Bowie in 1952, when asked his opinion of Stevenson, "Adlai has a third-rate mind that he can't make up."[30]

Although Acheson was asked to help draft the party platform on foreign policy for the 1956 Democratic convention, little of his words appeared in the final version. His language was too vehement, although some of his advice, such as urging a new administration to pursue a policy of "intelligent neglect" toward Communist China, was adopted. Acheson nonetheless attacked Eisenhower in a speech that he gave in September to a Democratic club in Maryland, which was printed in *The New York Times*. "This administration has been playing Russian roulette with an atomic pistol," he said of Eisenhower's policy of massive retaliation.[31]

For Acheson, the central axis of American foreign policy ran through Europe. Despite his concerns over the cohesiveness of the Atlantic Alliance, he was highly encouraged by the political direction of European affairs. With the formal creation of the Common Market—when France, Belgium, the Netherlands, Germany, Luxembourg, and Italy signed the Treaties of Rome in 1957—Acheson believed that Jean Monnet's vision of a unified Europe was fast coming into being. "The success of the movement toward unity in the West is no longer in doubt," Acheson wrote in 1957.[32]

Just at the time that these signs of a true West European political community were appearing, George Kennan, now a visiting professor at Oxford University, delivered the prestigious Reith Lectures over the BBC in six half-hour sessions beginning November 10, 1957. Because of his reputation as the foremost American Soviet scholar, Kennan's talks received wide publicity. Moreover, they were delivered at a time when NATO was considering whether or not to deploy tactical nuclear weapons in Western Europe, and in response to the first successful Russian testing of an intercontinental ballistic missile.

In essence, Kennan called for a joint Anglo-American and Soviet withdrawal of troops from central Europe. He supported a reunified, neutral Germany and urged both superpowers to adopt a hands-off policy in Europe as the most effective way of assuring European stability in the nuclear age.

For Kennan, the continued division of Europe was a central cause of instability. He had opposed the rearmament of Germany within NATO when Acheson was in power and believed that Washington's insistence that even a fully unified Germany would be free to become a member of NATO was totally unrealistic. (He surely must have been astonished to see a reunified Germany come into being in 1990, and then indeed become a member of NATO—and with the acquiescence of the Russians.[33])

Many in West Germany, especially members of the Social Democratic Party, welcomed Kennan's plan; and due to a misperception in Europe that Kennan exerted strong influence within the Democratic Party, his words carried great weight. Spurred on by pro-NATO forces in the United States, Acheson struck back.

His first riposte came in January 1958, in response to a request by the American Council on Germany. Acheson's "Reply to Kennan" was widely disseminated, along with statements supporting Acheson from, among others, Truman, Stevenson, Lyndon Johnson, and John F. Kennedy.

Acheson sharply dissociated himself and the Democratic Party from Kennan's proposal for a withdrawal of American and Soviet troops from Europe. He rested his case mainly on the contention that without an American military presence to counter the Soviet military threat, a united, pro-Western Germany would not be possible. For Acheson a mutual American-Soviet withdrawal would also lead to a new wave of U.S. isolationism. There was no guarantee that the Soviets would not put pressure on a neutral Germany to adhere to Soviet policies and no assurance that the United States would do anything to prevent this.

Acheson minced no words in attacking Kennan directly. After paying tribute to Kennan's deep knowledge of Russian history, he declared: "Mr. Kennan has never, in my judgment, grasped the realities of power relationships but takes a rather mystical attitude toward them. To Mr. Kennan there is no military threat in Europe."[34]

The severity of Acheson's criticisms hurt Kennan, who wrote Frank Altshul, a pillar of the Council on Foreign Relations, that Acheson and he "had always been friends; and mere disagreements about policy have never been occasions for public personal attacks in the world of human relations to which I thought we both belonged."[35]

Acheson felt compelled to explain himself to his friends, many of whom agreed with him on substance but were troubled by the tone of his attack. "I can quite understand that the Kennan-Acheson brawl causes pain to our mutual friends," he wrote to Philip Jessup. "George always engenders more solicitude in others than he shows for others. But . . . I was not writing for our friends nor to put forward a gentle caveat. I was writing for the Germans to destroy as effectively as I could the corroding effects of what he said and the belief that he was a seer in such matters."[36]

Acheson published a second, more measured response to Kennan in an article, which appeared in *Foreign Affairs* in April 1958. Acheson argued that disengagement from Europe was a synonym for isolationism: "the same futile—and lethal—attempt to crawl back into the cocoon of history. For us there is only one disengagement possible—the final one, the disengagement from life, which is death."

Acheson's argument rested also on the expectation that if the United States withdrew its troops from Europe, it was likely that soon they would be withdrawn from bases in the Far East and Middle East. Moreover, it was hard to believe that Russia could "undertake so hazardous a course" as withdrawal. "For, if physical force were permanently removed from eastern Europe, who can believe that even one of the Communist regimes would survive?"

In Acheson's mind, a neutralized Germany posed a deadly risk. History showed that no country as large and powerful as a united Germany could be successfully isolated, situated as it was "between two power systems and with ambitions and purposes of its own." Yet "there would be no Power in Europe capable of opposing Russian will after the departure of the United States from the Continent and the acceptance of a broad, missile-free area."

As for the future unification of Germany, Acheson shared Konrad Adenauer's view that a rich and democratic West Germany would act as a magnet to the East in some undefined future: "Finally, a thriving Western Europe would continue its irresistible pull upon East Germany and Eastern Europe. This would, in turn, have its effect upon the demands of the Russian people on their government." The pressures for a higher standard of living in Russia would ultimately diminish "the Russian need for the forced communization and iron control of Eastern Europe." At that point, meaningful negotiations "looking toward a united Germany" and "the return of real national identity to the countries of Eastern Europe" could take place, which "has been the goal of Western policy for the past decade."[37]

What Acheson predicted with regard to a unified Germany and a national identity for the East European countries came to pass after Mikhail Gorbachev came to power in Moscow in the mid-1980s.

Shortly before the article was to appear in *Foreign Affairs,* Acheson made a gesture to ease the pain he had earlier inflicted on Kennan by sending him the proofs. After praising Kennan's historical scholarship, he wrote: "As to our difference over current policy, I shall save the argument for public utterance. The enclosed proofs I send along are not to harass you but so that, should you choose, you can see the whole thing rather than mere snatches, often misquoted. We have differed on this subject for too long for it to affect my deep regard and affection for you."[38]

Kennan himself never retreated from his own position on German neutralization and withdrawal of U.S. and Soviet forces from the center of Europe.[39] Yet in the second volume of his memoirs, published after Acheson's death, Kennan cited the criticisms of his own position in 1958 of Raymond Aron. Although the French political analyst admitted that the "present situation in Europe is abnormal," a fluid situation was far more risky.[40]

Shortly after Eisenhower's reelection in 1956, the Democratic National Committee was determined to reorganize itself and mount a forceful challenge to the Republicans before the 1960 election, when Eisenhower would not be running. By an executive committee resolution, a Democratic Advisory Council (DAC) was formed on November 27, 1956, to act as the party's policy arm.

Acheson, who by now had published another book, *A Citizen Looks at Congress*, was approached to become the chairman of the DAC's foreign policy committee, an appointment that was urged by Truman. To mollify the Stevenson wing of the party, Harvard economist John Kenneth Galbraith was named chairman of the DAC's economic policy committee.

With Paul Nitze serving as Acheson's vice chairman, the tone and substance of the Democratic Party's foreign policy positions changed from the softer Stevensonian line to a tougher approach toward the Soviet Union. Although the foreign policy committee included twenty-seven members, many of whom were Stevensonians, Acheson soon became the intellectual powerhouse of the group, largely because he had done his homework, whereas the others were often sadly unprepared. The Stevenson wing, which placed great emphasis on economic aid to underdeveloped countries, soon found that its views were given less weight than those of the Acheson-Nitze bloc, which placed greater emphasis on the United States developing its military strength in conventional arms and maintaining a strong Atlantic alliance.

During Eisenhower's second term, nothing disturbed Acheson more than the president's support for Chiang Kai-shek and his handling of the 1958 crisis over the two offshore islands of Quemoy and Ma-tsu. Four years earlier Eisenhower had withdrawn the U.S. Seventh Fleet from the Taiwan Strait. As the tiny Taiwanese islands of Quemoy and Ma-tsu were only a few miles off the Chinese mainland, Chiang began to use them as bases for commando raids against the mainland. When the Communist Chinese started shelling the islands in the autumn of 1954, Eisenhower defended the Nationalists' right to use these outposts; he accepted the connection between Quemoy's defense and that of Taiwan and let it be known that he was contemplating the use of nuclear weapons as a last resort if the mainland Chinese did not desist.[41]

Acheson was horrified that the administration would ever threaten nuclear retaliation on behalf of two useless islands. By late May 1955 an informal cease-fire went into effect. Then, in August 1958, the mainland Chinese began once again shelling the islands. The Eisenhower administration responded with another show of support for Chiang. Once again the Chinese backed off.

Acheson, in his role as the Democratic Party's foreign policy spokesman, denounced the president's "horrendous" handling of the crisis. "We seem to be drifting, either dazed or indifferent, toward war with China," he said on September 6, "a war without friends or allies and over issues which the Administration has not presented to the people and which are not worth a single American life."[42]

Acheson's general approach to foreign policy had been supported in the mid-1950s by Senator Lyndon Johnson, and by Sam Rayburn, the Speaker of the

House. For Johnson, who became Senate majority leader in 1957, Acheson represented a most valuable asset as the doyen of the eastern establishment; in preparing his run for the presidency in 1960, he could use Acheson to define himself as something more than a parochial southern politician. Johnson, who knew no bounds in flattering those he needed, sent Acheson frequent notes—on his birthday, when his mother died in 1958, and on holidays such as Christmas and Easter.[43]

The Democrats won a stunning victory in the 1958 congressional elections. Within the Democratic Advisory Council, the split between the Achesonians and the Stevensonians widened. As Acheson saw them, Chester Bowles and William Benton, founders of a successful advertising agency and longtime supporters of Stevenson's, were too softheaded. Eleanor Roosevelt, also a firm supporter of Stevenson's, was too much a "do-gooder." By now Acheson was fully convinced that an expanding American economy could afford additional defense expenditures.

In December 1959 Senator John F. Kennedy of Massachusetts, who was quietly seeking the Democratic nomination and whose views were closer to Acheson's than to Stevenson's, joined the Democratic Advisory Council. Acheson was cautious in his dealings with Senator Kennedy. Like Truman, Acheson distrusted Kennedy because of the behavior of Kennedy's father, an isolationist prior to World War II and later a supporter of Joe McCarthy's.

Acheson followed Truman's lead and supported the candidacy of Missouri's senator Stuart Symington in the 1960 primaries, but he actually believed that a Johnson-Kennedy ticket would be the best combination to win the presidency. "Lyndon is the ablest man in public life today," Acheson wrote to Truman in August 1959. "He has thousands of faults. But . . . he is a giant among pygmies." If Johnson took on the campaign, "especially with Kennedy, we would have a chance for a fight in which I could join wholeheartedly."[44] Nevertheless, during the 1960 primaries, Acheson was instrumental in persuading Truman not to hold a press conference at which he was planning to be extreme in his opposition to Kennedy's candidacy. Kennedy, who went on to win the nomination and select Johnson as his running mate, learned this and was grateful.

During the presidential campaign, Kennedy and Johnson voiced many of the foreign policy positions developed by Acheson in the Democratic Advisory Committee. Acheson, however, played no active role in the campaign. Whatever his doubts about Kennedy prior to the convention, Acheson fully supported him in his successful run for the presidency against Vice President Nixon.

At one point during the campaign, Kennedy's headquarters issued a statement calling for the strengthening of the "non-Batista democratic anti-Castro forces in exile, and in Cuba itself, who offer eventual hope of overthrowing Castro," who had toppled Fulgencio Batista in 1959. It went on to lambaste the Eisenhower administration for not supporting these "fighters for freedom." This was an effort to counter Nixon's charge that Kennedy would turn Quemoy and Ma-tsu over to communism.

The reaction of the press to the Kennedy statement on Cuba was highly negative, and Kennedy called Acheson to ask if he should raise this issue in an upcoming debate with Nixon. Acheson replied that he should stop talking about Cuba immediately, so that he would not get himself "hooked into positions which would be difficult afterwards." Kennedy thereafter dropped Cuba from his campaign speeches.[45]

At the end of the year, with a Democrat who seemed to sympathize with many of his policy prescriptions about to enter the White House, Acheson was hopeful. The traditional Acheson Christmas caroling party at P Street presaged better times ahead.

CHAPTER THIRTY-ONE

"A SORT OF ANCIENT MARINER"

"I WOULD NOT SAY in any way that we were friends—we were acquaintances," Acheson said of his relationship with John F. Kennedy. "And he was extremely deferential to me, which made me feel even older than I otherwise would have felt."[1] As they both lived in Georgetown, Senator Kennedy occasionally drove Acheson home from Capitol Hill when the former secretary of state was speaking to groups of liberal lawmakers.

Both during the 1960 campaign and after he became president, Kennedy consulted seriously with Acheson. On European matters, and especially on Berlin, over which the Russians would soon create another crisis, Acheson significantly affected Kennedy's thinking. But even on issues over which the two men differed sharply, Kennedy took Acheson's criticisms to heart. So powerful was Acheson's logic, Kennedy believed, that it was no easy task to counter his argument except at the highest intellectual level. As Robert Kennedy, who often tangled with Acheson, wrote after listening to Acheson's presentation to the president on the Berlin crisis, "I thought to myself that I had never heard anyone so lucid and convincing and would never wish to be on the other side of an argument with him."[2]

Shortly after he was elected president, Kennedy came by Acheson's house on P Street to discuss possible cabinet appointments. Acheson was somewhat put out when a host of photographers arrived and began hooking up electrical equipment in and around the house. This meant the meeting would garner maximum publicity. When he and Kennedy were finally alone in the living room, Acheson, as was his custom with his guests, offered him a martini, but Kennedy said he preferred tea. This did not go down well with Acheson; a friend noted in an interview that Acheson "never trusted a man who wouldn't have a drink with him."[3] This was the first of "the famous teas I had with him," Acheson recalled ruefully.[4]

Kennedy wanted to discuss three major cabinet appointments—the secretaries of state, defense, and the Treasury. He began the conversation by informing Acheson that he had no intention of naming Adlai Stevenson and Chester Bowles to any of these posts; knowing of Acheson's antipathy toward them, he did not want to waste any time hearing Acheson's vituperative objections to them. In fact, Kennedy had no one firmly in mind for any of the positions, telling Acheson that "he had spent so much time in the last few years on knowing people who could help him become President that he found he knew very few people who could help him be President." Acheson found that comment "both true and touching."

Kennedy then asked him his opinion of Senator J. William Fulbright, chairman of the Senate Foreign Relations Committee, for secretary of state. Acheson responded that Fulbright was more valuable where he was. (Later, Kennedy decided that Fulbright's segregationist position on civil rights would damage his effectiveness in the State Department.)

Acheson's first choice was David Bruce, whose career as a diplomat was one of the most distinguished in the department and who had served as Acheson's under secretary. Then Acheson mentioned John J. McCloy; though he had served two Democratic presidents, McCloy was nonetheless a Republican, and Kennedy thought he should appoint someone from his own party. At that point, Acheson brought up Dean Rusk, who was then president of the Rockefeller Foundation.

Kennedy did not know Rusk, so Acheson told him how impressed he had been with Rusk's loyalty. He explained that at the time of the Korean War, when Acheson was most under attack from McCarthy and other Republicans, Rusk, then deputy under secretary of state, had offered to take a demotion to assistant secretary in charge of the Far East. Acheson admitted to Kennedy that there was always "a chance one takes that somebody who had been good as a second or third in command would not be as good when the whole responsibility was upon him"—which was precisely how Acheson came to regard Rusk in the Kennedy and Johnson years.

Kennedy suggested Robert Lovett for Treasury; but Acheson was sure that Lovett, who was "hardly a banker," would be uninterested in the post. Acheson preferred him as secretary of defense. Kennedy, however, put aside this suggestion and later appointed Robert McNamara, the Ford Motor Company president, to head the Pentagon.

For Treasury, Acheson suggested Douglas Dillon, a Wall Street Republican whose father had founded the investing banking house of Dillon, Read & Co.

and who had also served in the State Department in the Eisenhower administration and therefore "ought to have had a good idea of foreign policy." This was a suggestion that Kennedy welcomed.

When Kennedy brought up the idea that his brother Robert serve as deputy secretary of defense, Acheson warned him that it would be a great mistake for any cabinet officer to have the president's brother as his second in command. If he was going to put his brother anywhere, "he should put him at the head of a department" or "be brought into the White House and be close to the president himself." When Kennedy proposed that Robert become attorney general, Acheson pointed out that this was a poor idea. In the public mind, "Bobby and the president would be one person." It would be far wiser politically to have an attorney general who "should be able to take the blame for things without having it go directly to the president."

As the conversation drew to a close Kennedy asked Acheson if he would accept an appointment as ambassador to NATO. Acheson thanked him but firmly declined the offer. There was nothing that he wanted, he said, although he "would be glad to help him in any way that [he] could with advice." In fact, the only post he would have accepted was that of secretary of state.

But this was not to be. When Kennedy later asked Robert Lovett who should be secretary of state, Lovett said that Dean Acheson ought to have that job. Kennedy said that he couldn't do that—that it would upset a lot of people in his own party, to say nothing of the Republicans. Then Lovett suggested that the next best man for the position was Dean Rusk.[5] When Kennedy said he wanted to play a major role in the making of foreign policy, Lovett asked: "Do you want to have a Secretary of State, or do you want an *Under Secretary?*" Kennedy laughed and replied, "Well, I guess I want an Under Secretary." In that case, said Lovett, Rusk, the ideal staff man, would be perfect.[6] Rusk got the job.

On matters affecting NATO and the West European allies, both Rusk and Kennedy considered Acheson an invaluable adviser. Rusk met with Acheson frequently in the early months of the Kennedy administration to discuss the Atlantic Alliance and especially the precarious position of Berlin. "At times he had a sharp tongue," Rusk said later, "but you learned to get around that. He was always willing to pitch in and help out in a difficult situation. Kennedy had total respect for him. It was always worth listening to what Acheson had to say. This does not mean that we always followed his advice."[7]

In January 1961, the very month of Kennedy's inauguration, Soviet party chief Nikita Khrushchev reiterated his intention to sign a separate peace treaty with East Germany. At Kennedy's behest, Rusk asked Acheson if he would review the whole NATO situation for the president. Believing that Eisenhower's policy of "massive retaliation" was not appropriate for NATO, Kennedy wanted Acheson to become the administration's chief consultant on NATO policy. Acheson readily accepted this role, as long as it meant that he would not be officially appointed to anything. He wanted to be free to stay in his law firm and also free to gather information from wherever he chose. Under these conditions, he went straight to work, even though that meant giving up his customary winter vacation with the MacLeishes in Antigua.

In an earlier Berlin crisis of 1958–59, fearing West Germany's possible acquisition of nuclear weapons, Khrushchev had demanded a nuclear-free Germany, that East and West Germany negotiate unification, and that the four powers end the occupation of Berlin. If the Western powers refused to negotiate within six months, Moscow threatened to sign a separate peace treaty with East Germany, and the Western allies would have to deal directly with East Germany for access to Berlin. Khrushchev apparently believed that the policy of massive nuclear retaliation was a bluff. As Eisenhower and Dulles had not beefed up NATO's ground forces in West Germany, Khrushchev's demands seemed a serious threat to Western cohesion.

Acheson hastened to write a piece stressing the strategic importance of Berlin and the need for a buildup of conventional forces. On March 7, 1959, his article "Wishing Won't Hold Berlin" appeared in the *Saturday Evening Post.* Writing as head of the DAC's foreign policy committee, Acheson was determined to resist any withdrawal of the Western powers from Berlin. He also recognized that an airlift could no longer "maintain Berlin's economic life" as it had in 1948. But to "respond to a blockade of Berlin with a nuclear strategic attack would be fatally unwise. To threaten this attack would be even more unwise."[8]

Acheson was convinced that Khrushchev would not risk war—either conventional or nuclear—over Berlin. But in this contest of wills, the West need not negotiate in the face of Soviet threats. Confronted by a unified Western determination to hold the line, Khrushchev would back down. Both German chancellor Konrad Adenauer and French president Charles de Gaulle shared his assessment.

Nonetheless, five days after the article appeared, Eisenhower repeated his policy that the United States would defend Berlin without increasing the level of conventional forces in Europe.

A month later the Big Four foreign ministers met in Geneva in an effort to settle the German and Berlin questions. The Americans were now willing to talk with the Russians, and Eisenhower invited Khrushchev to come to the United States in September 1959, at which time Khrushchev did drop his deadline for negotiations over Berlin. In return, the president agreed to a June 1960 summit meeting in Paris to decide on the future status of the former German capital. The four-power summit turned out to be a diplomatic disaster, however, as it coincided with the downing of an American U-2 spy plane over the Soviet Union. Khrushchev refused to allow the meeting to continue unless Eisenhower apologized. He refused to do so, and the summit collapsed.[9]

With the help of Paul Nitze and William Bundy, as well as Secretary of Defense Robert McNamara and his "whiz kids," Acheson's advisory committee on NATO came up with possible responses to Khrushchev's new threats to sign a peace treaty with East Germany and make Berlin a "free city," ostensibly independent of any controls by the four powers.

The Acheson committee's report on NATO, widely known as the Acheson Report, was formally submitted to the State Department and the White House in late March 1961. It contained the essence of what the administration would christen its "Grand Design"—the idea of a united Europe within an Atlantic partnership with the United States and Canada.

Once again Acheson urged a significant buildup of NATO conventional forces in Europe. It was not that he believed the American nuclear deterrent was a hollow threat—on the contrary. But he thought that the ability of the West to resist a Soviet attack by using non-nuclear forces would give the Russians time to fully understand the risks they were running that a conventional war could escalate into a nuclear one.[10]

On April 21 Kennedy adopted the Acheson Report as the basis for official policy toward NATO and the Atlantic nations. Later, Kennedy increased defense spending for both nuclear and conventional weapons—reflecting the need for a flexible response to any Soviet attack in central Europe.

The White House had also asked Acheson to draw up a list of actions the allies might take if Khrushchev forced the Berlin issue. On April 3 he gave the president what McGeorge Bundy termed "a first-rate memorandum."[11]

"All courses are dangerous and unpromising," Acheson wrote, but "inaction is even worse." If the Soviets should provoke an actual crisis, then "a bold and dangerous course may be the safest." With so much at stake, "a willingness to fight for Berlin" was essential. "Economic and political measures" would not be enough, "nor would threatening to initiate a general war be a solution. The threat would not carry conviction; it would invite a preemptive strike; and it would alienate allies and neutrals alike. The fight for Berlin must begin, at any rate, as a local conflict. The problem is how and where it will end. This uncertainty must be accepted."[12]

Impressed by Acheson's toughness, and eager to prove his mettle, Kennedy asked Acheson to repeat his arguments a few days later at a briefing in the White House for British prime minister Harold Macmillan and his foreign secretary, Alec Douglas-Home. It was Kennedy's second encounter with Macmillan, whom historian and White House adviser Arthur Schlesinger Jr. described as that "languid Edwardian, who looked back to the sunlit years before the First World War as a lost paradise." Macmillan feared Kennedy would think of him as "a museum piece." Kennedy in turn hoped to impress Macmillan by demonstrating his strong commitment to European security, and what better way to do so than to let the great architect of European recovery, Dean Acheson, hold forth on these issues?[13]

Acheson asserted that if the Russians moved to cut off Berlin, the allies must be prepared to demonstrate their resolve. Brushing aside diplomatic and economic measures, Acheson outlined a range of military actions, including what he tentatively favored as the sending of a NATO division eastward along the autobahn to test the West's access rights to Berlin. If the Russians dared repulse this probe, the West at least would know where it stood and could rally and rearm as it did in Korea.

At the end of what Schlesinger called a "rather bloodcurdling recital," delivered with the customary Achesonian self-confidence, the British were shaken. Home pointed out that the allies were in Berlin by right of conquest, but that right was wearing thin. Acheson countered by replying coolly that perhaps "it was Western resolve that was wearing thin."

The UN ambassador Adlai Stevenson, who was present, was also dismayed by Acheson's emphasis on a military showdown. But Kennedy, who had remained diffident during Acheson's presentation, was seemingly not put off by Acheson's belligerence. Within a few months much of what Acheson had advised regarding the need for a military buildup in Europe would be followed.[14]

Not long after Acheson's briefing, Kennedy asked the elder statesman to pay courtesy calls on Charles de Gaulle and Konrad Adenauer and inform them that the administration was evaluating NATO policy and wanted to solicit their opinions. Acheson was planning to go to Europe anyway to argue a private case for his law firm at the World Court in The Hague.

A few days before Acheson was to leave, Kennedy called him in for a last consultation. It was the first warm spring day, and, as Acheson recalled, Kennedy suddenly changed the subject from NATO. "I want to talk to you about something else—come on out here in the garden and sit in the sun." So they went into the Rose Garden and sat on a bench, and the president said, "Do you know anything about this Cuba proposal?"

Acheson replied that he didn't even know there was one. The president then outlined the CIA plan, which had been started under the Eisenhower administration, to land Cuban exiles at what was called the Bay of Pigs, where they would be joined by other Cuban guerrillas in order to overthrow Fidel Castro. Alarmed by what he was hearing, Acheson said that he hoped the president wasn't serious about it.

"I don't know if I'm serious or not," Kennedy replied, "but this is the proposal and I've been thinking about it and it is serious—in that sense, I've not made up my mind, but I'm giving it very serious thought."

Appalled, Acheson said that it wasn't necessary to call in Price, Waterhouse, the big accounting firm, to discover that 1,500 invading Cubans weren't as good as 25,000 Cuban army regulars.

On April 17 the anti-Castro exiles waded ashore at the Bay of Pigs, only to find that the beachhead they established was indefensible. Castro's forces easily crushed the doomed expedition.

Acheson was in Europe when reports of the Bay of Pigs disaster reached him. The news shattered the confidence of the European leaders in the new men in Washington. Acheson recalled later: "It was such a completely unthought out irresponsible thing to do. They had tremendously high expectations of the new administration, and when this thing happened they just fell miles down with a crash."

The Bay of Pigs fiasco also temporarily damaged Acheson's relations with the president. In a speech to the Foreign Service Association in June, shortly after his return from Europe, Acheson spoke of how the Europeans were watching "a gifted young amateur practice with a boomerang, when they saw, to their horror, that he had knocked himself out." Upon hearing of Acheson's speech, not surprisingly the president was highly irritated.[15]

To Harry Truman, Acheson wrote, "Why we ever engaged in this asinine Cuban adventure, I cannot imagine. Before I left it was mentioned to me and I told my informants how you and I turned down similar suggestions for Iran and Guatemala and why. I thought that this Cuban idea had been put aside, as it should have been. . . . Brains are no substitute for judgment."[16]

Even before the Bay of Pigs disaster, Acheson's trip to Europe had entailed reassuring rather than simply briefing allied leaders. When Acheson arrived in Bonn on April 9, the old chancellor decided to take him up to his own house for the meeting. The ride through the flowering hills of the Rhine Valley was harrowing, with the car going at top speed to the right and left, up on the sidewalks, or on the wrong side of the road. Adenauer was imperturbable, as they arrived at his home, located about one hundred feet up the side of a hill, at the top of an intimidating line of steps that zigzagged up to the entrance. The eighty-four-year-old Adenauer said, "My friend, you are not as young as you were the first time we met and I must urge you not to take these steps too fast."

After a delicious lunch and a stroll through the chancellor's rose garden, Acheson told him that Kennedy would be steadfast over Berlin. Adenauer, however, was "worried to death," Acheson recalled, over the intentions of the new administration. He was fearful that JFK would strike a deal behind his back with the Russians over Germany, Berlin, or some kind of non-nuclear zone in central Europe.

After Acheson reassured him that there was no conspiracy against him in Washington and London, Adenauer ended their five-hour conversation by saying, "You have lifted a stone from my heart"—a phrase the American embassy used to start off its cable to Washington reporting on the interview. After that, the two men went outside to play the Italian bowling game of boccie, at which the chancellor was especially adept.[17]

Adenauer's first meeting with Kennedy at the White House two days after the boccie game was only modestly successful. Kennedy assured him that Acheson's recommendation for increased conventional forces in Europe was his primary goal. As for Berlin, Adenauer echoed Acheson's view that the Russians were testing Western resolve and that the Western allies must hold firm.

Despite Kennedy's assurances, Adenauer still feared that Kennedy would seek a belated understanding with Khrushchev over Berlin. He hoped that Acheson would continue to impress upon Kennedy's staff of "cooks," "whiz kids," and "prima donnas" the need to negotiate from positions of brute strength.[18]

Ten days after his visit with the German chancellor, Acheson met on April 20 for the first time with the French president. Acheson was deeply impressed by the general. He admired de Gaulle's toughness, his unwillingness to back down before Soviet threats, and his "authentic grand manner." De Gaulle received him, he wrote later, "with a grave courtesy that would have benefitted Louis XIV himself. We exchanged compliments in an eighteenth- or probably seventeenth-century solemnity and went to work."

Acheson was well aware that de Gaulle was unhappy with America's dominance of NATO, and he took the time to impress upon him Kennedy's deep commitment to the alliance and the need for a coordinated Western policy toward the Russians. While de Gaulle, as always, listened courteously, he made it quite clear he was going to develop his *force de frappe*, France's own independent nuclear force.

After Acheson proposed that NATO become the central point for allied consultation, de Gaulle, who preferred that all decisions be made jointly by America, Britain, and France, asked him whether the military alliance could actually be transformed into a transatlantic political mechanism. "Who knows," Acheson answered, "until we really try it?"

"But it is illogical," the general persisted. "NATO was conceived as a military alliance, now you are trying to make it a political mechanism."

"Quite right," Acheson said. "We Americans think less of logic in politics than you French do. With us the test is whether something works. If it does, logic conforms to a new verity."

De Gaulle conceded that "this was a point of view."

The interview finished in just fifty-eight minutes by the clock behind de Gaulle's desk. Acheson thought that at the very least he had put de Gaulle in a position "where he could not say that nobody let him know anything until he was faced with it."[19]

After briefing the NATO Council on American policy on Berlin on April 21, Acheson proceeded to Rome. With the passing from the political scene in 1953 of the tough-minded Italian premier Alcide de Gasperi, Acheson found the Italian politicians charming but ineffectual. Acheson had also been persuaded to attend "a meeting of intellectuals" in Bologna. To this end, he believed he would get the feeling of what was to come by reading D. H. Lawrence's *Twilight in Italy* and was pleased to pick up on Lawrence's assertion that Italian oratory "operates directly on the blood without any confusing interpolation of intellectual content." At Bologna, Acheson discovered that if he took off his earphones, "one got the full sonorous flow of sound, without being disturbed by the schoolmarmish twittering of the English interpreters trying to make sense out of it all."

The Italian trip ended well, however, when Acheson and his wife stopped over in Venice, where they looked at medieval and Renaissance documents, dined in a garden in the Giudecca, and had "a glorious lunch" on the island of Torcello.[20]

Upon his return to Washington, Acheson reflected on the Europeans he had encountered. He found them parochial, self-absorbed, and he came away with "a reluctant feeling that we perhaps are the only nation in the world which is capable of having a broad outlook on the world. . . . Therefore we must not be too delicate about being vigorous in our leadership."[21]

Acheson found that his success in mollifying Adenauer encouraged the president to ask him to write another report, this one focused solely on the gathering Berlin crisis. Acheson went to work on it with renewed zeal. According to his longtime secretary, Barbara Evans, who wrote to Marshall Shulman earlier that spring, "DA is buoyed up by it all and looks better and younger than I have seen him in years."[22]

* * *

On May 31 Kennedy took off for Paris and Vienna, first to meet with President de Gaulle and then with Khrushchev. Despite Acheson's reassurances about JFK's steadfastness, de Gaulle had been taken aback by Kennedy's ineptness over Cuba. In their first meeting, the French leader reminded Kennedy that Khrushchev had been setting deadlines over Berlin for two and a half years. Kennedy must make it clear to the Soviet leader that it was Khrushchev who wanted to change things, not the allies. If the Russians used force against the Western allies in Berlin, Khrushchev would have a general war on his hands. "That is the last thing he wants," de Gaulle said.

The meeting in Vienna went worse than Kennedy ever expected. Khrushchev was at his most belligerent, his most bullying; Kennedy was contained, cold, searching for common ground. The Soviet leader declared that only a treaty recognizing the existence of the two Germanys could be signed; otherwise he would sign a peace treaty with East Germany and "all commitments stemming from Germany's surrender will become invalid." West Berlin would be preserved as what Khrushchev called a "free city," but its links to the outside world would be controlled by a "sovereign" East Germany.

Kennedy rebuffed Khrushchev, but his words seemed to have no effect. By their last meeting, both men were grim faced. When Kennedy insisted on maintaining an access route to West Berlin, Khrushchev replied that that would be up to East Germany. He slammed his open hand down on the table. "I want peace. But if you want war, that is your problem."

Kennedy responded with what de Gaulle had recommended: "It is you, and not I, who wants to force a change."

Khrushchev retorted that the Soviet Union had no choice but to sign a treaty with East Germany. He would do so in December.

Kennedy, taut and tight-lipped, said, "If that is true, it's going to be a cold winter."

Back at the American residence, Kennedy told James Reston of *The New York Times* that he thought Khrushchev had tried to bully him so violently because of the Bay of Pigs. "I think he thought anyone who was so young and inexperienced as to get into that mess could be taken. And anyone who got into it and didn't see it through had no guts. So he just beat hell out of me."[23]

Upon his return from Vienna, the president called the National Security Council together on June 29 to listen to what Dean Acheson had to say about Berlin. He had announced two weeks earlier that Acheson would head a special task force to monitor the Berlin crisis, which Acheson insisted would include not only Paul Nitze, but also Averell Harriman.

Working on what he described as "a somber task," Acheson wrote to a friend that he had not yet been able to find out the answer to the predicament that FDR's longtime cabinet secretary Harold Ickes expressed to him some years earlier: "After he left the Truman Cabinet, I asked him one evening how it felt to be observing the government when, after so many years, he was not a part of it. He said he had been trying to figure that out and he could not decide whether he would rather be on the outside and be scared to death on account of what he did not know or be on the inside and terrified because of what he did know."[24]

Acheson had submitted his report on Berlin to the president the day before the meeting, and now in the Cabinet Room he gave what Arthur Schlesinger described as an "imperious and brilliant" oral presentation.

To Acheson West Berlin was not the real problem but rather a pretext to test America's will. American policy, at least at the outset, should not be to seek negotiations. Instead Kennedy must insist that the West retain access to Berlin. If Khrushchev were to block it, we must be prepared, first to launch a new airlift, and then, if the Russians interfered with that, to send a ground probe of two divisions.

Acheson did not believe Washington should threaten the Russians with nuclear retaliation. He rejected the suggestion of some in the military who called for the option of a "limited use of nuclear means." As he put it, "If you drop one bomb . . . it either indicated that you were going to drop more or you invited the other side to drop one back. This seemed to me to be irresponsible and not . . . adapted to the problem of Berlin."

Instead Acheson wanted Kennedy to declare a national emergency and order a rapid buildup of conventional and nuclear forces. Two or three additional divisions should be sent to Germany, with three to six more in reserve for transport overseas. If Kennedy demonstrated an American willingness to risk war, then he could afford to offer Khrushchev face-saving concessions, such as barring espionage from West Berlin or perhaps even recognition of the Oder-Neisse line as the boundary between Germany and Poland.

In the meantime, while the conventional forces were being readied, Acheson proposed that the administration carry on conversations with the Russians at a lower level. There were plenty of "elderly unemployed" who could "converse indefinitely without negotiating at all," and he volunteered himself to do so "for three months on end."[25]

In later years McGeorge Bundy recalled a conversation that took place at the end of a meeting in the Cabinet Room on contingency plans for Berlin. Only Kennedy, Acheson, and Bundy were left, and the president asked Acheson just when he thought America might have to use nuclear weapons.

Acheson reflected and spoke quietly, deliberately. According to Bundy, he told the president that he should give that question "the most careful and most private consideration, well before the time when the choice might present itself, that he should reach his own clear conclusion in advance as to what he should do, and that he should tell no one at all what that conclusion was."

On reflection, Bundy believed that Acheson had a further meaning than simply advising the president to be thoughtful. Or "at least that he had a view as to what his own answer to the president's question would be." The evidence lay in a passage toward the end of his 1959 article "Wishing Won't Hold Berlin." Bundy thought that unless Acheson had changed his mind since then, he believed "that the right final choice might be to accept defeat, and the loss of West Berlin, if the only remaining alternative were to start a nuclear war."

In the final analysis, Bundy wrote, "Eisenhower and Kennedy—and Acheson himself—all believed that their basic objective must be to persuade Khrushchev not to run nuclear risks.[26]

In another Cabinet Room meeting on July 13, Secretary of Defense Robert McNamara recommended that the president declare a national emergency, call up the reserves, and request an additional $4.3 billion for defense. Acheson was delighted that McNamara, whose self-confidence seemingly mirrored his own, echoed the recommendations in his Berlin crisis report. Rusk, however, wanted a quieter military buildup. Acheson then pointed out that if the president waited until late in the crisis to call up the reserves, this would not affect the Soviet leader's judgment any more than "dropping bombs after [Khrushchev] had forced the issue to the limit."[27]

The meeting had not gone as Acheson hoped, and he complained to Truman in a letter the next day of "a weakness in decision at the top—all but Bob McNamara, who impresses me as first class. The decisions are incredibly hard, but they don't, like Bourbon, improve with age. . . . As Holmes said, every day we must make decisions on imperfect knowledge."[28]

At the next NSC meeting on July 20, McNamara argued against an immediate declaration of a national emergency. He even convinced Acheson that if the crisis came to a head, six army and two marine divisions could be deployed rapidly to Europe. Kennedy then decided that calling for a national emergency would be premature at that time.[29]

Five days later the president addressed the nation over television. He accepted most of what Acheson had suggested: that Khrushchev was testing American resolve, that an immediate conventional forces buildup would take place; and while he did not declare a national emergency, he certainly presented the program as tantamount to that.

Although Acheson grumbled that Kennedy's speech was not forceful enough,

Khrushchev certainly found it so and declared on August 7 that no one should create "a war psychosis."

On August 1, just before setting out for a vacation on the island of Martha's Vineyard, Acheson submitted to the president his final report on Berlin. Basically it called for stabilizing Berlin along the lines of the status quo, trying to restore a semblance of national identity to the countries of Eastern Europe, and limiting armaments on the European continent to reduce the likelihood of armed conflict.

On August 13 Acheson and his wife were vacationing on the beaches of the Vineyard, along with his daughters, Jane and Mary, and the grandchildren, when the news broke that Khrushchev had ordered the erection of a barbed-wire barricade around the 104-mile perimeter of East Berlin, presumably to stanch the flow of refugees to the West. Three days later the first concrete slabs of what would become known as the Berlin Wall dividing East and West Berlin were in place.

It was Michael Janeway, the son of a noted political economist, who raced to the restaurant where Acheson was breakfasting with a copy of the *New York Herald-Tribune* bearing the front-page story on Berlin. Acheson turned "beet-red" when he saw the headline and "was just boiling over with indignation at Kennedy."

Janeway believed that Acheson's reaction came from not having been informed by anyone in the administration about this shocking development. The head of the president's task force on Berlin should not have to learn of it from a newspaper. So disturbed was Acheson by the incident that he finally had to excuse himself from the breakfast table.[30]

Kennedy, in fact, had turned to Acheson's final report on Berlin when the news of the wall reached him at the Kennedy summer cottage in Hyannisport, Massachusetts. He and his wife had just attended services at St. Francis Xavier Church and had boarded his sailboat, the *Marlin*, when he was called back to the dock for a high-priority message from Washington. Kennedy scanned the yellow Teletype copy of the message informing him of what had happened in Berlin, at which point he telephoned Rusk with the angry question "What the hell is this?"

Both men decided not to inflame the situation and perhaps spark an East German uprising, as the Russians had not yet blocked the access routes to West Berlin.[31]

On the following day, August 14, JFK sent a handwritten note to Acheson, thanking him for his report and asking him to discuss the new developments in Berlin after he returned from his "well-earned holiday."[32] Nonetheless, it may have been poor leadership for Kennedy to remain silent before the American people at this time; McGeorge Bundy later wrote that it would have been better "if Kennedy himself had publicly denounced the wall more quickly than he did."[33]

The president announced on August 18 that he would not use force to break through the barricade. He did order Vice President Lyndon Johnson and General Lucius Clay, the hero of the 1948 Berlin blockade, to go to Berlin; and after Johnson arrived, 1,500 men of the First Battle Group, Eighth Infantry, rolled down the autobahn to West Berlin. No one interfered with the American troop movement, and the vice president greeted the soldiers on their arrival in the former German capital.

In addition, Kennedy put into effect some of the measures Acheson had proposed by deploying another division to West Germany; some National Guard and reserve units were also called up, and a general posture of preparedness for conventional action was taking place.

Acheson felt vindicated. "This, I think, had a really profound effect on the Russians," he said later, "far more than blustery talk would have had about using nuclear weapons which would not impress them. When we were actually making life uncomfortable for a quarter of a million American citizens, they were quite aware the Government wouldn't have done this just for fun."[34]

Effectively, the crisis was over, and by October Khrushchev told the 22nd Congress of the Soviet Communist Party that he would no longer insist on signing a peace treaty with East Germany that year.

On the whole, Kennedy had hewed to Acheson's tough line on Berlin. Nonetheless, Acheson often saw himself in the Kennedy years as "a rather pampered and tolerated ghost among the bright new spirits . . . a sort of ancient mariner whose warnings only take on meaning *ex post facto*."[35] The ancient mariner soon found himself at the epicenter of the greatest crisis in the Cold War since the outbreak of the Korean War.

CHAPTER THIRTY-TWO

"THE SURVIVAL OF STATES"

FOR SEVERAL MONTHS after his involvement with the Berlin crisis, Acheson had little direct contact with the Kennedy administration. As the new year dawned, he and Alice spent the month of January 1962 in the Far East, where he met with Prince Norodom Sihanouk, Cambodia's head of state. His visit to that small Asian country, until 1954 part of French Indochina, was occasioned by his role as the chief counsel representing Cambodia in a dispute over the ninth-century Temple of Preah Vihear, whose ownership was claimed by both Cambodia and Thailand. Acheson had already made preliminary arguments before the World Court in April 1961; a year later, in March 1962, oral testimony was given, and in June the Court decided in favor of Cambodia, which was not expected to win. Acheson became a national hero in Cambodia and was awarded the Grand Cross of the Royal Cambodian Order.[1]

The Achesons' stay in Cambodia was filled with exotic entertainments as well as lengthy meetings with Sihanouk and visits to ancient temples, including a memorable stopover at the most famous temple of them all, Angkor Wat. In letters sent to his assistant, Barbara Evans, Acheson told how very much he liked the prince. One evening he attended an *audience populaire* at the Pagoda de Danse, where he had seen a performance by the Royal Ballet the previous day. The prince's "audience" consisted of six hours of petitioners who came before the prince to ask him to right wrongs that had been done them and to adjudicate disputes. Later, Acheson remarked that the prince's audience reminded him of Saint Louis, or Henry II "under his oak."

At the end of a long, rich dinner with the prince, Sihanouk toasted Acheson "as the greatest international lawyer since Grotius." After Acheson had responded with what he described as "a three Martini speech" that "nearly reduced the Prince to tears," it was time to go to another ballet, and after two hours of watching the dancing, Acheson needed "a stiff nightcap" at the embassy before returning to his hotel.[2]

His ten days in Cambodia gave Acheson a special interest in that country and in the prince; in 1963 he wrote to the newly arrived American ambassador to Cambodia that Sihanouk "has done a superb job with his little country, in holding it together and guiding it steadily along."[3]

After exiting through Singapore, the Achesons spent a few days in Sydney, Australia, which seemed after Cambodia "rather like some English food, sustaining but uninteresting," and then returned to Washington.[4]

On April 5, 1962, Acheson's great friend and mentor, Felix Frankfurter, was felled by a stroke, the first in a series that would finally cause his death three years later. Acheson, now almost seventy, was in apparently good health, even after his tiring journey to Asia and Australia. Later in the 1960s Acheson suffered from severe eye trouble brought on by a thyroid condition, as well as a small stroke; but in 1962 he was far more concerned over Frankfurter's failing health than his own ailments.

After Frankfurter's second stroke in July, President Kennedy made a generous gesture that warmed Acheson's feelings toward him. He arranged to call on the Supreme Court justice and asked Acheson to accompany him. At the meeting, Frankfurter suggested that the most outstanding presidents in American history were bound together by one factor—their conception of the office. It was idle to look to them for guidance in modern problems, but not idle to see how they conceived of the nature of their office. Kennedy enthusiastically agreed with this and then, after a brief tea, took his leave. Acheson was deeply gratified at how bucked up Frankfurter was by the visit. Once again the ailing Supreme Court justice seemed to be an adviser to presidents.[5]

Among the issues about which Acheson came to care deeply at this time was the State Department's policy toward southern Africa. He made it clear to Kennedy, as he would later to Presidents Lyndon Johnson and Richard Nixon, that he advocated more understanding for the position of a colonial power like Portugal and for the white governments of Rhodesia and South Africa.

Although he was working on problems of European security for Kennedy, he nevertheless took time out to urge the president not to put too much pressure on the colonial powers to hasten what Acheson believed to be the inevitable transition from colonial rule to independence.[6]

His advice had no near term effect. On April 20, 1961, the United States voted in favor of an unsuccessful UN resolution demanding that Portugal immediately move toward granting Angola independence. For Acheson, it was partly that he thought most Africans were not prepared to govern themselves, but more that he disapproved of antagonizing allies like Portugal and Britain. (In France's case, he believed—correctly, as it turned out—that General de Gaulle could control the pace of the independence movements in sub-Sahara, francophone Africa.) Moreover, in the case of Portugal he was convinced that Washington should not lean too hard on Salazar, lest the United States lose its rights to bases in the Azores.[7]

In April 1962 Kennedy and McGeorge Bundy called him over to the White House to ask him to take on the negotiations with Portugal for an extension of the lease Washington held for basing rights in the Azores. Once again Acheson vehemently criticized American policy toward Portugal, explaining that if the United States went ahead and denounced Lisbon's colonial policies, Washington would not get an extension anyway: "Nobody can get it. I can't. Nobody can."

In light of Acheson's objections to U.S. policy, Kennedy realized that it would be foolish to ask him to do something that he thought government policy was rendering impossible. Nevertheless, since Acheson was lunching the next day with the Portuguese ambassador, Kennedy suggested that perhaps he could at least broach the possibility of a more cooperative attitude on the part of the Portuguese toward the base's negotiations. Acheson said that he would.[8]

Despite Kennedy's reservations, Acheson's arguments did affect the president's thinking. Kennedy began looking for ways to "balance" support for the Angolan nationalists and for Lisbon. It soon became clear to him that he could not risk losing access to the Azores for his African policy.

Reversing American policy, Kennedy rerouted secret arms shipments intended for the Angolan nationalists to Salazar. He ceased urging Lisbon to grant independence to its African territories, even going so far as to offer Salazar a half billion dollars in aid in return for a promise to pull out of southern Africa within five years; Salazar turned down the proposition. In December 1962 the United States voted against two UN Security Council resolutions denouncing Portuguese colonialism. But when the Azores lease expired on December 31, 1962, no new lease was signed. Salazar simply permitted the Americans to remain there on a day-to-day basis.

Kennedy had finally sided with Acheson and the Europeanists. A decade of guerrilla warfare ensued in Portuguese Africa, the overseas Portuguese army became radicalized, and the dictatorship Salazar had installed in his own country was overthrown. Only then were Angola and Mozambique granted their independence in 1975 by a military government in Lisbon.[9]

* * *

Despite Kennedy's eagerness to consult him on European affairs, Acheson knew that he was not a member of the president's inner circle. Nonetheless, Acheson had become increasingly worried that JFK's obsession with Castro's Cuba was a distraction from the central strategic concerns of the United States—the containment of the Soviet Union in Europe and providing for the security of Japan. Acheson was, however, worried that Cuban-style revolution might spread throughout Latin America and threaten U.S. interests there.

On Sunday, October 14, 1962, two American U-2 aircraft returned with the damning pictures showing that Moscow was installing medium-range ballistic missiles and constructing sites for intermediate-range missiles, both of them capable of delivering nuclear weapons, in the woods near San Cristóbal, Cuba. The medium-range missiles could reach Washington, D.C., and the intermediate-range missiles could destroy every American city with the exception of Seattle and cities in Alaska and Hawaii. On Monday evening, October 15, the photographs were developed and marked, and at eight-thirty that evening the CIA phoned McGeorge Bundy to inform him of the ballistic missile installation.[10]

On Tuesday morning the president convened a small group of advisers, named the Executive Committee of the National Security Council, or ExCom, to discuss what should be done. The following day he asked Acheson to join the group.

Kennedy decided not to attend the ExCom meetings regularly because he believed that discussion would be inhibited with him present. "During all the deliberations," Attorney General Robert Kennedy wrote later, "we all spoke as equals. There was no rank, and in fact we did not even have a chairman. Dean Rusk, who as Secretary of State might have assumed that position, had other duties and responsibilities during this period of time and frequently could not attend our meetings." (Acheson commented later: "One wonders what those 'other duties and responsibilities' were, to have been half so important as those they displaced.")

For Robert Kennedy, "the conversations were completely uninhibited and unrestricted . . . a tremendously advantageous procedure that does not frequently occur within the Executive branch of the Government." (To which Acheson wrote acidly, "One can be devoutly thankful that this is so."[11])

Out of what Acheson called "a leaderless, uninhibited group, many of whom had little knowledge in either the military or diplomatic field," the chief advice reaching the president "came to him through his brother." Robert Kennedy's was the dominant influence on his brother's thinking. Acheson, who owed nothing to the president, became Robert Kennedy's most forceful antagonist.

When Acheson joined the ExCom on October 17, he found the group already divided between those who wanted to launch an immediate air strike to take out the missile sites and those who believed, as did Secretary of Defense McNamara, that a naval blockade, later called a quarantine, was the more appropriate response. Robert Kennedy was in the latter group; he believed that if Washington launched an air strike, the United States would be acting as the Japanese did when they bombed Pearl Harbor.

Acheson strongly disagreed with the attorney general. He supported those who favored an air strike to take out the missile sites, for he believed that a blockade would give the Russians time to make the missiles operational, and then it would be far more dangerous to try to eliminate them. Moreover, if the United States government should take a passive stance, "it would forfeit—and rightly so—all confidence and leadership in the Western Hemisphere (also under threat of these Soviet missiles) and in Western Europe."

Acheson was contemptuous of Robert Kennedy's analogy to Pearl Harbor. Bombing the missile sites, Acheson wrote later, would not be a sneak attack, for the president had repeatedly warned the Russians not to install "weapons that were capable of lethal injury to the United States." How much warning, he asked, was necessary to avoid the stigma of a "Pearl Harbor in reverse"? "Was it necessary to adopt the early nineteenth-century method of having a man with a red flag walk before a steam engine to warn cattle and people to stay out of the way?"[12]

In urging an air strike directed only at the missile locations, Acheson saw himself as sticking to a middle ground between those who opposed an early military response and the Joint Chiefs of Staff, who wanted to take out the airfields in Cuba before bombing the missile sites. Acheson believed such an action would likely lead to a full-scale invasion of the island. As he later described the arguments of the military, "The airfields were all right near Havana and other cities—you would have caused terrific casualties of Cubans, which would be a very, very bad idea. Then other military people said, 'Well, if you're going to do all that, why don't we put six divisions in and take over the Island.' This could be done quite easily," Acheson admitted. "The obvious danger was, once you got in, how were you ever going to get out?"[13]

Acheson dueled throughout the afternoon of October 17 with Robert Kennedy. He told him that the Pearl Harbor analogy was "thoroughly false and pejorative." Finally the ExCom split into two broad groups: those who wanted to destroy the missile sites (the Acheson view) and those who believed that a naval blockade of the island would be the best way to apply pressure for their removal (the Robert Kennedy line).

Later that day, in a private meeting with John Kennedy in the Oval Office, Acheson repeated the arguments he had made in the ExCom meetings. The president listened carefully to his presentation for about an hour. When Kennedy brought up his brother's Pearl Harbor analogy, Acheson recalled telling the president that this was not the way to handle the problem. It was a question of Soviet nuclear weapons in Cuba and what he was going to do about it. To talk about an air strike on missile sites as a Pearl Harbor in reverse seemed to him unworthy of people charged with the government of a great country.

As the conversation came to an end, the president walked over to the French windows overlooking the Rose Garden. He looked out for a long time. Then he turned to Acheson and said, "I guess I'd better earn my salary this week."

"I'm afraid you have to," Acheson replied. "I wish I could help more."

With that they parted.[14]

The next day President Kennedy asked Acheson and Under Secretary of State George Ball, as international lawyers, to explain the issues associated with either taking out the missile sites or instituting a naval blockade. Acheson discounted "legal niceties" when the security of the nation was threatened. "No law," he later declared, "can destroy the state creating the law. The survival of states is not a matter of law." Ball responded that an air attack on Cuba would be an "unlawful blunder" that would damage America's standing with the international community. A naval blockade would at least have the "color of legality."[15]

Both during and after the crisis, Acheson defended his position. While he acknowledged the possibility of a Soviet military response against the United States or West Berlin, or against Greece or the American Jupiter missile bases in Turkey, he dismissed Soviet retaliation as highly improbable. A sudden air attack by the United States on "a nonpopulated area of Cuba would have been an attack not on the Soviet Union but on something—not people—in Cuba." He said later, "This would hardly call for a reflex attack on the United States at the expense of reciprocal destruction of the Soviet Union."[16]

But in the discussions in the ExCom, according to McGeorge Bundy, who was present at all the meetings, the differences between Acheson's call for sharply limited air strikes against missile sites and the Joint Chiefs' air war were never adequately explored.[17]

For thirty years after the crisis, no one believed there had been any tactical nuclear weapons in Cuba. But in 1993 a Soviet general revealed that Khrushchev had authorized the Soviet commander in Cuba to use tactical nuclear warheads against invading American troops—*if* an attack were under way and *if* he could not reach Moscow to confirm permission. (Khrushchev, however, rescinded the oral order in writing on October 22, after learning that Washington had discovered the Soviet missile emplacements.)

Other Soviet documents revealed that sixty nuclear warheads for medium- and intermediate-range missiles had already arrived in Cuba prior to the blockade, in addition to ninety-eight tactical nuclear warheads. Furthermore, there were in Cuba Soviet expeditionary forces totaling more than forty thousand men, three times as many as Washington estimated at the start of the crisis. Any U.S. invasion would have proved a disaster.[18]

On Friday, October 19, when the ExCom met again, Acheson stressed his belief that the United States and the Soviet Union were involved in "a test of wills." After a lengthy meeting at which the participants once again repeated their positions, the ExCom broke into two groups, each to write out the diplomatic and military steps that the president would have to take to implement its respective recommendations.

Acheson joined those who favored a limited air strike, but then asked to be excused from further attendance at the ExCom. He believed it was no longer the place for a person like himself who did not hold an official government position; it was one thing for an outsider to give advice, but it was quite another to participate in writing the most secret strategic and tactical plans of a vital military operation that might be put into effect.The next day he and his wife drove to Harewood for the weekend.

Acheson was at peace with himself, for he had tried to persuade the president to take firm, decisive action. Now he believed that his role in the crisis was over. Moreover, he was convinced that the blockade—Robert Kennedy's choice—would probably be the president's choice as well.[19]

That Saturday evening, October 20, as the Achesons were preparing to retire, Dean Rusk called with an urgent message from the president. He told Acheson that Kennedy had decided not to take the steps Acheson favored, but he nonetheless wanted Acheson to go to Europe the next day to brief General de Gaulle. Acheson responded that he remembered Justice Holmes saying to him once that we all belonged to a club that was the least exclusive and the most expensive, the United States of America. "I guess if I belong to that club I better do what I'm asked to do. Sure I'll go."

Rusk asked, "You don't mind that your advice isn't being followed?"

"Of course not," Acheson replied. "I'm not the President." He figured he was enough of a lawyer to do a good job for his client, even though he thought the client had made the wrong decision.

Early Sunday morning as Acheson was preparing to fly to Paris, he found that he had just $7, no valid passport, and only country clothes to wear. His personal secretary, Barbara Evans, was sent to the passport office, which was opened especially for her. At State, where Acheson was being briefed, members of the department passed the hat to collect $50 for the special envoy. Acheson then rushed to P Street, packed a bag with appropriate clothes, and had his son-in-law, William Bundy, drive him to a waiting Air Force 707 destined for Paris.

On the plane were Walter "Red" Dowling, American ambassador to Germany; Sherman Kent of the CIA, who was carrying the aerial photographs of the missile sites; two other CIA men; and three armed bodyguards. Unfortunately the VIP room on the plane had a small hole in the fuselage that emitted a shrill scream that was like a squeaky chalk on a blackboard; no one could stand it, so they all sat in the larger part of the plane, looking at the photographs and making sure that no crew member could see what they were doing.

Arriving first at an American air base in England, Acheson was met by his old colleague David Bruce, now U.S. ambassador to the Court of St. James's. In one pocket he had a bottle of Scotch, which he shared with Acheson; in the other was a revolver. Acheson was stunned when he saw the gun. "Why?" he asked.

"I don't know," Bruce answered. "I was told by the Department of State to carry this when I went to meet you."

As Bruce was supposed to see Prime Minister Harold Macmillan the next day, Acheson told him of the intended blockade and then bade farewell after dropping off a CIA man and a guard with a set of photographs. Then Acheson flew on to Paris and spent a few restless hours trying to sleep at the house of the chargé d'affaires, Cecil Lyon.

The next day, Monday, the question was how to approach de Gaulle. Acheson suggested that Lyon tell his *chef de cabinet* that Acheson had come into town in the middle of the night on a very important secret mission from the president of the United States to the president of France. It would also be best if no one knew he was in the French capital.

At five P.M. a staff car arrived to take Acheson, Lyon, and Sherman Kent to the Elysée Palace. Once in the courtyard, they did not mount the main staircase but went to a side entrance, where they were led through winding passages past musty wine closets and steel doors with little eyelets in them.

Halfway through this maze, Kent said to Acheson, "D'Artagnan, is that rapier loose in its scabbard?"

Acheson replied, "Aye, Porthos," and added, "Be on the alert. The cardinal's men may be waiting."

Arriving outside the president's office, Acheson was told that the general would see only him and his interpreter, Cecil Lyon. As they entered the private office with photographs in hand, de Gaulle was standing just to the left of his desk to greet him: "Your President has done me great honor by sending so distinguished an emissary."

Acheson handed him a letter from Kennedy and a text of the speech the president would be delivering in about eight hours, telling the American people of the Soviet missile shipments and the intended blockade. After reading through the papers—for his reading knowledge of English was excellent—the general asked: "Do I understand that you have come from the president to inform me of some decision taken by the President—or have you come to consult me about a decision which he should take?"

Acheson explained that he had come solely to inform him. "I am in favor of independent decisions," de Gaulle replied. Acheson then offered to show him the photographs. "Not at all. Not now," said the general. "This is mere evidence, and great nations such as yours would not take a serious step if there was any doubt about the evidence at all. Later, it would be interesting to see these, and I will look at them."

De Gaulle asked, "Do you think the Russians will attempt to force this blockade?"

Acheson said, "No, I do not."

The general then asked, "Do you think they would have reacted if your President had taken even sharper action?"

Acheson said, "No, I do not think they would have done that."

De Gaulle agreed. Both men believed the Russians would not blockade Berlin or take any action in regard to the American missile bases in Turkey.

But then the general asked him a more difficult question: "Suppose they don't do anything—suppose they don't try to break the blockade—suppose they don't take the missiles out—what will your President do then?"

No one in Washington had told Acheson the answer to that question. He had no idea whether or not a plan existed. But he thought it unwise to let de Gaulle know that the Americans were absolutely unclear as to what they would do in the next stage; so he said, "We will immediately tighten this blockade."

De Gaulle nodded. "That's very good."

Acheson finally added, "If we have to go further, why, of course, we'll go further."

They then proceeded to examine the photographs with a magnifying glass, as the general's eyesight was especially poor. He was deeply impressed that the photographs were taken at sixty-five thousand feet. "*C'est formidable,*" he declared. "*C'est formidable.*" When they finished, de Gaulle said quite simply, "You may tell your President that France will support him in every way in this crisis."

As the general walked Acheson to the door, he spoke his only words of English during the whole session: "It would be a pleasure for me if these things were all done through you."

Despite his later differences with the general over France's role in NATO, Acheson always thought de Gaulle a man of great character, "a kind of 'hero as king' that Carlyle wrote about and everyone now, except me, makes fun of." He was especially pleased when Henry Kissinger, at the time a professor at Harvard, later reported to him that de Gaulle said of Acheson at the time of the missile crisis, "*Voilà un homme.*"[20]

Acheson then flew to Bonn after receiving an urgent telegram from Kennedy telling him to calm down Adenauer, who had learned of the crisis from American ambassador Dowling. It seemed the German chancellor feared that Khrushchev had sent the missiles to Cuba in order to use them as a bargaining chip to force the United States out of Berlin. When Acheson met Adenauer, the latter seemed puzzled at the use of a blockade, which would not in itself remove the missiles. When Adenauer asked what was Kennedy's rationale for this, Acheson shrugged and said, "Faith moves mountains." Despite this rather weak defense of Kennedy's actions, Adenauer gave full support to the president.[21]

With his European mission accomplished, Acheson flew back to Washington on Wednesday afternoon, October 24, where a showdown with the Russians seemed at hand. By this time Kennedy had publicly announced the decision to put in place the naval blockade or "quarantine" in order to prevent additional missiles from reaching Cuba. The president had also warned the Russians that any missile launched from Cuba would require the United States to launch "a full retaliatory response" against the Soviet Union. He then urged Khrushchev "to move the world back from the abyss of destruction."[22]

Upon his arrival at the State Department, Acheson reported to Rusk on the results of his mission. The following day he spoke directly with the president. The missiles were still in Cuba, and a week's collection of photographs showed "alarming progress" in deploying them. Time was running out, Acheson remembered telling the president. "The air strike remained the only method of eliminating them and hourly it was becoming more dangerous." Other members of the ExCom were now shifting to the need for military action.

Then, on Friday evening, October 26, Rusk showed Acheson a "confused, almost maudlin message" from Khrushchev that admitted the presence of nuclear weapons in Cuba but denied that they had been put there to attack the United States. They were there, the Soviet leader said, solely to protect Cuba against American attempts to overthrow Castro's government. The letter suggested that if the United States gave assurances that it would not attack Cuba, the removal of the missiles might be "an entirely different question."

At breakfast with McNamara on Saturday morning, Acheson learned of a second, more formal Russian note from Khrushchev, which may have been drafted by the Foreign Ministry in ignorance of Khrushchev's earlier message. The new note linked the withdrawal of the Cuban missiles to America's withdrawal of its missiles from Turkey. Formal linkage of this kind was rejected by the White House, though Kennedy was perfectly prepared to take out the Turkish missiles, which were now obsolete, at a later date.[23]

That Saturday a majority of the members of the ExCom (Acheson not participating) were in favor of an air attack on the Cuban surface-to-air missile sites. An American U-2 had been shot down over Cuba, and the Joint Chiefs of Staff were urging an air strike on Monday, followed by an invasion.[24]

The president balked. There would be no attack yet. They would try again to find a solution without bloodshed.

The missile crisis was resolved when the president, at his brother's suggestion, decided to reply to Khrushchev's first letter, which suggested that the missiles would be removed if the United States promised that it would not invade Cuba. Private assurances that the American missiles in Turkey would eventually be dismantled once the Cuban crisis was resolved would be given by Robert Kennedy to Moscow through Soviet ambassador Anatoly Dobrynin.[25]

Khrushchev accepted the deal that Kennedy offered. The Soviet leader could now say that he had saved Cuba from an invasion. To Acheson's amazement, Robert Kennedy's ploy of ignoring Khrushchev's second, hard-line letter—which Acheson later called a "one-hundred-to-one shot"—paid off. As Acheson reflected in later years, "It does not detract from President Kennedy's laurels in handling the Cuban crisis that he was helped by the luck of Khrushchev's befuddlement and loss of nerve. The fact was, as the Duke of Wellington said of Waterloo, it was 'a damned near thing.'"[26]

Despite American superiority of at least seventeen to one in strategic nuclear weaponry, the Soviets possessed enough missiles outside of Cuba—50 on land, 100 on submarines—and 150 strategic bombers, to make it almost certain that in any nuclear exchange, some of their missiles and bombers would be able to reach the United States. More decisive in Khrushchev's retreat was the overwhelming superiority of U.S. conventional forces—air, ground, and sea—in the Cuban region.[27]

Why then did Khrushchev put the missiles in Cuba in the first place? There were probably two main reasons: to narrow the missile gap and, above all, to protect Cuba from an American invasion. Even if the missiles in Cuba did not overturn the actual balance of power, if they remained, as Kennedy said at the end of the year, "it would have politically changed the balance of power. It would have appeared to, and appearances contribute to reality."[28]

As for Khrushchev's statement that the missiles were deployed in order to prevent the United States from invading Cuba, the testimony of Khrushchev's speechwriter, Fyodor Burlatsky, as well as of Sergo Mikoyan, son of Anastas Mikoyan, a close asociate of Khrushchev's, backs up the Soviet leader's contention. Despite differences of emphasis, both men agreed that Khrushchev felt he had genuine responsibilities toward Cuba.[29]

Acheson's air strike would certainly have damaged U.S.-Soviet relations more severely than the naval blockade did. But in McGeorge Bundy's view, it would not have posed a greater risk of nuclear war than did the quarantine. Under either scenario, a nuclear exchange would have been a wholly unacceptable option for Khrushchev.[30]

Acheson sent Kennedy a handwritten note on October 28 congratulating him on his "leadership, firmness and judgment" and pointing out, "Only a few people know better than I how hard these decisions are to make, and how broad the gap is between the advisers and the decider."[31]

Despite Acheson's words of praise, he always believed that the president lacked decisiveness, the quality that he had most admired in Harry Truman and always found wanting in his successors.

After the missile crisis, Acheson no longer played a significant role in the Kennedy administration's consultations. But he was too restless to remain inactive in public affairs, especially during the sharpening debates over America's relations with Europe. In one instance he became the center of controversy. Invited to deliver a keynote address at a student conference at West Point on December 5, 1962, Acheson for the most part sounded his familiar refrain on the importance of America's role in the Atlantic Alliance. About halfway through the talk, however, he singled out Great Britain as the country that had most consistently impeded European unity.

"Great Britain has lost an empire and has not yet found a role," he asserted. "The attempt to play a separate power role, that is, a role apart from Europe, a role based primarily on a 'special relationship' with the United States, a role based on being head of the Commonwealth"—is "about played out."[32]

The next day his words were on the front pages of British newspapers. Although Acheson had spoken as a private citizen—and his support for British entry into the European Common Market was official U.S. policy—his speech was seen as reflecting government policy. Moreover, Acheson's reputation as a strong friend of Britain's made his words cut even more deeply into the fragile British psyche.

Kennedy's press secretary, Pierre Salinger, was forced to declare that the president had no prior knowledge of Acheson's speech. Acheson's old friend, Oliver Franks, recalled, "He had stung us and we were temporarily numb."[33]

Acheson was himself quite taken aback by the notoriety his words caused, but he did not disavow them. For many years he had been discouraged when Britain refused to play a leading role in the creation of a West European union; even while in office he had deplored British unwillingness to join the Coal and Steel Community and refusal to become a member of the proposed European Defense Community. The speech also surprised those who saw Acheson as an Anglophile because of his bearing and dress. But Acheson was, above all, a pragmatist, and while he may have admired British style and institutions, he never promoted the idea of an Anglo-American connection.

Acheson's West Point speech underlined how greatly British influence on American policy had declined since the days when Acheson, Bevin, and Eden coordinated their efforts on the Marshall Plan and the creation of NATO. Not only had an American president not bothered to consult Macmillan over the Cuban missile crisis (which put Europe as well as America at risk, should the Russians have struck back militarily), but Kennedy, like Acheson, was hostile to the existence of a separate British nuclear force.

While Acheson was convinced that Britain's pretensions to being a world power were vastly overdone, he was angry that de Gaulle should persuade the French people to believe that France should also play a global role. Ironically, de Gaulle's stout support for the United States during the Cuban missile crisis, which Acheson had so admired, also led the general to the conclusion that the United States would risk European interests for American interests. It was therefore all the more important that France possess its own independent nuclear deterrent. In addition, de Gaulle was searching for a relaxation of tensions with the Soviet Union that would eventually allow Europe—led by France—to play a more independent role in the struggle between the two superpowers.

Acheson's views ran squarely counter to the Gaullist vision. He espoused European unity, but in a setting that would militarily and economically bind together Western Europe and the United States. At this point in history, the United States would be the decisive player, but over time he expected a more equal partnership to emerge.

On January 20, 1963, convinced that England, with its emphasis on its "special relationship" with America, was not sufficiently "European," de Gaulle vetoed Britain's entry into the Common Market. A week before, the general had signed a bilateral treaty establishing closer ties with West Germany. This was designed in part to counter American predominance in Western Europe while at the same time inaugurating a new era of better relations with the Soviet Union, with the long-term view of establishing a Europe, free of the Iron Curtain, that de Gaulle envisaged stretching "from the Atlantic to the Urals."

Acheson was now determined to lead the struggle against de Gaulle's efforts to manipulate Adenauer's Germany into becoming a tool of the general's plan to reduce America's power in Europe. To a member of the Foreign Affairs Committee of the Bundestag, he wrote, "The Chancellor has never understood General de Gaulle's design for the undignified and demeaning role designed for him and for Germany." He urged him to have the German parliament "attach a reservation" to the Franco-German treaty, stating German determination to hew to the North American connection.[34]

In an article in April 1963, Acheson paid homage to de Gaulle's personal qualities: "Among men now living and active, no one's personality makes as great, and generally beneficial, an impact on his environment as the General's. This is as good a definition of greatness as I know." Precisely because of these great qualities, Acheson concluded that it was not possible "to persuade, bribe or coerce de Gaulle from following a course upon which he is set." Only when the general recognized "the inevitable" would he adjust his conduct to it. In this respect, the "power of the U.S. to shape the inevitable for de Gaulle is immense."[35]

At a speaking tour in the West, he warned at the University of California at Berkeley that de Gaulle should not expect American protection of a Europe that excluded American influence. His words resonated in the European press, and by the summer of 1963 it was clear that Bonn did not want to weaken its ties to Washington, while nonetheless preserving close relations with Paris.

Kennedy's trip to Berlin in June 1963, when he affirmed America's willingness to defend Berlin from any Communist threat—uttering the famous phrase "*Ich bin ein Berliner*"—dampened Bonn's enthusiasm for a Franco-German entente. Shortly thereafter the West German government inserted a preamble into the Franco-German treaty that reaffirmed Germany's ties to Washington and NATO, just as Acheson had suggested.

Acheson never wavered from his core beliefs. In a letter to John Cowles that summer, he quoted Justice Holmes: "Deep seated principles cannot be argued about. You cannot argue a man into liking a glass of beer." As he insisted to Cowles, "The way to win the cold war may be difficult and unclear—though I am confident enough to believe that to plug away at the policies I have advocated since the end of the war will do it—but one thing seems to me as clear as day. That is that the one sure way to lose the cold war, is to lose Germany."[36]

As it did the rest of the country, the assassination of President Kennedy on November 22, 1963, saddened and shocked Acheson. "Surely there was sorrow for the death of a brave young man and an inexpressibly gallant young widow and two utterly pathetic and heartbreaking children," he wrote to an English friend. But Kennedy's death in office was not comparable to Roosevelt's: "It was not bewilderment at the loss of a great and tried leader, as with FDR, for JFK was not that. It was fear from the utter collapse of all sense of security which lay at the bottom of the emotion. . . . If he is old and should die of a heart attack, as Ike might have, we would be upset. But where in the person of a young and vibrant man he becomes a corpse within an hour, the vast factor of chance and insecurity in all our separate lives as well as our collective life becomes oppressive and paralyzingly terrifying."[37]

What Acheson admired most of all in JFK, as he did in Mrs. Kennedy in the aftermath of the assassination, was a certain stoicism and grace under pressure. Kennedy had always treated him with courtesy and thoughtfulness, and Acheson had responded to Kennedy's wry humor and ironic wit. The president was "attractive" and "blessed with real charm," Acheson said in an interview with the BBC in 1971. But "he didn't seem to me to be in any sense a great man."[38]

Kennedy, however much he may have disagreed with Acheson at times, always respected his intellect and powers of persuasion. "Acheson would have made a helluva Supreme Court Justice," he said to Ben Bradlee, the editor of the *Washington Post.*[39] George Ball, who worked closely with both men, may have best summed up Kennedy's relationship with the intimidating former secretary of state. "Kennedy was very impressed with Acheson," he said. "He retained that throughout, although they would occasionally get cross-wired. Jack was a little bit afraid of Dean. After all, Jack was a very young man and Acheson was a titan."[40]

CHAPTER THIRTY-THREE

CONTENDING WITH LBJ

LYNDON JOHNSON "[has done] an almost incredible job," Acheson wrote almost a year to the day after Kennedy was killed. Johnson had just been elected president in his own right by an overwhelming majority in November 1964, and Acheson had written to congratulate him, as he put it to an English friend, "upon the achievement which was his alone of pulling together a shattered country and bringing us through grave troubles to a new unity."

Yet Acheson went on to acknowledge Johnson's flaws: "Like all powerful men, he has his faults, and some are not small, including his vanity." The election, Acheson hoped, "will not, I think, feed his vanity, but will give him assurance, which he sometimes lacks, and bring home to him the vast responsibility which has been placed upon him." Acheson was not displeased that the new president "has encouraged me to annoy him with advice, which I shall do in moderation."[1]

Lyndon Johnson genuinely liked and admired Dean Acheson. They had worked together in the late 1950s when Acheson was the foreign policy spokesman for the Democratic Advisory Council and Johnson was the Senate majority leader. In addition to listening to Acheson's views on foreign affairs, with which Johnson generally agreed, LBJ had asked Acheson to help him in the drafting of the Civil Rights Act of 1957, then the most comprehensive civil rights legislation since Reconstruction.

Acheson had defended Johnson against those who accused the Senate majority leader of playing politics and watering down the bill; in fact, Acheson had worked together with Johnson's friend and later Supreme Court justice Abe Fortas to make the bill acceptable to southern politicians. To those who attacked Johnson for this, Acheson assured LBJ: "To regard the phrase 'playing politics' as a dirty phrase is silly." The two places where "politics have no honorable place" are "the security of the United States and in securing to our negro fellow citizens the basic right which we have promised them for nearly a century—the right to speak for themselves."[2]

Johnson was hurt that Acheson did not support him in his quest for the Democratic presidency in 1960. In 1959, when asked what type of person he would appoint as secretary of state if he were elected president, Johnson had said that he "would like to see another Dean Acheson." Acheson's reluctance to back Johnson in the campaign against Kennedy—largely because Acheson believed Kennedy, not Johnson, could win—cooled their friendship. But no sooner was Johnson installed as president in the wake of Kennedy's assassination than he called on Acheson for his advice on forming a commission to investigate the killing. Also in those first weeks in office, he solicited Acheson's views on Germany. On December 5, 1963, Acheson presented him with a memorandum that reiterated his long-held opinion that the president should do nothing to help de Gaulle with his nuclear striking force and should discourage talks with Russia over Germany.[3]

In a cover memo to Acheson's memorandum, McGeorge Bundy, who remained as LBJ's national security adviser, summed up Acheson's foreign policy views for Johnson: "Re your lunch with Acheson: He is a determined believer in the 'hard line.' . . . Acheson believes in action even during an election year (he remembers what Truman accomplished in '48) and has little patience for less developed countries, the UN, Adlai Stevenson, George Kennan, etc."[4]

Johnson's relationship with Acheson, like that with other members of the foreign policy elite, was characterized by both envy and disdain. He was convinced that men such as Bundy and Ball and Acheson would get the credit for any foreign policy successes, yet he was proud that his "intellectuals" were working for him. His insecurity showed when he told a columnist for *Time* magazine, "I don't believe I'll ever get credit for anything I do in foreign affairs, no matter how successful it is, because I didn't go to Harvard."[5]

LBJ once mocked Acheson's imperious manner by giving a pantomime performance of the former secretary of state testifying before a congressional committee, yet he badly wanted to be admired and respected by Acheson. His letters to the former secretary of state were often fawning, as he tried to seduce him with effusive compliments. (Acheson was deluged with autographed pictures of the president, with the usual flattering inscriptions such as "To Dean Acheson, a master logician and dedicated patriot"; "To Dean Acheson, an American I admire most." Writing to a friend in December 1963, Acheson dismissed his own "budding reputation as an 'elder statesman.'"[6])

To Acheson, Johnson's behavior became more and more irritating. At a meeting in the Oval Office on December 6, 1963, Acheson found Johnson in a nearly uncontrollable rage because the Soviet Union had just denied permission for an American theatrical company to perform the musical *Hello, Dolly!* in Moscow.

Moreover, the leading lady was a friend of the president's. Johnson cursed out the Russians, and then an aide rushed in with a "crisis update." "The damn State Department," Johnson railed, had strongly advised him not to take any action against the Soviets. What should he do?

Acheson snapped back that such a trivial issue wasn't worthy of the attention of the president of the United States. He had come over to talk about European issues. "I don't care what the Russians think about *Hello, Dolly!*" he said. "And neither should you."[7]

Acheson's preoccupation with European affairs was clearly not what mainly interested Johnson. He knew where Acheson stood, and he also believed he could count on Acheson to defend the administration's European policies, which largely reflected Acheson's views, against any and all critics.

What Johnson definitely needed from Acheson was his willingness to become a member of a panel of consultants on major foreign policy issues during and after the 1964 presidential campaign. The Vietnam War was worsening, and Johnson was presenting himself as the peace candidate against the avowedly hawkish Republican senator from Arizona, Barry Goldwater. At last, through the ministrations of McGeorge Bundy, Acheson joined with other senior statesmen, such as John J. McCloy, Douglas Dillon, and Robert Lovett, in a group that Bundy somewhat ironically referred to as "the Wise Men."

Socially, the Acheson that Washingtonians knew from dinner parties in Georgetown during this period was often irascible, his luminous wit often assuming a tone of exasperation or mockery. Acheson had always been something of a performer, and on social occasions guests would often goad him into making extreme remarks, particularly after he had had a second martini. He came from a hard-drinking, hardworking generation. It might be said of him, as Gibbon said of the great general Belisarius: "His vices were the vices of his time; his virtues were his own."

Except for his regular winter holidays in Antigua, he preferred to remain at his Maryland farm. In 1960 in Harewood a studio was built for Alice to paint in, while Acheson was most happy to stand over a lathe in his well-equipped carpentry shop, where he built stylish furniture. "The great thing about this hobby," he said with infinite satisfaction, "is that when I have finished a table or a chair and I put it down, it either stands or falls. It's not like foreign policy, you don't have to wait for twenty years to see whether it works."[8]

George Ball, the under secretary of state, was one member of the Johnson administration with whom Acheson was especially comfortable. Even when they disagreed, Ball had a direct and forthright manner that appealed to Acheson. Moreover, they were close allies in believing that Europe was the theater of action most important for the United States.

In February 1964 Ball came up with the idea that Acheson might prove to be the indispensable mediator between Greece and Turkey, two NATO allies, in the latest phase of the simmering Cyprus conflict. Ball knew that Acheson was not interested in the pomp of high office but that he very much enjoyed tackling difficult jobs (even with scant chance of credit).

In this case, he would be more than a consultant called in to stiffen the president's back; instead he would be a key player in a dispute that threatened to tear apart the Atlantic Alliance and offer Moscow an opportunity to meddle in the crisis. As a legendary figure in both Athens and Ankara because of his role in creating the Truman Doctrine, Acheson might just be the man who could bring off a successful negotiation.[9]

For three centuries under rule by the Ottoman empire, the two Cypriot communities, Greek and Turkish, lived in relative harmony on the eastern Mediterranean island. The Ottomans did not impose Islam on the Greek Cypriots, and this peaceful state of affairs lasted until 1878, when Cyprus became a British possession; the British continued to allow each group to retain its cultural identity. Nonetheless, Greek Cypriots (making up about 80 percent of the population) periodically agitated for union (*enosis*) with Greece, and in the 1930s *enosis* became a powerful and continuous movement. In turn, a Turkish Cypriot movement for partition (and presumably for double annexation) was created in the mid-1950s, in large part stimulated by London and Ankara as a counterpoint to *enosis*.

With the winds of decolonization then sweeping throughout the world, it was inevitable that Britain, progressively less concerned with the island's strategic value, would grant independence to the island; this in fact occurred in 1960, at which time it was agreed that the Republic of Cyprus would be governed jointly by the two ethnic groups, with Britain, Greece, and Turkey acting as guarantors of the new nation. However, by giving the Turkish Cypriot minority a virtual veto over all major policy decisions, the governing system was almost bound to fail.

The struggle between the Greek and Turkish Cypriots intensified after the Greek Cypriot leader and first president of Cyprus, Archbishop Makarios, took power in 1960. In November 1963 he proposed amendments to the constitution that would limit Turkish Cypriot participation in government, and by Christmas a civil war had erupted on the island.[10]

To calm things down, a United Nations peacekeeping force was created in March 1964, but the situation worsened. Turkey, convinced that the Turkish-speaking enclaves on the island might be attacked, was ready to launch an invasion of the island. In the meantime, the archbishop was discussing the situation with Khrushchev and outlining his strategy, which also involved gaining support from "neutralists" in the East-West conflict. In June 1964 Lyndon Johnson decided to summon the Greek and Turkish prime ministers, George Papandreou and Ismet Inonu, to Washington.

Despite a meeting on the president's yacht, *Sequoia*, that included LBJ and the two prime ministers, as well as Acheson and Ball, it was impossible to make real progress. The seventy-seven-year-old Papandreou insisted on Cyprus's right to self-determination, and he would not negotiate directly with the Turkish government.

Now was the moment for Acheson to step forward as the essential mediator in a conference scheduled for July in Geneva under the auspices of the United Nations. At first, UN secretary-general U Thant refused to let Acheson take over the mediation, but when he arrived with his wife in Switzerland on July 5, that was exactly what he did.

By the end of the month the so-called Acheson Plan had taken shape. It called for union of part of Cyprus with Greece, the cession of one of the Greek Dodecanese islands to Turkey, two or three Turkish Cypriots "cantons" with local authority, and the establishment of a Turkish military base on Cyprus.[11]

Since the plan called for the disappearance of an independent Cyprus, Archbishop Makarios, earlier a fervent advocate of *enosis*, was now resolutely opposed to union with Greece. For Acheson, however, an independent Cyprus was an invitation to a new Graeco-Turkish war. The task for Acheson was to sell the plan to the Greek prime minister as well as to Ankara.

While the Turkish delegation was willing to use Acheson's proposals as the basis for a settlement, Athens proved intractable. Makarios had no intention of giving up his presidency of an independent Cyprus, and he stirred up as much opposition as possible to the plan in Greece. In the end, the Greek prime minister rejected the Acheson Plan, even though Acheson had managed to convince most of the negotiators on both sides who were in Geneva to accept his proposal in principle.

Acheson was furious with Makarios, whom he regarded as that "bloody and bearded old reprobate."[12] By mid-August he was ready to go home. Ball, however, begged him to stay on. If the Geneva enterprise must die, Ball contended in a series of telexes to Acheson, its burial should be conducted not "by an orthodox Archbishop but by the son of an Episcopal bishop." Yet on August 31 the State Department announced that the negotiations had indeed collapsed and Acheson was coming back to Washington.

For the next ten years the Acheson Plan remained the basis for negotiations over Cyprus. The Turks did not invade, and Greek Cypriots did not overwhelm the Turkish Cypriots. A UN peacekeeping force remained in place until the ultra-nationalistic Greek colonels' junta, in power in Athens since mid-1967, mounted a coup to overthrow Makarios in July 1974. The Turkish army then did invade, occupying over one-third of the island. Partition of Cyprus did take place, but by force. No further agreements were forthcoming, and the island would remain tense for years to come. In retrospect, the Acheson Plan may have been the best way to avoid ethnic conflict.[13]

Despite Acheson's failure to bring peace to Cyprus, 1964 ended well for him. In September Johnson conferred on him the highest civilian honor, the Presidential Medal of Freedom. Johnson's election that November also cheered Acheson, but shortly thereafter he grew more and more distressed by LBJ's manner and style. At one meeting that Acheson attended a few weeks into the new term, Johnson ridiculed his top foreign policy advisers. He put down George Ball for compiling a "disgraceful" list of ambassadorial candidates, abused McNamara for his ignorance of congressional affairs, and even insulted Acheson by calling him "the man who got us into war in Korea," adding, "[we had to] get Eisenhower to get us out of that."

This was too much for Acheson, who interrupted him by saying, "Mr. President, you don't pay these men enough to talk to them that way—even with the federal pay raise." His comment broke the tension, and when discussion resumed, Johnson took a more respectful tone.[14]

With the new year Acheson continued to send the president memorandums, which usually dealt with the need to preserve the Atlantic Alliance and the urgency of concluding tariff reductions with the other industrialized nations. But by mid-1965 Lyndon Johnson was consumed with the deepening American military involvement in Vietnam, and Acheson's urging him to pay more attention to Europe received only perfunctory attention.

The death of Felix Frankfurter on February 22, 1965, was especially hard on Acheson. As he wrote to Erwin Griswold, dean of Harvard Law School, "I find it hard to realize that it is all over. Almost every day something happens which I immediately remind myself to tell Felix about."[15] Acheson's memoir, *Morning and Noon,* published that October, was dedicated to Frankfurter.

Frankfurter, it turned out, had made no arrangements for his funeral, so Acheson took on the responsibility and organized a memorial service much in the pattern of Brandeis's in 1941. "It was very simple," Acheson wrote to Archibald MacLeish, "small and in the apartment, no casket or ashes; a trio from the National Symphony. . . . a beautiful Hebrew magnificat for the dead. That was it. . . . Felix would have approved. The President came and was very moved."[16]

Acheson felt the stirrings of his own mortality when he attended the fiftieth reunion of his class at Yale that June. At first he was reluctant to go, and his worsening thyroid condition and chronic stomach ailments seemed reason enough to stay home. For a vigorous man to feel so continuously bad was hard indeed. But, as he wrote MacLeish after the affair, he enjoyed the talk with his old classmates—which on this occasion was the "undirected, drifting, casual sort of talk which only comes with intimacy and quiet. This to me was the priceless product of this reunion. . . . For this I am very grateful."[17]

Acheson continued to worry about LBJ's priorities. Even though he supported the American effort in Vietnam, he was appalled by the degree to which Vietnam crowded out attention to European problems.

The 1966 NATO crisis turned out to be even more severe than he had envisaged. On March 7 de Gaulle informed Johnson that he was removing all French troops from the integrated NATO military organization and insisted that all foreign troops, including the Americans, quit French soil. NATO headquarters would have to be removed from outside Paris to Belgium. Although France was pulling out of NATO's military organization, it would nevertheless remain a member of the Atlantic Alliance.

Johnson immediately called on Acheson to head a NATO crisis management group to study the long-term implications of the French withdrawal. At a meeting in the White House in mid-March the collective wisdom of Johnson's advisers was to respond to de Gaulle's "fervent nationalism" with "restraint and patience." With this Acheson concurred, but he minimized the military damage that the French withdrawal would cause. His main worry was that de Gaulle's assertion of independence would affect Germany and other members of the alliance.

LBJ largely shared the views of his advisers, and he did not attack de Gaulle personally. Acheson, however, was not bound by diplomatic restraint. He lambasted de Gaulle in a television interview that April. Asked about de Gaulle's belief that the integrated NATO command under an American general served only to enhance American predominance over Europe, Acheson responded: "It's a curious situation of a recovered patient, a convalescent who has been weak, who has been ill and has finally been built up and had good food and good care, been in a warm house and warm bed and suddenly he says, 'I'm a big man, I don't need any more food, no more doctors, no more house, I want to get out in the wind and the rain, the ice and the snow. I don't need any of this protection.'"[18]

On April 17, 1966, Acheson testified as the lead witness at congressional hearings on the Atlantic Alliance. His was a commanding presence, and most of his testimony was devoted to reassuring the senators that NATO would survive France's defection from the military organization. De Gaulle's France was not now "a dependable or an effective ally," he said. The best policy in a bad situation was the policy of the "empty chair," meaning the alliance should wait for a time when a successor to President de Gaulle would decide to rejoin the integrated command structure of NATO.

Acheson did not publicly relate de Gaulle's desire to speed up the American withdrawal from France and his unwillingness to remain within the integrated command to the Cuban missile crisis. He could imagine, however, de Gaulle's thinking on this score, for the Cuban missile crisis could have involved Western Europe in a conflict with Russia, even though Europe's vital interests were not at stake.

In June, after nearly four months of "unrequited toil," Acheson resigned from the NATO crisis management group. It had not been a very agreeable experience to work with either the White House or the State Department. He felt that the White House had sometimes been conducting a "press leak campaign against George Ball, Jack McCloy and me as anti–de Gaulle extremists." As he wrote to Anthony Eden on June 29, 1966, "This all blew up at a White House meeting when, at some crack of LBJ's, I lost my temper and told him what I thought of his conduct and that I was not prepared to stand for any more of it. Rusk and McNamara dove for cover while Ball and I slugged it out with Mr. Big. . . . It was exhilarating and did something to clear the air. Since then I have been inundated with action photographs of LBJ and me, and—more important—he has approved of my recommendations. Whether anything will be *done* about them, is doubtful. I have not seen the Department so disorganized since the end of the Hull regime."[19]

His disillusion with Dean Rusk was now almost total. In a letter in early October thanking Truman for his condolences on the death of his younger brother, Ted Acheson, of a sudden heart attack, Acheson summed up his views of Rusk and Johnson. Regretting his recommendation to JFK to appoint Rusk as secretary of state, he described him as being "no good at all. For some reason, unknown to me, he will not disclose his mind to anyone. The Department is totally at a loss to know what he wants done or what he thinks."

As for LBJ, "Now-a-days his preoccupations are Vietnam and the balance of payments. So Europe is forgotten. . . . He could be so much better than he is. He creates distrust by being too smart. He is never quite candid. He is both mean and generous, but the meanness too often predominates."[20]

Acheson was right that Johnson was preoccupied with Vietnam, and soon Acheson himself shared that obsession.

CHAPTER THIRTY-FOUR

INTO THE QUAGMIRE

By the spring of 1965, the American involvement in Vietnam had deepened. Thirty-five thousand American troops were now there; the shaky South Vietnamese regime, torn by internal political strife, was almost wholly dependent on American economic and military aid. In response to Communist Viet Cong attacks against U.S. military facilities at Pleiku on February 6 and 7, Johnson had ordered a series of retaliatory air strikes against North Vietnam and then a sustained bombing effort, which was christened Operation Rolling Thunder; during a three-year period Rolling Thunder would drop over four hundred thousand tons of bombs on North Vietnam.

Acheson had supported the American effort to contain what he saw as Communist expansionism in Southeast Asia. He was convinced that after having committed itself to helping the non-Communist South Vietnamese government, Washington had to back up its commitment or lose credibility with its allies elsewhere. But he nonetheless believed that the Soviet Union, not China, was the chief American adversary, and he feared that the United States would find itself mired in a part of the world of secondary importance to the national interest.

Disturbed at the escalation of the war in the months following Johnson's election in 1964, George Ball pointed out the following April that Rolling Thunder had not forced Hanoi to drop its support for the Communist Viet Cong in the south. On April 21 the president listened carefully to Ball and then urged him to get some people together to do nothing for a few days but ponder the political alternatives in Southeast Asia.

At this point, Ball recalled, "I desperately needed at least one high-level confrere on my side; how could the President be expected to adopt the heresies of an

Under Secretary against the contrary views of his whole top command? But since no top-level official shared my view, I decided to seek help outside." He called Dean Acheson.

Together with Lloyd Cutler, another prominent Washington lawyer, Acheson expanded Ball's memorandum into a detailed program for "the social and political reconstruction of South Vietnam." By early May the Acheson-Ball peace plan was ready. Acheson had rewritten almost entirely Ball's original proposal. In his memorandum to the president, he set aside his worries over how America would be perceived by other nations if it should pull out of Vietnam and stuck to Ball's premise that the war was unwinnable. Lloyd Cutler later recalled that "Acheson was convinced that the war in Vietnam was going nowhere and we had to have a settlement."

The Acheson-Ball plan called for an immediate halt to the bombing; a phased withdrawal of all foreign troops, including American and North Vietnamese forces, from South Vietnam; a general amnesty for "all Viet Cong adherents who cease fighting"; and the holding of local elections to include Viet Cong participation.

The plan, reflecting Acheson's skepticism over negotiations with the Communists, required no negotiations, but rather unilateral action by the South Vietnamese government, although Washington should be willing "to hold discussions with any government concerned."

Meeting with Johnson and Rusk on May 16, Acheson presented the Acheson-Ball plan. The purpose of the plan, his memorandum stated, was to achieve U.S. objectives in the South Vietnam "by shifting the struggle from the military to the political arena" before there was further escalation of the conflict. Rusk suggested that Ball's deputy, Thomas Ehrlich, go to Saigon to present the peace plan to U.S. ambassador Maxwell Taylor, the former chairman of the Joint Chiefs of Staff, and get his opinion on whether the South Vietnamese government would go along with it.[1]

"A giveaway program of the worst sort," was Taylor's reaction. As far as Taylor was concerned, the Acheson-Ball plan was equal to a stamp of approval for Hanoi to take over South Vietnam. To Ball, Taylor's reaction showed that "America had become a prisoner of whatever Saigon military clique was momentarily in power. Like a heroine in an eighteenth-century novel who got her own way by fainting if anyone spoke crossly, each clique understood how to exploit its own weakness. If we demanded anything significant of it, it would collapse; so we never made any serious demands."[2] The plan was stillborn.

Whatever Acheson's doubts about Johnson's policy in Vietnam, he now bucked up the president at a July 8, 1965, meeting of "the Wise Men," which now included Robert Lovett, John J. McCloy, retired army general Omar Bradley, and John Cowles. The group said that whatever forces were required, Johnson should have no hesitation in providing them. Vietnam was a crucial test of America's willingness to stand up to Communist "wars of liberation," and withdrawal was an "unacceptable alternative."[3]

That evening Johnson met the group at the White House, where he began complaining about his problems in Europe, Latin America, and Vietnam. He was whining about how everyone was against him. Here was a president, Acheson realized as he recalled his days with General Marshall and Truman, who would spend hours "fighting the problem," endlessly reconsidering decisions, or feeling sorry for himself. Finally Acheson "blew his top," as he wrote to Truman, and told LBJ to stop complaining and that in Vietnam "he had no choice but to press on." It was like Korea, when America stepped in not so much to save the South Koreans as to demonstrate to America's allies as well as to the Communists that the United States stood firm against Communist aggression.

He told LBJ that "explanations were not as important as successful action; and that the trouble in Europe (which was more important than either of the other spots) came about because under him and Kennedy there had been no American leadership at all." With this lead, "my colleagues came thundering in like the charge of the Scots Greys at Waterloo. They were fine; old Bob Lovett, usually cautious, was all out, and, of course, [General Bradley] left no doubt that he was with me all the way. I think . . . we scored."[4]

They clearly did. Three weeks later Johnson announced the critical decision to commit American combat troops to fight an aggressive, open-ended ground war in South Vietnam.

Acheson, after his peace plan went nowhere, felt he had to take an uncompromising position. As Ball recalled later, "Acheson was an all-or-nothing man. [After Korea] he was uncomfortable with the notion of limited war."[5] Yet despite Acheson's apparently bare-knuckled support for carrying on in Vietnam, the very day after the meeting with LBJ, he wrote to Erik Boheman, a former Swedish ambassador to Washington, "If we take over the war, we defeat our purpose and merely take the place of the French."[6]

For the next two years polls continued to show that most Americans supported the war in Vietnam, but the antiwar movement was gaining in ferocity. Acheson, however, gave full public support to the president in his conduct of the war. He signed manifestos that were often published as full-page advertisements in *The New York Times*, endorsing Johnson's measures "to meet the increased aggression against South Vietnam." Like many men and women of his generation, he was disturbed by the vehemence of the antiwar protesters.

Despite upbeat reports from the military commanders in Vietnam, reporters on the scene saw little evidence that the United States was winning "the hearts and minds" of the Vietnamese people. In addition, the bombing of North Vietnam—including its capital, Hanoi—did not seem to be bringing the North Vietnamese leaders closer to the conference table. In a series of devastating reports in *The New York Times* in December 1966 by Harrison Salisbury, the military's contention that the air force was not bombing civilian targets or, indeed, any part of the city of Hanoi at all was shown to be untrue. The destruction was enormous and "right in the center of town."

By 1967 there were mass demonstrations against the war in American cities: on April 15, between 125,000 and 400,000 protesters (depending on who was doing the counting) gathered in New York City; on the same day, 75,000 demonstrators marched in San Francisco. In the fall, in Washington, D.C., almost 100,000 people arrived for a march on the Pentagon, and when it got dark, dozens of draft cards began to burn like candles in the night.[7]

Acheson took no part in policymaking during this period. Seeing a parallel to Korea, he reflexively adopted the hard line. In any case, if he depended on optimistic reports by generals from the field supplied by the administration, he was hardly likely to change his mind. In addition, his earlier meetings with McNamara in 1965 had convinced him that the secretary of defense's self-confident and hawkish tone meant that the war was progressing far better than the reports in the press portrayed it. What he did not know was that by 1966 McNamara was becoming increasingly tortured by self-doubt.

For Johnson, beleaguered, unpopular, filled with a sense of his own martyrdom, a new session of the "Wise Men" seemed in order. On November 1 and 2, 1967, eleven members of a new senior advisory group responded to the president's summons. Along with Acheson came Clark Clifford, one of LBJ's advisers and an avowed war hawk; Abe Fortas, another close friend of LBJ's; George Ball, now out of office; McGeorge Bundy, who had resigned as national security adviser in February 1966 to head the Ford Foundation; Generals Maxwell Taylor and Omar Bradley; Arthur Dean, U.S. armistice negotiator in Korea under Dulles; Robert Murphy, General Clay's political adviser in Berlin; Henry Cabot Lodge, former ambassador to Saigon; Douglas Dillon, Kennedy's Treasury secretary; Arthur Goldberg, ambassador to the United Nations; and Averell Harriman, now LBJ's ambassador-at-large.

Gathering for cocktails on the eighth floor of the State Department on November 1, the group was briefed by General Earle Wheeler, chairman of the Joint Chiefs of Staff. Everything looked rosy: the statistics, the body counts, the captured documents, all showed the United States winning the war. Nonetheless,

Wheeler told the group that the enemy would not collapse within the next fifteen months.

The "Wise Men" were unaware of a memo that McNamara had given the president earlier that day. Noting that it contained his "personal views" on the direction of U.S. policy in Vietnam, which "may be incompatible with your own," McNamara's memo had proposed a policy of stabilization of the American military effort that included freezing force levels (then standing at half a million troops in Vietnam) and no further expansion of air operations against North Vietnam. Air bombardment had not broken the will of the North Vietnamese or the Viet Cong in the south. McNamara favored a bombing halt because he believed the air war was preventing a political settlement. According to McNamara, public opinion would force the president into the following alternatives: step up the air war in the north while expanding the ground war in the south, or withdraw from Vietnam. To avoid these harsh extremes, it was necessary to stabilize the war and seek negotiations.[8]

Meeting with the "Wise Men" later that evening, McNamara admitted that "perhaps [his] and Rusk's efforts since 1961 have been a failure"—but he did not spell out the recommendations he had given to the president.

The next morning Johnson met with the group in the Cabinet Room. He called first on Acheson. Buoyed by General Wheeler's briefing, Acheson said, "I got the impression that this is a matter we can and will win." However, he did not believe that bombing would bring Hanoi to the negotiating table: "The bombing has no effect on negotiations. When these fellows decide they can't defeat the South, then they will give up."

He recalled the dark days in the winter of 1950, when the Chinese attacked in Korea and the military had become defeatist. Dean Rusk and George Kennan and General Marshall had persuaded Truman to hold fast, to buck up the military, and thus a humiliating defeat was avoided.

McGeorge Bundy fully backed Acheson, adding his view that negotiations were no longer viable: "Getting out of Vietnam is as impossible as it is undesirable." The main thing was to persuade the public that there were "light at the end of the tunnel instead of the battles, deaths and danger."[9]

The doubters, Harriman and Ball, sat silent or said very little. Harriman, who was stone-faced throughout the meeting, straightened up and weighed in only to advise the president that negotiations with the Communists were both "inevitable and necessary."[10]

A month later, on a dark evening in December, Averell Harriman walked over from his house to Acheson's. Over the years the two elderly men, though they were never close, had grown to respect each other deeply. Even when Harriman had longed for Acheson's job as secretary of state, he had remained loyal to him. Now, as they settled down for cocktails in Acheson's book-lined study, Harriman was determined to share with him his doubts on the conduct of the war in Vietnam.

Harriman did not mince words. He told Acheson that Vietnam was not like Korea. This time around, Russia and China were bitter enemies, and Moscow wanted to end the war. Moreover, Vietnam was not a conventional war, as was Korea, but a guerrilla war. A war of attrition, which was the Pentagon's strategy, would not work.

To Harriman's surprise, Acheson listened quietly. Recalling MacArthur's exaggerated expectations of victory prior to the Chinese invasion, he told Harriman that he was indeed suspicious of the military's claims. This was one lesson from Korea that certainly did apply: distrust the predictions of the military.

At the end of their lengthy conversation, Harriman urged Acheson to tell Johnson about his doubts. But Acheson did not believe he had much influence over the president anymore, especially after his blowup with LBJ over NATO. Nonetheless, while making no promises, he seemed interested in helping.

Harriman returned home filled with new hope. "I found he was not as rigid as I supposed," he wrote of his talk with Acheson.[11]

He was right. Acheson was deeply worried about the effect of the war on American society and on America's image abroad. "Vietnam plus the riots is very bad," he wrote to Anthony Eden at the end of December. "It spells frustration and a sense of feebleness at home and abroad. . . . Americans aren't used to this, and LBJ is not a lovable type. He is the one to blame."[12]

In the early hours of January 31, 1968—the Vietnamese New Year, or Tet, the Year of the Monkey—about eighty thousand North Vietnamese regulars and Viet Cong guerrillas attacked over one hundred cities and towns throughout South Vietnam. In addition, they attacked the American compound in Saigon, Saigon's Tan Son Nhut airport, the presidential palace, and the headquarters of South Vietnam's general staff. In Hue, 7,500 Viet Cong and North Vietnamese troops occupied the ancient Citadel, the interior town that had been the seat of the emperors of the kingdom of Annam. It took nearly three weeks for the U.S. Marines to retake Hue, street by street, house by house. The Communist attacks were supposed to achieve a popular uprising against the South Vietnamese government as well as to demonstrate to the Americans that there was no security in the South.

From an American military standpoint the Tet offensive was a failure. The Communist losses were horrendous; over half of their committed forces were destroyed. The popular uprising did not materialize. But if the military offensive was a failure, psychologically it was a decisive success for the Communists. It demonstrated their ability to strike at the very heart of South Vietnamese government strongholds and put in doubt recent predictions of the U.S. military command of imminent success in the field. The defeat of the Communist forces did not spell victory for the United States and the government of South Vietnam.[13]

"If this is a failure," said Senator George Aiken of Vermont, "I hope the Viet Cong never have a major success." The mainstream American media turned against the war, and the White House felt under siege.[14]

Shaken by the Communist offensive, Johnson summoned Acheson to the White House on February 27. Acheson had just returned from his holiday in Antigua, where he had found John Cowles and his other friends had wholly turned against the war. Acheson was now determined not to be used by the president: he suspected that he and the other "Wise Men" had not been given enough information on which to base their judgments. Acheson, more than ever, searched for the facts that would allow him to make the kind of case that would stand up in a courtroom.

The president was exhausted after spending much of the night in the basement of the West Wing, where a scale model of the besieged marine base at Khe Sanh had been built. He feared another defeat there like the French collapse at Dien Bien Phu. Moreover, his commander in Vietnam, General William Westmoreland, had called for 200,000 more troops to add to the 542,000 American troops already in South Vietnam—"a whole new ball game." For forty-five minutes Johnson went on with his tirades. Finally, when Acheson concluded that LBJ was less interested in his advice than in venting his spleen, he excused himself and returned to his law office two blocks from the White House.

The phone rang almost immediately. It was Walt Rostow, now the national security adviser, who asked Acheson why he had left so abruptly. "You can tell the president—and you can tell him in precisely these words," Acheson said coldly, "that he can take Vietnam and stick it up his ass."

The president soon came on the line and asked him to come back. Acheson walked back to the White House and was polite in his next encounter with the commander in chief; but he spoke no less bluntly. "With all due respect, Mr. President, the Joint Chiefs of Staff don't know what they're talking about." When Johnson replied that this was a "shocking" statement, Acheson said, "Then maybe you should be shocked."

Asked to give his candid view of what he thought of the American military strategy of fighting a war of attrition to wear out the enemy, Acheson retorted that it would be impossible to do that unless he could conduct his own inquiry. He wanted "full run of the shop" and no more canned briefings.

Johnson agreed: he could have complete access to all top-secret intelligence information and the full cooperation of State, Defense, and the CIA, so that he could conduct a Vietnam investigation of his own.[15] Acheson's insistence on private meetings and cross-examination of officials was a real breakthrough.

Writing that very day to John Cowles in Antigua, Acheson began his letter with the statement "The situation in VN is very bad." He concluded his letter by declaring, "We must always be aware that we are there in the role of helpers of the [South Vietnamese government]. If that collapses, we have no future there and must be able to extricate ourselves. This is [a] dark picture, but the way I see it."[16]

Acheson got to work right away, interrogating officials at his Georgetown house, especially three individuals who proved most illuminating. These were Philip Habib, a tough-talking diplomat back from two years in Saigon; George Carver, a CIA analyst who held the raw intelligence data; and General William DuPuy, former chief of operations in Saigon and now with the JCS, a man who could supply him with the combat field reports.

He was preparing himself as though he were to go to trial, night after night questioning assumptions and asking not just for the summaries, but for the raw data on enemy troop strength and the actual battle reports from commanders in the field.[17]

On March 14, his Vietnam study complete, Acheson met alone with the president to discuss his findings. LBJ began the session with another one of his long speeches. He spoke in an upbeat manner about the estimate of General William Westmoreland, the U.S. commander in Vietnam, that he could make do with an additional 80,000 to 90,000 troops rather than 200,000 and that Johnson would therefore not have to mobilize the reserves.

Finally Acheson let loose. "Mr. President, you're being led down the garden path." He said he gravely doubted a figure of Westmoreland's that Johnson had mentioned, to the effect that 60,000 Communist troops had been killed or captured during the Tet offensive. Based on the information Acheson had gathered, Westmoreland's strategy of attrition would take unlimited resources and at least five more years. He told the president that Westmoreland reminded him of General George McClellan in the Civil War, who had finally been relieved by Lincoln after nearly ruining the Union Army.

America's objective after Tet, Acheson went on, should be to allow the South Vietnamese government to survive long enough "to be able to stand alone, at least for a period of time, with only a fraction of the foreign support it had now." If this could not be done, "the operation was hopeless and . . . a method of disengagement should be considered." He still believed that negotiations were not possible at this time, for the North Vietnamese would never allow a government in the south that they could not control.

At that point Walt Rostow came into the room, and the president asked Acheson to summarize for Rostow what he had said and to give Rostow the names of those he should consult. "Walt," Acheson wrote in a memo for his files, "listened to me with the bored patience of a visitor listening to a ten-year-old playing the piano."[18]

That same day Acheson wrote to John Cowles: "I have completed the second stage [high school] of my Vietnam education . . . which has confused some of my earlier simple conclusions and shown the difficulties to be even greater than I thought."[19]

Like a drowning man clinging to wreckage, Johnson looked for salvation and hoped that the "Wise Men" might provide it. Robert McNamara, ridden with anxiety and self-doubt, had left the Pentagon on March 1 to become head of the World Bank. His successor, Clark Clifford, was perceived as an unreconstructed hawk. But Clifford, like Acheson, had made his own investigation and had privately turned against the war. At the urging of both Acheson and Clifford, the senior advisers met at the State Department on March 25; it was the same group that had met with Johnson in November, with two additions: Cyrus Vance, former deputy secretary of defense, and General Matthew Ridgway, who had succeeded MacArthur in Korea after the Chinese invasion. Also present were four government officials: Vice President Hubert Humphrey, Generals Earl Wheeler and Maxwell Taylor, and former U.S. ambassador to South Vietnam Henry Cabot Lodge. Lovett and McCloy were absent. After carefully reading the documents that had been assembled for them in a small library in the State Department, the group gathered on the eighth floor for a dinner and a formal briefing.

The president, who had not planned to meet with them until the next morning, dropped by during dinner and shook hands all around, then left to go pick bombing targets in the White House Situation Room. With Johnson absent, Clifford gave a briefing in which he called for a "reduced strategy" of a bombing halt or a reduction in bombing of the north, abandonment of isolated military positions, and a new ground strategy that used U.S. troops as a shield around populated areas in order to give the South Vietnamese time to assume the burden of the war.

After hearing the secretary of defense, the group went down to the State Department Operations Center on the seventh floor, where they were briefed by Acheson's main instructors, Philip Habib, George Carver, and General DuPuy.

The tone of the evening was far different from that of the earlier gatherings. When asked by Clifford if a military victory could be won, Habib answered, "Not under the present circumstances."

"What would you do?" Clifford asked.

"Stop bombing and negotiate," Habib replied.

To General DuPuy's claim that eighty thousand of the enemy had been killed during the Tet offensive, Arthur Goldberg asked the general what the normal ratio of wounded to killed was. "Ten to one; three to one conservatively," he answered.

How many Communist troops and guerrillas were in the field? Goldberg asked. "Two hundred and thirty thousand."

Goldberg did the arithmetic on the spot: "Well, General, I am not a great mathematician, but with 80,000 killed and with a wounded ratio of three to one, or 240,000, for total of 320,000, who the hell are we fighting?"

The group reconvened the next morning in the Cabinet Room. General Wheeler, who had just returned from Saigon, gave an optimistic assessment of the situation. The United States was "back on the offensive." When Wheeler declared that "this was the worst time to negotiate," Cabot Lodge whispered to Acheson, "Yes, because we are in worse shape militarily than we have ever been."

General Maxwell Taylor, however, vigorously supported an escalation of the bombing and sending more combat troops. The "Wise Men" were unmoved.

At lunch LBJ dismissed everyone in the government from the table, even Secretary of State Dean Rusk. After the plates had been cleared, the president asked McGeorge Bundy to summarize the group's conclusions. He reported that there had been a "significant shift" in views since their last meeting in November. In Bundy's estimation Dean Acheson had best stated "the majority feeling when he said that we can no longer do the job we set out to do in the time we have left, and we must begin to take steps to disengage."

When Bundy finished, Acheson spoke up immediately: the process of disengagement must begin no later than this summer.

LBJ went around the table, asking for other comments, but Acheson remained the dominant presence. When Abe Fortas protested that Bundy's summary did not accurately represent the group's view, Acheson cut in sharply. "It represents my view," he said.

As Acheson spoke of the impossibility of gaining a military victory, General Wheeler tried to correct him. The Pentagon was not bent on a "classic military victory," the general said, but only helping the Vietnamese to avoid a Communist victory. This enraged Acheson, and he answered with a characteristic flash of his old style: "Then what in the name of God are five hundred thousand men out there doing—chasing girls? This is not a semantic game, General; if the deployment of all those men is not an effort to gain a military solution, then words have lost all meaning."

The president knew from his meeting with him two weeks earlier that Acheson had changed his views. But, as Clifford recalled, "Speaking almost ex officio as the leader of the foreign policy establishment, and with his customary authority, Acheson had an unquestionable impact on the President," even though nearly half the participants were still giving the military full or partial support.[20] Lyndon Johnson never again sought the counsel of Dean Acheson.

* * *

On March 31, in a televised speech to the nation, Lyndon Johnson took the advice of the "Wise Men." He ordered a bombing halt above the twentieth parallel in North Vietnam in order to give Hanoi an opportunity to agree to negotiate. The escalation of the war had ended.

The president also announced that he would not seek reelection.

Acheson, too, had to recant. In a letter to his daughter Jane Acheson Brown on April 13, he wrote, "We had been wrong in believing that we could establish an independent, non-communist state in South Vietnam."[21]

In questioning the American presence in Vietnam, Acheson, without being fully aware of it, was questioning the nation's expansive definition of its national interests. In the end, however, as Clark Clifford put it: "I don't think Acheson changed his philosophy about America's role in the world. Rather, he was always a realist."[22]

Despite his often bullying manner, Lyndon Johnson could make a generous gesture toward those who disagreed with him. After Acheson's apostasy regarding Vietnam, Johnson took the time to send him an especially thoughtful letter on April 11, 1968, his seventy-fifth birthday: "You and I both know there have been a number of times when I did not like the advice you gave me. I am aware that you were aware I would not like it when you gave it to me—and I am aware that as you define your duty, my dislike was, and had to be, an irrelevancy."

Acheson was moved by Johnson's letter, and in his reply he acknowledged the president's understandable reactions to his criticisms over the years. "What touches me most deeply is that you should not only have known that I knew that on occasion the advice I brought you was unwelcome but that you should not have attributed it to opinionated obstinacy. . . . You have borne with me with great patience and, you encourage me to believe, not without some profit. I shall always be at your service and will strive to keep the perversity of age strictly disciplined."[23]

That discipline was to be sorely tried, in ways that Acheson could not have imagined, during the presidency of his once great antagonist, Richard Nixon, elected to the White House in November 1968.

CHAPTER THIRTY-FIVE

SEDUCTIONS AND BETRAYALS

THE ANNUAL GRIDIRON CLUB white-tie dinners were meant to be an affair at which prominent politicians and members of the administration were mocked by members of the White House press corps with silly songs and drag costumes. Moreover, the president himself was expected to participate by making remarks that were supposed to be both humorous and self-deprecating. It was at the March 1969 dinner that Dean Acheson, who had never met Richard Nixon, first encountered the new president.

Acheson attended the dinner with his publisher friend John Cowles, and after what both men considered a rather long evening for the material available, they went to the suite in the Statler Hotel, where the Cowles publishers were entertaining friends. There, to Acheson's surprise, was Nixon surrounded by well-wishers. After talking with Thomas Dewey and other friends for a bit, Acheson strode over to the president, who was, for the moment, alone. He decided to make the first gesture "to deescalate our ancient feud." He formally introduced himself as Dean Acheson, which surely took Nixon aback. He then congratulated the president on his decision to go ahead with an antiballistic missile program. Nixon was highly courteous in response and said that he hoped he would have a chance to see him privately sometime soon.[1]

Three days later Henry Kissinger, Nixon's national security adviser, called and told him the president wished to see him the next day. Kissinger wrote in his memoirs that "Nixon's shabby treatment of Acheson in the 1952 campaign did not keep Acheson from assisting the president when he was needed almost two decades later. His loyalty ran to the office, not the man." In his portrait of Acheson, Kissinger praised him more than any other public official, writing of Acheson's "moral integrity," which, as a realist, he never used "as a device for avoiding the attainable."[2]

Nixon himself later wrote in his memoirs that he regretted calling Adlai Stevenson a graduate of Acheson's "Cowardly College of Communist Containment" in the 1952 presidential campaign. As Nixon recalled, Acheson's "clipped moustache, his British tweeds, and his haughty manner made him the perfect foil for the snobbish kind of foreign service personality and mentality that had been taken in hook, line and sinker by the Communists."[3] Although he could write after his years in the presidency that he regretted the intensity of his attacks, at the time he had rivaled Senator McCarthy in the virulence of his criticisms of Acheson's personality and policies.

Acheson had certainly opposed Nixon during the 1968 presidential campaign against Hubert Humphrey and thought that the country would be "going to hell in a hack with Mr. Nixon as our inspiring leader."[4] But he came to favor Nixon's program of Vietnamization—which meant to Acheson the steady withdrawal of American troops from Indochina and turning over the war to the South Vietnamese. Kissinger may well have encouraged Nixon to seek Acheson's advice in order to soften any criticism that Acheson might be tempted to make of Nixon's policies. Acheson's gesture after the Gridiron Club dinner opened the way, and on March 19 the two met in the Oval Office, with only Kissinger also present.

The serious business of that day was Vietnam. They talked for an uninterrupted hour, which Acheson found a pleasing contrast to his meetings with Johnson, when people would come running in and out of the room, sometimes handing LBJ a note, sometimes a telephone, while Johnson motioned his guest to continue talking as he himself listened and spoke into the phone. With Nixon, Acheson got "a feeling of orderliness and concentration rather than of Napoleonic drive and scattered attention."

Acheson first went over his own involvement with Vietnam. He explained that from 1951 on, "the Truman administration had been opposed to putting any troops whatever in Indochina, that we had been practically blackmailed by the French to contribute funds for equipment for the war until we were bearing about forty percent of it. This was necessary to keep France in NATO."

Acheson told the president that the turning point in American policy came when Johnson decided to put in substantial American troops in 1965, which was a "great mistake." Acheson readily admitted that he had supported it at the time and also thought that "we had been wrong." (Nixon added that he had done the same.) Acheson explained that "the source of error for me had come from relying upon the statements from the Pentagon, which I had done until February of 1968." He was now "completely leery of military information."

When Nixon asked him what the policy should be now, Acheson replied that he thought it would be best to build up a strong South Vietnamese military, not to resume bombing "of any sort in North Vietnam," to keep withdrawing troops to "serve notice on the Russians and the North that we were, in fact, making a beginning of de-escalation," and to make sure that Saigon was kept in line. The American objective at the present time should be "to so reduce the belligerency in Vietnam that with minimum, competent help from us the South Vietnamese could survive in an attempt to reach a political modus vivendi with the Vietcong."

When asked whether or not it was a good time to negotiate with the Russians, Acheson thought that the only negotiation with Moscow worth pursuing was to see if the Russians were willing to seek some progress on disarmament. Nixon then asked his views on a proposed summit meeting with the Russians, as they were having trouble, including border clashes, with the Chinese.

Acheson, not surprisingly, thought that this was a poor idea: "Russians do not negotiate under pressure—only when the 'correlation of forces' makes it seem to their advantage." Nixon, however, reserved judgment on this issue. Determined personally to sit down with the Soviets, he never again solicited Acheson's advice on whether or not to negotiate with them.

The meeting ended with Acheson pressing Nixon not to support an African-Asian move in the United Nations to put an end to South Africa's mandate over Southwest Africa (Namibia). He found both Nixon and Kissinger receptive to the notion that the internal policies of southern African nations were not matters for American or UN intervention.

Upon returning home, Acheson told his wife that his opinion of Nixon had "been moved toward a more favorable one and in this process I am quite conscious that a change in his attitude from abusive hostility to respect with a dash of flattery played a part." Alice Acheson, however, remained skeptical.[5]

In the following months, Acheson particularly supported Nixon's decision to push ahead with the development of an antiballistic missile (ABM) system, which he believed would prove an excellent bargaining chip to convince Moscow to limit its ABM program and perhaps its placement of intercontinental ballistic missiles (ICBMs). Along with Paul Nitze and Albert Wohlstetter, a leading nuclear theorist, Acheson founded the Committee to Maintain Prudent Defense Policy, essentially a lobbying organization to promote ABM development and deployment. On this issue, Acheson broke—not for the first time—with the dovish wing of the Democratic Party, which believed that the ABM system would escalate the arms race and therefore hurt the chances of negotiating with the Russians.

Nixon later believed that the efforts of Acheson and Nitze helped garner the votes in the Senate to proceed with the ABM program and were thus crucial for the successful negotiations of arms control agreements that Nixon signed in

Moscow in May 1972. These agreements—the Strategic Arms Limitation Talks, or SALT I—capped the number of antiballistic missiles that either side could deploy and instituted a five-year freeze on offensive strategic ballistic missiles.[6]

With the publication of *Present at the Creation* in September 1969, Acheson found himself an enormous critical success. Five years earlier, at the age of seventy, he had put together some of his autobiographical writings in *Morning and Noon*, his memoir, published the following year, of growing up in Middletown and his formative years in Washington. His initial decision not to write about his government experience gave way before the encouragement he received from critics and friends for *Morning and Noon* and his own conclusion that it was right to go on to describe a "time of larger events."

He had feared, as he wrote in his preface to *Present at the Creation*, that "detachment and objectivity" would become suspect. In the late 1960s, however, widespread protests over America's deadly involvement in Vietnam and racial unrest in the streets brought the country to what Acheson saw as "a mood of depression, disillusion, and withdrawal from the effort to affect the world around us." He decided that detachment and objectivity were "less important than to tell a tale of large conceptions, great achievements, and some failures, the product of enormous will and effort."[7]

Acheson started writing of his years in the State Department in 1966 mostly in longhand on yellow legal pads, and the work served as a needed tonic for him to relive what he called the "splendid years."[8] The book, remarkably free of self-congratulation, was dedicated to Harry S. Truman, "the captain with the mighty heart."

Elegantly written, with arresting portraits of the great figures of that time, as well as of less well known individuals who worked with him in the State Department, the book earned great praise even from those, like George Kennan and John Kenneth Galbraith, whom Acheson might have supposed would be highly critical of his description of his dealings with them. It remained on most best-seller lists until well into the spring of 1970, with sales that surprised both author and publisher. In May 1970 the book won the Pulitzer Prize for History. "I was delighted to hear the news of your Pulitzer Award but I must confess I was not surprised," Robert Lovett wrote Acheson. "If you keep on at that rate you will probably collect an Oscar, an Emmy—and anything else that is not nailed down."[9]

Acheson had been disappointed that under the Johnson administration American policy toward southern Africa had hardened. The United States had joined

Britain and the other members of the UN Security Council in voting to impose economic sanctions on Rhodesia, whose white government had unilaterally declared independence from Britain in 1965 rather than accede to a timetable for black majority rule. Acheson's firm position was that the political system in Rhodesia was an internal matter.

After his first meeting with Nixon and Kissinger, Acheson found the new administration more willing to align American policy toward Africa with his own views. Nixon and his senior advisers saw the white-ruled governments as islands of order and stability. A national security study memorandum, while not endorsing what it called the "Acheson approach" of noninterference in internal affairs of the white regimes in southern Africa, did call for a more conciliatory approach and defense ties with those regimes.[10]

In this same period, his old colleague and sometime antagonist George Kennan expressed similar views. In an article in *Foreign Affairs* in January 1971, Kennan attacked efforts by "white liberals" to put pressure on the South African economy in order to force an end to the South African policy of apartheid.

Neither Acheson nor Kennan saw himself as a racist; nor did either approve of apartheid. Their attitude might best be described as paternalistic. Above all, they were Europeanists who distrusted the ability of Africans (as well as other so-called Third World or postcolonial regimes) to govern themselves effectively. Toward the Portuguese colonies of Angola and Mozambique, Kennan joined Acheson in his wariness of too quickly pushing Lisbon to decolonization.[11]

To Acheson, most African leaders were politically unreliable, often corrupt, and unable to create "a modern territorial state."[12] Acheson, however, found himself at odds with many of his family and friends, who did not want to see him defending anachronistic and racist regimes. "My daughters—natural and by marriage—think I am an old reactionary," Acheson complained in May 1971. "They are wrong about that."[13]

His thyroid ailment had prevented Alice and him from taking a trip to southern Africa in November 1969. Whether his trip would have modified his views is impossible to know. Despite his writings during these last years on the issues of decolonization and southern Africa, he never managed to visit the region. Nor did he live to see the sudden collapse of the Portuguese empire in the mid-1970s or, a decade after his death, the birth of Zimbabwe out of the ruins of Rhodesia.

Meetings with Nixon, however, did not address postcolonial Africa: it was Vietnam that dominated their discussions, and Acheson determinedly reminded the president that he must pull out of Indochina as quickly as possible. On October 20, 1969, he wrote to Kissinger in regard to the president's scheduled television address for November 4, at which time, Acheson believed, Nixon should make a special plea to the American people for their support.[14]

A week later Acheson met with the president. Just before the meeting, Kissinger informed him that some of Acheson's ideas had been incorporated into the speech. When the meeting began, Nixon asked Acheson if he should include in the upcoming talk a schedule of troop withdrawals and a deadline for completion. Acheson was emphatically against this, as it could be seen as a sign of "weakness and yielding to pressure." The main objective should be to reassure the American public that he was in command of the situation and was operating under "a definitive plan."[15]

Nixon did what Acheson suggested. Not only did he heed Acheson's advice not to provide specific numbers and dates for troop withdrawals, but he also incorporated parts of Acheson's letter to Kissinger in his speech. Nixon's address, which came to be known as the "silent majority" speech, ended by his pledging to carry out his Vietnam policy with "all the strength and wisdom I can command, in accordance with your hopes, mindful of your concerns, sustained by your prayers."[16]

Acheson had very much laid out the tone of the speech. The president, he had written to Kissinger, should address the American people with "a Lincolnian touch of patience and sadness, of understanding beneath determination; and above all an indication that the goal is a common one." He should ask "for strength and wisdom to achieve this common goal in accordance with the hopes, mindful of the interests, and aided by the prayers of all."

Nixon called Acheson after delivering the speech and, Acheson recorded, "most touchingly expressed his gratitude."[17]

In a letter in December to his former colleague Lincoln MacVeagh, Acheson wrote, "I have, I believe, propelled the president in the right direction in his Vietnam policy."[18]

The pleasure of being listened to by the White House—which, Acheson admitted to Anthony Eden, was "seductive"—continued for some time longer. Twenty years later Alice Acheson still believed that "Nixon was wooing Dean for his own political purposes" and regretted very much that her husband had succumbed to the campaign of flattery waged by Nixon and Kissinger. At one point the White House even set up a special communications link to Acheson through the U.S. Marine station on Antigua when Acheson was on vacation there.[19]

As long as Nixon seemed to be following Acheson's prescription for a steady withdrawal from Vietnam, their improbable relationship remained intact. But when the president, on April 26, 1970, expanded the war by ordering U.S. forces across the border into neutral Cambodia to destroy North Vietnamese sanctuaries and arms depots, the Nixon-Acheson honeymoon came to an abrupt end.

* * *

With Acheson's old friend Prince Sihanouk in exile after a coup that brought to power the anti-Communist general Lon Nol, Acheson nonetheless saw no reason to hesitate in withdrawing American troops from all of Indochina. Nixon's decision to invade Cambodia to prevent Communist attacks from that country on South Vietnam, while at the same time bolstering the Lon Nol regime, seemed to Acheson a profound error.

"This new version of the search-and-destroy strategy, I think, is bound to lead us a chase around Cambodia," he wrote to John Cowles on May 5, 1970. "The chances of cornering any substantial number of enemy forces seems small." As for Nixon's statement that he did not intend to keep U.S. troops there, that made absolutely no sense, since "the enemy is likely to come back when the troops leave." The Cambodian incursion led Acheson to conclude that Nixon's judgment was "very bad." He now refused to see the president, "making it clear" that he disagreed "strongly with the policy."[20]

Moreover, policies in Cambodia were contributing to further turmoil at home. On May 4, 1970, nettled by demonstrators at Kent State University in Ohio, National Guardsmen had fired into the crowd, killing four youths. The Kent State tragedy sparked demonstrations across the country. More than four hundred universities and colleges shut down in protest, and nearly one hundred thousand demonstrators marched on Washington, encircling the White House and other government buildings.[21]

In early June 1970 Acheson suffered what he was told was a "mini" stroke, "although it didn't seem so very mini at the time," he wrote to a friend. "I am using the excuse of my illness—no mere excuse at that—not to be drawn into the White House for a so-called consultation in any way."[22] After a two-week stay in the hospital, he spent the summer at Harewood, relaxing, reading, swimming, gardening, and seeing only a few close friends.

By the beginning of the New Year, Acheson wrote to John Cowles from Antigua that he had not changed his views of Nixon's poor performance: "My sad, current conclusion is that the present administration is the most incompetent and undirected group I have seen in charge of the U.S. government since the closing years of the Wilson administration."[23]

Acheson might have never worked closely with Nixon and Kissinger again; certainly he was unwilling to serve as a prop for policies he did not support. To Acheson, as he wrote to an English friend in April 1971, Nixon "has so lost confidence within the country that other policies, more important than Southeast Asia, will be harmfully affected."[24]

But when the cause seemed just, Acheson was still willing to support the administration. And nothing was more calculated to arouse his ire than any threat to the NATO alliance. He was already profoundly disturbed by the new West German chancellor, Willy Brandt, whose efforts to reduce East-West tensions by establishing friendly relations with East Germany, Poland, and the Soviet Union would undermine, he believed, the solidarity of the Western alliance. Brandt's policy, known as *Ostpolitik*, was also encouraging efforts in the U.S. Senate to reduce American military deployments in Europe.

In May 1971, in the shadow of America's failure in Vietnam, the Senate majority leader, Mike Mansfield, proposed to cut in half the U.S. troop commitment to NATO. Moreover, the passage of the Mansfield amendment seemed highly probable, especially in view of America's worsening balance of payments.

When Kissinger asked Acheson to help defeat Mansfield's proposal, Acheson could not refuse. He offered to call up any senators and gave Kissinger a list of "Wise Men," such as McGeorge Bundy, Robert Lovett, Cyrus Vance, George Ball, and John J. McCloy. But Kissinger reported back to Acheson that he had had only fair luck in garnering their support. Acheson therefore decided to lead the battle. "It seems to me," he said to Kissinger, "what we want is a little volley firing and not just a spluttering of musketry."

Acheson rounded up former secretaries of defense, high commissioners for Germany, NATO commanders, and chairmen of the Joint Chiefs of Staff. He even persuaded McCloy to fly to Germany to get Chancellor Brandt's support. For Nixon, as Kissinger recalled, it was "the first, and in the event the only, time in his public life that he would have the Establishment on his side—the men he revered and despised, whose approbation he both cherished and scorned."

On May 13 the "Old Guard" met with the president in the Cabinet Room. While everyone agreed that the Mansfield amendment must be beaten, some felt that a compromise was possible. Acheson, whom Kissinger described as having "none of Nixon's reluctance to engage in face-to-face confrontations," effectively squelched any possibility that the consensus that existed among the "Old Guard" would evaporate. Acheson insisted on a press release as soon as possible. Nixon then asked Acheson to be the one who would report on the meeting to the press.

Acheson, accompanied by George Ball, went directly to the White House briefing room to speak to the media about the Mansfield amendment. He gave his impression that the president was adamant against any variation of the Mansfield proposal. It would be "asinine," Acheson said, and "sheer nonsense" to reduce forces without a cut in Soviet forces. He described how the president had called on the people who created NATO and saw it through for two decades. And they came out, Acheson said, with their "fighting gloves on." Asked why the meeting took so long, he joked: "We are all old and we are all eloquent."[25]

Less than a week later the Mansfield amendment failed in the Senate by an overwhelming vote of sixty-one to thirty-six. "It has been great fun," Acheson wrote to John Cowles, "and resulted in a most satisfying victory."[26]

* * *

That autumn Acheson seemed to have recovered from his small stroke. His worst fear was that another stroke would disable him, as had happened to Felix Frankfurter, whose long decline had included a progressive loss of his faculties and personality.[27] Now he decided to spend much of the fall at Harewood, working in the garden and at his cabinetmaking, on articles on Berlin, the Middle East, and China. With improving health, he was also planning a long-delayed tour of southern Africa in January with Anthony Eden.

His letters that September reflected his own autumnal feelings, for they were often filled with reminiscences of his Connecticut boyhood. At seventy-eight Acheson saw in his peers a generation of great moral fiber. Writing in mid-September to Averell Harriman, one of those men whom he had always valued despite their differences in temperament, he set down his feelings about their life and their struggles.

They had met, he recalled, sixty-six years ago that month, as schoolboys at Groton. "In most of the years that have passed," he wrote, "we have joined in activities that sometimes have been pretty strenuous, first of all on the water, where we both rowed, and later in government, where we both struggled." Referring to their dismissal as Yale rowing coaches, he recalled: "The first time that I was ever fired was in company with you. . . . I have been fired since, and so have you. I hope we can both say, 'Never in such good company.'"

For all his ambition, Harriman had stood by Acheson in the darkest days of the Korean War and the McCarthy era; he had always been among the most loyal of his comrades, so Acheson ended his letter with boyish imagery: "I . . . hope you will let an old friend say that there is no one with whom I would rather go tiger-shooting than with you. Your aid and your steadfastness are one hundred percent reliable."[28]

During those last weeks of September and early October, in the soft Maryland fall, Acheson's temperament seemed to mellow as his health and spirits improved. On October 12, 1971, a particularly bright day that Acheson had earlier spent preparing his garden for winter, Edward Youter Johnson, his butler of forty years, noticed that he was walking all about the farm, as though it might be one of the last times he would see it. About five o'clock Acheson went into his study and wrote Anthony Eden a long and enthusiastic letter about their upcoming trip together. An hour later Johnson had a premonition that something was wrong, and though it was not his habit, he entered the study, where he found Acheson slumped over his desk, dead in seconds of a massive stroke.[29]

Three days after Dean Acheson's death, more than one thousand persons attended his funeral at the Washington Cathedral. As Acheson had requested, there was no eulogy. It was, as he preferred, a brief service for the burial of the dead from the Episcopal Church's Book of Common Prayer.

Among the mourners who stood by as the American flag and blue banner of the secretary of state were carried by were those who seemed to step from the pages of Acheson's own memoir—George Ball, David Bruce, Charles Bohlen, Clark Clifford, Averell Harriman, Robert Lovett, and Archibald MacLeish. Paul Nitze read Psalm 49: "O hear ye this, all ye people; ponder it with your ears, all ye that dwell in the world: High and low, rich and poor, one with another. My mouth shall speak of wisdom; and the meditation of my heart shall muse of understanding."

On that perfect fall day, Acheson's casket was lowered into a grave on a grassy knoll in Oak Hill Cemetery, only a few blocks from the redbrick house on P Street.[30]

A little over a quarter century later, Madeleine Albright had the official portrait of Dean Acheson prominently placed in the large outer office of the Secretary of State.

CODA

"A BLADE OF STEEL"

THE MEASURE OF GREATNESS is the ability to seize the moment and to create out of chaos the enduring structures of success. Acheson, the pragmatic realist always distrustful of universal solutions, cited time and again Oliver Wendell Holmes's advice that "if you want to hit a bird on the wing, one must have all your will in focus. You must not be thinking about yourself . . . you must be living with your eye on that bird. Every achievement is a bird on the wing."

With perseverance and resolute conviction, that is precisely what Acheson did. In the twelve months following the victory over the Axis powers, he made every effort to seek common ground with the Soviet Union as a great power. He offered to work with Moscow to control the destructive power of the atom bomb and persuaded the administration to get the Russians to withdraw from Iran through negotiation and firmness, but nonetheless to give them "a graceful way out." Moreover, he forcefully opposed those who urged a preventive strike against an increasingly truculent Soviet Union. At this time he was far from being an intractable Cold Warrior.

But when he became convinced that Stalin's Russia, like the Russia of the czars, was an expansive power that could threaten Europe, Turkey, and the eastern Mediterranean, he struck back. First, he urged the president to risk an armed conflict, if necessary, to force the Soviet Union to abandon its demands over the control of the Dardanelles; then in 1947 he helped devise the Truman Doctrine to shore up Greece and Turkey. Although it was a doctrine of limited containment—not intended to become a global system that would extend beyond the confines of Europe and the eastern Mediterranean—it was nonetheless the beginning of a larger strategy to frustrate any overweening ambitions of the Soviet Union in the West.

Both the Marshall Plan to rebuild the faltering economies of Western Europe and the NATO military alliance were designed to put in place a system in which Western Europe and the United States would align and preserve their political and economic values. Acheson believed that over time, through patience and unflinching determination, the West would be a magnet to Eastern Europe and the Soviet Union.

Above all, for Acheson, even while he often deferred to the needs and sensibilities of America's principal allies, American leadership was essential. As he grew older and became increasingly skeptical of Europe's ability to evolve into a common political and economic polity, he embraced even more fully the notion of American purpose; he said in his later years, "In the final analysis, the United States [is] the locomotive at the head of mankind, and the rest of the world the caboose."[1]

While Acheson's success in welding together a Western alliance—economic, military, and political—is incontestable, he was less surefooted in Asia. The Japanese peace treaty and Japan's mutual security treaty with the United States were enduring achievements. And his desire to recognize Mao was surely the correct approach, once again revealing his essential pragmatism; if Mao had taken Taiwan, as Acheson expected, before the Korean War broke out, then he might have been able to carry through with his plans to establish formal ties to Beijing.

On the other hand, he was never able to resolve the contradiction between his view that French policy in Vietnam was mainly responsible for the success of Ho Chi Minh and his unwillingness to urge the French to negotiate a settlement directly with Ho. In office, he was resolutely opposed to use of American combat troops in Vietnam, yet he did not deny the French the economic aid they demanded to fight on in Southeast Asia, lest they fail to play their part in providing troops for Western Europe.

Truman's decision—largely on Acheson's advice—to stand up to the North Korean attack on South Korea, which was indeed backed by Stalin, astonished the Kremlin and ensured the durability of the Japanese-American alliance. But Truman, Marshall, and Acheson's reluctance to challenge MacArthur's decision to strike north toward the Yalu River undermined the successful effort to prevent Communist expansion south. Had the American and South Korean offensive halted at or near the thirty-eighth parallel, the Chinese would almost surely not have intervened. The Truman-Acheson policy of repelling aggression would have been hailed as a triumph of firmness and restraint.

Too often Acheson's rhetoric betrayed the prudence of his policies. He felt compelled to make things "clearer than truth"—in trying to garner support from the Congress for aid to Greece and Turkey; in branding the Chinese Communists as tools of Moscow in the covering letter to the *White Paper*, thus contributing to the congressional and public hostility to China he was seeking to overcome; and in trying to "bludgeon the mass mind" of top government to urge a greater American buildup in conventional forces rather than rely on atomic weapons.

Despite Acheson's often strained relations with Congress, which reached a crescendo after he declared in a spirit of Christian compassion that he would not turn his back on Alger Hiss, Congress usually gave the administration what he proposed and urged: the Bretton Woods agreements, foreign aid to Greece and Turkey, the Marshall Plan, NATO, and military action in Korea. Perhaps he would not have succeeded in gaining congressional and popular backing for these policies without employing the tactic of universalizing threats in order to attain limited goals. Nevertheless, these rhetorical devices laid the groundwork for an expansive American policy of global containment, which would be carried out by his successors.

In retrospect, even though the Soviet Union was possessed of a deep sense of insecurity, made greater by the American response to postwar Soviet intransigence, the opening up of Soviet archives after the Cold War make it all but impossible to imagine Stalin's Russia to have acted in a benign fashion. As historian Arthur Schlesinger Jr. asked on the occasion of Acheson's death: "Could the Western democracies really have relied upon Premier Stalin's self-restraint if there had been no Western response—no Truman Doctrine, no Marshall Plan, no NATO, no rearmament, no reaction to the Berlin blockade or to the invasion of South Korea?"[2]

As head of the State Department, Acheson was a towering figure. And he had in Truman a president who rarely questioned his advice. No other department of government could compete with State for the control of American foreign policy. In later years, when asked his opinion of the growing power of such White House national security advisers as McGeorge Bundy and Henry Kissinger, Acheson replied that under similar circumstances he would simply have had to resign.

His logical presentation, his marshaling of facts, his meticulous preparation for his meetings with Truman, these talents were put in the service of receiving the president's backing for the policies Acheson proposed. As both men shared a disposition for decisive action, their teamwork lent an extraordinary dynamism to the furthering of American foreign policy goals. No secretary of state in this century possessed the power Truman granted to Acheson.

Moreover, Acheson knew well the Foreign Service officers who served under him. At his famous nine-thirty meeting with his assistant secretaries, problems were identified and actions proposed. Everyone was aware of his or her responsibilities, and Acheson made it clear to his subordinates that he was speaking for the White House.[3]

Even in his later years his brilliance in argument did not falter. He always wanted to show his panache, the grand manner, a D'Artagnan who grew up to become a Richelieu, the foreign statesman he most admired. Above all, he was a builder, and it is not surprising that his most rewarding avocation was his cabinetmaking and the architectural drawings and designs he made for his renovations at Harewood and at P Street. Like those of John Quincy Adams, the secretary of state whose portrait hung in his office, Acheson's achievements were enshrined in the structures he built. He was not merely present at the creation, he was the prime architect of that creation.

In the end, his actions not only defined American power and purpose in the postwar era, but also laid the foundations for American predominance at the end of the twentieth century and beyond. He was, as his great friend and confidant Oliver Franks described him, "a pure American type of a rather rare species," imbued "with a love of cabinet making and gardening, never forgetting and ever going back to the roots from which it all sprang"—but above all and always, "a blade of steel."[4]

NOTES

PROLOGUE: THE CUSTOM OF THE COUNTRY

1. David McCullough, *Truman* (New York: Simon & Schuster, 1992), p. 524.
2. Dean Acheson, *Present at the Creation: My Years in the State Department* (New York: W. W. Norton, 1969), p. 200.
3. Ibid., p. 41.
4. From a talk by David McCullough, Acheson Conference, SAIS, Washington, D.C., April 8, 1989.
5. Quoted in "Mr. Secretary," part I, by Philip Hamburger, *The New Yorker*, November 12, 1949.
6. Dean Acheson, *Morning and Noon* (New York: Houghton Mifflin, 1965), p. 18.
7. Acheson, *Present at the Creation*, p. 200.
8. House Committee on Foreign Affairs 80:1, *Assistance to Greece and Turkey* hearings, pp. 32–33.

ONE: *ET IN ARCADIA EGO*

1. Acheson quote from the profile of Dean Acheson, "Mr. Secretary, II," by Philip Hamburger in *The New Yorker*, November 19, 1949, p. 40.
2. Ibid., p. 40.
3. Ibid., p. 41.
4. See Elizabeth Warner, *A Pictorial History of Middletown* (Norfolk/Virginia Beach. Va.: The Donning Co., 1989).
5. Acheson, *Morning and Noon*, p. 2.
6. Ibid., p. 5.
7. Interview, David Acheson, December 20, 1988; Acheson, *Morning and Noon*, p. 9.
8. Interview, David Acheson, December 20, 1988; Mary Acheson Bundy, October 12, 1991.
9. Letter from Lieutenant Colonel W. T. Barnard, Queen's Own Rifles of Canada, March 1949, Dean Acheson Papers, Yale University Library, series I, box 23, f. 293.
10. David S. McLellan, *Dean Acheson: The State Department Years* (New York: Dodd, Mead & Company, 1976), p. 1.

11. See obituary in *The New York Times,* January 29, 1934.
12. "A History of Wycliffe College," printed in *The Calendar [of] Wycliffe College* (Toronto, Ontario, Canada: 1991–1994). The year 1881 marked the five hundredth anniversary of the traditional date of the first English Bible, which had been inspired by the teachings of the Oxford priest John Wycliffe, so the building was named Wycliffe College.
13. McLellan, *Dean Acheson,* p. 1.
14. Acheson, *Morning and Noon,* p. 10.
15. Interview with Alice Acheson (Mrs. Dean Acheson), January 2, 1988.
16. Raymond Baldwin, "Reminiscences of Middletown," cited in Walter Isaacson and Evan Thomas, *The Wise Men: Six Friends and the World They Made: Acheson, Bohlen, Harriman, Kennan, Lovett, McCloy* (New York: Simon & Schuster/Touchstone, 1986), p. 53.
17. Interview with Mary Acheson Bundy, October 12, 1991.
18. David C. Acheson, *Acheson Country* (New York: W. W. Norton, 1993), p. 38.
19. Quoted in McLellan, *Dean Acheson,* p. 5.
20. Acheson, *Morning and Noon,* p. 16.
21. Ibid.
22. Ibid., p. 18.
23. Ibid.
24. Ibid., p. 23.
25. Interview with Mary Acheson Bundy, October 12, 1991.

TWO: A WORLD APART

1. Acheson, *Morning and Noon,* p. 24.
2. Ibid., p. 23.
3. Lawton quotations found in McLellan, *Dean Acheson,* p. 7, and Isaacson and Thomas, *The Wise Men,* p. 53.
4. Joseph Alsop (with Adam Platt), *"I've Seen the Best of It"* (New York: W. W. Norton, 1992), p. 59.
5. Quoted in George Biddle, "As I Remember Groton School," *Harper's* magazine, August 1939, p. 295.
6. On Peabody's choice of students, an interview with social historian Nelson Aldrich, August 15, 1991.
7. Cited in Isaacson and Thomas, *The Wise Men,* p.48.
8. Kenneth S. Davis, *FDR* (New York: Putnam, 1972), p. 110.
9. Biddle, "As I Remember Groton School," pp. 293–294.
10. Ibid., p. 297.
11. Frank Davis Ashburn, *Fifty Years On: Groton School, 1884–1934* (New York: privately printed, 1934), p. 97.
12. Joseph Alsop, *"I've Seen the Best of It,"* p. 61.
13. Isaacson and Thomas, *The Wise Men,* p. 48.
14. Davis, *FDR,* p. 105.
15. Biddle, "As I Remember Groton School," p. 293.
16. Groton School Archives.
17. Interview with Alice (Mrs. Dean) Acheson, January 2, 1988; see also David C. Acheson, *Acheson Country,* pp. 40–41.
18. Acheson Papers, Yale University, series I, box I, f. 1.
19. Acheson Papers, Yale University, series I, box 37, f. 481.
20. Hamburger, "Mr. Secretary," *The New Yorker,* November 12, 1949.

21. Ibid., p. 26.
22. Dean Acheson, "The Snob in America," the *Grotonian*, 1911, pp. 262–265.
23. Acheson, *Morning and Noon*, p. 27.
24. Nelson Aldrich, *Old Money: The Mythology of America's Upper Class* (New York: Alfred A. Knopf, 1988), pp. 159, 163.
25. Acheson, *Morning and Noon*, p. 37.
26. All the preceding citations: ibid., ch. 2, pp. 25–39.
27. DGA to his mother, December 14, 1911, private collection.
28. DGA to Endicott Peabody, February 26, 1918, private collection.
29. Ibid., February 21, 1934.

THREE: THE MOST DASHING OF YALE MEN

1. Owen Johnson, *Stover at Yale* (New York, 1912), pp. 182; 242–44.
2. Quoted in Godfrey Hodgson, *The Colonel* (New York: Alfred A., Knopf, 1990), p. 37.
3. Cited in Brooks Mather Kelley, *Yale: A History* (New Haven and London: Yale University Press, 1974), p. 303.
4. Kelley, *Yale*, p. 313.
5. Wilmarth S. Lewis, *One Man's Education* (New York: Alfred A. Knopf, 1967), p. 95.
6. Ibid., p. 87.
7. Kelley, *Yale*, pp. 343–344.
8. Ibid., p. 345.
9. Lewis, *One Man's Education*, p. 102.
10. Hamburger, *The New Yorker*, November 19, 1949, p. 41; McLellan, *Dean Acheson*, p.10; Gaddis Smith, *Dean Acheson* (New York: Cooper Square Publishers, 1972), p. 4 (in the American Secretaries of State series, vol. XVI).
11. Quoted in Hamburger, *The New Yorker*, November 19, 1949, p. 41.
12. Interview with Alice (Mrs. Dean) Acheson, January 2, 1988. For MacLeish at Yale, see Scott Donaldson, *Archibald MacLeish* (Boston: Houghton Mifflin, 1992), ch. 4.
13. Interview with Archibald MacLeish, cited in McLellan, *Dean Acheson*, p. 10.
14. On Harriman's rowing career at Yale, see Rudy Abramson, *Spanning the Century: The Life of Averell Harriman, 1891–1986* (New York: Morrow, 1992), ch. 4, "Yale: Bones, a Boathouse, and a Bride."
15. Acheson Papers, Yale University Library, series III, box 48, f. 20.
16. Ibid.
17. From an interview with Acheson, cited in McLellan, *Dean Acheson*, p. 10.
18. Dean Acheson, *A Democrat Looks at His Party* (New York: Harper & Brothers, 1955), p. 13.
19. Interview with David C. Acheson, December 20, 1988.
20. Interview with Mary Acheson Bundy, October 12, 1991.
21. Interviews with Alice (Mrs. Dean) Acheson, April 25, 1988; March 22, 1991.
22. Excerpt from the log, July 28, 1915, private collection. The log was written by various hands at various times, so that it is impossible to know who wrote what. The six travelers were A. B. Dick Jr. ("June"), Huntington Morse ("Turnie"), T. Philip Swift ("Phil"), M. D. Truesdale ("Bud"), Charles Farwell Winston ("Far"), and, of course, Dean Acheson. There are said to be two copies of the log, one "expurgated" and another "unexpurgated." The only log available is the expurgated version, and all citations are from that copy. The log runs from July 4, 1915, to September 13, 1915.
23. Letter from DGA to his mother, undated, Yokohama, Japan, July 1915, private collection.
24. Quoted in Isaacson and Thomas, *The Wise Men*, p. 87.

FOUR: "THIS WONDERFUL MECHANISM, THE BRAIN"

1. Letter from T. Gaillard Thomas to DGA, January 8, 1949, Acheson Papers, Yale University Library, series I, box 29, f. 381.
2. Interview with David C. Acheson, May 14, 1992. Though Acheson and Cole Porter were never close friends, Porter often sent him tickets for the openings of his shows; but when they encountered each other decades later in an elevator in the Waldorf-Astoria Hotel in New York City, their greetings were casual, almost perfunctory. (Interview with Alice Stanley Acheson, March 22, 1991.)

   For Porter at Harvard Law School, see Charles Schwartz, *Cole Porter* (New York: Dial Press, 1977), p. 38.
3. Dean Acheson, *Grapes from My Thorns* (New York: W. W. Norton, 1972), pp. 38–39.
4. Ibid., p. 40.
5. Dean Acheson to Michael Janeway, November 14, 1963, Acheson Papers, Yale University Library, series I, box 16, f. 209.
6. Quoted in Hamburger, *The New Yorker,* November 12, 1949, p. 39.
7. Lewis, *One Man's Education,* p. 356.
8. Oliver Wendell Holmes, *The Common Law* (1881), cited in Sheldon M. Novick, *Honorable Justice: The Life of Oliver Wendell Holmes* (Boston: Little, Brown, 1989), p. 158.
9. Felix Frankfurter (recorded in talks with Dr. Harlan B. Phillips), *Felix Frankfurter Reminisces* (New York: Reynal & Co., 1960), p. 172.
10. Quoted in Hamburger, *The New Yorker,* November 12, 1949, p. 39.
11. Acheson, fragments from an unpublished manuscript, "The Administration of Justice in Industry."
12. Quoted in McLellan, *Dean Acheson,* p.13.
13. Letter from Acheson to Felix Frankfurter, December 9, 1918, in *Among Friends: Personal Letters of Dean Acheson,* ed. David S. McLellan and David C. Acheson (New York: Dodd, Mead, 1980), p. 2.

FIVE: THE HEROES

1. Acheson, *Morning and Noon,* p. 47.
2. Interview with Dean Acheson, June 20, 1960, cited in McLellan, *Dean Acheson,* p. 16.
3. See Leonard Baker, *Brandeis and Frankfurter* (New York: Harper & Row, 1984), ch. 5.
4. Ibid., p. 95.
5. Louis D. Brandeis, "The Living Law," cited in Baker, *Brandeis and Frankfurter,* pp. 95–96.
6. Acheson, *Morning and Noon,* p. 58.
7. Ibid., p. 80.
8. Ibid., p. 81.
9. Ibid., p. 96.
10. Ibid., p. 94.
11. Ibid., p. 52.
12. Ibid., pp. 49–50.
13. Baker, *Brandeis and Frankfurter,* pp. 183–184.
14. Interview with Alice (Mrs. Dean) Acheson, January 2, 1988.
15. Acheson, *Morning and Noon,* p. 47.
16. Dean Acheson, *Fragments of My Fleece* (New York: W. W. Norton, 1971), p. 215.
17. Sheldon M. Novick, *Honorable Justice: The Life of Oliver Wendell Holmes* (New York: Little, Brown, 1989), p. 310.

18. McLellan and Acheson, *Among Friends*, letter to Michael Janeway, May 24, 1960.
19. Acheson, *Morning and Noon*, p. 64.
20. Ibid., p. 62.
21. From *The Common Law*, cited in Novick, *Honorable Justice*, p. 158.
22. See Novick, *Honorable Justice*, p. 250.
23. Acheson, *Morning and Noon*, p. 69.
24. McLellan and Acheson, *Among Friends*, letter from Acheson to Eelco Van Kleffens, September 6, 1961, p. 211.
25. Acheson, *Morning and Noon*, p. 65.
26. Ibid., p. 112.
27. Quoted in Acheson, *Morning and Noon*, p. 115.
28. Novick, *Honorable Justice*, pp. 329–330.
29. *Abrams* v. *United States*, 250 U.S. 616 (1919); cited in Novick, *Honorable Justice*, pp. 331–332; in Acheson, *Morning and Noon*, p. 120.
30. Acheson, *Morning and Noon*, p. 121.

SIX: "THE REGULAR CONNECTION OF IDEAS"

1. McLellan and Acheson, *Among Friends*, letter to John H. Vincent, p. 4.
2. Ibid., p. 8. In the August 15, 1920, issue of the *New Republic*, Acheson published an article on labor/management relations at the Rock Island Arsenal. In essence, Acheson praised the initiative taken by the workers during the war to cooperate with management in setting production standards through the formation of a Works Council and subsidiary shop committees; he lamented the fact that after the war, management rejected "cooperation through joint committees."
3. Acheson, *Morning and Noon*, 43.
4. Interview with Alice (Mrs. Dean) Acheson, March 22, 1991.
5. Acheson, *Morning and Noon*, p. 43.
6. Ibid., p. 45.
7. McLellan and Acheson, *Among Friends*, p. 12; letter from DGA to Felix Frankfurter, April 20, 1921.
8. See Howard C. Westwood, *Covington and Burling 1919–1984* (privately printed by Covington and Burling, 1986), p. 5.
9. Ibid., ch. 1; see also Westwood, "Something of C & B's History," pamphlet published by Covington and Burling, November 19, 1973.
10. Acheson, *Morning and Noon*, p. 126.
11. Ibid., pp. 125–130. After Acheson and others became partners in the 1920s, the firm was expanded into Covington, Burling, Rublee, Acheson and Shorb; after Acheson became secretary of state in 1949, it was renamed Covington, Burling, Rublee, O'Brian & Shorb; today it has reclaimed its first title, Covington and Burling, and that is the name used throughout this biography.
12. Acheson, *Fragments*, p. 208.
13. Westwood, *Covington and Burling*, p. 37.
14. Acheson, *Morning and Noon*, ch. 7, "Starting at the Top."
15. Acheson, *Morning and Noon*, p. 134.
16. Ibid., pp. 135–136.
17. Ibid., pp. 138–139.
18. Ibid., p. 140.
19. Ibid., pp. 140–141; Westwood, *Covington and Burling*, p. 47; see also Isaacson and Thomas, *The Wise Men*, p. 130, and Hamburger, *The New Yorker*, November 19, 1949, p. 42.

20. Interview with Felix Frankfurter, June 17, 1960; cited in McLellan, *Dean Acheson*, p. 21.
21. Isaacson and Thomas, *The Wise Men*, p. 132.
22. Interview with Mary A. Bundy, October 4, 1997.
23. Cited in Isaacson and Thomas, *The Wise Men*, p. 131.
24. Cited in Hamburger, *The New Yorker*, November 19, 1949, p. 44.
25. Interview with William P. Bundy, October 12, 1991.
26. Acheson, *Morning and Noon*, pp. 144–145.
27. Acheson, *Fragments*, p. 120; *Morning and Noon*, p. 145.
28. Acheson, *Fragments*, pp. 127–128; *Morning and Noon*, pp. 146–147.
29. Acheson, *Morning and Noon*, p. 147.
30. See Acheson, *Fragments*, p. 117.

SEVEN: "A LOW LIFE BUT A MERRY ONE"

1. Acheson, *A Democrat Looks at His Party*, p. 15.
2. Ibid., p. 15.
3. Isaacson and Thomas, *The Wise Men*, p. 133; McLellan, *Dean Acheson*, p. 22.
4. Letter to Mary Acheson Bundy, June 8, 1945, cited in Dean Acheson, *Present at the Creation* (New York: W. W. Norton, 1969), pp. 107–108.
5. Acheson, *Morning and Noon*, p. 155.
6. Ibid., p. 159.
7. James A. Farley, *Jim Farley's Story: The Roosevelt Years* (New York: Whittlesey House, 1948), pp. 19–27. The number of votes actually recorded does not always correspond to the number of votes officially required to nominate; some delegates simply do not vote.
8. See Frank Freidel, *Franklin D. Roosevelt: A Rendezvous with Destiny* (Boston: Little, Brown, 1990), ch. 5; Ted Morgan, *FDR* (New York: Simon & Schuster, 1985), ch. 13.
9. Acheson, *Morning and Noon*, p. 159.
10. Ibid., p. 160.
11. Ibid., p. 161.
12. Acheson's old friend, Budget Director Lewis W. Douglas, may also have urged the president to appoint Acheson as attorney general. (Hamburger, *The New Yorker*, November 19, 1949, p. 44.)
13. Acheson, *Morning and Noon*, p. 162.
14. Ibid.
15. Ibid.
16. Ibid., p. 164.
17. Ibid., pp. 164–165.
18. Ibid.
19. See Arthur M. Schlesinger Jr., *The Coming of the New Deal* (Boston: Houghton Mifflin, 1959), ch. 12.
20. McLellan, *Dean Acheson*, pp. 26–27. While FDR's executive order of March 4, 1933, had put the United States theoretically "off the gold standard"—meaning that the dollar was not redeemable in gold—this was accepted by the public as a provisional measure to protect the government's gold reserve during the banking crisis.
21. Acheson, *Morning and Noon*, p. 174.
22. Ibid., pp. 174–175; see also Schlesinger, *Coming of the New Deal*, p. 234.
23. Schlesinger, *Coming of the New Deal*, pp. 243–244; John Morton Blum, *From the Morgenthau Diaries: Years of Crisis, 1928–1938* (Boston: Houghton Mifflin, 1959), part I.
24. Davis, *The New Deal Years*, p. 290; Schlesinger, *Coming of the New Deal*, p. 234; Acheson, *Morning and Noon*, pp. 174–175.

25. Acheson, *Morning and Noon*, p. 178.
26. McLellan, *Dean Acheson*, p. 27; Schlesinger, *Coming of the New Deal*, p. 238–239.
27. Quoted in Acheson, *Morning and Noon*, p. 181.
28. Acheson, *Morning and Noon*, p. 181.
29. Blum, *From the Morgenthau Diaries: Years of Crisis, 1928–1938*, p. 67.
30. For FDR quotations, see McLellan, *Dean Acheson*, p. 27; see also Schlesinger, *Coming of the New Deal*, p. 239.
31. Cited in Blum, *From the Morgenthau Diaries*, pp. 67–68.
32. Acheson, *Morning and Noon*, p. 189.
33. Cited in Schlesinger, *Coming of the New Deal*, p. 242.
34. In effect, the Gold Act of 1934 retroactively endorsed what FDR had already done.
35. Cited in Acheson, *Morning and Noon*, p. 192.
36. Some years later one of Acheson's successors in office resigned in a letter bristling with criticism of the president's policies. FDR read it through and then said to his press secretary, "Return it to him and tell him to ask Dean Acheson how a gentleman resigns." (Acheson, *Morning and Noon*, pp. 193–194.)
37. Grace Tully, *F.D.R., My Boss* (New York: Scribner's, 1949), p. 178.
38. Acheson, *Morning and Noon*, p. 191.
39. Interview with Mary Acheson Bundy, October 12, 1991.
40. Acheson, Princeton Seminar transcript, July 2, 1953.

EIGHT: "FORCES STRONGER THAN REASON"

1. Letter from Dean Acheson to Ranald MacDonald, September 29, 1937, Acheson Papers, Yale University Library, series I, box 21, f. 263.
2. Cited in David C. Acheson, *Acheson Country: A Memoir* (New York: W. W. Norton, 1993), p. 46.
3. Acheson, *Morning and Noon*, pp. 198–199.
4. See *Fortune* magazine, April 1949.
5. Interview with Felix Frankfurter, June 17, 1960, quoted in David McLellan, *Dean Acheson*, p. 31.
6. Acheson, *Fragments*, "Roger Brooke Taney," p. 133.
7. Ibid., p. 143.
8. Norman Hapgood to FDR, July 7, 1936. Cited in McLellan, *Dean Acheson*, p. 32.
9. Dean Acheson, letter to Ranald MacDonald, March 11, 1937, Yale University Library, series I, box 21, f. 263.
10. McLellan and Acheson, *Among Friends*, letter to James P. Warburg, March 12, 1937, p. 31.
11. Dean Acheson, "Mr. Justice Cardozo and Problems of Government," address in the proceedings of the bar and officers of the Supreme Court of the United States, November 26, 1938, Washington, D.C.; see also McLellan, *Dean Acheson*, p. 34.
12. Dean Acheson, letter to Ranald MacDonald, September 29, 1937, Acheson Papers, Yale University Library, series I, box 21, f. 263.
13. David Acheson, *Acheson Country*, pp. 82–83.
14. Ibid., pp. 75–76.
15. Ibid., pp. 27–28.
16. Ibid., p. 157.
17. Ibid., pp. 163–164.
18. Acheson, *Morning and Noon*, pp. 199–200.
19. Letter from Felix Frankfurter to Dean Acheson, dated Thanksgiving Day 1937, Acheson Papers, Yale University Library, series I, box 11, f. 141.

20. Letter to Richard Goodwin, August 14, 1957, Acheson Papers, Yale University Library, series I, box 12, f. 155.
21. Letter from Dean Acheson to George Rublee, January 17, 1939. Acheson Papers, Yale University Library, series I, box 27, f. 340.
22. Acheson, *Morning and Noon,* pp. 207–208.
23. For a description of the Ashurst lunch and the Roosevelt visit, see Acheson, *Morning and Noon,* pp. 208–212.
24. See David Acheson, *Acheson Country,* p. 170.
25. Letter from Acheson to Roosevelt, February 6, 1939, cited in Acheson, *Morning and Noon,* p. 213.
26. For FDR's offer and Acheson's reaction, see Acheson, *Morning and Noon,* pp. 212–214; see also McLellan, *Dean Acheson,* p. 37.
27. Draft Letter to the Attorney-General from Walter Gellhorn, December 21, 1939, Acheson Papers, Truman Library, box 1.
28. See Dean Acheson, *Morning and Noon,* pp. 214–215; Acheson, address before the American Bar Association, Philadelphia, Pennsylvania, September 10, 1940, Acheson Papers, Truman Library, box 1. See also *The New York Times,* January 25, 1941; the *Washington Post,* January 25, 1941; *Journal of Commerce,* January 25, 1941; *Wall Street Journal,* January 25, 1941. See also McLellan, *Dean Acheson,* p. 36.
29. Acheson, *Morning and Noon,* p. 215. Harvard Law School offered a prize to the committee in 1946, which Acheson insisted go for a scholarship to the law school in the field of administrative law.
30. Dean Acheson, "An American Attitude Toward Foreign Affairs," address given at the annual dinner of Davenport College of Yale University, November 28, 1939. Reprinted in *Morning and Noon,* pp. 267–275. See also Gaddis Smith, *Dean Acheson,* p. 14.
31. Dean Acheson, "Do You Mean Those Words?" address before the annual convention of the International Ladies' Garment Workers Union, New York City, June 4, 1940. (Excerpts reprinted in *Morning and Noon,* pp. 218–222.)
32. Cited in Richard M. Ketchum, *The Borrowed Years 1938–1941: America on the Way to War* (New York: Random House, 1989), pp. 474–479.
33. See *The New York Times,* August 11, 1940.
34. Stimson letter cited in McLellan, *Dean Acheson,* p. 41.
35. Roosevelt also had assurances that the Republican presidential nominee, Wendell Willkie, would back him up on the destroyer-for-bases deal. See also Acheson, *Morning and Noon,* pp. 222–224; and McLellan, *Dean Acheson,* pp. 39–41.
36. Letter from Dean Acheson to John J. McCloy, September 12, 1940, reprinted in McLellan, *Dean Acheson,* p. 41 fn.
37. Letter from FDR to Dean Acheson, October 2, 1940; letter from Dean Acheson to Franklin Delano Roosevelt, October 4, 1940, Roosevelt Library, P.P.F. file no. 6906.
38. Citations from Acheson, *Morning and Noon,* pp. 226, 175.
39. Ibid., pp. 226–227.

NINE: MOST UNSORDID ACTS

1. Grew's letter of December 14, 1940, to Roosevelt is quoted in Joseph Grew, *Ten Years in Japan* (New York: Simon & Schuster, 1944), pp. 359–363.
2. See Godfrey Hodgson, *The Colonel: The Life and Wars of Henry Stimson, 1867–1950* (New York: Alfred A. Knopf, 1991); see also James Chace and Caleb Carr, *America Invulnerable: The Quest*

for Absolute Security from 1812 to Star Wars, "A Reckoning in the East, 1921–1941" (New York: Summit Books, 1988).

3. Acheson, *Present at the Creation,* p. 62.
4. Blum, John Morton, *From the Morgenthau Diaries: Years of Urgency, 1938–1941* (Boston: Houghton Mifflin, 1964), p. 332.
5. Acheson, *Present at the Creation,* p. 23.
6. Ibid.
7. Ibid.
8. Polls, May 20–25, 1939, January 22–17, 1940, October 2–7, 1940, Gallup Poll; cited in Jonathan G. Utley, "Diplomacy in a Democracy: The United States and Japan, 1937–1941," *World Affairs* 139, no. 2 (fall 1976).
9. See Jonathan Utley, *Going to War with Japan, 1937–1941,* "The Hull-Nomura Talks" (Knoxville: University of Tennessee Press, 1985); see also Utley, "Upstairs, Downstairs at Foggy Bottom: Oil Exports and Japan, 1940–41," *Prologue, the Journal of the National Archives* 8, no. 1 (spring 1976) (Washington, D.C.: National Archives and Records Service of the General Services Administration); Waldo Heinrichs, *Threshold of War: Franklin D. Roosevelt and American Entry into World War II,* "July: The Containment of Japan," "August–September: Crossing the Threshold" (New York: Oxford University Press, 1988).
10. See Utley, *Going to War with Japan,* p. 153.
11. Memo for secretary's files, July 30, 1941, Morgenthau diary, cited in Waldo Heinrichs, *Threshold of War,* p. 141; Acheson, *Present at the Creation,* p. 26.
12. Warren Kimball, ed., *Churchill and Roosevelt: The Complete Correspondence,* vol. 1, *Alliance Emerging* (Princeton, N.J.: Princeton University Press, 1984), p. 225.
13. Cited in Herbert Feis, *The Road to Pearl Harbor* (New York: Atheneum, 1967 [paper]), p. 248.
14. Quoted in Heinrichs, *Threshold of War,* p. 177.
15. Acheson, *Present at the Creation,* p. 26.
16. Daniel Yergin, *The Prize* (New York: Simon & Schuster, 1991), p. 318.
17. Heinrichs, *Threshold of War,* p. 177.
18. See Robert Dallek, *Franklin D. Roosevelt and American Foreign Policy, 1932–1945* (New York: Oxford University Press), p. 275.
19. Acheson, *Present at the Creation,* p. 27.
20. Ronald H. Spector, *Eagle Against the Sun* (New York: Vintage, 1985), p. 77.
21. Acheson, *Present at the Creation,* p. 35.
22. U.S. Department of State, *Foreign Relations of the United States* (FRUS), 1940, vol. III (U.S. Government Printing Office), p. 36.
23. John Morton Blum, *Roosevelt and Morgenthau: A Revision and Condensation of "From the Morgenthau Diaries"* (Boston: Houghton Mifflin, 1970), "Years of Urgency," p. 343.
24. Warren F. Kimball, *Churchill and Roosevelt: The Complete Correspondence,* vol. 1, *Alliance Emerging, October 1933–November 1942* (Princeton, N.J.: Princeton University Press, 1984), pp. 108–109.
25. Blum, *Roosevelt and Morgenthau,* p. 347.
26. Robert E. Sherwood, *Roosevelt and Hopkins* (New York: Harper, 1948), p. 225.
27. Blum, *Roosevelt and Morgenthau,* p. 348; Burns, *Roosevelt: The Soldier of Freedom,* p. 26; Sherwood, *Roosevelt and Hopkins,* p. 225;
28. See Kimball, *The Most Unsordid Act,* p. 137.
29. Acheson, *Present at the Creation,* p. 29.
30. R. F. Harrod, *The Life of John Maynard Keynes* (New York: Harcourt Brace, 1951), p. 556. Lydia Lopokova quote cited in Robert Heilbroner, *The Worldly Philosophers* (New York: Simon & Schuster, 1967), p. 234.

31. Acheson, *Present at the Creation*, p. 29.
32. The British system of Imperial Preference was embodied in the Ottawa agreements of 1930, which were promulgated in reaction to the notoriously restrictive Smoot-Hawley tariff act, which the U.S. Congress had passed in the same period. According to the Ottawa agreements, tariffs were to be lowered for those countries operating within the system of Imperial Preference.
33. Cited in Harrod, *John Maynard Keynes*, p. 512.
34. Quoted in Acheson, *Present at the Creation*, p. 30.
35. See Richard N. Gardner, *Sterling-Dollar Diplomacy* (New York: McGraw-Hill, 1969), pp. 59–60.
36. Acheson, *Present at the Creation*, p. 33.
37. Kimball, *Churchill and Roosevelt: The Complete Correspondence*, vol. 1, p. 351, Churchill to Roosevelt, February 7, 1942.
38. Ibid., pp. 357–358, Roosevelt to Churchill, February 11, 1942.
39. Winston S. Churchill, *Their Finest Hour* (Boston: Houghton Mifflin, 1949), p. 569.

TEN: THE NEW ECONOMIC WORLD ORDER

1. Acheson, *Present at the Creation*, p. 17.
2. For the story of economic welfare abroad, see Ibid., pp. 47–61.
3. Ibid., p. 68.
4. Ibid.
5. Ibid., pp. 68–69.
6. Ibid., pp. 70–71.
7. On Vandenberg, see Dean Acheson, *Sketches from Life of Men I Have Known* (New York: Harper & Brothers, 1959), "Arthur Vandenberg and the Senate," ch. 6; see also Acheson, *Present at the Creation*, pp. 71–72; McCullough, *Truman*, pp. 529–530.
8. Acheson, *Sketches from Life*, p. 124.
9. Ibid., p. 125.
10. Acheson, *Present at the Creation*, p. 72; *Sketches from Life*, p. 127.
11. Quoted in Thomas G. Paterson, J. Gary Clifford, and Kenneth J. Hagen, *American Foreign Policy: A History/1900 to the Present*, 3rd ed. (Lexington, Mass.: D. C. Heath, 1988), p. 405.
12. Letter from Dean Acheson to Eleanor C. Acheson, November 27, 1943, Acheson Papers, Yale University Library, series I, box 1, f. 4.
13. Acheson, *Present at the Creation*, p. 78.
14. Letter from Dean Acheson to Eleanor C. Acheson, November 27, 1943, Acheson papers, Yale University Library, series I, box 1, f. 4.
15. Paterson et al., *American Foreign Policy: A History/1900 to Present*, p. 405.
16. Letter from Dean Acheson to David Acheson, reprinted in *Among Friends*, p. 46.
17. See Armand Van Dormael, *Bretton Woods: Birth of a Monetary System* (New York: Holmes & Meier, 1978), p. 168.
18. Letter to David Acheson, August 1, 1944, Acheson papers, Yale University Library, series I, box 1, f. 4.
19. Cited in Blum, *Roosevelt and Morgenthau*, p. 461.
20. Blum, *Roosevelt and Morgenthau*, p. 461. White was certainly initially sympathetic to Soviet experiments in economic planning; and he also appointed some assistants who, according to Morgenthau's biographer, John Morton Blum, "were almost certainly members of the Communist Party, though Morgenthau did not know they were, and those assistants, in White's view, were as free to pass along information about Treasury policy to the Russians as was

Averell Harriman [acting as FDR's lend-lease "expeditor"], for example, free to talk to the British." See also Alfred E. Eckes, *Search for Solvency: Bretton Woods and the International Monetary System, 1941–1971* (Austin: University of Texas, 1975), pp. 44–45.

21. On the provisions of Bretton Woods, see Robert Lekachman, *The Age of Keynes* (London: Penguin, 1967), ch. 7; Gardner, *Sterling-Dollar Diplomacy*, part II; Fred L. Block, *The Origins of International Economic Disorder* (Berkeley: University of California Press, 1977); Van Dormael, *Bretton Woods*, ch. 16; G. John Ikenberry, "The Political Origins of Bretton Woods," in *A Retrospective on the Bretton Woods System: Lessons for International Monetary Reform* (Chicago: University of Chicago Press, 1993).
22. See Acheson, *Present at the Creation*, pp. 83–84; Eckes, *A Search for Solvency*, pp. 160–162; Paterson et al., *American Foreign Policy*, p. 406.
23. For the Acheson, Morgenthau, and White discussion, see Van Dormael, *Bretton Woods*, pp. 198–200.
24. Harrod, *John Maynard Keynes*, pp. 583–584; Van Dormael, *Bretton Woods*, pp. 219–220.
25. Long quoted in Acheson, *Present at the Creation*, p. 87.
26. Acheson, *Present at the Creation*, p. 88.
27. Gregory A. Fossedal, *Our Finest Hour: Will Clayton, the Marshall Plan, and the Triumph of Democracy* (Stanford, Calif.: Hoover Institution Press, 1993), ch. 6.
28. Quoted in Fossedal, *Our Finest Hour*, p. 138.
29. See U.S. Congress, Senate Committee on Banking and Currency, Bretton Woods Agreements Act. First Session on HR 3314, "An Act to Provide for the Participation of the United States in the IMF and IBRD." Seventy-ninth Congress, June 12, 1945, p. 27; see also Fossedal, *Our Finest Hour*, pp. 137–138.
30. Senate Hearings on HR 3314, p. 45; see also Gardner, *Sterling-Dollar Diplomacy*, p. 135.
31. Cited in Fossedal, *Our Finest Hour*, pp. 140–141.
32. See Acheson's testimony before the Subcommittee on Foreign Trade and Shipping—Special Subcommittee on Postwar Economic Policy and Planning of the House of Representatives. Seventy-ninth Congress, first session, November 30, 1944; see also Block, *The Origins of International Monetary Disorder*, p. 40; William Appleton Williams, *The Tragedy of American Diplomacy* (New York: Dell, 1962), pp. 235–236.
33. See Block, *The Origins of International Monetary Disorder*, p. 41; see also Gardner, *Architects of Illusion*, p. 204, where he cites Acheson's testimony before the Senate Banking and Currency Committee on the "Anglo-American Financial Agreement" (second session on S. J. Res. 138, Seventy-ninth Congress, March 13, 1946, p. 313) regarding the postwar British loan: "We are interested not primarily in lending money to keep good relations with the British, but in an economic system which is the very basis of our life—the system of free, individual enterprise."
34. U.S. Bureau of the Census, "Historical Statistics of the United States from Colonial Times to 1970," part 2 (Washington, D.C.: U.S. Government Printing Office, 1975).
35. *State Department Bulletin* 12 (April 22, 1945), p. 738.

ELEVEN: "THE GOOD LIFE IS VERY HARD"

1. Acheson, *Present at the Creation*, p. 103.
2. Ibid.
3. Letter from Dean Acheson to David Acheson, April 30, 1945, Acheson Papers, Yale University Library, series I, box 1, f. 4.
4. Ibid.
5. Letter from Dean Acheson to Mary A. Bundy, May 23, 1945, Acheson Papers, Yale University Library, series I, box 4, f. 52.

6. Dean Acheson to Mary A. Bundy, May 26, 1945, Acheson Papers, Yale University Library, series I, box 4, f. 52.
7. Letter from Dean Acheson to Mary A. Bundy, May 28, 1945, Acheson Papers, Yale University Library, series I, box 4, f. 52.
8. Ibid.
9. Letter to Mary A. Bundy, May 12, 1945, Acheson Papers, Yale University Library, series I, box 4, f. 52.
10. Dean Acheson to Mary A. Bundy, May 16, 1945, Acheson Papers, Yale University Library, series I, box 4, f. 52.
11. Acheson, *Present at the Creation*, pp. 111–112.
12. Acheson, *Fragments*, "Random Harvest," p. 23.
13. Oliver Wendell Holmes, in *The Mind and Faith of Justice Holmes*, edited by Max Lerner (Boston: Little, Brown, 1943), p. 19. Cited in McLellan, *Dean Acheson*, p. 51.
14. Acheson, *Present at the Creation*, pp. 111–112.
15. Dean Acheson to Mary A. Bundy, June 28, 1945, Acheson Papers, Yale University Library, series I, box 4, f. 52.
16. Acheson, *Present at the Creation*, p. 114.

TWELVE: "AN ARMAMENT RACE OF A RATHER DESPERATE NATURE"

1. For the story of his appointment, see Acheson, *Present at the Creation*, pp. 119–121; see also Isaacson and Thomas, *The Wise Men*, p. 322.
2. Reprinted in Acheson, *Present at the Creation*, p. 121.
3. David Holloway, *Stalin and the Bomb: The Soviet Union and Atomic Energy, 1939–1956* (New Haven, Conn.: Yale University Press, 1994), p. 127; Richard Rhodes, *Dark Sun: The Making of the Hydrogen Bomb* (New York: Simon & Schuster, 1995), p. 176.
4. For a description of Stimson's experience at Ausable, see Hodgson, *The Colonel: The Life and Wars of Henry Stimson*, ch. 8.
5. Cited in Gregg Herken, *The Winning Weapon* (New York: Alfred A Knopf, 1980), p. 26.
6. According to Barton J. Bernstein in his article "Understanding the Atomic Bomb and the Japanese Surrender: Missed Opportunities, Little-Known Near Disasters, and Modern Memory," Stimson hoped that "a guarantee of the emperor, *together* with the A-bomb and heavy conventional bombing, as well as the blockade, might produce a surrender" before the U.S. invasion of the Japanese islands, set for November 1, 1945 (emphasis added). *Diplomatic History* 19, no. 2 (spring 1995), p. 238.
7. The interim committee consisted of Henry Stimson, chairman; George L. Harrison, former chairman of the New York Federal Reserve Bank; Vannevar Bush, chairman of the National Defense Research Committee; James Bryant Conant, president of Harvard University; Ralph Bard, assistant secretary of the navy; Will Clayton, assistant secretary of state; and James F. Byrnes, Truman's personal representative and known to be Truman's choice for secretary of state.
8. Stimson diary, June 19, 1945. Cited in Herken, *The Winning Weapon*, p. 17.
9. Stimson diary, May 15, 1945. See Herken, *The Winning Weapon*, pp. 17–18.
10. FRUS, *The Conference of Berlin*, II, cited in Martin J. Sherwin, *A World Destroyed: The Atomic Bomb and the Grand Alliance* (New York: Alfred A. Knopf, 1975), p. 224.
11. Herken, *The Winning Weapon*, pp. 19–20.
12. G. K. Zhukov, *Vospominaniia i razmyshlenia*, vol. 3, 10th ed. (Moscow: Novosti, 1990), p. 334; cited in David Holloway, *Stalin and the Bomb: The Soviet Union and Atomic Energy 1939–1956* (New Haven, Conn.: Yale University Press, 1994), p. 117.

13. See Kai Bird, *The Chairman: John J. McCloy: The Making of the American Establishment* (New York: Simon & Schuster, 1992), pp. 244–249.
14. Quoted in Herken, *The Winning Weapon*, p. 25.
15. McCloy diary, September 2, 1945, box 1, f. 18, JJM, Amherst College, McCloy collection, cited in Bird, *The Chairman*, pp. 261–262.
16. Stimson diary, September 4, 1945, cited in Hodgson, *The Colonel*, p. 352.
17. The quotes from the covering letter of September 11, 1945, are from Hodgson, *The Colonel*, pp. 357.
18. Quoted in Bundy, *Danger and Survival*, p. 138; see also Henry L. Stimson and McGeorge Bundy, *On Active Service in Peace and War* (New York: Harper & Brothers, 1948), pp. 644–645.
19. Quoted in Hodgson, *The Colonel*, p. 358.
20. Herken, *The Winning Weapon*, p. 27.
21. Stimson diary, Yale Library, September 12, 1945. Cited in Hodgson, *The Colonel*, p. 359.
22. Acheson, *Present at the Creation*, p. 113; see also Robert L. Messer, "Acheson, the Bomb, and the Cold War," in *Dean Acheson and the Making of U.S. Foreign Policy* (New York: St. Martin's Press, 1993), p. 56.
23. Acheson, *Present at the Creation*, p. 123.
24. See Hodgson, *The Colonel*, p. 339.
25. Herken, *The Winning Weapon*, p. 30.
26. Walter Millis, ed., *The Forrestal Diaries* (New York: The Viking Press, 1951), pp. 94–86; see also Robert Beisner, "Patterns of Peril: Dean Acheson's Cold War Conversion, 1945–1946," unpublished paper.
27. Acheson, *Present at the Creation*, p. 124.
28. Herken, *The Winning Weapon*, p. 31.
29. Acheson, *Present at the Creation*, p. 124.
30. Acheson memorandum, September 25, 1945, in FRUS, 1945, 2:48–50; Acheson, *Present at the Creation*, pp. 124–125; see also Bundy, *Danger and Survival*, p. 141.
31. Cited in Bundy, *Danger and Survival*, pp. 141–142.
32. Ibid., p. 142.
33. Herken, *The Winning Weapon*, p. 33.
34. Bundy, *Danger and Survival*, pp. 142–143; Herken, *The Winning Weapon*, pp. 34–35.
35. Herken, *The Winning Weapon*, p. 35; see also Acheson, *Present at the Creation*, p. 125.
36. Quoted in Herken, *The Winning Weapon*, p. 36.
37. Ibid., pp. 35–39; Bundy, *Danger and Survival*, pp. 143–145.
38. Bundy, *Danger and Survival*, pp. 146–147.
39. Acheson, *Present at the Creation*, pp. 125, 132.
40. Bundy, *Danger and Survival*, pp. 150–155.
41. Cited in Herken, *The Winning Weapon*, p. 83.
42. Cited in Patricia Dawson Ward, *The Threat of Peace: James F. Byrnes and the Council of Foreign Ministers, 1945–1946* (Kent, Ohio: Kent University Press, 1979), p. 22.
43. Melvyn P. Leffler, *A Preponderance of Power: National Security, the Truman Administration, and the Cold War* (Stanford, Calif.: Stanford University Press, 1992), pp. 94–99; Daniel Yergin, *Shattered Peace* (New York: Penguin Books, 1990), pp. 147–151.
44. Cited in Herken, *The Winning Weapon*, p. 86.
45. Acheson, *Present at the Creation*, pp. 151–152.
46. See Murray Kempton, "The Ambivalence of Robert Oppenheimer," pp. 118–135, in *Rebellions, Perversities and Main Events* (New York: Times Books, 1994).
47. *In the Matter of J. Robert Oppenheimer* (U.S. Government Printing Office, 1954; MIT Press,

1971), p. 59; cited in "Were the Atomic Scientists Spies?" *The New York Review of Books,* June 9, 1994.

48. In 1954 Oppenheimer would have his security clearance stripped from him for refusing to support with any enthusiasm the hydrogen bomb program.
49. Acheson, *Present at the Creation,* p. 153.
50. Quoted in David Lilienthal, *The Journals of David E. Lilienthal,* vol. 2, *The Atomic Energy Years, 1945–1950* (New York: Harper & Row, 1964), p. 13.
51. Lilienthal, *Journals,* vol. 2, pp 28–29.
52. Ibid., p. 27.
53. Acheson, *Present at the Creation,* p. 153; Bundy, *Danger and Survival,* pp. 159–161; Robert L. Messer, "Acheson, the Bomb, and the Cold War," in *Dean Acheson and the Making of Foreign Policy,* ed. Douglas Brinkley (New York: St. Martin's Press, 1993); U.S. Department of State, Committee on Atomic Energy, *A Report on the International Control of Atomic Energy,* pp. 5, 21.
54. Harry S. Truman, *Off the Record: The Private Papers of Harry S. Truman,* edited by Robert Ferrell (New York: Harper & Row, 1980), p. 87.
55. Lilienthal, *Journals,* vol. 2, p. 30.
56. Quoted in Lilienthal, *Journals,* vol. 2, p. 32; see also Lincoln Gordon, "Oral Memoir," Washington, D.C., July 17, 1975, courtesy of Mr. Gordon, and available as well at the Truman Library, Independence, Missouri.
57. Quoted in Herken, *The Winning Weapon,* p. 172.
58. Acheson, *Present at the Creation,* p. 155.
59. Messer, "Acheson, the Bomb, and the Cold War," p. 62.
60. Acheson, *Present at the Creation,* p. 155; Bundy, *Danger and Survival,* p. 165.
61. Herken, *The Winning Weapon,* p. 185.
62. Lilienthal, *Journals,* vol. 2, p. 59.
63. Cited in Messer, "Acheson, the Bomb, and the Cold War"; Acheson interview, February 16, 1955, Presidential Papers, Truman Library, box 1.
64. Cited in Herken, *The Winning Weapon,* p. 170.
65. Bundy, *Danger and Survival,* p. 176.
66. Cited in Bundy, *Danger and Survival,* p. 177, from David Holloway, "Entering the Nuclear Arms Race: The Soviet Decision to Build the Atomic Bomb, 1939–45," *Social Studies of Science* II (1981), p. 183.
67. Bundy, *Danger and Survival,* pp. 186–187.

THIRTEEN: NO GRAND STRATEGY

1. Acheson recollections, Truman Library, Post-Presidential Memoirs, box 1.
2. Ibid.; Acheson, *Present at the Creation,* p. 129; McLellan, *Dean Acheson,* p. 59.
3. Acheson, *Present at the Creation,* p. 129.
4. The Central Intelligence Agency as such was not set up until July 1947 after Acheson was temporarily out of government. In *Present at the Creation,* Acheson wrote: "I had the gravest forebodings about this organization and warned the President that as set up neither he, the National Security Council, nor anyone else would be in a position to know what it was doing or to control it" (p. 214).

   On the struggle to control the State Department in 1945–46, see Acheson, *Present at the Creation,* pp. 160–163.
5. Acheson, *Present at the Creation,* p. 163; David Robertson, *Sly and Able: A Political Biography of James F. Byrnes* (New York: W. W. Norton, 1994), pp. 489–490.

6. Acheson, *Present at the Creation*, p. 169.
7. Alonzo L. Hamby, *A Man of the People: A Life of Harry S. Truman* (New York: Oxford University Press, 1995), p. 407.
8. Quoted in Hamby, *Man of the People*, p. 405.
9. Acheson, *Present at the Creation*, p. 176; Hamby, *Man of the People*, pp. 407–408.
10. Acheson, *Present at the Creation*, p. 179.
11. Ibid., p. 259; Smith, *Dean Acheson*, p. 331.
12. See Yergin, *Shattered Peace*, p. 148.
13. Ibid.
14. Leffler, *A Preponderance of Power*, pp. 47–48; Yergin, *Shattered Peace*, pp. 149–150.
15. Charles E. Bohlen, *Witness to History* (New York: W. W. Norton, 1973), p. 250.
16. Acheson, *Present at the Creation*, p. 136.
17. Harry S. Truman, *Memoirs: Year of Decisions*, vol. I (Garden City, N.Y.: Doubleday, 1955), p. 550.
18. Yergin, *Shattered Peace*, p. 158; McCullough, *Truman*, p. 479.
19. Acheson, *Present at the Creation*, p. 136; Robertson, *Sly and Able*, p. 456; Yergin, *Shattered Peace*, p. 158.
20. Yergin, *Shattered Peace*, p. 159.
21. McCullough, *Truman*, p. 480.
22. Quoted in Acheson, *Present at the Creation*, p. 137.
23. Acheson, "The American People and Their State Department," address to the Maryland Historical Society, Baltimore, November 19, 1945, quoted in McLellan, *Dean Acheson*, p. 66.
24. Acheson, *Present at the Creation*, p. 189.
25. Ibid., pp. 130–131. Acheson was viewed at this time by liberal columnists such as I. F. Stone writing in *The Nation* as one who "has been pro–de Gaulle, anti-Franco, strongly opposed to the admission of Argentina to the U.N., and friendly to the Soviet Union." See I. F. Stone, "Shake-up in the State Department," *The Nation*, August 25, 1945.
26. Acheson, *Present at the Creation*, p. 131.
27. Summary of Acheson's remarks to the American Platform Guild Conference, State Department, January 3, 1946: Acheson Papers, files as assistant secretary of state, 1941–1945, and undersecretary of state, 1945–1947, Truman Library. Cited in Robert Beisner, "Patterns of Peril: Dean Acheson Joins the Cold Warriors, 1945–46," *Diplomatic History*, 20, no. 3 (summer 1996), pp. 324–325.
28. Acheson, *Present at the Creation*, p. 726.

FOURTEEN: "A GRACEFUL WAY OUT"

1. Mark Lytle, *The Origins of the Iranian-American Alliance, 1941–1953* (New York: Holmes & Meier, 1987), pp. 57–58.
2. Ibid., pp. 56–57.
3. For an analysis of Washington's views of Middle Eastern oil reserves during World War II, see Daniel Yergin, *The Prize: The Epic Quest for Oil, Money and Power* (New York: Simon & Schuster, 1991), pp. 391–408.
4. Quoted in Yergin, *The Prize*, p. 401.
5. Kimball, *Churchill-Roosevelt Correspondence: Alliance Declining*, letter from FDR to Churchill, March 3, 1944, p. 14.
6. Ibid., letter from Churchill to Roosevelt, March 4, 1944, p. 17.

   These wartime exchanges tended to reflect an understanding between the two countries that was generally respected. By 1947 American companies were actually being invited by the

British to invest in Anglo-Iranian, largely because of Anglo-Iranian's need to build up a large refining and marketing system of its own in Europe, coupled with its fears of being shut out by the cheap and ever more abundant oil flowing from the Arabian-American oil company in Saudi Arabia. Along with growing fears of Soviet encroachment in Iran, the chairman of Anglo-Iranian believed that its interests would be best served by obtaining American partners. (See Yergin, *The Prize*, pp. 420–422.)

7. Memorandum to the secretary and under secretary of state from Dean Acheson, assistant secretary for economic affairs, January 28, 1944, State Department National Archives, 891.00/1-28-44. For the Rostow anecdote, see Lytle, *Origins of the Iranian-American Alliance*, fn. p. 62; see also Acheson, *Present at the Creation*, p. 133.
8. George F. Kennan, *Sketches from Life* (New York: Pantheon Books, 1989), p. 165.
9. George F. Kennan, *Memoirs: 1925–1950* (New York: Pantheon Books, paper, 1967), p. 4.
10. See Wilson Miscamble, *George F. Kennan and the Making of American Foreign Policy, 1947–1950* (Princeton, N.J.: Princeton University Press, 1992), pp. 15–17.
11. See Kennan, "Russia—Seven Years Later," September 1944, annex in Kennan's *Memoirs*, vol. I, pp. 503–531.
12. Kennan, *Memoirs*, vol. I, p. 209.
13. See Kuniholm, *Origins of the Cold War*, p. 276.
14. Quoted in Lytle, *Origins of the Iranian-American Alliance*, p.142; FRUS, 1945, vol. 8, pp. 410, 410n.
15. FRUS, 1945, vol. 8, p. 424, Kennan to secretary of state, October 1, 1945.
16. Eben Ayers diary, December 17, 1945, Truman Library, cited in Deborah Welch Larson, *Origins of Containment: A Psychological Explanation* (Princeton, N.J.: Princeton University Press, 1985), p. 239.
17. FRUS, 1945, vol. VIII, Iran, p. 500.
18. Ibid., p. 508.
19. Truman to Byrnes, January 5, 1946, Truman Papers: PSF, "Longhand Memos," Truman Library.
20. McLellan, *Dean Acheson*, p. 92.
21. Quoted in Kuniholm, *Origins of the Cold War*, p. 321; see also Larson, *Origins of Containment*, pp. 267–268.
22. Kuniholm, *Origins of the Cold War*, pp. 321–323; Lytle, *Origins of the Iranian-American Alliance*, pp. 163–164; McLellan, *Dean Acheson*, pp. 91–92.
23. Letter from Kennan to Bruce Kuniholm, in Kuniholm, *Origins of the Cold War*, pp. 320–321.
24. For the denouement of the Iranian crisis, see Leffler, *A Preponderance of Power*, p. 110; Lytle, *Origins of the Iranian-American Alliance*, pp. 165–168; Yergin, *Shattered Peace*, pp. 187–190.
25. FRUS, 1946, vol. VII, pp. 732–736.
26. Quoted in Beisner, "Patterns of Peril," p. 325.
27. War College speech, September 16, 1948, Acheson Papers, Truman Library, box 69, pp. 26–27. Cited in Beisner, "Patterns of Peril," p. 335.

FIFTEEN: RISKING WAR

1. For Churchill speech, see *Major Problems in American Foreign Policy*, edited by Thomas G. Paterson (Lexington, Mass.: D. C. Heath, 1989), pp. 288–292; see also Larson, *Origins of Containment*, pp. 263–264.
2. McCullough, *Truman*, p. 488.
3. Quoted in Ronald Steel, *Walter Lippmann and the American Century* (New York: Vintage Books, 1981), pp. 428–429.

4. For an account of the dinner party and its aftermath, see Isaacson and Thomas, *The Wise Men*, p. 363; McLellan, *Dean Acheson*, p. 88; Steel, *Walter Lippmann*, pp. 428–429.
5. Acheson, *Sketches from Life*, pp. 62–63.
6. Quoted in McCullough, *Truman*, pp. 489–490.
7. *The New York Times*, March 1, 1946; address to the Overseas Press Club of America, February 28, 1946.
8. *The New York Times*, March 17, 1946; speech by Byrnes in New York City to members of the Society of the Friendly Sons of Saint Patrick, March 16, 1946.
9. Quoted in Yergin, *Shattered Peace*, pp. 166–167; see also Beisner, "Patterns of Peril," pp. 13–14; Leffler, *Preponderance of Power*, pp. 336–337.
10. Quoted in Walter Millis, ed., *The Forrestal Diaries* (New York: Viking Press, 1951), p. 134.
11. Quoted in Larson, *Origins of Containment*, pp. 253–254; Steel, *Walter Lippmann*, p. 427.
12. Quoted in Larson, *Origins of Containment*, p. 254.
13. See Isaacson and Thomas, *The Wise Men*, pp. 350–351; Paul Nitze, *From Hiroshima to Glasnost: A Memoir of Five Perilous Decades* (New York: Weidenfeld & Nicolson, 1989), p. 77.

    In his memoirs, *Present at the Creation*, written in the 1960s and published in 1969, Acheson takes the view that Stalin's speech was an offensive aimed at the United States and the West, but this is hindsight, for there is no record that Acheson believed this at the time. All available evidence points to the opposite conclusion.
14. The "Long Telegram" was intended for high government officials; it later became the genesis for the more nuanced "X" article, "The Sources of Soviet Conduct," which appeared in *Foreign Affairs* in July 1947 and articulated for a broader public the policy of the containment of the Soviet Union.
15. Kennan, *Memoirs, 1925–1950*, p. 293.
16. "The Kennan 'Long Telegram,'" February 22, 1946, reprinted in *Origins of the Cold War: The Novikov, Kennan, and Roberts "Long Telegrams" of 1946*, edited by Kenneth M. Jensen, published by United States Institute of Peace, Washington, D.C., 1991.
17. Quotes in Isaacson and Thomas, *The Wise Men*, p. 355.
18. Kennan, *Memoirs, 1925–1950*, p. 295.
19. Acheson, *Present at the Creation*, p. 151.
20. Larson, *Origins of Containment*, p. 257; Robert Messer, "Paths of Containment," *Diplomatic History* (fall 1977); Yergin, *Shattered Peace*, pp. 164–165.
21. Acheson, *Fragments*, "Random Harvest," address delivered at a dinner of the Associated Harvard Clubs, Copley Plaza Hotel, Boston, June 4, 1946, pp. 17–26.
22. Harry N. Howard, *Turkey, the Straits, and U.S. Policy* (Baltimore: Johns Hopkins Press, 1974), p. 255.
23. Ibid., p. 214.
24. Kuniholm, *Origins of the Cold War*, pp. 262–264.
25. Nikita Khrushchev, *Khrushchev Remembers: The Last Testament* (Boston: Little, Brown, 1974), pp. 295–296.
26. William Hillman, *Mr. President: The First Publication from the Personal Diaries, Private Letters, Papers and Revealing Interviews of Harry S. Truman* (New York: Farrar, Straus & Young, 1952), pp. 22–23.
27. Howard, *Turkey, the Straits*, p. 233.
28. Kennan to James F. Byrnes, March 20, 1946, FRUS, 1946, vol. VI, p. 723; see also John Lewis Gaddis, *We Now Know: Rethinking the Cold War* (New York: Oxford University Press, 1997), ch. 1, "Dividing the World."
29. Kuniholm, *Origins of the Cold War*, p. 356.

30. Memorandum of Hottelet interview with Litvinov to the secretary of state, Moscow, June 21, 1946, FRUS, 1946, vol. VI, pp. 763–764.
31. On August 9 the Yugoslavs forced down an unarmed U.S. Army transport plane; after Acheson dispatched an ultimatum to Belgrade on August 15, the Yugoslavs released the U.S. crew. (Acheson, *Present at the Creation*, p. 195.)
32. FRUS, 1946, vol. VII, pp. 840–842.
33. Quoted in Isaacson and Thomas, *The Wise Men*, p. 371.
34. Acheson, *Present at the Creation*, pp. 195–196; Jones, *The Fifteen Weeks*, pp. 63–64; Truman, *Years of Trial and Hope*, p. 97. Other accounts say that Eisenhower was not present at the August 15 meeting, but he was nonetheless worried that any Soviet occupation of the Straits would lead to war. (See Kuniholm, *The Origins of the Cold War in the Near East*, p. 362, fn. 166; Millis, *The Forrestal Diaries*, p. 192; Eduard Mark, "The War Scare of 1946 and Its Consequences," *Diplomatic History* [summer 1997], p. 383, fn. 1.)
35. James Reston, "The No. 1 No. 2 Man in Washington," *The New York Times Magazine*, August 25, 1946; see also Beisner, "Patterns of Peril," pp. 343–345.
36. Interview with Dean Acheson, Post-Presidential Memoirs, February 17, 1955, Truman Library, box 1.

SIXTEEN: "CLEARER THAN TRUTH"

1. See David E. Lilienthal, *The Journals of David E. Lilienthal*, vol. 2, *The Atomic Energy Years 1945–1950* (New York: Harper & Row, 1964), p. 215.
2. Clifford, *Counsel to the President*, pp. 109–129; see also McCullough, *Truman*, pp. 543–545; Yergin, *Shattered Peace*, p. 241–243.

   According to Clifford, the report became known twenty years later in 1968, when Arthur Krock, a former Washington bureau chief, approached Clifford in the course of gathering material for his memoirs. Apparently Truman had told Krock of the existence of this report, and he asked Clifford if he had a copy. As it happened, he had kept one copy of the draft from which the final report had been printed, and "since it was no longer sensitive, I showed it to him on what I thought was a background basis." Krock published the 26,000-word document in 1968 as an appendix to his memoirs. Sixteen of the original twenty are now at the Truman Library. The others have never turned up. (Clifford, *Counsel to the President*, p. 124.)
3. Yergin, *Shattered Peace*, p. 247.
4. John Morton Blum, ed., *The Price of Vision: The Diary of Henry A. Wallace, 1942–1946* (Boston: Houghton Mifflin, 1973), pp. 588–601; Yergin, *Shattered Peace*, pp. 249–25.
5. Blum, *Diary of Henry A. Wallace*, pp. 661–669; Yergin, *Shattered Peace*, pp. 251–252.
6. Quoted in Clifford, *Counsel to the President*, p. 119.
7. Ibid., pp. 121–122.
8. Acheson, *Present at the Creation*, pp. 192–193.
9. Ibid., p. 213.
10. For Acheson's description of his encounter with Marshall, see Acheson, *Present at the Creation*, pp. 213–216; see also Acheson, *Sketches from Life*, p. 154.
11. Forrest C. Pogue, *George C. Marshall: Education of a General, 1880–1939* (New York: Viking Press, 1963), p. 5; see also Charles L. Mee Jr., *The Marshall Plan* (New York: Simon & Schuster, 1984), p. 39.
12. Pogue, *Education of a General*, pp. 19–20.
13. For the description of life at the Virginia Military Institute: ibid., ch. 3.
14. Mee, *The Marshall Plan*, pp. 41–42.
15. Acheson, *Sketches from Life*, p. 147.

16. Isaacson and Thomas, *The Wise Men*, p. 387.
17. Acheson, *Present at the Creation*, p. 217; Princeton Seminars, February 18, 1955, Truman Library, box 1; Isaacson and Thomas, *The Wise Men*, p. 387; Joseph Marion Jones, *The Fifteen Weeks (February 21–June 5, 1947)* (New York: Harvest/HBJ, 1955), pp. 3–4.
18. Acheson, *Present at the Creation*, pp. 217–218; Jones, *The Fifteen Weeks*, pp. 4–6.
19. For Stalin's policy toward the Greek Communist Party, see Peter J. Stavrakis, "Soviet Policy in Areas of Limited Control: The Case of Greece, 1944–1949," in John O. Iatrides and Linda Wrigley, eds., *Greece at the Crossroads: The Civil War and Its Legacy* (University Park, Pa.: Pennsylvania State University Press, 1995 [paper]).
20. For the description of the December 1944 "battle of Athens" and its aftermath, see John O. Iatrides, "Greece at the Crossroads: 1944–1950," in Iatrides and Wrigley, *Greece at the Crossroads: The Civil War and Its Legacy.*
21. Iatrides, "Greece at the Crossroads: 1944–1950."
22. Ibid.
23. Stavrakis, "Soviet Policy in Areas of Limited Control," p. 250.
24. Ibid.
25. See Iatrides, "Greece at the Crossroads"; Stavrakis, "Soviet Policy in Greece"; Ivo Banac, "The Tito-Stalin Split," in Iatrides and Wrigley, *Greece at the Crossroads: The Civil War and Its Legacy.*
26. Quoted in Isaacson and Thomas, *The Wise Men*, p. 393.
27. Notes on interview with Dean Acheson, February 24, 1947, Louis Fischer Papers, Princeton; Larson, *Origins of Containment: A Psychological Explanation*, pp. 303–304.
28. Jones, *The Fifteen Weeks*, pp. 90–99.
29. Quoted in Isaacson and Thomas, *The Wise Men*, p. 394.
30. Jones, *The Fifteen Weeks*, p. 139.
31. Acheson, *Present at the Creation*, p. 219.
32. Jones, *The Fifteen Weeks*, p. 141.
33. Acheson, *Present at the Creation*, p. 219; see also the Princeton Seminars, February 18, 1955, HSTL.
34. Acheson, *Present at the Creation*, pp. 220–221.
35. Jones, *The Fifteen Weeks*, pp. 154–155.
36. Ibid., p. 159.
37. For Will Clayton memorandum of March 5, 1947, see Fossedal, *Our Finest Hour*, pp. 217–219.
38. Jones, *The Fifteen Weeks*, pp. 17–23, 269–274.
39. Acheson, *Present at the Creation*, pp. 225, 375; see also John Lewis Gaddis, *Strategies of Containment: A Critical Appraisal of Postwar American National Security Policy* (New York: Oxford University Press, 1982), ch. 1.
40. Senate Committee on Foreign Relations, Eightieth Congress, first session, *Hearings on S. 938 to Provide for American Assistance to Greece and Turkey;* see also Acheson, *Present at the Creation*, p. 225; Jones, *The Fifteen Weeks*, pp. 190–193.
41. Richard M. Freeland, *The Truman Doctrine and the Origins of McCarthyism: Foreign Policy, Domestic Politics, and Internal Security, 1946–1948* (New York: New York University Press, 1971), pp. 112–113.
42. Quoted in Acheson, *Present at the Creation*, p. 225.
43. Steel, *Walter Lippmann*, pp. 439–440.
44. Milovan Djilas, *Conversations with Stalin* (New York: Harcourt, Brace, & World, 1962), pp. 181–182.
45. Stavrakis, "Soviet Policy in Areas of Limited Control."

SEVENTEEN: REVEILLE IN MISSISSIPPI

1. Acheson, Post-Presidential Memoirs, Truman Library, February 18, 1955, p. 38.
2. Acheson, *Present at the Creation*, p. 227.
3. Ibid., p. 230.
4. Ibid., p. 228.
5. Jones, *The Fifteen Weeks*, p. 26.
6. Ibid., p. 27.
7. Acheson, *Present at the Creation*, pp. 228–229; Acheson, Post-Presidential Memoirs, Truman Library, February 18, 1955, p. 39; Jones, *The Fifteen Weeks*, pp. 26–27.
8. Under Secretary of State Dean G. Acheson's address before the Delta Council, Cleveland, Mississippi, May 8, 1947, reprinted in Jones, *The Fifteen Weeks*, pp. 274–281.
9. Acheson, *Present at the Creation*, p. 230.
10. See Leonard Miall, Truman Library Oral History Collection, cited in Mee, *The Marshall Plan*, pp. 95–96.
11. Acheson, *Present at the Creation*, p. 133.
12. *Anglo-American Financial Agreement*, hearings before the Committee on Banking and Currency, U.S. Senate, Seventy-ninth Congress, second session, March 13, 1946. See also McLellan, *Dean Acheson*, p. 93.
13. *The New York Times*, April 23, 1946.
14. McLellan, *Dean Acheson*, pp. 94–95.
15. Michael J. Hogan, *The Marshall Plan: America, Britain, and the Reconstruction of Western Europe, 1947–1952* (New York: Cambridge University Press, 1989), pp. 21, 26–35; McLellan, *Dean Acheson*, pp. 70–73.
16. Acheson, *Present at the Creation*, p. 226; Jones, *The Fifteen Weeks*, pp. 199–202.
17. Acheson, Post-Presidential Memoirs, Truman Library, February 18, 1955, p. 41.
18. Acheson, *Present at the Creation*, p. 226; March 5, 1947, memorandum in Fossedal, *Our Finest Hour*, pp. 216–219.
19. Hearings of the Senate Committee on Foreign Relations, *Origins of the Truman Doctrine*, p. 95, quoted in Yergin, *Shattered Peace*, p. 296. Even before departing for the Russian capital, a senior State Department official—possibly Charles Bohlen, who was to accompany Marshall to Moscow—told a reporter from *Time* magazine, "Our experience with [the Russians] has proved by now that it is impossible to negotiate with them. It is to yield to them or tell them 'no.'" (Quoted in Yergin, *Shattered Peace*, p. 296.)
20. Hogan, *The Marshall Plan*, pp. 26–35; Jones, *The Fifteen Weeks*, pp. 214–220.
21. Cited in Yergin, *Shattered Peace*, p. 300.
22. Bohlen, *Witness to History*, pp. 262–263.
23. FRUS, 1947, vol. II, pp. 337–344.
24. Department of State *Bulletin*, May 11, 1947, p. 919; cited in McLellan, *Dean Acheson*, p. 129.
25. Quoted in George F. Kennan, *Memoirs: 1925–1950* (New York: Pantheon Books, 1967), p. 326; see also Miscamble, *George F. Kennan*, p. 11.
26. Acheson, *Present at the Creation*, p. 230; Jones, *The Fifteen Weeks*, p. 236.
27. Kennan, *Memoirs: 1925–1950*, p. 328.
28. From Kennan's address to the National War College, May 6, 1947, cited in his *Memoirs*, p. 330.
29. Bohlen, *Witness to History*, pp. 264–265; Kennan, *Memoirs: 1925–1950*, pp. 330–342.
30. Kennan, *Memoirs: 1925–1950*, p. 342.
31. Paul Nitze, with Steven L. Rearden and Ann M. Smith, *From Hiroshima to Glasnost* (New York: Weidenfeld & Nicolson, 1989), pp. 51–52.

32. Clayton memorandum of May 27, 1947, printed in Fossedal, *Our Finest Hour*, pp. 228–230.
33. Acheson, *Present at the Creation*, p. 231.
34. Ibid., p. 232.
35. Acheson, Post-Presidential Memoirs, Truman Library, February 18, 1955, p. 42.
36. See Price interviews with Bohlen, HSTL Bohlen Oral History; see also Bohlen, *Witness to History*, pp. 263–264; Jones, *The Fifteen Weeks*, p. 255; Mee, *The Marshall Plan*, p. 99.
37. Mee, *The Marshall Plan*, p. 98.
38. Acheson, *Present at the Creation*, p. 233; Mee, *The Marshall Plan*, p. 100.
39. Acheson, the Princeton Seminars, HSTL, February 18, 1955, p. 43.
40. Address by Secretary of State George C. Marshall at the commencement exercises of Harvard University, Cambridge, Mass., June 5, 1947, reprinted in Jones, *The Fifteen Weeks*, pp. 281–281; see also Mee, *The Marshall Plan*, pp. 102–104.
41. See Mee, *The Marshall Plan*, p. 101.
42. For Bevin speech to the National Press Club, Washington, D.C., April 1, 1949, see Bullock, *Ernest Bevin*, p. 405.
43. Jones, *The Fifteen Weeks*, p. 256.
44. Mee, *The Marshall Plan*, pp. 124–126.
45. Ibid., pp. 130–137.
46. Bullock, *Ernest Bevin*, p. 422.
47. Quoted in Miscamble, *George F. Kennan*, p. 57.
48. Acheson, *Present at the Creation*, p. 375.
49. Acheson, *Sketches from Life*, pp. 147–148.
50. On Lovett, see Isaacson and Thomas, *The Wise Men*, ch. 3 and 7.
51. Cited by Acheson in *Present at the Creation*, p. 237.
52. Acheson, *Present at the Creation*, p. 238.

EIGHTEEN: THE HABIT-FORMING DRUG OF PUBLIC LIFE

1. Acheson, *Present at the Creation*, p. 238.
2. Letter to Jane Acheson Brown, May 3, 1947, in *Among Friends: Personal Letters of Dean Acheson*, p. 66.
3. Acheson, *Present at the Creation*, p. 239.
4. Ibid.
5. Interview with Dean Rusk in Daniel Yergin, *Shattered Peace*, p. 278.
6. Quoted in Mee, *The Marshall Plan*, p. 237.
7. Quoted in Richard Freeland, *The Truman Doctrine and the Origins of McCarthyism: Foreign Policy, Domestic Politics, and Internal Security, 1945–1948* (New York: W. W. Norton, 1977), p. 255.
8. Quoted in Theodore A. Wilson and Richard D. McKinzie, "White House versus Congress: Conflict or Collusion? The Marshall Plan as a Case Study" (paper delivered at the annual meeting of the Organization of American Historians, 1973), cited in Thomas G. Paterson, *On Every Front: The Making of the Cold War* (New York: W. W. Norton, 1979), p. 135.
9. Acheson, *Present at the Creation*, pp. 240–241.
10. On the Hoover Commission, see Acheson, *Present at the Creation*, pp. 242–244.
11. Acheson, Post-Presidential Memoirs, Truman Library, February 18, 1955, pp. 46–47; see also Acheson, *Present at the Creation*, pp. 241–242. For quotation of Paul Hoffman as a salesman, see Mee, *The Marshall Plan*, p. 247.
12. Quoted in Yergin, *Shattered Peace*, p. 327.
13. Kennan, "The Sources of Soviet Conduct," *Foreign Affairs* (July 1947), reprinted in Walter Lippmann, *The Cold War* (New York: Harper Torchbooks, 1972), pp. 74, 76.

14. Kennan, *Memoirs: 1925–1950*, p. 358.
15. See the reprints of Lippmann articles and the introduction by Ronald Steel in Lippmann, *The Cold War.*
16. Quoted in Yergin, *Shattered Peace*, p. 328.
17. See Hogan, *The Marshall Plan*, p. 83.
18. Yergin, *Shattered Peace*, pp. 333–335.
19. Truman quote from Yergin, *Shattered Peace*, pp. 343–354.
20. Yergin, *Shattered Peace*, pp. 354–355.
21. Isaacson and Thomas, *The Wise Men*, p. 441.
22. Ibid., p. 461; Leffler, *A Preponderance of Power*, pp. 217–219; for Truman quote, see Yergin, *Shattered Peace*, p. 377.
23. McCullough, *Truman*, p. 631; Truman quote in Yergin, *Shattered Peace*, p. 392.
24. Isaacson and Thomas, *The Wise Men*, p. 462.
25. Acheson, the Princeton Seminars, HSTL, July 2, 1953.

NINETEEN: IN MARSHALL'S CHAIR

1. Quoted in Allen Weinstein, *Perjury: The Hiss-Chambers Case* (New York: Knopf, 1978), p. 5; see also ch. 2, "Alger and Whittaker: The Crucible of Family," and *The New York Times*, Hiss obituary, November 16, 1996.
2. Nomination of Dean G. Acheson, hearings before the Senate Committee on Foreign Relations, Eighty-first Congress, January 13, 1949.
3. Executive sessions of the Senate Foreign Relations Committee, January 14, 1949.
4. Berle's testimony in the hearings of the House Un-American Activities Committee, I, August–September 1948, pp. 1,291–1,300 (quote on p. 1,293).
5. For Berle's statement before HUAC, see hearings of the House Un-American Activities Committee, I, August–September 1948, p. 1,296.
6. Acheson, *Present the Creation*, pp. 251–252.
7. Quoted in McLellan, *Dean Acheson*, pp. 138–139.
8. See Acheson, testimony at the confirmation hearings, executive session, Senate Committee on Foreign Relations, vol. II, Eighty-first Congress, January 14, 1949, pp. 6–8.
9. Testimony of Dean Acheson, January 14, 1949, executive session, the Senate Foreign Relations Committee, vol. II, Eighty-first Congress, first and second sessions 1949–1950, pp. 12, 368.

   J. Edgar Hoover needed Attorney General Tom Clark's permission to institute physical surveillance of Hiss and his wife during his final year at the State Department and made known his suspicion of Hiss to Acheson, Byrnes, and Truman both verbally and in a memorandum that "reached Truman, Byrnes, and Clark as well as other leading government officials from January to March 1946." See Allen Weinstein, *Perjury: The Hiss-Chambers Case* (New York: Knopf, 1978), p. 357.
10. Weinstein, *Perjury*, p. 10.
11. Quoted in Isaacson and Thomas, *The Wise Men*, p. 467.
12. Acheson, *Present at the Creation*, p. 254.
13. Ibid., pp. 250, 254–257.
14. Quoted in Philip Hamburger, "Mr. Secretary," part I, *The New Yorker*, pp. 39–53; Interview with Alice Acheson, January 2, 1988.
15. For a description of Acheson's office, see Philip Hamburger, *The New Yorker*, November 12, 1949.
16. Interview with Lucius D. Battle, October 19, 1989.
17. Ibid.
18. Quoted in Hamburger, *The New Yorker*, November 12, 1949.

19. Interview with Joseph Alsop, October 6, 1988.
20. See David C. Acheson, *Acheson Country*, p. 157.
21. Quoted in Hamburger, *The New Yorker*, November 12, 1949.
22. Interview with Lucius D. Battle, October 19, 1989; see also Hamburger, *The New Yorker*, November 11, 1949.
23. Interview with Marshall Shulman, December 20, 1994.
24. Hamburger, *The New Yorker*, November 19, 1949.
25. Miscamble, *George F. Kennan*, pp. 115–116; see also Richard A. Best Jr., *"Co-operation with Like-Minded Peoples": British Influences on American Security Policy, 1945–1949* (Westport, Conn.: Greenwood Press, 1986), p. 156; Herbert Feis, *From Trust to Terror: The Onset of the Cold War* (New York: W. W. Norton (1970), pp. 375–377.
26. Miscamble, *George F. Kennan*, ch. 4, pp. 132–140.
27. Acheson, *Present at the Creation*, pp. 267–275.
28. Acheson, *Sketches from Life*, "Ernest Bevin"; see also Alan Bullock, *Ernest Bevin, Foreign Secretary* (London: Heinemann, 1983).
29. Acheson, *Sketches from Life*, "Robert Schuman."
30. Acheson in an off-the-record talk in London, June 16, 1952, said, "We have been deeply guided by those who know that problem [Germany] far better than we do." And therefore, "We have deferred to our friends. . . . We have supported plans which they have supported." Cited in Harper, *American Visions of Europe*, p. 280.
31. Acheson, *Present at the Creation*, pp. 282–283.
32. Ibid., p. 285.
33. Plan A represented a radical change of position for Kennan, who had written four years earlier: "Better a dismembered Germany in which the West, at least, can act as buffer to the forces of totalitarianism than a united Germany which again brings these forces to the North Sea." (Kennan, *Memoirs: 1925–1950*, p. 258.)
34. Kennan, *Memoirs: 1925–1950*, pp. 423–424; Miscamble, *George F. Kennan*, pp. 148–149.
35. Thomas Schwartz, *America's Germany: John J. McCloy and the Federal Republic of Germany* (Cambridge, Mass.: Harvard University Press, 1991), p. 38.
36. For the Bohlen and Clay reactions, see Miscamble, *George F. Kennan*, pp. 152–153.
37. Robert Murphy memorandum, conversation with Acheson, March 9, 1949, FRUS, 1949, vol. III, pp. 102–105; see also Miscamble, *George F. Kennan*, pp. 161–162.
38. Jessup cited in Miscamble, *George F. Kennan*, p. 166.
39. Acheson proposal to Bevin and Schuman, cited in Miscamble, *George F. Kennan*, p. 169.
40. Johnson to Acheson, FRUS, May 14, 1949, vol. III, pp. 875–876.
41. Jessup letter to Kennan, May 24, 1949, cited by Miscamble, *George F. Kennan;* Kennan comment on Acheson in letter to Miscamble, August 10, 1979, both found on p. 171.
42. Miscamble, *George F. Kennan*, p. 171.
43. Acheson, *Sketches from Life*, pp. 9–10.
44. Miscamble, *George F. Kennan*, p. 173.
45. Acheson, *Sketches from Life*, pp. 14–15.
46. Acheson, *Present at the Creation*, p. 301.
47. Kennan, *Memoirs: 1950–1963*, p. 344.
48. Aron quote cited in Kennan, *Memoirs: 1950–1963*, p. 253.

TWENTY: LETTING THE DUST SETTLE

1. John Leighton Stuart, *Fifty Years in China* (New York: Random House, 1954), pp. 216, 218, 237, 240–242; Acheson, in *Present at the Creation*, pp. 305–306, writes: "'The ridiculously easy

Communist crossing of the Yangtze,' reported our embassy in Nanking, 'was made possible by defections at key points, disagreements in the High Command, and the failure of the Air Force to give effective support.'"

2. See Thomas J. Christensen, *Useful Adversaries: Grand Strategy, Domestic Mobilization, and Sino-American Conflict, 1947–1958* (Princeton, N.J.: Princeton University Press, 1996 [paper]), pp. 77–78.
3. The *China White Paper*, August 1949, originally issued as *United States Relations with China, with Special Reference to the Period 1944–1949*, Department of State Publication 3573, Far Eastern Series 30, reissued with the original letter of transmittal to President Truman from Secretary of State Dean Acheson and with a new introduction by Lyman P. Van Slyke (Stanford, Calif.: Stanford University Press, 1967).
4. Interview with Dean Acheson, Post-Presidential Memoirs, Truman Library, February 17, 1955, box 1.
5. See Theodore H. White and Annalee Jacoby, *Thunder Out of China* (New York: William Sloane Associates, 1946), "The Rise of the Kuomintang" and "Chiang Kai-shek—The People's Choice?"
6. White and Jacoby, *Thunder Out of China*, "Patrick J. Hurley"; also "Chiang Kai-shek—The People's Choice?"
7. Cited in Patterson et al., *American Foreign Policy Since 1900*, p. 400.
8. Acheson, *Present at the Creation*, pp. 134–135.
9. The *White Paper*, p. 132; "Letter from President Harry S. Truman to General George C. Marshall, December 15, 1945," reprinted in Acheson, *Present at the Creation*, pp. 744–745.
10. The *White Paper*, pp. 136–145; Acheson, *Present at the Creation*, pp. 144–148.
11. Acheson, *Present at the Creation*, pp. 204–205; Tang Tsou, *America's Failure in China: 1941–50* (Chicago: University of Chicago Press, 1990), pp. 426–427.
12. Testimony of Hon. Dean G. Acheson, "Military Situation in the Far East," *Hearings before the Committee on Armed Services and Committee on Foreign Relations*, United States Senate, Eighty-second Congress, first session, part 3, June 4, 1951.
13. Acheson, *Present at the Creation*, p. 304; Walter Judd cited in Tsou, *America's Failure in China*, p. 363.
14. Stuart, *Fifty Years in China*, pp. 178–179.
15. *Military Situation in the Far East*, p. 1,955; the *White Paper*, p. 354.
16. The *White Paper*, pp. 257–258.
17. Thomas Christensen, *Useful Adversaries: Grand Strategy, Domestic Mobilization, and Sino-American Conflict, 1947–1958* (Princeton, N.J.: Princeton University Press, 1996 [paper]), pp. 65–66.
18. *Military Situation in the Far East*, p. 1,671–1,672.
19. Nancy Bernkopf Tucker, *Patterns in the Dust: Chinese-American Relations and the Recognition Controversy, 1949–1950* (New York: Columbia University Press, 1983), p. 14. The meeting with the thirty Republican congressmen took place on February 7, 1949. Acheson, *Present at the Creation*, p. 306.
20. NSC 34/1, FRUS, 1949, vol. IX, pp. 474–475.
21. Quoted in Christensen, *Useful Adversaries*, p. 78.
22. NSC 41, FRUS, 1949, vol. IX, pp. 826–834.
23. On July 16, 1949, Shanghai consul general John Cabot, who had been in the U.S. diplomatic service in Belgrade, believed that the situation in China was even more favorable to the West than it had been in Yugoslavia. See Tucker, *Patterns in the Dust*, pp. 30, 223, fn. 62.
24. Memorandum of Acheson-Bevin conversation, April 4, 1949, FRUS, vol. VII, pp. 1138–1141.
25. Quoted in Sergei N. Goncharov, John W. Lewis, Xue Litai, *Uncertain Partners: Stalin, Mao, and the Korean War* (Stanford, Calif.: Stanford University Press, 1993), p. 44.

26. Quoted in Goncharov et al., *Uncertain Partners*, p. 49.
27. See Christensen, *Useful Adversaries*, pp. 91–92.
28. Frankfurter quotation in Acheson, *Present at the Creation*, p. 302.
29. The *White Paper*, pp. xiv–xvi.
30. The *China White Paper*, p. xvi; see also McLellan, *Dean Acheson*, p. 196.
31. In his oral history, Melby recalls that Acheson "didn't believe a word of that Letter of Transmittal. The Letter of Transmittal was one of those products of a committee. . . . Still, the letter was all anyone ever read, and Acheson had signed it thinking that it didn't make any difference. . . . That was his mistake, because it was what people latched on to." Melby citation from Christensen, *Useful Adversaries*, p. 96, fn. 79. Christensen also reveals in the same footnote that the China scholar Allen Whiting told him that Philip Jessup claimed authorship of the letter of transmittal in a conversation he had with Whiting.
32. The *White Paper*, p. xvi.
33. Cited in Tsou, *America's Failure in China*, p. 509.
34. Ibid.; Senator Wherry characterization in Isaacson and Thomas, *The Wise Men*, p. 475.
35. Butterworth's and Kennan's plans cited in Warren Cohen, "Acheson, His Advisers, and China," in Dorothy Borg and Waldo Heinrichs, eds., *Uncertain Years: Chinese-American Relations, 1947–1950*, pp. 27–28.
36. In the spring of 1949 Acheson had sent State Department official Livingston Merchant to Taiwan to investigate conditions on the island. He came back with the recommendation that America do nothing to prevent the island from falling to the Communists. (See memorandum from Livingston T. Merchant to the director of the Office of Far Eastern Affairs [Butterworth], FRUS, 1949, vol. IX, May 24, 1949, pp. 337–341.)
37. Acheson, *Present at the Creation*, p. 350.
38. Letter from Dean Acheson to Archibald MacLeish, in *Among Friends*, edited by McLellan and David C. Acheson, p. 68.
39. Quoted in Christensen, *Useful Adversaries*, p. 108.
40. Cited in Cohen, "Acheson, His Advisers, and China," pp. 29–30.
41. *The New York Times*, January 6, 1950; see also McLellan, *Dean Acheson*, p. 206.
42. Bruce Cumings, *The Origins of the Korean War*, vol. 2, *The Roaring of the Cataract, 1947–1950* (Princeton, N.J.: Princeton University Press, 1990).
43. Acheson's top-secret memorandum for Ambassador Philip Jessup, July 18, 1949, as reprinted in *Nomination of Jessup*, p. 603; hearings, Senate Foreign Relations Committee, Eighty-first Congress, second session.
44. Acheson testimony before the U.S. Senate Committee on Foreign Relations, Eighty-first Congress, *Historical Series: Reviews of the World Situation, 1949–1950* (Washington, D.C.: U.S. Government Printing Office, 1974), January 10, 1950, pp. 131–134, 137, 149.
45. Dean Acheson, "Relations of the Peoples of the United States and the Peoples of Asia: We Can Only Help Where We Are Wanted," *Vital Speeches of the Day*, January 12, 1950.
46. *The New York Times*, March 2, 1949.
47. His statements about being "fresh and eager and inexperienced" can be found in the Princeton Seminars, HSTL, February 13–14, 1954.
48. Acheson testimony in executive session before the Senate Foreign Relations Committee, January 13, 1950, *Historical Series*, Eighty-first Congress. See also Acheson, *Present at the Creation*, p. 764.
49. Steel, *Walter Lippmann*, pp. 466–467.
50. For Soviet and Chinese sources, see Goncharov et al., *Uncertain Partners*, ch. 3, "The Making of the Alliance," pp. 101–104.
51. See, for example, Acheson's remarks on January 23, 1950, quoted in Christensen, *Useful Ad-*

versaries, p. 117, fn. 166, when he argued: "For 50 years, it has been the fundamental belief of the American people . . . that the control of China by a foreigner was contrary to American interest." While the administration was also interested "in stopping the spread of communism," he declared that it would create "more misrepresentation in the Far East by stating that our national interest is merely to stop the spread of communism than any other way."

According to Christensen, John Melby in his oral history reported that "even the Sino-Soviet pact did not disabuse Acheson and many China experts in the State Department of their beliefs about [Chinese Communist Party] independence from Moscow." (Christensen, *Useful Adversaries*, p. 119, fn. 172.)

52. Acheson testimony in executive session before the U.S. Senate Committee on Foreign Relations, Eighty-first Congress, *Historical Series*, March 29, 1950, p. 273.
53. Acheson testimony in executive session, U.S. Senate Committee on Foreign Relations, March 29, 1950, pp. 273–276.

TWENTY-ONE: "THAT MOMENT OF DECISION"

1. Quoted in McLellan, *Dean Acheson*, pp. 172–173.
2. Ibid., p. 173.
3. Letter from Dean Acheson to Mary A. Bundy, January 4, 1950, in Acheson, *Present at the Creation*, p. 354.
4. Private notes of W. P. Bundy, March 12, 1987.
5. Interview with Lucius Battle, October 19, 1989.
6. Isaacson and Thomas, *The Wise Men*, p. 401.
7. Letter from Dean Acheson to Mary A. Bundy, January 25, 1950, cited in Acheson, *Present at the Creation*, pp. 359–360.
8. Acheson, *Present at the Creation*, p. 360.
9. Interview with William P. Bundy, May 11, 1997.
10. Acheson, *Present at the Creation*, p. 360; letter to Mary Acheson Bundy, January 27, 1950.
11. McLellan, *Dean Acheson*, p. 220; see also Sam Tanenhaus, *Whittaker Chambers: A Biography* (New York: Random House, 1997), ch. 34.
12. McLellan, *Dean Acheson*, p. 221.
13. See Isaacson and Thomas, *The Wise Men*, pp. 493–494.
14. Acheson, *Present at the Creation*, p. 361.
15. Cited in McCullough, *Truman*, pp. 760–761.
16. McCullough, *Truman*, p. 761.
17. David E. Lilienthal, *The Atomic Energy Years*, p. 569. See also Rhodes, *Dark Sun*, p. 372.
18. Lilienthal, *The Atomic Energy Years*, p. 570.
19. Rhodes, *Dark Sun*, pp. 252, 332.
20. Holloway, *Stalin and the Bomb*, pp. 294–299; Rhodes, *Dark Sun*, pp. 332–334.
21. Bundy, *Danger and Survival*, p. 204; see also Rhodes, *Dark Sun*, pp. 384–385.
22. Bundy, *Danger and Survival*, p. 206.
23. Other members of GAC were Enrico Fermi, I. I. Rabi, and Glenn Seaborg, all nuclear scientists of the first rank. Also serving on the GAC were two scientists who were now college presidents, Harvard's Conant and Cal Tech's Lee DuBridge; Cyril Smith, a metallurgist; Hartley Rowe, an engineer who had worked on the Manhattan Project; and Oliver E. Buckley, president of Bell Laboratories. See Bundy, *Danger and Survival*, pp. 207–208; also Rhodes, *Dark Sun*, pp. 388–389; James Hershberg, *James B. Conant* (New York: Knopf, 1993), p. 476.
24. Lilienthal, *The Atomic Energy Years*, p. 581.

25. Quoted in Rhodes, *Dark Sun*, pp. 397–398, citing David Lilienthal, *The Atomic Energy Years*, p. 581.
26. Bundy, *Danger and Survival*, p.208; see also Lilienthal, *The Atomic Energy Years*, pp. 580–583.
27. Bundy, *Danger and Survival*, p. 208; Rhodes, *Dark Sun*, pp. 401–402.
28. Quoted in Rhodes, *Dark Sun*, p. 403.
29. Lilienthal, *The Atomic Energy Years*, pp. 584–585.
30. Ibid., pp. 583–584.
31. Bundy, *Danger and Survival*, p. 209; Lilienthal, *The Atomic Energy Years*, p. 594; Rhodes, *Dark Sun*, 404.
32. Holloway, *Stalin and the Bomb*, p. 301.
33. FRUS, 1949, vol. 1, p. 595.
34. McCullough, *Truman*, pp. 741–742.
35. Isaacson and Thomas, *The Wise Men*, p. 488. Acheson remarks to the National War College, December 21, 1949, Acheson Papers, Truman Library.
36. Kennan, *Memoirs: 1925–1950*, p. 466.
37. Miscamble, *George F. Kennan*, pp. 302–303.
38. Ibid., p. 303.
39. Kennan, *Memoirs: 1925–1950*, p. 472.
40. Ibid., pp. 473–474.
41. In 1963, in an oral interview with David McLellan, Acheson said that he told Kennan, as regards his memorandum, that "if that was his view he ought to resign from the Foreign Service and preach his Quaker gospel but not push it within the Department." However, I find Wilson Miscamble's view more convincing, when he writes: "As with much Acheson later claimed to have said to and about Kennan, there is not the slightest evidence to support his recollection." Whatever his private comments, Miscamble suggests "Acheson found the critiques in Kennan's paper much more persuasive." Nor did Acheson want Kennan to resign; he kept him on as counsellor to the department until June 1950, offered him a one-year leave of absence, and expected he would return. By the 1960s, however, Kennan and Acheson had tangled openly on questions of German rearmament and unification, and Acheson tended to speak far more harshly of those of Kennan's earlier views with which he disagreed. Kennan, moreover, had published the first volume of his memoirs, and Acheson doubtless found much to quarrel with in Kennan's exposition. (Miscamble, *George F. Kennan*, p. 306; McLellan, *Dean Acheson*, p. 176.)
42. Nitze memorandum to Acheson, January 17, 1950, FRUS, 1950, vol. 1, pp. 13–17.
43. R. Gordon Arneson, "The H-Bomb Decision," *Foreign Service Journal* 46 (May 1969), p. 29.
44. See Miscamble, *George F. Kennan*, pp. 305–306. Oppenheimer's reflections are drawn from notes given to Warner Schilling, June 11, 1957.
45. Rhodes, *Dark Sun*, p. 405.
46. Acheson, *Present at the Creation*, p. 346.
47. Acheson, *Grapes from My Thorns*, "Morality, Moralism, and Diplomacy," pp. 125–140; see also Robert L. Messer, "Acheson, the Bomb, and the Cold War," in *Dean Acheson and the Making of U.S. Foreign Policy* (New York: St. Martin's Press, 1993).
48. Lilienthal, *The Atomic Energy Years*, p. 630–633.
49. Rhodes, *Dark Sun*, p. 407; see also Bundy, *Danger and Survival*, pp. 228–229; McCullough, *Truman*, p. 763.
50. FRUS, 1950, vol. I, p. 513.
51. Rhodes, *Dark Sun*, p. 407.
52. André Sakharov, *Memoirs* (New York: Knopf, 1990), pp. 98–100.
53. Richard M. Fried, *Men Against McCarthy* (New York: Columbia University Press, 1976), pp. 40–43.

54. Richard Rovere, *Senator Joe McCarthy* (New York: Harcourt, Brace, 1959), p. 125.
55. Rovere, *Senator Joe McCarthy*, pp. 129–131.
56. McCullough, *Truman*, p. 766.
57. Cited in Thomas C. Reeves, *The Life and Times of Joe McCarthy* (New York: Stein & Day, 1982), p. 263; Taft denied that he had made any such comment. See also Rovere, *Senator Joe McCarthy*, pp. 134–140.
58. Fried, *Men Against McCarthy*, p. 63.
59. Ibid., p. 86.
60. Letter to the editor from Armistead M. Lee, Foreign Service officer from 1942 to 1967, published in the *Washington Post*, July 31, 1995; see also Rovere, *Senator Joe McCarthy*, pp. 169–170.
61. McLellan, *Dean Acheson*, p. 234.
62. Acheson, *Present at the Creation*, pp. 364–365.
63. When the session ended for lunch, the two governors took the secretary of state off for a reviving drink and then to lunch with them at a center table in the dining room. Acheson had been Tom Dewey's friend for a number of years, though he had never before met Warren. After that episode, his gratitude to both of them never wavered. (Acheson, *Present at the Creation*, p. 368.)
64. Interview with Archibald MacLeish by David S. McLellan, July 2, 1964, in McLellan, *Dean Acheson*, p. 228.
65. Acheson, *Present at the Creation*, pp. 367–368.

TWENTY-TWO: THE GERMAN QUESTION, THE BRITISH CONNECTION, AND THE FRENCH SOLUTION

1. See John Maynard Keynes, *The Economic Consequences of the Peace* (New York: Harcourt, Brace & Howe), 1920.
2. Acheson, *Present at the Creation*, p. 326; Thomas Alan Schwartz, *America's Germany: John J. McCloy and the Federal Republic of Germany* (Cambridge, Mass.: Harvard University Press, 1991), pp. 70–73. In discussions among Acheson, Bevin, and Schuman in Washington in September, nothing had been decided about dismantling German industry for reparations, and they agreed to discuss it further in Paris in November.
3. Quotations in Schwartz, *America's Germany*, pp. 71, 74.
4. Schwartz, *America's Germany*, pp. 74–76.
5. Ibid., pp. 31–32; 77–78.
6. Ibid., pp. 51–52.
7. Acheson, *Present at the Creation*, pp. 340–341.
8. Acheson, *Sketches from Life*, pp. 168–171; FRUS, 1949, vol. III, pp. 309–311.
9. Schwartz, *America's Germany*, pp. 53–56.
10. Acheson, *Present at the Creation*, pp. 341–342; *Sketches from Life*, pp. 171–172; Schwartz, *America's Germany*, pp. 79–80.
11. Acheson, *Sketches from Life*, pp. 172–173.
12. FRUS, 1949, vol. 3, pp. 600–601.
13. Acheson, the Princeton Seminars, October 10, 1953; McLellan, *Dean Acheson*, p. 244.
14. Acheson, *Present at the Creation*, p. 387–388.
15. McLellan, *Dean Acheson*, pp. 245–246.
16. Schwartz, *America's Germany*, pp. 84–90.
17. Ibid., pp. 92–95.

18. Ibid., p. 96.
19. Ibid., pp. 96–100; see also Theodore White, *In Search of History: A Personal Adventure* (New York: Harper & Row, 1978), p. 334.
20. Jean Monnet, *Memoirs* (London: Collins, 1978), pp. 284–294; cited in Schwartz, *America's Germany*, p. 102.
21. Schwartz, *America's Germany*, pp. 102–103.
22. For a description of Bruce, see White, *In Search of History*, p. 283.
23. Acheson, *Sketches from Life*, pp. 36–37; for Bruce cable, see Acheson, *Present at the Creation*, p. 382.
24. Acheson, *Present at the Creation*, pp. 384–385.
25. Acheson, *Sketches from Life*, pp. 39–40.
26. Acheson, *Present at the Creation*, pp. 391–393.
27. Ibid., pp. 396–399.
28. Ibid., letter to Mary A. Bundy, May 31, 1950, p. 400.

TWENTY-THREE: PUTTING OUR HAND TO THE PLOW

1. Letter from HST to Dean Acheson, November 28, 1949, and letter from Dean Acheson to HST, December 5, 1949, collection of David Acheson.
2. See Alonzo M. Hamby, *Man of the People: A Life of Harry S. Truman* (New York: Oxford University Press, 1995), pp. 510–511.
3. See Tony Smith, *America's Mission: The United States and the Worldwide Struggle for Democracy in the Twentieth Century* (Princeton, N.J.: Princeton University Press, 1994), pp. 146–176.
4. Figures on the Japanese economy in 1946, as well as quotation from State Department official, from Ronald L. McGlothlen, *Controlling the Waves: Dean Acheson and U.S. Foreign Policy in Asia* (New York: W. W. Norton, 1993), "Acheson and the American Reconstruction of Japan," pp. 23–25.
5. Ibid., pp. 29–36; Miscamble, *George F. Kennan*, pp. 252–258.
6. Miscamble, *George F. Kennan*, p. 249.
7. Kennan, *Memoirs*, vol. I, p. 382.
8. Ibid., pp. 382–390; Miscamble, *George F. Kennan*, pp. 258–263.
9. Kennan, *Memoirs*, vol. I, pp. 391–395; Miscamble, *George F. Kennan*, pp. 264–270.
10. McGlothlen, *Controlling the Waves*, pp. 36–37.
11. Acheson, *Present at the Creation*, pp. 428–433; McGlothlen, *Controlling the Waves*, pp. 40–43.
12. Warren I. Cohen, *Dean Rusk* (Totowa, N.J.: Cooper Square Publishers, 1980), pp. 33–35.
13. Townsend Hoopes, *The Devil and John Foster Dulles* (New York: Atlantic–Little, Brown, 1973), p. 85; McGlothlen, *Controlling the Waves*, pp. 43–44; Leonard Mosley, *Dulles: A Biography of Eleanor, Allen, and John Foster Dulles and Their Family Network* (New York: Dial Press, 1978), p. 248.
14. From Dulles's book, *War or Peace* (New York: Macmillan, 1950), cited in Hoopes, *The Devil and John Foster Dulles*, p. 83.
15. McGlothlen, *Controlling the Waves*, "Acheson and the American Commitment to Vietnam," pp. 164–165.
16. *The Pentagon Papers: The Defense Department History of United States Decisionmaking on Vietnam* (Boston: Beacon Press, 1971), Senator Gravel ed., vol. I, p. 10.
17. Ibid., p. 2.
18. Ibid., p. 15.
19. For Acheson's offer in December to Henri Bonnet, see *Pentagon Papers*, vol. I, pp. 29–30.
20. Ibid., pp. 28–31.
21. McGlothlen, *Controlling the Waves*, pp. 175–176.

22. Cited in Young, *The Vietnam Wars*, p. 23.
23. FRUS, 1949, vol. VII, I, p. 8; see also McGlothlen, *Controlling the Waves*, pp. 179–180.
24. *Pentagon Papers*, vol. I, pp. 58–63.
25. McGlothlen, *Controlling the Waves*, pp. 180–181.
26. Ibid., pp. 179–183.
27. Ibid., pp. 185–186.
28. Ibid., pp. 185–187.
29. Ibid., pp. 186–187.
30. Acheson, *Present at the Creation*, p. 673.
31. Acheson testimony before the U.S. Senate, Committee on Foreign Relations, executive session, Historical Section, Eighty-first Congress, October 12, 1949, pp. 90, 182.
32. *Pentagon Papers*, vol. I, pp. 64–65.
33. Acheson memorandum of conversation with the French ambassador, Henri Bonnet, February 16, 1950, Truman Library, box 65.
34. *Pentagon Papers*, vol. I, pp. 76–77.
35. See Acheson interview with Gaddis Smith, *The New York Times Book Review*, October 12, 1969.
36. Acheson testimony before the Senate Foreign Relations Committee, executive session, Eighty-first Congress, first and second sessions, March 28–29, 1950, *Review of the World Situation: 1949–1950*, pp. 266–267.
37. Acheson, *Present at the Creation*, pp. 673–674.
38. Special Interdepartmental Committee on Korea to Marshall, February 25, 1947, FRUS, 1947, vol. VI, pp. 608–616. See also Bruce Cumings, *The Origins of the Korean War: The Roaring of the Cataract*, vol. II, pp. 46–47; McGlothlen, *Controlling the Waves*, pp. 52–53.
39. U.S. Congress, Senate Committee on Foreign Relations, *Legislative Origins of the Truman Doctrine: Hearings before the Committee on Foreign Relations in Executive Session on S. 938*, Historical Section, Eightieth Congress, first session, 1973, pp. 21–22.
40. For Eisenhower quote, see McGlothlen, *Controlling the Waves*, p. 60; Acheson interview, Post-Presidential Memoirs, February 18, 1955, Truman Library, box 1.
41. Cited in McGlothlen, *Controlling the Waves*, p. 63.
42. NSC 8/2, March 23, 1949, FRUS 1949, vol. VII, pp. 969–978. Both Paul Nitze and Dean Rusk opposed the total military withdrawal from Korea. Acheson, however, did nothing to oppose withdrawal of U.S. troops on schedule. (McGlothlen, *Controlling the Waves*, p. 230, fn. 26.)

    Any thoughts that the South Koreans should be given help in creating a sizable army above the sixty-five thousand men in place on June 20, 1949, was put to rest by General Bradley, chairman of the JCS, and General MacArthur in Japan.

    See also McGlothlen, *Controlling the Waves*, pp. 67, 71.

TWENTY-FOUR: SITUATIONS OF STRENGTH

1. Acheson, remarks made at a meeting of the Advertising Council at the White House, February 16, 1950, in Bundy, *The Pattern of Responsibility*, pp. 30.
2. Cited in Melvyn Leffler, "Negotiating from Strength: Acheson, the Russians and American Power," in *Dean Acheson and the Making of U.S. Foreign Policy*, edited by Douglas Brinkley, p. 9.
3. Acheson, remarks made at a press conference, February 8, 1950, in Bundy, *The Pattern of Responsibility*, p. 30.
4. Acheson, address at the University of California at Berkeley, March 16, 1950, cited in Bundy, *The Pattern of Responsibility*, p. 23.
5. Address before the United Nations General Assembly, September 20, 1950; address at the

University of California, Berkeley, March 16, 1950; address to the American Society of Newspaper Editors, April 22, 1950; address before the Harvard Alumni Association, Cambridge, Mass., June 22, 1950, cited in Bundy, *The Pattern of Responsibility*, pp. 31–35.

6. Miscamble, *George F. Kennan*, pp. 288–291.
7. Kennan to Harriman, December 29, 1949, cited in Miscamble, *George F. Kennan*, p. 295.
8. Cited in an interview with the author, September 6, 1979, in Miscamble, *George F. Kennan*, p. 292.
9. Acheson remarks, December 21, 1949, papers of James E. Webb, Truman Library, box 20, cited in Miscamble, *George F. Kennan*, p. 295. Acheson's differences with Kennan over policy did not become acute until the mid-1950s over American policy toward Germany.
10. Letter from George F. Kennan to Dean Acheson, December 21, 1949, Truman Library, DGA memoranda, box 64.
11. David Callahan, *Dangerous Capabilities: Paul Nitze and the Cold War* (New York: HarperCollins, 1990), pp. 60–61; Miscamble, *George F. Kennan*, p. 297.
12. Isaacson and Thomas, *The Wise Men*, pp. 482–485.
13. Acheson, *Present at the Creation*, p. 373.
14. For Battle, Tufts, and Fosdick citations, see Callahan, *Dangerous Capabilities*, pp. 94–98.
15. Paul Nitze, "Recent Soviet Moves," February 8, 1950, cited in Samuel F. Wells Jr., *International Security* (fall 1979), "Sounding the Tocsin: NSC 68 and the Soviet Threat," p. 125.

    A CIA analysis, issued two days after Nitze finished his own paper, took a different tack. To the intelligence specialists, Soviet foreign policy was motivated not by messianic faith, but by a terrible insecurity. The CIA analysts nonetheless concluded that no one could assume that Russia would or would not attack the United States. (CIA report cited in Callahan, *Dangerous Capabilities*, pp. 98–99.)
16. Paul Nitze, *International Security* (spring 1980), "The Development of NSC 68," pp. 170–176.
17. Paul Nitze (with Steven L. Rearden and Ann M. Smith), *From Hiroshima to Glasnost: A Memoir of Five Perilous Decades* (New York: Weidenfeld & Nicolson, 1989), p. 92.
18. Acheson, *Present at the Creation*, p. 374.
19. All citations from NSC 68 are found in FRUS, 1950, vol. I, pp. 237–290.
20. Wells, "Sounding the Tocsin," pp. 152–153.
21. Nitze, "The Development of NSC 68," p. 169.
22. Gaddis, *Strategies of Containment*, "NSC–68 and the Korean War," p . 94.
23. For the parallel to Hamilton, see John Lewis Gaddis, *The United States and the End of the Cold War: Implications, Reconsideration, Provocations* (New York: Oxford University Press, 1992), pp. 54–55; see also Gaddis, *Strategies of Containment*, pp. 94–98.
24. Acheson, *Present at the Creation*, p. 373.
25. Ibid., pp. 373–374; Callahan, *Dangerous Capabilities*, pp. 113–115.
26. See Wells, "Sounding the Tocsin," p. 136; Nitze anecdote, see Isaacson and Thomas, *The Wise Men*, pp. 498–499.
27. Wells, "Sounding the Tocsin," pp. 129.
28. Acheson, *Present at the Creation*, pp. 374–376.
29. Acheson testimony, U.S. Congress, Senate Committee on Foreign Relations, executive session, Historical Section, *Reviews of the World Situation, 1949–1950*, p. 292.

TWENTY-FIVE: "AN ENTIRELY NEW WAR"

1. Kennan, *Memoirs, 1925–1950*, pp. 484–485.
2. Acheson, *Present at the Creation*, p. 402.
3. Muccio cable quoted in Truman, *Memoirs*, vol. 2, *Years of Trial and Hope*, pp. 33–334.

4. Lie, cited in Smith, *Dean Acheson*, p. 179.
5. Acheson, *Present at the Creation*, pp. 404–405; Truman, *Years of Trial and Hope*, p. 332.
6. Acheson, *Present at the Creation*, p. 404.
7. Kennan, *Memoirs, 1925–1950*, p. 486.
8. Acheson, *Present at the Creation*, p. 405.
9. Acheson interview by Charles Collingwood, Edward R. Murrow, Bancroft Gidding, September 10, 1950, State Department Release #922, September 8, 1950; cited in McLellan, *Dean Acheson*, p. 275 fn.
10. Truman, *Memoirs: Years of Trial and Hope*, pp. 332–333.
11. Acheson, *Present at the Creation*, p. 406; on the effect of sending the Seventh Fleet to the Taiwan Strait, see Chen Jian, "The Sino-Soviet Alliance and China's Entry into the Korean War," pp. 21–22, Working Paper No. 1, Chinese documents cited in the Cold War International History Project, published by the Woodrow Wilson International Center for Scholars, Washington, D.C., June 1992; see also Warren I. Cohen, *America's Response to China* (New York: John Wiley & Sons, 1971), p. 202; McLellan, *Dean Acheson*, fn. p. 277.
12. Acheson, *Present at the Creation*, pp. 407–408.
13. See Thomas G. Paterson, ed., *Major Problems in American Foreign Policy*, vol. 2, *Since 1914*, "Documents and Essays," 3rd ed. (Lexington, Mass.: D. C. Heath, 1989), pp. 400–404.
14. Truman, *Memoirs: Years of Trial and Hope*, pp. 338–339; Acheson, *Present at the Creation*, p. 409.
15. Cited in McLellan, *Dean Acheson*, p. 276, fn. p. 276.
16. Rudy Abramson, *Spanning the Century: The Life of W. Averell Harriman, 1891–1986* (New York: W. W. Morrow, 1992), pp. 440–446.
17. Acheson, *Present at the Creation*, pp. 411–412
18. Memo of a meeting at Blair House, July 3, 1950, cited in McLellan, *Dean Acheson*, p. 281.
19. McLellan, *Dean Acheson*, pp. 281–282.
20. The Princeton Seminars, February 13–14, 1954.
21. Acheson's memorandum "Authority of the President to Repel the Attack on Korea," Department of State *Bulletin*, July 31, 1950, pp. 173–178; see also Louis Fisher, *Presidential War Power* (Lawrence, Kans.: University of Kansas Press, 1995), p. 89.
22. See Chace, *America Invulnerable: The Quest for Absolute Security from 1812 to Star Wars*, pp. 225–226.
23. Douglas MacArthur, *Reminiscences* (New York: McGraw-Hill, 1964), p. 327.
24. On MacArthur's movements in the first days after the outbreak of the Korean War, see William Manchester, *American Caesar, Douglas MacArthur 1880–1964* (Boston: Little, Brown, 1978), pp. 546–555.
25. *The New York Times*, July 9, 1950.
26. See Rosemary Foot, *The Wrong War: American Policy and the Dimensions of the Korean Conflict, 1950–1953* (Ithaca, N.Y.: Cornell University Press, 1985), p. 87.
27. Document VI: Ciphered telegram from [Soviet ambassador to Pyongyang Terentii] Shtykov to [Soviet foreign minister Andrè] Vyshinsky, 19 January 1950, Cold War International History Project *Bulletin* 5 (spring 1995), p. 8.
28. Document VII: Ciphered telegram from Stalin to Shtykov, 30 January 1950, Cold War International History Project *Bulletin*, p. 9.
29. Goncharov, Lewis, and Litai, *Uncertain Partners*, pp. 139–140.
30. Some years later, Marshal Peng Dehuai, who was in charge of the Chinese troops that would eventually rescue Kim's army, recalled that Mao was not happy with Kim's proposed plan but could not find a way of opposing it openly. As the Chinese were still pursuing unification of their own country, how could they deny the Koreans an opportunity to do the same? (See Goncharov, Lewis, and Litai, *Uncertain Partners*, p. 146.)

31. For preparations for the war, see Goncharov, Lewis, and Litai, *Uncertain Partners*, pp. 136–154.
32. Manchester, *American Caesar*, pp. 560–561.
33. Smith, *Dean Acheson*, pp. 194.
34. Acheson, *Present at the Creation*, pp. 334–336.
35. Ibid., pp. 416–420.
36. Ibid., pp. 448–449.
37. Ibid., pp. 451–452.
38. Ibid., p. 454; McLellan, *Dean Acheson*, pp. 282–283.
39. Acheson, *Present at the Creation*, p. 451.
40. NSC 81/1, Foot, *The Wrong War*, p. 74; see also Acheson, *Present at the Creation*, p. 452.
41. Acheson, *Present at the Creation*, p. 445.
42. Ibid., pp. 445–446.
43. Ibid., pp. 422–423; Manchester, *American Caesar*, pp. 562–565.
44. Abramson, *Spanning the Century*, pp. 451–452.
45. Harriman memorandum reprinted in Truman, *Memoirs: Years of Trial and Hope*, pp. 351–352.
46. Acheson, *Present at the Creation*, pp. 423–424.
47. Abramson, *Spanning the Century*, pp. 456–457.
48. For a description of the Inchon operation, see Manchester, *American Caesar*, pp. 577–581.
49. Acheson, *Present at the Creation*, pp. 447–448; Isaacson and Thomas, *The Wise Men*, p. 532.
50. For instructions from the JCS, see Acheson, *Present at the Creation*, p. 452–453.
51. For Battle anecdote, see Isaacson and Thomas, *The Wise Men*, pp. 532–533.
52. Acheson, *Present at the Creation*, p. 453; Manchester, *American Caesar*, p. 584.
53. Acheson, *Present at the Creation*, pp. 453–454; Manchester, *American Caesar*, pp. 584–585.
54. Acheson, *Present at the Creation*, pp. 454–455.
55. Ibid., p. 452.
56. Isaacson and Thomas, *The Wise Men*, pp. 533–534.
57. Cited in Foot, *The Wrong War*, p. 79; FRUS, 1950, vol. 7, p. 868 (October 4).
58. Manchester, *American Caesar*, pp. 590–591; Truman, *Memoirs: Years of Trial and Hope*, pp. 365–370.
59. Truman, *Memoirs: Years of Trial and Hope*, pp. 364–367.
60. McLellan, *Dean Acheson*, p. 287.
61. Alexandre Y. Mansourov, "Stalin, Mao, Kim, and China's Decision to Enter the Korean War, September 16–October 15, 1950: New Evidence from the Russians' Archives," Cold War International History Project *Bulletin* (winter 1995–1996), pp. 98–99; document 10: Ciphered telegram, Filippov (Stalin) to Mao Zedong and Zhou Enlai, 1 October 1950.
62. Document 12: Ciphered telegram from Roshchin in Beijing to Fillipov [Stalin], 3 October 1950, conveying October 2 message from Mao to Stalin, CWIHP *Bulletin* (winter 1995–1996), pp. 114–115.
63. Document 13: letter, Fyn Si [Stalin] to Kim Il Sung (via Shtykov), 8 [7] October 1950, CWIHP *Bulletin* (winter 1995–1996), p. 116. Stalin's letter to Mao quoted by Stalin in this letter to Kim Il Sung.
64. See Mansourov, *China's Decision to Enter the Korean War*, CWIHP *Bulletin* (winter 1995–1996), pp. 102–103. The account of the Stalin-Zhou talks is based on a June 1995 interview by Mansourov with Nikolai Fedorenko, one of the Soviet participants in the talks who interpreted them and later composed minutes thereof. Other accounts maintain that Stalin reneged on the deal to send air cover (see especially Goncharov et al., *Uncertain Partners*, pp. 187–192).

    Mao's telegram to Zhou Enlai in Moscow in Christensen, *Useful Adversaries*, p. 159, fn. 75, pp. 159–160, and appendix B, "Mao's Korean War Telegrams," pp. 273–274.

65. Kathryn Weatherby, "New Russian Documents on the Korean War," CWIHP *Bulletin* (winter 1995–1996), p. 32.
66. Manchester, *American Caesar,* p. 599.
67. Acheson, *Present at the Creation,* p. 775, fn. 4 to ch. 48.
68. Ibid., p. 462; U.S. Congressional Hearings, the "Military Situation in the Far East" (henceforth, MacArthur hearings), part 2, p. 1,241.
69. Letter from Acheson to Richard Neustadt, May 9, 1960, Acheson Papers, Yale University Library, box 23; Acheson, *Present at the Creation,* pp. 463–465.
70. Acheson, *Present at the Creation,* p. 467.
71. Ibid., pp. 467–468.
72. Ibid., p. 469.

TWENTY-SIX: THE SUBSTITUTE FOR VICTORY

1. Acheson, *Present at the Creation,* pp. 469–471; minutes of NSC meeting, White House, November 28, 1950, Acheson Papers, memorandum of conversation, Truman Library, box 65.
2. Truman, *Memoirs: Years of Trial and Hope,* pp. 395–396; McCullough, *Truman,* pp. 821–822.
3. Acheson, *Present at the Creation,* pp. 472–275; Isaacson and Thomas, *The Wise Men,* p. 542; notes on a meeting in JCS Conference Room, December 1, 1950, Acheson Papers, memorandum of conversation, Truman Library, box 65.
4. Report on meeting at the White House, December 3, 1950, Acheson Papers, memorandum of conversation, Truman Library, box 65.
5. Matthew B. Ridgway, *The Korean War* (Garden City, N.Y.: 1967), pp. 61–62; Acheson, *Present at the Creation,* p. 475.
6. Ridgway, *The Korean War,* pp. 76–77.
7. Draft paper, "Soviet Intentions in the Current Situation," December 2, 1950, Acheson Papers, Truman Library, box 65.
8. Letter from George Kennan to Dean Acheson, December 4, 1950, Acheson Papers, Yale University Library, Manuscripts and Archives, series I, box 17, f. 222; Isaacson and Thomas, *The Wise Men,* pp. 542–544.
9. Notes by George Kennan on his meeting with General Marshall, December 4, 1950, Acheson Papers, Truman Library, box 65; Acheson, *Present at the Creation,* pp. 476–477.
10. Acheson, *Present at the Creation,* p. 477.
11. Ibid., p. 479; Isaacson and Thomas, *The Wise Men,* p. 544.
12. Acheson, *Present at the Creation,* pp. 480–485; Bullock, *Ernest Bevin,* pp. 820–824; meeting in Secretary Acheson's office, December 5, 1950, memorandum of conversation, Truman Library, box 65; Truman, *Years of Trial and Hope,* pp. 395–413.
13. Ridgway, *The Korean War,* pp. 79–83.
14. Acheson, *Present at the Creation,* pp. 512–516; Manchester, *American Caesar,* pp. 624–625; McLellan, *Dean Acheson,* pp. 302–304.
15. Acheson, *Present at the Creation,* p. 365.
16. Acheson, *Sketches from Life,* pp. 134–135.
17. Interview with Alice Acheson, February 21, 1975, in McLellan, *Dean Acheson,* p. 228.
18. Acheson, *Present at the Creation,* p. 365.
19. Cited in Richard M. Fried, *Men Against McCarthy* (New York: Columbia University Press, 1976), p. 102.
20. McCarthy quote cited in Fried, *Men Against McCarthy,* p. 156.
21. Steel, *Walter Lippmann,* pp. 474–475. Lippmann's biographer, Ronald Steel, points out that "the problem with hitting Acheson was that the criticism would seem to lend aid to the Mc-

Carthyites." Lippmann himself was well aware of this and especially how deeply his attacks on Acheson disturbed his closest friends. In this respect he felt compelled to write Judge Learned Hand that throughout "this whole wretched business all my personal inclinations were and still are in his favor."

22. Isaacson and Thomas, *The Wise Men*, p. 546.
23. Cited in Acheson, *Present at the Creation*, p. 366.
24. Interview with Alice Acheson, January 2, 1988.
25. Acheson, *Present at the Creation*, p. 518.
26. MacArthur statement reprinted in Acheson, *Present at the Creation*, pp. 755–756; see also Manchester, *American Caesar*, pp. 633–634.
27. Acheson, *Present at the Creation*, pp. 521–522; Truman, *Years of Trial and Hope*, pp. 445–446.
28. Comments by William P. Bundy, March 12, 1987.
29. Acheson, *Present at the Creation*, pp. 521–522.
30. The Princeton Seminars, February 14, 1954, p. 1,343.
31. Acheson, *Present at the Creation*, pp. 521–522; Manchester, *American Caesar*, pp. 644–646.
32. The Princeton Seminars, February 14, 1954, p. 1,342.
33. Acheson, *Present at the Creation*, pp. 523–524.
34. Manchester, *American Caesar*, pp. 649–651.
35. Ibid., pp. 661–665.
36. MacArthur, *Reminiscences*, pp. 400–405.
37. Merle Miller, *Plain Speaking: An Oral Biography of Harry S. Truman* (New York: Berkley Publishing, 1973), pp. 312–313.
38. *Hearings to Conduct an Inquiry into the Military Situation in the Far East* [MacArthur hearings], Senate Committees on Armed Services and Foreign Relations, Eighty-second Congress, first session, part II (Washington, D.C.: U.S. Government Printing Office, 1951), pp. 731–732.
39. MacArthur hearings, p. 1,216.
40. Ibid., pp. 729–730, 1,782–1,783.

    In June 1952, Acheson, during ministerial talks in London, discussed what might be done in the event of Chinese aggression in Indochina. He said that Washington was at least thinking in terms of a "blockade of the coast of China, combined with air action designed to . . . lessen the will of Chinese Communists to continue their aggression." He believed that if this were done, the Soviet Union would not enter the conflict as long as it believed Washington was not planning to try to overthrow the Chinese regime. As Professor Rosemary Foot points out, "No longer would Acheson argue that an expansion of hostilities into China risked world war. In a sense, he had reverted to his pre–Korean War position, that the 'basic interests' of Moscow conflicted with those of Peking." (Foot, *The Wrong War*, p. 198.)
41. Acheson, *Present at the Creation*, p. 527.
42. The Princeton Seminars, March 14, 1954, pp. 1,493, 1,501–1,502, 1,505, 1,514.
43. Ibid., pp. 1,494–1,498.
44. Ibid., p. 1,491.
45. Acheson, *Present at the Creation*, pp. 542–543.
46. The Princeton Seminars, March 14, 1954, pp. 1,510–1,511.
47. Battle interview with the author, cited in McGlothlen, *Controlling the Waves*, p. 47.
48. The Princeton Seminars, March 14, 1954, p. 1,512; Acheson, *Present at the Creation*, p. 546.
49. Rusk interview with the author in McGlothlen, *Controlling the Waves*, p. 47.
50. Acheson, *Present at the Creation*, pp. 548–549.
51. FRUS, 1951, vol. VII, pp. 241–243.
52. Acheson, *Present at the Creation*, pp. 532–533; the Princeton Seminars, March 14, 1954, pp. 1,384–1,385.

53. Smith, *Dean Acheson*, pp. 280–285; the Princeton Seminars, March 14, 1954, p. 1,403; Truman, *Years of Trial and Hope*, pp. 460–461.
54. Quoted in McLellan, *Dean Acheson*, p. 321.

TWENTY-SEVEN: ENTANGLING ALLIANCES

1. Quoted in Kaplan, *The United States and NATO*, p. 154.
2. Acheson, *Present at the Creation*, pp. 435–442; Kaplan, *The United States and NATO*, p. 160; McLellan, *Dean Acheson*, pp. 327–330.
3. Acheson, *Present at the Creation*, p. 444.
4. Ibid., pp. 457–458; McLellan, *Dean Acheson*, pp. 332–33; Schwartz, *America's Germany*, pp. 141, 230; Theodore H. White, *Fire in the Ashes: Europe in Mid-Century* (New York: William Sloane, 1953), p. 263. The European Defense Community (EDC) was also known as the Pleven Plan after French premier René Pleven.
5. Cited in McLellan, *Dean Acheson*, p. 335.
6. Acheson, *Present at the Creation*, pp. 485–488; Schwartz, *America's Germany*, pp. 151–153.
7. See Bundy, *The Pattern of Responsibility*, pp. 83–87.
8. Acheson, *Present at the Creation*, p. 488.
9. McLellan, *Dean Acheson*, pp. 340–341; Bundy, *The Pattern of Responsibility*, pp. 83–84; the Princeton Seminars, December 11, 1963, p. 994.
10. Acheson, *Present at the Creation*, pp. 489–490.
11. Ibid., pp. 491–492; McLellan, *Dean Acheson*, pp. 341–342.
12. Bundy, *The Pattern of Responsibility*, p. 89.
13. Acheson, *Present at the Creation*, pp. 493–495; Bundy, *The Pattern of Responsibility*, pp. 89–90.
14. "Assignment of Ground Forces of the United States to Duty in the European Area," *Hearings before the Committee on Foreign Relations and the Committee on Armed Services, United States Senate*, Eighty-second Congress, February 1, 15, 16, 20, 21, 22, 23, 24, 26, 27, 28, 1951, pp. 78–79, 84–85, 88–93, 94, 103–107, 122–123. See also Bundy, *The Pattern of Responsibility*, pp. 90–100.
15. Acheson, *Present at the Creation*, pp. 552–553; McLellan, *Dean Acheson*, p. 383; Smith, *Dean Acheson*, p. 319; *The Pentagon Papers: The Defense Department History of United States Decision-making on Vietnam* (Boston: Beacon Press, 1971), vol. 1, p. 66.
16. Schwartz, *America's Germany*, p. 210.
17. Ibid., p. 212.
18. Stephen E. Ambrose, *Eisenhower* (New York: Simon & Schuster, 1982), vol. 1, pp. 500–509; Schwartz, *America's Germany*, pp. 216–219.
19. Schwartz, *America's Germany*, pp. 222–234.
20. Acheson, *Present at the Creation*, pp. 554–555.
21. The Princeton Seminars, December 12, 1953, p. 1,028.
22. Ibid., pp. 1,042–1,043.
23. Acheson, *Present at the Creation*, pp. 569–571; McLellan, *Dean Acheson*, pp. 353–355.
24. Interview with Marshall Shulman, December 20, 1994.
25. Bullock, *Ernest Bevin*, p. 86.
26. The Princeton Seminars, December 13, 1953, pp. 6–8; Acheson, *Sketches from Life*, pp. 176–177.
27. Acheson, *Present at the Creation*, pp. 584–585; the Princeton Seminars, December 1, 1953, p. 1,086.
28. Acheson, *Present at the Creation*, p. 586.

29. Ibid., pp. 592–593.
30. Ibid., pp. 595–596.
31. Ibid., pp. 598–599.
32. Acheson, *Sketches from Life*, pp. 65–69.
33. Ibid., pp. 69–70.
34. Acheson, *Present at the Creation*, pp. 608–609.
35. Ibid., pp. 612–614.
36. Ibid., pp. 620–621; *Sketches from Life*, pp. 70–71.
37. Acheson, *Sketches from Life*, pp. 107–110.
38. Ibid., pp. 115–118; the Princeton Seminars, March 14, 1954, pp. 1,527–1,533.
39. Cited in McLellan, *Dean Acheson*, p. 365.
40. Kaplan, *The United States and NATO*, p. 171. According to Kaplan, "By the end of 1953 there were no more than fifteen NATO divisions."
41. Acheson, *Present at the Creation*, pp. 625–626; the Princeton Seminars, March 14, 1954, pp. 1,041–1,043.

TWENTY-EIGHT: ENDGAME

1. Schwartz, *America's Germany*, pp. 265–266.
2. FRUS, 1952–1954, vol. VII, the Soviet note of March 10, 1952, pp. 169–172; Schwartz, *America's Germany*, p. 262.
3. Schwartz, *America's Germany*, p. 266.
4. Quotation from Stalin's 1952 monograph, *Economic Problems of Socialism in the U.S.S.R.*, cited in Schwartz, *America's Germany*, p. 263.
5. Schwartz, *America's Germany*, p. 263; Alexei Filitov, "The Soviet Policy and Early Years of Two German States, 1949–1961," Cold War International History Project Conference Paper, Essen, June 1994, p. 6, cited in Gaddis, *We Now Know: Rethinking Cold War History* (New York: Oxford University Press, 1997), "The German Question," p. 127.
6. Letter from Acheson to Truman, March 11, 1953, Acheson Papers, Truman Library, cited in McLellan, *Dean Acheson*, p. 37.
7. Acheson's aide Marshall Shulman wrote in his reappraisal of Soviet foreign policy years later, by 1952, "the Soviet Union was less worried about the revival of a German military menace than about the strengthening of the Western alliance" (Marshall Shulman, *Soviet Foreign Policy Reappraised* [Cambridge, Mass.: Harvard University Press, 1963], p. 191).
8. Schwartz, *America's Germany*, p. 264.
9. Acheson summary of Eden's views, FRUS, 1952–1954, vol. VII, pp. 176–177; Schwartz, *America's Germany*, p. 265.
10. Acheson, *Present at the Creation*, p. 631. According to Ronald Steel, even Walter Lippmann, who had previously stressed the neutralization of Germany, wrote in March and April American and British forces could not be withdrawn from Europe "in the presence of a reunited, a rearmed, Germany bound to no European system of law and treaty, and under Russian patronage." (Steel, *Walter Lippmann*, p. 489.)
11. Acheson to U.S. embassy in London, April 30, 1952, FRUS, 1952–1954, vol. VII, pp. 218–219; see also Gaddis, *We Now Know*, pp. 126–127.
12. Kennan to State Department, FRUS, 1952–1954, vol. VII, pp. 252–253.
13. Shulman, *Stalin's Foreign Policy Reappraised*, p. 194.
14. Albert Resis, ed., *Molotov Remembers: Inside Kremlin Politics: Conversations with Felix Chuev* (Chicago: Ivan R. De, 1993), p. 36; Gaddis, *We Now Know*, "The German Question," p. 128.
15. Acheson, *Present at the Creation*, p. 633.

16. Ibid., pp. 651–657; Smith, *Dean Acheson*, pp. 283–286.
17. Richard Whelan, *Drawing the Line: The Korean War 1950–1953* (Boston: Little, Brown, 1990), pp. 353–362.
18. Acheson, *Present at the Creation*, pp. 642–644.
19. Ibid., pp. 644–646.
20. Ibid., p. 647.
21. The Princeton Seminars, March 14, 1954, pp. 1576–1568.
22. See Gaddis, *We Now Know*, "The German Question"; see also McLellan, *Dean Acheson*, p. 366.

TWENTY-NINE: "THAT CANDLES MAY BE BROUGHT"

1. Acheson, *Present at the Creation*, pp. 659–660.
2. Ibid., pp. 673–678; Smith, *Dean Acheson*, pp. 321–329.
3. Acheson, *Present at the Creation*, pp. 562–567; Smith, *Dean Acheson*, pp. 348–352; McLellan, *Dean Acheson*, p. 392.
4. The Princeton Seminars, May 15, 1954, p. 1,607.
5. Ibid., p. 1,620; Yergin, *The Prize*, p. 457.
6. Yergin, *The Prize*, pp. 463–464.
7. Acheson, *Present at the Creation*, p. 508.
8. The Princeton Seminars, May 15, 1954, p. 1,607–1,608.
9. Acheson, *Present at the Creation*, p. 504.
10. The Princeton Seminars, May 15, 1954, p. 1,629.
11. McLellan, *Dean Acheson*, p. 320.
12. Acheson, *Present at the Creation*, pp. 683–685; the Princeton Seminars, May 15, 1954, pp. 1,660–1,662.
13. Yergin, *The Prize*, pp. 470, 478.
14. Acheson, *Present at the Creation*, p. 649.
15. Acheson, *Sketches from Life*, pp. 181–198.
16. Smith, *Dean Acheson*, pp. 359–361.
17. Acheson, *Present at the Creation*, p. 690.
18. Ibid., p. 691. Press conference, September 26, 1952, cited in Acheson, *Present at the Creation*, pp. 763–765. Acheson tried once again to set the record straight by referring to the exact language he had used in his now famous January 12, 1950, press conference, in which he spoke of "the Aleutian Islands, Japan and the Ryukyus, and the Philippines being our 'defensive perimeter' in the Pacific area." His point was that "if this line were attacked we would defend it alone if necessary—just as we would our continental area." On the other hand, responsibility for defending Korea lay first of all with the Koreans themselves and then with other nations, including the United States, under the charter of the United Nations.
19. Acheson, *Present at the Creation*, p. 693.
20. Ibid., pp. 693–695.
21. Memorandum of conversations, Acheson Papers, Truman Library, box 67A; Acheson, *Present at the Creation*, pp. 706–707; Truman, *Years of Trial and Hope*, pp. 514–521.
22. Acheson, introduction to Louis J. Halle, *Civilization and Foreign Policy*, cited in Smith, *Dean Acheson*, p. 395.
23. Memoranda to and from the president to the secretary of state, January 3, 1953, Elsey Papers, Truman Library, box 101; Acheson, *Present at the Creation*, pp. 710–713.
24. Acheson, *Present at the Creation*, pp. 713–714.
25. Memorandum of conversations, meeting of Secretary Acheson with Jean Monnet, December 14, 1952, Acheson Papers, Truman Library, box 67A.

26. Acheson, *Present at the Creation*, pp. 709–710.
27. Ibid., pp. 715–716.
28. Ibid., pp. 716–720; 732–733; 735.
29. Ibid., pp. 720–721; Emmet John Hughes, *The Ordeal of Power: A Political Memoir of the Eisenhower Years* (New York: Atheneum, 1963), pp. 55–56; McCullough, *Truman*, pp. 922–923.

THIRTY: REJOINING THE FRAY

1. Letters of Dean and Alice Acheson to Archibald and Ada MacLeish, March 26, 1953, Acheson Papers, Yale University Library, series I, box 21, f. 270.
2. On life in Antigua, see Scott Donaldson, *Archibald MacLeish: An American Life* (Boston: Houghton Mifflin, 1992), pp. 417–421.
3. Letters from Acheson to Truman, February 10, 1953; to David Acheson, February 19, 1953; to Jeffrey Kitchen, February 13, 1953; in McLellan and Acheson, *Among Friends*, pp. 78–80.
4. Letter from Acheson to MacLeish, March 26, 1953, Acheson Papers, Yale University Library, series I, box 21, f. 270.
5. Cited in Douglas Brinkley, *Dean Acheson: The Cold War Years* (New Haven, Conn.: Yale University Press, 1992), p. 15.
6. Cabell Phillips, "Dean Acheson Ten Years Later," *New York Times Magazine*, January 18, 1959.
7. Letter from Dean Acheson to George Rublee, September 11, 1953, Acheson Papers, Yale University Library, series I, box 27, f. 340.
8. Interview with Alice Acheson, January 2, 1988.
9. Letter from Acheson to Jake Podoloff, March 29, 1962, Acheson Papers, Yale University Library, series I, box 25, f. 316; see also Howard Westwood, *Covington and Burling, 1919–1984* (Washington, D.C.: Covington and Burling, 1986).
10. Letter from Acheson to Sir Oliver Franks, July 20, 1955, Acheson Papers, Yale University Library, series I, box 12, f. 150.
11. The anecdote was given by Eugene Rostow at an Acheson conference at Yale University, April 24, 1982; cited in Brinkley, *Dean Acheson: The Cold War Years*, fn. 4, p. 339.
12. For an account of Seymour's presidency, see Brooks Mather Kelley, *Yale: A History* (New Haven, Conn.: Yale University Press, 1974), pp. 393–421.
13. Acheson, *Present at the Creation*, pp. 371–372.
14. Letter from Acheson to Griswold, December 30, 1957, Yale University Library, YRG-2-A-16, box 4, f. 29.
15. Letter from Acheson to Charles Seymour, September 19, 1939, Yale University Library, YRG-2-A-15, box 1, f. 1–3.
16. Cited in Dan A. Oren, *Joining the Club: A History of Jews and Yale* (New Haven, Conn.: Yale University Press, 1985), p. 127.
17. Letter from Acheson to Griswold, December 18, 1953, Yale University Library, YRG–2A–16, box 136, f. 1237.
18. Oren, *Joining the Club*, pp. 270–271, fn. 23, p. 390; letter from Acheson to Griswold, April 13, 1955. Yale University Library, YRG-2-16, box 136, f. 1,240.
19. Letter from Truman to Acheson, February 18, 1953, collection of David Acheson.
20. Letter from Acheson to Truman, May 28, 1953, in *Among Friends*, pp. 84–85.
21. Acheson, memorandum of conversation, June 23, 1953, collection of David Acheson.
22. Letter from Acheson to Battle, August 6, 1953, in *Among Friends*, p. 89.
23. See Brinkley, *Dean Acheson: The Cold War Years*, pp. 20–21.
24. Acheson, "Instant Retaliation: The Debate Continued," *New York Times Magazine*, March 28,

1954, reprinted in Acheson, *This Vast External Realm* (New York: W. W. Norton, 1973), pp. 29–41.

25. Quoted in Isaacson and Thomas, *The Wise Men*, p. 561.
26. Letter from Acheson to Truman, February 5, 1954, in *Among Friends*, p. 92. In this same letter he wrote that he had put down these thoughts during a day "spent without food or water having my insides X-rayed." He hoped that this would be "the wind-up of almost a year of trying to get rid of some amoebae that I collected somewhere probably in Africa or South America." (p. 93)
27. Acheson, *Power and Diplomacy* (Cambridge, Mass.: Harvard University Press, 1958), pp. 34–35, 43, 106–108, 137. The book was drawn from lectures Acheson delivered at the Fletcher School of Law and Diplomacy on October 1957.
28. Cited in Brinkley, *Dean Acheson: The Cold War Years*, p. 45.
29. Acheson, *A Democrat Looks at His Party* (New York: Harper & Brothers, 1955), pp. 53, 79.
30. Bowie quote in Brinkley, *Dean Acheson: The Cold War Years*, p. 47; "staff officer" citation in a letter from Acheson to Lord Stow Hill, April 21, 1971, Yale University Library, series I, box 29, f. 377.
31 *The New York Times*, September 27, 1956.
32. Acheson, *The Illusion of Disengagement*, p. 379.
33. Kennan, *Memoirs: 1950–1963* (New York: Pantheon, 1972), pp. 235–245.
34. Acheson, "Reply to Kennan," January 11, 1958, Acheson Papers, Yale University Library, series I, box 9, f. 123; see also Brinkley, *Dean Acheson: The Cold War Years*, pp. 79–82.
35. Letter from Kennan to Frank Altshul, January 26, 1958, cited in Wilson Miscamble, "Rejected Architect and Master Builder: George Kennan, Dean Acheson and Postwar Europe," *Review of Politics* (summer 1996), p. 463.
36. Letter from Acheson to Philip Jessup, March 25, 1958, Acheson Papers, Yale University Library, series I, box 17, f. 213.
37. Acheson, "The Illusion of Disengagement," *Foreign Affairs*, April 1948.
38. Acheson to Kennan, March 13, 1958, Acheson Papers, Yale University Library, series I, box 17, f. 222.
39. On his ninetieth birthday in 1994, he commented that "we will never know who was right and who was wrong in this disagreement. The one course was tried. Its consequences, good and bad, are now visible. The other course remained hypothetical. Its results will never be known." (Quoted in Miscamble, "Rejected Architect and Master Builder: George Kennan, Dean Acheson and Postwar Europe," p. 467.)
40. Kennan, *Memoirs: 1950–1963*, pp. 252–255; see also the perceptive comments of Wilson Miscamble in "Rejected Architect and Master Builder: George Kennan, Dean Acheson and Postwar Europe," pp. 466–467.
41. Bundy, *Danger and Survival*, p. 277–283.
42. Acheson, "Statement on Quemoy Crisis," Acheson Papers, Speeches and Articles, 1936–1971, Truman Library, box 139; see also Brinkley, *Dean Acheson: The Cold War Years*, pp. 62–64.
43. See Brinkley, *Dean Acheson: The Cold War Years*, pp. 54–58.
44. Letter from Acheson to Truman, August 31, 1959, in *Among Friends*, pp. 170–171.
45. Acheson Oral History Interview, April 27, 1964, JFK Library; see also Brinkley, *Dean Acheson*, pp. 111–112; Arthur M. Schlesinger Jr., *A Thousand Days* (New York: Fawcett, 1965), pp. 74–75.

THIRTY-ONE: "A SORT OF ANCIENT MARINER"

1. Acheson, Oral History Interview, JFK Library, April 27, 1964.
2. Robert F. Kennedy, *Thirteen Days: A Memoir of the Cuban Missile Crisis* (New York: New American Library [paper], 1969), p. 38.

3. Cited in Brinkley, *Dean Acheson*, p. 113.
4. Acheson, Oral History, JFK Library, April 27, 1964.
5. Acheson's version of the conversation with Kennedy can be found in Acheson's Oral History, JFK Library, April 27, 1964.
6. Isaacson and Thomas, *The Wise Men*, p. 594.
7. Interview with Dean Rusk, March 1988, in Brinkley, *Dean Acheson*, p. 117.
8. Acheson, "Wishing Won't Hold Berlin," *Saturday Evening Post*, March 7, 1959.
9. See Stephen Ambrose, *Eisenhower: Soldier and President* (New York: Simon & Schuster, 1990), pp. 474–475; Brinkley, *Dean Acheson*, pp. 93–101.
10. Dean Acheson, "A Review of North Atlantic Problems for the Future," March 1961, Acheson Papers, Post-Administration Files, State Department and White House Advisor, April–June 1961, Truman Library, box 85.

    Unlike some members of the State Department who were calling for the creation of an allied multilateral nuclear force under NATO command that would presumably end any competition among the West Europeans to develop their own nuclear arsenals, Acheson showed no desire for the United States to share its nuclear weaponry with any West European country, not even with Great Britain.
11. McGeorge Bundy, "Memorandum for the President," April 4, 1961, NSF/84, JFK Library.
12. Acheson, "Memorandum for the President," April 3, 1961, Declassified Documents Collection, 1985 2547, Center for Research Libraries, Chicago.
13. Arthur Schlesinger Jr., *A Thousand Days: John F. Kennedy in the White House* (New York: Fawcett, 1965), p. 349.
14. Schlesinger, *A Thousand Days*, pp. 354–355.
15. Acheson, Oral History, JFKL, pp. 13–14.
16. Letter from Acheson to Truman, May 3, 1961, in *Among Friends*, pp. 206–207.
17. Acheson, Oral History, JFKL, pp. 16–17, 19.
18. Michael R. Beschloss, *The Crisis Years: Kennedy and Khrushchev, 1960–1963* (New York: HarperCollins, 1991), p. 241; Brinkley, *Dean Acheson*, p. 130.
19. Acheson, Oral History, JFKL, p. 16; Acheson, *Grapes from My Thorns*, pp. 70–71.
20. Acheson, *Grapes from My Thorns*, pp. 71–72.
21. Acheson, remarks at Foreign Service lunch, June 29, 1961, Acheson Papers, Yale University Library, series 3, box 51, f. 51.
22. Cited in Isaacson and Thomas, *The Wise Men*, p. 609.
23. Beschloss, *The Crisis Years*, pp. 223–225; Bundy, *Danger and Survival*, pp. 363–366; Schlesinger, *A Thousand Days*, pp. 340–348; Theodore C. Sorensen, *Kennedy* (New York: Harper & Row), 1965.
24. Letter from Acheson to John Cowles, June 28, 1961, Yale University Library, series I, box 6, f. 82.
25. Acheson, Oral History, JFKL, pp. 19–20; Beschloss, *The Crisis Years*, pp. 242–244; Brinkley, *Dean Acheson*, pp. 141–144; Schlesinger, *A Thousand Days*, pp. 355–357; NSC memorandum, June 29, 1961, JFKL.
26. Bundy, *Danger and Survival*, pp. 375–376.
27. Memorandum, NSC meeting, July 13, 1961, JFKL.
28. Letter to Truman, July 14, 1961, in *Among Friends*, p. 208.
29. Memorandum, NSC meeting, July 20, 1961, JFKL.
30. Interview with Eliot Janeway, May 1990, in Brinkley, *Dean Acheson*, p. 149.
31. Beschloss, *The Crisis Years*, pp. 272–273.
32. Brinkley, *Dean Acheson*, p. 149.
33. Bundy, *Danger and Survival*, p. 370.

34. Acheson, Oral History, JFKL, p. 21.
35. Acheson to John Cowles, June 8, 1951, Acheson Papers, Yale University Library, series I, box 6, f. 82.

THIRTY-TWO: "THE SURVIVAL OF STATES"

1. Howard C. Westwood, *Covington and Burling, 1919–1984* (Washington, D.C.: Covington and Burling, 1986), pp. 142–143.
2. Letters from Acheson to Barbara Evans, January 16, 17, 18, 21, 29, 1962, Acheson Papers, Yale University Library, series I, box 10, f. 126.
3. Letter from Acheson to Philip Sprouse, January 21, 1963, Acheson Papers, Yale University Library, series I, box 29, f. 370.
4. Letter from Acheson to Barbara Evans, January 29, 1962, Acheson Papers, Yale University Library, series I, box 29, f. 370.
5. Memorandum on the president's call on Justice Frankfurter, July 26, 1962, Acheson Papers, Yale University Library, series I, box 12, f. 148.
6. Letter from Acheson to John F. Kennedy, March 19, 1961, in *Among Friends*, pp. 205–206; see also Brinkley, *Dean Acheson*, pp. 305–308.
7. Acheson, Oral History, JFKL, p. 15.
8. Acheson, memorandum of conversation with the president, April 2, 1962, in *Among Friends*, pp. 225–228.
9. See Brinkley, *Dean Acheson*, pp. 312–314.
10. Bundy, *Danger and Survival*, p. 391; Isaacson and Thomas, *The Wise Men*, pp. 619–620; Robert Kennedy, *Thirteen Days* (New York: New American Library, 1969), pp. 26–27; Schlesinger, *A Thousand Days*, pp. 732–733.
11. Acheson, "Dean Acheson's Version of Robert Kennedy's Version of the Cuban Missile Affair: Homage to Plain Dumb Luck," *Esquire*, February 1969, p. 45.
12. Acheson, "Dean Acheson's Version . . . ," p. 76.
13. Acheson, Oral History, JFKL, p. 23.
14. Kenneth Harris, "Pungent Memories from Mr. Acheson," *Life*, July 23, 1971; Acheson, "Dean Acheson's Version . . . ," *Esquire*, p. 77; Acheson, Oral History, JFKL, p. 24.
15. Quoted in George Ball, *The Past Has Another Pattern: Memoirs* (New York: W. W. Norton, 1982), p. 291.
16. Acheson, "Dean Acheson's Version . . . ," p. 77.
17. Bundy, *Danger and Survival*, p. 400.
18. Raymond L. Garthoff, "Some Reflections on the History of the Cold War," Society for Historians of American Foreign Relations *Newsletter*, 26:3 (September 1995), pp. 6–8; see also John Lewis Gaddis, *We Now Know: Rethinking Cold War History*, "The Cuban Missile Crisis," p. 276.
19. James G. Blight and David A. Welch, *On the Brink: Americans and Soviets Reexamine the Cuban Missile Crisis* (New York: Hill & Wang, 1989), pp. 47–50; Laurence Chang and Peter Kornbluh, eds., *The Cuban Missile Crisis, 1962* (New York: New Press, 1992), "Minutes of the October 19, 1962, Executive Committee Meeting," pp. 124–125.
20. Acheson, Oral History, JFKL, pp. 24–29; Harris, "Pungent Memories from Mr. Acheson"; Letter from Acheson to Michael Janeway, October 31, 1962, Acheson Papers, Yale University Library, series I, box 16, f. 209; letter from Acheson to John Cowles, January 7, 1963, Acheson Papers, Yale University Library, series I, box 6, f. 83; see also Elie Abel, *The Missile Crisis* (New York: Bantam [paper]), pp. 95–97.
21. Brinkley, *Dean Acheson*, p. 169.

22. Radio-TV address of the president to the nation, October 22, 1962, document 28, in Chang and Kornbluh, *The Cuban Missile Crisis,* pp. 151–154.
23. Acheson, "Dean Acheson's Version . . . ," p. 44.
24. Kennedy, *Thirteen Days,* pp. 97–99.
25. Anatoly Dobrynin, *In Confidence: Moscow's Ambassador to America's Six Cold War Presidents (1962–1986)* (New York: Times Books, 1995), pp. 86–91; Gaddis, "The Cuban Missile Crisis," pp. 270–271.
26. Acheson, "Dean Acheson's Version . . . ," p. 45.
27. Bundy, *Danger and Survival,* pp. 447–448; Gaddis, *We Now Know,* "The Cuban Missile Crisis," p. 268.
28. Quoted in Bundy, *Danger and Survival,* p. 452.
29. Blight and Welch, *On the Brink,* pp. 229; 234.
30. Bundy, *Danger and Survival,* p. 456.
31. Letters from Acheson to Kennedy, October 28, 1962, Acheson Papers, Yale University Library, series I, box 18, f. 223; Oral History, pp. 30–31, JFKL.
32. Acheson, "Our Atlantic Alliance: The Political and Economic Strands," December 5, 1962, reprinted in *Vital Speeches of the Day,* no. 6, January 1, 1963, pp. 162–166; see also Douglas Brinkley, "Dean Acheson and the 'Special Relationship': The West Point Speech of December 1962," in the *Historical Journal* 33:3 (1990), pp. 599–608.
33. See Brinkley, *Dean Acheson,* p. 177.
34. Letter from Acheson to Kurt Birrenbach, February 19, 1963, in *Among Friends,* p. 242.
35. Acheson, "De Gaulle and the West," *New Leader,* New York, April 1, 1963, pp. 17–22.
36. Letter from Acheson to John Cowles, August 15, 1963, in *Among Friends,* p. 251.
37. Acheson, "Thoughts Written to a British Friend on the Assassination of President Kennedy," in *Grapes from My Thorns,* pp. 81–82.
38. Harris, "Pungent Memories from Mr. Acheson, *Life,* July 23, 1971.
39. Benjamin C. Bradlee, *Conversations with Kennedy* (New York: W. W. Norton, 1975), pp. 224–225.
40. Interview with George Ball, cited in Brinkley, *Dean Acheson,* p. 200.

THIRTY-THREE: CONTENDING WITH LBJ

1. Letter from Acheson to Lady Pamela Berry, November 20, 1964, in *Among Friends,* pp. 262–263.
2. Letter from Acheson to Lyndon Johnson, August 13, 1957, in *Among Friends,* pp. 128–129.
3. Brinkley, *Dean Acheson,* pp. 206–207.
4. Bundy memo of December 6, 1963, cited in Isaacson and Thomas, *The Wise Men,* p. 645.
5. Cited in Isaacson and Thomas, *The Wise Men,* p. 643.
6. Ibid., p. 646.
7. John Franklin Campbell, *The Foreign Affairs Fudge Factory* (New York: Basic Books, 1971), pp. 70–74, cited in Brinkley, *Dean Acheson,* pp. 207–208.
8. Henry Brandon, *Special Relationships: A Foreign Correspondent's Memoirs from Roosevelt to Reagan* (New York: Atheneum, 1988), p. 68.
9. George W. Ball, *The Past Has Another Pattern: A Memoir* (New York: W. W. Norton, 1982), pp. 355–358; interview with George Ball, March 27, 1992.
10. Tad Szulc, "Peacekeeping and Diplomacy in Cyprus, 1964–1993," Carnegie Council Case Study on Ethics and International Affairs 16 (New York: Carnegie Council on Ethics and International Affairs, 1993); see also K. C. Markides, *The Rise and Fall of the Cyprus Republic* (New Haven, Conn.: Yale University Press, 1977), chap. 4 passim, pp. 126–129.

11. Specifically, the original Acheson Plan provided for a large Turkish military base (this would be located in the northeastern part of Cyprus, which was an area almost one-fifth of the island); two or three Turkish Cypriot "cantons" with local autonomy; the cession of the rest of Cyprus to Greece; and of the island of Castelliorizo (part of the Greek Dodecanese) to Turkey.
12. Letter from Acheson to Ranald MacDonald, September 6, Acheson Papers, Yale University Library, series I, box 21, f. 264.
13. Ball, *The Past Has Another Pattern*, pp. 356–359.
14. See Brinkley, *Dean Acheson*, p. 220–221.
15. Letter from Acheson to Erwin Griswold, March 22, 1965, in *Among Friends*, p. 267.
16. Letter from Acheson to Archibald MacLeish, March 3, 1965, MacLeish correspondence, Library of Congress.
17. Letter from Acheson to Archibald MacLeish, June 24, 1965, in *Among Friends*, p. 269.
18. Acheson television interview with Marvin Kalb, CBS News, April 4, 1966, Acheson Papers, Yale University Library, series 3, box 53, f. 70; see also Brinkley, *Dean Acheson*, pp. 226–231.
19. Letter from Acheson to the earl of Avon (Anthony Eden), June 29, 1966, in *Among Friends*, p. 279.
20. Letter from Acheson to Harry Truman, October 3, 1966, in *Among Friends*, pp. 282–282.

THIRTY-FOUR: INTO THE QUAGMIRE

1. William Conrad Gibbons, *The U.S. Government and the Vietnam War: Executive and Legislative Roles and Relationships* (Princeton, N.J.: Princeton University Press, 1989), part III, pp. 259–262.
2. Ball, *The Past Has Another Pattern*, pp. 392–395; Brinkley, *Dean Acheson*, pp. 243–247; Acheson and Ball, "A Plan for a Political Resolution in South Vietnam," given to the author by George Ball.
3. Gibbons, *The U.S. Government and the Vietnam War*, part III, p. 348.
4. Letter from Acheson to Harry Truman, July 10, 1965, in *Among Friends*, pp. 272–273; Isaacson and Thomas, *The Wise Men*, pp. 650–652.
5. Interview with George Ball, 1988, in Brinkley, *Dean Acheson*, p. 248.
6. Letter from Acheson to Erik Boheman, July 7, 1965, in *Among Friends*, p. 271.
7. Marilyn B. Young, *The Vietnam Wars, 1945–1990* (New York: HarperPerennial, 1991), pp. 192–201.
8. See Larry Berman, *Lyndon Johnson's War* (New York: W. W. Norton, 1989), pp. 93–95.
9. Berman, *Lyndon Johnson's War*, pp. 96–113; Isaacson and Thomas, *The Wise Men*, 679.
10. Clark Clifford with Richard Holbrooke, *Counsel to the President: A Memoir* (New York: Random House, 1991), p. 455.
11. On Acheson-Harriman conversation, see Isaacson and Thomas, *The Wise Men*, pp. 681–682.
12. Letter from Acheson to Anthony Eden, December 31, 1967, Acheson Papers, Yale University Library, series I, box 9, f. 118.
13. On Tet, see Berman, *Lyndon Johnson's War*, pp. 145–146; George Herring, *America's Longest War: The United States and Vietnam, 1950–1975* (New York: John Wiley, 1979), pp. 186–187.
14. Young, *The Vietnam Wars*, pp. 216–225.
15. Brinkley, *Dean Acheson*, p. 256–257; Isaacson and Thomas, *The Wise Men*, pp. 686–687.
16. Letter from Acheson to John Cowles, February 27, 1968, in *Among Friends*, pp. 289–291; Acheson Papers, Yale University Library, series I, box 7, f. 84.
17. Brinkley, *Dean Acheson*, p. 257; Isaacson and Thomas, *The Wise Men*, pp. 687.

18. Acheson memorandum, "Meeting with the President," March 14, 1968, in *Among Friends*, pp. 292–294; Acheson Papers, Yale University Library, series 4, box 68, f. 173; see also Isaacson and Thomas, *The Wise Men*, p. 694.
19. Letter from Acheson to John Cowles, March 14, 1968, Acheson Papers, Yale University Library, series I, box 7, f. 84.
20. On the March 25–26 Wise Men meetings, see Acheson memorandum "DA's Views Regarding Vietnam, as of March 26, 1968," in *Among Friends*, pp. 295–296; Berman, *Lyndon Johnson's War*, pp. 194–199; Clifford, *Counsel to the President*, pp. 511–519; Isaacson and Thomas, *The Wise Men*, pp. 698–702.
21. Letter from Acheson to Jane Acheson Brown, April 13, 1968, in *Among Friends*, pp. 296–297, Acheson Papers, Yale University Library, series I, box 5, f. 69.
22. Cited in Isaacson and Thomas, *The Wise Men*, p. 697.
23. Letter from Lyndon Johnson to Acheson, April 11, 1968, Acheson Papers, Yale University Library, series I, box 17, f. 215; letter from Acheson to Johnson, April 15, 1968, Acheson Papers, Yale University Library, series I, box 17, f. 215.

THIRTY-FIVE: SEDUCTIONS AND BETRAYALS

1. Letter from Acheson to J. H. P. Gould, March 21, 1969, in *Among Friends*, p. 302,
2. Henry Kissinger, *White House Years* (Boston: Little, Brown, 1979), pp. 942–943.
3. Richard Nixon, *RN: The Memoirs of Richard Nixon* (New York: Warner Books, 1978), p. 136.
4. Letter from Acheson to Jane Acheson Brown, April 13, 1968, in *Among Friends*, p. 297.
5. Acheson memorandum, meeting at the White House, March 19, 1969, Acheson Papers, Yale University Library, series 4, box 68, f. 173; letter from Acheson to J. H. P. Gould, March 21, 1969, in *Among Friends*, pp. 302–304; Stephen Ambrose, *Nixon: The Triumph of a Politician: 1962–1972* (New York: Simon & Schuster, 1989), pp. 259–260; Brinkley, *Dean Acheson*, pp. 268–271; Gregory T. D'Auria, *Presidential Studies Quarterly*, 17:2 (spring 1988), "Present at the Rejuvenation: The Association of Dean Acheson and Richard Nixon," pp. 393–396.
6. Brinkley, *Dean Acheson*, pp. 271–275; D'Auria, "Present at the Rejuvenation," pp. 396–397.
7. Acheson, *Present at the Creation*, "Apologia pro Libre Hoc," p. xvii.
8. Letter from Acheson to Truman, August 12, 1969, Acheson-Truman correspondence, 1965–1971, Truman Library, box 166.
9. Letter from Robert Lovett to Acheson, May 5, 1970, Acheson Papers, Yale University Library, series I, box 20, f. 248.
10. Brinkley, *Dean Acheson*, pp. 321–322.
11. George F. Kennan, "Hazardous Courses in Southern Africa," *Foreign Affairs*, January 1971.
12. Cited in Brinkley, *Dean Acheson*, p. 325.
13. Letter from Acheson to John Cowles, May 29, 1971, Acheson Papers, Yale University Library, series I, box 7, f. 86.
14. Letter from Acheson to Henry Kissinger, October 20, 1969, Acheson Papers, Yale University Library, series I, box 13, f. 226.
15. Acheson, memorandum of conversation with the president, October 27, 1969, Acheson Papers, Yale University Library, series IV, box 68, f. 173.
16. Nixon address to the nation, *The New York Times*, November 4, 1969.
17. Letter from Acheson to Sir Roy Welensky, November 5, 1969, Acheson Papers, Yale University Library, series I, box 33, f. 430.
18. Letter from Acheson to Lincoln MacVeagh, December 2, 1969, Acheson Papers, Yale University Library, series IV, box 22, f. 276.

19. Letter from Acheson to Anthony Eden, November 3, 1969, Acheson Papers, Yale University Library, series I, box 9, f. 117; interview with Alice Acheson, December 1987, cited in Brinkley, *Dean Acheson*, pp. 282–283.
20. Letter from Acheson to John Cowles, May 5, 1970, Acheson Papers, Yale University Library, series I, box 7, f. 86.
21. Karnow, *Vietnam*, pp. 611–612.
22. Letter from Acheson to Desmond Donnelly, June 22, 1970, Acheson Papers, Yale University Library, series I, box 8, f. 108.
23. Letter from Acheson to John Cowles, January 21, 1971, Acheson Papers, Yale University Library, series I, box 7, f. 86.
24. Letter from Acheson to Lord Stow Hill, April 21, 1971, Acheson Papers, Yale University Library, series I, box 29, f. 377.
25. Kissinger, *White House Years*, pp. 943–945.
26. Letter from Acheson to John Cowles, May 21, 1971, Acheson Papers, Yale University Library, series I, box 7, f. 86.
27. David Acheson, *Acheson Country*, pp. 214–215.
28. Letter from Acheson to Averell Harriman, September 15, 1971, Acheson Papers, Yale University Library, series I, box 15, f. 193. For his last days at Harewood, see David Acheson, *Acheson Country*, p. 215; Brinkley, *Dean Acheson*, p. 329; Isaacson and Thomas, *The Wise Men*, p. 719; *The New York Times*, October 13, 1971.
29. Interview with Mary A. Bundy, October 5, 1997.
30. The account of Acheson's funeral is drawn from Marilyn Berger's report in the *Washington Post*, October 16, 1971.

CODA: "A BLADE OF STEEL"

1. Quoted in Brinkley, *Dean Acheson*, p. 133.
2. Arthur Schlesinger Jr., "The Style Was Always Bravura," *The New York Times*, October 17, 1971.
3. See Gaddis Smith, *Dean Acheson*, p. 399.
4. Quoted in John Harper, *American Visions of Europe*, p. 236.

SELECTED BIBLIOGRAPHY

This book would not have been possible without the path-breaking works on the life and career of Dean Acheson that preceded this biography. Foremost is Acheson's own prize-winning masterwork, *Present at the Creation: My Years in the State Department.* A work remarkably free of self-congratulation, it is invaluable for any scholar of Acheson or the period of the early Cold War. In addition, any biographer is grateful to Acheson for being a stylist of the highest order in his memoir, *Morning and Noon,* and in his other books and essays.

Three other works have also provided this author with inspiration and understanding. Gaddis Smith's early biographical work, *Dean Acheson,* was published in 1972 in the series "The American Secretaries of State and Their Diplomacy." His many insights remain undimmed by time. In 1976 David S. McLellan's *Dean Acheson: The State Department Years* appeared, a richly detailed study of the most productive years of Acheson's public life. Last but not least, Douglas Brinkley wisely wrote on Acheson's years after his retirement in *Dean Acheson: The Cold War Years, 1953–71,* which appeared in 1992. An additional work brimming with revealing anecdotes and interviews is *The Wise Men: Six Friends and the World They Made: Acheson, Bohlen, Harriman, Kennan, Lovett, McCloy,* by Walter Isaacson and Evan Thomas (1986).

Invaluable to the writing of this full-scale biography have been the documents from the former Soviet Union, Eastern Europe, and the People's Republic of China that have been appearing under the auspices of the Cold War International History Project of the Woodrow Wilson International Center for Scholars in Washington, D.C. Sadly, Acheson did not live to see the end of the Cold War and how the institutions he did so much to create helped bring this about.

Abramson, Rudy. *Spanning the Century: The Life of Averell Harriman, 1891–1986.* New York: Morrow, 1992.

Acheson, David C. *Acheson Country: A Memoir.* New York: W. W. Norton, 1993.

Acheson, Dean. *A Citizen Looks at Congress.* New York: Harper & Brothers, 1957.

———. *A Democrat Looks at His Party.* New York: Harper & Brothers, 1955.

———. *Fragments of My Fleece.* New York: W. W. Norton, 1971.

———. *Grapes from My Thorns.* New York: W. W. Norton, 1972.

———. *Morning and Noon.* New York: Houghton Mifflin, 1965.

———. *Power and Diplomacy.* Cambridge, Mass.: Harvard University Press, 1958.

———. *Present at the Creation: My Years in the State Department.* New York: W. W. Norton, 1969.

———. *Sketches from Life of Men I Have Known.* New York: Harper & Brothers, 1959.

———. *This Vast Eternal Realm.* New York: W. W. Norton, 1973.

Aldrich, Nelson. *Old Money: The Mythology of America's Upper Class.* New York: Alfred A. Knopf, 1988.

Ambrose, Stephen. *Eisenhower: Soldier and President.* New York: Simon & Schuster, 1990.

———. *Nixon: The Triumph of a Politician: 1962–1972.* New York: Simon & Schuster, 1989.

Baker, Leonard. *Brandeis and Frankfurter.* New York: Harper & Row, 1984.

Ball, George. *The Past Has Another Pattern: Memoirs.* New York: W. W. Norton, 1982.

Berman, Larry. *Lyndon Johnson's War.* New York: W. W. Norton, 1989.

Beschloss, Michael R. *The Crisis Years: Kennedy and Khrushchev, 1960–1963.* New York: HarperCollins, 1991.

Bird, Kai. *The Chairman: John J. McCloy: The Making of the American Establishment.* New York: Simon & Schuster, 1992.

Blight, James G., and David A. Welch. *On the Brink: Americans and Soviets Re-examine the Cuban Missile Crisis.* New York: Hill & Wang, 1989.

Block, Fred L. *The Origins of International Economic Disorder.* Berkeley: University of California Press, 1977.

Blum, John Morton. *Roosevelt and Morgenthau: A Revision and Condensation of "From the Morgenthau Diaries."* Boston: Houghton Mifflin, 1970.

———, ed. *The Price of Vision: The Diary of Henry A. Wallace, 1942–1946.* Boston: Houghton Mifflin, 1973.

———. *From the Morgenthau Diaries: Years of Crisis, 1928–1938.* Boston: Houghton Mifflin, 1959.

———. *From the Morgenthau Diaries: Years of Urgency, 1938–1941.* Boston: Houghton Mifflin, 1964.

Bohlen, Charles E. *Witness to History.* New York: W. W. Norton, 1973.

Borg, Dorothy, and Waldo Heinricks, eds. *Uncertain Years: Chinese American Relations, 1947–1950.* New York: Columbia University Press, 1980.

Bradlee, Benjamin C. *Conversations with Kennedy.* New York: W. W. Norton, 1975.

Brandon, Henry. *Special Relationships: A Foreign Correspondent's Memoirs from Roosevelt to Reagan.* New York: Atheneum, 1988.

Brinkley, Douglas. *Dean Acheson: The Cold War Years, 1957–1971.* New Haven, Conn.: Yale University Press, 1992.

———, ed. *Dean Acheson and the Making of U.S. Foreign Policy.* New York: St. Martin's Press, 1993.

Bullock, Alan. *Ernest Bevin, Foreign Secretary.* London: Heinemann, 1983.

Bundy, McGeorge, and Henry L. Stimson. *On Active Service in Peace and War.* New York: Harper & Brothers, 1948.

Bundy, McGeorge, ed. *The Pattern of Responsibility.* Boston: Houghton Mifflin, 1968.

Burns, James M. *Roosevelt: The Soldier of Freedom.* Orlando, Fla.: Harcourt & Brace, 1970.

Callahan, David. *Dangerous Capabilities: Paul Nitze and the Cold War.* New York: HarperCollins, 1990.

Chace, James, and Caleb Carr. *America Invulnerable: The Quest for Absolute Security from 1812 to Star Wars.* New York: Summit Books, 1988.

Chang, Laurence, and Peter Kornbluh. *The Cuban Missile Crisis, 1962.* New York: The New Press, 1992.

China White Paper, August 1949. Stanford, Calif: Stanford University Press, 1967.

Christensen, Thomas J. *Useful Adversaries: Grand Strategy, Domestic Mobilization, and Sino-American Conflict, 1947–1958.* Princeton, N.J.: Princeton University Press, 1996.

Churchill, Winston S. *Their Finest Hour.* Boston: Houghton Mifflin, 1949.

———. *The Second World War,* vol. 6, *Triumph and Tragedy.* Boston: Houghton Mifflin, 1989.

Clifford, Clark M., with Richard Holbrooke. *Counsel to the President: A Memoir.* New York: Anchor Books, 1992.

Clifford, J. Gary, and Kenneth J. Hagen. *American Foreign Policy: A History/1900 to the Present.* Lexington, Mass.: D. C. Heath, 1988.

Cohen, Warren I. *America's Response to China.* New York: John Wiley & Sons, 1971.

———. *Dean Rusk.* Totowa, N.J.: Cooper Square Publishers, 1980.

Cumings, Bruce. *The Origins of the Korean War,* vol. 2, *The Roaring of the Contract, 1947–1950.* Princeton, N.J.: Princeton University Press, 1990.

Dallek, Robert. *Franklin Roosevelt and American Foreign Policy, 1932–1945.* New York: Oxford University Press, 1995.

Davis, Kenneth S. *FDR: The Beckoning of Destiny, 1882–1928.* New York: Putnam, 1972.

Djilas, Milovan. *Conversations with Stalin.* New York: Harcourt, Brace, & World, 1962.

Dobrynin, Anatoly. *In Confidence: Moscow's Ambassador to America's Six Cold War Presidents (1962–1986).* New York: Times Books, 1995.

Donaldson, Scott. *Archibald MacLeish: An American Life.* Boston: Houghton Mifflin, 1992.

Eckes, Alfred E. *Search for Solvency: Bretton Woods and the International Monetary System, 1941–1971.* Austin: University of Texas Press, 1975.

Farley, James A. *Jim Farley's Story: The Roosevelt Years.* New York: Whittlesey House, 1948.

Feis, Herbert. *From Trust to Terror: The Onset of the Cold War.* New York: W. W. Norton, 1970.

———. *The Road to Pearl Harbor.* New York: Atheneum, 1967.

Ferrell, Robert. *Off The Record: The Private Papers of Harry S. Truman.* New York: Harper & Row, 1980.

Fisher, Louis. *Presidential War Power.* Lawrence: University of Kansas Press, 1995.

Foot, Rosemary. *The Wrong War: American Policy and the Dimensions of the Korean Conflict, 1950–1953.* Ithaca, N.Y.: Cornell University Press, 1985.

Fossedal, Gregory A. *Our Finest Hour: Will Clayton, the Marshall Plan, and the Triumph of Democracy.* Stanford, Calif.: Hoover Institution Press, 1993.

Frankfurter, Felix. *Felix Frankfurter Reminisces.* New York: Reynal & Co., 1960.

Freeland, Richard M. *The Truman Doctrine and the Origins of McCarthyism: Foreign Policy, Domestic Politics, and Internal Security, 1946–1948.* New York: New York University Press, 1971.

Freidel, Frank. *Franklin D. Roosevelt: A Rendezvous with Destiny.* Boston: Little, Brown, 1990.

Fried, Richard M. *Men Against McCarthy.* New York: Columbia University Press, 1976.

Gaddis, John L. *Strategies of Containment: A Critical Appraisal of Postwar American National Security Policy.* New York: Oxford University Press, 1982.

———. *The United States and the End of the Cold War: Implications, Reconsideration, Provocations.* New York: Oxford University Press, 1992.

———. *We Now Know: Rethinking Cold War History.* New York: Oxford University Press, 1997.

Gardner, Richard N. *Sterling-Dollar Diplomacy.* New York: McGraw-Hill, 1969.

Gibbons, William Conrad. *The U.S. Government and the Vietnam War: Executive and Legislative Roles and Relationships.* Princeton, N.J.: Princeton University Press, 1989.

Goncharov, Sergei N., John W. Lewis, and Xue Litai. *Uncertain Partners: Stalin, Mao, and the Korean War.* Stanford, Calif.: Stanford University Press, 1993.

Grew, Joseph. *Ten Years in Japan.* New York: Simon & Schuster, 1944.

Hamby, Alonzo L. *Man of the People: A Life of Harry S. Truman.* New York: Oxford University Press, 1995.

Harper, John L. *American Visions of Europe: Franklin D. Roosevelt, George F. Kennan, and Dean G. Acheson.* New York: Cambridge University Press, 1994.

Harrod, R. F. *The Life of John Maynard Keynes.* New York: Harcourt Brace, 1951.

Heilbroner, Robert. *The Worldly Philosophers.* New York: Simon & Schuster, 1967.

Heinrichs, Waldo. *Threshold of War: Franklin D. Roosevelt and American Entry into World War II.* New York: Oxford University Press, 1988.

Herken, Gregg. *The Winning Weapon.* New York: Alfred A. Knopf, 1980.

Herring, George. *America's Longest War: The United States and Vietnam, 1950–1975.* New York: John Wiley, 1979.

Hershberg, James. *James B. Conant.* New York: Alfred A Knopf, 1993.

Hillman, William. *Mr. President: The First Publication from the Personal Diaries, Private Letters, Papers, and Revealing Interviews of Harry S. Truman.* New York: Farrar, Straus, & Young, 1952.

Hodgson, Godfrey. *The Colonel: The Life and Wars of Henry Stimson, 1867–1950.* New York: Alfred A. Knopf, 1990.

Hogan, Michael J. *The Marshall Plan: America, Britain, and the Reconstruction of Western Europe, 1947–1952.* New York: Cambridge University Press, 1989.

Holloway, David. *Stalin and the Bomb: The Soviet Union and Atomic Energy, 1939–1956.* New Haven, Conn.: Yale University Press, 1994.

Hoopes, Townsend. *The Devil and John Foster Dulles.* New York: Atlantic–Little, Brown, 1973.

Howard, Harry N. *Turkey, the Straits, and U.S. Policy.* Baltimore: Johns Hopkins University Press, 1974.

Iatrides, John O., and Linda Wrigley, eds. *Greece at the Crossroads: The Civil War and Its Legacy.* University Park: Pennsylvania State University Press, 1995.

In the Matter of J. Robert Oppenheimer. U.S. Government Printing Office, 1954.

Isaacson, Walter, and Evan Thomas. *The Wise Men: Six Friends and the World They Made: Acheson, Bohlen, Harriman, Kennan, Lovett, McCloy.* New York: Simon & Schuster/Touchstone, 1986.

Jensen, Kenneth M. *Origins of the Cold War: The Novikov, Kennan, and Roberts "Long Telegrams" of 1946.* Washington, D.C.: United States Institute of Peace, 1991.

Johnson, Owen. *Stover at Yale.* New York: Frederick A. Stokes Company, 1912.

Jones, Joseph M. *The Fifteen Weeks (February 21–June 5, 1947).* New York: Harvest/HBJ, 1955.

Kaplan, Lawrence S. *The United States and NATO: The Formative Years.* Lexington: University of Kentucky Press, 1984.

Kelly, Brooks Mather. *Yale: A History.* New Haven, Conn.: Yale University Press, 1974.

Kempton, Murray. *Rebellions, Perversities, and Main Events.* New York: Times Books, 1994.

Kennan, George F. *Memoirs: 1925–1950.* New York: Pantheon Books, 1967.

———. *Sketches from Life.* New York: Pantheon Books, 1989.

Kennedy, Robert F. *Thirteen Days: A Memoir of the Cuban Missile Crisis.* New York: New American Library, 1969.

Keynes, John Maynard. *The Economic Consequences of the Peace.* New York: Harcourt, Brace, & Howe, 1920.

Khrushchev, Nikita. *Khrushchev Remembers: The Last Testament.* Boston: Little, Brown, 1974.

Kimball, Warren F. *The Most Unsordid Act: Lend Lease, 1939–1941.* Baltimore: Johns Hopkins University Press, 1969.

———, ed. *Churchill and Roosevelt: The Complete Correspondence*, vol. 1, *Alliance Emerging.* Princeton, N.J.: Princeton University Press, 1984.

Kissinger, Henry. *White House Years.* Boston: Little, Brown, 1979.

Kuniholm, Bruce R. *The Origins of the Cold War: Great Power Conflict and Diplomacy in Iran, Turkey and Greece.* Princeton, N.J.: Princeton University Press, 1994.

Larson, Deborah W. *Origins of Containment: A Psychological Explanation.* Princeton, N.J.: Princeton University Press, 1985.

Leffler, Melvyn P. *A Preponderance of Power: National Security, the Truman Administration and the Cold War.* Stanford, Calif.: Stanford University Press, 1992.

Lekachman, Robert. *The Age of Keynes.* London: Penguin, 1967.

Lerner, Max, ed. *The Mind and Faith of Justice Holmes.* Boston: Little, Brown, 1943.

Lilienthal, David E. *The Journals of David E. Lilienthal,* vol. 2, *The Atomic Energy Years, 1945–1950.* New York: Harper & Row, 1964.

Lippmann, Walter. *The Cold War.* New York: Harper Torchbooks, 1972.

Lytle, Mark. *The Origins of the Iranian-American Alliance, 1941–1953.* New York: Holmes & Meier, 1987.

MacArthur, Douglas. *Reminiscences.* New York: McGraw Hill, 1964.

Manchester, William. *American Caesar, Douglas MacArthur 1880–1964.* Boston: Little, Brown, 1978.

Markides, K. C. *The Rise and Fall of the Cyprus Republic.* New Haven, Conn.: Yale University Press, 1997.

McCullough, David. *Truman.* New York: Simon & Schuster, 1992.

McGlothlen, Ronald L. *Controlling the Waves: Dean Acheson and U.S. Foreign Policy in Asia.* New York: W. W. Norton, 1993.

McLellan, David S. *Dean Acheson: The State Department Years.* New York: Dodd, Mead & Company, 1976.

McLellan, David S., and David C. Acheson, eds. *Among Friends: Personal Letters of Dean Acheson.* New York: Dodd, Mead, 1980.

Mee, Charles L. Jr. *The Marshall Plan.* New York: Simon & Schuster, 1984.

Miller, Merle. *Plain Speaking: An Oral Biography of Harry S. Truman.* New York: Berkley Publishing, 1973.

Millis, Walter, ed. *The Forrestal Diaries.* New York: Penguin, 1951.

Miscamble, Wilson. *George F. Kennan and the Making of American Foreign Policy, 1947–1950.* Princeton, N.J.: Princeton University Press, 1992.

Monnet, Jean. *Memoirs.* London: Collins, 1978.

Morgan, Ted. *FDR.* New York: Simon & Schuster, 1985.

Mosley, Leonard. *Dulles: A Biography of Eleanor, Allen, and John Foster Dulles and Their Family Network.* New York: Dial Press, 1978.

Oren, Dan A. *Joining the Club: A History of Jews and Yale.* New Haven, Conn.: Yale University Press, 1985.

Nitze, Paul. *From Hiroshima to Glasnost: A Memoir of Five Perilous Decades.* New York: Weidenfeld & Nicolson, 1989.

Nixon, Richard. *RN: The Memoirs of Richard Nixon.* New York: Warner Books, 1978.

Novick, Sheldon M. *Honorable Justice: The Life of Oliver Wendell Holmes.* Boston: Little, Brown, 1989.

Patterson, Thomas G. *American Foreign Policy: A History Since 1900.* Lexington, Mass.: D. C. Heath, 1988.

———, ed. *Major Problems in American Foreign Policy,* vol. 2, *Since 1914,* 3rd ed. Lexington, Mass.: D. C. Heath, 1989.

———. *On Every Front: The Making of the Cold War.* New York: W. W. Norton, 1979.

The Pentagon Papers: The Defense Department History of United States Decisionmaking on Vietnam (the Gravel edition). Boston: Beacon Press, 1971.

Pogue, Forrest C. *George C. Marshall: Education of a General, 1880–1939.* New York: Viking, 1963.

Reeves, Thomas C. *The Life and Times of Joe McCarthy.* New York: Stein & Day, 1982.

Resis, Albert, ed. *Molotov Remembers: Inside Kremlin Politics: Conversations with Felix Chuev.* Chicago: Ivan R. Dee, 1993.

Rhodes, Richard. *Dark Sun: The Making of the Hydrogen Bomb.* New York: Simon & Schuster, 1995.

Ridgway, Matthew B. *The Korean War.* Garden City, N.Y.: Doubleday, 1967.

Robertson, David. *Sly and Able: A Political Biography of James F. Byrnes.* New York: W. W. Norton, 1994.

Rovere, Richard. *Senator Joe McCarthy.* New York: Harcourt, Brace, 1959.

Sakharov, Andrei. *Memoirs.* New York: Alfred A. Knopf, 1990.
Schlesinger, Arthur M. Jr. *A Thousand Days: John F. Kennedy in the White House.* New York: Fawcett, 1965.
———. *The Coming of the New Deal.* Boston: Houghton Mifflin, 1959.
Schwartz, David. *Cole Porter.* New York: Dial Press, 1977.
Schwartz, Thomas. *America's Germany: John J. McCloy and the Federal Republic of Germany.* Cambridge, Mass.: Harvard University Press, 1991.
Sherwin, Martin J. *A World Destroyed: The Atomic Bomb and the Grand Alliance.* New York: Alfred A. Knopf, 1975.
Sherwood, Robert E. *Roosevelt and Hopkins.* New York: Harper, 1948.
Shulman, Marshall. *Soviet Foreign Policy Re-appraised.* Cambridge, Mass.: Harvard University Press, 1963.
Smith, Gaddis. *American Secretaries of State and Their Diplomacy,* vol. 16, *Dean Acheson.* New York: Cooper Square Publishers, 1971.
Smith, Tony. *America's Mission: The United States and the Worldwide Struggle for Democracy in the Twentieth Century.* Princeton, N.J.: Princeton University Press, 1994.
Sorensen, Theodore C. *Kennedy.* New York: Harper & Row, 1965.
Spector, Ronald H. *Eagle Against the Sun.* New York: Vintage, 1985.
Steel, Ronald. *Walter Lippmann and the American Century.* New York: Vintage Books, 1981.
Stuart, John Leighton. *Fifty Years in China.* New York: Random House, 1954.
Tanenhaus, Sam. *Whittaker Chambers: A Biography.* New York: Random House, 1997.
Truman, Harry S. *Memoirs: Years of Decision.* Garden City, N.Y.: Doubleday, 1955.
———. *Memoirs,* vol. 2, *Years of Trial and Hope.* Garden City, N.Y.: Doubleday, 1955.
Tsou, Tang. *America's Failure in China: 1941–50.* Chicago: University of Chicago Press, 1990.
Tucker, Nancy Bernkopf. *Patterns in the Dust: Chinese-American Relations and the Recognition Controversy, 1949–1950.* New York: Columbia University Press, 1983.
Tully, Grace. *F.D.R., My Boss.* New York: Scribner's, 1949.
Utley, Jonathan G. *Going to War with Japan, 1937–1941.* Knoxville: University of Tennessee Press, 1985.
Van Dormael, Armand. *Bretton Woods: Birth of a Monetary System.* New York: Holmes & Meier, 1978.
Ward, Patricia D. *The Threat of Peace: James F. Byrnes and the Council of Foreign Ministers, 1945–1946.* Kent, Ohio: Kent University Press, 1979.
Warner, Elizabeth. *A Political History of Middletown.* Norfolk/Virginia Beach, Va.: The Donning Co., 1989.
Weinstein, Allen. *Perjury: The Hiss-Chambers Case.* New York: Alfred A. Knopf, 1978.
Westwood, Howard C. *Covington and Burling 1919–1984.* Washington, D.C.: Covington and Burling, 1986.
White, Theodore. *In Search of History: A Personal Adventure.* New York: Harper & Row, 1978.
White, Theodore H., and Annalee Jacoby. *Thunder Out of China.* New York: William Sloane Associates, 1946.
Williams, William Appleton. *The Tragedy of American Diplomacy.* New York: Dell, 1962.
Yergin, Daniel H. *Shattered Peace: The Origins of the Cold War.* New York: Penguin Books, 1990.
———. *The Prize: The Quest for Oil, Money and Power.* New York: Simon & Schuster, 1991.
Young, Marilyn B. *The Vietnam Wars, 1945–1990.* New York: HarperPerennial, 1991.
Zhukov, G. K. *Vospominaniia i razmyshlenia,* vol. 3. Moscow: Novosti, 1990.

ACKNOWLEDGMENTS

My thanks are due, first of all, to Mary Acheson Bundy and David C. Acheson for their unstinting support of this project and helping me to understand the background and character of Dean Gooderham Acheson. I also owe a vast debt of thanks to those historians who have given me aid and insights in the reading of this manuscript, most especially to Wilson D. Miscamble, C.S.C., and William P. Bundy. Other historians who have commented on parts of the book were McGeorge Bundy, William Diebold, Lincoln Gordon, John Iatrides, Mark Lytle, and John Morton Blum. Invaluable editorial suggestions were also made by Harvey Ginsberg. Research assistance was provided by Sean O'Neill and Sarah Chace.

I have further benefited from a discussion of chapters of this book at the Foreign Policy Roundtable of the Council on Foreign Relations, under the chairmanship of Nicholas X. Rizopoulos. Frequent conversations with Caleb Carr, David Fromkin, Tony Smith, and Ronald Steel have been of immense help to me in thinking through the history of the period.

My thanks to the dedicated staffs of the Manuscripts and Archives room of Yale University's Sterling Memorial Library, the Harry S. Truman Library (and especially to Dennis Bilger), the Franklin D. Roosevelt Library, and the Library of Congress. I wish to thank James Silberman for his suggestions, and F. Joseph Spieler for his commitment to the project.

Alice Mayhew has been unfailingly supportive and a wise and acute editor throughout the writing of this biography. Roger Labrie has been a skillful craftsman at all times.

There are three people to whom I am deeply indebted. Sarah Rothenberg has provided help and commitment beyond measure. Peter Collias has mightily supported my work throughout the long years of our friendship. And Jack Sherman has read the entire manuscript and offered vital encouragement and advice at every twist and turning.

INDEX

Abbott, George M., 265
Abrams, Jacob, 49
Acheson, Alexander (grandfather), 17
Acheson, Alice Stanley (wife):
  Acheson as viewed by, 312, 345, 431, 434
  Acheson's courtship of, 34–35, 36, 37
  Acheson's marriage to, 39, 40, 46, 55–56, 62, 64–65, 109, 113, 114, 147–48, 155, 182, 200, 252, 313, 367–68, 395
  paintings by, 39, 46, 51, 147–48, 200, 339–40, 368, 412
Acheson, David (son), 27–28, 51, 72, 73, 97
Acheson, Dean Gooderham:
  as acting secretary of the Treasury, 62–68
  ancestry of, 17–18
  anticommunism of, 11, 172–73, 184
  in Antigua, 367–68, 384, 412, 434
  articles by, 372, 375–77, 384, 392
  as assistant secretary of state for congressional relations and international conferences, 101–9, 114, 183
  as assistant secretary of state for economic affairs, 81, 83–101
  as author, 373, 374, 375–77, 378, 432
  birth of, 18
  cabinetmaking by, 368, 412, 437, 442
  in Cambodia, 395–96
  Canada visited by, 26–27, 62, 64–65, 73, 77, 159, 182
  childhood of, 15–28
  confirmation hearings of, 193–96
  congressional testimony of, 183–84, 222, 223, 224, 266, 317, 416–17
  correspondence of, 106, 198, 255, 437
  daily routine of, 196–201
  death of, 437
  education of, 21–39
  in England, 33, 246–47, 251–54, 337–39, 349–51, 402
  family life of, 55–56, 72–73
  foreign affairs as viewed by, 155, 170–72, 182, 270–71, 323, 372–73, 412, 441
  in France, 73, 207–9, 242–43, 247–51, 265–66, 333–34, 388–89, 401–3
  funeral of, 437–38
  gardening of, 281, 437, 442
  Georgetown home of, 55, 72–73, 162, 197, 381–82, 438, 442
  in Germany, 243–46, 346–47, 387–88, 404
  Harewood farm of, 55–56, 59, 72, 87, 182, 189, 200, 280–81, 367, 368, 401, 412, 435, 437, 442
  health of, 396, 415–16, 433, 435, 437
  horsemanship of, 72
  as internationalist, 77–81, 87, 326–29
  in Italy, 389
  in Japan, 35–36
  labor relations as viewed by, 39, 40, 48, 50–51, 52, 59, 70, 447*n*
  as law clerk, 40–52
  law practice of, 51–58, 59, 69, 70, 72, 74, 105, 180, 183, 189, 338, 368–69, 371, 384, 401
  legacy of, 10–12, 348, 439–42
  legal opinions of, 38–39, 40, 44, 48, 77
  legal training of, 37–40
  liberalism of, 48, 51, 52

Acheson, Dean Gooderham (*cont.*)
in Lisbon, 339–41
loyalty of, 10, 256, 361–62, 363
Medal of Merit awarded to, 181
memoirs of, 63, 197, 267, 298, 315, 317, 334, 361, 432, 438
military service of, 37–40
in Minnesota, 184–85
in Mississippi, 170–72
nonconformity of, 19, 20, 21, 24–26, 28
office of, 93, 197–98
Oxford honorary degree awarded to, 349–50
personality of, 19, 53, 73, 239
personal philosophy of, 10, 16, 19–20, 34, 95
physical appearance of, 31, 282, 389, 407
political activities of, 59–61, 70–71, 74, 81, 185, 373–75, 378–80
political views of, 34, 59–60, 74, 81, 185, 373–75, 378–80
Presidential Medal of Freedom awarded to, 415
press coverage of, 171, 199, 217, 226–28, 239–40, 311, 312
as public servant, 22, 31, 61, 62, 70, 76–77, 182–83, 189
Pulitzer Prize awarded to, 432
as railroad worker, 26–27, 73
reading by, 189, 199–200, 281, 368, 369
as realist, 12, 47, 71, 107–8, 127, 168, 205, 225–26, 233, 271, 273, 322, 356, 372–73, 407, 428, 430, 439
resignations of, 67–68, 105, 108–9, 113–14, 131, 159, 228, 310–12, 362
retirement of, 159, 182–90
in Rio de Janeiro, 355–56
on rowing crew, 25, 32–33, 437
in San Francisco, 319–21
as secretary of state, 10, 12, 80, 189–90, 193–363, 439–42
social life of, 31, 32, 72–73, 199, 412
solicitor general appointment desired by, 61–62, 105
speeches of, 70–71, 78, 135–36, 145, 151, 170–72, 173, 176, 178, 184–85, 222–23, 226, 239–40, 254, 269, 326, 356–57, 406–7, 408
staff of, 93, 196–97, 442
as statesman, 58, 357–58, 411, 442
strokes suffered by, 396, 435, 437
thyroid condition of, 396, 415–16, 433
as under secretary of state, 9, 113–81, 182, 213–14, 257, 263–64
as under secretary of the Treasury, 62
in Vienna, 354–55
Acheson, Edward Campion (father), 10, 16, 17–20, 34, 36, 62, 68, 151, 372
Acheson, Edward "Ted" (brother), 19, 417
Acheson, Eleanor Gooderham (mother), 18–19, 25, 27, 34, 72
Acheson, Jane Stanley (daughter), 40, 114
Acheson, Margaret "Margo" (sister), 18–19, 34, 39
Acheson, Mary Campion (grandmother), 17
Acheson, Mary Eleanor (daughter), 55, 105–6, 108, 109, 113, 313
Acheson Plan, 414–15
Acheson Report, 385
Adams, John, 27, 368
Adams, John Quincy, 12, 197, 361–62, 442
Adenauer, Konrad, 242–47, 333–34, 337–39, 342, 344, 346, 347, 377, 384, 386, 387–88, 389, 404, 408–9
Africa, 396–97, 431, 432–33, 437
Aiken, George, 424
Ala, Hussein, 143
Albright, Madeleine, 438
Aldrich, Nelson, 26
Alsop, Joseph, 23, 199, 281
Altshul, Frank, 376
Amerasia, 238
Anderson, Vernice, 300
Anglican Church, 17–18
Angola, 397
antiballistic missile (ABM) system, 431–32
anticommunism, 48, 49, 74, 75, 98, 107, 187
Acheson's views on, 11, 172–73, 184
loyalty reviews and, 238, 359–60
McCarthy's role in, 228, 236–40, 369, 371, 372
anti-Semitism, 74
Arneson, Gordon, 234
Aron, Raymond, 209, 377
Ashurst, Henry, 75
Atherton, Maude, 77
Atherton, Ray, 77, 109, 159
Atlantic Alliance, 262–63, 335–37, 383, 406, 413, 415, 416
Atlantic Charter, 262–63

atomic bomb, 114–29
Acheson-Lilienthal report on, 124–27, 128, 129, 147, 234
Acheson's views on, 120–23, 129
arms race in, 115, 158, 231, 234
Byrnes's views on, 117–18, 122, 126, 129
conventional forces vs., 269, 271, 274–79, 323–24, 328–29, 372, 384, 385, 391, 441
deployment of, 108, 114–15, 372, 378
development of, 115–17, 124, 128
FDR's policy on, 128–29
international control of, 117, 118, 120, 126
Korean War and, 305, 308–9, 346
massive retaliation with, 372, 374, 375, 383–84
scientific information on, 117–23, 124, 125, 129, 146
Soviet development of, 225–26, 229–30, 232, 239, 247, 270, 328–29
Stalin's policy on, 116–17, 118, 122–23, 127, 128
Stimson's memorandum on, 114–23, 129
Truman's policy on, 114–29
U.S.-Soviet relations and, 114–29, 151
Atomic Energy Commission (AEC), 229, 230, 231, 232, 235–36
Attlee, Clement, 108, 122–23, 131, 203, 251, 305, 308–9, 335
Attorney General's Committee on Administrative Procedure, 77
Austin, Warren, 295
Australia, 319
Austria, 170, 174, 202, 209
Ayers, Eben, 236
Azerbaijan, 142, 143–44, 145

Baillie, Hugh, 312
Baker, Newton D., 60
Ball, George, 400, 409, 412–13, 414, 415, 417, 418–19, 420, 421, 422
Ballantine, Arthur, 62
Bao Dai, 264, 265, 266
Barkley, Alben, 254
Barr, David, 215
Baruch, Bernard, 126–28, 187
Baruch Plan, 127–28
Batista, Fulgencio, 379
Battle, Lucius D., 197, 198, 199, 200, 226, 227, 260–61, 273, 297–98, 320, 368, 372
"battle of the notes," 342–45
Bay of Pigs invasion, 386–87, 390
Beneš, Eduard, 188
Benét, Stephen Vincent, 30
Benton, William, 379
Beria, Lavrenti, 152
Berle, Adolf A., 195
Berlin airlift, 188–89, 193, 201, 202, 203, 239, 384, 441
Berlin crisis (1961), 383–94, 408
Berlin Wall, 393–94
Bevin, Ernest, 123, 133, 139, 178, 179, 187, 201, 203–4, 206–9, 218, 242–43, 246, 248, 251, 252, 253, 324, 326, 332, 407
Bidault, Georges, 179, 263
Biddle, Francis, 76, 81
Biddle, George, 23
Bilbo, Theodore, 170
Bingham, Hiram, 359
Bishop, Max, 259
Blair House Group, 283–85, 287
Bliss, Robert Woods, 126
Bohlen, Charles "Chip," 131, 134, 140, 144, 147, 151, 175, 177, 178, 206, 207, 228, 233, 238, 273, 277, 278, 285, 306–7
Bohr, Niels, 125
Bolivia, 355
"bomb in the Waldorf," 324
bonds, government, 63, 65
Bonnet, Henri, 263
Bowie, Robert, 342, 374
Bowles, Chester, 356, 379, 382
Bradlee, Ben, 409
Bradley, Omar, 207, 231, 277, 278, 282, 284, 303, 304, 306, 314, 317, 324, 335, 420, 421
Brandeis, Louis D., 40–52, 53, 57, 59, 62, 65, 81, 131, 415
Brandt, Willy, 436
Brazil, 355
Bretton Woods conference (1944), 10–11, 78, 97–103, 180, 225, 441
Brewster, Owen, 215
Bridges, Styles, 166, 220, 315
Browning, Robert, 239–40
Bruce, David, 196, 249–51, 265–66, 331, 382, 402
Bulgaria, 123, 133, 156, 163
Bullitt, William C., 141
Bunche, Ralph, 132

Bundy, Harvey, 105
Bundy, Mary Eleanor Acheson, 55, 105–6, 108, 109, 113, 313
Bundy, McGeorge, 128, 385, 391–92, 393, 397, 400, 406, 412, 421, 422, 427, 441
Bundy, William Putnam, 105–6, 226, 313, 385, 402
Burlatsky, Fyodor, 405–6
Burling, Edward B., 52, 53, 54, 55, 57
Burlingham, Charles C., 79, 80
Burma, 263
Burns, James, 274–75, 277–78
Bush, Vannevar, 122, 124, 126, 231
Business Week, 148
Butler, Hugh, 229
Butterworth, Walton, 221, 265–66
Byrnes, James Francis:
  Acheson's relationship with, 130–31
  Acheson's resignations and, 105, 108, 109, 113–14, 131
  atomic policy and, 117–18, 122, 126, 129
  Iran crisis and, 142–43, 144, 148
  resignation of, 131, 156, 159
  as secretary of state, 113–14, 130–31, 134, 135, 158, 159, 160, 182, 260, 263
  Stalin's meetings with, 123, 124, 128, 133, 134–35
  Truman and, 61, 129, 130, 134–35, 159

Caffery, Jefferson, 264, 265
Cambodia, 12, 262, 265, 266, 369, 395–96, 434–35
Campbell, Ronald, 86
Cannon, Joe, 34
Cardozo, Benjamin N., 71
Carver, George, 425, 426
Casey, Richard, 147
Castro, Fidel, 379–80, 387, 404
Central Intelligence Agency (CIA), 278, 387, 456*n*
Century Group, 77–78, 79
Chamberlain, Neville, 73
Chambers, Whittaker, 193, 194, 195, 226, 228
Chen Mingshu, 219
Chiang Kai-shek, 159, 201, 210, 211, 212, 215, 216–17, 220, 221, 222, 224, 265, 269, 285, 287, 294, 296, 359, 378
China:
  Acheson's views on, 213–14, 217, 219–20, 221
  civil war in, 133, 136, 159, 168, 193, 201, 210–17
  Communist government of, 201, 213, 216, 217–24, 247, 375
  congressional policy on, 215, 217, 218, 220, 224
  European recovery and, 211, 215–16, 218
  Japanese occupation of, 212, 213
  Japanese relations with, 218
  in Korean War, 287, 290–91, 294, 297–306, 313, 316, 317, 322, 325, 327, 422, 423
  "loss" of, 211, 224, 238, 260, 261, 270
  Marshall's views on, 214, 215, 216
  Marshall's visit to, 214, 215, 352
  Nationalist government of, 211, 212–13, 215, 216, 217, 219, 220, 221–22
  "Open Door" policy on, 211–12
  Soviet alliance with, 212, 218–20, 221, 223–24, 255, 262, 290
  Truman's policy on, 211, 215–16, 217, 221–22, 225
  U.S. aid to, 165, 215–16, 218, 219
  U.S. public opinion on, 211, 219, 441, 468*n*
  U.S. recognition of, 217, 219, 220, 222, 223, 224, 241, 319, 440
  U.S. trade with, 211–12, 219, 322
China White Paper, 211, 219–20, 222, 223, 441
Churchill, Winston S.:
  Acheson and, 147–48, 322, 334–37, 339
  FDR's meetings with, 86, 91–92
  Iron Curtain speech of, 146–48
  paintings by, 147–48
  at Potsdam conference, 108, 116, 152
  Stalin and, 152, 163
  at Tehran conference, 138, 139
  Truman's meetings with, 116, 146, 334–37
  wartime leadership of, 73, 79, 80, 85, 87, 88, 104, 108, 203
  at Yalta conference, 152
Citizen Looks at Congress, A (Acheson), 378
Citizens Committee for the Marshall Plan, 184–85
civil rights, 48, 410–11
Civil Rights Act (1957), 410–11
Clay, Lucius D., 175, 206, 207, 241, 394
Clayton, Will, 101–2, 103, 167, 170, 174, 177, 272, 273
Clifford, Clark, 157, 158, 167, 361, 421, 426, 427, 428

Coal and Steel Community, 249, 250, 251, 325, 407
Cohen, Benjamin V., 79
Cold War:
  ideology in, 261, 275, 372–73
  limited wars in, 286, 289, 373, 420
  nuclear arms in, 129, 279
  polarization in, 166, 219, 226
  as term, 187
Collingwood, Charles, 283
Collins, J. Lawton "Joe," 285, 304, 306, 308, 309, 310, 317
Committee to Defend America, 77
Committee to Maintain Prudent Defense Policy, 431
Common Market, 251, 361, 375, 406–7
Compton, Karl, 236
Conant, James Bryant, 123, 124, 231, 235, 278
congressional elections:
  of 1942, 94
  of 1946, 9, 156, 158, 159, 215, 363
  of 1948, 379
Connally, Tom, 121, 166, 168–69, 194
Connors, W. Bradley, 281
Constitution, U.S., 49, 57, 71, 371
Conway, Rose, 189
Coolidge, Calvin, 59
Covington, J. Harry, 52, 53, 61, 199
Covington and Burling, 51–58, 59, 72, 105, 183, 338, 368–69
Cowles, John, 367–68, 420, 424, 425, 426, 429
Cox, Oscar, 89
Cripps, Sir Stafford, 252
Crocker, Willie, 31, 34
Cuba, 379–80, 386–87
Cuban missile crisis, 398–406
  Acheson's role in, 11, 394, 398–406, 417
  air strikes considered in, 398–401, 404–5, 406
  de Gaulle and, 401–3, 417
  ExCom meetings in, 398–401, 404–5
  JFK in, 398–406
  Khrushchev in, 400, 404, 405–6
  naval blockade in, 398–403, 404, 406
Cummings, Homer, 62, 65, 66
Cut Knife Creek, battle of, 17
Cutler, Lloyd, 419
Cyprus, 413–15
Czechoslovakia, 188, 202
Dalton, Hugh, 203
Dardanelles, 133, 145, 152, 153, 154–55, 156, 162, 166, 439
Davenport, Abraham, 349–50
Davenport, John, 349
Dean, Arthur, 421
Dean, Gordon, 231, 232
de Gasperi, Alcide, 389
de Gaulle, Charles, 248, 384, 386, 388–89, 390, 397, 401–3, 411, 416–17
Delta Council, 170–72, 173, 176, 178
Democratic Advisory Committee, 61
Democratic Advisory Council (DAC), 377–78, 379, 384, 410
Democratic National Convention (1932), 60–61
Democratic Party:
  Acheson as member of, 59–61, 74, 81, 185, 373–75, 378–80
  McCarthyism and, 238–39
  Truman as leader of, 9, 170
Democrat Looks at His Party, A (Acheson), 374
Democrats for Landon, 74
Denegre, Bayne, 34
Depression, Great, 63–68
de Tocqueville, Alexis, 57, 371
Dewey, Thomas E., 157, 188, 189, 239, 261, 429
Dillon, Douglas, 382–83, 412, 421
Dixon, Pierson, 179
Dobrynin, Anatoly, 405
Dodge, Joseph, 259, 358
Donne, John, 240
Donnelly Garment Company, 70
Douglas, James, 62
Douglas, Lewis, 63, 64, 68, 74
Douglas, William O., 148
Douglas-Home, Alec, 386
Dowling, Walter "Red," 402, 404
Draper, William H., Jr., 259
Dubinsky, David, 70
Dulles, John Foster, 79, 200, 248, 260–62, 289, 315, 318, 356, 358–60, 371–74
Dumbarton Oaks, 125–26
DuPuy, William, 425, 426–27
Dutch East Indies, 84

Early, Steve, 75
Eden, Anthony, 91, 196, 333, 334, 335, 337, 339, 344, 346, 350, 351, 352–53, 374, 407, 423, 437

Egypt, 351, 373–74
Ehrlich, Thomas, 419
Eisenhower, Dwight D.:
  Acheson and, 328, 331, 350
  Khrushchev and, 384–85, 392
  as military commander, 107, 154, 159, 161, 267, 269, 290, 325, 328, 331, 334
  as president, 346, 371, 372, 378
  as president-elect, 358, 362
  presidential campaign of (1952), 328, 356–58, 429–30
  Truman and, 358, 362, 371
elections:
  of 1932, 60–61
  of 1936, 70
  of 1940, 79, 81
  of 1942, 94
  of 1946, 9, 156, 158, 159, 215, 363
  of 1948, 188, 189, 193, 245, 379
  of 1952, 328, 356–58, 429–30
  of 1956, 374–75
  of 1960, 379–80, 381
Eliot, T. S., 178
Elizabeth II, Queen of England, 252, 337, 339
Elsey, George, 157
Elysée Agreements, 265, 266
Emerson, Ralph Waldo, 47
Episcopal Church, 20, 62, 243, 438
Ertegun, Mehmet Munir, 153
Euripides, 312
Europe, Eastern, 141, 152, 374, 377
Europe, Western:
  German recovery and, 241–54
  reconstruction of, 171–72, 176–80, 184, 185–86, 201, 211, 215–16, 218
  Soviet threat to, 254, 327, 328–29, 348, 376
  unification of, 249–51, 325, 360–61, 406–7
  U.S. military commitments to, 323–24, 326–29, 331, 341, 361, 375–77
  see also individual countries
European Defense Community (EDC), 325, 329–31, 335, 337–38, 339, 341, 342, 343, 344, 346, 347–48, 360
European Recovery Program, 185–86, 188, 211, 215–16, 218
Evans, Barbara, 93, 104, 197, 198, 389, 401
Executive Committee of the National Security Council (ExCom), 398–401, 404–5
Export Control Office, 85, 86
Farley, James, 60
Farm Credit Administration, 64, 65
Fechteler, William, 335, 336
Federal Reserve Bank of New York, 64
Federal Reserve Board, 44
Federal Trade Commission, 44
Fermi, Enrico, 231–32, 235
Figl, Leopold, 354
Finletter, Thomas, 372
Fischer, Louis, 165
Fisher, Adrian, 93, 239, 311, 359
Fisher, Walter L., 54
Foley, Edward, 89
Folliard, Edward, 305
Fontaine, André, 248
Foreign Funds Control Committee, 84, 85, 86
Forrestal, James V., 120, 149, 150, 153, 154, 173, 174, 232, 273
Fortas, Abe, 410, 421, 427
Fosdick, Dorothy, 273
Foster, John, 261
France:
  colonies of, 262–67, 353–54, 397
  communism in, 165, 166, 168, 187
  in NATO, 389–90, 403, 407–8, 416–17, 430
  nuclear weapons of, 407, 411
Frankfurter, Felix, 38, 39, 40, 44, 45, 48, 50, 55, 59, 61–62, 70, 74–76, 81, 131, 194, 197, 201, 219, 227, 357, 358, 368, 396, 415, 437
Franks, Oliver, 247, 308–9, 336, 369, 406, 442
Friends of Roosevelt, 62
Fuchs, Klaus, 225, 230, 236, 239
Fulbright, J. William, 382

Gaddis, John Lewis, 345
Galbraith, John Kenneth, 378, 432
Garner, John Nance, 60–61
General Theory of Employment, Interest and Money, The (Keynes), 89
George, VI, King of England, 252, 337–38
Germany:
  demilitarization of, 205, 207–8, 209, 323, 331
  occupied zones of, 175, 187, 202, 207, 241, 245, 250, 253, 268, 338–39, 342, 344
  Plan A for, 205–8
  reparations by, 174–75, 187, 242
  reunification of, 205, 207, 208, 244, 245, 271, 326, 342–45, 375, 377, 384

Soviet policy on, 170, 174, 175, 202–3, 208–9, 342–48
Truman's policy on, 241–54
U.S. policy on, 83–84, 93–94, 165, 171
Weimar Republic of, 243, 244, 343
in World War II, 73, 83–84, 93–94
Germany, East, 345, 377, 383, 384, 385, 390
Germany, West:
Anglo-French relations with, 242–54, 267, 324–26, 329–31, 360–61, 407–8
Bundestag of, 241–42
creation of, 187, 188, 202, 205–9, 346–47, 348
economic recovery of, 241–54
industrial production of, 242–43, 244
rearmament of, 323–26, 329–34, 337, 342–48, 360, 375–77
sovereignty of, 347–48
Gesell, Gerhardt, 189
Goldberg, Arthur, 421, 427
gold standard, 63–68, 99
Goldwater, Barry, 412
Gonzalez, Donald, 281
Gooderham, George (grandfather), 18
Gorbachev, Mikhail, 377
Gottwald, Klement, 188
Graham, Wallace, 320
Grand Trunk Pacific Railway, 26–27
Grant, Ulysses S., 303
Great Britain:
Commonwealth of, 251–52, 406
empire of, 90–92, 103, 251–52, 263, 351–53, 360, 406
Greek civil war and, 163, 164, 169
international role of, 136, 140, 143, 151, 155, 165, 166, 173, 174, 251–52, 333, 335–36, 351, 406–7
Iran crisis and, 142, 143, 151
as nuclear power, 123
U.S. aid to, 172–73
U.S. relations with, 136, 145, 146, 147, 151, 246–47, 251–53, 305, 360, 406, 407
in World War II, 79, 80, 85, 86, 87–92, 98
Great Debate, 326–29
Great Depression, 63–68
Greece, 156, 162–69, 170, 173, 180, 268, 332, 400, 413–15, 439, 441
Greek Communist Party, 163, 164, 169
Green, Marshall, 258
Grew, Joseph, 82, 86, 101, 106–7
"Grief" (MacLeish), 32
Griswold, Whitney, 370–71
Gromyko, Andrei, 144, 209, 319, 320, 321, 331
Groton School, 21–28, 31, 52, 73, 437
Groves, Leslie, 124, 125, 126, 127
Gruber, Karl, 354
Guatemala, 356

Habib, Philip, 425, 426
Hadley, Arthur, 31
Halifax, Edward Wood, Lord, 94–95, 139
Hamilton, Alexander, 276
Hamilton, John, 74
Hamlet Lodge, 21
Hand, Learned, 359, 360
Hannevig, Christoffer, 54, 55
Hapgood, Norman, 51, 71
Harding, Warren, 59
Harriman, Averell, 22, 32–33, 34, 107, 138, 140, 141, 143, 149, 150, 250, 286–87, 295–99, 314, 351–52, 371, 421, 422–23, 437
Harriman, Daisy, 312
Harrison, Benjamin, 261
Harvard Law School, 27, 32, 35, 36, 37–39
Henderson, Loy W., 140, 142, 163, 166
Herridge, Mildred, 65
Herridge, William Duncan, 65
Heusinger, Adolf, 330
Hickenlooper, Bourke, 205
Hickerson, John, 206, 281, 282, 284
Hilldring, John, 173
Hirohito, Emperor of Japan, 106–7
Hiroshima bombing, 108, 114–15, 128
Hiss, Alger, 193–96, 225, 226–29, 236, 237, 441, 464*n*
Hiss, Donald, 93, 195, 196, 227
Hiss, Priscilla, 194
Hitler, Adolf, 73, 84, 102, 125, 244, 245, 284
Ho Chi Minh, 255, 262, 264, 265, 330, 440
Hoffman, Paul, 185–86
Holmes, Fanny, 49
Holmes, Oliver Wendell, 38, 44, 47–48, 49, 58, 77, 81, 107–8, 180, 194, 195, 279, 368, 392, 401, 439
Hoover, Herbert, 60, 61, 185, 326, 327, 328
Hoover, J. Edgar, 195, 464*n*
Hoover Commission, 185, 189
Hopkins, Harry, 69, 81, 88, 334

Hottelet, Richard C., 153
House Foreign Relations Committee, 311
House Un-American Activities Committee (HUAC), 193–96
Hudson, Manley, 45
Hughes, Charles Evans, 288
Hull, Cordell, 74, 81, 83, 84, 85, 86, 87, 90, 93, 94, 96, 100, 106, 160, 254, 263, 417
Humelsine, Carlisle, 197, 198
Humphrey, Hubert, 184–85, 426, 430
Hungary, 133, 168, 374
Hurley, Patrick J., 140, 213–14, 220
Hu Shih, 95
hydrogen bomb, 229–36

Ickes, Harold L., 69, 82, 83, 391
Imperial Preference, 90–92
Indochina, 201, 255, 262–67, 285, 354
Indochina War, 262, 264, 267, 329–30, 350, 358, 440, 477*n*
Indonesia, 201
Inonu, Ismet, 414
International Ladies' Garment Workers Union, 70
International Monetary Fund, 97, 98–99, 102, 103, 149
Inverchapel, Lord, 162, 179
Iran, 123, 133, 137, 138–45, 146, 147, 148, 151, 152, 166, 351–53, 358, 439, 457*n*–58*n*
Iron Curtain, 146–48, 180, 268, 275, 279
isolationism, 59, 80, 84, 94, 95, 107, 193, 326–29, 376
Israel, 131–32, 201
Italy, 187, 389

Jackson, Andrew, 71
Jackson, Robert H., 80
Jacobson, Eddie, 132
James, William, 56
Janeway, Michael, 393
Japan:
  demilitarization of, 256
  industrial production of, 256–60
  reparations by, 318–19
  surrender of, 106–7, 109, 113, 115, 117, 256
  Truman's policy on, 256–60
  U.S. bases in, 318–19
  U.S. occupation of, 106–7, 201, 255, 256–60, 262, 269, 315
  U.S. relations with, 165, 171, 262, 299, 317–21, 323, 398, 440
  in World War II, 82–87
Jefferson, Thomas, 368
Jenner, William, 311
Jessup, Philip C., 197, 198, 200, 203, 207, 208, 219, 222, 238, 281, 282, 283, 284, 299, 300, 347, 376
Johnson, Edward Youter, 437
Johnson, Louis, 207, 232–33, 235, 256, 274, 277–78, 282, 284, 287, 296, 311, 324
Johnson, Lyndon B., 378–79, 394, 410–28
  Acheson's relationship with, 410–28, 430
  foreign policy of, 411–17
  Vietnam War policy of, 11–12, 412, 415, 416, 417, 418–28
Johnson, Owen, 29
Joint Chiefs of Staff (JCS), 221, 222, 231, 232, 236, 267, 269, 399, 400, 405, 424
  in Korean War, 289–90, 292, 293, 297, 298, 302–3, 304, 305–6, 310, 314, 316–17, 345
Jones, Joseph, 167
Judd, Walter, 168, 215
Jupiter missile bases, 400, 403, 404, 405

Karsh, Yousuf, 104
Kennan, George F., 140–41
  Acheson's relationship with, 150–51, 196–97, 198, 200, 205, 206, 207, 208, 209, 233–34, 271–72, 375–77, 432, 433, 469*n*
  China as viewed by, 221
  Germany as viewed by, 375–77
  hydrogen bomb as viewed by, 231, 233, 234
  Indochina as viewed by, 265
  Iran crisis and, 141, 143, 144
  Japan as viewed by, 257–59
  in Korean War, 280, 283, 284, 285, 306–8, 321–22
  "Long Telegram" of, 149–51, 157
  Marshall Plan and, 175–77, 178, 179–80
  NATO opposed by, 200, 202
  Soviet Union as viewed by, 141, 149–51, 153, 167, 179–80, 277, 278, 344–45
Kennedy, John F., 381–409
  Acheson's relationship with, 11, 260, 379, 380, 381–409
  assassination of, 408–9, 411
  Berlin crisis and, 383–94, 408
  cabinet of, 381–82

foreign policy of, 256, 383, 385
Khrushchev and, 390, 400, 404, 405–6
presidential campaign of (1960), 379–80, 381
Truman and, 379
Kennedy, Joseph P., 327, 379
Kennedy, Robert F., 381, 383, 398–99, 401, 405
Kent, Sherman, 402
Kent State shootings, 435
Keynes, John Maynard, 89–91, 98–100, 103, 241
Keynes, Lydia Lopokova, 89
Keyserling, Leon, 276
Khrushchev, Nikita, 152, 383, 384–85, 388, 390, 391–94, 400, 404, 405–6, 413
Kim Il Sung, 268, 290–91, 300
King, William Lyon Mackenzie, 80, 122
Kissinger, Henry A., 403, 429–30, 433–34, 435, 441
Kitchen, Jeffrey, 368
Knowland, William, 215, 220
Koerner, Theodor, 354
Korean War, 11, 80, 200, 280–322
Acheson's role in, 280–322, 323, 357, 415, 440, 441
atomic bomb and, 305, 308–9, 346
Blair House Group in, 283–85, 287
cease-fire in, 292, 307, 308, 312, 313, 317, 321–22, 334, 345–46
Chinese intervention in, 287, 290–91, 294, 297–306, 313, 316, 317, 322, 325, 327, 422, 423
congressional support for, 286, 287–88, 310–12
Inchon landing in, 294–97, 300, 311, 318
JCS in, 289–90, 292, 293, 297, 298, 302–3, 304, 305–6, 310, 314, 316–17, 345
Kennan's role in, 280, 283, 284, 285, 306–8, 321–22
Korean unification and, 293, 297, 298, 312, 345–46
as limited war, 285, 286, 289, 302, 303, 304, 310, 373
MacArthur's insubordination in, 294, 295–300, 312–17
MacArthur's strategy in, 289–310, 311, 312–17, 327, 423, 440
Mao's role in, 290–91, 300–301
map of, 284
Marshall's role in, 296, 298, 299, 302, 303, 304, 308, 311, 314, 322
North Korean offensive in, 280–96, 323, 440
press coverage of, 281, 282, 297, 305, 311, 312
prisoners of war in, 322, 346, 358
Pusan perimeter in, 291–92, 295, 297, 310
Pyongyang-Wonsan line in, 298, 301–2, 303
South Korean army in, 281, 282, 285, 289, 291–92, 302, 317
Soviet involvement in, 222–23, 268, 269, 283, 284–85, 287, 290–91, 293, 297, 298, 300–301, 304, 305, 307, 308–9, 317, 321–22, 327, 440
Stalin's role in, 290–91, 300–301, 440
Truman's policy on, 282, 283–88, 293, 295–300, 305, 308–12, 422, 440
UN involvement in, 281–82, 284, 285–86, 288, 291, 292–93, 294, 296, 298, 309
U.S. air support in, 285, 287
U.S. intervention in, 283, 284–322, 420
U.S. troop withdrawals and, 268–69, 280, 290
Vietnam War compared with, 420, 421, 422
Krock, Arthur, 460*n*
Kurchatov, Igor, 117, 128

Landis, James M., 46
Landon, Alf, 74
Landon, Truman "Ted," 275, 277
Lansing, Robert, 261
Laos, 262, 265, 266
Laski, Harold, 75, 368
Latin America, 355–56
Lattimore, Owen, 238
Lawrence, D. H., 389
Lawrence, Ernest, 230
Lawton, Joe, 21
League of Nations, 59
LeHand, Marguerite "Missy," 76
Lehman, Herbert H., 96, 260
Lend-Lease Act (1941), 89
Lend-Lease program, 79–80, 87–92, 103
Letter of Transmittal, 219–20, 467*n*
Lewis, Fulton, 239
Lewis, Grace Hegger, 51
Lewis, John L., 51
Lewis, Sinclair, 51
Lewis, W. S., 30, 31, 370
Liberty bonds, 65

Lie, Trygve, 282
Lilienthal, David, 124, 126, 127, 229–30, 231, 232, 233, 234, 235, 271
Lincoln, Abraham, 235, 303, 334, 355, 425
Lippmann, Helen, 146–47, 186–87
Lippmann, Walter, 146–47, 148, 169, 199, 220, 223, 312, 476–77*n*
Litvinov, Maxim, 95, 153
Lodge, Henry Cabot, 358, 421, 426, 427
Long, Breckinridge, 101
Lon Nol, 435
Los Alamos laboratory, 125
Lothian, Lord, 80, 88, 94
Louis XIV, king of France, 63
Lovett, Robert A., 180–81, 188, 196, 201, 202, 228, 276, 278–79, 305, 308, 309, 312, 313, 320, 321, 325, 336, 345, 382, 412, 420, 426, 432
Loy, Myrna, 313
Loyalty Review Board, 238, 359–60
Lucas, Scott, 288
Luce, Clare Boothe, 140
Lyon, Cecil, 402

McAdoo, William, 61
MacArthur, Douglas, 201, 222
  insubordination of, 11, 294, 295–300, 312–17
  in Japan, 256–60
  Korean War strategy of, 289–310, 311, 312–17, 327, 423, 440
  reputation of, 289–90, 303, 315–16
  Truman's dismissal of, 11, 313–17
  Truman's meeting with, 299–300, 302
McCardle, Carl, 260
McCarran, Patrick, 75, 76, 220, 228, 315
McCarthy, Joseph R., 11, 48
  Acheson attacked by, 228, 237, 239–40, 281, 311–12, 368, 369, 382, 430
  anticommunist campaign of, 228, 236–40, 369, 371, 372
McClellan, George, 425
McCloy, John J., 80, 117, 124, 228, 241, 242, 243, 247, 248, 331, 333–34, 342–43, 382, 412, 417, 420, 426
MacColl, René, 171, 178
McCormack, James, Jr., 229
MacDonald, Ranald, Jr., 71
McGrigor, Roderick Robert, 335–36
McKellar, Kenneth, 311
MacLeish, Ada, 87, 367–68
MacLeish, Archibald, 30, 32, 39, 50, 81, 87, 106, 108, 239, 367–70, 384
McMahon, Brien, 232, 236
Macmillan, Harold, 386, 402, 407
McNamara, Robert, 382, 392, 398, 404, 415, 417, 421, 422, 426
MacVeagh, Lincoln, 339, 434
Main Street (Lewis), 51
Makarios, Archbishop, 413, 414
Malik, Jacob, 203, 285, 292, 321–22
Manhattan Project, 115–16, 117, 124, 125, 231
Manley, John, 231
Mansfield, Mike, 436
Mao Zedong:
  as Communist leader, 159, 193, 201, 211, 212, 213, 217–19, 221, 224, 239, 262, 285, 440
  Korean War and, 290–91, 300–301
  Stalin and, 218, 219, 220, 223–24, 290–91, 300–301
Marks, Herbert, 121
Marshall, George Catlett, 47, 119, 130, 131
  Acheson's relationship with, 159–60, 162, 181
  China as viewed by, 214, 215, 216
  China visit of, 214, 215, 352
  Greek and Turkish aid supported by, 164–67
  Harvard University speech of, 178–79
  in Korean War, 296, 298, 299, 302, 303, 304, 308, 311, 314, 322
  military career of, 159, 160–61, 290
  personality of, 160
  press coverage of, 178–79
  as secretary of defense, 296, 298, 299, 302, 303, 304, 308, 311, 314, 322, 324–25, 328, 440
  as secretary of state, 159–61, 162, 164–67, 170, 182, 186, 187, 188, 189, 196, 215, 256, 257, 260, 264, 271
  Stalin and, 175
  Truman and, 161, 256
Marshall, John, 160
Marshall Plan, 10, 78, 102, 173–88, 193, 202, 216, 225, 241, 242, 272, 286, 323, 346, 361, 440, 441
Martin, Joseph W., 165, 166, 313
Marxism, 150
Masaryk, Jan, 188
Massigli, René, 251

Matthews, H. Freeman "Doc," 131, 283
Maugham, Somerset, 349
Melby, John, 220
Merz, Charles, 79
Mexico, 355
Miall, Leonard, 171, 178, 179
Middle East, 133, 139, 143, 145, 154, 155, 166, 201, 353–54
Middletown, Conn., 15–16, 18, 21, 55, 199, 243
Mikoyan, Anastas, 405
Mikoyan, Sergo, 405–6
Military Aid Program, 218
Molotov, Vyacheslav, 117, 139, 152, 175, 179, 223, 345
Monnet, Jean, 248–49, 250, 251, 325, 329, 360–61, 375
Montreux Convention, 152, 154, 155
Moore, Douglas, 32
Morgenthau, Elinor, 64
Morgenthau, Henry, Jr., 64, 65, 66, 67, 82, 83, 84, 88, 98, 99, 100
Morning and Noon (Acheson), 63, 415, 432
Morocco, 353–54
Morrison, Herbert, 332–33
Mosadeq, Mohammed, 351–53
Mozambique, 397
Muccio, John J., 281
Muggeridge, Malcolm, 171, 178
Murphy, Robert, 206, 421
Mutual Aid Agreement, 92

Nagasaki bombing, 115, 126
Namibia, 431
Nasser, Gamal Abdel, 374
National Council of Soviet-American Friendship, 135–36
National Liberation Front (EAM), 163, 164
National Military Establishment, 185
National Popular Liberation Army (ELAS), 163
National Security Council (NSC), 205, 208, 217, 218, 235, 259, 266–67, 274–79, 304–5, 390–92, 398–401, 404–5
Naval Overseas Transportation Service, 39–40
Neely, Matthew M., 75
Nehru, Jawaharlal, 292
Neutral Nation Commission, 346
New Deal, 9, 61–62, 69–70, 71, 74, 81, 89, 96, 165, 229, 256, 374
New York Times, 79–80, 142, 155, 178, 179, 207, 238, 297, 375, 420, 421
New York Times Magazine, 372
New Zealand, 319, 320
Niebuhr, Reinhold, 372–73
Nitze, Paul, 149, 177, 197, 198, 226, 234, 271, 272–74, 276, 277, 279, 378, 385, 391, 431, 438
Nixon, Richard M.:
  Acheson attacked by, 228, 429–30
  Acheson's relationship with, 428, 429–36
  foreign policy of, 256
  in Hiss case, 194
  presidential campaign of (1960), 379, 380
  "silent majority" speech of, 434
  Vietnam War policy of, 12, 430–31, 433–35, 436
Norstad, Lauris, 294
North Atlantic Treaty (1949), 219, 225, 241, 329, 347, 361
North Atlantic Treaty Organization (NATO):
  Acheson's support for, 10, 102, 200, 201–5, 218, 224, 305, 312, 323, 375, 440, 441
  congressional approval of, 102, 201–5, 218
  Council of, 253–54, 324–25, 334, 341, 360–61, 389
  Eisenhower as commander of, 325, 328, 331, 334
  French participation in, 389–90, 403, 407–8, 416–17, 430
  U.S. military commitment to, 323, 324, 328, 329, 331, 341, 435–36
North Korea, 222–23, 280–96, 323, 440
Norway, 53–55, 338
NSC 64 document, 266
NSC 68 document, 274–79, 323, 329

Office of Strategic Services, 131
Oliphant, Herman, 65, 66
One Man's Education (Lewis), 30
Operation Rolling Thunder, 418
Oppenheimer, J. Robert, 124, 125, 126, 229, 231, 232, 234, 278

Pace, Frank, 282, 287, 314
Page, Frank, 60
Palestine, 131–32
Palmer, A. Mitchell, 48
Panikkar, Kavalam, 299

Papandreou, George, 414
Patterson, Robert, 76, 165, 173, 174
Peabody, Endicott, 22–25, 27–28, 73
Pearl Harbor attack, 87, 91, 95, 212, 399
Pendergast, Tom, 228
Peng Dehuai, 291
Penguin Club, 59
Pershing, John J., 161
Petersberg formula, 330–31
Philippines, 285
Pleven, René, 329–30, 331
Poland, 116, 136, 145
Policy Planning Staff, 175–77, 200, 207, 233, 265, 271, 272, 273, 275, 343
Porter, Cole, 37, 73
Portugal, 340, 396–97
Potsdam conference (1945), 108, 113, 116–17, 122, 133, 152, 263, 358
Pound, Roscoe, 39, 50
Power and Diplomacy (Acheson), 373
Present at the Creation (Acheson), 432
Prohibition, 45
Public Works Administration, 69

Qavam, Ahmed, 144
Quemoy and Ma-tsu crisis, 378, 380

Rabi, I. I., 231–32, 235
Rayburn, Sam, 166, 254, 319, 378
Reader's Digest, 186
Reciprocal Trade Agreements Program, 74, 106
Reconstruction Finance Corporation (RFC), 65, 66, 101
Reed, Charles, 265
Reed, James A., 70
Reed, Stanley, 65, 66
"Reply to Kennan" (Acheson), 375–76
Republican Party:
- Acheson attacked by, 228, 310–12, 315–16, 326–29, 356, 368, 369, 373, 382, 429–30
- anticommunism in, 107, 228, 237–38, 239
- China issue and, 211, 224, 238, 260, 261, 270
- isolationism in, 59, 94, 107, 193, 326–29
- progressive wing of, 59

Reston, James, 155, 162, 172, 178, 199, 207–8, 228, 290, 390
Rhee, Syngman, 268, 285, 290, 291
Rhodesia, 396, 433
Ridgway, Matthew B., 306, 310, 312, 314, 317, 426
Riel, Louis, 17
Robeson, Paul, 136
Romania, 123, 133, 156, 163
Roosevelt, Eleanor, 64, 379
Roosevelt, Franklin D.:
- Acheson's relationship with, 62–68, 69, 71, 73–76, 104–5
- atomic policy and, 128–29
- China policy of, 212
- Churchill's meetings with, 86, 91–92
- colonialism opposed by, 262–63
- congressional opposition to, 80, 88, 95–96, 101–2
- death of, 104–5, 263, 408
- economic policies of, 63–68, 74
- foreign policy of, 73–74, 77–81, 84–85, 130, 138–40, 141, 167, 256, 261, 358
- Marshall and, 161
- political leadership of, 9, 104–5
- presidential campaign of (1932), 60–61
- presidential campaign of (1936), 70
- presidential campaign of (1940), 79, 81
- Stalin and, 104, 116, 128–29, 138–39, 152, 212
- at Tehran conference, 138–39
- Truman compared with, 114, 256
- war policy of, 87–89
- at Yalta conference, 152

Roosevelt, Theodore, 34, 52, 59, 221
Rosenman, Samuel, 81, 121
Rossow, Robert, 143
Rostow, Eugene, 140, 371
Rostow, Walt, 424, 425–26
Rowe, Hartley, 231
Rublee, George, 52–53, 54, 56, 59, 74, 79, 369
Rusk, Dean, 183, 196, 198, 260, 262, 281, 282, 283, 284, 299, 318, 321, 382, 383, 393, 401, 404, 417, 419, 422, 427
Russell, Donald, 131
Russell, Francis, 171

Sakharov, Andrei, 230, 236
Salazar, Antonio de Oliveira, 340, 397
Salinger, Pierre, 406
Salisbury, Harrison, 421
Santayana, George, 56

Schlesinger, Arthur, Jr., 386, 391, 441
Schumacher, Kurt, 245
Schuman, Robert, 203, 204, 206–9, 242–43, 246, 247–51, 252, 253, 324, 325, 333, 337–38, 344, 346, 347, 350
Schuman Plan, 250, 251
Schuyler, Cortlandt Van Rensselaer, 258
Scroll and Key, 30, 32
Seaborg, Glenn, 231
Semyonov, Vladimir, 343
Senate Foreign Relations Committee, 95–96, 168, 174, 184, 222, 223, 224, 237, 266
Sergeant, Howland, 313
Service, John, 238
Seventh Fleet, U.S., 285, 294, 378
Seymour, Charles, 370
Shah of Iran, 141–42, 353
Shulman, Harry, 370–71
Shulman, Marshall, 332, 345
Sihanouk, Norodom, 395–96, 435
Sino-Soviet Treaty of Friendship, 224, 255, 262, 290
Smith, Al, 60
Smith, Alexander, 329
Smith, Kingsbury, 202
Smith, Margaret Chase, 239
Smith, Merriman, 305
Smith, Walter Bedell, 145, 175
Smyth, Henry, 231
"Snob in America, The" (Acheson), 26
Society of Pilgrims, 247, 253
Souers, Sidney, 277, 278
"Sources of Soviet Conduct, The" (Kennan), 186–87
South Africa, 396, 431, 433
South Korea, 165, 222–23, 255, 268–69, 281, 282, 285, 289, 291–92, 302, 317
Soviet Union:
  Acheson's views on, 136, 150–51
  atomic bomb developed by, 225–26, 229–30, 232, 239, 247, 270, 328–29
  Chinese alliance with, 212, 218–20, 221, 223–24, 255, 262, 290
  containment of, 10, 11, 150, 168, 176, 186–87, 261, 262, 270–71, 275, 276–77, 279, 289, 323, 356–57, 398, 439–40, 441
  expansionism of, 141, 145, 146–51, 154, 156, 157, 166, 180, 186, 201, 262, 270–71, 274
  hydrogen bomb developed by, 230–36
  in Korean War, 222–23, 268, 269, 283, 283–85, 287, 290–91, 293, 297, 298, 300–301, 304, 305, 307, 308–9, 317, 321–22, 327, 440
  military strength of, 136, 153, 275–76
  as nuclear power, 117–29
  oil supplies of, 139, 144
  U.S. public opinion on, 135, 149
  U.S. recognition of, 95, 141
  U.S. relations with, *see* U.S.-Soviet relations
  Western Europe threatened by, 254, 327, 328–29, 348, 376
  World Bank and, 99–100
Spain, 94
"Special relationship between the United States and Great Britain," 246
Speidel, Hans, 330
Spofford, Charles, 323
Stalin, Josef:
  atomic policy of, 116–17, 118, 122–23, 127, 128
  Byrnes's meetings with, 123, 124, 128, 133, 134–35
  China policy of, 212, 223–24
  Churchill and, 152, 163
  death of, 346, 371
  FDR and, 104, 116, 128–29, 138–39, 152, 212
  foreign policy of, 141, 145, 153, 156, 163, 164, 169, 441
  German policy of, 175, 202–3, 208–9, 342–45, 348
  "gradualist policy" of, 163
  Greek civil war and, 163, 164, 169
  hydrogen bomb development supported by, 230, 236
  Iran crisis and, 142–45
  Korean War and, 290–91, 300–301, 440
  Mao and, 218, 219, 220, 223–24, 290–91, 300–301
  Marshall Plan and, 179–80
  at Potsdam conference, 108, 116–17, 122, 152
  as realist, 133
  speeches of, 148–49
  at Tehran conference, 138, 139
  Truman and, 116–17, 144, 148–49, 152
  Turkish crisis and, 152–53
  at Yalta conference, 104, 152

Stanley, Alice English, 35
Stanley, Jane Caroline Mahon, 35
Stanley, John Mix, 35, 198
Stanley, Louis, 35
Stark, Harold "Betty," 85
State, War and Navy Coordinating Committee, 170, 173–74
State Department, U.S., 83, 87, 90, 96, 97, 99, 100, 130–31, 139, 149, 159–62, 167, 234, 236–40, 241
Steel, Ronald, 169
Stephens, Harold, 66
Stettinius, Edward R., Jr., 101, 105, 106, 263
Stevenson, Adlai, 356–58, 372, 373, 374, 378, 379, 382, 386, 430
Stimson, Henry L., 29, 38, 184, 196, 197
  Acheson and, 119–23
  atomic bomb memorandum of, 114–23, 129
  as secretary of war, 80, 82–83, 128
Stimson, Mabel, 115
Stokes, Richard, 352
Strategic Arms Limitation Talks (SALT I), 432
Strauss, Lewis, 230, 231, 232
Stuart, John Leighton, 210, 216, 219
Sudan, 351
Suez Canal, 351, 373–74
Suez crisis, 373–74
Sun Yat-sen, 211, 213
Supreme Commander of the Allied Powers (SCAP), 256
Supreme Court, U.S., 40–52, 56–57, 61, 70–71, 183, 238, 288, 369
Swan, Thomas W., 50
Sweden, 94
Switzerland, 94
Symington, Stuart, 379

Taft, Robert A., 73, 101–2, 166, 172, 193, 237, 287, 288, 296, 311, 326–27, 328, 368, 371
Taft, William Howard, 34, 57, 288
Taiwan, 217, 220, 221–22, 224, 269, 285, 286, 291, 294, 295, 319, 378, 440
Taney, Roger Brooke, 70–71
tariffs, 59, 91
Taylor, Maxwell, 419, 421, 426, 427
Tehran conference (1943), 138–39, 142
Tehran Declaration, 138, 139, 142
Teller, Edward, 230
Thacher, Thomas, 79
Thailand, 369, 395
Thurmond, Strom, 189
Time, 148, 158, 193, 194, 411
Tito, Marshal (Josip Broz), 164, 169, 218, 224, 262
"total diplomacy," 270–71
trade, international, 90–92, 99, 102, 103, 106
Treasury Department, U.S., 64, 97, 149
Tripartite Pact, 84
Truman, Bess, 345
Truman, Harry S.:
  Acheson's relationship with, 9–11, 12, 63, 109, 114, 162, 181, 185–86, 189–90, 198, 199, 226, 255–56, 312, 320, 345, 361–63, 371, 432, 441
  anticommunism of, 188, 238
  atomic policy of, 114–29
  budget of, 165
  Byrnes and, 61, 129, 130, 134–35, 159
  cabinet of, 189
  China policy of, 211, 215–16, 217, 221–22, 225
  Churchill's meetings with, 116, 146, 334–37
  congressional opposition to, 165–66, 176, 177, 185–86, 215–16, 260, 288, 310–12, 315–16, 326–29
  as Democratic leader, 9, 170
  Dulles and, 260–62
  Eisenhower and, 358, 362, 371
  FDR compared with, 114, 256
  foreign policy of, 11, 12, 136, 145, 150, 151, 156–59, 166–69, 172, 184, 189, 193, 226, 256, 261, 318, 326, 346, 348, 441
  German policy of, 241–54
  Greek and Turkish aid supported by, 165–169
  hydrogen bomb supported by, 229–36
  Indochina policy of, 263, 266–67
  Iran crisis and, 142, 144
  Israel supported by, 132
  Japan policy of, 256–60
  Kennedy and, 379
  Korean War policy of, 282, 283–88, 293, 295–300, 305, 308–12, 422, 440
  MacArthur dismissed by, 11, 313–17
  MacArthur's meeting with, 299–300, 302
  Marshall and, 161, 256
  memoirs of, 283–84
  personality of, 105, 362

at Potsdam conference, 108, 113, 116–17, 122, 152, 263, 358
presidential campaign of (1948), 188, 189, 193, 245
press coverage of, 121–22, 158
second term renounced by, 345
speeches of, 166–68, 188, 345
Stalin and, 116–17, 144, 148–49, 152
Turkish crisis and, 152, 154–55
Truman, Margaret, 362–63
Truman Doctrine, 10, 166–69, 170, 173, 174, 187, 222, 225, 268, 279, 346, 413, 439, 441
trusts, 43, 44, 52
Tufts, Robert, 273
Tully, Grace, 68
Tunisia, 353–54
Turkey, 133, 145, 152–55, 156, 162, 164–69, 170, 173, 180, 268, 332, 400, 403, 404, 405, 413–15, 439, 441
Twilight in Italy (Lawrence), 389
Tydings, Millard, 237–38

UN Atomic Energy Commission, 118, 119, 121, 122, 123, 124, 127–28, 133
United Mine Workers, 51
United Nations:
Acheson's views on, 107–8
charter of, 106, 107, 222
China issue and, 221, 223, 282, 292, 309
Cyprus conflict and, 413, 414
founding of, 104, 105, 106, 107, 261
General Assembly of, 124, 298, 333
German question and, 344
influence of, 97, 168
Iran crisis and, 143, 144
in Korean War, 281–82, 284, 285–86, 288, 291, 292–93, 294, 296, 298, 309
origins of, 91, 94–97
Security Council of, 123, 127, 128, 143, 144, 281–82, 285–86, 292, 352, 433
Soviet boycott of, 282, 285, 292
United Nations Relief and Rehabilitation Administration (UNRRA), 94–97
United States:
defense budget of, 247, 255, 274–79, 323, 327, 328, 379, 385
defense perimeter of, 222–23, 269, 288–91, 357, 480*n*
economy of, 78, 92
foreign aid by, 162–80
foreign trade of, 90, 103
"grand strategy" of, 136–37
international influence of, 10–11, 78, 92, 168–69, 174, 225–26, 241, 440
national security of, 174, 225, 271, 288–89
as nuclear power, 114–29, 483*n*
oil supplies of, 139
USS *Missouri*, 153–54
U.S.-Soviet relations:
atomic bomb and, 114–29, 151
confrontation in, 123, 143–45, 153–54, 157
Iran crisis and, 133, 137, 138–45, 148
spheres of influence in, 138, 155, 158, 163, 202, 343
see also Soviet Union
U Thant, 414
U-2 spy planes, 385, 398, 405

Vance, Cyrus, 426
Vandenberg, Arthur, 95–96, 124, 165–66, 173, 178, 184, 185–86, 193, 196, 215, 216, 261, 326
Van Fleet, James, 314
Vaughan, Harry, 199
Versailles Treaty, 262
Viet Cong, 418, 419, 423–24
Viet Minh, 262, 263, 267, 330
Vietnam, 262, 265, 266–67, 351
Vietnam War, 418–28, 433–35
Acheson-Ball plan for, 418–19, 420
Acheson's views on, 11–12, 418–28, 430–431
bombing campaigns in, 418, 419, 421, 422, 427, 428, 431
Johnson's policy on, 11–12, 412, 415, 416, 417, 418–28
Korean War compared with, 420, 421, 422
Nixon's policy on, 12, 430–31, 433–35, 436
opposition to, 420, 435
peace negotiations in, 418–19, 425, 427
Tet offensive in, 423–24, 425, 426–27
Vietnamization in, 430, 433–34
"Wise Men" and, 419–22, 424, 426–28
Vincent, John Carter, 263, 359–60
Vinson, Fred M., 196, 361
Virginia Military Institute (VMI), 160
Vishinsky, Andrei, 208–9

Walker, Frank, 81
Walker, Joe, 31
Walker, Walton, 302, 309–10
Wallace, Henry A., 120, 121, 147, 156–59, 188, 189
Wallace Plan, 121
Walsh, Edmund A., 236
Warburg, James, 71, 74
Ward, Angus, 220
Warren, Earl, 239
Warren, George F., 64
Washington, George, 253, 355
Webb, James, 196, 198, 261, 271, 284, 307
Wedemeyer, Albert, 210, 216
Weimar Republic, 243, 244, 343
Wei Tao-ming, 95
Welles, Sumner, 83, 84, 85
Wellesley College, 34, 36, 39
Wesleyan University, 15–16
Westmoreland, William, 424, 425
Wheeler, Earl, 421–22, 426, 427
Wherry, Kenneth, 220, 288, 311, 327–28
White, Harry Dexter, 98–99, 100, 101, 452*n*–53*n*
White, William Allen, 77
Wierblowski, Stefan, 320
Wiley, Alexander, 321
Willkie, Wendell, 81, 89, 101
Wilson, Woodrow, 34, 37, 43–44, 49, 52, 59, 108, 261, 288
Wise Men, 412, 419–22, 424, 426–28, 436
"Wishing Won't Hold Berlin" (Acheson), 384, 392
Wohlstetter, Albert, 431
Woodin, William, 62, 66, 67
Works Projects Administration (WPA), 69
World Bank, 97, 99–100, 103, 149
World Court, 53–55, 369, 386, 395
World War I, 35, 37–39, 45, 49, 52–53, 161, 289–90
World War II, 73, 77–109, 148, 322
Wrong, Hume, 62
Wycliffe College, 17
Wynne, William T., 170, 171

Yale College, 27, 28, 29–35, 37, 415–16, 437
Yale Corporation, 78, 369–70
Yale Law School, 370–71
Yale Literary Renaissance, 30
Yalta conference (1945), 104, 152, 187, 193, 194, 263
Yergin, Daniel, 139
Yoshida, Shigeru, 315, 319
Yugoslavia, 164, 169

Zahariadis, Mikos, 164, 169
zaibatsu, 256–60
Zhou Enlai, 213, 219, 299, 300, 301
Zionism, 131–32